More Praise for *Divine Stories*, Part 2

"These stories are vivid reminders that Buddhism is much more than a collection of philosophical abstractions or a bare-bones meditative technique for altering our neurobiology. Here we see the Buddha's teachings firmly anchored in their natural habitat, shaping lives by opening us up to the sorrows and joys of others. In pondering the depths of the human soul, they invite us to examine our assumptions about the hidden springs of desire and fear, and what motivates us to think, speak, and act in the way we do."

—C. W. Huntington Jr., author of *Maya*

"The *Divyāvadāna* interrupts the assumption that Buddhist literature is technical and devoid of drama. These stories are full of big questions—of choice and consequence, love and power—harrowing events, and unexpected turns. These Buddhist texts reveal storytelling and teaching at its narrative best, and Andy Rotman has translated them with unparalleled love and dedication."

—Akincano M. Weber, guiding teacher, Atammaya Cologne

"Those who devoured the first volume of *Divine Stories* will delight in this fresh batch of adventures and misadventures, each illustrating the twisting karmic bonds of a host of comic, tragic, evil, mundane, and divine characters. Pairing profundity with playfulness, Rotman's precise translations of these historically important tales not only captivate, they also remind us of the power of stories to shape humans and the worlds they inhabit. An exhilarating storytelling tour de force!"

—Sara McClintock, Emory University

Classics of Indian Buddhism

The flourishing of Buddhism in South Asia during the first millennium of the Common Era produced many texts that deserve a place among the classics of world literature. Exploring the full extent of the human condition and the limits of language and reason, these texts have the power to edify and entertain a wide variety of readers. The *Classics of Indian Buddhism* series aims to publish widely accessible translations of important texts from the Buddhist traditions of South Asia, with special consideration given to works foundational for the Mahāyāna.

Editorial Board

Andy Rotman (chair), *Smith College*
Paul Harrison, *Stanford University*
Jens-Uwe Hartmann, *University of Munich*
Sara McClintock, *Emory University*
Parimal Patil, *Harvard University*
Akira Saitō, *University of Tokyo*

The Divyāvadāna

The *Divyāvadāna* is a large collection of Indian Buddhist stories written in Sanskrit from the early centuries of the Common Era. These stories have frequently been used in the moral education of monastics and laypeople, and they have often been considered to be the word of the Buddha himself. These stories have since spread throughout Asia, as both narrative and narrative art, leaving an indelible mark on Buddhist thought and practice. Representations of these stories can be found across Asia, from Kizil in China to Sanchi in India to Borobudur in Indonesia. It is not hyperbole to say that these are some of the most influential stories in the history of Buddhism. This volume contains stories from the second half of the collection.

CLASSICS OF INDIAN BUDDHISM

Divine Stories

Divyāvadāna

PART 2

Translated by Andy Rotman

Wisdom

Wisdom Publications, Inc.
199 Elm Street
Somerville MA 02144 USA
www.wisdompubs.org

Library of Congress Cataloging-in-Publication Data for Part 1
Tripiṭaka. Sūtrapiṭaka. Avadāna. Divyāvadāna. English.
Divine stories : Divyāvadāna / translated by Andy Rotman.
p. cm.
Translated from Sanskrit.
Includes bibliographical references and index.
ISBN 0-86171-295-1 (pbk. : alk. paper) ISBN 978-0-83171-831-3 (ebook)
1. Buddhist literature, Sanskrit—Translations into English. I. Rotman, Andy, 1966–
II. Title.
BQ1562.E5R68 2008
294.3'823—dc22

2008016709

ISBN 978-1-61429-470-2 ebook ISBN 978-1-61429-490-0

21 20 19 18 17
5 4 3 2 1

Cover photo courtesy of the Huntington Archive and the Bharat Kala Bhavan in Varanasi, India. For more information, see page 350, note 16.
Cover and interior design by Gopa&Ted2, Inc. Typeset by James D. Skatges.
Set in Diacritical Garamond Pro 11.75/15.75.

Wisdom Publications' books are printed on acid-free paper and meet the guidelines for permanence and durability of the Production Guidelines for Book Longevity of the Council on Library Resources.

This book was produced with environmental mindfulness. For more information, please visit wisdompubs.org/wisdom-environment.

Printed in the United States of America.

FSC www.fsc.org MIX Paper from responsible sources FSC® C011935

Please visit fscus.org.

To Ida Rose and Janna Rose,
sublime gifts for the world

Publisher's Acknowledgment

The publisher gratefully acknowledges the generous help of the Hershey Family Foundation in sponsoring the production of this book.

Contents

Preface ix

Map of Indian Places in the *Divyāvadāna* xvi

Technical Notes xix

A Summary of the Stories xxvii

THE DIVYĀVADĀNA

18. The Story of Dharmaruci 3
    Dharmaruci-avadāna

19. The Story of Jyotiṣka 45
    Jyotiṣka-avadāna

20. The Story of Kanakavarṇa 83
    Kanakavarṇa-avadāna

21. The Story of Sahasodgata 95
    Sahasodgata-avadāna

22. The Story of the Deeds of the Bodhisattva Candraprabha 117
    Candraprabhabodhisattvacaryā-avadāna

23. The Story of Saṅgharakṣita, part 1 135
    Saṅgharakṣita-avadāna

24. The Story of a Young Nāga 157
    Nāgakumāra-avadāna

25. The Story of Saṅgharakṣita, part 2 163
Saṅgharakṣita-avadāna

31. The Story of Five Hundred Farmers 167
Pañcakārṣakaśata-avadāna

32. The Story of Rūpāvatī 181
Rūpāvatī-avadāna

34. The Mahāyāna Sūtra on the Topic of Giving 197
Dānādhikaraṇa-mahāyānasūtra

35. The Story of a Lonesome Fool 201
Cūḍāpakṣa-avadāna

36. The Story of Mākandika 241
Mākandika-avadāna

37. The Story of Rudrāyaṇa 287
Rudrāyaṇa-avadāna

APPENDIX

The Cosmos According to the *Divyāvadāna* 345

Notes 349

Glossary 445

Bibliography 467

Index 487

About the Translator 507

Preface

Actions never come to naught,
even after hundreds of millions of years.
When the right conditions gather and the time is right,
then they will have their effect on embodied beings.
—The *Divyāvadāna*

THE *Divyāvadāna* is a classic, and it is a pleasure that this second installment of translations from the collection can likewise find a home in Wisdom Publications' *Classics of Indian Buddhism* series. The title of the text notwithstanding, the "divine stories" in this collection are also deeply human, recording the trials and successes of ordinary people as they struggle to live good lives, with special attention given to their spiritual development. But these are also stories of charlatans, sages, and sea monsters, feasts and famines, the miraculous and the mundane, deadly sacrifices and stupendous gifts, incest and celibacy, evil ministers and wise rulers, wise ministers and evil rulers. These stories deal with big, meaningful questions: poverty and moral agency, political power and corruption, love and lust, death and the afterlife. They are stories to ponder deeply.

While one can claim, as I do in the introduction to *Divine Stories, Part 1*, that "these are some of the most influential stories in the history of Buddhism" and talk about their importance to the fields of art, law, literature, and the like,[1] here I want to make a more provocative claim:

these stories can be life-changing. Sara McClintock (2017) makes a convincing case for this when she describes how encountering these stories can facilitate one's own ethical transformation. She describes reading these stories not simply to understand the logic behind particular actions or principles but as an ethical practice in its own right. This kind of ethical reading allows individuals to "fashion and refashion their subjectivity in relation to both self and world through a process of more or less conscious reflection on issues of moral significance" (2017: 185).[2] The stories in the *Divyāvadāna*, McClintock argues (and I wholeheartedly agree), are a perfect vehicle for this exercise.

This volume contains translations of many, but not all, of the stories in the second half of the *Divyāvadāna*. The original plan was that Joel Tatelman would translate these other stories, but owing to unforeseen circumstances, this plan couldn't come to fruition. *Divine Stories, Part 1*, contained stories 1–17. Contained here are stories 18–25, 31–32, and 34–37. Missing are stories 26–30, 33, and 38. Fortunately, however, the stories not translated in this collection are mostly available elsewhere. Stories 26–29 constitute a narrative cycle about King Aśoka, and these have been translated by John Strong (1983) in his pathbreaking work. Story 30, "The Story of the Youth Sudhana" (*Sudhanakumāra-avadāna*), was translated by Joel Tatelman (2005: 219–308) in his excellent volume for the Clay Sanskrit Library. There is no English translation of story 33, "The Story of Śārdūlakarṇa" (*Śārdūlakarṇa-avadāna*), although Joel Tatelman is working on one. It is a fascinating drama of love, caste, class, and astrology, with an equally fascinating history of transmission.[3] There is also no English translation of story 38, "The Story of Maitrakanyaka" (*Maitrakanyaka-avadāna*), but there is an excellent German translation (Klaus 1983). There is, nevertheless, good reason to omit this story. It is likely a later composition taken from Gopadatta's *Jātakamāla* that, according to Michael Hahn (1992: 5), somehow "found its way into the *Divyāvadāna*, where it does not belong at all."[4]

I have been reading and pondering these stories for two decades, and this process has been transformative. These stories make good teachers: they're smart, challenging, entertaining, surprising, and insightful. I hope my translations allow them to continue to work their magic.

Acknowledgments

This book is the result of a collective effort. It would not have been possible without the help of friends, family, and teachers, although these categories often, and fortuitously, overlap.

I first began working with the stories in the *Divyāvadāna* more than two decades ago when I was a graduate student at the University of Chicago. My analysis of the stories turned into a dissertation and later a book, and my translations of the first half of the stories were released with Wisdom Publications in 2008. My debts from those formative years in Chicago are numerous. Special thanks go to Sheldon Pollock, Steven Collins, Wendy Doniger, and A. K. Ramanujan for all they taught me about Sanskrit and translation, and for helping me to love both.

In India, I received great help from scholars in Sarnath and Pune, my two primary homes during my years of research as a graduate student. In Sarnath, at the Central Institute of Higher Tibetan Studies (now the Central University of Tibetan Studies), I read stories from the *Divyāvadāna* in Sanskrit with K. N. Mishra and Ram Shankar Tripathi, and in Tibetan (to help decipher and occasionally correct the Sanskrit) with Ramesh Negi, Geshe Ngawang Samten, Lobsang Norbu Shastri, and Pema Tenzin. They were immensely generous with their knowledge, and immensely patient with my mistakes, and I owe each a debt of gratitude.

In Pune, I read more stories from the *Divyāvadāna* with M. G. Dhadphale, whose brilliance at unraveling linguistic knots and whose love for Sanskrit and the subtleties of language continue to inspire me, and also with the late J. R. Joshi. Professor Joshi spent untold afternoons reading with me, and his care and humility were humbling. I last saw him on Guru Purnima in 2009, shortly before he died. I brought him a copy of *Divine Stories, Part 1*, and thanked him profusely, and he offered me his blessing. I learned more than just Sanskrit from Professor Joshi; his gentleness and conscientiousness are teachings I am still trying to master.

The catalyst for producing this second volume of translations from the *Divyāvadāna* was a National Endowment for the Humanities Scholarly Editions and Translations grant in 2011. My thanks to them, and also to the American Institute of Indian Studies and the Fulbright-Nehru program, whose support for other projects also allowed me to finish this one. And a special thank you to Smith College, whose faculty research grants have been enormously helpful.

Since 2011, I have been fortunate to travel to India each year to work on this project. In Goa, I met with few distractions besides a lovely beach. Each year there I was offered the support of various friends, especially Sophia Preza and Ira Mastaram Schepetin, and in 2013 I was fortunate to spend time with Shyamdas, just before he passed away. His enthusiasm for reading texts and translation was truly infectious. Special thanks also go to Rob Phillips, whose food is a genuine lifesaver.

In Banaras, I was the recipient of astounding hospitality. My deepest thanks to Rabindra Goswami, who welcomed me into his home for months and whose sitar would wake me each day and thrill me to work; to Ramu Pandit, whose caring and conscientiousness have guided me for decades; and to Hari Paudyal, an elder statesman in the guise of a younger brother. Thanks also to Abhishek Agrawal, Arun Himatsingka, Dhrub Kumar Singh, and Virendra Singh, whose longstanding friendship has helped make Banaras my second home; and to Rakesh Singh, for making Harmony Books the best hangout in India.

In America, my first thanks go to my colleagues in the Religion Department and the Buddhist Studies program at Smith College and to the members of the Five College Buddhist Studies faculty seminar. The unstinting support and collective wisdom of this incredible community has made me a much better teacher, scholar, translator, and human being. My thanks to Jay Garfield, Peter Gregory, Jamie Hubbard, Connie Kassor, Ruth Ozeki, and Marilyn Rhie; Sue Darlington, Maria Heim, Susanne Mrozik, and Rafal Stepien; Mark Blum, Benjamin Bogin, Georges Dreyfus, Reiko Ohnuma, Andrew Olendzki, Kristin Scheible, and many others. Special thanks as well to Sandy Huntington and Sara McClintock, old friends whose care, comments, and suggestions have made this a much better book.

The extended community of Buddhist scholars has likewise been helpful. Thanks to Stefan Baums, Johannes Bronkhorst, José Cabezón, Chris Clark, John Dunne, Michael Hahn, Jens-Uwe Hartmann, Satoshi Hiraoka, Timothy Lenz, Kazunobu Matsuda, Dieter Maue, Jason McCombs, James McHugh, Richard Salomon, Dieter Schlingloff, Johannes Schneider, Jonathan Silk, John Strong, Akincano Marc Weber, and Monika Zin for their helpful advice. A special thanks, too, to Joel Tatelman, who began work on this volume with me and whose insights have been enormously beneficial. I am especially grateful to Shrikant Bahulkar for helping me to finalize this book; to Peter Skilling, the outside reviewer, whose comments were immensely helpful; and to Paul Harrison, who reviewed the book on behalf of the board of the *Classics of Indian Buddhism* series. His careful reading helped me make many corrections to the manuscript.

Additional thanks also to the rest of the CIB board, for their wise counsel, and to Wisdom Publications, for their consummate professionalism. David Kittelstrom is an extraordinary editor, with an uncanny ability to make my translations both more accurate and more literary. Tim McNeill, Daniel Aitken, Kestrel Slocombe, Lydia Anderson, Gopa Campbell, Lindsay D'Andrea, Ben Gleason, and the rest of the staff at Wisdom Publications also merit special recognition for all that they've done for the field of Buddhist studies. Thank you for your indefatigability.

This book also owes a great debt to friends and scholars outside the field of Buddhist studies. Ernie Alleva, Nalini Bhushan, Arin Brenner, Lewis Davis, Laura Desmond, Jamal Elias, William Elison, Rick Fantasia, Jack Hawley, Arvind Krishna Mehrotra, Phoebe McKinnell, the friendly folks at Northampton Coffee, Christian Novetzke, Davin Pasek, Andrea Pinkney, April Strickland, Twobert, and James Wilson have been crucial interlocutors and consigliere.

Thanks, too, to my parents, Arline and Barry; my brothers, Dave and Al; my grandmother Ida; and the rest of the clan. Your love has been an inspiration.

And my deepest thank you to Janna Rose White—partner, editor, muse, and sage.

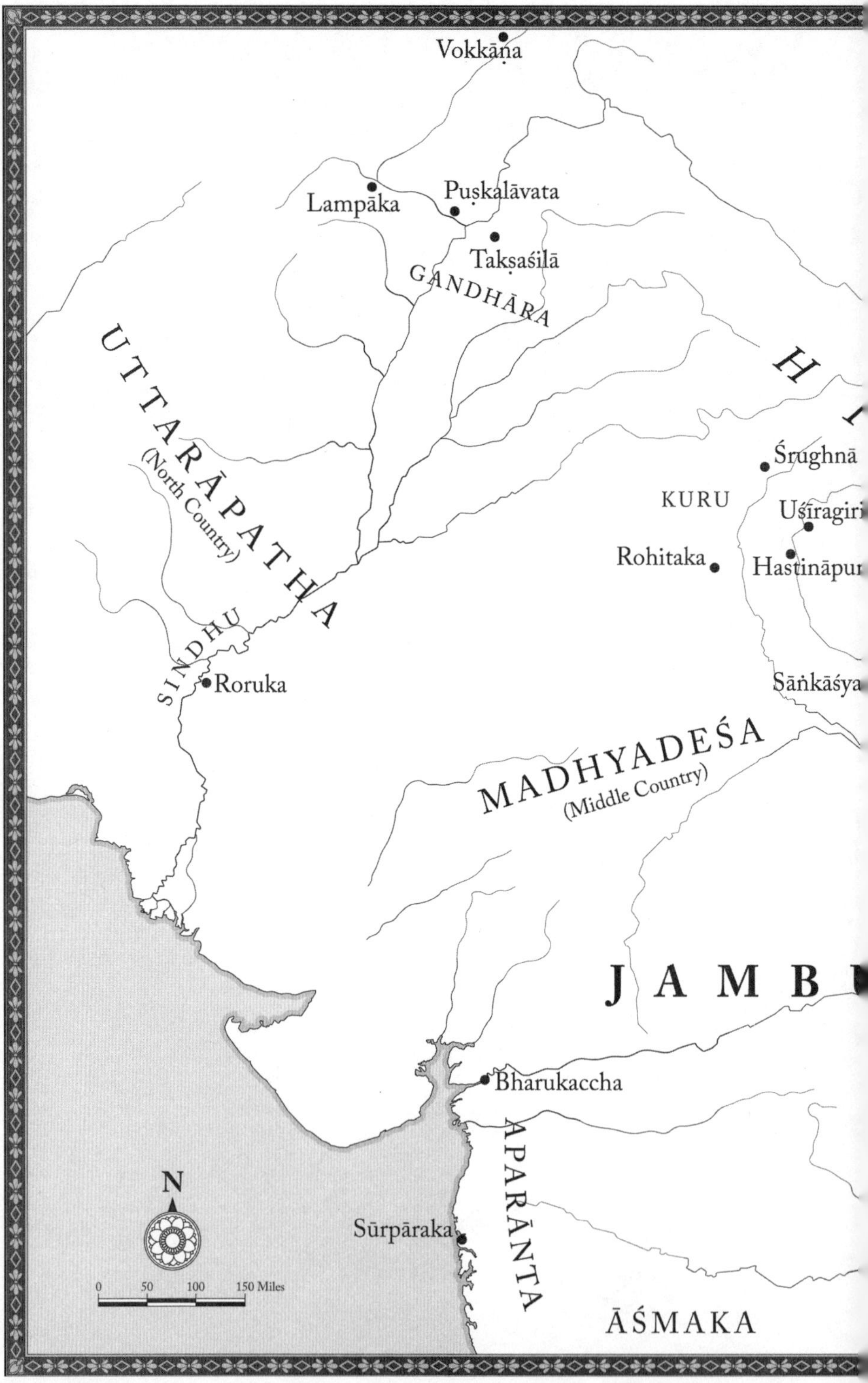

Vokkāṇa
Lampāka
Puṣkalāvata
Takṣaśilā
GANDHĀRA
UTTARĀPATHA
(North Country)
SINDHU
Roruka
KURU
Śrughnā
Uśīragiri
Rohitaka
Hastināpur
Sāṅkāśya
MADHYADEŚA
(Middle Country)
JAMB
Bharukaccha
APARĀNTA
Sūrpāraka
ĀŚMAKA
N
0
50
100
150 Miles

Map of Indian Places in the DIVYĀVADĀNA

CHINA
PAKISTAN
TIBET (China)
NEPAL
BHUTAN
New Delhi
Karachi
BANGLADESH
INDIA
Kolkata
Mumbai
Arabian Sea
Chennai
Bay of Bengal
SRI LANKA
Mandākinī
MĀLAYA
Śrāvastī
Kapilavastu
Jeta Grove
Kuśinagarī
Mithilā
Gaṅgā
KOŚALA
ŚĀKYA
LICCHAVI
PŪRVADEŚA
MALLA
Vaiśālī
KĀŚI
Pāṭaliputra
Gaṅgā
Campā
Vārāṇasī
Nairañjanā
Rājagṛha
Puṇḍravardhana
Kauśāmbī
Śuśumāragiri
MAGADHA
PUṆḌRAVARDHANA
BHARGA
Uruvilvā
DVĪPA
KALIṄGA

Technical Notes

Sources

THE FOLLOWING translation is based on the Sanskrit edition of the *Divyāvadāna* compiled by E. B. Cowell and R. A. Neil in 1886 (= Divy). Cowell and Neil made use of seven manuscripts in compiling their edition (mss. A–G).[5] I also consulted two manuscripts from the Nepal-German Manuscript Preservation Project, labeled 5819, A120/5–121/1 (ms. H) and A874/3 (ms. I). In addition, I refer to the edition by P. L. Vaidya from 1959 (= Divy-V), which is primarily a rendering of Cowell and Neil's Roman-script edition into Devanāgarī. Vaidya's edition contains some welcome emendations as well as some unfortunate mistakes. I indicate the former in my notes and, on occasion, the latter. Page numbers to Cowell and Neil's edition are included in square brackets within the translation. This pagination is retained in the margins of Vaidya's edition but not in the online versions available through the Göttingen Register of Electronic Texts in Indian Languages (http://gretil.sub.uni-goettingen.de/).

In instances when versions of the stories from the *Divyāvadāna* are also contained in the *Mūlasarvāstivāda-vinaya*, I note some of the major discrepancies and preferable readings. I rely on the Sanskrit of the *Gilgit Manuscripts* (= MSV), the facsimile edition of the *Gilgit Buddhist Manuscripts* (GBM; cf. Clarke 2014), and critical editions of portions of the text when available (e.g., GM-Saṅgh; GM-Nāga). I also make reference to the *Mūlasarvāstivāda-vinaya* in its Tibetan recensions, generally to both the Peking (= P) and Derge (= D) editions of the Tripiṭaka, which I cite in that order in the notes. Full citations are offered at the beginning of each story and abbreviated ones in what follows. For many of the Tibetan variants, I rely on the excellent work of Satoshi Hiraoka, who translated the text into Japanese and compiled a list of suggested emendations, first as an appendix to his translation (HA) and then in two articles published in English (HC, HD). His work supplements the work of D. R. Shackleton Bailey (1950, 1951), who likewise compiled a list of preferable readings in the Tibetan as well as their Sanskrit equivalents.

I have also benefited enormously from the labor of previous scholars, particularly the work of Stefan Baums (2002, 2016) on the *Jyotiṣka-avadāna*, Eugene Burnouf (1844: 90–98, 2010: 130–37) on the *Kanakavarṇa-avadāna*, Jens-Uwe Hartmann (1980) on the *Candraprabhabodhisattvacaryā-avadāna*, Dieter Maue (1996, 2010) on the *Cūḍāpakṣa-avadāna*, Johannes Nobel (1955) on the *Rūdrāyaṇa-avadāna*, Jonathan Silk (2008a) on the *Dharmaruci-avadāna*, Joel Tatelman (2005) on the *Mākandika-avadāna*, Claus Vogel and Klaus Wille (1996, 2002) on the *Saṅgharakṣita-avadāna*, and James R. Ware (1929) on the *Dānādhikaraṇa-mahāyānasūtra*. In addition, Cowell and Neil as well as Vaidya provided useful addenda to their editions, such as glossaries and notes, J. S. Speyer (1902) published critical remarks and corrections to the *Divyāvadāna*, and Franklin Edgerton (BHSD) compiled a monumental dictionary of Buddhist Hybrid Sanskrit that contains many references to the text.

In the first note to each story in this volume, I provide references to the various editions, translations, studies, and parallels that I consulted to make my translation of that story. Each story is then annotated with numerous notes that record grammatical peculiarities, philological conundrums, textual issues, and possible alternate readings and reconstructions. This critical apparatus, which is much more extensive than the one I provided in *Divine Stories, Part 1*, is intended for specialists—for those already interested in these stories and for those who, after reading through these translations, one day might be.

Conventions

In my translation, I have tried to be consistent in following certain conventions, particularly in terms of methodology. Whenever possible I privilege the text of the *Divyāvadāna*, even when I think a reading preserved in the Sanskrit or Tibetan of the *Mūlasarvāstivāda-vinaya* might sound a little better or make a little more sense. My default, in other words, is to translate the text as written, erring on the side of minimal intervention. Many of the stories in the *Divyāvadāna* appear to be revised versions of their counterparts in the *Mūlasarvāstivāda-vinaya*, so to "return" to a reading preserved in the latter may be an instance of bad faith or even bad philology.[6] Nevertheless, there are plenty of instances when a copyist has apparently made a mistake, be it a revision or a transcription error, that renders the text obscure, if not opaque. In these cases, I follow the *Mūlasarvāstivāda-vinaya*, another source, or even a best guess. In cases when I simply can't make sense of a passage, whether this be the fault of a copyist or my own limited abilities, I follow the same protocol. Most of the notes in this volume contain critical notations of this kind: variant readings, followed or simply noted, and the consequent issues of translation. These notes are primarily intended for specialists.

These notes, in total, are not intended to constitute a kind of critical edition; they are not comprehensive. The *Divyāvadāna* contains, for example, many abbreviated (and sometimes obscure) passages that occur in longer form in the *Mūlasarvāstivāda-vinaya*. I note only some of these.[7] Sometimes the text also plays a bit loose with classical Sanskrit grammar and syntax. I note these issues only when particularly egregious or relevant.

In terms of style, I try to translate prose as prose and verse as verse, and I offset certain stereotypical passages for ease of reading. I do not translate proper names and place names, although the first time they occur in each story I include a translation in parentheses (if a translation is helpful or possible). Some of these names are found in the glossary, but not place names or the names of the heavens and hells. The former, when identifiable, are included in the "Map of Indian Places in the *Divyāvadāna*." The latter are included in a table of the various realms of existence in the appendix.

Technical terms have been translated when possible, and when not, they have been left in the original Sanskrit and italicized. There are, however, some exceptions. Terms that have been adopted in vernacular English, such as *dharma*, *brahman*, and *saṃsāra*, have been left untranslated and unitalicized, as have terms that appear frequently and are part of the naturalized lexicon of the text, such as *arhat*, *bodhisattva*, and *tathāgata*. Conversely, some rather technical terms have been translated, such as *antigod* (for *asura*), *celestial musician* (for *gandharva*), and *great snake* (for *mahoraga*). Although all of these terms could be usefully glossed, I think the vernacular understanding of the former and the translations of the latter are sufficient for the reader to understand these stories in their complexity. These technical terms, whether translated or not, can be found in the glossary.

I have added subheadings within the stories to guide the reader. These interpolations, while not part of the text itself, nonetheless appear without brackets. As I noted in the introduction to *Divine Stories, Part 1*, these stories were meant to be recited orally; hence, I understand abbreviations such as "and so on as before" (*pūrvavat yāvat*) to be instructions to the reciter to fill in the requisite missing words. I therefore translate abbreviated passages in full. In my efforts to remain faithful to the voice of the text, I have also retained the repetitions and some of the idiosyncrasies of style in the Sanskrit text in my English translation.

In the Sanskrit, Pāli, and Tibetan passages in my notes, the use of [ ] brackets indicates a gap in the text that has been filled. The use of < > brackets indicates a restoration or reconstruction based on another source.

Abbreviations

Aśokāv	*Aśokāvadāna*. See Mukhopadhyaya 1963.
BHSD	*Buddhist Hybrid Sanskrit Dictionary*. See Edgerton 1993, vol. 2.
D	Derge edition of the Tibetan Tripiṭaka
Divy	*Divyāvadāna*. See Cowell and Neil 1886.
Divy-V	*Divyāvadāna*. See Vaidya 1959a.
DPPN	*Dictionary of Pāli Proper Names*. See Malalasekera 1995.
DS	*Divine Stories, Part 1*. See Rotman 2008.
GBM	*Gilgit Buddhist Manuscripts*. See Vira and Chandra 1995.
G1	GBM, folios 1474–83
G2	GBM, folios 1354–58
GM-Saṅgh	"The Final Leaves of the Pravrajyāvastu Portion of the Vinayavastu Manuscript Found near Gilgit: Part 1, Saṅgharakṣitāvadāna." See Vogel and Wille 1996.
GM-Nāga	"The Final Leaves of the Pravrajyāvastu Portion of the Vinayavastu Manuscript Found near Gilgit: Part 2, Nāgakumārāvadāna." See Vogel and Wille 2002.
HA	"Appendix A." See Hiraoka 2007: ii, 1–32.
HC	"Text Critical Remarks on the *Divyāvadāna* (1)." See Hiraoka 2009.
HD	"Text Critical Remarks on the *Divyāvadāna* (2)." See Hiraoka 2010.
ms.	manuscript

mss.	manuscripts
MSV	*Mūlasarvāstivāda-vinaya* (= *Gilgit Manuscripts*, vol. 3, parts 1–4). See Dutt 1984.
P	Peking edition of the Tibetan Tripiṭaka
PTSD	*The Pāli Text Society's Pāli-English Dictionary*. See Rhys Davids and Stede 1986.
Skt.	Sanskrit
SWTF	*Sanskrit-Wörterbuch der buddhistischen Texte aus den Turfan-Funden und der kanonischen Literatur der Sarvāstivāda-Schule*. See Waldschmidt et al. 1973–.
Tib.	Tibetan

Sanskrit Pronunciation

The vowels and consonants in Sanskrit listed below are pronounced much like the italicized letters in the English words that follow them. Note that an *h* after a consonant is not a separate letter. It signifies instead that the consonant it follows is to be aspirated. The Sanskrit letters are listed in Sanskrit alphabetical order.

Vowels

a	b*u*t
ā	f*a*ther
i	p*i*t
ī	s*ee*
u	f*oo*t
ū	dr*oo*l
ṛ	*ri*g
ṝ	no obvious English equivalent; lengthened *ṛ*
e	r*a*y
ai	h*i*gh

o   h*o*pe
au   r*ou*nd

Gutturals (pronounced by slightly raising the back of the tongue and closing off the throat)

k   *k*ick
kh   blo*ckh*ead
g   *g*o
gh   do*gh*ouse
ṅ   ri*n*g

Palatals (pronounced with the tongue lying on the bottom of the mouth)

c   *ch*ip
ch   mat*chh*ead
j   *j*ob
jh   he*dge*hog
ñ   i*n*jury

Retroflex (pronounced by curling the tip of the tongue to touch the roof of the mouth)

ṭ   *t*ry
ṭh   *t*art
ḍ   *d*rum
ḍh   no obvious English equivalent; strongly aspirated *ḍ*
ṇ   ti*n*t

Dentals (pronounced by placing the tip of the tongue against the back of the upper teeth)

t s*t*ick
th an*th*ill
d *d*inner
dh roun*dh*ouse
n *n*ice

Labials (pronounced with the lips together)

p s*p*in
ph u*ph*eaval
b *b*in
bh clu*bh*ouse
m *m*other

Semivowels, sibilants, and additional sounds

y *y*es
r d*r*ama
l *l*ife
v a sound between English *v* and *w* (e.g., between *v*ine and *w*ine)
ś *sh*ip
ṣ retroflex *ś*
s *s*ip
h *h*ope
ṃ *anusvāra:* nasalizes the preceding vowel
ḥ *visarga:* an aspiration with an echoing of the preceding vowel (e.g., *devaḥ* as *devaha*)

A Summary of the Stories

18. The Story of Dharmaruci
Dharmaruci-avadāna
A huge sea creature named Timiṅgila is about to devour a boatload of merchants when he hears an invocation of the Buddha's name and vows to refrain from eating. After his death, he is reborn in a brahman family and given the name Dharmaruci. Perpetually hungry, he eventually goes forth as a monk, whereby his hunger is finally satisfied and he attains arhatship. At the monks' request, the Buddha recounts how he and Dharmaruci had previously met three times—long ago during the respective eras of Kṣemaṅkara Buddha, Dīpaṅkara Buddha, and Krakucchanda Buddha.

19. The Story of Jyotiṣka
Jyotiṣka-avadāna
A householder questions the Buddha about his pregnant wife, and the Buddha foretells that she will give birth to a boy who will become a Buddhist monk and arhat. An evil Nirgrantha overhears this prediction and, to spite the Buddha, convinces the householder that his future son will bring him to ruin. Frightened, the householder kills his wife. During her cremation, a lotus arises from her stomach, and perched upon it is a boy, who is given the name Jyotiṣka and raised by

King Bimbisāra. Jyotiṣka goes on to achieve great wealth, which he then renounces, becoming a Buddhist monk and arhat. Questioned by the monks, the Buddha recounts Jyotiṣka's past life during the time of Vipaśyin Buddha.

20. The Story of Kanakavarṇa
Kanakavarṇa-avadāna
King Kanakavarṇa rules all of Jambudvīpa, and it thrives until it is beset by a drought destined to last twelve years. The king has all the food in the kingdom collected and then distributed to the people, gradually and equally, but during the twelfth year the food runs out. Many people die. A solitary buddha arises and arrives before the king, asking for alms. Only a single serving of food remains in the kingdom; the king offers it to him nonetheless. As a result of that deed, rains of goodness fall upon the kingdom, illustrating the importance of charity.

21. The Story of Sahasodgata
Sahasodgata-avadāna
A boy visits a monastery and sees a wheel of existence in the entrance hall. A monk explains to him the actions that lead to the various realms of existence, and the boy decides to feed the monastic community so he will be reborn among the gods. He gets a job as a day laborer, manages to feed the monastic community and please a group of merchants, and because of his merit is appointed guildmaster. He again feeds the monastics and, instructed by the Buddha, has a vision of truth. The Buddha then recounts the boy's interactions in a previous lifetime with a solitary buddha that led to his present success.

22. The Story of the Deeds of the Bodhisattva Candraprabha
Candraprabhabodhisattvacaryā-avadāna
King Candraprabha rules an enormous and prosperous kingdom, and he gives away so much that everyone in Jambudvīpa comes to possess

treasures and look like kings themselves. His ministers begin to have nightmares about the king's demise, and bad omens abound. Hearing that the king has vowed to give away everything, a brahman comes before the king and asks for his most prized possession: his head. The king is pleased; everyone else, aghast. To attain perfect awakening, the king then gives his head to the brahman. Witnessing his demise, many beings die and achieve a divine rebirth.

23. The Story of Saṅgharakṣita, part 1
Saṅgharakṣita-avadāna
Stories 23–25 constitute a cycle about the monk Saṅgharakṣita. While he is the resident dharma teacher on an overseas voyage with five hundred merchants, his boat is seized by nāgas, who implore him to come to their watery realm and teach the four Āgamas. Teach them he does, and then he returns to the ship, which soon arrives ashore. Saṅgharakṣita then encounters various hell-beings suffering for the misdeeds they committed as monastic disciples of the Buddha Kāśyapa. Then he encounters five hundred seers, whom he converts, and the five hundred merchants from before, all of whom he brings to the Buddha for ordination.

24. The Story of a Young Nāga
Nāgakumāra-avadāna
The monks question the Buddha about a young nāga, and he tells them how, in a previous lifetime, a nāga eventually became a monk under the Buddha Kāśyapa and attained arhatship. Thereby able to remember his past lives, he then goes to the nāga realm to visit his former parents, who are still mourning his death. At their request, he returns each day to consume a meal of divine ambrosia that they serve him. One day his novice attendant surreptitiously accompanies him and then becomes angry when he is served ordinary food instead of divine ambrosia. He curses the nāgas and vows to be reborn there.

25. The Story of Saṅgharakṣita, part 2
Saṅgharakṣita-avadāna
The Buddha tells how Saṅgharakṣita also became a monk under the Buddha Kāśyapa but never attained spiritual distinction. On his deathbed, he makes a fervent aspiration to be reborn during the time of the Buddha Śākyamuni, to become a monk in his order, and to attain arhatship. His students and the citizens of his town make the same aspiration. The Buddha then reveals the present identities of those characters from the past.

31. The Story of Five Hundred Farmers
Pañcakārṣakaśata-avadāna
The Buddha magically transforms a brahman's offering of rice gruel such that it can feed the entire community, and the brahman becomes a stream-enterer. The Buddha then teaches and initiates five hundred farmers, who become arhats, and also teaches their cattle, who see the truth. The Buddha then travels to Toyikā and there, sitting upon the spot where the Buddha Kāśyapa lies buried, creates a site that is doubly venerable. Pilgrims venerate the shrine, and the Buddha explains the value of their offerings. A festival known as the Toyikāmaha is established there.

32. The Story of Rūpāvatī
Rūpāvatī-avadāna
The Buddha offers a discourse on charity and then tells the story of Rūpāvatī. Seeing a starving mother about to eat her newborn child, Rūpāvatī cuts off her own breasts and feeds them to the mother to satisfy her hunger. She then performs two vows of truth, one that restores her breasts and a second that transforms her into a man—Rūpāvata. The Buddha then recounts Rūpāvata's next two births: first as Candraprabha, who offers his eyes and body to a flock of birds, and then Brahmaprabha, who feeds himself to a starving tigress.

34. The Mahāyāna Sūtra on the Topic of Giving
Dānādhikaraṇa-mahāyānasūtra
This sūtra enumerates thirty-seven gifts that a wise person may offer and the results that they generate.

35. The Story of a Lonesome Fool
Cūḍāpakṣa-avadāna
Two brothers, Panthaka and Mahāpanthaka, become Buddhist monks, and while the latter flourishes, the former is disparaged as an idiot, unable to memorize even a single verse in three months. Pondering a single couplet, however, Panthaka attains arhatship and surpasses his seemingly wiser brother. The Buddha then recounts deeds from three of Panthaka's past lives that led to his present situation. Jīvaka Kumārabhūta then disrespects Panthaka, which leads the Buddha to tell a story about a thoroughbred horse and a potter, who turn out to be Panthaka and Jīvaka in past lives.

36. The Story of Mākandika
Mākandika-avadāna
Mākandika tries to marry his beautiful daughter Anupamā to the Buddha. The Buddha refuses her, and a lecherous old monk tries in vain to gain her hand. Then the Buddha tells two past-life stories about Anupamā and the old man. Anupamā then marries King Udayana and, jealous of her virtuous co-wife Śyāmāvatī, convinces her father Mākandika to arrange for Śyāmāvatī's death while the king is away quelling a rebellion. The Buddha tells various past-life stories about Anupamā, Śyāmāvatī, and others involved to explain what led to the present circumstances.

37. The Story of Rudrāyaṇa
Rudrāyaṇa-avadāna
Two kings, Bimbisāra and Rudrāyaṇa, exchange precious gifts, culminating with a gift of an image of the Buddha to Rudrāyaṇa, which

leads him onto the Buddhist path. He becomes a monk, and his son Śikhaṇḍin takes the throne. The latter, under the influence of evil ministers, rules unjustly and oppresses the people. Rudrāyaṇa, now a monk, comes to intercede, and just as he attains arhatship is killed by assassins sent by his son. King Śikhaṇḍin then has the noble Mahākātyāyana buried alive, which leads to his entire capital being buried under a rain of dirt. The noble Mahākātyāyana nonetheless survives and continues to propagate the dharma. The Buddha then tells past-life stories about Rudrāyaṇa, Śikhaṇḍin, and others involved to explain what led to the current events.

The Divyāvadāna

(STORIES 18–25, 31–32, 34–37)

18. The Story of Dharmaruci

DHARMARUCI-AVADĀNA[8]

Five Hundred Merchants and a Sea Monster

THUS have I heard. At one time the Blessed One was staying in the city of Śrāvastī at the Jeta Grove in the park of Anāthapiṇḍada (Almsgiver to the Poor).

At that time five hundred merchants gathered up their goods, and after passing through marketplaces, villages, towns, trading centers, and capitals, one after another, arrived at the shore of the great ocean. There they carefully chose an ocean-going ship, [229] but when the merchants saw the great ocean, they were of two minds. They couldn't bring themselves to go down to the water.

"Friend," the merchants said to the captain, "proclaim for us the true glory of the great ocean!"[9]

"Listen, honorable men of Jambudvīpa (Black Plum Island)!" the captain proclaimed. "In the great ocean there are treasures such as these—jewels, pearls, beryl, and conch, quartz, coral, silver, and gold, emeralds, sapphires, red pearls, and right-spiraling conch shells. Whoever wants to make himself happy with such treasures, and to delight his mother, father, wife, and children, servants, maids, workers, and laborers, friends, counselors, kinsmen, and relatives, and whoever wants, from time to time, to present to those worthy of offerings—ascetics and brahmans—gifts that guide one upward, bring good fortune, result in pleasure, and lead to heaven in the future, he should set sail in this great ocean to find that wealth."

Since all beings, without exception, desire wealth and spurn poverty, everyone who heard him decided to set sail in the great ocean. As a result, the ship was overcome by all those people and the heavy load. It began to sink on the spot.

"The ship can't take it!" the captain said.

"So whom should we tell to disembark?" the merchants asked.

Then those merchants said to the captain, "Proclaim for us the true infamy of the great ocean!"[10]

"Listen, honorable men of Jambudvīpa!" he proclaimed again. "In the great ocean there are also great, great dangers—the danger of sea monsters like the Timi and the Timiṅgila, the danger of waves, the danger of turtles, the danger of going aground, the danger of sinking, the danger of running into reefs, and the danger of hurricanes. Dark-clothed pirates may also come and steal your riches. Whoever is prepared[11] to give up his very life and to give up his mother, father, wife, and children, servants, maids, workers, and laborers, friends, counselors, kinsmen, and relatives, as well as wonderful Jambudvīpa, he should set sail in the great ocean."

Few men are brave. Many are cowards. [230]

Hearing this, those who had clambered on board expressed their agreement—"So be it, so be it"—and then most of them disembarked from the ship. Only a small number remained. Thereafter the merchants cut one of the ship's ropes, then a second and a third and so on, until all the ropes were cut. Once the ropes were cut, the great captain launched the ship, and urged on by powerful winds, it sailed off quickly, like a cloud in the sky blown by a cylone. It soon arrived in Ratnadvīpa (Treasure Island).

When they arrived there, the captain said to the merchants, "There are glass jewels just like diamonds here in Ratnadvīpa. You should examine them carefully, one by one, as you collect them. Let's not have any regrets after you've returned to Jambudvīpa. And here there are also females called *krońca* maidens. If they come across a man, they'll attack him with stones, and he'll straightaway meet with his death.[12] There are also intoxicating fruits here. Whoever eats them stays asleep for seven days and nights. And here in Ratnadvīpa, nonhumans don't put up with men after seven days. They'll stir up headwinds that will carry off a ship, even if one's work isn't finished. If you find any of these fruits, don't eat them!"

After listening to this, the merchants remained mindful and on their guard. When they arrived at Ratnadvīpa, they diligently looked for treasures, examining one after another, and they filled their ship with these treasures as one would with barley or barleycorn, mung beans or black gram. Once they'd filled the ship, they departed with favorable[13] winds leading them back to Jambudvīpa.

Now in the great ocean, creatures are dispersed across the three water levels. In the first level, creatures have bodies one hundred leagues long, though sometimes their bodies are two or three hundred leagues long.[14] In the second level, they have bodies eight hundred leagues long, though sometimes their bodies are nine, ten, or up to fourteen hundred leagues long. In the third level, they have bodies fifteen hundred leagues long, though sometimes their bodies are sixteen hundred leagues long, or even up to twenty-one hundred leagues long.

And in the great ocean, these species of animals are intent on devouring each other. Those who live in the first level are eaten by those in the second level, and those who live in the second level are eaten by those in the third level. Now it was for this reason that the sea creature Timiṅgila arose from the third water level, [231] brought himself to the uppermost water level,[15] and began to roam about. Then he opened his jaws, and in that moment water from the great ocean was sucked into his mouth with great speed. Pulled by that mass of water, a great variety of sea creatures such as fish, tortoises, *vallabhaka*s, crocodiles, and *makara* monsters flowed down through his mouth and into his belly. As Timiṅgila was doing this, his head from far away appeared to be separate from the rest of his body, like a mountain touching the sky. And his eyes from far away looked like two suns in the sky.[16]

The merchants reflected on this from far away, and as they reflected on the form of the great churning ocean, they began to think, "Friends, what is this? The rising of two suns?" As they were occupied with such thoughts, their ship began to be swept toward Timiṅgila's mouth. Watching their ship[17] being swept away and reflecting on the two suns that had arisen, they were panicked. "Friends," they said to each other, "have you heard it said that seven suns will rise up at the destruction of an age? Well, now it seems that they have arisen."

Then the captain spoke to the men, engaged as they were in such thoughts: "Friends, you have heard of the sea monster Timitimiṅgila. Well, *this* is the danger of Timitimiṅgila. Friends, look at that! What appears like a mountain rising from the water is his head. And look! Those dark ruby-red streaks are his lips. And see there! That dazzling white strip is a row of his teeth. And look at those two things that appear like suns from far away! Those are the pupils of his eyes."

Again the captain addressed the merchants. "Listen, my friends! There is no way now that we can save ourselves, no way to be free from this danger.[18] Death stands before us all. So what should you do now? Each of you should pray to the god in whom you have faith. Perhaps by these prayers some deity will free us from this great danger. There is no other means of survival."

Those merchants, afraid as they were of dying, [232] began praying to gods such as Śiva, Varuṇa, Kubera, the great Indra, and Upendra to save their lives. Despite their prayers, nothing happened to save them from the mortal danger they faced. Just as before, their ship was being pulled by the current and carried off toward the mouth of the Timiṅgila monster.

There was, however, a lay disciple of the Buddha on board. He said, "Friends, there is no escape for us from this mortal danger. Every single one of us will die. Still, let all of us raise our voices together and say, 'Praise to the Buddha!' If we have to face death, let us die with our awareness focused on the Buddha. This way there will be a good fate for us after death."

Then every single one of the merchants, with their hands respectfully folded, raised their voices together and said, "Praise to the Buddha!"

Now the Blessed One, who was staying in the Jeta Grove, heard those words with his divine hearing, which is faultless and superhuman. And upon hearing them, the Blessed One exercised his power so that the Timiṅgila monster could hear that outcry. When Timiṅgila heard that cry "Praise to the Buddha!" an unease arose in his mind, and he became worried: "Oh no! A buddha has arisen in the world. It wouldn't be right for me to eat any food after hearing an invocation of the Lord Buddha's name." Then he began to think, "If I close my mouth suddenly, this ship will be driven back by the swell and destroyed. Many people will lose their lives. I should close my mouth gently and ever so slowly." Then the Timiṅgila monster closed his mouth gently and ever so slowly.

Freed from the jaws of that great monster, the merchants' ship found a favorable wind and soon arrived at shore. When the merchants came to shore, they loaded their goods on carts, camels, bulls, donkeys, and so on, and after passing through marketplaces, villages, towns, and trading centers, one after another, they arrived in Śrāvastī. Once there, they reflected, "It's only proper that if a ship successfully completes its voyage because of the power of someone's name, all its treasures should go to him. We really should give these treasures to the Lord Buddha."

Then they collected those treasures and went before the Blessed One. Having each, in turn, placed their heads in veneration at the Blessed One's feet, they said to him: "Blessed One, we set sail on the ocean in a ship, and then when our ship was being carried off by the Timiṅgila monster [233] and the end of our lives was before us, we spoke the name of the Blessed One, concentrating our awareness on him, and were thus freed from the jaws of that great monster. Now that we have successfully completed our voyage, Blessed One, we have come here, safe and sound. It's only proper that if people successfully complete a voyage on a ship[19] because of the power of someone's name, the treasures of that ship should go to him. By speaking the name of the Blessed One, we escaped from that mortal danger. Therefore the Blessed One should take these treasures of ours."

The Blessed One said, "I have obtained the treasures of the [five] spiritual faculties, their corresponding powers, and the [seven] factors of awakening. What can ordinary gems do for the Tathāgata beyond this? My sons, if you want to go forth as monks in my order, come with me."

The merchants reflected, "Whatever life we have is completely due to the power of the Lord Buddha. Let us abandon these treasures and go forth as monks under[20] the Blessed One."

Then they distributed their treasures, according to custom, to their mothers, fathers, wives, and children, servants, maids, and workers, friends, counselors, kinsmen, and relatives, and went forth as monks. After going forth as monks, they strived, struggled, and strained until they directly experienced arhatship.

Some monks in doubt asked the Lord Buddha, the remover of all doubts, "Blessed One, what deeds did those merchants perform and accumulate that resulted in them pleasing and not displeasing the Blessed One?"

"Long ago, monks," the Blessed One said, "the perfectly awakened Kāśyapa arose in the world, and those very merchants went forth as monks into his order. After going forth as monks into his order, they didn't amass any particular collection of virtues[21] that was different from what those who had followed the religious life with them—and who had learned, studied, and recited the teachings—had come to possess. At the time of their death, they made this fervent aspiration: 'Although we have come to the perfectly awakened Kāśyapa, and we have learned, studied, and recited the teachings, we still haven't amassed any great collection of virtues. Still, as a result of those actions, may we please and not displease the one whom the perfectly awakened

Kāśyapa has foretold will be a perfectly awakened buddha in the future, the one named Śākyamuni.'"

"What do you think, monks?" the Blessed One said. [234] "Those five hundred monks who in the past went forth as monks into the order of the perfectly awakened Kāśyapa were none other than[22] these five hundred monks. Their senses have finally matured, and now they have directly experienced arhatship."

Dharmaruci and His Insatiable Appetite

Now in the great ocean, once the sea monster named Timitimiṅgila heard the word *buddha*, he resolved not to take any food. Unable to endure the hunger pains that occurred because of his naturally inflamed digestive fire, he died and passed away. He then took rebirth in Śrāvastī in a brahman family that was devoted to the six duties of a brahman. That former body of his, now a corpse, floated along in the great ocean. The nāgas were unable to bear the smell of this corpse near their homes, so they cast it off to another place. Near where it was cast, however, was the home of another nāga. He too couldn't bear the smell, so he cast it off as well. Cast off again and again in this way, that corpse was gradually brought close to the great ocean's shore. Then it was immediately cast out by the tide and thrown onto the waterfront. The decomposed flesh on that mass of bones was consumed by many, like crows, vultures, dogs, jackals, tigers, and birds, and even by worms that were produced from it, until the bones of the corpse lay there stripped white.

Back in Śrāvastī,[23] as soon as that brahman's wife became pregnant,[24] she was afflicted with severe hunger pains from the formation of the fetus. She said to her husband, "Dear husband, I'm suffering from terrible hunger pains."

Since she spoke to him like this, her husband said, "My dear, whatever there is to eat and drink in our home is all yours to consume."

Then she began to indulge herself. She consumed all that there was to eat and drink, but she still wasn't satisfied. Once again, she asked her husband for help: "Dear husband, I'm still not satisfied."

He asked his neighbors, friends, family, and others for food and drink and then gave whatever he got to her. She consumed all this as well,[25] but she still wasn't satisfied. Once again, she said to her husband, "Dear husband, I'm still not satisfied."

Then the brahman, already disturbed, began to worry.

"Friends," he said, "what could this be? A being has come to life in her womb, and as a result of its formation, she is never satisfied."

Then the brahman had sign readers look at her, and to remove any doubts, he also spoke to physicians and others, and to those learned in the mysteries of the spirits. [235] "Look, gentlemen," he said. "Could it be that my wife is consumed by a serious illness? Or maybe she is possessed by spirits or demons? Or maybe it's some other kind of illness that's fatal? Should some treatment be given?"

Hearing this, they treated her accordingly, but they didn't observe any change in the brahman woman's senses or faculties.[26] When they didn't observe any change in the brahman woman's senses or faculties, the doctors, sign readers, physicians, and those learned in the mysteries of the spirits questioned her.

"When did the fire of your digestion start to blaze like this?"

"This condition of mine developed when the fetus first formed."[27]

"There isn't any known illness of the kind that she has," the sign readers, doctors, and physicians said, "nor is there any kind of affliction like this that arises because one is possessed by spirits or demons.[28] An inflamed digestive fire such as hers is due to the influence of the fetus."

When the brahman received this news, he was relieved, but still the brahman's wife was never satisfied from what she ate or drank.

Eventually, in due time, a son was born. As soon as that boy was born, the brahman woman's hunger pains subsided. But from the moment he was born, the boy himself was pained by intense hunger.

Since he was pained by hunger, his mother began to breastfeed him. Even after the boy drank every drop of milk from her breasts, he still wasn't satisfied. The brahman and his wife requested help from the young women among their neighbors and relatives,[29] and then they too began to breastfeed the boy. The boy drank from the breasts of all those women as well, but he still wasn't satisfied. Then the brahman got a goat for him. The boy drank the goat's milk in addition to the milk from his mother's breasts, but he still wasn't satisfied.

From time to time monks and nuns would enter that house for alms and tell a roundabout story. The boy would listen to that roundabout story, and at that time he wouldn't cry. He'd listen attentively and silently to their stories about listening to the dharma.[30] When the monks and nuns would depart, he would again experience the suffering of thirst and begin to cry.[31] [236]

"This child relishes the dharma," his parents reflected. And so they gave him the name Dharmaruci (Relishes the Dharma).[32]

Gradually, after months and fortnights passed, the boy began to take solid food, but he still never got his fill of food and drink. Finally, when the boy reached the right age, his mother and father gave him a begging bowl. "Go, my son," they said. "This is your begging bowl. Take it, wander through Śrāvastī for alms, and eat whatever food you get."[33] The boy took the begging bowl and went wandering through Śrāvastī for alms. Wandering on and on, and eating and eating, he still came home unsatisfied.

"What deed have I done," he reflected, "that's resulted in my never being satisfied with the food I get?" Feeling distraught, he began to think, "Should I throw myself in a fire, drown myself, or jump off a cliff?" He stood there with such thoughts in mind.

A lay disciple of the Buddha saw him and said, "Why do you stand there like that, lost in thought? Go! Great is the order of the Buddha, full of magic and power. You should go forth as a monk into it. Once you've done so, you'll accumulate good qualities, and any bad qualities that you may have accumulated in this life will diminish. If you go on to amass a great collection of virtues, the course of your existence in saṃsāra will be brought to an end."

Urged on by the lay disciple, that great being went to the Jeta Grove. Having gone to the Jeta Grove, he saw monks there diligently engaged in reading, recitation, and concentration, and he became filled with intense faith.

He approached a monk and said, "Noble one, I want to go forth as a monk."

"Have you received permission from your parents?" some monks asked him.

"No," he said. "I haven't received permission from my parents."

"Go, my son," they said. "Seek your parents' permission."

So he set out to seek permission from his parents. His parents told him, "Go, son. Do as you wish."

Having obtained their permission, he went back to the monks. Thereafter one of the monks initiated him.

Now in the monastery, sometimes there was almsfood for the monks, and sometimes there was an invitation to eat at someone's home. On one particular day when there was almsfood, his instructor said to him, "Son, are you satisfied or not?"

"No, I'm not satisfied," he said to his instructor. [237]

Then the instructor made this observation[34] about him: "Dharmaruci went forth as a monk while still of a young age. His digestive fire is inflamed, so he's never satisfied." The instructor then began to share with him the food from his own bowl.

"My son," he asked again, "are you satisfied now?"

"No, I'm still not satisfied," he said to the instructor.

After the instructor heard this, he began to speak with some kind-hearted monks and some other students also living in the monastery. Those monks who had the same instructor as Dharmaruci, those who had the same teacher, and others who were kindhearted began to make special provisions of food and drink for him. But even after receiving those provisions from them, he still wasn't satisfied. When there was an invitation for a meal, they would make provisions for him in just the same way. A particular donor also knew about Dharmaruci's condition. He would come and give Dharmaruci whatever extra food he had. And if there was anything extra to drink, he'd do likewise. Anything extra at all was given to him. Nevertheless, from the time Dharmaruci had gone forth as a monk, his stomach had not once been full with food and drink.

One time a householder invited the community of monks led by the Buddha for a meal. In the morning the Blessed One got dressed, took his bowl and robe, and along with the community of monks, went to the man's home to eat. [In the interim,] Dharmaruci was appointed as the acting caretaker of the monastery.

At that time in Śrāvastī there lived a certain householder. He came to understand that whoever feeds the community of monks led by the Buddha, without informing them beforehand, will immediately prosper. And so he collected food for five hundred monks. He filled up a cart with this fresh and exceptionally fine food and went to the monastery at the Jeta Grove. "Assisted by my friends and family," he thought, "and on behalf of all my family members,[35] I will feed the community of monks led by the Buddha." In the Jeta Grove, he saw that there weren't any monks. Wandering about, he saw the acting caretaker Dharmaruci.

"Noble one," the householder asked him, "where have the monks gone?"

"They were invited for a meal and have gone to someone's home to eat," he said.

When the householder heard this, he became upset. "Oh no! My efforts are in vain!" He thought about this and then said to Dharmaruci, "Noble one, at least you can eat."

"If, gracious sir, you have any food to spare," he said.

Then the householder reflected on how much food was enough for one monk, [238] took that much food and drink from the cart, and began to serve it to Dharmaruci. Dharmaruci ate until there was nothing left, but he still wasn't satisfied.

"He isn't satisfied," the householder reflected. So he said, "Noble one, will you eat some more?"

"If, gracious sir, you have any food to spare," Dharmaruci said.

Then, once again, the householder took food and drink from the cart, this time what should have been enough food for two monks, and began to feed him. Dharmaruci ate this as well, but he still wasn't satisfied.

"He still isn't satisfied," the householder reflected once again. So he said, "Noble one, will you eat some more?"

"If, gracious sir, you have any food to spare," Dharmaruci said.

The householder took food and drink from his cart and, thinking, "This should be enough for three monks," began to serve him again. Dharmaruci ate this as well, but he still wasn't satisfied.

"Noble one, will you eat some more?" he asked.

"If you have any food to spare," Dharmaruci said.

The householder then took food and drink from his cart and, thinking, "This should be enough for four monks," began to serve him once again.

Dharmaruci ate this as well, but he still wasn't satisfied.

"Noble one, will you eat some more?" he asked.

"If you have any food to spare," he said once again.

Again he took food and drink from his cart, this time what should have been enough to satisfy five monks, and again he began to serve him. Dharmaruci consumed this as well, but he still wasn't satisfied. This happened again and again. Finally he consumed what should have been enough food and drink for ten monks, and yet he still wasn't satisfied.

Then the householder reflected, "This isn't a man. This isn't any kind of man at all! It's said that the Jeta Grove is filled with five hundred dark-clothed yakṣas.[36] This must be one of them!" With this in mind, he began to send home his young family: "Go right home, quickly! I'll deal with this myself, whether I live or die." After he sent off his family, the householder, afraid as he was to die, took more food and drink from his cart and began to serve Dharmaruci. Dharmaruci ate as much as he liked.

The householder said, "Noble one, quickly—accept this food."

So Dharmaruci immediately accepted the food and began to eat. [239] The householder served him faster and faster, giving him all that there was to eat and drink from his cart. Then, so seized was he with terror, that without even waiting to hear the assignment of the reward from the offering, he said, "Noble one, I praise you!" and then set out for the city as fast as he could, never looking back.

A monk whose task it was to bring almsfood from the city returned with alms he had brought specially for Dharmaruci. Dharmaruci ate that food as well. Since birth, Dharmaruci's stomach had never been full. And yet, on this day, that food satisfied him.

Meanwhile the Blessed One, surrounded by the community of monks, came face to face with that householder as he was entering the city. The householder said to the Blessed One, "Blessed One, for the sake of the community of monks led by the Buddha, I filled up my cart with enough food and drink to satisfy five hundred monks. Then I went to the Jeta Grove with the intention of feeding the community of monks led by the Buddha. But I didn't find those monks there. Instead I saw only one monk. He explained to me that the community of monks led by the Buddha had been invited for a meal and had gone off to eat at someone's home. This thought occurred to me: 'At least this one monk may eat.' Then, by and by, I gave him all the food and drink from my cart. He consumed every single bit of it. Blessed One, was he a human being or not?"

"Householder," the Blessed One said, "he is a monk named Dharmaruci. You should be pleased. From your food and drink, he is now satisfied, and soon he will directly experience arhatship."

When the Blessed One returned to the Jeta Grove, he reflected, "What donor could ever support Dharmaruci with this much food every day?"

Therefore the Blessed One said to Dharmaruci, "Dharmaruci, have you seen the great ocean?"

"No, Blessed One, I haven't," he said.

"Take hold of the edge of my robe," the Blessed One said. "I will show you the great ocean."

Dharmaruci grabbed hold of the edge of the Buddha's robe. Then, like a royal goose with outstretched wings, the Blessed One made use of his magical powers, and in the space of a single thought, he arrived at the seashore with Dharmaruci in tow. The Blessed One brought Dharmaruci to that place where the skeleton of what had been the sea monster Timitimiṅgila still remained and set him down. [240]

Then he said to him, "Go, my son. Concentrate on this object."

Dharmaruci began to look it over. "What is this," he thought, "a piece of driftwood or a mass of bones?[37] Or is it a plank of wood?" Not getting a clear sense of its size, he began to look for its endpoints. But he just couldn't grasp its size.[38] And while trying to determine its size, moving here and there and on both sides of the thing, he became exhausted. He couldn't find an end to it.

It occurred to him: "I'm not about to understand what it was that was this big by asking myself, 'What is this?' Nor will I reach its end. I'll go and ask the Blessed One himself about it." Then he went before the Blessed One and asked him, "Blessed One, what is this? I can't figure out what it was that was this big."

"My son," the Blessed One said to him, "this is a skeleton."

"Blessed One," he asked, "is there such a being with a skeleton like this?"

Then the Blessed One said, "Rejoice, Dharmaruci, in the different states of existence! Rejoice in the means that lead to these states of existence![39] This is your skeleton."

When Dharmaruci heard these words of the Blessed One, he was perplexed and said, "A skeleton like this is mine?"

"Dharmaruci," he said to him, "this is your skeleton."

Hearing this, Dharmaruci was shocked.[40]

Then the Blessed One gave him these instructions: "Dharmaruci, concentrate on this and this alone."

With that said, the Blessed One, like a royal goose with outstretched wings, made use of his magical powers and arrived back at the Jeta Grove.

Then Dharmaruci, thinking and practicing concentration, passed through [the four stages of the path of application]—the heat stage, the summit stage, and the tolerance stage, followed by the highest worldly dharma stage—and then through the path of seeing and the path of cultivation. He obtained the reward of the stream-enterer, then the reward of the once-returner, followed by the reward of the nonreturner, and finally he obtained arhatship. Becoming an arhat,[41]

> he was free from attachment in the three realms;
> he regarded clods of earth and gold as equal in value;
> he possessed equanimity toward the sky
> and the palm of his hand;
> he cast off passion and repugnance;
> the eggshell [of his ignorance] was broken by knowledge;[42]
> he obtained the special knowledges, superhuman faculties,
> and analytic insights;
> he was averse to worldly attainments, temptations, and honors;
> and he didn't distinguish between being cut by a blade
> and being anointed with sandalwood paste.
> He became worthy of respect, honor, and obeisance
> from the gods, including Indra and Upendra.

He began to focus his attention on his previous lives—"From where did I die and pass away? Where was I reborn?" He saw many hundreds of his lives. He had died and passed away from the realms of hell, the animal realm, and the realm of hungry ghosts and been reborn once again. It occurred to him, "If the Blessed One hadn't turned his attention to me, [241] I'd still have more lives to pass through in the future." Then he reflected on what would have been the continuous flow of his life in the future, a constant, uninterrupted cycle of rebirths in hell realms and the realm of hungry ghosts. Having reflected in this way, he thought, "Oh! The Blessed One has done for me something that is very difficult to do. If the Blessed One had achieved unsurpassed perfect awakening just for my sake, it would have been a very great deed. Yet he has led many thousands of beings away from rebirth in the terrible realms of existence!" Then, making use of his magical powers, Dharmaruci arrived at the Jeta Grove to see the Blessed One.

At that time the Blessed One was sitting down in front of an assembly of many hundreds of monks and discoursing on the dharma. Meanwhile Dharmaruci approached the Blessed One. Having approached, he placed his head in veneration at the Blessed One's feet and then sat down at a respectful distance. Sitting down at a respectful distance, he was addressed by the Blessed One.

"It's been a long time [since we met], Dharmaruci."

"Yes, it's been a long time, Blessed One," Dharmaruci said.

"It's been a very long time, Dharmaruci," the Blessed One said.

"Yes, it's been a very long time, Blessed One," Dharmaruci said.

"It's been an incredibly long time, Dharmaruci," the Blessed One said.

"Yes, it's been an incredibly long time, Blessed One." Dharmaruci said.

Some monks in doubt asked the Lord Buddha, the remover of all doubts, "Blessed One, Dharmaruci was born right here in Śrāvastī, and in this very place, the Jeta Grove, he went forth as a monk. He didn't come from someplace else and never went anyplace else. And yet, while Dharmaruci was standing right here, the Blessed One said, 'It's been a long time [since we met], Dharmaruci. It's been a very long time,

Dharmaruci. It's been an incredibly long time, Dharmaruci.' What was the Blessed One talking about?"

In response, the Blessed One addressed the monks: "Monks, I wasn't talking about the present. I was talking about the past. What I said was about the past. Monks, do you want to hear a dharma story about the former karmic bonds of Dharmaruci?"

"Yes, Blessed One. It is the right time and the right occasion, Sugata, for the Blessed One to tell the monks a dharma story about Dharmaruci. Hearing such a story from the Blessed One, the monks will keep it in mind." [242]

Kṣemaṅkara Buddha, the Guildmaster, and the Powerful Fighter

Long ago, monks, in a time gone by, in the first incalculable age, there arose in the world a tathāgata named Kṣemaṅkara (Safety Maker),

> who was perfect in knowledge and conduct,
> a sugata,
> a knower of the world,
> an unsurpassed guide for those in need of training,
> a teacher of gods and humans,
> a buddha,
> and a blessed one.

He stayed near the capital called Kṣemāvatī (Safe Place). And in Kṣemāvatī there ruled a king named Kṣema (Safety). And in the capital Kṣemāvatī there also resided a certain guildmaster[43] of the merchants. He provided the perfectly awakened Kṣemaṅkara and the community of monks with all their necessities for sixty[44] rainy seasons.

The guildmaster reflected, "I will go to the great ocean. I'll gather up my goods, sell them in exchange for jewels, and arrange a quinquennial festival for the community." After thinking this over, he gathered up his goods, and after passing through marketplaces, villages, towns, trading centers, and capitals, one after another, arrived at the ocean. There he had bells rung to proclaim his intention and then set sail in the great ocean on an ocean-going ship.

As he set sail in the great ocean, the perfectly awakened Kṣemaṅkara, who had finished performing all the duties of a buddha, passed into the realm of remainderless nirvāṇa. After he had passed into final nirvāṇa, those monks who were in complete control of themselves also passed into final nirvāṇa. Seven days after the perfectly awakened Kṣemaṅkara passed into final nirvāṇa, his doctrine disappeared.

Now that guildmaster, after successfully completing his voyage, which had been favored by deities and spirits, returned from the great ocean. Having come ashore, he loaded up his goods on carts, camels, cows, and donkeys and in due course set off. Going along the road, he asked some people coming in the opposite direction, "Friends, do you know what's happening in the capital Kṣemāvatī?"

"Yes, we know," they said.

"Is the perfectly awakened buddha named Kṣemaṅkara there?" he asked.

"The Blessed One, the perfectly awakened Kṣemaṅkara, has passed into final nirvāṇa," they said.

When he heard this, the guildmaster was grief-stricken. He fainted and fell to the ground. Splashed with water, he regained his senses and was revived.[45] Then he got up and asked, "Friends, do you know if at least the disciples of the Blessed One are still there?"

"Those monks were also in complete control of themselves," they said. "They too passed into final nirvāṇa. Seven days after the Lord Buddha Kṣemaṅkara passed into final nirvāṇa,[46] [243] his doctrine disappeared. Then King Kṣema had a simple shrine constructed for the perfectly awakened Kṣemaṅkara."[47]

The guildmaster then went to the capital and asked some people, "Friends, has any stūpa been constructed for the Lord Buddha?"

"Yes," they said. "King Kṣema had a simple shrine constructed for him."

Then it occurred to the guildmaster, "I brought this gold for the perfectly awakened Kṣemaṅkara, but he has passed into final nirvāṇa. I really should use this gold to renovate the Blessed One's shrine so that it's even more special." With this thought in mind, he informed King Kṣema, "Your majesty, I brought this gold for the perfectly awakened Kṣemaṅkara, but the Blessed One has passed into final nirvāṇa. Now, your majesty, if you permit, I will use this gold to renovate the Blessed One's shrine so that it is even more special."

"Do as you wish," the king said.

Then all the brahmans who lived in the city came together and approached the great guildmaster. "Great guildmaster," they said, "before Kṣemaṅkara Buddha had arisen in the world, we alone were worthy of people's offerings. But after he arose, he became the one worthy of offerings. Now that he has passed into final nirvāṇa, we are the only ones worthy of offerings. This gold belongs to us."

"No," he said to them, "I won't give this gold to you."

"If you don't give it to us," they said, "we won't cooperate with you."

There were many brahmans; the guildmaster, on the other hand, had few supporters. Since they were so resistant, he wasn't able to use the gold and renovate the shrine as he wished.

The guildmaster then went before the king and said, "Your majesty, I haven't succeeded as I intended in renovating the shrine because of some brahmans."

The king gave him one of his own men—a powerful fighter who was capable of battling a thousand men. The king ordered his man as follows: "If anyone harasses the great guildmaster while he is renovating the stūpa, you should punish that person severely."

"Yes, my lord," the powerful fighter replied, consenting to the king's request, and then he departed. Having departed, he spoke to those brahmans as follows: [244] "Listen, gentlemen. I am one of the king's men, and he has given me to the great guildmaster with the following orders—'If anyone prevents the great guildmaster from renovating the stūpa, you should punish that person severely.' So if you make any trouble here, I will punish you severely."

Hearing such words from the man who was a powerful fighter, those brahmans were afraid.

Now the great guildmaster, thinking that the gold should be placed in the inner chamber of the stūpa,[48] began to build four stairways, one at each of the four sides of the stūpa, [leading to the level] where the upper circumambulatory terrace would surround the stūpa's dome.[49] And so, in succession, a first terrace was built, and this was followed by a second and a third terrace, until they reached the domed top. Accordingly, a larger domed top was then built, and into it was placed a shaft for a central post.[50] Then above this brand-new dome,[51] a top enclosure was built. Following this, the central post was erected. And then precious jewels and treasures were mounted on the stūpa's rain receptacle.

While this was being done, it occurred to the powerful fighter, "Now no one will attack this place." Then, confidently, he went out into the countryside on some business.

Meanwhile the great guildmaster constructed four gateways on the four sides of the stūpa, and on those four sides he built four great shrines, marking the Blessed One's birth, perfect awakening, setting in motion the wheel of dharma, and final nirvāṇa. The courtyard of the stūpa was also covered with slabs of stone inlaid with jewels, and four adjacent compounds were constructed in the four directions. Also in the four directions, along the sides of the stūpa, lotus pools were constructed, and in them were planted various aquatic flowers, such as blue, red, and white waterlilies, white lotuses,[52] the [sweet-smelling] *saugandhika*, and the [fragrant] *mṛdugandhika*. And in the ground on the banks of the lotus pools, various kinds of flowers were likewise planted, such as the *atimuktaka*, *campaka*, *pāṭalā*, *vārṣikā*, Arabian jasmine, *sumanā*, needle-nose jasmine, and *dhānuṣkārī*.[53] Trees perennially filled with flowers and fruit were also planted there to honor the stūpa.[54] Furthermore, permanent arrangements were made for its upkeep.[55] Stūpa attendants were appointed.[56] Conch, drums, and other musical instruments were presented. And at the shrine, offerings began to be made of perfume, incense, [245] flowers, and aromatic powders.

People came from the town and region to offer perfume, garlands, incense, and aromatic powders at the shrine. When the wind was blowing from the south, that southerly wind suffused the shrine and its courtyard with the smells of all the varieties of flowers that were there. And it was the same with a westerly wind, as well as with winds from the other directions. As those winds would blow, the shrine and its courtyard would become suffused with the smells of various kinds of flowers.

When everything to be done at the stūpa was done, the powerful fighter approached. Seeing that everything to be done at the stūpa was done, he said, "What does one get from making offerings at this shrine?"

Then the guildmaster began to offer an account of buddhas. "Straining valiantly in this way for three incalculable ages," he explained, "one obtains unsurpassed awakening."[57]

Hearing this, the powerful fighter was dejected, for he lacked perserverance. "I can't attain unsurpassed perfect awakening," he said.

Then the guildmaster offered an account of solitary buddhas. When the powerful fighter heard an account of their glory as well, he became depressed and said, "I can't attain awakening as a solitary buddha either."

Then the great guildmaster offered an account of the glory of disciples. "At least for now," he said, "make a fervent aspiration in your mind for this."

"Great guildmaster," the powerful fighter said, "for which awakening have you made a fervent aspiration?"

"I have set my mind on attaining unsurpassed awakening," the great guildmaster said.

"If you have set your mind on attaining unsurpassed awakening," the powerful fighter said, "then I shall be your disciple. You'll look after me."

"But you've done many terrible things!" the guildmaster said to him. "Nevertheless, when you hear that a buddha has arisen in the world, you must remain mindful of this."[58] Then the guildmaster, who had built the shrine, regarded it, fell before it, and made this fervent aspiration:

> By virtue of this gift to a great one,
> may I become a buddha, a sugata,[59] a self-made one.
> Having crossed, may I help multitudes of people to cross,
> those not taken to the other shore by previous great victors.

Then the Blessed One said, "That guildmaster in the past was none other than me, following the path of the bodhisattva at that time. That powerful fighter was none other than Dharmaruci [246] at that time and at that juncture. I saw Dharmaruci in that first incalculable age. It is with reference to this that I said, "It's been a long time [since we met], Dharmaruci." And when Dharmaruci came to understand, he said, "Yes, it's been a long time, Blessed One."

Dīpaṅkara Buddha and the Wise Brahmans Sumati and Mati

In the second incalculable age, there arose in the world a perfectly awakened buddha named Dīpaṅkara (Illuminator),

> who was perfect in knowledge and conduct,[60]
> a sugata,
> a knower of the world,
> an unsurpassed guide for those in need of training,
> a teacher of gods and humans,
> a buddha,
> and a blessed one.

After traveling through the countryside, the perfectly awakened Dīpaṅkara arrived in the capital Dīpāvatī (Full of Light). In the capital Dīpāvatī, a king named Dīpa (Light) ruled a kingdom that was thriving, prosperous, and safe, with plenty of food and throngs of people. Following the proper formalities,[61] King Dīpa invited the perfectly awakened Dīpaṅkara to enter the city.

Now there was a neighboring king[62] of King Dīpa named Vāsava. King Dīpa sent a messenger to him with the following message: "Please come. Following the proper formalities, I have invited the perfectly awakened Dīpaṅkara to enter the city so that I can honor him with offerings."

Then King Vāsava, who had just finished performing a twelve-year sacrifice, arranged for five great gifts to be given at the sacrificial site—a golden water-pitcher, a golden food-bowl, a four-jeweled bed, five hundred *kārṣāpaṇa* coins, and a girl adorned with all kinds of ornaments.

Meanwhile two young brahmans were living at that time in another region. They had completed their study of the Veda under an instructor and were pondering the fact that one should give a gift to one's teacher that is appropriate for a teacher and a gift to one's instructor that is appropriate for an instructor. They heard that King Vāsava had collected five great gifts at the sacrificial site and that whichever brahman was most adept at Vedic recitation would receive them. It occurred to them, "Let's go there and receive those gifts. Who there will be more learned and more capable of reciting the Veda than we are?" With this in mind, they set out for the great city of King Vāsava.

In the meantime, a deity informed the king, [247] "Two young brahmans are coming, Sumati (Very Wise) and Mati (Wise). Of these two, give the gifts to Sumati. Your majesty, you have performed a twelve-year sacrifice. As a result of the merit from this sacrifice, you should give these great gifts to the young brahman Sumati, for he is of the highest standing."

"Surely these two must be great souls," the king reflected, "if even deities speak on their behalf." Then the king saw the two young brahmans coming from a distance.[63] They were attractive and handsome.

The two went to the sacrificial site, climbed up to the highest seat among the rows of seats reserved for brahmans, and sat down.

When King Vāsava saw the two young brahmans, he thought, "The one named Sumati, the one the deities told me about, that must be him." The king approached the highest seat and asked the young brahman Sumati, "Are you Sumati?"

"Yes, I am," he said.

Then King Vāsava fed the young brahman Sumati while he sat in the highest seat and offered him the five gifts. The young brahman Sumati accepted the first four of the great gifts, beginning with the water pitcher, but he didn't accept the final gift of a girl. "I am a celibate follower of the religious life," he said. When the girl saw the young brahman Sumati, who was attractive and handsome, she felt full of desire and love.

"Accept me, brahman," she said to the young brahman Sumati.

"I can't accept you," he said.

Since the king had surrendered the girl with the intention of giving her away as a gift, he wouldn't take her back again. And since the young brahman Sumati wouldn't accept her either, she went to King Dīpa's city of Dīpāvatī. Once there, she removed the jewelry from her body and offered it to a garland-maker. "Against the value of this jewelry," she said, "give me blue waterlilies every day for honoring the Lord." With that agreement, she gave him her golden ornaments and became a devotee of the Lord.

Meanwhile the young brahman Sumati took those four great gifts and went to his instructor. Having gone to his instructor, he offered him those four great gifts. The instructor accepted three of those gifts but gave the five hundred *kārṣāpaṇa* coins back to Sumati. That night, Sumati had ten dreams—he saw himself (1) drinking the great ocean; (2) flying through the air; (3) touching and stroking with his hand the sun and the moon, which are full of magic and power;[64] [248] (4) harnessing a royal chariot; and he also saw (5–10) sages, white elephants, geese, lions, a great rock, and mountains. After having these dreams, he woke up. And when he woke up, it occurred to him, "Who can interpret these dreams for me?"

Not far from there lived a seer who possessed the five superhuman faculties. To clear away his doubts, the young brahman Sumati went to the seer. Once there he greeted the seer, described his dreams to him, and then said, "Interpret these dreams for me."

"I can't interpret these dreams," the seer said. "Go to the capital Dīpāvatī. There King Dīpa, following the proper formalities, has invited a perfectly awakened buddha named Dīpaṅkara to enter the city. He will interpret these dreams for you."

In the meantime, King Vāsava, having accepted King Dīpa's invitation, arrived at the capital Dīpāvatī surrounded by eighty thousand ministers. At the same time, King Dīpa had this thought: "Following the proper formalities, I will arrange for the perfectly awakened Dīpaṅkara to enter the city after seven days." Then he began to gather all the flowers from every town and region. On the same day that King Dīpa, following the proper formalities, began to arrange for the perfectly awakened Dīpaṅkara to enter the city, Sumati also arrived there. Soon the king had all the available flowers gathered together in the city.

Meanwhile the girl, now an attendant of the Lord, went to the garland-maker. "Give me some blue waterlilies. I will honor the Lord."

"The king has gathered all the available flowers for Dīpaṅkara's entrance into the city today," the garland-maker said.

"Go," she said. "If, because of my meritorious deeds, there are once again blue waterlilies[65] in the lotus pond that haven't been plucked, then get them for me."

By the power of Sumati's merit,[66] seven blue waterlilies appeared in the lotus pond. The garland-maker went there and saw them. After he saw them, the girl said to him, "Pick those waterlilies."

"I'm not going to pick them," the garland-maker said. "The king's men will punish me." [249]

"No," she said. "You already picked all the flowers and gave them to the king."

"Yes, I did," the garland-maker said.

"Well, it's because of my meritorious deeds that they have appeared," the girl said. "So give whatever you pick to me."

"How will they be taken away[67] without the king's men noticing?" the garland-maker asked.

"You just pluck them," the girl said. "I'll take them away hidden in a water pot."

After the garland-maker heard all this, he plucked those waterlilies and gave them to the girl. She took them, hid them in a water pot, filled the pot with water, and then set out for the city.

Meanwhile Sumati also arrived at that place, and it occurred to him, "How can I see the Lord Buddha and not honor him with an offering?" He wandered around the garland-makers' homes, searching diligently for any flowers, but he didn't come across even a single flower. Then he went to the outskirts of town and wandered from garden to garden in search of flowers, but still he didn't come across a single flower. As he was wandering about, he arrived at that park. Just then the girl left the park and came face to face with the young brahman. By the power of his merit, those blue waterlilies rose up out of her water pot. When Sumati saw them, he said to the girl, "Give me those waterlilies. And take these five hundred *kārṣāpaṇa* coins from me as a reward."

"Back then you didn't want to accept me," the girl said to Sumati, "and now you're begging me for waterlilies. I won't give them to you!" With that, she then said to the young brahman Sumati, "What will you do with them?"

"I will honor the Lord Buddha," Sumati said.

"But what use are *kārṣāpaṇa* coins to me?" the girl asked. "I'll give these waterlilies to the Buddha, unless as a result of giving them to you, you'll seek me[68] as your wife in every rebirth to come—that is, at the time of giving this gift to the Buddha, you make the following fervent aspiration: 'May she be my wife in every rebirth to come.'"

"We're both intent on giving. Both of us would sacrifice our own family members, even our own flesh," Sumati said.

"Make the fervent aspiration!" the girl said to Sumati. "Afterward, you may offer me to whomever you wish."[69] [250] After the girl had said this, she gave five waterlilies to Sumati and took two herself. Then she uttered this verse:

> Wherever you make a fervent aspiration,
> having accepted the Buddha as your guide,
> there, always, I shall be your wife,
> helping you perform religious rites.

In town, following the king's orders, all the pebbles, stones, and potsherds were removed; flags, banners, and welcoming arches were raised; silk banners were hung up; and fragrant water and powder were sprinkled about. And from the main gate of the city, along the span between the monastery and the city, pebbles, stones, and potsherds were removed; flags, banners, and welcoming arches were raised; silk banners were hung up; and fragrant water and powder were sprinkled about.

Then King Dīpa took a hundred-ribbed umbrella and went out to meet the perfectly awakened Dīpaṅkara. His ministers did likewise, as did King Vāsava, who went out to meet him accompanied by his own ministers. King Dīpa fell prostrate at the Lord Buddha's feet and made this request: "Blessed One, please enter the city."

Then the Blessed One, leading the community of monks, set out toward the entrance to the city. King Dīpa held up his hundred-ribbed umbrella for the perfectly awakened Dīpaṅkara. His ministers did likewise, as did King Vāsava, accompanied by his own ministers. Making use of his magical powers, the Blessed One exercised his power so that each one reflected, "I am carrying the Blessed One's umbrella!"

Then the Blessed One, in all his splendor, entered among the people. And there, with his mind focused,[70] the Blessed One put his foot down on the threshold to the city. At that moment when the Blessed

One put his foot down on the threshold to the city, the earth began to move in six different ways: it quivered, quavered, and quaked; it shifted, shuddered, and shook.

It is a law of nature that whenever lord buddhas, with their minds focused, put their feet down on a threshold, various wonderful and fantastic things occur:

the mad recover their senses;
the blind recover their sight;
the deaf can hear;
the mute can speak;
the crippled can walk;
breech babies of pregnant women are straightened out;
the bonds of those beings bound with wooden fetters and
  iron shackles are loosened;
those who are filled with enmity in birth after birth immediately
  regain thoughts of loving-kindness; [251]
calves break their tethers and reunite with their mothers;
elephants trumpet;
horses neigh;
bulls bellow;
parrots, mynahs, cuckoos, and peacock pheasants coo sweetly;
musical instruments make sweet music without being played;
jewelry boxes make sweet music as well;
raised portions of the earth sink down, and sunken ones rise up;
pebbles, stones, and potsherds disappear;
deities throw divine blue waterlilies from the sky;
they also throw red waterlilies, white waterlilies, and
  white lotuses; pounded agarwood, sandalwood, and *tagara*;
  tamāla leaves and flowers from the divine coral tree;
the east rises up and the west sinks down;
the west rises up and the east sinks down;

the south rises up and the north sinks down;
the north rises up and the south sinks down;
the middle rises up and the ends sink down;
and the ends rise up and the middle sinks down.

And there in the capital Dīpāvatī, many hundreds of thousands of beings made offerings of flowers, incense, and perfume. Sumati and the girl, holding their waterlilies, also followed the perfectly awakened Dīpaṅkara. But they were engulfed by a great mass of people who wanted to honor him with offerings, and they couldn't get close to the Blessed One. Then the Blessed One reflected, "The young brahman Sumati will earn more merit than this great mass of people." With this in mind, he magically created a great tempest of wind and rain. The crowd began to disperse.

Given room, the young brahman Sumati saw the Blessed One—a sight one never tires of seeing—and was filled with intense faith. Filled as he was with faith, he tossed those five waterlilies toward the Buddha. The perfectly awakened Lord Dīpaṅkara then exercised his power so that those waterlilies circled his head like a small wagon wheel.[71] Wherever he went, it would follow. Wherever he stood, it would remain.

Seeing all this, the girl was filled with faith, and she tossed her two waterlilies toward the Blessed One. The Blessed One exercised his power as before so that those two waterlilies circled near his ears, also like small wagon wheels.

Now because of that tempest of wind and rain, that place became muddy. So the young brahman Sumati then approached the Lord Buddha, [252] and at that muddy place in front of the Blessed One, he spread out the locks of his matted hair[72] and uttered this verse:

If I am to become a buddha for the sake
of awakening others, O awakener to wisdom,

may you tread with your feet on my matted hair,
which will bring an end to birth and old age.[73]

Then the perfectly awakened Dīpaṅkara placed his feet on the matted hair of the young brahman Sumati. Meanwhile the young brahman Mati, who was standing close behind Sumati, angrily addressed Lord Dīpaṅkara: "Hey! Look here! The perfectly awakened Dīpaṅkara tramples on the matted hair of the young brahman Sumati with his feet, just like an animal."

Then the perfectly awakened Dīpaṅkara made this prediction about the young brahman Sumati:

You will be freed from human existence, liberated,[74]
powerful, a teacher for the benefit of the world,
the scion of the Śākyas with the name Śākyamuni,
best in the three worlds and a light for the universe.

At that very moment when the perfectly awakened Dīpaṅkara made this prediction about the young brahman Sumati, Sumati rose up into the air the height of seven palm trees. Then his matted hair fell off, and even more impressive matted hair appeared in its place. A large crowd of people saw him hovering in midair, and upon seeing him, they made this fervent aspiration: "When he attains supreme knowledge, may we be his disciples."

The girl also made a fervent aspiration:

"Whenever you make a fervent aspiration,
taking the Buddha as your guide,
I shall be there as your wife,
a constant companion in the dharma.

When you are perfectly awakened,
the best instructor in the world,

at that time, when it comes,
I will be your disciple."

Seeing the young brahman floating in the air,
hundreds and thousands of beings
all long to be his disciples,
in that time still to come.

[And they said,]
"When you are perfectly awakened,
the best guide in the world,
at that time, when it comes,
we'll be your disciples." [253]

After the perfectly awakened Dīpaṅkara had made his prediction about the young brahman Sumati, King Dīpa took hold of the matted hair that had fallen from Sumati's head.

"Give his matted hair to me," King Vāsava said.

Then King Dīpa gave it to him. King Vāsava took it and counted the hairs—there were eighty thousand.

"My lord, give each of us a single hair," the ministers said to King Vāsava. "We will make shrines for them." So the king gave each of those officials a single hair. The ministers then went back to their respective territories and established shrines for them.

After it had been predicted that the young brahman Sumati would attain unsurpassed perfect awakening, King Dīpa, King Vāsava, and many townsmen and villagers offered all kinds of provisions in expectation of good things in the future.

Meanwhile Sumati addressed the young brahman Mati: "It has been predicted that I will attain unsurpassed perfect awakening. What have you set your mind on?"

"Sumati, I have been spiritually damaged," he said.

"How is that you've been spiritually damaged?" he asked.

Then he said, "When the perfectly awakened Dīpaṅkara trampled on your matted hair, I became angry and these words slipped out: 'The perfectly awakened Dīpaṅkara tramples on the matted hair of a learned brahman, just like an animal.'"

"Come," Sumati said to him. "Let's go forth as monks in the presence of the Lord Buddha."

Then Sumati and Mati went forth as monks, following the teaching of the perfectly awakened Dīpaṅkara. After Sumati had gone forth as a monk, he learned [the threefold collection of scripture known as] the Tripiṭaka and won the favor of the assembly of monks with his righteousness. The young brahman Sumati eventually died and passed away and was reborn among the gods of Tuṣita (Content). When the young brahman Mati died and passed away, he was reborn in the realms of hell.

The Blessed One said, "King Vāsava at that time and at that juncture is now King Bimbisāra (Precious as Gold). Those eighty thousand ministers at that time and at that juncture are now these eighty thousand deities. Those people from Dīpavatī [at that time and at that juncture are now these people of Śrāvastī].[75] That girl is now none other than Yaśodharā. Sumati is none other than me, who at that time was following the path of the bodhisattva. And Mati is none other than Dharmaruci. I saw Dharmaruci in that second incalculable age. [254] It is with reference to this that I said, 'It's been a long time [since we met], Dharmaruci. It's been a very long time, Dharmaruci.'"

The Three Deadly Sins[76]

After that time, in the third incalculable age, there arose in the world a perfectly awakened buddha named Krakucchanda (Destroyer of Saṃsāra),[77]

> who was perfect in knowledge and conduct,
> a sugata,

a knower of the world,
an unsurpassed guide for those in need of training,
a teacher of gods and humans,
a buddha,
and a blessed one.

[He stayed near the capital Śobhāvatī].[78] And in the capital there lived a great guildmaster. He brought home a girl from an appropriate family as his wife, and with his wife[79] he fooled around, enjoyed himself, and made love. From fooling around, enjoying himself, and making love with her, a son was born.

Now the householder was a man of faith, and he had an instructor for his family who was a monk and an arhat.

"This son of ours will bring us debt and take away our wealth," the householder said to his wife. "I will go now, dear wife. I'll take my goods to another country as merchants do."[80] And so, driven by the greed that consumes merchants,[81] he took his goods and went far away. He wouldn't return home for a long time.[82]

In the meantime, his son grew up, and he was handsome, good-looking, and attractive. "Mom," he asked his mother, "what is our traditional family business?"[83]

"Son," she said, "your father used to run a shop."

So the son then began to run a shop. As for his mother, she was tormented with desire for him, and began to think, "Is there any way for me to get rid of these desires without anyone knowing this about me?" Thinking it over, she came to this resolution: "Because of this desire for my son, I'll make love with him. It's only this way, by being with him, that I can rid myself of this lust.[84] And my relatives will never suspect it." Then she invited over a madam,[85] fed her two or three times, and later offered her new clothes.

The old woman asked her, "Why are you trying to get me to take kindly to you, doing all these nice things for me?"

Now feeling confident, she said to the the old woman, "Madam, listen to my request.[86] I am terribly tormented by desire. Have some affection for me. Find me a man, probably an insider, who people won't suspect." [255]

"A man like that won't be found here in this house," the old woman said. "And there isn't anyone who desires you who could enter without people becoming suspicious. Is there any such man to speak of?"

"If there is no other man we can involve in such a plan,"[87] the merchant's wife said to the old woman, "there is still my son.[88] People won't be suspicious of him."

"How can you go in for making love with your son?" the old woman asked her. "It would be okay, though, for you to enjoy making love with another man."

"If no other man who is an insider is found," the merchant's wife said, "my son will do just fine."

"Do as you wish," the old woman said.

Then the madam came to that merchant's son and asked, "Son, you're young and handsome. Are you set up or not?"[89]

"What are you saying?" he said to her.

"You're young and handsome," the old woman said. "At this age, it would suit you to fool around, enjoy yourself, and make love with a young girl in the prime of her youth.[90] Why be deprived of sexual pleasure?"

The merchant's son heard the old woman's proposal, but at heart he was shrinking from shame and modesty, and so he didn't consent.

The old woman spoke likewise to the boy a second time and a third as well. "There is a young girl tormented with desire for you," she said.

After being addressed a second time and a third as well, the merchant's son said to the old woman, "Madam, did you say anything to the young girl about me?"[91]

"I spoke to her about you,"[92] the old woman replied. "She didn't consent readily to the situation.[93] The girl is extremely bashful and modest and won't say anything. But she won't cover her body completely.[94] In return, you shouldn't make any effort to seek her out."[95]

"Where will we meet?" the merchant's son asked the old woman.

"In my house," she replied.

"Where is your house located?" he asked.

The old woman gave him directions to her house. Then she went to the merchant's wife and said, [256] "I got this boy of yours to agree."[96]

"Where will this meeting of ours take place?" she asked.

"In my house."

Now when the boy finished his work, he went home. In due course he ate dinner, and then he said to his mother, "I'm going out. I'll be sleeping at a friend's house."

Then his mother gave him permission: "Okay, you can go."

Having received permission, the boy then went to the old woman's house. After the boy arrived at her house, he waited for the time of lovemaking to come. In the nighttime, at that hour when forms can't be recognized,[97] the merchant's son's mother went there, to that very house, to enjoy the pleasures of making love. And after going to that house at that odd hour when the shape of forms is not clearly seen,[98] she secretly began to enjoy making love with her son, which was wicked and illicit. And as the night wore away, after she had enjoyed making love, in the pitch-black darkness of the night, at that time when the shape of forms is not seen, she went back to her own home. As for the merchant's son, after enjoying making love, at daybreak he went to his warehouse and took care of the family business. It went on like this a second time and a third as well.

The boy continued enjoying making love there in the old woman's house, and this routine of their lovemaking went on in the same way for a long time.[99] Meanwhile the boy's mother began to think, "How much longer will I have to go to someone else's house and in this way, without being seen, enjoy making love? Suppose I gradually let my son know about the true arrangement of our lovemaking. That way we could enjoy making love right here in our own house?"[100] Having considered this, she went right to the old woman's house and once again enjoyed making love with her son. Just as planned,[101] as the night wore away, at that time when it was pitch black, she put on the boy's upper garment, left behind her own headscarf, and went back to her home. At daybreak the boy saw her scarf resting on the head of the bed. Not finding his own upper garment,[102] he realized that her scarf was there in its place. Leaving it behind, he went to his warehouse, put on another set of clothes, and then went home. When he went there, he clearly saw that it was his own garment covering his mother's head. [257] Seeing this, he asked his mother, "Mother, how did this garment come to be on your head?"

"Am I still your mother, even now?" she asked. "Considering that you've been satisfying your own desires with me for such a long time, am I still your mother, one and the same, even now?"

When the merchant's son heard his mother say such things, he was stunned and shocked, and collapsed on the ground. Then his mother splashed him with some water from a pot. Even after the boy was splashed with water, it took him a long time to come back to his senses. Then his mother consoled him, "Why are you so depressed? Listen to what I have to say and compose yourself. Don't despair."

"Why shouldn't I be depressed or confused!"[103] the boy said to her. "I've done something so evil."

"Don't create stress[104] for yourself about this," she said to him. "Women are like a path, for whichever one a father travels, a son also travels the very same one. The son is not faulted for following the path, and it's the same thing with regard to women.[105] Women are also like fords, for whichever ford a father bathes in, a son also bathes in the same one. The son is not faulted for bathing in it, and it's the same thing with regard to women. In the border areas, it's very common that whomever a father approaches for illicit sex, the son also approaches the same woman."

In this way, his mother's many passionate words[106] assuaged the merchant's son's grief, and he began to take great pleasure, over and over again, in that sinful, illicit behavior with his mother.

Then the guildmaster sent a letter back to his house. "Dear wife," it said, "gather your strength and rest assured. Shortly after you receive this letter, I will be returning home."

When the merchant's wife heard the content of the letter, she became dejected and began to think, "For a long time I was looking forward to his return. Then he didn't come. It's only now, with things going as they are, when I'm already making love with my son, that he is going to return. Is there any way that I can have him killed before he arrives here?" After giving it some thought, she called on her son and said, "Your father has sent a letter saying that he is coming home.[107] [258] Do you know what we should do now? Go, arrange for your father's death before he arrives here."

"How could I kill my own father?" he asked.

When he wouldn't dare murder his own father, his mother spoke to him repeatedly with rousing words. Being addressed with these stirring words and being addicted to sexual pleasures, he finally resolved to kill his father.

I say, there is no evil act that a person who indulges in sexual pleasures won't commit.[108]

"How should I kill him?" he asked.

"I'll make all the arrangements," she said. With that said, she took poison, mixed it with flour, and made some *maṇḍīlaka* cakes. She also made some others without poison. Then she called the boy and said, "Go. These are the poisonous *maṇḍīlaka* cakes, and these are the ones without poison. Take them, go to your father, and when he is confidently eating together with you, offer him the poisonous *maṇḍīlaka* cakes, and eat the ones without poison yourself."

Then the boy took the *maṇḍīlaka* cakes and departed, along with the man carrying the letter. When he approached his father, his father saw that his son was handsome, attractive, and powerful, and he was very happy. He asked about his health, and then said to the merchants there, "This, gentlemen, is my son."

When the boy was sure that his father fully recognized him, he said to his father, "Father, Mother sent some *maṇḍīlaka* cakes as a gift. You should eat them."

While he was eating with his father off the same plate,[109] he gave his father the poisonous *maṇḍīlaka* cakes and ate the ones without poison himself. His father ate those poisonous *maṇḍīlaka* cakes and promptly died. Though his father's life had now come to an end, no one considered or suspected that the boy had done anything wrong. Later, after those merchants who were his dear and loving friends had finished grieving, they gave the boy whatever goods, gold, and valuables[110] that the merchant possessed. The boy took the goods, gold, and valuables that belonged to his father and then went back home.

After he returned home,[111] his mother continued having secret and illicit sex with him, her son, but she was never satisfied. And in that unsatisfied condition, she said to her son, "How long will we [259] have to make love in secret like this? We really should leave this place, go to some other place, and live happily, declaring ourselves husband and wife, openly and without inhibitions."

So the two left their home, leaving behind their friends, relatives, and relations, and leaving those maids, servants, and workers who had long served them. They took what they could of their wealth, gold, and valuables, and went to another district. After going there, they openly declared themselves in the region as husband and wife and settled down, enjoying the pleasure of making love.

Then, one day, an arhat monk journeying through the region arrived at that town. While wandering there for alms, he came and sat down in the marketplace. There he saw the boy carrying on business as merchants do. Seeing him, he offered greetings, they conversed, and then he said, "Is your mother well?" When the boy heard the arhat say such a thing, his mind snapped. Fearful because of his own terrible act, he began to think, and after giving it some thought,[112] he went and informed his mother, "An ascetic has arrived here—it's the one who used to come to our house. Now that he's here in town, he'll recognize you and think, 'She is the boy's mother.' But we're well known here as husband and wife. How can he be killed?"

Then the two decided: "We'll invite him to our home for a meal, and while he's eating, we'll kill him."[113] Having thought this over, they invited that arhat monk into their home for a meal and began to feed him. The boy, carrying a concealed knife, fed the arhat, with the help of his mother. He then made sure that there was no one else in the house. After the arhat monk had finishing eating, he left the house and walked away unsuspectingly. Then the boy watched him unsuspectingly walking away from the house,[114] and getting behind him as he departed, he plunged the knife into the arhat's body and took his life.

Sexual pleasure is like salt water. The more you indulge in it, the more your thirst increases.

While the boy's mother was behaving illicitly with her son, she was also having a secret love affair with a guildmaster's son in town. [260] She became obssessed with those illicit pleasures. The boy came to know of her affair.

"Mom," he said to his mother, "refrain from such sin." But her mind was so attached to that guildmaster's son that even when she was asked a second time and a third as well, she didn't refrain. Then, unsheathing his sword, the boy killed his mother.

After he had committed his third deadly sin, deities announced throughout the region, "This boy is a sinner! He has killed his father, he has killed an arhat, and he has killed his mother. He has committed three deadly sins. These deeds, once performed and accumulated, lead to the sufferings of hell."

When the townspeople heard this, they banished him from town. After he was banished from town, he began to think, "There must be some expiation from this in the Buddha's order." He contemplated the possibilities. "I'll go now. I'll go forth as a monk." He went to a monastery, approached a monk, and said, "Noble one, I would like to be initiated as a monk."

The monk asked, "You haven't killed your father, have you?"

"Yes, I killed my father," he said to the monk.

Then he asked, "Have you killed your mother?"

"Yes, noble one," he said. "I killed my mother,"

Then he asked, "Have you killed an arhat?"

"I killed an arhat as well," he said.

"Committing any single one of these actions," the monk said to him, "would make you unworthy of initiation, let alone all of them combined. Go away, my son. I won't initiate you."

Then the man[115] approached another monk and said, "Noble one, I would like to be initiated." That monk also asked the same series of questions and then refused him. Then he went to another monk and in just the same way requested initiation. That monk also asked the same series of questions and then, likewise, refused him. After he had requested initiation a second time and a third as well, and the monks would not initiate him, he became angry and began to think, "I request initiation, which is there for everyone, yet I don't receive it."

Then, when the monks were asleep, he set that monastery on fire. [261] After setting that monastery on fire, he went to another monastery. There too he went and approached the monks and requested initiation. They also asked the same series of questions and then refused him. With his mind full of hate, he likewise started another fire there. In that monastery too, many monks, both students and masters, were burned. As he continued in this way, burning many monasteries, word about him spread all over: "Such and such a man, a doer of evil deeds, not receiving initiation from monks, sets fire to their monasteries and burns those monks alive."

Meanwhile the man set off for another monastery. In that monastery there lived a monk with the character of a bodhisattva who knew the Tripiṭaka, the threefold collection of scripture. He heard that a man, a doer of truly evil deeds, was coming there, so the monk went out to meet the man before he arrived at the monastery. Approaching the man, he said, "Friend, what's the problem?"

"Noble one," the man said to him, "I can't take initiation as a monk."

"Come, my son," the monk said to him, "I will initiate you."

Thereafter the monk shaved the man's head and offered him ochre robes.

"Noble one," the man said, "administer the precepts to me."

"What use are the precepts to you?" the monk replied. "All the time just say, 'Praise to the Buddha! Praise to the dharma! Praise to the community!'"[116] Then the monk began to give that man instructions in the dharma. "You have committed such-and-such evil deeds. So if you ever hear the word *buddha*, you must remain mindful of this."[117]

Then that monk who knew the Tripiṭaka died and passed away and was reborn among the gods. That man also died and passed away. He was reborn in the realms of hell.

"What do you think, monks?" the Blessed One said. "That monk who in the past knew the Tripiṭaka was none other than me at that time and at that juncture. That being who was the doer of evil deeds, killing his mother, father, and an arhat, was none other than Dharmaruci. I saw Dharmaruci in that third incalculable age. It is with reference to this that I said, 'It's been a long time [since we met], Dharmaruci. [262] It's been a very long time, Dharmaruci. It's been an incredibly long time, Dharmaruci.' Monks, for three incalculable ages while I fulfilled the six perfections and performed hundreds of thousands of difficult deeds to earn unsurpassed perfect awakening, Dharmaruci spent most of that time in the realms of hell and in the animal realm."

This was said by the Blessed One. With their minds uplifted, the monks rejoiced at the words of the Blessed One.

So ends the *Dharmaruci-avadāna*, the eighteenth chapter in the glorious *Divyāvadāna*.

19. The Story of Jyotiṣka

JYOTIṢKA-AVADĀNA[118]

Subhadra, Bhūrika, and the Nirgranthas

THE LORD BUDDHA was staying in the city of Rājagṛha at the bamboo grove in Kalandakanivāpa (Squirrel Feeding Place). In the city of Rājagṛha there lived a householder named Subhadra (Very Good Man), who was rich, wealthy, and prosperous and who had great faith in the Nirgranthas. He brought home a girl from an appropriate family as his wife, and with her he fooled around, enjoyed himself, and made love. After some time, from fooling around, enjoying himself, and making love, his wife became pregnant.

Now one morning the Blessed One got dressed, took his bowl and robe, and entered Rājagṛha for alms. While he was wandering through Rājagṛha for alms, he approached the home of the householder Subhadra. The householder Subhadra saw the Blessed One from a distance, and upon seeing him, he took his wife and approached the Blessed One. Having approached, he said this to him: "Blessed One, my wife here is pregnant. What will she give birth to?"

"Householder," the Buddha said, "she will give birth to a boy. He will make the family shine; he will experience divine-like[119] glory as a result of his actions; and he will go forth as a monk in my order, where by ridding himself of all defilements, he will directly experience arhatship."

Then the householder filled the Blessed One's bowl with hard and soft foods, both fresh and fine. The Blessed One, in turn, wished him good health, took his almsfood, and departed. [263]

Meanwhile, not very far from the householder stood [a non-Buddhist ascetic named] Bhūrika (Clever). He reflected, "If even one household gives me alms, the ascetic Gautama goes and converts it! I'll go and see what the ascetic Gautama has predicted." So he went there and said, "Householder, has the ascetic Gautama come here?"

"Yes, he's come."

"What did he predict?"

"Noble one, I showed him my wife and asked him what she will give birth to. He said that she will give birth to a boy; that he will make the family shine; that he will experience divine-like glory as a result of his actions; and that he will go forth as a monk in his order, where by ridding himself of all defilements, he will directly experience arhatship."

Now Bhūrika was an expert in making astrological calculations.[120] He took a piece of chalk and began to calculate. He saw that everything would happen just as the Blessed One had predicted. "If I verify all this," he reflected, "the householder will have even greater faith[121] in the ascetic Gautama. Some of what he said should be affirmed and some rejected." With this in mind, he began to wring his hands and make a face.

"Noble one," the householder Subhadra said, "why are you wringing your hands and making a face?"

"Householder," he said, "some of what has been said is true and some false."

"Noble one, what part is true and what part false?"

"Householder, he said that your wife will give birth to a son. Here he tells the truth. It is also true that the boy will make the family shine. His name will be Agrajyoti (Highest Light).[122] But this being is ill fated. As soon as he is born, he will cause your family to burn in flames. The ascetic Gautama also said that he will experience divine-like glory as a result of his actions. This is false. Householder, have you ever seen any human being experience divine-like glory as a result of his actions? In addition, he said that he will go forth in his order. This is true. When he has no food and no clothing, he will certainly go forth as a monk under the ascetic Gautama. That he will rid himself of all defilements and thereby directly experience arhatship—this is false. The ascetic Gautama hasn't rid himself of all defilements and directly experienced arhatship, so how will it happen for your son?"

Subhadra became dejected. "Noble one," he said, "what should I do next?"

"Householder," Bhūrika said, "those of us who've gone forth as monks are constrained by religious vows,[123] but you'll know what to do." With that said, he departed.

Subhadra reflected, [264] "The boy must be gotten rid of altogether." With this in mind, he began to administer the remedy. But that being was in his final existence, [destined to be reborn no more].

"This will be the remedy for him," he thought, as he began to push on the left side of his wife's stomach. The fetus then went to the right side. Then Subhadra began to push on the right side of her stomach. It went to the left side.

Now it is impossible and inconceivable that a being in his final existence would leave course and die before his corruptions were destroyed.

Meanwhile, as her stomach was being pushed on, the householder's wife began to wail. The neighbors heard and came quickly.

"Friends," they asked, "why is the householder's wife crying out?"

"She's pregnant," Subhadra said. "It must be time for her to give birth."

Then the neighbors departed, and Subhadra reflected, "I can't force her to miscarry here. I'll bring her to the forest." So he led her to the forest, where he attacked her and she died.[124] Then he brought her back home secretly and told his friends, relations, relatives, and neighbors,

"Friends, my wife has died." They began to wail. Still wailing, they adorned a funeral bier with pieces of blue, yellow, red, and white cloth, put her on it, and brought her to the cremation ground known as Śītavana (Cool Forest).

When the Nirgranthas heard this, they were happy, satisfied, and delighted. They raised umbrellas and banners, and roaming through the roads, marketplaces, squares, and crossroads of the city of Rājagṛha, they announced, "Listen, friends! The ascetic Gautama predicted that the householder Subhadra's wife would give birth to a boy; that he would make the family shine; that he would experience divine-like glory as a result of his actions; and that he would go forth as a monk in his order, where by ridding himself of all defilements, he would directly experience arhatship. But now she has died and been taken to the Śītavana cremation ground. If a tree has no roots, how will it have branches, leaves, and fruit?"

Meanwhile there is nothing that lord buddhas do not know, see, realize, and understand. It is a law of nature that lord buddhas have great compassion,

> they are intent on doing good deeds for mankind,
> they have a single guardian [which is mindfulness],
> they abide in the meditative states of tranquility and insight,
> they are expert in the three objects for self-control,
> they have crossed the four floods [of corruptions],
> they have planted the soles of their feet
> on the [four][125] bases of success,
> they have long since developed an expertise in the four means
> of attracting beings to the religious life,
> they are confident with the four confidences, [265]
> they have destroyed the five [bad] qualities,
> they have crossed over the five realms of existence,
> they have acquired the six [good] qualities,

they have fulfilled the six perfections,
they reside alone,[126]
they are replete with the flowers of the seven factors
of awakening,
they are teachers of the eightfold path,
they are expert in attaining the nine successive states
of quiescence meditation,
they are powerful with the ten powers,
they have fame that fills up the ten directions,
and they are superior to the thousand gods who have control
over others.

As lord buddhas observe the world with their buddha vision, three times in the night and three times in the day, knowledge and insight arise as to the following:

Who will get worse?
Who will get better?
Who will encounter trouble?
Who will encounter difficulty?
Who will encounter danger?
Who will encounter trouble, difficulty, and danger?
Who is inclined toward a terrible realm of existence?
Who is drawn toward a terrible realm of existence?
Who is disposed toward a terrible realm of existence?
Whom shall I lift up from a terrible realm of existence
and establish in heaven and liberation?
For whom with roots of virtue unplanted shall I plant them?
For whom with roots of virtue already planted
shall I cause them to mature?
For whom with roots of virtue already matured
shall I cause them to be released?

And it is said,

Although the sea, home to monsters,
may allow the time of the tides to pass,
the Buddha never allows the time to pass
for training his beloved children.

Then in a certain place the Blessed One displayed his smile.

The Buddha's Smile

Now it is a law of nature that whenever lord buddhas manifest their smiles, rays of blue, yellow, red, and white light emerge from their mouths, some going downward and some going upward. Those that go downward enter various hells[127]—Sañjīva (Reviving), Kālasūtra (Black Thread), Saṃghāta (Crushing), Raurava (Shrieking), Mahāraurava (Loud Shrieking), Tapana (Heat), Pratāpana (Extreme Heat), Avīci (Ceaseless Torture), Arbuda (Blistering), Nirarbuda (Blisters Bursting), Aṭaṭa (Chattering Teeth), Hahava (Ugh!), the Huhuva (Brrr!), Utpala (Blue Waterlily), Padma (Lotus), and Mahāpadma (Great Lotus). Becoming cold, they descend into the hot hells, [and becoming hot, they descend into the cold hells.][128] In this way, those rays of light alleviate the particular torments of those beings who dwell in these various hells. And so they think, "Friends, have we died and passed away from this place? Have we been reborn somewhere else?"

Then, in order to engender their faith, the Blessed One manifests a magical image of himself.[129] Seeing this magical image, they think, "Friends, we haven't died and passed away from this place, nor have we been born someplace else. Instead, it's this person who we've never seen before; it's by his power that our particular torments are alleviated." Cultivating faith in their hearts toward this magical image, they cast off that karma still to be suffered in these hells [266] and take rebirth among gods and humans, where they become vessels for the [four noble] truths.

Those rays of light that go upward enter the various divine realms[130]—Cāturmahārājika (Four Groups of the Great Kings), Trāyastriṃśa (Thirty-Three), Yāma (Free from Conflict), Tuṣita (Content), Nirmāṇarati (Delighting in Creation), Paranirmitavaśavartin (Masters of Others' Creations), Brahmakāyika (Brahmā's Assembly), Brahmapurohita (Brahmā's Priests), Mahābrahmaṇa (Great Brahmā), Parīttābha (Limited Splendor), Apramāṇābha (Immeasurable Splendor), Ābhāsvara (Radiant), Parīttaśubha (Limited Beauty), Apramāṇaśubha (Immeasurable Beauty), Śubhakṛtsna (Complete Beauty), the Anabhraka (Unclouded), the Puṇyaprasava (Merit Born), Bṛhatphala (Great Result),[131] Atapa (Serene), Sudṛśa (Good-Looking), Sudarśa (Clear Sighted), and finally Akaniṣṭha (Supreme). There they proclaim the truth of impermanence, suffering, emptiness, and no-self. And they utter these two verses:

Strive! Go forth!
Apply yourselves to the teachings of the Buddha!
Destroy the army of death
as an elephant would a house of reeds.

Whoever diligently follows
this dharma and monastic discipline
will abandon the endless cycle of rebirth
and put an end to suffering.

Then those rays of light, having circulated through the billionfold world-system, come together directly behind the Blessed One.

In this case, those rays of light vanished into the Blessed One's mouth.

The venerable Ānanda then respectfully cupped his hands together and addressed the Blessed One:

A bundle of diverse light rays,
variegated with a thousand colors,
comes forth from your mouth.
They illuminate every direction,
as though the sun were rising.

And he uttered these verses:

Without pride, free from grief and passion,
buddhas are the cause of greatness in the world.
Not without reason do victors, defeaters of the enemy,
display a smile, white like the conch or lotus root.

O you who are resolute, an ascetic, and an excellent victor,[132]
you know at once with your mind the desires of your listeners.
Destroy their doubts that have arisen, O best of sages,
with words excellent, enduring, and virtuous. [267]

Resolute awakened ones,
those with the patience of an ocean or great mountain,
do not display a smile without reason.
Masses of people yearn to hear why it is
that masters display a smile.

"It is so, Ānanda," the Blessed One said. "It is so. Perfectly awakened tathāgatha arhats do not manifest a smile, Ānanda, without proper cause and reason. Ānanda, go and inform the monks as follows: 'The Tathāgata, monks, wants to travel to a cremation ground. Whoever among you is eager to travel to a cremation ground with the Tathāgata should take up his robes.'"

"Yes, Bhadanta," the venerable Ānanda replied, consenting to the Blessed One's request, and then he announced to the monks, "Venerable ones, the Tathāgata wants to travel to a cremation ground.

Whoever among you is eager to travel to a cremation ground with the Tathāgata should take up his robes."

"Yes, venerable one," all the monks replied in consent, and then they approached the Blessed One.

Now the Blessed One was self-controlled
and his followers were self-controlled,
he was calm and his followers were calm,
he was liberated and his followers were liberated,
he was confident and his followers were confident,
he was disciplined and his followers were disciplined,
he was an arhat and his followers were arhats,
he was without attachment
and his followers were without attachment,
and he instilled faith and his followers instilled faith.

He was like a bull surrounded by a herd of cows,
like a royal elephant surrounded by a herd of elephant cubs,
like a lion surrounded by a pack of wild animals,
like a royal goose surrounded by a gaggle of geese,
like an eagle surrounded by a flock of birds,
like a learned brahman surrounded by an assembly of students,
like an eminent doctor surrounded by a group of patients,
like a warrior surrounded by a troop of soldiers,
like a guide surrounded by a group of travelers,[133]
like a caravan leader surrounded by a company of merchants,
like a guildmaster surrounded by townspeople,
like a vassal king surrounded by a cabinet of ministers,
like a wheel-turning king surrounded by a thousand sons,
like the moon surrounded by a constellation of stars,
like the sun surrounded by thousands of rays,
like the great king Dhṛtarāṣṭra surrounded by a group
of celestial musicians,

like the great king Virūḍhaka surrounded by a group
of *kumbhāṇḍa*s,[134]
like the great king Dhanada surrounded by a group of yakṣas,
like Vemacitri surrounded by a group of antigods,
like Śakra surrounded by a group of gods,
and like Brahmā surrounded by the gods of Brahmakāyika.

He was like an ocean but calm,
like a cloud but full of water,
and like a mighty elephant but without pride or passion.
His senses were well restrained, [268]
his deportment and demeanor were unflappable,
he was adorned with the thirty-two marks of a great man,
and his body was radiant with the eighty minor marks.
His form was adorned with a halo extending an arm's length,
his brilliance was greater than a thousand suns,
and like a mountain of jewels that moved,
he was beautiful from every side.

He was endowed with the ten powers,
the four confidences,
the three special applications of mindfulness,
and great compassion.

Showdown at the Śītavana Cremation Ground

The Blessed One, surrounded by great disciples such as Ājñāta Kauṇḍinya, Aśvajit, Bāṣpa, Mahānāma, Bhadrika, Śāriputra, Maudgalyāyana, Kāśyapa, and Yaśaḥpūrṇa, and together with a large community of monks and many hundreds of thousands of beings, set out for the great cremation ground known as Śītavana. Knowing that there are eighteen benefits in traveling with a buddha,[135] many hundreds of thousands of deities followed close behind the Blessed One. And then, in the direction of the Śītavana, winds began to blow.

In the meantime, two young boys, a brahman and a kṣatriya, left Rājagṛha and began to play. The kṣatriya boy was immersed in faith, but not so the brahman boy.

"Friend," the brahman boy said to the kṣatriya boy,[136] "the Blessed One predicted that the householder Subhadra's wife would give birth to a boy; that he would make the family shine; that he would experience divine-like glory as a result of his actions; and that he would go forth as a monk in his order, where by ridding himself of all defilements, he would directly experience arhatship. But now the householder Subhadra's wife has died. She has met her end and been taken to the Śītavana cremation ground. I hope the Blessed One hasn't spoken falsely."[137]

Then the kṣatriya boy uttered this verse:

> The sky with the moon and stars may fall down,
> the earth with its mountains and forests may fly away,
> the water of vast oceans may dry up,
> but great seers never speak falsely.

"Friend, if that's the case," the brahman boy said, "let's go[138] to the great Śītavana cremation ground and see."

"Yes, my friend. Let's go."

Then the two set out.

At that time the Blessed One was also leaving Rājagṛha. The kṣatriya boy saw the Blessed One from a distance, and upon seeing him, he uttered these verses:[139] [269]

> Though surrounded by crowds of people,
> this humble sage proceeds without anxiety.

Surely he will crush the rival teachers
and roar[140] the highest roar of the lion.

These winds, cool like snow dust,[141]
eagerly blow toward Śītavana.
Many gods must be going
to see the miracle of Śākyamuni.

King Bimbisāra (Precious as Gold) heard that the Blessed One had predicted that the householder Subhadra's wife would give birth to a boy; that he would make the family shine; that he would experience divine-like glory as a result of his actions; and that he would go forth as a monk in his order, where by ridding himself of all defilements, he would directly experience arhatship. And he heard that now the householder Subhadra's wife had died; that she had met her end and been taken to the Śītavana cremation ground; and that the Blessed One, along with the community of his disciples, had also set off for Śītavana. Hearing this, it occurred to him, "The Blessed One wouldn't go to Śītavana without a reason. No doubt the Blessed One will want to perform a great feat in connection with the householder Subhadra's wife to gain new disciples. I'll see for myself." So, surrounded by the women of the palace, and by princes, ministers,[142] townspeople, and villagers, he set out from Rājagṛha.

The kṣatriya boy saw the king of Magadha, Śreṇya Bimbisāra, from a distance, and upon seeing him, he uttered this verse:

Since Śreṇya himself, the king of Magadha,
has left Rājagṛha with his entourage,
in my heart I am sure of this—
many people will soon be uplifted.

When the crowd of people saw the Blessed One, they made way for him. The Blessed One, with a smile on his face, entered the large crowd. When the Nirgranthas saw the Blessed One with a smile on his face, they reflected, "Since the ascetic Gautama has entered this large crowd with a smile on his face, that being[143] must not have died." They spoke to the householder Subhadra.

"Householder," they said, "perhaps that ill-fated being didn't pass away." [270]

"Noble one, if that's the case," he said, "what should I do next?"

"Householder," they said, "we're constrained by religious vows,[144] but you'll know what to do."

The householder then placed his wife on the funeral pyre and set it ablaze. Her entire body burned except for the area around her stomach. Then her stomach split open and a lotus appeared. Sitting on top of the pericarp of the lotus[145] was a young boy who was handsome, good-looking, and attractive. Seeing him, many hundreds of thousands of beings were filled with awe. The Nirgranthas, in turn, had their pride and arrogance destroyed, as well as their influence.[146]

Then the Blessed One said to the householder Subhadra, "Householder, take the boy." The householder began to scan the faces of the Nirgranthas.

"Householder," they said, "if you enter this burning pyre, you'll be completely consumed."[147]

The householder Subhadra wouldn't accept[148] the boy.

Then the Blessed One addressed [the doctor,] Jīvaka Kumārabhūta (Forever Young). "Jīvaka, take the little boy."

Jīvaka reflected, "It is impossible and inconceivable that the Blessed One would order me to do something that isn't right. I'll take him." Without doubt or hesitation, he plunged into the funeral pyre and took the boy.

As he plunged into the pyre at the Victor's command
and accepted[149] the young boy, enveloped in flames,
the fire, through the Victor's great power,
at once became cool like snow dust.

Then [the Blessed One][150] said this to Jīvaka Kumārabhūta: "Jīvaka, you aren't hurt or injured, are you?"

"Bhadanta," he said, "I was born in a palace, and I've grown up in a palace, but I've never known such coolness, not even from *gośīrṣa* sandalwood [paste], like I felt in this funeral pyre that the Blessed One transformed with his power."

Then the Blessed One addressed the householder Subhadra. "Householder, take the boy now."

The householder, however, was under the influence of false views, so he didn't comply. Again he scanned the faces of the Nirgranthas.

"Householder," they said, "this being is extremely ill-fated. He wasn't even burned by this all-consuming fire. What more is there to say? If you take him into your home now, you'll surely bring it to ruin,[151] and you'll die."

There is no love equal to that which one has for oneself. [271] The householder didn't accept the boy.

Then the Blessed One addressed King Bimbisāra: "Your majesty, take the boy."

With excitement, King Bimbisāra stretched out his hands and took him.[152] He then looked all around and asked, "Blessed One, what should this boy's name be?"[153]

"Your majesty, since this boy was delivered from the middle of a fire, let the boy's name be Jyotiṣka (Fiery One)."

And so he was given the name Jyotiṣka.[154]

Then the Blessed One, knowing the inclinations, propensities, makeup, and nature of that crowd of people, gave them a discourse on the dharma such that when they heard it, many hundreds of beings attained great distinction. Some directly experienced the reward of the stream-enterer; some the reward of the once-returner; some the reward of the nonreturner; and some, by ridding themselves of all defilements, directly experienced arhatship. Some produced roots of virtue for the weak and medium levels of the heat stage, the summit stage, and the tolerance stage. Some set their minds on attaining awakening as a disciple, some awakening as a solitary buddha, and some unsurpassed perfect awakening. Some accepted the taking of the refuges, and others the precepts. Almost the entire assembly became favorably inclined toward the Buddha, drawn toward the dharma, and well disposed toward the community.

Jyotiṣka and His Paternity

King Bimbisāra gave the boy Jyotiṣka over to eight nurses—two shoulder nurses, two wet nurses, two nursemaids, and two playtime nurses. Raised by these eight nurses, who nourished him with milk, yogurt, fresh butter, clarified butter, buttercream, and other special provisions that were very pure, he grew quickly like a lotus in a lake.

During this time, Jyotiṣka's maternal uncle had taken his goods and gone abroad. There he heard that his sister had become pregnant; that the Blessed One had predicted that she would give birth to a boy; that he would make the family shine; that he would experience divine-like glory as a result of his actions; and that he would go forth as a monk in his order, where by ridding himself of all defilements, he would directly experience arhatship. He disposed of his goods, took the goods that he received in exchange, and came to Rājagṛha. Then he heard that his sister had died, and upon hearing this, he reflected, "The Blessed One [272] predicted that she would give birth to a boy; that he would make the family shine; that he would experience divine-like glory as a result of his actions; and that he would go forth as a monk in his order, where by ridding himself of all defilements, he would directly experience arhatship. I hope the Blessed One hasn't spoken falsely." So he went and questioned his neighbors: "I heard that my sister was pregnant; that the Blessed One predicted that she would give birth to a boy; that he would make the family shine; that he would experience divine-like glory as a result of his actions, and that he would go forth as a monk in his order, where by ridding himself of all defilements, he would directly experience arhatship. I was very pleased when I heard this, but now I hear that she has died, that she has met her end. I hope the Blessed One hasn't spoken falsely."

Then the neighbors uttered this verse:

The sky with the moon and stars may fall down,
the earth with its mountains and forests may fly away,
the water of vast oceans may dry up,
but great seers will never speak falsely.

"The Blessed One hasn't spoken falsely," they said. "How could the Blessed One speak falsely? It's because your sister's husband attacked her as he did that she died.[155] The boy, however, possesses great magic and great power. He wasn't burned by the fire. Even now he grows up in the palace."[156]

Jyotiṣka's maternal uncle went to the householder Subhadra and said, "Householder, what you've done isn't right."

"What did I do?"

"Taken in by those Nirgranthas, you attacked my pregnant sister and she died.[157] The boy, however, possesses great magic and great power. He wasn't burned by the fire. Even now he grows up in the palace. But what's done is done. Now it would be best if you take the boy in. If you don't, we'll throw you out of the community and make you an outcast.[158] We'll have your infamy proclaimed on the streets, roads, squares, and crossroads. We'll say, 'Our sister was killed by the householder Subhadra! He's a killer of women! No one should speak to him!' And then in the royal court we'll bring about your ruin."

When the householder Subhadra heard this, he was distraught. He'd been rebuked, and he realized that he'd have to do as he'd been told. So he fell prostrate at the king's feet and said, "My lord, my relatives have rebuked me. They say that it would be best if [273] I take the boy in, and that if I don't take him in, they'll throw me out of the community and make me an outcast. They'll have my infamy proclaimed on the streets, roads, squares, and crossroads. They'll say, 'Our sister was killed by the householder Subhadra! He's a killer of women! No one should speak to him!' And in the royal court they'll bring about my ruin. So please give the boy Jyotiṣka to me."[159]

"Householder," the king said, "I didn't take the boy Jyotiṣka from you; he was entrusted to me by the Blessed One. If you want the boy, go to the Blessed One."

The householder Subhadra then went to the Blessed One. He fell prostrate at his feet and said, "Blessed One, my relatives reprimand me. They say that it would be best if I take the boy in, and that if I don't take him in, they'll throw me out of the community and make me an outcast. They'll have my infamy proclaimed on the streets, roads, squares, and crossroads. They'll say, 'Our sister was killed by the householder Subhadra! He's a killer of women! No one should speak to him!' And in the royal court they'll bring about my ruin. So please have the boy Jyotiṣka given to me."

The Blessed One reflected, "If Subhadra doesn't get the boy Jyotiṣka, given the situation, he'll cough up hot blood and die." With this in mind, he addressed the venerable Ānanda. "Ānanda, go and offer my greetings to King Bimbisāra. Then say this to him: 'Your majesty, give the boy Jyotiṣka to the householder Subhadra. If the householder Subhadra doesn't get the boy Jyotiṣka, given the situation, he'll cough up hot blood and die.'"

"Yes, Bhadanta," the venerable Ānanda replied, consenting to the Blessed One's request. Then he approached King Bimbisāra and, having approached, said this to him: "Your majesty, the Blessed One offers you his greetings and says that your majesty should give the boy Jyotiṣka to the householder Subhadra. He says that if the householder Subhadra doesn't get the boy Jyotiṣka, given the situation, he'll cough up hot blood and die."

"Bhadanta Ānanda," the king said, "I pay homage to the Lord Buddha. I will do as the Blessed One instructs." [274]

Pleasantries were then exchanged, and the venerable Ānanda departed.

King Bimbisāra then addressed the householder Subhadra. "Householder, I've raised this boy. He's dear and beloved to me. I'll give him up only on the condition that he comes to see me three times each and every day."

"Yes, my lord," he said, "he'll come to you. Who else would he come to see?"

The king then adorned Jyotiṣka with all kinds of ornaments, placed him on the back of an elephant, and sent him off.

Jyotiṣka and the Sandalwood Bowl

Now it is common knowledge that a son doesn't make a name for himself as long as his father is still alive.[160]

Time passed, and one day the householder Subhadra died. The boy Jyotiṣka was put in charge of the house. He developed faith in the Buddha and faith in the dharma and the community. He took refuge in the Buddha and took refuge in the dharma and the community. In that place where Subhadra killed his wife, he had a monastery built, filled it with all the necessary provisions, and offered it to the noble community of monks who arrived from all four directions.

The place is also referred to by the elders in a sūtra: "The Blessed One was staying in the city of Rājagṛha in the Mṛditakukṣika Forest (Where a Woman's Womb Was Squeezed) . . ."[161]

Those servants of the householder Subhadra who had taken their goods and gone abroad heard that the householder Subhadra had died, that the boy Jyotiṣka was put in charge of the home, that he developed faith in the Buddha and faith in the dharma and the community, and that he had also taken refuge in the Buddha and taken refuge in the dharma and the community. They procured a bowl made of *gośīrṣa* sandalwood, filled it with jewels, and offered it as a gift to the [new] householder Jyotiṣka. He, in turn, mounted it on top of a tall pillar. Then he had bells rung for the following proclamation: "No one is to retrieve this bowl of jewels using a rope, ladder, or hook.[162] But whoever retrieves it using magical powers, whether he be an ascetic, a brahman, or one possessed of great magic or great power, may do with it as he likes."

Now some non-Buddhist renunciants got up very early the next morning and went to take their ritual baths in sacred waters.[163] They saw the bowl full of jewels, and upon seeing it, they spoke to the householder Jyotiṣka.

"Householder, what is this?"

He explained the situation to them in detail.

"Householder," they said, "you have faith in the followers of that ascetic from the Śākya clan. Let them retrieve it in this way." With that said, they departed.

Just then some very senior monks entered Rājagṛha for alms. [275] They saw the bowl full of jewels, and they too asked the householder Jyotiṣka, "What is this?"

He explained the situation to them in detail as well.

"Householder," they said, "why should we expose ourselves just for a bowl? The Blessed One has said that monks should live with their virtues concealed and their sins cleansed."[164] And with that said, they departed.

Meanwhile the venerable Daśabala (Possessing the Ten Powers) Kāśyapa arrived there.[165] "Householder, what is this?" he asked.

Jyotiṣka explained to him just what had happened.

The venerable Daśabala Kāśyapa reflected, "I have spewed up, spit out, abandoned, and driven away a mass of defilements collected from time immemorial, and yet the householder challenges[166] a person such as myself to make use of a magical power common even among heretics.[167] I will fulfill this desire of his." Stretching out his arm like the trunk of an elephant, he took the bowl. Having taken it, he went to the monastery. There he was addressed by the monks.

"Elder, where did you get this bowl made of *gośīrṣa* sandalwood?"

He explained to them what had happened.

"Elder," the monks asked, "is it permissible for you to display your magical powers just for a bowl?"

"Venerable ones," he said, "it may be permissible and it may not. What's done is done. What is there to do now?"

The monks related this incident to the Blessed One. The Blessed One said, "A monk is not to display magical power in front of a lay person. Whoever does so commits a transgression. Furthermore, there are four bowls to be considered—those of gold, silver, beryl, and crystal. And there are four other bowls as well—those of brass, copper, bronze, and camphor.[168] Regarding those first four bowls, if they haven't yet been presented as an offering, then they shouldn't be presented. And if they've already been presented, then they should be discarded. Regarding those latter four bowls, if these haven't yet been presented as an offering, then they shouldn't be presented. And if they've already been presented, then they should be used as containers for medicine. However, as for those that are most desirable,[169] there are two kinds of bowls—those made of iron and clay."

Divine-Like Glory Appears

One day, divine-like glory appeared to the householder Jyotiṣka.

Now on the way between Rājagṛha and Campā there is a customs house, and in it the customs officer had died. Thereafter he was reborn among the serpent yakṣas.[170] He then appeared to his sons in a dream saying, "Sons, in this place build a yakṣa abode for me, [276] and in it hang a bell. Whenever someone goes through without paying customs tax on his goods, the bell will clang until he is made to come back and pay up."[171] The sons told their relatives and relations about the dream, and at the right day, date, and time, they built a yakṣa abode in that place and in it hung a bell.

Meanwhile, in Campā there lived a certain brahman. He brought home a girl from an appropriate family as his wife. The brahman girl reflected, "My husband earns a living by doing this and that. I only eat. It isn't right that I should be without a job." So she went to the marketplace and bought some cotton. She worked it until it was soft, and then she spun it into thread. From that thread, a skilled weaver wove twin pieces of cloth that were worth thousands of *kārṣāpaṇa* coins. She then said to her husband, "Brahman, these twin pieces of cloth are worth thousands of *kārṣāpaṇa* coins. Take them and go to the marketplace. If anyone inquires, they should be sold for thousands of *kārṣāpaṇa* coins. If not, you should declare, 'This isn't a real trading center!' and then go somewhere else."

He took the twin pieces of cloth and went to the marketplace. No one was willing to spend thousands of *kārṣāpaṇa* coins for them. "This isn't a real trading center!" he declared. Then he placed the twin pieces of cloth inside the handle of his umbrella and set out with a caravan for Rājagṛha.

Eventually he arrived at the customs house. A customs officer taxed the caravan. The caravan paid its customs tax and set off. The bell began to ring. "Gentlemen," the customs officers said, "since the bell is ringing, the caravan must not have been taxed correctly. Let's tax it again." They made the caravan return and once again they taxed it.

"Nothing is left untaxed," they thought, and yet the bell still rang. They had the caravan return once more and they inspected it. "There's absolutely nothing!"

The merchants from the caravan began to complain: "Do you want to rob us, making us return again and again?" The customs officers divided the caravan into two groups, and let one group go through. Those whom the brahman wasn't among went ahead, but as the others went through, the bell began to ring as it had before. The customs officers examined them once again. They divided them into two groups, again and again, following the same procedure, until just the brahman remained. Then they grabbed him.

"Look and see if I have anything," he said. The customs officers examined everything and then released him. [277] The bell continued to ring. They then had the brahman return and said, "Hey brahman, speak up! We won't force you to pay any customs tax, but the deity [in the yakṣa abode] has made his presence known."

"Truthfully," he said, "you won't force me to pay?"

"No, we won't force you to pay."

He then took out the twin pieces of cloth from the handle of his umbrella and showed them to the customs officers. They were in awe.

"Friend, something like this belongs to the deity!" Then they unfolded one of the pieces of cloth and cloaked the deity with it.

"You told me that you wouldn't force me to pay any customs tax," the brahman said, "and now you take away all my possessions!"

"Brahman, we didn't take anything," they said. "This is a divine possession, so we have used it to cloak the deity. Now you can take it and go."

He took it back, once again placed it in the shaft of his umbrella, and set off. Eventually he arrived at Rājagṛha. In the marketplace, he spread out those pieces of cloth and waited. There too no one who was willing to spend thousands of *kārṣāpaṇa* coins for the pair inquired about them. "Rājagṛha isn't a real trading center either!" he declared.

Just then Jyotiṣka,[172] who had left the palace mounted on the back of an elephant, was going through the middle of the marketplace on his way back home. He heard what the brahman had declared and said, "Gentlemen, why does this brahman declare that this isn't a real trading center? Summon him. I shall ask him."

They summoned him.

"Brahman," Jyotiṣka said, "why do you declare that this isn't a real trading center?"

"Householder, these twin pieces of cloth are worth thousands of *kārṣāpaṇa* coins, but no one inquires about them."

"Bring them here," he said. "Let me see them."

The brahman showed him the two pieces of cloth.

"It's just as you say," Jyotiṣka said. "But one piece of material is used and one is unused. The value of the unused one is five hundred *kārṣāpaṇa* coins. The used one is worth only two hundred and fifty."

"Why is that?" the brahman asked.

"Brahman," Jyotiṣka said, "I'll let you see it with your own eyes. Look here."

He threw the unused one high into the air. It remained there like a canopy. Then he threw the used one. Right after it was thrown, it fell down.

The brahman saw this and was in awe. "Householder," he said, "you possess great magic and great power."

"Brahman," Jyotiṣka said, "show me the unused one again." [278] Jyotiṣka then took the unused piece of cloth and threw it on top of a thorny hedge. It passed over without getting caught. He threw the other, and it got stuck on a thorn.

The brahman was even more inspired and said, "Householder, you possess great magic and great power. Offer what you wish for the two pieces of cloth."

"Brahman, you are a guest," he said. "You yourself are to be honored. I'll offer you exactly one thousand." He gave him one thousand *kārṣāpaṇa* coins. The brahman took the coins and departed. Jyotiṣka gave the used cloth to a boy, and the unused one he made into a bathing garment.

Now one day King Bimbisāra went out on the roof of his palace and stood there surrounded by his cabinet of ministers. Jyotiṣka's bathing garment was on top of his house drying in the open air when it was carried off by the wind. It then fell on top of King Bimbisāra.

"Gentlemen," the king said, "this garment is worthy of a king! Where is it from?"

"My lord," they said, "it's been heard that for a week, a rain of gold fell for King Māndhātā.[173] And now for my lord, a rain of fine garments has begun to fall. Soon there will be a rain of gold."

"Gentlemen," the king said, "the Blessed One predicted that the householder Jyotiṣka would experience divine-like glory as a result of his actions. And now this divine garment has fallen from the sky. Put it aside. When he comes in person, I'll give it to him."

As they were talking, Jyotiṣka arrived.

"Young man," the king said, "the Blessed One predicted that you would experience divine-like glory as a result of your actions. And now I have here this divine garment that has fallen from the sky. Take it."

Jyotiṣka stretched out his hand and said, "My lord, allow me to see it." He began to examine it and found that it was his bathing garment. Astonished,[174] he said, "My lord, this is my bathing garment! The wind must have carried it away and brought it here."

"Young man, has divine-like glory appeared to you?"

"Yes, my lord, it has appeared to me."

"Young man, if that's the case, why didn't you invite me over?"

"My lord, consider yourself invited."

"Go then. And have food prepared."

"My lord, what does someone to whom divine-like glory has appeared need to prepare?"

"Of course! It's already prepared. Let's go."[175]

Jyotiṣka's Home

The king went to Jyotiṣka's home, and when he saw the outdoor attendants, he averted his eyes.

"My lord, why do you avert your eyes?"

"Young man," he said, "these are the women of the house." [279]

"My lord, these aren't the women of the house. They are only outdoor attendants."

The king was in awe. Further along, when he saw some indoor attendants, he once again began to avert his eyes. Jyotiṣka questioned him as before, and the king replied as before. Jyotiṣka then said, "My lord, these aren't the women of the house either. They are indoor attendants." The king was in even greater awe.

Now in the interior entrance hall of Jyotiṣka's home a jeweled floor had been constructed. Fish could be seen moving about on the surface of the floor by means of a mechanical device, as though the floor were filled with water.[176] Thinking it was a pool, the king wanted to enter it, so he began to take off his sandals.

"My lord," Jyotiṣka said, "why are you taking off your sandals?"

"Young man," he said, "for entering the water."

"My lord, this isn't water," Jyotiṣka said. "It's a jeweled floor."

"Young man," he said, "there are fish clearly visible moving about on the surface."[177]

"My lord, they move about by means of a mechanical device."

The king didn't believe him, so he dropped his seal ring. It fell to the ground with a clink. In awe, he then entered the hall and sat on the lion throne. The women of the house approached to venerate his feet. Tears began to fall from their eyes.

"Young man," the king said, "why do the women of the house cry?"

"My lord, they aren't crying. Garments were made fragrant for my lord with wood smoke, and from this they shed tears."

Served there with divine-like glory, the king lost his senses and didn't leave. Royal functions and royal duties were neglected. The ministers prevailed upon Prince Ajātaśatru (Without Enemies).[178]

"Prince," they told him, "my lord has entered Jyotiṣka's home and lost his senses. Go and inform him of the situation."

Prince Ajātaśatru went there and said, "My lord, how is it that you've come here and stayed on? The ministers say that the royal functions and royal duties are being neglected."

"Prince," he asked, "can't you rule for a single day?"

"Does my lord think that only one day has passed since he's come here? Today is the seventh day that my lord stays here."

The king scanned Jyotiṣka's face and said, "Young man, is this true?"

"It's true, my lord. It's been a full seven days."

"Young man, how do you know whether it's day or night?"

"My lord, from the flowers as they bloom and wither, from the jewels as they glow and dim, and from the birds as they chirp and fall silent. Aren't there flowers that bloom at night and wither by day? [280] Aren't there those that bloom by day and wither at night? Aren't there jewels that glow at night and not by day? Aren't there those that glow by day and not at night? Aren't there birds that chirp at night and not by day? And those that chirp by day and not at night?"

In awe, the king said, "Young man, the Blessed One tells the truth. Exactly what the Blessed One predicted for you has happened and nothing else." With that said, he left Jyotiṣka's home.

Jyotiṣka and Prince Ajātaśatru

Meanwhile Prince Ajātaśatru stole a jewel that belonged to Jyotiṣka and placed it in the hands of a boy. The jewel magically returned to the place from where he took it.

"Boy," Ajātaśatru said, "bring me the jewel so I can see it."

The boy opened his fists and said, "Prince, I don't know where it went."

Prince Ajātaśatru began to beat him.

"Prince, why are you beating him?" Jyotiṣka asked.

"Householder, I'm a thief, but he's a bigger thief. I stole a jewel from you, and then he stole it from me!"

"Prince," he said, "you didn't steal it, and neither did he. It has come right back to where you took it from. Nevertheless, Prince, this is your home. Take as many jewels as you like or whatever else you need."

Humiliated, the prince reflected, "When my father dies and I become king, then I'll take what I want."

Ajātaśatru, under the evil influences of Devadatta, eventually killed his father, a just and virtuous king, and then crowned himself and put himself on the throne. Then he said to Jyotiṣka, "Householder, you are my brother. Let's divide up your house."[179]

Jyotiṣka reflected, "Why would someone who kills his father, a just and virtuous king, have mercy on me? He'll come to my house, for sure. I'll offer him whatever he likes." With this in mind, he said, "My lord, it's already been divided up. What's left to be divided? You come to my house, and I'll come to your house."

"Very well," Ajātaśatru said. "Do as you wish." He then went to Jyotiṣka's house, and Jyotiṣka went to Ajātaśatru's house. The glory from Jyotiṣka's house disappeared and followed Jyotiṣka wherever he went. It went on like this until that glory had disappeared and reappeared seven times.

Then Ajātaśatru reflected, "Even switching houses like this, I can't[180] steal Jyotiṣka's jewels! I'll try something else."[181] He then hired [281] some thieves and told them, "Go and steal the jewels from Jyotiṣka's house." They began to climb into his house using ladders and hooks.

One of the women of the house was standing on the roof and saw them. "Thief! Thief!" she screamed.

Jyotiṣka heard this and called out from his bedroom, "Stop! Thieves!"

They stopped instantly, right where they were, and stayed there until night became dawn. Then many people saw them and said, "Friends, this evil king killed his father, a just and virtuous king. Now he even gets thieves to rob people's homes for him. Why wouldn't he get someone to rob my home?" There was a lot of agitation.

Ajātaśatru sent a messenger to Jyotiṣka to say, "Stop making me out to be a villain!"

Jyotiṣka called out from his bedroom, "Get lost, thieves!" And they left. Jyotiṣka then reflected, "Why wouldn't someone who kills his father kill me as well? The Blessed One has predicted that I will definitely go forth in his order, where by ridding myself of all defilements, I will directly experience arhatship. I'm leaving. I'm going forth as a monk."

Jyotiṣka gave away whatever riches he had to the poor, the orphaned, and the destitute, making the unwealthy wealthy. The householder Jyotiṣka then said farewell to his friends, relations, and relatives and approached the Blessed One. Having approached the Blessed One, he placed his head in veneration at the Blessed One's feet and then sat down at a respectful distance. Sitting down at a respectful distance, the householder Jyotiṣka then said this to the Blessed One: "Bhadanta, may I renounce, take ordination, and become a monk according to the dharma and monastic discipline that have been so well expressed. May I follow the religious life in the presence of the Blessed One."

Then the Blessed One addressed him, uttering the "Come, O monk" formula for ordination: "Come, O monk! Follow the religious life!" As soon as the Blessed One finished speaking, there Jyotiṣka stood—head shaved, garbed in monastic robes, bowl and water pot in hand,[182] with a week's growth of hair and beard and the disciplined deportment of a monk who had been ordained for one hundred years.

"Come," the Tathāgata said to him.
With head shaved and body wrapped in robes,
he instantly attained tranquility of the senses,
and so he remained by the will of the Buddha.[183]

Then the Blessed One gave him instructions. After striving and straining, he came to understand that ever-turning five-spoked wheel of saṃsāra; he dealt a final blow to rebirth in all realms of saṃsāra, since they are subject to decay and decline, scattering and destruction; and by ridding himself of all defilements, he directly experienced arhatship. [282] Becoming an arhat,

he was free from attachment in the three realms;
he regarded clods of earth and gold as equal in value;
he possessed equanimity toward the sky
  and the palm of his hand;
he didn't distinguish between being cut by a blade
  and being anointed with sandalwood paste;
the eggshell [of his ignorance] was broken by knowledge;
he obtained the special knowledges, superhuman faculties,
  and analytic insights;
and he was averse to worldly attainments, temptations,
  and honors.
He became worthy of respect, honor, and obeisance
  from the gods, including Indra and Upendra.

Some monks in doubt asked the Lord Buddha, the remover of all doubts, "Bhadanta, what deed did the venerable Jyotiṣka do such that he was placed on a funeral pyre, divine-like glory appeared to him, and he eventually went forth as a monk in the Blessed One's order, where by ridding himself of all defilements, he directly experienced arhatship?"

"Monks," the Blessed One said, "the deeds that Jyotiṣka himself has performed and accumulated have now come together,[184] and their conditions have matured. They remain before him like an oncoming flood and will certainly come to pass. Those deeds were performed and accumulated by Jyotiṣka. Who else will experience their results? For those deeds that are performed and accumulated, monks, do not mature outside of oneself—neither in the element of earth nor in the element of water, in the element of fire or in the element of wind. Instead, those deeds that are performed and accumulated, both good and bad, mature in the aggregates, the elements, and the sense bases that are appropriated when one is reborn.

> Actions never come to naught,
> even after hundreds of millions of years.
> When the right conditions gather and the time is right,
> then they will have their effect on embodied beings.

Vipaśyin, King Bandhumān, and the Householder Anaṅgaṇa

Long ago, monks, in the ninety-first age, there arose in the world a teacher named Vipaśyin (Insightful),

> who was a tathāgata,
> an arhat,
> a perfectly awakened being,
> perfect in knowledge and conduct,
> a sugata,

a knower of the world,
an unsurpassed guide for those in need of training,
a teacher of gods and humans,
a buddha,
and a blessed one.

Wandering through the countryside surrounded by sixty-two thousand monks, he arrived at the capital Bandhumatī (Ancestral Home), and in Bandhumatī he stayed in the Bandhumatīyaka (Ancestral Homeland) Forest.

At that time in the capital Bandhumatī, a king named Bandhumān (Rich in Relations) ruled a kingdom that was thriving, prosperous, and safe, with plenty of food and throngs of people, that was free from quarrel and strife, with no hustle and bustle, thieves, or diseases, that was rich in rice, sugarcane, cattle, and buffalo. He was a just and virtuous king, and he ruled according to dharma. [283]

And in that capital there was a householder named Anaṅgaṇa (Sinless),[185] who was rich, wealthy, and prosperous, with vast and extensive holdings, who had amassed a wealth like the god Vaiśravaṇa. Truly, he rivaled Vaiśravaṇa in wealth. "I have invited the perfectly awakened Vipaśyin to my home many times and served him food," the householder Anaṅgaṇa reflected, "but I've never offered him all the necessary provisions for the three months of the rainy season. I really should offer the perfectly awakened Vipaśyin all the necessary provisions for the three months of the rainy season." With this in mind, he approached the perfectly awakened Vipaśyin and, having approached, placed his head in veneration at the perfectly awakened Vipaśyin's feet and then sat down at a respectful distance.

The perfectly awakened Vipaśyin instructed, incited, inspired, and delighted the householder Anaṅgaṇa, who was seated at a respectful distance, with a discourse on the dharma. After he instructed, incited, inspired, and delighted him in many ways with this discourse on the dharma, he became silent.

The householder Anaṅgaṇa then got up from his seat, properly arranged his robe on one shoulder, bowed toward the perfectly awakened Vipaśyin with his hands respectfully folded, and said this to him: "May the Blessed One, along with the community of monks, accept my offering of enough provisions of robes, begging bowls, bedding and seats, and medicines to cure the sick to last the three months of the rainy season."

With his silence, the perfectly awakened Vipaśyin accepted the householder Anaṅgaṇa's invitation. Then the householder Anaṅgaṇa, realizing that by his silence the Blessed One had accepted his invitation, placed his head in veneration at the perfectly awakened Vipaśyin's feet, got up from his seat, and departed.

King Bandhumān heard that the perfectly awakened Vipaśyin, after wandering through the countryside surrounded by sixty-two thousand monks, had now arrived at Bandhumatī, and that in Bandhumatī he was staying in the Bandhumatīyaka Forest. When he heard this, it occurred to him, "I have invited the Blessed One to my home many times and served him food, but I've never offered him all the necessary provisions for the three months of the rainy season. I really should offer the perfectly awakened Vipaśyin all the necessary provisions [for those three months]."[186] With this in mind, he approached the perfectly awakened Vipaśyin and, having approached, placed his head in veneration at the perfectly awakened Vipaśyin's feet and then sat down at a respectful distance. [284]

The Blessed One instructed, incited, inspired, and delighted King Bandhumān, who was seated at a respectful distance, with a discourse on the dharma. After he instructed, incited, inspired, and delighted the king in many ways with this discourse on the dharma, he became silent.

King Bandhumān then got up from his seat, properly arranged his robe on one shoulder, bowed toward the perfectly awakened Vipaśyin with his hands respectfully folded, and said this to him: "May the Blessed One, along with the community of monks, accept my offering of enough provisions of robes, begging bowls, bedding and seats, and medicines to cure the sick to last the three months of the rainy season."

"Your majesty, the householder Anaṅgaṇa invited me before you did."

"Then may the Blessed One accept that I will do as the householder Anaṅgaṇa permits."

"Your majesty, if the householder Anaṅgaṇa gives you permission, then I will give you permission as well."

King Bandhumān then placed his head in veneration at the perfectly awakened Vipaśyin's feet, got up from his seat, and departed. He returned to his home. King Bandhumān then had a messenger say this to the householder Anaṅgaṇa: "Householder, please be informed that I will feed the perfectly awakened Vipaśyin before you. Afterward, there won't be any problem for you to feed him."

"My lord," the householder Anaṅgaṇa replied, "I invited the perfectly awakened Vipaśyin before you. I myself will feed him."

"Householder, that may be the case," the king said, "but you still live in my kingdom. Shouldn't I be entitled to feed him before you?"

"My lord, although I live in your kingdom, whoever invited him first should still feed him. In this instance, my lord's demand isn't proper."

"Householder, I'm not giving you a choice. Nevertheless, whoever can defeat the other by preparing better food can feed the perfectly awakened Vipaśyin for the rest of the rainy season."

"As you wish," the householder Anaṅgaṇa replied, consenting to his proposal.

That very night the householder Anaṅgaṇa prepared hard and soft foods, both fresh and fine, and then at daybreak he got up, [prepared the seats,][187] and set out pitchers of water. Then he had a messenger inform the Blessed One that it was now the appropriate time: "It is time, Bhadanta. The food is ready. Now the Blessed One may do as the time permits." [285]

Later in the morning the perfectly awakened Vipaśyin got dressed, took his bowl and robe, and surrounded by the community of monks, approached the place where the householder Anaṅgaṇa was offering food. Having approached, he sat down in front of the community of monks in the seat specially prepared for him.

Now when the householder Anaṅgaṇa was sure that the community of monks led by the Buddha was comfortably seated, he served and indulged them, with his own hands, with hard and soft foods, both fresh and fine. When he had served and indulged them, with his own hands, with many courses of hard and soft foods, both fresh and fine, and was sure that the Blessed One had finished eating, washed his hands, and set aside his bowl,[188] he then sat down in front of the Buddha, taking a lower seat, to listen to the dharma.

The perfectly awakened Vipaśyin then instructed, incited, inspired, and delighted the householder Anaṅgaṇa with a discourse on the dharma. After he instructed, incited, inspired, and delighted him in many ways with this discourse on the dharma, Anaṅgaṇa departed.

King Bandhumān likewise fed him—and here the very same text is to be supplied in full.[189] Yet in no way did King Bandhumān defeat the householder Anaṅgaṇa by preparing better food. King Bandhumān sat lost in thought, with cheek in hand.

"My lord," the ministers said, "why do you sit there lost in thought, with cheek in hand?"

"Gentlemen," he said, "why shouldn't I sit here lost in thought? I can't even defeat an ordinary householder who lives in my kingdom by preparing better food!"

"My lord," they said, "this householder doesn't own any firewood. Just prevent any firewood from being sold."

The king had bells rung for the following proclamation: "Friends, no one is to sell firewood to the inhabitants of my kingdom. Whoever sells it to them shall be banished from my kingdom."

The householder Anaṅgaṇa began to prepare food with [luxurious] fragrant wood.[190] He also drenched some cloth in fragrant oil and with it rubbed the cakes [that he had prepared to give them a nice fragrance].[191] The entire city of Bandhumatī was suffused with a sweet smell.

"Gentlemen," King Bandhumān asked, "where does that pleasing smell come from?"

They explained the situation to him in detail.

"I shall do the same as well," he said. "Can't I afford to do so?" [286]

"My lord," his ministers said, "what's the use of doing that? This householder will soon die, and he has no son. All that he has earned and inherited will belong to my lord. Allow firewood to be sold."

So the king allowed firewood to be sold.

The householder Anaṅgaṇa heard that the king once again allowed firewood to be sold. Polluting his mind with bad thoughts, he uttered harsh words: "Now that there's firewood for cooking food, I can stick him and his ministers on a funeral pyre and torch them both!"

Meanwhile, with cheek in hand, the king sat lost in thought.

"My lord," the ministers said, "why do you sit there lost in thought, with cheek in hand?"

He explained the situation to them in detail.

"My lord," they said, "don't despair. We'll fix it so that my lord defeats the householder Anaṅgaṇa."

The next day the ministers had the capital Bandhumatī cleared of stones, pebbles, and gravel; sandalwood-scented water was sprinkled about; small pots of fragrant incense were lined up; rows of silk banners were hung; flags and banners were raised; and various flowers were scattered about so that it looked like the divine Nandana Grove or a heavenly park. A circular courtyard[192] was also built, which was as beautiful as what it enclosed, and in it seats were prepared, which were made beautiful by seat covers that were adorned with many kinds of jewels. In addition, the ministers had food prepared that was soft, pure, and sweet smelling, as well as various rice dishes and condiments, all of which were pleasing like divine ambrosia and fit for the teacher of the three worlds.

The ministers then informed King Bandhumān, "My lord, the food is now as beautiful as the city. Rejoice!"

When King Bandhumān saw all this, he was in awe. His mind was overcome with astonishment. Then he had a messenger announce to the perfectly awakened Vipaśyin that it was now the appropriate time: "It is time, Bhadanta, the food is ready. Now the Blessed One may do as the time permits."

Later in the morning the perfectly awakened Vipaśyin got dressed, took his bowl and robe, and leading the community of monks that surrounded him, approached the place where King Bandhumān was offering food. Having approached, he sat down in front of the community of monks in the seat specially prepared for him. King Bandhumān's auspiciously anointed elephant [287] carried a hundred-ribbed umbrella over the perfectly awakened Vipaśyin's head, and the remaining elephants did likewise for the monks. King Bandhumān's chief queen fanned the perfectly awakened Vipaśyin with a golden yak-tail fan encrusted with jewels, and the remaining women of the palace did likewise for the remaining monks.

The householder Anaṅgaṇa sent a spy with these instructions: "My friend, go and see what kind of food King Bandhumān is feeding the community of monks led by the Buddha." When the spy went and saw those riches, he stood there transfixed, his mind filled with wonder. Anaṅgaṇa likewise sent a second spy, and then a third, who also went and stood there transfixed.

The householder Anaṅgaṇa then went in person. When he saw those riches, he was despondent. "I could arrange another feast," he reflected, "but I don't have elephants or a palace full of women. Where would I find that kind of wealth?" With this in mind, he went home and addressed his gatekeeper: "My friend, if any supplicant comes, give him what he asks for but don't let him enter." With that said, he entered the grieving chamber to console himself, and there he remained.

Now Śakra, lord of the gods, can look and come to know what is below him.[193] He reflected, "The perfectly awakened Vipaśyin is the best of those who are worthy of offerings in the world, and the householder Anaṅgaṇa is the best of donors. The householder should be helped."

With this in mind, Kauśika magically transformed himself so that he had the appearance of a brahman and then approached the householder Anaṅgaṇa's home. Having approached, he addressed the gatekeeper: "Sir, go and tell the householder Anaṅgaṇa that a brahman from the Kauśika clan is standing at the door and wants to see him."

"Brahman," he said, "the householder has posted me [here with instructions that] any supplicant who comes should be given what he asks for but can't enter. Take what you want and go. What good will it do you to see the householder?"

"My friend," he said. "I don't need anything. I just want to see the householder in person. Now go."

He went and informed the householder Anaṅgaṇa, "Sir, a brahman from the Kauśika clan is standing at the door. He wants to see you."

"Go, my friend," he said. "Give him whatever he wants. What good will it do him to enter here?"

"Sir," he said, "I told him that. He said that he wasn't asking for anything but that he just wants to see the householder in person." [288]

"My friend," he said, "if that's the case, then send him in."

He sent him in.

Then the brahman asked, "Householder, why do you sit here lost in thought, with cheek in hand?"

The householder uttered this verse:

> One shouldn't disclose one's grief to someone
> who won't release him from that grief.
> One should only disclose one's grief
> to someone who'll fully release him from that grief.

"Householder," Śakra said, "what grief do you have? Tell me. I can release you from that grief."

He explained the situation to him in detail.

Then Śakra, lord of the gods, cast off his appearance as a Kauśika brahman and, standing in his natural form, said, "Householder, the divinely born Viśvakarman will offer you assistance." With that said, he departed.

Then Śakra, lord of the gods, went to the gods of Trāyastriṃśa (Thirty-Three) and addressed the divinely born Viśvakarman: "Viśvakarman, go and offer assistance to the householder Anaṅgaṇa."

"Yes, Kauśika," the divinely born Viśvakarman replied, consenting to the request of Śakra, lord of the gods. "And all the best to you." Then he came to Bandhumatī.

He magically transformed the city so that its beauty was even more sublime; he created a divine circular courtyard; he set aside a divine seat; and he prepared divine food. [The householder then fed the community of monks led by the Buddha. Indra's mount,] the elephant-king Airavaṇa, carried a hundred-ribbed umbrella over the perfectly awakened Vipaśyin's head, and the remaining elephants did likewise for the remaining monks. [Indra's wife,] the divine maiden Śacī, fanned the perfectly awakened Vipaśyin with a golden yak-tail fan encrusted with jewels, and the remaining nymphs did likewise for the [remaining] monks.

King Bandhumān sent a spy with these instructions: "My friend, go and [see][194] what kind of food the householder is serving to the community of monks led by the Buddha." When the man went there and saw those riches, he stood there transfixed. The king then sent a minister. He too stood there transfixed. He sent the prince. He too stood there transfixed. Then King Bandhumān went in person and stood at the gate.

The perfectly awakened Vipaśyin said, "Householder, King Bandhumān has seen the truth.[195] You committed an act of harsh speech toward him.[196] Now he stands in person at the gate. Go and ask for forgiveness."

He went out, asked for forgiveness, and then said, "Your majesty, please come in. You may serve the food with your own hands."

The king entered and saw the divine wealth, [289] and upon seeing it, he was in awe. "Householder," he said, "you yourself should feed the community of monks led by the Buddha every day, not me."

The householder Anaṅgaṇa then satisfied the perfectly awakened

Vipaśyin with that wealth and those fine foods for the three months of the rainy season. Then he fell prostrate at the perfectly awakened Vipaśyin's feet and made this fervent aspiration: "Since I have made offerings to someone so righteous and worthy of offerings, by this root of virtue may I be born in a family that is rich, wealthy, and prosperous; may I experience divine-like glory as a result of my actions; and may I obtain such virtues so that I may please and not displease a teacher just like this!"

"What do you think, monks? The householder Anaṅgaṇa was none other than the nobly born Jyotiṣka at that time and at that juncture. Since he uttered harsh words toward King Bandhumān, who had seen the truth, as a result of that action, he was placed on a funeral pyre and burned along with his mother five hundred times. Even in this lifetime he was placed on a funeral pyre and burned. As a result of the act of making offerings to the Tathāgatha Vipaśyin and then making a fervent aspiration, he was born in a family that was rich, wealthy, and prosperous; divine-like glory appeared to him; and he went forth as a monk in my order, where by ridding himself of all defilements, he directly experienced arhatship. And as his teacher—who is equal in speed and equal in strength with the perfectly awakened Vipaśyin, who is equally dedicated to religious duties, and who has attained an equal universality—I have been pleased and not displeased by him.

"And so, monks, the result of absolutely evil actions is absolutely evil, the result of absolutely pure actions is absolutely pure, and the result of mixed actions is mixed. Therefore monks, because of this, one should reject absolutely evil actions and mixed ones as well and strive to perform only absolutely pure actions. It is this, monks, that you should learn to do."

This was said by the Blessed One. With their minds uplifted, the monks rejoiced at the words of the Blessed One.

So ends the *Jyotiṣka-avadāna*, the nineteenth chapter in the glorious *Divyāvadāna*.

20. *The Story of Kanakavarṇa*

KANAKAVARṆA-AVADĀNA[197]

THUS have I heard. [290] At one time the Blessed One was staying in the city of Śrāvastī at the Jeta Grove in the park of Anāthapiṇḍada (Almsgiver to the Poor), together with a large community of monks, 1,250 in number. There the Blessed One was respected, honored, revered, and venerated by monks, nuns, male and female lay devotees, kings, royal ministers, various non-Buddhist renunciants, ascetics, brahmans, roaming and wandering mendicants, gods, nāgas, yakṣas, antigods, heavenly birds, celestial musicians, kinnaras, and great snakes. In addition, the Blessed One received an abundance of excellent provisions, both divine and human, of robes, begging bowls, bedding and seats, and medicines to cure the sick. And the Blessed One was unsullied by these, like a lotus by water.

And in every direction and quarter, the Blessed One gained great fame through praises of his virtue. It was said:

The Blessed One is just like this—

a tathāgata,
an arhat,
a perfectly awakened being,
perfect in knowledge and conduct,
a sugata,
a knower of the world,

an unsurpassed guide for those in need of training,
a teacher of gods and humans,
a buddha,
and a blessed one.

In this lifetime, he has directly understood and experienced this world with its gods, [evil] Māra, and [lord] Brahmā, and the inhabitants of this world with their ascetics, brahmans, gods, and humans, and now having become a monk, he holds forth. He teaches the dharma that is excellent in the beginning, excellent in the middle, and excellent in the end and good in both meaning and letter. He makes perfectly clear the religious life that is complete, perfect, pure, and chaste.

Then the Blessed One addressed the monks: "If, monks, beings were to know the result of charity and the consequence of offering charity as I know the result of charity and the consequence of offering charity, then they would never eat the very last remaining morsel of food without giving it away or sharing it, if a worthy recipient of that food were to be found.[198] And the stingy thoughts that arise would not seize hold of their minds.[199] But monks, those beings who do not know the result of charity and the consequence of offering charity [291] as I know the result of charity and the consequence of offering charity eat with a mind that is miserly, without giving their food away or sharing it. And the stingy thoughts that arise do seize hold of their minds. Why is this?"

King Kanakavarṇa and the Famine

Long ago, monks, in a time gone by, there was a king named Kanakavarṇa (Golden in Color) who was handsome, good-looking, and attractive, with a brilliant golden complexion. King Kanakavarṇa, monks, was rich, wealthy, and prosperous, his subjects were affluent,[200] and his sources of income were many. He had an abundance of riches, grain, gold and golden things, jewels, pearls, beryl, conch, quartz, coral, silver, and precious metals; an abundance as well of elephants, horses, cows, and rams; and his treasuries and granaries were completely full.

King Kanakavarṇa, monks, had a capital called Kanakāvatī (Possessing Gold) that was twelve leagues wide east to west and seven leagues long south to north. It was thriving, prosperous, pleasant, and safe, with plenty of food and throngs of people. King Kanakavarṇa also possessed eighty thousand cities, containing 180 million families, that were thriving, prosperous, and safe, with plenty of food and throngs of people; 570 million villages that were thriving, prosperous, pleasant, and safe, with plenty of food and throngs of people; and sixty thousand market towns that were thriving, prosperous, and safe, with plenty of food and throngs of people. In addition, King Kanakavarṇa had eighteen thousand ministers and a harem of twenty thousand wives. King Kanakavarṇa was virtuous, monks, and he ruled his kingdom according to dharma.

Now at one time when King Kanakavarṇa was all alone in a secluded place, absorbed in meditation, this thought arose in his mind: "I really should exempt all the merchants [in my dominion] from customs and transit fees. I should exempt all the people of Jambudvīpa (Black Plum Island) from taxes and duties." Then King Kanakavarṇa addressed his accountants, chief advisors, ministers, gatekeepers, and counselors: "From now on, officers, I exempt all merchants from customs and transit fees.[201] I exempt all the people of Jambudvīpa from taxes and customs fees." [292]

After ruling his kingdom for many years according to this plan,[202] eventually the constellations became misaligned so that the heavens would produce no rain for twelve years. Those brahmans who could read signs and interpret omens and were skilled in mantras controlling the earth and sky observed this prospect in the movements of the constellations and the planet Venus. They approached King Kanakavarṇa and, having approached, said this to him: "May my lord be informed that the constellations are misaligned. The heavens will not produce rain for twelve years."

When King Kanakavarṇa heard this terrible pronouncement, tears began to flow. "Oh no! The poor people of my Jambudvīpa! Oh no! My poor Jambudvīpa! Now thriving, prosperous, pleasant, and safe, with plenty of food and throngs of people, very soon it will be empty, without any inhabitants." After grieving for a moment, it occurred to King Kanakavarṇa, "Those who are rich, wealthy, and prosperous will be able to survive. But those who are poor, with little wealth, and with little in the way of food, drink, and comforts, how will they survive?" Then it occurred to him, "I really should collect all the rice and other means of subsistence from Jambudvīpa and count all of Jambudvīpa's inhabitants. Then, after counting them, make the necessary calculations, and after making the necessary calculations, establish a single granary for all the marketplaces, hamlets, villages, market towns, and capitals. After establishing a single granary, I can distribute equal amounts of food to all the people of Jambudvīpa."

And so King Kanakavarṇa addressed his accountants, chief advisors, ministers, gatekeepers, and counselors: "Officers, go and collect all the rice and other means of subsistence in Jambudvīpa and then count it, and after counting it, make the necessary calculations, and after making the necessary calculations, establish a single granary for all the marketplaces, hamlets, villages, market towns, and capitals."

"Yes, my lord," the accountants, chief advisors, ministers, gatekeepers, and counselors replied, consenting to King Kanakavarṇa's request. And then they counted all the rice and other means of subsistence collected from Jambudvīpa, and after counting it, they made the necessary calculations, and after making the necessary calculations, they stored everything in a single granary for the benefit of all the marketplaces, hamlets, villages, market towns, and capitals. When they had stored everything in a single granary, they approached King Kanakavarṇa[203] and, having approached, said this to him: [293] "My lord, please be informed that all the rice and other means of subsistence from all the marketplaces, hamlets, villages, market towns, and capitals have been collected, and after everything was collected, it was counted, and after it was counted, the necessary calculations were made, and after the necessary calculations were made, it was stored in a single granary for the benefit of all those marketplaces, hamlets, villages, market towns, and capitals. Now my lord may do as he sees fit."[204]

King Kanakavarṇa then summoned his financial advisors, accountants, scribes, and workers and said this: "Officers, go and count all the people in Jambudvīpa. And officers, after counting them, offer all the people in Jambudvīpa equal amounts of food."

"Yes, my lord," his financial advisors, accountants, scribes, and workers replied, consenting to King Kanakavarṇa's request. And then they counted all the people in Jambudvīpa and, having counted them, distributed equal amounts of food to of them, beginning with King Kanakavarṇa.

The people survived eleven years like this, but they couldn't make it through the twelfth. As the first month of the twelfth year passed, many women and men and boys and girls, suffering from hunger and thirst, passed away. At that time the rice and other means of subsistence that had been collected from Jambudvīpa were completely exhausted except for a single measure[205] of food that remained in King Kanakavarṇa's possession.

The Bodhisattva and the Power of Charity

At that time a certain bodhisattva, who had set out forty eons before, arrived in this world-system. The bodhisattva saw a son committing incest with his mother in a forest. Seeing this, he thought, "These beings are so impure! These beings are so defiled! Hers was the womb in which he passed nine months, and hers were the breasts that he suckled. How can he now do such things with her![206] I've had enough of beings like this! They lack virtue. They're inflamed by immoral passions, perverse in their views, and overcome by coarseness and greed. They don't honor their mothers[207] or ascetics or brahmans, and they don't revere the elders of their families. Who could be eager to follow the path of the bodhisattva for the benefit of beings like this? [294] I really should focus on my own obligations."

Then the bodhisattva approached the base of a tree and, having approached, sat down there. Crossing his legs and holding his body upright, he made his mindfulness fully present and observed the rising and falling of the five aggregates, which are the basis of clinging to existence—namely,

this is matter, this is the arising of matter,
and this is the cessation of matter;
this is feeling;
this is recognition;
this is conditioning;
this is consciousness, this is the arising of consciousness,
and this is the cessation of consciousness.[208]

Observing in this way the rising and falling of the five aggregates, which are the basis of clinging to existence, he quickly came to know that everything that has the nature of arising has the nature of cessation. And right then he attained awakening as a solitary buddha.

At that moment the lord solitary buddha, having observed that all things arise depending on conditions,[209] uttered this verse:

From longing arises love,
then sorrow is born, for in this world it follows from love.
Knowing that misery comes from love,
one should wander alone like the rhinoceros.[210]

Then it occurred to the him, "I have performed difficult deeds for the sake of many beings, but I have yet to benefit a single being [since my awakening]. For whom should I now have compassion? Whose alms should I now accept and consume?"

Then the lord solitary buddha, with his pure and superhuman divine sight, looked over all of Jambudvīpa from every angle, and he saw that the rice and other means of subsistence in Jambudvīpa were completely exhausted except for a single measure of food that remained in King Kanakavarṇa's possession. It occurred to him, "I really should have compassion for King Kanakavarṇa. I really should accept and consume alms from King Kanakavarṇa's home."

Just then the lord solitary buddha made use of his magical powers and rose up into the sky. And with his magical powers, with his body looking like a bird, he approached the capital Kanakāvatī.

At that time King Kanakavarṇa was standing on the roof of the palace [295] surrounded by five thousand ministers. One of the chief advisors saw that lord solitary buddha coming from a distance, and upon seeing him, he addressed the other chief advisors: "Look! Look, officers! Far in the distance a bird with red wings is coming toward us!"

A second chief advisor said, "No, officers. It's not a bird with red wings. It's a strength-stealing demon that's coming here. He's going to eat us!"

Then King Kanakavarṇa, rubbing his face with both hands, addressed his chief advisors: "No, officers. It's not a bird with red wings nor is it a strength-stealing demon. It's a seer coming here, out of compassion for us."

Then the lord solitary buddha landed on top of King Kanakavarṇa's palace. At once King Kanakavarṇa got up from his seat and went to meet him. He placed his head in veneration at the lord solitary buddha's feet and then brought him to the seat specially prepared [for the king himself]. Then King Kanakavarṇa said to that lord solitary buddha, "What is the reason, seer, for your coming here?"

"For food, your majesty."

Thus addressed, King Kanakavarṇa began to cry. With tears flowing, he said, "Oh! How terrible is my poverty! How terrible poverty is!

I established lordship and dominion over Jambudvīpa, and now I can't even offer alms to a single seer!"

Then the resident deity of the capital Kanakāvatī uttered this verse in front of King Kanakavarṇa:

> What is sorrow? Poverty.
> What is greater sorrow?
> This very poverty,
> poverty like death.

Then King Kanakavarṇa addressed the guardian of the granary: "Sir, is there any food in my home that I can give to this seer?"

"My lord," he said, "there is something you should know. All the grain and other means of subsistence in Jambudvīpa are completely exhausted except for a single measure of food that belongs to my lord.

Then it occurred to King Kanakavarṇa, "If I eat this food, I'll live. If I don't eat it, I'll die. [296] But whether I eat or don't eat," he reflected, "it is certain that death will come to me. I've had enough of this life. How can I let such an honest and virtuous seer as the one now in my home leave with a clean bowl, not having received any alms?"[211]

Then King Kanakavarṇa assembled his accountants, chief advisors, ministers, gatekeepers, and counselors, and said, "Permit me, officers, to grant this last bit of rice that I, King Kanakavarṇa, possess. By this root of virtue may all the people in Jambudvīpa be completely freed from poverty." Then King Kanakavarṇa took the great seer's bowl and in it placed that single measure of food. He then grasped the bowl with both hands, fell to his knees, and placed the bowl into the right hand of that lord solitary buddha.

As a rule, solitary buddhas teach the dharma through deeds, not words.

The lord solitary buddha took those alms from King Kanakavarṇa and, making use of his magical powers, immediately set off up into the sky. King Kanakavarṇa stood there, with his hands folded respectfully, watching without blinking, until the lord solitary buddha had vanished from sight.

King Kanakavarṇa then addressed his accountants, chief advisors, ministers, gatekeepers, and counselors: "Officers, go back to your own homes. I don't want you all to die from hunger and thirst right here in the palace."

"When my lord had an abundance of wealth and good fortune," they said, "we indulged and enjoyed ourselves with my lord.[212] How could we abandon my lord now, at this last time, this last moment?"

Then King Kanakavarṇa began to cry, and the tears flowed. Wiping away his tears, he again said to his accountants, chief advisors, ministers, gatekeepers, and counselors: "Officers, go back to your own homes. I don't want you all to die from hunger and thirst right here in the palace."

Thus addressed, the accountants, chief advisors, ministers, gatekeepers, and counselors also began to cry and shed tears. Wiping away their tears, they approached King Kanakavarṇa. [297] Having approached, they placed their heads in veneration at King Kanakavarṇa's feet, folded their hands respectfully, and said this to him: "Forgive us for any sins we may have committed against you. Now is the last time we will see my lord."

Just then, the lord solitary buddha ate his almsfood, and at that very moment, four masses of clouds arose in each of the four directions. Cold winds began to blow, removing the impurities from Jambudvīpa, and then the clouds sent forth rain, calming the dust. And then, during the latter half of that very day, it rained various kinds of hard and soft foods. There were soft foods such as boiled rice, barleymeal, lentils and rice, fish, and meat[213] and hard foods made from roots, stalks, leaves, flowers, fruits, sesame seeds, candied sugar, molasses, and flour.

King Kanakavarṇa, now pleased, satisfied, excited, uplifted, delighted, and full of joy and pleasure, addressed his accountants, chief advisors, ministers, gatekeepers, and counselors: "Look, officers! Right now the sprout, [the first result] of offering that single portion of alms, has appeared. Other fruits will surely come."

On the second day it began to rain down grains—sesame seeds, rice, mung beans, and black gram, barley, wheat, masoor beans, and white rice. This lasted a week. And then clarified butter rained for a week, and then sesame oil rained for a week,[214] and then cotton rained for a week, and then various kinds of fine cloth rained for a week, and then for a week there was a rain of seven treasures—gold, silver, beryl, crystal, red pearls, emeralds, and sapphires. Thanks to King Kanakavarṇa, all this occurred, and the people of Jambudvīpa were completely freed from poverty.

Coda

"You may have some doubt or uncertainty, monks, as to the identity of King Kanakavarṇa at that time and at that juncture. Ponder no further. [298] At that time and at that juncture I was King Kanakavarṇa. Monks, understand it in this way:

> If, monks, beings were to know the result of charity and the consequence of offering charity, then they would never eat the very last remaining mouthful of food without giving it away or sharing it, if a worthy recipient of that food were to be found. And the stingy thoughts that arise would not seize hold of their minds. But monks, those beings who do not know the result of charity and the consequence of offering charity as I know the result of charity and the consequence of offering charity eat with a mind that is miserly, without giving their food away or sharing it. And the stingy thoughts that arise do seize hold of their minds.

Previous actions, both good and bad, don't perish,
services offered to the wise don't perish,
words spoken among the noble don't perish,
and what is done among the grateful doesn't ever perish.

Whether a good deed done well
or an evil deed done maliciously,
both will inevitably mature
and bear fruit.

This was said by the Blessed One. With their minds uplifted, the monks, nuns, male and female lay devotees, gods, nāgas, yakṣas, celestial musicians, antigods, heavenly birds, kinnaras, great snakes, and so on, as well as the entire assembly, rejoiced at the words of the Blessed One.

So ends the *Kanakavarṇa-avadāna*, the twentieth chapter in the glorious *Divyāvadāna*.

21. The Story of Sahasodgata

SAHASODGATA-AVADĀNA[215]

THE LORD BUDDHA was staying in the city of Rājagṛha at the bamboo grove in Kalandakanivāpa (Squirrel Feeding Place).

Mahāmaudgalyāyana and the Five-Sectioned Wheel

As was his practice, from time to time the venerable Mahāmaudgalyāyana would journey through the realms of hell, journey through the animal realm, and journey through the realms of hungry ghosts, gods, and humans. [299] There he saw many kinds of suffering, such as hell beings being pulled, plucked, cut, and pierced; animals being devoured by each other;[216] hungry ghosts being tormented by hunger and thirst; gods passing away and falling, undergoing ruin and destruction; and humans pained by longing and misfortune. And having seen all this, he would come to Jambudvīpa (Black Plum Island) and address the four assemblies.

Whoever had a student[217] or pupil who didn't eagerly follow the religious life would take him and approach the venerable Mahāmaudgalyāyana with the thought that the venerable Mahāmaudgalyāyana would properly admonish him and properly instruct him. Then the venerable Mahāmaudgalyāyana would indeed properly admonish him and properly instruct him. In this way, again and again, those who were properly admonished[218] and properly instructed by the venerable Mahāmaudgalyāyana would eagerly follow the religious life, and later they would attain distinction.

At that time the venerable Mahāmaudgalyāyana was always surrounded by the four assemblies—monks, nuns, and male and female lay devotees.

Now lord buddhas will ask questions even though they know the answers. And so the Lord Buddha questioned the venerable Ānanda: "Why is the venerable Mahāmaudgalyāyana always surrounded by the four assemblies?"[219]

"Bhadanta," the venerable Ānanda said, "as is his practice, from time to time the venerable Mahāmaudgalyāyana journeys through the realms of hell and journeys through the realms of animals, hungry ghosts, gods, and humans. There he sees many kinds of suffering, such as hell beings being pulled, plucked, cut, and pierced; animals being devoured by each other; hungry ghosts being tormented by hunger and thirst; gods passing away and falling, undergoing ruin and destruction; and humans pained by longing and misfortune. And having seen all this, he comes to Jambudvīpa and addresses the four assemblies.

"Whoever has a student or pupil that doesn't eagerly follow the religious life takes him and approaches the venerable Mahāmaudgalyāyana with the thought that the venerable Mahāmaudgalyāyana will properly admonish him and properly instruct him. Then the venerable Mahāmaudgalyāyana [300] does properly admonish him and properly instruct him. In this way, again and again, those who are properly admonished and properly instructed by the venerable Mahāmaudgalyāyana eagerly follow the religious life, and later they attain distinction.

"This is the cause, Bhadanta, this is the reason that the venerable Mahāmaudgalyāyana is always surrounded by the four assemblies—monks, nuns, and male and female lay devotees."

"But Ānanda, the monk Mahāmaudgalyāyana or even someone like

Mahāmaudgalyāyana can't be everywhere. Therefore a five-sectioned wheel should be made in the entrance hall[220] of the monastery."

[Then Ānanda replied:] "The Blessed One has said that a five-sectioned wheel should be made in the entrance hall of the monastery, but the monks won't know what sort of wheel should be made."

"The five realms of existence are to be depicted," the Blessed One said, "the realms of hell beings, animals, hungry ghosts, gods, and humans.[221] Down below, various hell beings are to be depicted, as well as animals and hungry ghosts; up above, gods and humans. The four continents are to be depicted—Pūrvavideha (Eastern Videha), Aparagodānīya (Western Godānīya), Uttarakuru (Northern Kuru), and Jambudvīpa. In the middle, attachment, hate, and delusion are to be depicted—attachment in the form of a dove, hate in the form of a serpent, and delusion in the form of a pig. And images of the Buddha are to be depicted overlooking the circle of nirvāṇa. Spontaneously generated beings are to be depicted passing away and being reborn by a set of enclosures that resemble the buckets of a waterwheel. Nearby, the twelve links of interdependent arising are to be depicted, both forward and backward. Everything is to be depicted as in the grip of impermanence. And these two verses are to be inscribed:

> Strive! Go forth!
> Apply yourselves to the teachings of the Buddha!
> Destroy the army of death
> as an elephant would a house of reeds.
>
> Whoever diligently follows
> this dharma and monastic discipline
> will abandon the endless cycle of rebirth
> and put an end to suffering."

The Blessed One said that a five-sectioned wheel should be made in the entrance hall, and so the monks made one. Brahmans and householders would come and ask, "Noble one, what is this that's drawn here?"

"Friends," they would say, "we also don't know."

Then the Blessed One said, "A monk is to be appointed in the entrance hall who can explain the five-sectioned wheel to those brahmans and householders who visit." [301]

The Blessed One said that a monk should be appointed, so they appointed monks but did so indiscriminately, choosing ones who were childish and foolish, immature and lacking virtue. They themselves didn't understand the five-sectioned wheel—how could they explain it to the brahmans and householders who would visit?

So the Blessed One said, "A competent monk is to be appointed."

A Householder's Son, the Five-Sectioned Wheel, and the Gift of a Meal

A certain householder lived in Rājagṛha. He brought home a girl from an appropriate family as his wife, and with her he fooled around, enjoyed himself, and made love. From fooling around, enjoying himself, and making love, a son was born. For three weeks—that is, twenty-one days[222]—the occasion of his birth was celebrated in full, and then a name was selected for him that was appropriate to his family.

The householder then addressed his wife: "My dear, this son of ours will bring us into debt and take away our wealth.[223] So I'm going. I'll take my goods and set sail in the great ocean."

"Yes, dear husband," she said. "Do as you wish."

After saying goodbye to his friends, relations, and relatives and consoling those closest to him, he gathered up his goods for export and, at an opportune day, date, and time, set sail in the great ocean. And right there [in the great ocean,] he succumbed to death.

The boy was protected, supported, and nourished by the man's wife, with her own hands and with the help of her relatives. He was also entrusted [to a teacher to learn] writing, and he became an expert scribe.

One day he went with a friend to the bamboo grove [in Kalandakanivāpa]. He entered the monastery there and saw the five-sectioned wheel inscribed in the entrance hall.

"Noble one," he asked, "what is this that's inscribed here?"

"Friend," the monk said, "these are the five realms of existence—the realms of hell beings, animals, hungry ghosts, gods, and humans."

"Noble one, what deed did these [hell beings] do to experience such suffering?"

"They killed, stole, or engaged in sexual misconduct; told lies, spoke maliciously, spoke harshly, or chattered idly; coveted, had malicious thoughts, or perverse views," he said. "To a great degree, they practiced, developed, and cultivated the tenfold path of evil actions, and as a result they experience such suffering as being pulled, plucked, cut, and pierced."

"Noble one, I understand. And what deed did these [animals] do to experience such suffering?"

"Friend, they also practiced, developed, and cultivated the tenfold path of evil actions, and as a result they experience such suffering as being devoured by each other." [302]

"Noble one, this too I understand. And what deed did these [hungry ghosts] do to experience such suffering?"

"Friend, they were stingy, mean,[224] and miserly with their possessions. From stingily practicing, developing, and cultivating such deeds,[225] they experience as a result such sufferings as hunger and thirst."

"Noble one, this too I understand. And what deed did these [gods] do to experience such pleasures?"

"Friend, they abstained from killing, stealing, and engaging in sexual misconduct; from telling lies, speaking maliciously, speaking harshly, and chattering idly; and they didn't covet or have malicious thoughts, and they had right views. To a great degree, they practiced, developed, and cultivated the tenfold path of virtuous actions, and as a result they experience such pleasures as parks, floating mansions, and consorting with divine women."

"Noble one, this too I understand. And what deed did these [humans] do to experience such pleasures?"

"Friend, they also practiced, developed, and cultivated the tenfold path of virtuous actions, although in a weaker and lighter form, and so they experience such pleasures as elephants, horses, chariots, food, drink, bedding, seats, parks, and consorting with women."

"Noble one, of these five realms of existence, these three realms—those of hell beings, animals, and hungry ghosts—don't seem good to me. But these—those of gods and humans—do seem good. So, after adopting this tenfold path of virtuous actions, how is one to live?"

"Friend, go forth as a monk according to the dharma and monastic discipline that have been so well expressed, and if in this lifetime you attain perfect knowledge, then in this lifetime your suffering will end. If you die with some bonds to existence still remaining, you will be reborn among the gods. It has been said by the Blessed One that a wise person who properly understands the five benefits should be fully intent on becoming a renunciant.[226] Which five?

[1] 'I will attain my own special objectives.'
Understanding this, a wise person should be fully intent on becoming a renunciant.

[2] 'Whether I am someone's slave, messenger, attendant, servant, or bonded laborer,[227] I shall be worthy of his honor and praise.'
Understanding this, a wise person should be fully intent on becoming a renunciant.

[3] 'I will obtain the supreme security that is nirvāṇa.' [303]
Understanding this, a wise person should be fully intent on becoming a renunciant.

[4] 'While striving[228] for the supreme security that is nirvāṇa, if no offense is committed, [I] will be reborn among the gods.'

Understanding this, a wise person should be fully intent on becoming a renunciant.

[5] 'Renunciation has been praised in many way by buddhas and the disciples of buddhas.'"

"Noble one, this sounds good. But what does one do as a renunciant?"

"Friend, for as long as one lives, one follows the religious life."

"Noble one, this isn't possible for me. Is there another way?"

"Yes, friend, there is. Be a lay disciple."

"Noble one, what does one do then?"

"Friend, for as long as one lives, one abstains from killing and stealing, from engaging in sexual misconduct, and from becoming intoxicated from liquor, spirits, or wine."

"Noble one, this too isn't possible. Tell me another way."

"Friend, feed the community of monks led by the Buddha."

"Noble one, how many *kārṣāpaṇa* coins does it take to feed the community of monks led by the Buddha?"

"Friend, it takes five hundred *kārṣāpaṇa* coins."

"Noble one, this is possible." He then venerated his feet and departed.

He approached his house and, having approached, said this to his mother: "Mother, today I went to the bamboo grove. There I saw a five-sectioned wheel inscribed in the entrance hall of the monastery. On it were the five realms of existence—the realms of hell beings, animals, hungry ghosts, gods, and humans. As a result of their actions, hell beings experience such suffering as being pulled, plucked, cut, and pierced; animals are devoured by each other; and hungry ghosts are tormented by hunger and thirst. Gods experience such pleasures as parks, floating mansions, and consorting with divine women. Humans experience [those of] elephants, horses, chariots, food, drink, bedding, seats, parks, and consorting with women. The first three of these realms of existence I didn't like, but I liked the last two. Do you want me to be reborn among the gods?"

"Son, I want all beings to be reborn among the gods, especially you."

"Mother, if that's the case, give me five hundred *kārṣāpaṇa* coins. I'll feed the community of monks led by the Buddha."

"Son, I nurtured,[229] supported, and nourished you with my own hands and with the help of my relatives. Where could I find five hundred *kārṣāpaṇa* coins? That's a fortune!"

"Mother, if you don't have it, I'll get a job as a day laborer."

"Son, you're too young and frail. You can't work as a day laborer." [304]

"Mother, I'm going. I can do it."

"Son, if you can do it, then go."

With her permission, he went and stood in the marketplace for day laborers. Brahmans and householders chose other men as day laborers, but no one asked him. He spent the whole day there, then went home at night.

"Son," his mother asked, "did you get a job as a day laborer?"

"Mother, what could I do? No one asked me."

"Son, men who are day laborers aren't like this. Son, they're ragged and rugged,[230] they have coarse hair, and they wear dirty clothes. If it's necessary for you to work as a day laborer, take on that appearance and then go and stand in the marketplace for day laborers."

"All right then, Mother. I'll do as you say."

The next day he took on that appearance and then went and stood in the marketplace for day laborers.

Now, a certain householder was building a house, so he went to the marketplace to get some day laborers. The householder rejected the boy and then chose other men as day laborers.

"Householder," the boy said, "I also work as a day laborer."

"Son," the householder said, "you're too young and frail. You can't work as a day laborer."

"Uncle, do you pay wages in advance or after work?"

"After work, son."

"Uncle, let me work today. If you're satisfied, pay me my wages."

"He speaks sensibly," the householder reflected. "Now I'll test him. If he can work, I'll pay him. If he can't, I won't give him anything." With this in mind, he said, "Son, come on. Let's go!" Then he brought him home.

The other day laborers worked irresponsibly, but the boy worked very quickly. He also instructed the other day laborers: "Because of our bad deeds in the past, we were born in the houses of the poor. If we work irresponsibly now, when we die and pass away from here, what will be our destiny?"

"Hey junior," they said, "you've just been trained. You're supposed to follow us. Come on. Let's have a look."

The boy was an expert in popular stories.[231] He regaled the other day laborers with popular stories that captivated them while they listened. They followed his every footstep, though he went very quickly,[232] so that they wouldn't miss hearing his story. That day the day laborers did twice as much work as usual. When the householder was examining the work that had been finished, [305] he came to that place where twice as much work had been done.

"Hey," he asked the supervisor, "did you take on extra day laborers?"

"No, sir, I didn't."

"Then why was twice as much work done today?"

The supervisor explained to him what had happened.

Hearing this, the householder began to give the boy double wages.

"Uncle," he said, "why are you giving me twice the daily wage?"

"Son," he said, "I'm not giving you twice the daily wage. Rather, since I have faith, I'm doing the duty of one who has faith [and offering a gift]."[233]

"Uncle," he said, "if you have faith in me, then hold on to it yourself until the work on your house is done."

"Okay, son, as you wish."

When the householder's house was finished, the boy began to count his wages, but they didn't amount to five hundred *kārṣāpaṇa* coins. He began to cry.

"Son," the householder said, "why are you crying? I hope I didn't cheat you."

"Uncle, you are a great person, why would you cheat me? I'm just unlucky. I began working as a day laborer to earn five hundred *kārṣāpaṇa* coins so that I could feed the community of monks led by the Buddha and later be reborn among the gods. But I haven't earned enough. Now I'll have to work as a day laborer somewhere else."

The householder was filled with even more faith. "Son, if that's the case," he said, "I'll provide the rest."

"Uncle, but I won't be reborn among the gods."

"Son, do you believe in the Blessed One?"

"Uncle, I believe."

"Son, go and ask the Blessed One."

He approached the Blessed One and, having approached, placed his head in veneration at the Blessed One's feet and then sat down at a respectful distance. The householder's son said this to the Blessed One: "Blessed One, I worked for a certain householder as a day laborer to earn five hundred *kārṣāpaṇa* coins so that I could feed the Blessed One along with the community of his disciples. But I haven't earned enough. That householder says that he'll provide the rest. Blessed One, what should I do?"

"Son," he said, "take it. The householder is a man of faith."

"Blessed One, I'll still be reborn among the gods, won't I?"

"Son, you will be reborn there. Just take it."

Fully satisfied, he placed his head in veneration at the Blessed One's feet, left the Blessed One's presence, and then approached the householder. [306] Having approached, he took [the rest of] the five hundred *kārṣāpaṇa* coins from the householder and then went to his mother.

"Mother," he said, "here are the five hundred *kārṣāpaṇa* coins. Prepare the food! I'll feed the community of monks led by the Buddha."

"Son," she said, "I don't have pots and utensils or bedding and seats. That householder has lots of pots and utensils, and he's a man of faith. Go and ask him. He can help us out."

He then went to the householder, bowed his head respectfully, and said, "You've already given me five hundred *kārṣāpaṇa* coins. But in our house there aren't pots and utensils or bedding and seats. So please, out of compassion for me, prepare the food. I'll return and, with my own hands, feed the community of monks led by the Buddha."

"This house of mine is only recently built," the householder reflected. "If the community of monks led by the Buddha will eat here, I'll make the food." With this in mind, he said, "Son, it's okay. Place the *kārṣāpaṇa* coins here. Go and invite the community of monks led by the Buddha for a meal tomorrow. I'll prepare the food."

In good spirits, the boy bowed his head respectfully and left. Then he approached the Blessed One and, having approached, stood in the area of the elders and said, "I would like to invite the community of monks led by the Buddha for a meal."

With his silence, the Blessed One accepted this invitation from the householder's son. Then the householder's son, realizing that by his silence the Blessed One had accepted his invitation, left the Blessed One's presence.

That very night the householder prepared hard and soft foods, both fresh and fine, and then at daybreak he got up, cleaned the house, spread a fresh[234] layer of cow dung, prepared the seats, and set out pitchers of water. Then the householder's son went and informed the Blessed One, "It is time, Bhadanta. The food is ready. Now the Blessed One may do as the time permits."

Later in the morning the Blessed One got dressed, took his bowl and robe, and leading the community of monks that surrounded him, approached the householder's home.

The group of six monks asked, "Who has invited the community of monks led by the Buddha for a meal?"

"Such-and-such householder's son," others answered. [307]

Then they conversed among themselves: "Nanda, Upananda—he's a day laborer.[235] What can he give? Let's go. We can go to those houses that usually provide for us[236] and have breakfast."[237] They then approached those houses that usually provided for them.

"Noble ones,"[238] the householders said, "please have breakfast."

"Yes, we'll do so," they said. Then they took their breakfast.

Now in that householder's home, the Blessed One sat down in front of the community of monks in the seat specially prepared for him. The group of six monks, having already had breakfast, sat down among the community of monks.

Now when the householder's son was sure that the community of monks led by the Buddha was comfortably seated, he served and indulged them, with his own hands, with hard and soft foods, both fresh and fine. Constantly serving everyone, he saw the group of six monks eating the food without doing justice to it. Having seen this, when he was sure that the Blessed One had washed his hands and set aside his bowl, he stood in front of the Blessed One and said, "Blessed One, some of the noble ones here ate the food without doing justice to it. I'll still be reborn among the gods, no?"

"Son," the Blessed One said, "by providing bedding and seats you would be reborn among the gods, much less by providing food and drink." Then the Blessed One, having instructed, incited, inspired, and delighted the householder's son with a discourse on the dharma, got up from his seat and went out.

Five Hundred Merchants and the Duty of Faith

Meanwhile five hundred merchants, having successfully completed their voyage, left the great ocean and arrived in Rājagṛha. In Rājagṛha it was a holiday, so there was nothing to be had, regardless of money.

One merchant there was a provider of food for the monks. "Gentlemen," he said, "come with me. In that person's home where the community of monks led by the Buddha has eaten today, there is sure to be some extra food."

Asking person after person, and following the trail of advice, they came before that householder.

"Householder," they said, "considering that the community of monks led by the Buddha ate in your [home][239] today, and considering that it's a holiday here, so that there's nothing to be had, regardless of money, if you have any extra food, please sell it to us."

"This isn't my food. It's the food of that son of a householder. You should ask him."

The five hundred merchants approached him and said, [308] "Householder's son, please give us whatever food is left over. We'll pay for it."

"I won't offer it to you for a price," he said. "Instead, I'll offer it in just the same way [as I did to the community of monks led by the Buddha]."[240]

After they were satisfied with that food and drink, the five hundred merchants went to the householder and said, "Householder, you have profited and gained much—with food and drink you have satisfied in your home the community of monks led by the Buddha as well as five hundred merchants."

"The householder's son has profited and gained much," he said. "He, not I, has satisfied the community of monks led by the Buddha with food and drink."

"Which householder is he the son of?" they asked.

"Of such-and-such caravan leader."

"Gentlemen," the caravan leader said, "he is the son of a friend of mine! His father set sail in the great ocean and straightaway met his death. It is possible for many to rescue one but not for one to rescue many. This cloth has been spread out before you.[241] Offer whatever you have to spare by placing it here."

Since they already had great faith [in the householder's son] and since they were encouraged by the caravan leader, the five hundred merchants gave as many jewels, such as gems and pearls, as they could. A great collection was amassed.

"Son, take it," the caravan leader said.

"Uncle," he said, "I didn't sell you [that food and drink]."

"Son, nor are we paying you," the caravan leader said. "And if you calculate the value [of all this, you'll see that] many hundreds of meals like this can be had with just a single one of these jewels. Since we have full faith in you, we're doing the duty of one who has faith [and offering a gift]. Take it."

"Uncle," he said, "I fed the community of monks led by the Buddha so that I could be reborn among the gods. That's why whatever was left over was simply given to all of you. If I take this, it stands to reason that I won't be reborn among the gods."

"Son," the caravan leader said, "do you believe in the Blessed One?"

"Yes, uncle, I believe in him."

"Then go and ask the Blessed One."

The householder's son then approached the Blessed One and, having approached, placed his head in veneration at the Blessed One's feet and then sat down at a respectful distance. The householder's son said this to the Blessed One: "Blessed One, after feeding the community of monks led by the Buddha, I gave the leftover food and drink to some merchants. Having faith in me, they do the duty of one who has faith [and offer a gift]. Am I permitted to take it or not?" [309]

"If they have faith and do the duty of one who has faith [and offer a gift]," the Blessed One said, "then take it."

"Blessed One, I'll be reborn among the gods, won't I?"

"Son," the Blessed One said, "this is just the flower. The fruit will be something else entirely."

Due to his complete confidence in the words of the Blessed One, he went away satisfied and took the jewels.

The New Guildmaster

Meanwhile the guildmaster in Rājagṛha died without a son. The citizens of Rājagṛha assembled and conferred: "Gentlemen, the guildmaster has died. Whom should we appoint as the new guildmaster?"

"One who is very powerful because of his merit,"[242] some among them said.

"How are we to know?" others replied.

"Let's put different varieties of seeds in a well-fired pot, and whoever can take out just one variety of seed we'll appoint as guildmaster."

So they put different varieties of seeds in a well-fired pot and announced, "Gentlemen, whoever can take out just one variety of seed from this pot will be appointed as guildmaster. Whoever among you wants to be guildmaster, come and take them out."

People came and began to take out the seeds. Everyone took out a mix of varieties, but the householder's son took out just one variety.

"Gentlemen," the townspeople and villagers said, "this person is very powerful because of his merit. Let's all appoint him as guildmaster."

"Gentlemen," one among them said, "this man is a day laborer. How can we appoint him as guildmaster?"

"Let's test him once again," others said.

Three times in a row he took out just one kind of seed.

"Gentlemen, these wretches[243] insult him," they said. "Come, we'll appoint him just as we said we would." So they appointed him as guildmaster.

The householder reflected, "Although he worked for me as a day laborer, he is a very powerful being because of his merit. I should establish a close connection with him." With this in mind, he gave him his daughter, adorned with all kinds of ornaments, as a wife. And he gave him a house and an abundance of wealth.[244] As a result, because of his sudden material success, he came to be known as the householder Sahasodgata (Upstart).

"Whatever glory and good fortune I possess," he reflected, "all that is due to the Lord Buddha. I really should invite the community of monks led by the Buddha for a meal once again, and this time I'll feed them in my own house." With this in mind, [310] he approached the Blessed One and, having approached, placed his head in veneration at the Blessed One's feet and then sat down at a respectful distance. The Blessed One instructed, incited, inspired, and delighted the householder Sahasodgata, who was seated at a respectful distance, with a discourse on the dharma. After he instructed, incited, inspired, and delighted him in many ways with this discourse on the dharma, he became silent.

The householder Sahasodgata then got up from his seat, properly arranged his robe on one shoulder, bowed toward the Buddha with his hands respectfully folded, and said this to him: "May the Blessed One, along with the community of monks, accept this invitation to eat at my home tomorrow."

The Blessed One accepted the householder Sahasodgata's invitation with his silence. Then the householder Sahasodgata, realizing that by his silence the Blessed One had accepted his invitation, placed his head in veneration at the Blessed One's feet and then left the Blessed One's presence.

That very night the householder Sahasodgata prepared hard and soft foods, both fresh and fine, and then at daybreak he got up, prepared the seats, and set out pitchers of water. Then he had a messenger inform the Blessed One that it was now the appropriate time: "It is time, Bhadanta. The food is ready. Now the Blessed One may do as the time permits."

Later in the morning the Blessed One got dressed, took his bowl and robe, and surrounded by a group of monks, approached the householder Sahasodgata's home. Having approached, he sat down in front of the community of monks in the seat specially prepared for him.

Now when the householder Sahasodgata was sure that the community of monks led by the Buddha was comfortably seated, he served and indulged them, with his own hands, with hard and soft foods, both fresh and fine. When he had served and indulged them, with his own hands, with many courses of hard and soft foods, both fresh and fine, and was sure that the Blessed One had finished eating, washed his hands, and set aside his bowl, he then sat down in front of the Blessed One, taking a lower seat, to listen to the dharma.

Then the Blessed One, knowing the householder Sahasodgata's inclinations, propensities, makeup, and nature, gave him a discourse on the dharma that elucidated the four noble truths. When the householder Sahasodgata heard this, with his thunderbolt of knowledge he broke through that mountain, which is the false view of individuality that arises with its twenty peaks of incorrect views, and directly experienced the reward of the stream-enterer. Having seen the truth, three times he uttered this inspired utterance:

> What the Blessed One has done for the likes of me, Bhadanta, [311]
> neither my mother nor my father have done,
> nor any dear one,
> nor any kinsmen or relatives,
> nor any king,
> nor any deities or deceased ancestors,
> nor ascetics or brahmans.
> Oceans of blood and tears have dried up!
> Mountains of bones have been scaled!
> The doors to the lower realms of existence have been closed!
> The doors to heaven and liberation have been opened!
> We have been established among gods and humans!

> I have crossed over, Bhadanta! I have crossed over![245] And so, I take refuge in the Lord Buddha, in the dharma, and in the community of monks. Hereafter, and for as long as I live and breathe, consider me a faithful disciple.

Then the Blessed One [instructed, incited, inspired, and delighted] the householder Sahasodgata with a discourse on the dharma. After he instructed, incited, inspired, and delighted him [in many ways with this discourse on the dharma],[246] he got up from his seat and departed.

Some monks in doubt asked the Lord Buddha, the remover of all doubts, "Bhadanta, what deed did the householder Sahasodgata do so that he worked as a day laborer, suddenly prospered, and then had a vision of truth?"

"Monks," the Blessed One said, "the deeds that the householder Sahasodgata has performed and accumulated have now come together, and their conditions have matured. They remain before him like an oncoming flood and will certainly come to pass. Those deeds were performed and accumulated by the householder Sahasodgata. Who else will experience their results? For those deeds that are performed and accumulated, monks, do not mature outside of oneself—neither in the element of earth nor in the element of water, in the element of fire or in the element of wind. Instead, those deeds that are performed and accumulated, both good and bad, mature in the aggregates, the elements, and the sense bases that are appropriated when one is reborn.

> Actions never come to naught,
> even after hundreds of millions of years.
> When the right conditions gather and the time is right,
> then they will have their effect on embodied beings."

The Householder Balasena and the Solitary Buddha

Long ago, monks, in a market town there lived a householder named Balasena, who was rich, wealthy, and prosperous, with vast and extensive holdings, who had amassed a wealth like the god Vaiśravaṇa.

Truly, he rivaled Vaiśravaṇa in wealth. He brought home a girl from an appropriate family as his wife, and with her he fooled around, enjoyed himself, and made love. From fooling around, enjoying himself, and making love, his wife became pregnant. After eight or nine months, she gave birth. A son was born. For three weeks—that is, twenty-one days—the occasion of his birth was celebrated in full, [312] and then a name was selected for him that was appropriate to his family. Raised and nourished, in time he grew up.

One time when spring had arrived and the trees were blossoming, that householder, accompanied by his immediate family, went out to a place in the forest where there was a park that resounded with the calls of geese, herons, peacocks, parrots, mynahs, cuckoos, and peacock pheasants.

When no buddhas are born, solitary buddhas can arise in the world. They have compassion for the poor and neglected, they live in remote areas, and they alone are worthy of people's offerings.

Meanwhile a certain solitary buddha, after traveling through the countryside, arrived at that market town. As one who inhabits remote areas,[247] he didn't enter the market town but approached the park instead. The householder Balasena saw the solitary buddha, who instilled faith through his body and was calm in his comportment, entering the park. Seeing him, the householder was pleased and delighted and hurriedly went out to meet him.

"This park is crowded," the solitary buddha reflected, "I'll go somewhere else." With this in mind, he began to turn back.

The householder fell prostrate at his feet and said, "Noble one, why are you turning back? You are in want of food and I of merit. Take up residence here in this park and I'll offer you a steady supply of alms."

Great beings are intent on helping others. Maintaining a compassionate mind for him, the solitary buddha took up residence in that park, and the householder began to support him with alms.

After a time some work became necessary for that householder in another market town.

"My dear," he said to his wife, "some work has become necessary for me in such-and-such market town. I'm going there. Offer a steady supply of food and drink to that great man who has gone forth as a renunciant." With that said, he departed.

The next day the householder's wife got up at daybreak and began to prepare food and drink for the solitary buddha.

"Mother," her son said to her, "who are you preparing this food and drink for?"

"Son," she said, "it's for that calm man who has gone forth as a renunciant and now stays in the park."

He became angry and said, "Mother, why doesn't he get work as a day laborer and feed himself?"

"Son, don't speak like that!" she said. "The result of this deed will be terrible."

Even after being dissuaded he didn't comply. Then the householder returned. [313]

"My dear," he asked his wife, "did you offer a steady supply of alms to that solitary buddha?"

"Yes, dear husband, I did. However, this son of ours uttered harsh words toward him."

"My dear," he said, "what are you saying?"

She explained to him in detail what had happened.

"That poor fellow has been hurt,"[248] the householder reflected. "I'll go and ask that great man for forgiveness. I hope he isn't very hurt." With this in mind, he took his son and approached the solitary buddha.

The solitary buddha saw the householder coming with a second person and reflected, "The householder never comes with a second person.[249] What is the reason for this?"

Now the knowledge and insight of disciples and solitary buddhas does not operate unless they focus their attention. So he began to focus his attention and, having focused his attention, came to know.

Those great beings teach the dharma through deeds, not words. Out of compassion for the householder's son, like a royal goose with outstretched wings, he flew up high into the sky and began to perform the miraculous deeds of causing fire and heat, making rain and lightning.

Magic quickly wins over the ordinary person. Like trees cut down at the roots,[250] the householder and his son[251] fell prostrate at the solitary buddha's feet.[252] With gooseflesh bristling, the boy said, "Come down! Come down, O you who are righteous and worthy of offerings![253] Offer me a helping hand, for I am mired in the mud of desire!"

Out of compassion for him, the solitary buddha came down. The householder's son, with heartfelt sincerity, fell prostrate at his feet and made this fervent aspiration: "Although I have uttered harsh words at someone so righteous and worthy of offerings, may I not suffer from this deed. Since my mind is now full of faith, by this root of virtue may I be born in a family that is rich, wealthy, and prosperous, and may I obtain such virtues so that I may please and not displease a teacher even more distinguished than this one!"

"What do you think, monks? That householder's son was none other than the householder Sahasodgata. Since he uttered harsh words toward that solitary buddha, for five hundred births he was born to be a day laborer. Even up until recently he worked as a day laborer. Yet, having cultivated faith in his heart toward that solitary buddha, [314] he made a fervent aspiration, and because of this he suddenly became materially successful. Then, under me, he had a vision of truth. And as his teacher, who is more distinguished than hundreds of thousands of millions of solitary buddhas, I have been pleased and not displeased by him.

"And so, monks, the result of absolutely evil actions is absolutely evil, the result of absolutely pure actions is absolutely pure, and the result of mixed actions is mixed. Therefore monks, because of this, you should reject absolutely evil actions and mixed ones as well, and strive to perform only absolutely pure actions. Monks, it is this you should learn to do."[254]

This was said by the Blessed One. With their minds uplifted, the monks rejoiced at the words of the Blessed One.

So ends the *Sahasodgatasya prakaraṇāvadānam*,[255] the twenty-first chapter in the glorious *Divyāvadāna*.[256]

22. *The Story of the Deeds of the Bodhisattva Candraprabha*

CANDRAPRABHABODHISATTVACARYĀ-AVADĀNA[257]

THUS have I heard. At one time the Blessed One was staying in the city of Rājagṛha on Vulture's Peak together with a large community of monks, 1,250 in number.

Some monks in doubt asked the Lord Buddha, the remover of all doubts, "Look, Bhadanta. How is it that the venerable Śāriputra and Maudgalyāyana passed into the realm of remainderless nirvāṇa without waiting for the death of their [spiritual] father?"[258]

"What a wonder it is, monks, that in the here and now Śāriputra and Maudgalyāyana were monks, free from attachment, hate, and delusion; that they were liberated from the irritations of birth, old age, sickness, and death, sorrow, lamentation, suffering, and grief; that they were without craving or clinging to existence; that they were permanently rid of all evil propensities and the false beliefs of 'me,' 'mine,' and 'I am'; and that they were the very first in the community of monks led by the Buddha to pass into the realm of remainderless nirvāṇa without waiting for the death of their [spiritual] father. Yet, in a time gone by, Śāriputra and Maudgalyāyana were filled with attachment, hate, and delusion; [315] and they weren't liberated from the irritations of birth, old age, sickness, and death, sorrow, lamentation, suffering, and grief. But they cultivated faith in me, and when they died, they transcended the desire realm and were reborn in the Brahmā world without waiting for the death of their [spiritual] father. Listen to this."

King Candraprabha and His People's Royal Pleasures

Long ago, monks, in a time gone by, there was a capital city in the North Country called Bhadraśilā (Beautiful Stones) that was thriving, prosperous, and safe, with plenty of food and throngs of people. The city was twelve leagues long and twelve leagues wide; it was foursquare with four symmetrically arranged[259] gates; it was adorned with high arched doorways,[260] vents shaped like bulls' eyes, windows, and railings; and it was teeming with a variety of treasures. There were homes belonging to extremely wealthy merchants who had every amenity[261] as well as residences[262] of the king and his ministers, householders, guildmasters, governors, and politicians.[263] The city resounded with the sounds of veenas, flutes, *paṇava* drums, *sughoṣaka*s, *vallarī*s, mridangams, kettledrums, war drums, and conchs.

And in that capital there was the smell of agarwood, sandalwood, and aromatic powders, as well as the perennial smell of flowers in bloom.[264] These were stirred by flurries of wind, so that magnificent breezes blew through the marketplaces, squares, and crossroads. In addition, the city had armies of elephants, horses, chariots, and foot soldiers; it was graced with vehicles and the animals to draw them; it had marketplaces and main roads that were wide and magnificent; it had colorful flags and banners raised up high; and it was covered with arched doorways, vents shaped like bulls' eyes, and crescent-shaped windows.[265] Truly, the city shined like the abode of the gods.

And the city was adorned with blue, red, and white waterlilies, white lotuses,[266] and wonderfully fragrant aquatic flowers;[267] it was resplendent with lotus pools, tanks, ponds, and springs, each filled with water that was very sweet, pure, and cold; it was blanketed with many kinds of flowers—*śāla*, palmyra, *tamāla*,[268] *karṇikāra*, *aśoka*, *tilaka*, *punnāga*, *nāgakeśara*, *campaka*, *bakula*, *atimuktaka*, and *pāṭalā*;[269] and it was adorned with forests and parks, echoing with the calls of flocks of sparrows, parrots, mynahs, cuckoos, and peacocks as well as peacock pheasants.

And in the capital Bhadraśilā there was a royal park called Maṇiratnagarbha (Containing the Most-Treasured Jewel)[270] that was resplendent with various flowers, fruits, trees, and shrubs and had a lovely pond that resounded with the delightful songs of geese, herons, peacocks, and parrots, mynahs, cuckoos, peacock pheasants, and pariah kites.[271] As such, the capital Bhadraśilā was truly beautiful.

In the capital Bhadraśilā there was a king named Candraprabha (Moonlight) who was handsome, good-looking, and attractive and who possessed divine sight. He was a wheel-turning king ruling over the four quarters of the earth [316] and a just and virtuous ruler who had established kingship, lordship, and dominion over Jambudvīpa (Black Plum Island). King Candraprabha was radiant,[272] so wherever he would go there would be no darkness, though he was led by neither jewel, lamp, nor torch. Light emerged from King Candraprabha's body like rays from the disk of the moon. For this reason, King Candraprabha was given the name Candraprabha.

At that time in Jambudvīpa there were 68,000 cities, the foremost of which was the capital Bhadraśilā, and all of them were thriving, prosperous, and safe, with plenty of food and throngs of people. Furthermore, the people of Jambudvīpa were exempt from taxes, customs, or freight fees; the districts were peaceful and well cultivated with farms; and the marketplaces, villages, districts, and capitals were so close together that a cock could jump from one to the next. And at that time in Jambudvīpa, people lived for 44,000 years.

Now King Candraprabha was a bodhisattva who gave away everything, who sacrificed everything, and who did so without attachment. He lived in a state of great renunciation. Leaving the capital Bhadraśilā and going outside the city, he established four great sacrificial sites at the four gates to the city, and at each umbrellas, flags, sacrificial posts, and banners were raised. Then golden kettledrums were beaten,[273] gifts were given, and meritorious deeds were performed, such that there was food for the hungry, water for the thirsty, as well as hard and soft foods; garlands, creams, and clothes; bedding, seats, and bolsters;[274] homes, lamps, and umbrellas; carriages, finery, and ornaments; golden bowls filled with silver powder; silver bowls filled with gold;[275] and cows with golden horns that yielded milk whenever one desired.[276] Young men and women were also adorned with all kinds of ornaments. When this was done, clothes of various colors, produced in various countries and having various patterns, were given as gifts—clothes of woven silk, Chinese silk, Indian silk, and bleached silk;[277] beautiful clothes made of wool and *dukūla*; those made of bark from Aparānta; crocheted shawls;[278] cloaks made with gold and jewels; silken cloth from Vārāṇasī; linen; and so on.

King Candraprabha [317] gave so many gifts that all the people of Jambudvīpa became rich, wealthy, and prosperous. King Candraprabha gave away so many elephants, horses, carriages, and umbrellas as gifts that not even a single person in Jambudvīpa traveled on foot. All the people of Jambudvīpa traveled from park to park and village to village on the backs of elephants or in carriages drawn by four horses, with umbrellas overhead made of gold and silver.

Then it occurred to King Candraprabha, "What is the use of my giving such petty gifts? I really should offer gifts of clothes, ornaments, and finery just like my own so that all the people of Jambudvīpa may enjoy royal pleasures."

So King Candraprabha offered crowns, diadems, clothes, ornaments, and finery to the people of Jambudvīpa—that is, he offered gifts of bracelets,[279] armlets, strings and necklaces of pearls, and the like. King Candraprabha offered so many gifts of clothes, jewelry, crowns, and diadems, all of which were fit for kings, that all the people of Jambudvīpa came to wear crowns and diadems. All the people of Jambudvīpa came to look just like King Candraprabha!

Then King Candraprabha had bells rung in his 68,000 cities for the following proclamation: "Friends, all the people of Jambudvīpa shall enjoy royal pleasures for as long as I live!"

When the people of Jambudvīpa heard King Candraprabha's

proclamation, every one of them began to enjoy royal pleasures. Thousands of veenas, flutes, *paṇava* drums, *sughoṣakas*, *vallarīs*, kettledrums, war drums, mridangams, cymbals,[280] and conchs were played, hundreds of horns were sounded, and the people of Jambudvīpa, wearing armlets, necklaces, jewels, pearls, finery, and earrings, and surrounded by groups of beautiful young women adorned with all kinds of ornaments, experienced royal glory.

And at that time, as the people of Jambudvīpa enjoyed those royal pleasures, the sounds of veenas, flutes, *paṇava* drums, *sughoṣakas*, *vallarīs*, kettledrums, mridangams, and war drums as well as the melody of cymbals and bamboo pipes arose in all 68,000 cities. And as golden kettledrums were beaten at [King][281] Candraprabha's four great sacrificial sites, sweet and pleasing sounds emerged.[282] As such, all of Jambudvīpa [318] resounded with pleasing sounds. Even [Sudarśana], the divine city of the gods of Trāyastriṃśa (Thirty-Three), reverberated with the sounds of dancing, singing, and the playing of musical instruments. In this way, at that time and at that juncture, owing to the sounds of singing and music, all the people living in Jambudvīpa were filled with intense pleasure and enjoyed themselves greatly.

Now at that time in the capital Bhadraśilā there lived seventy-two thousands of millions of billions of people.[283] To them, King Candraprabha was cherished, dear, and beloved, and they never tired of gazing upon his complexion, characteristics, form, and figure.[284] Whenever King Candraprabha would go to one of the great sacrificial sites, hundreds and thousands and millions and billions of beings would look at him and say, "What a wonder! King Candraprabha is born from the gods, yet he rules here in Jambudvīpa. No other man has a complexion and form like that of Lord Candraprabha." And whichever way King Candraprabha would look, thousands of women would be looking at him and thinking, "Lucky are those women who have him for a husband!" And this thought that occurred in their minds was pure, not otherwise. Truly King Candraprabha was someone to be seen.

King Candraprabha's Ministers and Their Alarming Dreams

King Candraprabha had 12,500 ministers, and among them were two chief ministers—Mahācandra (Great Moon) and Mahīdhara (Supporting the Earth). They were wise, learned, and intelligent; distinguished from the rest of the cabinet of ministers by their virtues; authorities for everyone; and managers and protectors of the king.[285] The king had few worries about any of his affairs, for the chief minister Mahācandra repeatedly urged the people of Jambudvīpa to follow the tenfold path of virtuous actions. "People of Jambudvīpa," he would say, "adhere to the tenfold path of virtuous actions!" The minister Mahācandra would admonish and instruct them just as would a wheel-turning king. To the chief minister Mahācandra, King Candraprabha was cherished, dear, and beloved, and he never tired of gazing upon the king's complexion, form, characteristics, and figure.

One day the chief minister Mahācandra had a dream that *piśāca*s the color of smoke carried off King Candraprabha's crown. When he woke up, [319] he was afraid, he was alarmed, and his hair stood on end. "Oh no!" he thought. "Don't let anyone come begging for Lord Candraprabha's head! My lord is all-giving. He gives away everything.[286] There isn't anything that he hasn't given away to the poor, the destitute, orphans, mendicants, and beggars."

Then he had an idea. "I won't tell King Candraprabha about this dream. Instead, I'll commision some heads to be made out of jewels and I'll store them in the treasury.[287] If someone comes begging for my lord's head, I'll entice him with these jeweled heads." With this in mind, he commisioned some jeweled heads and stored them in the treasury.

Then one day the chief minister Mahīdhara had a dream that a child[288] made completely of jewels, who was inside King Candraprabha's palace,[289] shattered into hundreds of pieces. Having had this dream, he was frightened, scared, and terrified. "Oh no!" he thought. "Don't let King Candraprabha's kingdom come to an end! Don't let there be any obstacle to his life!"

He then summoned some brahman soothsayers[290] who could interpret omens. "Gentlemen," he said, "I have had such-and-such a dream. Interpret it for me."[291]

Then those brahman soothsayers[292] who could interpret omens explained it to him: "This dream that you have had indicates that very soon someone will come begging for King Candraprabha's head. He will come down from on high, right here to the capital Bhadraśilā."

When chief minister Mahīdhara heard this interpretation of his dream, he sat lost in thought, cheek in hand. "King Candraprabha is kind at heart, compassionate, and treats all beings as his children. Yet very soon he will experience the force of impermanence."

Then one day all 12,500 ministers had a dream that *karoṭapāṇi* ("bowl in hand") yakṣas threw down the umbrellas, flags, and banners and broke the golden kettledrums at King Candraprabha's four great sacrificial sites. Having had this dream, they became frightened, scared, and terrified. "Oh no!" they thought. "King Candraprabha is a protector of the great earth. He is kind at heart, compassionate, and treats all beings as his children. Don't let him come under the force of impermanence! Don't let us become deprived, detached, and disconnected from our lord! Don't let Jambudvīpa become unsafe and unprotected!" [320]

King Candraprabha heard about all this and, having heard, had bells rung in his 68,000 cities for the following proclamation: "Friends, all the people of Jambudvīpa shall enjoy royal pleasures for as long as I live. Why worry about things like dreams and illusions?"[293]

After hearing King Candraprabha's proclamation, all of the people of Jambudvīpa once again began to enjoy royal pleasures. Thousands of veenas, flutes, *paṇava* drums, *sughoṣaka*s, *vallarī*s, kettledrums, mridangams, cymbals, and conchs were played, hundreds of horns were sounded, and the people of Jambudvīpa, wearing armlets, necklaces, jewels, pearls, finery, and earrings, and surrounded by groups of beautiful young women adorned with all kinds of ornaments, experienced royal glory.

At that time, as the people of Jambudvīpa enjoyed those royal pleasures,[294] the sounds of veenas, flutes, *paṇava* drums, *sughoṣakas*, *vallarīs*, kettledrums, mridangams, war drums as well as the melody of cymbals and bamboo pipes[295] arose in all 68,000 cities. And as golden kettledrums were beaten at King Candraprabha's four great sacrificial sites, sweet and pleasing sounds emerged. As such, all of Jambudvīpa resounded with pleasing sounds. Even [Sudarśana], the divine city of the gods of Trāyastriṃśa, reverberated with the sounds of dancing, singing, and the playing of musical instruments.[296] In this way, at that time and at that juncture, owing to the sounds of singing, all the people living in Jambudvīpa were filled with intense pleasure and enjoyed themselves greatly.

Raudrākṣa and the Gift of a Head

At that time on Mount Gandhamādana (Intoxicated with Fragrance) there lived a brahman named Raudrākṣa (Cruel-Eyed)[297] who could perform magical spells. The brahman Raudrākṣa heard that in the capital Bhadraśilā there was a king named Candraprabha who had vowed to himself to give away everything.

"I really should go and beg for his head," he thought. Then it occurred to him, "If he'll give away everything, he'll give me his head. But it is difficult, impossible, and inconceivable that one would sacrifice the best part of one's body, that which is cherished, precious, dear, and beloved—namely, one's head. It simply isn't possible!" With this in mind, he came down from Mount Gandhamādana.

Then a deity living on Gandhamādana began to cry out: "It's so sad! King Candraprabha, who is kind at heart, greatly compassionate, and treats all beings as his children, will experience the force of impermanence!" [321]

At that time all of Jambudvīpa became very disturbed and darkened with smoke. There were meteor showers, the sky looked like it was on fire, and the drums of the gods thundered in the air.

Not far from the capital Bhadraśilā there lived a seer named Viśvāmitra (Friend to the World), who possessed the five superhuman faculties. He had five hundred followers, and he too was kind at heart, compassionate, and treated all beings as his children. Seeing that all of Jambudvīpa was disturbed, the seer addressed his young brahman disciples: "Young brahmans, as you know, at present all of Jambudvīpa is in disarray and darkened with smoke. The sun and the moon, powerful as they are, neither shine nor burn or illuminate. Certainly some great man will soon be no more.[298]

Hordes of kinnaras and forest deities are crying,[299]
the assemblies of the gods likewise call out in distress.[300]
The moon doesn't shine, and the thousand-rayed sun doesn't glow;
even the sound of instruments being played[301] is no longer heard.

Fruits and flowers covering the multitude of trees
fall to the ground when merely stirred by the wind.[302]
A foreboding sound fills the air.
A great[303] disaster will surely[304] befall the city!

All the devoted residents of Bhadraśilā are filled with sorrow;
struck by the arrow of intense grief, their faces and throats
quiver.[305]
Young women with faces like the moon cry in their fine homes;
everyone wails piteously as though at a cremation ground.[306]

Why[307] do all the city's residents
bear[308] such grief welled up in their minds?
For those incessantly crying, with fingers clenched,[309]
a matchless power[310] holds back their words.

Clouds thunder with no water,
and the ponds have almost dried up.[311]

Those tender breezes, over water as on land,[312]
now blow as fierce and dusty winds.

The inauspicious omens are now manifold![313]
It would be best[314] if we left here and went to a safer region.

"And there's this, young brahmans: golden kettledrums are being beaten at King Candraprabha's four great sacrificial sites, and pleasing sounds no longer emerge. [322] Alas! A great disaster will definitely befall Bhadraśilā."

Meanwhile the brahman Raudrākṣa arrived in the capital Bhadraśilā. A deity who resided in the city saw the brahman Raudrākṣa from a distance and then approached King Candraprabha. Having approached, she said this to him: "My lord, there is something you should know. Today a beggar will come to my lord. He is hostile and violent. He looks for weaknesses, seeking a point of attack. He will beg for my lord's head. For the sake of living beings, my lord should protect himself!"

When King Candraprabha heard that someone would come begging for his head, he was glad at heart, and his eyes opened wide with wonder. He spoke to the deity. "Deity, go away. If he comes, I will fulfill this long-held wish of his." The deity realized the strength of King Candraprabha's resolve and felt sad, dejected, and deeply disturbed. Then she vanished on the spot.

It occurred to King Candraprabha, "What a wonderful thing it is that I give food to the hungry, water to the thirsty, and clothes, gold and golden things, jewels, pearls, and the like to those who desire them. But to those who come begging, I really should sacrifice my own body as well."

Meanwhile, as the brahman Raudrākṣa was entering the southern gate to the city, the deity stopped him. "Go away, evil brahman," she said. "Don't enter! You deluded man, how can you cut off[315] King Candraprabha's head? He is kind at heart, compassionate, and treats all beings as his children; he is endowed with many virtues, a protector of Jambudvīpa, and he does no wrong and causes no harm. You vicious and evil brahman, don't enter here!"

In the meantime, King Candraprabha heard about this incident: "A deity has detained a man who wants to beg from me at a gate to the city!" After hearing about it, he addressed his chief minister Mahācandra: "Mahācandra, please be informed that a deity has detained a supplicant at a gate to the city. Go quickly and bring him to me."

"Yes, my lord," the chief minister Mahācandra replied, consenting to King Candraprabha's request. He then went to the city gate and spoke to the deity: "Deity, please be informed that this brahman is to be allowed to enter. King Candraprabha has summoned him." [323]

Then that deity residing in the city said this to the chief minister Mahācandra: "Mahācandra, please be informed that this brahman is vicious and without compassion. He has come to Bhadraśilā to destroy King Candraprabha. Why should someone evil at heart be allowed to enter? He will approach the king and ask for his head!"

Then the chief minister Mahācandra said to the deity, "Deity, I've thought of a plan so that the brahman won't be able to take the lord's head."

So the chief minister Mahācandra brought the brahman Raudrākṣa into the city and ordered the treasurers as follows: "Gentlemen, bring out the jeweled heads! I will give them to this brahman." The treasurers made a pile of the jeweled heads at the king's door. The chief minister Mahācandra showed the jeweled heads to Raudrākṣa. "Great brahman," he said, "take all these jeweled heads! I'll also give you so much gold that it will provide livelihoods for your children and grandchildren. What do you want with my lord's head, filled as it is with marrow, snot, and fat?"

Thus addressed, the brahman Raudrākṣa said this to the chief minister Mahācandra: "I have no use for jeweled heads, nor for gold and golden things. I have come to this all-giving protector of the great earth for the sake of his head."

Thus addressed, the chief ministers Mahācandra and Mahīdhara each sat lost in thought, with cheeks in hand: "What is to be done now?"[316]

When King Candraprabha heard what had happened, he had a messenger[317] convey these instructions to the chief ministers Mahācandra and Mahīdhara: "Bring that [brahman][318] before me. I will fulfill this desire of his."

Thus addressed, the chief ministers Mahācandra and Mahīdhara, their faces streaked with tears, lamented mournfully and cried out: "My lord is kind at heart, compassionate, and treats all beings as his children. He is endowed with many virtues, is wise and skillful, and possesses divine sight. Soon he will experience the force of impermanence. Today we will become deprived, detached, disconnected, and separated from my lord!" With this in mind, they fell prostrate at the king's feet and then sat down at a respectful distance.

Now since King Candraprabha desired to make a sacrifice that would be distinguished as the ultimate sacrifice,[319] he addressed the brahman while the latter was still a distance away. "Come here, brahman!" he said. [324] "Make a request. Take whatever you want."[320]

The brahman Raudrākṣa then approached King Candraprabha and, having approached, greeted him with wishes for his success and well-being. Then he said this to him:

> You are steadfast in the pure dharma, O excellent bodhisattva,[321]
> desiring omniscience with all your heart, O virtuous one.
> Great compassion being foremost in your mind,[322]
>   cast off your head to me!
> Give it to me! Satisfy me now![323]

When King Candraprabha heard the brahman utter such words, he was glad at heart and wide-eyed with pleasure. He then said to the brahman Raudrākṣa, "At last, brahman, freely and without interference, you may take this head of mine—it is the best part of my body." And he said,

Although it is as dear as an only son,
take this head[324] of mine nonetheless.
May the fruit of your desires come quickly.
And from this gift of my head, may I attain awakening.[325]

After he spoke, he removed the crown from his head. And at the very moment that King Candraprabha removed the crown from his head, the crowns on the heads of all the people of Jambudvīpa fell off.[326] And in the capital Bhadraśilā, there were meteor showers in the four directions, and the sky looked like it was on fire.

The deities of the city cried out: "This evil brahman will cut off King Candraprabha's head!" Hearing this, the chief ministers Mahācandra and Mahīdhara realized that King Candraprabha truly would make such a sacrifice of his body. Their faces streaked with tears, they embraced King Candraprabha's feet and said, "Fortunate are those men, my lord, who will again catch sight of your truly wonderful form."[327] Looking up toward King Candraprabha, the two cultivated faith in their hearts for him and produced thoughts of loving-kindness toward the brahman Raudrākṣa. "We can't watch the impermanence of my lord," they thought. "He is incomparably virtuous." And at that very moment, they died. Transcending the realm of desire, they were reborn in the Brahmā world.

When the yakṣas on the ground and in the air came to understand the strength of King Candraprabha's resolve and heard the pained cries of those deities residing in the city, they began to cry out. "How terrible! Now King Candraprabha will abandon his body."

Meanwhile, at the gate to the palace, many hundreds of thousands of people had assembled. [325] When the brahman Raudrākṣa saw this crowd of people, he spoke to King Candraprabha. "My lord, there is something you should know. I can't take my lord's head in front of a crowd of people. If your head is to be sacrificed, let us go to a secluded place."

Thus addressed, King Candraprabha said to the brahman Raudrākṣa,

"So be it, great brahman. Let it be done. May you have success in all that you desire, and may your wishes be fulfilled." Then King Candraprabha got up from his throne, took a sharp sword, and approached Maṇiratnagarbha Park.

Seeing the strength of King Candraprabha's resolve, many hundreds of thousands of people in the capital Bhadraśilā followed behind him, wailing. Seeing this large gathering of people wailing, King Candraprabha consoled them. "Don't be careless with virtuous things," he said.

After giving this brief dharma teaching, he took the brahman Raudrākṣa and entered Maṇiratnagarbha Park. As soon as King Candraprabha entered the park, the umbrellas, flags, and banners in Bhadraśilā bent over in that direction. King Candraprabha then shut the gate to Maṇiratnagarbha Park and addressed the brahman Raudrākṣa: "Brahman, please take my head, the best part of my body."

Thus addressed, the brahman Raudrākṣa said to King Candraprabha, "I can't cut off my lord's head."

Now in the middle of Maṇiratnagarbha Park there was a red amaranth tree as well as a *campaka* tree always in bloom.[328] King Candraprabha then took out his sharp sword and approached that ever-blossoming *campaka* tree.

Then the deities living in the park, realizing that King Candraprabha was about to make such a sacrifice of his own body, began to cry out. "Evil brahman!" they said. "King Candraprabha does no wrong and causes no harm, he treats all beings as his children, and he is endowed with many virtues. How can you cut off his head?"

Then King Candraprabha stopped the deities of the park. "Deities, don't obstruct this man who begs for my head! [326] Why is that? Deities, in the past a deity obstructed someone who begged for my best limb. That deity earned a lot of demerit. Why is that? If that deity had not obstructed that beggar, I would have attained supreme knowledge very quickly. It is for this reason that I say to you—don't obstruct this man who begs for my best limb! Right here, in this Maṇiratnagarbha

Park of yours, I have sacrificed my head thousands of times, and no one has ever obstructed me. So, deity, don't obstruct this man who begs for my best limb. Moreover, deity, it was right here that I sacrificed myself to a tigress and surpassed Maitreya. The bodhisattva Maitreya, who had set out for buddhahood forty eons before, was surpassed with a single sacrifice of my head!"[329]

Now as those deities came to understand the great majesty of King Candraprabha, they experienced great faith in the king and so remained silent. Then King Candraprabha made this proper fervent aspiration:

"Listen, honorable deities, antigods, heavenly birds, celestial musicians, and kinnaras living in the ten directions! Here in this park I will make a sacrifice, a great sacrifice,[330] a complete sacrifice of my own head. And I will sacrifice my own head,[331] not for the sake of royal power, not for reaching heaven, not for personal pleasure, not for becoming a Śakra, not for becoming a Brahmā, and not for the victory of a wheel-turning king.[332] It is for no other reason than that I may attain unsurpassed perfect awakening and so subdue those beings who are unsubdued, pacify the unpacified, help to cross over those who have not crossed over, liberate the unliberated, console the unconsoled, and lead to final nirvāṇa those who have not reached final nirvāṇa.

"By this truth, this vow of truth, may my efforts be successful! And when I have passed into final nirvāṇa, may there be relics the size of mustard seeds.[333] And here in the middle of Maṇiratnagarbha Park, may there be a great stūpa that is the most distinguished of all stūpas. And may those beings who are exhausted[334] and who want to venerate this great shrine go there, and when they see it—the most distinguished of all stūpas and filled with relics[335]—may their exhaustion cease. And when I have passed into final nirvāṇa, may crowds of people come to my shrines, make offerings, and become intent on heaven and liberation."

After making this proper fervent aspiration, King Candraprabha bound his topknot to the *campaka* tree and then said to the brahman Raudrākṣa, [327] "Come, great brahman. Take it! Don't obstruct me!"

Then King Candraprabha, generating strength and power in his body and producing thoughts of loving-kindness along with compassion for the brahman Raudrākṣa, cut off his head and presented it to him. And when he died, because of his virtuousness,[336] he transcended the Brahmā world and was reborn among the gods of Śubhakṛtsna (Complete Beauty).

As soon as King Candraprabha sacrificed his head, three times the billionfold world-system teetered, tottered, and tremored; quivered, quavered, and quaked; shifted, shuddered, and shook.[337] And the deities in the sky began to throw divine blue waterlilies as well as red waterlilies, white waterlilies, and white lotuses; agarwood, *tagara*, and sandalwood powders; *tamāla* leaves and flowers from the divine coral tree. They also began to play divine instruments and throw cloth streamers.

Then the brahman Raudrākṣa left the park, holding King Candraprabha's head.[338] Many hundreds of thousands of people let out the cry, "How terrible! My lord, who fulfilled everyone's wishes, has been killed!"

Some of those people writhed around and about on the ground; some cried out, flailing their arms; and some wept, their hair disheveled. Many hundreds of thousands of people gathered together. While there in that place, some of them attained meditative states, died right then and there, and were reborn among the Śubhakṛtsna gods—at the same level as King Candraprabha. Others attained [lower] meditative states, died right then and there, and were reborn among the gods of Ābhāsvara (Radiant). Others entered the first meditative state and then died and were reborn as inhabitants of the Brahmā world.

Still others gathered together, built a funeral pyre out of all all kinds of fragrant wood, and cremated King Candraprabha's body.[339] And when his bones were burned to ashes, they placed them in a golden pot and at the main crossroads built a stūpa for his relics. And there they raised umbrellas, flags, and banners. Then they honored the stūpa with offerings of fragrances, garlands, incense, oil lamps, and flowers, and having cultivated faith in their hearts for King Candraprabha, they died and were reborn among the gods in the six spheres of desire. And all of those who made offerings there became intent on heaven and liberation.

"You may have some doubt or uncertainty, [328] monks, as to the identity of the capital called Bhadraśilā in the North Country at that time and at that juncture. Ponder no further. Why is that? Because at that time and at that juncture Takṣaśilā itself was the capital called Bhadraśilā.

"You may have some doubt or uncertainty, monks, as to the identity of the king named Candraprabha at that time and at that juncture. Ponder no further. Why is that? Because at that time and at that juncture I myself was King Candraprabha.

"You may have some doubt or uncertainty, monks, as to the identity of the brahman named Raudrākṣa at that time and at that juncture. Ponder no further. Why is that? Because at that time and at that juncture Devadatta himself was [the brahman Raudrākṣa].[340]

"You may have some doubt or uncertainty, monks, as to the identity of the chief ministers Mahācandra and Mahīdhara at that time and at that juncture. Ponder no further. Why is that? Because the chief ministers Mahācandra and Mahīdhara were themselves Śāriputra and Maudgalyāyana. Back then, too, they died without waiting for the death of their [spiritual] father."[341]

This was said by the Blessed One. With their minds uplifted, the monks and others—gods, nāgas, yakṣas, antigods, heavenly birds, celestial musicians, kinnaras, great snakes, and so forth—rejoiced at the words of the Blessed One.

So ends the *Candraprabhabodhisattvacaryā-avadāna*, the twenty-second chapter in the glorious *Divyāvadāna*.

Addendum[342]

And so in the past, King Candraprabha had a wealth of jewels, gold, silver, beryl, sapphires, and the like; he had clothes, vehicles, food, and ornaments; and he also had a kingdom made up of marketplaces, villages, towns, and regions.[343] The stream of King Candraprabha's praise abounded in virtues; it was made great by his consecration as lord of the entire earth; and it was powerful because he offered protection to those people who were struck by the fear of sorrows falling upon them—sorrows such as[344] rebirth in a lower realm of existence, death, or old age; having deformed hands, feet, or sense organs; and encountering undesirable things or being separated from desirable ones.[345] Such a stream of praise could never be attained unless one had sacrificed everything—one's royal chariots, one's offspring, one's wife, one's flesh and blood, hands and feet, head, eyes, neck, and so on.

And so, when King Candraprabha—whose footrest was glowing with the rays of light from the crest gems of all the feudal kings who had bowed down before him, and who himself had fulfilled the desires of absolutely all the people of Jambudvīpa by giving away his horses, elephants, chariots, clothes, ornaments, and so on—resolved to pacify the suffering of the entire world out of his compassion, he sacrificed his head, which had been capturing everyone's thoughts and attention. If one should ask, "How?" this is the way the story goes.

23. The Story of Saṅgharakṣita, part 1

SAṄGHARAKṢITA-AVADĀNA[346]

Stories 23–25 constitute a cycle of stories about the monk Saṅgharakṣita, but their ordering and relation to each other require some explanation.[347] *Each of these stories has close parallels in the* Mūlasarvāstivāda-vinaya, *which can offer some context. Only some of the original Sanskrit for these materials is extant,*[348] *but Tibetan and Chinese translations are available.*[349] *Story 23 begins abruptly, including some of the frame story that precedes it in the* Mūlasarvāstivāda-vinaya. *Likewise in the* Mūlasarvāstivāda-vinaya, *story 23 is followed immediately by story 25, and story 24, which is a continuation of the framestory that preceded story 23, appears immediately after that.*[350]

[THOSE NĀGAS of the great ocean, in the guise of brahmans and householders, assembled there, and (another nāga, in the guise of a monk,) taught them the dharma. When they had heard the dharma from him, they gave all the necessities to those monks who had just arrived and those who were preparing to depart.

Then (some of) the group of six monks questioned (two of its members): "Nanda and Upananda,][351] [329] what does this monastic latecomer[352] know?"

"The *Gradual Sayings* (*Ekottarikā*)," Nanda and Upananda said.

"But he uses a *Gradual Sayings* that is faulty[353] to teach the dharma," the other monks said. "These monks [that come and go] know the [entire] Tripiṭaka, they can discourse on the dharma, and they are gifted with eloquence that is inspired yet controlled.[354] Why doesn't he ask them [to teach]?"[355]

"Hey, latecomer, what do you know?" those monks asked the old monk.

"The *Gradual Sayings*," he said.

"Latecomer," they said, "you use a *Gradual Sayings* that is faulty to teach the dharma. These monks [that come and go] know the Tripiṭaka, they can discourse on the dharma, and they are gifted with eloquence that is inspired yet controlled. Why don't you ask them [to teach]?"

"Noble ones," the old monk said, "why don't you teach? Do I prevent you?"

"Nanda and Upananda," they said, "this latecomer speaks against us. You should suspend him from the order!"

"If they suspend me from the order," the old monk reflected, "I won't even be received in the nāga realm." So, while they were sleeping, he made their monastery disappear and entered the great ocean. They remained asleep on the sandy shore.

"Nanda and Upananda," the six monks said, "get up! Prepare a lion throne. We will teach the dharma." Then they said, "That must have been a god, a nāga, or a yakṣa, full of faith in the Blessed One. While he was serving the Buddha, the dharma, and the community, we harassed him."

The monks related this incident to the Blessed One, and the Blessed One said, "Monks, if that being who magically appeared [in the guise of a monk][356] had not been harassed by the group of six monks, he would have gone on to serve the Buddha, the dharma, and the community as someone able to explain the full extent of the teachings."[357] And the Buddha said,[358] "It is a dangerous mistake, monks, for anyone to teach the dharma without being requested to do so. Therefore, unless requested, a monk is not to teach the dharma. [330] If a monk teaches the dharma without being requested to do so, he commits a transgression. But those monks invited into his presence [for a teaching of the dharma] depart without incurring an offense."[359]

Saṅgharakṣita Sets Sail in the Great Ocean

In Śrāvastī there lived a householder named Buddharakṣita (Protected by the Buddha) who was rich, wealthy, and prosperous. He brought home a girl from an appropriate family as his wife, and with her he fooled around, enjoyed himself, and made love. From fooling around, enjoying himself, and making love, his wife became pregnant.

At this time, the venerable Śāriputra approached their household in search of a new disciple. There he established the householder along with his wife in the taking of the refuges as well as in the precepts.

After some time, the householder's wife became pregnant [again].[360] The venerable Śāriputra, knowing that it was now time to get a new disciple, approached the household all alone.

"Doesn't the venerable Śāriputra have an attending disciple?" the householder asked.

"Householder," he said, "do you think that our attending disciples simply emerge from shoots of *kāśa* grass or *kuśa* grass?[361] It is those individuals we receive from people like you who become our attending disciples."

"Noble one," the householder Buddharakṣita said, "my wife is pregnant. If she gives birth to a son, I will offer him as an attending disciple to the noble one."

"Householder," he said, "that would be good."

[After][362] eight or nine months, the householder's wife gave birth. A boy was born who was beautiful, good-looking, and attractive, radiant with a golden complexion, who had a parasol-shaped head, lengthy arms, a broad forehead, joined eyebrows, and a prominent nose.

Then his relatives came together and assembled. For three weeks—

that is, twenty-one days—they celebrated the occasion of his birth in full, and then they selected a name for him.

"What should this boy's name be?"

"This boy is the son of the householder Buddharakṣita, so let the boy's name be Saṅgharakṣita (Protected by the Community)."

On the very day that Saṅgharakṣita was born, five hundred sons were also born to five hundred merchants. They were also given names that were appropriate to their families.

The boy Saṅgharakṣita was raised and nourished with milk, yogurt, fresh butter, clarified butter, buttercream, and other special provisions that were very pure. He grew quickly [331] like a lotus in a lake.

When the boy had grown up, the venerable Śāriputra, knowing that it was time to get a new disciple, approached their household all alone [without an attending disciple] and gave a sign of his presence.

"Son," the householder Buddharakṣita said to Saṅgharakṣita, "before you were born I offered you as an attending disciple to the noble Śāriputra."

That being, who was in his final existence, followed behind the venerable Śāriputra continuously.[363] The venerable Śāriputra initiated and ordained him and taught him the four Āgamas.

After some time, those [sons of the] five hundred merchants gathered up goods for export across the great ocean. Wanting to cross the great ocean, they said, "Friends, we need to get some young noble one to set sail with us who will teach us the dharma while we're crossing the great ocean."

"Gentlemen," they said, "the noble Saṅgharakṣita is our friend, brother, and childhood companion. Let's get him to set sail with us." So they approached him.

"Noble Saṅgharakṣita, you are our friend, brother, and childhood companion. We are setting out for the great ocean. You should set sail with us. While we're crossing the ocean, you can teach us the dharma."

"It is not mine to say. Ask my instructor for permission."

So they approached the noble Śāriputra. Having approached, they said, "Noble Śāriputra, the noble Saṅgharakṣita is our friend, brother, and childhood companion. We are setting out for the great ocean. Let him set sail with us. While we're crossing the great ocean, he can teach us the dharma."

"Ask the Blessed One for permission," he said.

So they approached the Blessed One. "Blessed One, we are setting out for the great ocean. The noble Saṅgharakṣita is our friend, brother, and childhood companion. Let him set sail in the great ocean with us. While we're crossing the great ocean, he can teach us the dharma."

Then the Blessed One reflected, "Do they have any roots of virtue? Yes, they do. Are they connected with someone? Yes—the monk Saṅgharakṣita." [332]

Considering this, the Blessed One addressed Saṅgharakṣita, "Go, Saṅgharakṣita, although you will have to withstand fear and dread."[364]

The venerable Saṅgharakṣita accepted the Blessed One's request with his silence.

Those five hundred merchants performed auspicious rituals and benedictions for a safe journey, loaded many goods in carts, carriers, containers, and baskets, and on camels, bulls, and donkeys, and then set out for the great ocean. They passed through marketplaces, hamlets, villages, towns, and trading centers, one after another, until they arrived at the seashore. Then they carefully outfitted an ocean-going ship[365] and set sail in the great ocean to find their fortune.

When they were crossing the great ocean, nāgas seized their ship. The merchants began to implore the guardian deity: "Whoever presides over this great ocean, whether god, nāga, or yakṣa, should tell us what he seeks."

Then a voice emerged from the great ocean: "Give us the noble Saṅgharakṣita!"

"The noble Saṅgharakṣita is our friend, brother, and childhood companion," they said. "He has been entrusted to us by Bhadanta Śāriputra, handed over to us by the Blessed One. It is better that we die with Saṅgharakṣita than that we abandon him."

The venerable Saṅgharakṣita heard what they were saying, and said, "Gentlemen, what are you saying?"

"Noble Saṅgharakṣita," they said, "a voice has emerged from the ocean saying, 'Give us the noble Saṅgharakṣita!'"

"So why don't you give me to them?" he said.

"Noble one," they said, "you are our friend, brother, and childhood companion. You were entrusted to us by Bhadanta Śāriputra and by the Blessed One. It is better that we die with you, noble Saṅgharakṣita, than that we abandon you."

The venerable Saṅgharakṣita reflected, "The Blessed One has said that I must withstand fear and dread. This must be that." Then he took his bowl and robe and began to lower himself into the great ocean.

The merchants saw him and said, "Noble Saṅgharakṣita, what are you doing? [333] Noble Saṅgharakṣita, what are you doing!" While they were crying out, he jumped into the great ocean. Then their boat was released.

Meanwhile the nāgas took the noble Saṅgharakṣita and led him to the nāga realm.[366] "Noble Saṅgharakṣita, this is the perfumed chamber of the perfectly awakened Vipaśyin. This is the perfumed chamber of Śikhin, and this of Viśvabhū, this of Krakucchanda, this of Kanakamuni, this of Kāśyapa, and this of the Blessed One. Noble Saṅgharakṣita, the sūtras and the *mātṛkā*s of the Blessed One have been established among gods and humans. We nāgas are debased creatures that have fallen [into a lower karmic realm].[367] How excellent it would be if the noble Saṅgharakṣita would establish the four Āgamas here as well."

"And so it shall be," he said.

He encouraged three young nāgas. "You read the *Connected Sayings* (*Saṃyuktaka*)," he said to the first. "You read the *Middle-Length Sayings* (*Madhyama*)," he said to the second. "And you read the *Longer Sayings* (*Dīrghāgama*)," he said to the third.

[Then a fourth nāga, who had previously appeared by magic in the guise of an old man,] said,[368] "I will recite and make clear the *Gradual Sayings*, for its form has become obscured."

And so the nāgas began to study. The first closed his eyes while receiving instruction.[369] The second turned his face away while receiving instruction. And the third sat at a distance while receiving instruction. Only that [fourth] one among them was respectful and courteous, and always ready to perform his duties.

"Noble one, get up!" [he would say to the others]. "Put aside that dental stick![370] Clear a spot for the Blessed One![371] Venerate his shrine! Eat! Prepare your bed!"

Meanwhile all the nāgas studied the Āgamas.

"Noble one," [the fourth nāga][372] said [to the noble Saṅgharakṣita], "they have studied the Āgamas. Will they remember them or not?"

"They are gifted with memory, so they will remember them. But there is a common fault among them."

"Noble one," he said, "what fault?"

"All of them lack respect and courtesy. The first one closes his eyes while receiving instruction. The second one turns his face away while receiving instruction. And the third one sits at a distance while receiving instruction. Only you are respectful and courteous, and always first to perform your duties."

"Noble one," he said, "it isn't that they lack respect and courtesy. The one who receives instruction with his eyes shut has a poisonous glance. The one who receives instruction with his face turned away has poisonous breath. And the one who receives instruction from a distance has a poisonous touch. As for me, I have poisonous fangs." [334]

The noble one was afraid. He became extremely pale and drawn, and he felt weak, faint, and unsteady.

"Noble one," he said, "why are you so pale and drawn? Why do you look weak, faint, and unsteady?"

"Friend," he said, "I am living among enemies. If one of you gets angry at another, I'll end up dead."

"We won't injure a noble one," he said. "Nevertheless, do you want to go back to Jambudvīpa (Black Plum Island)?"

"Friend, that is what I desire."

The boat arrived again, and they raised him to the surface.

The merchants saw him and said, "Welcome, noble Saṅgharakṣita!"

"Gentlemen, rejoice!" he said. "I have established the four Āgamas among the nāgas."

"Noble Saṅgharakṣita," they said, "we are delighted."

They then brought him on board and set out. Eventually they reached the seashore, and then all the merchants went to sleep. The venerable Saṅgharakṣita began to look out at the great ocean.

The Blessed One has said that there are five things one never tires of seeing:

> A mighty elephant and a king,
> an ocean and a tall mountain—
> one never tires from seeing these,
> or a buddha, the best of blessed ones.[373]

The venerable Saṅgharakṣita remained awake for a long time looking out at the great ocean. Then, in the last watch of the night, he became very tired, lay down, and fell asleep. The merchants got up while it was still night, loaded their cargo, and set off. When night turned into dawn they asked each other, "Where is the noble Saṅgharakṣita?"[374]

"He travels up front," some of them said.

"He brings up the rear," others said.

"He travels in the middle of the caravan," still others said.

"We've left the noble Saṅgharakṣita behind!" they said. "This isn't a good thing that we've done. We should turn back."

"Gentlemen," others said, "the noble Saṅgharakṣita has such great magic and great power that he didn't die crossing the ocean. How could he die now? He must have gone ahead. Come, let's go." So they continued on their way.

Saṅgharakṣita Learns the Deeds of Misbehaving Monks

At sunrise the venerable Saṅgharakṣita was struck by the sun's rays, woke up, and saw nothing around him. The merchants had left. [335] So he took up a narrow path and set out. After a while, in a particular forest of *śāla* trees, he saw a monastery that was adorned with raised benches on platforms,[375] railings, latticed windows, and vents shaped like bulls' eyes. He also saw monks properly clothed and covered who remained calm in their comportment. He approached them, and they said to him, "Welcome, venerable Saṅgharakṣita!" Then they had him rest, and after he was rested, they brought him into the monastery. There he saw that an excellent bed and place to sit had been specially prepared for him and that fine foods had been served.

"Bhadanta Saṅgharakṣita," they asked him, "aren't you thirsty? Aren't you hungry?"

"Noble ones," he said, "I'm thirsty and I'm hungry."

"Then you should eat, Bhadanta Saṅgharakṣita."

"I will eat along with the community," he said.

"Bhadanta Saṅgharakṣita," they said, "eat now. It's going to get dangerous here."

He ate and, after eating, stepped away and maintained a respectful distance. After some time, a gong was sounded [announcing the monks' mealtime].[376] They each took their bowls, [entered according to seniority,] and sat down in the order in which they arrived.[377] Immediately their monastery disappeared, and their begging bowls appeared as iron hammers.[378] With these iron hammers, they broke each other's skulls, everyone crying out in pain all the while. This continued on until night turned to day. Then, once again, their monastery appeared, as did those monks who remained calm in their comportment. The venerable Saṅgharakṣita approached them.

"Who are you, venerable sirs? What deed led you to be reborn here?"

"Bhadanta Saṅgharakṣita, the people of Jambudvīpa are difficult to convince. You won't believe us."

"I can see what's before my eyes. Why wouldn't I believe you?"

"Bhadanta Saṅgharakṣita," they said, "in the past we were the disciples of the perfectly awakened Kāśyapa. One day we caused a fight in the dining hall.[379] Since we caused a fight in the dining hall, we have been reborn here in our own individual hell realms.[380] And when we die and pass away from here, it is very likely that we will be reborn in the true realms of hell.

"Please, [Bhadanta][381] Saṅgharakṣita, go to Jambudvīpa and announce to those who follow the religious life with you: 'Venerable sirs, don't cause a fight within the community! [336] Otherwise, you will share in the same kind of suffering and sorrow as the ascetics of the Buddha Kāśyapa.'"

The venerable Saṅgharakṣita set out and continued on his way until he saw a second monastery that was surrounded by raised benches on platforms, railings, and latticed windows and adorned with vents shaped like bulls' eyes. And he saw monks properly clothed and covered, who were calm and remained calm in their comportment. He approached them, and they said to him, "Welcome, Bhadanta Saṅgharakṣita!" Then they had him rest, and after he was rested, they brought him into the monastery. There he saw that an excellent bed and a place to sit had been specially prepared for him and that fine foods had been served.[382]

"Bhadanta Saṅgharakṣita," they said to him, "you should eat."

Realizing the danger,[383] he ate, and after eating, he stepped away and maintained a respectful distance. After some time, a gong was sounded [announcing the monks' mealtime]. They each took their bowls, [entered according to seniority,] and sat down in the order in which they arrived. Immediately their monastery disappeared, and their food and drink appeared as molten iron. With this molten iron, they doused each other's bodies, everyone crying out in pain all the while. This continued on until night turned to day. Then, once again, their monastery appeared, as did those calm monks who remained calm in their comportment. He approached them.

"Who are you, venerable sirs? What deed led you to be reborn here?"

"Bhadanta Saṅgharakṣita, the people of Jambudvīpa are difficult to convince. They won't believe us."[384]

"I can see what's before my eyes. Why wouldn't I believe you?"

"Bhadanta Saṅgharakṣita," they said, "in the past we were the disciples of the perfectly awakened Kāśyapa. Once when the community received an offering [of food and drink] given out of love, some visiting monks arrived. Seized with ignoble thoughts,[385] we resolved that we wouldn't consume that offering until those visiting monks departed. And so we did just that. But for a week it was unseasonably rainy, and the food and drink we had received went bad. Since we wasted a gift given out of faith, we have been reborn here in our own individual hell realms. [337] And when we die and pass away from here, it is very likely that we will be reborn in the true realms of hell.

"Please, Bhadanta Saṅgharakṣita, go to Jambudvīpa and announce to those who follow the religious life with you: 'Venerable sirs, don't waste a gift given out of faith! Otherwise, you will experience the same kind of suffering and sorrow as the ascetic followers of the Buddha Kāśyapa.'"[386]

The venerable Saṅgharakṣita set out and continued on his way until he saw a third monastery that was adorned with raised benches on platforms, railings, latticed windows, and vents shaped like bulls' eyes. [And he saw monks properly clothed and covered, who were calm and remained calm in their comportment. He approached them, and they said to him, "Welcome, Bhadanta Saṅgharakṣita!" Then they had him rest, and after he was rested, they brought him into the monastery. There he saw that an excellent bed and a place to sit had been specially prepared for him and that fine foods had been served.

"Bhadanta Saṅgharakṣita," they said to him, "you should eat."

Realizing the danger, he ate],[387] and after eating, he stepped away and maintained a respectful distance. A gong was sounded [announcing the monks' mealtime]. Immediately the monastery caught on fire, then it burned and blazed, and merging into a single flame, it began to pour smoke. The monks in the monastery cried out in pain as their bodies burned. This continued on until night turned to day. Then, once again, their monastery appeared, as did those calm monks who remained calm in their comportment. He approached them.

"Who are you, venerable sirs? What deed led you to be reborn here?"

"Bhadanta Saṅgharakṣita, the people of Jambudvīpa are difficult to convince. You won't believe us."

"Gentlemen, I can see what's before my eyes. Why wouldn't I believe you?"

"Bhadanta Saṅgharakṣita," they said, "in the past we were the disciples of the perfectly awakened Kāśyapa. We were lacking virtue, and so the monks who were virtuous expelled us. We then took up residence in an empty monastery. One day a virtuous monk arrived there. The thought came to us that this monk should stay with us. All by himself he could sanctify the offerings made to us [and thereby help us receive gifts].[388] The monk did stay there in our monastery, and since it was affiliated with him,[389] once again many virtuous monks came there. And from there too we were expelled. Filled with resentment, we collected dried wood, dried grass, and dried cow dung and started a fire in the monastery.[390] Many people, both students and masters, were burned there. Since we caused those students and masters to burn, we have been reborn here in our own individual hell realms. [338] And when we die and pass away from here, it is very likely that we will be reborn in the true realms of hell.

"Please, Bhadanta Saṅgharakṣita, go to Jambudvīpa and announce to those who follow the religious life with you: 'Venerable sirs, don't entertain evil thoughts toward those who follow the religious life with you. Otherwise, you will experience the same kind of suffering and sorrow as the ascetic followers of the Buddha Kāśyapa.'"

Saṅgharakṣita Gives the Blessed One a Gift

The venerable Saṅgharakṣita set out and continued on his way once again. By and by, he saw beings—

having the form of pillars,
having the form of walls,
having the form of trees,
having the form of leaves,
having the form of flowers,
having the form of fruits,
having the form of ropes,
having the form of brooms,
having the form of mortars,
having the form of cups,[391]
and having the form of pots.

[He also saw beings walking about, cut in half at the waist and held together by string.][392]

Eventually, the venerable Saṅgharakṣita arrived in the countryside. There in a certain hermitage lived five hundred seers. They saw the venerable Saṅgharakṣita from a distance and said to each other, "Gentlemen, let's make an agreement. Since these ascetics who follow Śākyamuni are great talkers, no one is to say a word to him." They all agreed.

The venerable Saṅgharakṣita approached them and, having approached, began to ask them for shelter. No one uttered a word.

Now in the hermitage there was one seer with a virtuous character,[393] and he said, "Why isn't shelter given to you followers of Śākyamuni? It's because you have a fault. You're great talkers. I'll give you shelter on the condition that you don't say anything."

"Yes, seer," the venerable Saṅgharakṣita said. "And so it shall be."

There in the hermitage one seer had gone wandering in the countryside. His hut remained empty. So [the virtuous seer] said to Saṅgharakṣita,[394] "You may sleep in that hut." The venerable Saṅgharakṣita sprinkled water about the hut, swept and cleaned it, and then applied a fresh layer of cow dung.

The seers watched him and remarked, "Gentlemen,[395] these ascetics who follow Śākyamuni make a show of cleanliness."[396]

Meanwhile the venerable Saṅgharakṣita washed his feet outside the hut, then entered the hut and sat down. Crossing his legs and holding his body upright, [339] he made his mindfulness fully present.

In the first watch of the night, the deity who lived in that hermitage approached the venerable Saṅgharakṣita and, having approached, said, "Noble Saṅgharakṣita, teach the dharma."

"It's fine for you [to ask],"[397] the venerable Saṅgharakṣita said. "But don't you see that I received shelter by making an agreement? Do you want me to be sent away?"

"He is exhausted," she reflected. "He needs to sleep. I'll approach him again in the middle watch of the night."

So in the middle watch of the night she approached him again and, having approached, said, "Noble Saṅgharakṣita, teach the dharma."

Again the venerable Saṅgharakṣita said, "It's fine for you [to ask]." "But don't you see that I received shelter by making an agreement? Do you want me to be sent away?"

"He is still exhausted," she reflected. "He needs to sleep. I'll approach him again in the last watch of the night."

So in the last watch of the night she approached him again and, having approached, said, "Noble Saṅgharakṣita, teach the dharma."

Once again the venerable Saṅgharakṣita said, "It's fine for you [to ask]. But don't you see that I received shelter by making an agreement? Do you want me to be sent away?"

"Noble Saṅgharakṣita," she said, "it is daybreak now. If they send you away, you can go. Besides, didn't the Blessed One say that you would have to withstand fear and dread?"

"She speaks truly," the venerable Saṅgharakṣita reflected. "If that seer sends me away, I'll go. These seers are brahmans," he reflected further, "so verses concerning brahmans should be recited."[398] Then the venerable Saṅgharakṣita began to recite from the "Chapter on Brahmans" [in the *Udānavarga*]:[399]

Neither wandering about naked, nor matted hair, nor mud,
not fasting or sleeping on the bare ground,
not dust and dirt or squatting in ascetic postures—
none can purify an ignorant man[400] who has not overcome
desire.

Although well adorned, he who follows the dharma
is restrained, peaceful, subdued, and chaste
and relinquishes violence against all beings;
he is a brahman, he is an ascetic, he is a monk.

When the brahmans heard this, they reflected, "He utters verses concerning brahmans."[401] [340] So one brahman approached him, then a second and a third, until all of them had come to him. Then the deity exercised her power so that they couldn't see each other. After this, the venerable Saṅgharakṣita taught the sūtra known as the *Simile of the Town* (*Nagaropama*).[402] And then he uttered this verse:

May those beings assembled here,
on the ground or in the air,
always act with love for others
and practice the dharma day and night.[403]

While this explanation of the dharma was being delivered, all of them clearly grasped the truth and simultaneously achieved the reward of the nonreturner. They also acquired magical powers.[404] Then all of them in one voice exclaimed, "Well said, Bhadanta Saṅgharakṣita!"

The deity then released the effects of her magical powers, and they began to see each other again.

"You've come, too?" they said to each other.

"Yes, I've come."

"Excellent!"

Having seen the truth, they said, "Bhadanta Saṅgharakṣita, may we renounce, take ordination, and become monks according to the dharma and monastic discipline that have been so well expressed. May we follow the religious life under the Blessed One."[405]

"Do you want to renounce as monks in my presence or in the Blessed One's?" the venerable Saṅgharakṣita asked.

"In the Blessed One's," they said.

"If that's the case," the venerable Saṅgharakṣita said, "come and we'll go to the Blessed One."

"Bhadanta Saṅgharakṣita," they said, "should we go using our magical powers or using yours?"

The venerable Saṅgharakṣita reflected, "These men have amassed many virtues through my instruction.[406] I have become like a raft, [bringing them to the other shore]."[407] Then he said, "Gentlemen, wait just a moment."[408] The venerable Saṅgharakṣita then sat at the base of a tree, crossed his legs, held his body upright, and made his mindfulness fully present.

The Blessed One has said that there are five benefits in having great learning. Such a person is

well versed in the elements,
well versed in interdependent arising,
well versed in what is possible and impossible,[409]
and not dependent on another for instruction or admonition.[410]

After striving, struggling, and straining, the venerable Saṅgharakṣita rid himself of all defilements and thereby directly experienced arhatship. [341] Becoming an arhat,

he was free from attachment in the three realms;
[he regarded clods of earth and gold as equal in value;
he possessed equanimity toward the sky
  and the palm of his hand;
he didn't distinguish between being cut by a blade
  and being anointed with sandalwood paste;
the eggshell of his ignorance was broken by knowledge;
he obtained the special knowledges, superhuman faculties,
  and analytic insights;
and he was averse to worldly attainments, temptations,
  and honors].
He becomes worthy of respect, honor, and obeisance
  [from the gods, including Indra and Upendra].[411]

"Gentlemen," the venerable Saṅgharakṣita said to them, "take hold of the edge of my robe, and we shall go." So they clung to the edge of the venerable Saṅgharakṣita's robe. Then the venerable Saṅgharakṣita, like a royal goose with outstretched wings, made use of his magical powers and set off up into the sky.

Meanwhile those five hundred merchants [who had previously traveled with the venerable Saṅgharakṣita] were unloading their wares. A shadow fell on them from above. Then they saw him. "Noble Saṅgharakṣita," they said. "You've returned!"

"Yes, I've returned."

"Where are you going?"

"[To the Blessed One].[412] These five hundred noble sons want to renounce, take ordination, and become monks according to the dharma and monastic discipline that have been so well expressed," he said.

"Noble Saṅgharakṣita," they said, "we'd also like to go forth as monks. Please come down! We'll finish unloading our wares."

The venerable Saṅgharakṣita then descended, and the merchants finished unloading their wares. Then the venerable Saṅgharakṣita, with those one thousand noble sons in tow, set off toward the Blessed One.

At that time the Blessed One was seated in front of an assembly of many hundreds of monks, and he was teaching the dharma. The Blessed One saw the venerable Saṅgharakṣita from a distance, and upon seeing him, he addressed the monks once again: "That, monks, is the monk Saṅgharakṣita, and he is coming with a gift. For a tathāgata, there is no gift that compares with the gift of new disciples."

The venerable Saṅgharakṣita then approached the Blessed One. Having approached, he placed his head in veneration at the Blessed One's feet and then sat down at a respectful distance. Sitting down at a respectful distance, the venerable Saṅgharakṣita said this to the Blessed One: "Bhadanta, these one thousand noble sons want to renounce, take ordination, and become monks according to the dharma and monastic discipline that have been so well expressed. May the Blessed One, out of compassion for them, initiate and ordain them."

Then the Blessed One addressed them, uttering the "Come, O monk" formula for ordination: "Come, O monks! Follow the religious life!" As soon as the Blessed One finished speaking, there they stood—heads shaved, garbed in monastic robes, bowls and water pots in hand, with a week's growth of hair and beard and the disciplined deportment of monks who had been ordained for one hundred years. [342]

> "Come," the Tathāgata said to them.
> With heads shaved and bodies wrapped in robes,
> they instantly attained tranquility of the senses,
> and so they remained by the will of the Buddha.[413]

Then the Blessed One gave them instructions.

After striving, struggling, and straining, they rid themselves of all defilements and thereby directly experienced arhatship. Becoming arhats,

they were free from attachment in the three realms;
[they regarded clods of earth and gold as equal in value;
they possessed equanimity toward the sky
  and the palms of their hands;
they didn't distinguish between being cut by a blade
  and being anointed with sandalwood paste;
the eggshell of their ignorance was broken by knowledge;
they obtained the special knowledges, superhuman faculties,
  and analytic insights;
and they were averse to worldly attainments, temptations,
  and honors].
They became worthy of respect, honor, and obeisance
  [from the gods, including Indra and Upendra].[414]

Then the venerable Saṅgharakṣita asked the Lord Buddha, "Bhadanta, I saw beings

having the form of walls,
having the form of pillars,
having the form of trees,
having the form of leaves,
having the form of flowers,
having the form of fruits,
having the form of ropes,
having the form of brooms,
having the form of cups,[415]
having the form of mortars,
and having the form of pots.

I also saw one being walking about, cut in half at the waist and held together by string. As a result of what action has all this occurred?"

"Saṅgharakṣita," the Blessed One said,[416] "those beings you saw in the form of walls were disciples of the perfectly awakened Kāśyapa. They dirtied a monastery wall with their snot. As a result of that action, they have come to have the form of walls. Just as those beings have the form of walls, for the same reason those other beings have the form of pillars.

"Those beings you[417] saw having the form of trees, Saṅgharakṣita, they too were disciples of the perfectly awakened Kāśyapa. They used the flowering and fruit-bearing trees belonging to the monastery for personal use. As a result of that action, they have come to have the form of trees. Just as those beings have the form of trees, for the same reason those other beings have the form of leaves, fruits, and flowers.

"That being you saw having the form of rope, Saṅgharakṣita, he too was a disciple of the perfectly awakened Kāśyapa. He used the monastery's rope for personal use. As a result of that action, he has come to have the form of rope. Just as that being has the form of rope, for the same reason that other being has the form of a broom.

"That being you saw having the form of a cup,[418] Saṅgharakṣita, he was a novice disciple of the perfectly awakened Kāśyapa. [343] At one time he was put in charge of drinking vessels, and after he had washed the vessels,[419] some visiting monks arrived. 'Hey novice,' they asked him, 'is there still anything for the community to drink?'

"'No there isn't,' he said. Disappointed, they continued on their way. But there was still something for the community to drink.[420] As a result of that action, he has come to resemble a cup.[421]

"That being you saw who resembled a mortar, Saṅgharakṣita, he too was a disciple of the perfectly awakened Kāśyapa. He was put in charge of looking after bowls. Now, a certain novice there had become an arhat. 'Hey novice,' he said to the arhat, 'grind some rice paste in a mortar[422] and give it to me.'

"'Elder,' he said, 'wait just a moment. I'm busy. When I'm finished I'll give it to you.'

"The elder became furious and said, 'Novice, if you like,[423] I'll throw you in that mortar and grind you up, not just some rice paste!'[424] Since he committed an act of harsh speech toward an arhat, as a result of that action, he has come to resemble a mortar.

"Those beings you saw who resembled pots, Saṅgharakṣita, they were disciples of the perfectly awakened Kāśyapa. While decocting medicines for the monks, they broke the pots. This was a setback for those monks. As a result of that action, they have come to resemble pots.[425]

"That being, Saṅgharakṣita, you saw walking about, cut in half at the waist and held together by string, he had gone forth as a monk following the teaching of the perfectly awakened Kāśyapa, and he was greedy for profit. He would barter offerings received in the rainy season against those received in the winter, and those in the winter against those in the rainy season. As a result of that action, he walks about cut in half at the waist and held together by string."

So ends the *Saṅgharakṣita-avadāna*, the twenty-third chapter in the glorious *Divyāvadāna*. [344]

24. *The Story of a Young Nāga*

NĀGAKUMĀRA-AVADĀNA[426]

SOME MONKS in doubt asked the Lord Buddha, the remover of all doubts, "Where, Bhadanta, did the [shapeshifting] young nāga [who knew the *Gradual Sayings*][427] first gain faith?"

And the Blessed One spoke.

Long ago, monks, in this present auspicious age, when people lived for twenty thousand years, there arose in the world a teacher named Kāśyapa,

who was a tathāgata,
an arhat,
a perfectly awakened being,
perfect in knowledge and conduct,
a sugata,
a knower of the world,
an unsurpassed guide for those in need of training,
a teacher of gods and humans,
a buddha,
and a blessed one.

He taught the dharma to his disciples as such: "You should meditate, monks, in forests, in empty chambers, in mountains, valleys, hills, caves, heaps of straw, open spaces, cremation grounds, wooded plateaus, and in remote areas. Don't be careless, monks! Otherwise, later on, you'll be filled with regret. This is our teaching."

Accordingly, some monks went and meditated on the terraces of Mount Sumeru, some on the banks of lotus ponds filled with Gangetic waters, some on the shores of the great lake Anavatapta (Unheated), some on the seven golden mountains,[428] and some went and meditated in various villages, towns, and royal capitals.[429]

A Novice Accepts Alms in the Nāga Realm

A certain young nāga, not long after he was born,[430] was carried off by Suparṇin (Well-Winged), the king of birds, up onto the slopes of Mount Sumeru.[431] There he saw monks engaged in meditation, study, yoga, and contemplation. And seeing them, his mind was filled with faith. Possessed of faith, he reflected, "These noble ones are truly free from the various forms of suffering!"

He then died and passed away and was born in Vārāṇasī in a family of brahmans that was devoted to the six duties of a brahman. Raised and nourished, in time he grew up, and eventually he went forth as monk in the order of the perfectly awakened Kāśyapa. After striving, struggling, and straining, he rid himself of all defilements and thereby directly experienced arhatship. Becoming an arhat,

> he was free from attachment in the three realms;
> [he regarded clods of earth and gold as equal in value;
> he possessed equanimity toward the sky
>   and the palm of his hand;
> he didn't distinguish between being cut by a blade
>   and being anointed with sandalwood paste;
> the eggshell of his ignorance was broken by knowledge;
> he obtained the special knowledges, superhuman faculties,
>   and analytic insights;

and he was averse to worldly attainments, temptations,
and honors].
He became worthy of respect, honor, and obeisance
[from the gods, including Indra and Upendra].[432]

Then he reflected, "From where did I die and pass away? From among animals. Where was I reborn? Among humans. Where are my former parents?" He saw that now they stood crying in the nāga realm. [345] So he went there.

Having gone there, he asked, "Mother, Father, why are you crying?"

"Noble one," they said, "our nāga son, not long after he was born,[433] was carried off by Suparṇin, the king of birds."

"I am that very son," he said.

"Noble one, so wretched is the state of a nāga[434] that we wouldn't have imagined that he'd have a good rebirth, let alone that he'd come to possess such qualities."

He informed those two of all that had occurred. Then they fell prostrate at his feet and said, "Noble one, you have amassed many virtues. Noble one, you desire alms, and we desire merit. Come back here every day, have a meal, and then you can go."

So each day he would partake of divine ambrosia in the nāga realm, and then he would return [to the human realm].

There was a novice who was his attending student. Some monks addressed him: "Novice, this instructor of yours, where does he return from each day, having already eaten?"

"I don't know," he said.

"He returns from the nāga realm where each day he partakes of divine ambrosia. Why don't you go too?"

"He possesses great magic and great power," he said. "How can I go the way he goes?"

"When he does go, making use of his magical powers, take hold of the edge of his robe," they said.

"I hope I don't fall," he said.

"Friend," they said, "even if Sumeru, the king of mountains, took hold[435] of the edge of his robe, he wouldn't fall, much less you."

After determining exactly where his instructor would disappear,[436] he went to that place before [his instructor arrived] and waited. When he knew that his instructor would disappear, he took hold of the edge of his robe. The two of them set off up into the sky, and there they were seen by the nāgas, who then prepared two seats for them and cleared two spots on the ground.

"Why has another seat been prepared?" the instructor reflected. Then he turned around and saw the novice.

"Friend, you've come as well!" he said.

"Yes, instructor, I have come."

"Excellent!"

"This noble one possesses great magic and great power," the nāgas reflected. "He can digest[437] divine ambrosia. The other one can't."[438] So they gave divine ambrosia to the instructor and to the other, ordinary food.

Now the novice was his instructor's bowl-carrier. [346] So after the meal he took his instructor's bowl, and in it there remained a single grain of cooked rice.[439] He put it in his mouth. It tasted divine.

"These nāgas are so stingy," he reflected. "While the two of us are seated together, they give divine ambrosia to him, and to me only ordinary food."

He made this fervent aspiration:[440] "Since I have observed the religious life under the perfectly awakened lord Kāśyapa, who is unsurpassed and worthy of great offerings, by this root of virtue may I cause this nāga [before me] to die and fall from this realm, and may I be reborn here instead."

At that moment water began to trickle from his hands.[441] As for the nāga, he began to develop a headache.[442]

"Noble one," the nāga said, "this novice has set his mind on something terrible! Make him withdraw it."

"Friend," the instructor said to the novice, "these are terrible realms of existences [that await you]. Withdraw this terrible thought!"

Then the novice uttered this verse:

I am unable to withdraw this thought,
which is so inclined.
As I stand right here, Bhadanta,
water trickles from my hands.[443]

He thus caused that nāga to die and fall from that realm, and he was reborn there instead. And it was there, monks, that the [novice reborn as a] young nāga [who would later learn the *Gradual Sayings*] first gained faith.

So ends the *Nāgakumāra-avadāna*, the twenty-fourth[444] chapter in the glorious *Divyāvadāna*.

25. *The Story of Saṅgharakṣita, part 2*

SAṄGHARAKṢITA-AVADĀNA[445]

SOME MONKS in doubt asked the Lord Buddha, the remover of all doubts, "Bhadanta, what deed did the venerable Saṅgharakṣita do so that, as a result of that deed, he was born in a family that was rich, wealthy, and prosperous; went forth as a monk in the presence of the Blessed One, where by ridding himself of all defilements, he directly experienced arhatship; and also trained new disciples?"

"Monks," the Blessed One said, "the deeds that Saṅgharakṣita himself has performed and accumulated [have now come together, and their conditions have matured. They remain before him like an oncoming flood and will certainly come to pass. Those deeds were performed and accumulated by Saṅgharakṣita. Who else will experience their results? For those deeds that are performed and accumulated, monks, do not mature outside of oneself—neither in the element of earth nor in the element of water, in the element of fire or in the element of wind. Instead, those deeds that are performed and accumulated, both good and bad, mature in the aggregates, the elements, and the sense bases that are appropriated when one is reborn.

Actions never come to naught,
even after hundreds of millions of years.
When the right conditions gather and the time is right,
then they will have their effect on embodied beings.].[446]

Long ago, monks, in this present auspicious age, when people lived for twenty thousand years, [347] [there arose in the world] a teacher named Kāśyapa,

> [who was a tathāgata,
> an arhat,
> a perfectly awakened being,
> perfect in knowledge and conduct,
> a sugata,
> a knower of the world,
> an unsurpassed guide for those in need of training,
> a teacher of gods and humans,
> a buddha,
> and a blessed one]."[447]

A Servant of the Dharma and His Followers Make Fervent Aspirations

A man went forth as a monk into the perfectly awakened lord Kāśyapa's order, and there he served [the dharma].[448] He lived together with five hundred students, and nearly all the residents of the one [nearby] market town had faith in him. He followed the religious life there as long as he lived, but he still never amassed many virtues.

After a time, he became sick. Though treated with medicines made from roots, stalks, leaves, flowers, and fruits, he continued to get worse. Then, at the time of his death, he made this fervent aspiration: "Since I have followed the religious life my entire life under the perfectly awakened lord Kāśyapa, who is unsurpassed and worthy of great offerings, without amassing many virtues, by this root of virtue may I go forth as a monk in the order of the young brahman named Uttara (Superior). The perfectly awakened lord Kāśyapa, who is also unsurpassed, has predicted that when people live for one hundred years he will definitely be a buddha.[449] And may I then, by ridding myself of all defilements, directly experience arhatship."

Soon afterward, those students who lived with him approached and said, "Instructor, have you amassed many virtues?"

"No, I haven't," he said.

"What fervent aspiration did you make?"

"This and that."

They said, "Thanks to you, our instructor and our spiritual guide, may we rid ourselves of all defilements and thereby directly experience arhatship under that blessed one."

The residents of that market town heard that the noble one was sick. They too approached him and said, "Has the noble one amassed many virtues?"

"No, I haven't."

"What fervent aspiration did you make?"

"This and that."

They said, "Thanks to you, our noble one and spiritual guide, may we rid ourselves of all defilements and thereby directly experience arhatship under that blessed one."

"What do you think, monks? The one who served [the dharma] was none other than the monk Saṅgharakṣita. Those five hundred students who lived with him were none other than these five hundred monks. And those people who lived in the market town were none other than these five hundred merchants. Since he had served the dharma, as a result of that action, he was reborn in a family that was rich, wealthy, and prosperous. Since at the time of his death he made a fervent aspiration, [348] as a result of that action, he went forth as a monk in my presence, where by ridding himself of all defilements, he directly experienced arhatship, and also trained new disciples.

"And so, monks, the result of absolutely evil actions is absolutely evil, [the result of absolutely pure actions is absolutely pure, and the result of mixed actions is mixed. Therefore monks, because of this, you should reject absolutely evil actions and mixed ones as well and strive to perform only absolutely pure actions. It is this, monks, that you should learn to do]."[450]

31. *The Story of Five Hundred Farmers*

PAÑCAKĀRṢAKAŚATA-AVADĀNA[451]

ONE TIME the Blessed One addressed the venerable [Ānanda]:[452] "Come, Ānanda, let us go to Śrāvastī."

"Yes, Bhadanta," the venerable Ānanda replied, consenting to the Blessed One's request. Then the Blessed One set out on a journey to Śrāvastī.[453]

A Brahman and a Gift of Rice Gruel

Meanwhile, in a certain place a brahman who had missed his last meal was driving a plow. His daughter took some rice gruel and brought it to him. Just then the Blessed One arrived there. The brahman saw the Lord Buddha,

> who was adorned with the thirty-two marks of a great man,
> whose body was radiant with the eighty minor marks,
> who was adorned with a halo extending an arm's length,
> whose brilliance was greater than a thousand suns,
> and who, like a mountain of jewels that moved,
> was beautiful from every side.

As soon as the brahman saw him, he developed faith in the Blessed One.

Twelve years' practice of quiescence meditation
does not produce such peace of mind—
nor does the birth of a son for one who has no son,
the sight of a treasure trove for one who is destitute,
or a royal coronation for one who desires kingship.
None of these produce such well-being
as when a being who has accumulated roots of virtue
sees a buddha for the first time.

He took that rice gruel and quickly approached the Blessed One. Having approached, he said this to him: "Gautama, here is some rice gruel. If Lord Gautama has compassion for me, may he drink it."[454]

Then the Blessed One showed the brahman an old well. [462] "Brahman, if you have anything to spare, throw it into this old well." The brahman threw the rice gruel into that old well, and that old well became full of steaming[455] rice gruel. Such is the power possessed by all buddhas and the divine powers of deities.

Then the Blessed One said to the brahman, "Great brahman,[456] distribute this rice gruel." So the brahman began to distribute it. The Blessed One exercised his power over that rice gruel so that the whole community could partake of it. That old well remained just as full of steaming rice gruel as it was before.

The brahman, having even greater faith, placed his head in veneration at the Blessed One's feet and sat down in front of him to listen to the dharma. Then the Blessed One, knowing the brahman's inclinations, propensities, makeup, and nature, gave him a discourse on the dharma that elucidated the four noble truths. [When the brahman heard this,][457] with his thunderbolt of knowledge he broke through that mountain, which is the false view of individuality that has accumulated since time immemorial,[458] and directly experienced the reward of the stream-enterer.

"I have crossed over, Bhadanta! I have crossed over!"[459] he said. "And so, I take refuge in the Lord Buddha, in the dharma, and in the community of monks. Hereafter, and for as long as I live and breathe, consider me a faithful disciple who has taken the refuges."

Then the brahman, like a merchant with fortune found, like a farmer with a rich harvest, like a warrior victorious in battle, and like a patient released from every illness, rejoiced and delighted in the words of the Blessed One. He then placed his head in veneration at the Blessed One's feet, left the Blessed One's presence, and went back to his field. He saw that it was rich with golden grains of barley. Seeing this, with his eyes wide open with wonder, he uttered this verse:

> Oh! This field is so fertile and faultless!
> A seed sown today bears fruit today as well.

Then the brahman hurriedly approached the king. Having approached and greeted the king with wishes for his success and well-being, he then said this to him: "My lord, the barley that I've planted has turned to gold. Do me the favor of sending someone to oversee it."

So the king sent off an overseer.

The brahman piled together the barley and then divided it up. The king's share turned into ordinary barley. The overseer informed the king, and the king ordered that it be divided up once again. [463] So they divided it up again, and just as before the king's share turned into ordinary barley. In this way, they divided it up again and again seven times, but the results were always the same.[460] The king became curious, so he went there in person. He too saw the same results.

Then he said to the brahman, "Brahman, this occurs because of your merit. There's no need for a king's share. Give me as much as you like."[461] The brahman was satisfied, and then whatever barley he gave to the king turned to gold.

Five Hundred Farmers and Their Oxen

One day the Blessed One set out.

Meanwhile, in a certain place there were five hundred farmers dressed in rags of coarse cloth, looking very pale, their hands and feet cracked, driving their plows. As for the oxen that led the plows, their bodies were covered with cuts and bruises from the harnesses that bound them and the cattle prods that beat them, and they were constantly panting for breath. Then those farmers saw the Lord Buddha,

> who was adorned with the thirty-two marks of a great man,
> [whose body was radiant with the eighty minor marks,
> who was adorned with a halo extending an arm's length,
> whose brilliance was greater than a thousand suns,
> and who, like a mountain of jewels that moved,
> was beautiful from every side.

As soon as the farmers saw him, they developed faith in the Blessed One.

> Twelve years' practice of quiescence meditation
> does not produce such peace of mind—
> nor does the birth of a son for one who has no son,
> the sight of a treasure trove for one who is destitute,
> or a royal coronation for one who desires kingship.
> None of these produce such well-being][462]
> as when a being who has accumulated roots of virtue
> sees a buddha for the first time.

Then they approached the Blessed One.

The Blessed One saw the farmers from a distance, and upon seeing them, with the intention of obtaining new disciples, he stepped off the road and sat down in front of the community of monks in the seat specially prepared for him. Those farmers placed their heads in veneration at the Blessed One's feet and then sat down at a respectful distance. The Blessed One, knowing their inclinations, propensities, makeup, and nature, gave them a discourse on the dharma that elucidated the four noble truths.

[When the farmers heard this,][463] with their thunderbolts of knowledge they broke through that mountain, which is the false view of individuality that has accumulated since time immemorial, and directly experienced the reward of the stream-enterer. Having seen the truth, they bowed toward the Blessed One with their hands respectfully folded[464] and said this to him: "Bhadanta, may we[465] renounce, take ordination, and become monks according to the dharma and monastic discipline that have been so well expressed. May we follow the religious life in the presence of the Blessed One."

Then the Blessed One initiated them uttering the "Come, O monk" formula for ordination: ["Come, O monks! Follow the religious life!" As soon as the Blessed One finished speaking, there they stood—heads shaved, garbed in monastic robes, bowls and water pots in hand, with a week's growth of hair and beard and the disciplined deportment of monks who had been ordained for one hundred years.

"Come," the Tathāgata said to them.
With heads shaved and bodies wrapped in robes,
they instantly attained tranquility of the senses,][466]
and so they remained[467] by the will of the Buddha.

Then the Blessed One gave them instructions. After striving [and straining, they came to understand that ever-turning five-spoked wheel of saṃsāra; they dealt a final blow to rebirth in all realms of saṃsāra, since they are subject to decay and decline, scattering and destruction; and by ridding themselves of all defilements, they directly experienced arhatship. Becoming arhats,

they were free from attachment in the three realms;
they regarded clods of earth and gold as equal in value;
they possessed equanimity toward the sky
  and the palms of their hands;
they didn't distinguish between being cut by a blade
  and being anointed with sandalwood paste;
the eggshell of their ignorance was broken by knowledge;
they obtained the special knowledges, superhuman faculties,
  and analytic insights;
and they were averse to worldly attainments, temptations,
  and honors.
They became worthy of respect, honor,] and obeisance
  [from the gods, including Indra and Upendra].[468] [464]

As for the oxen, they broke through their harnesses and straps and approached the Blessed One. Having approached, they stood crowding around him. The Blessed One taught them the dharma with three principles, like when he crossed the Gaṅgā River and taught [five hundred] geese, fish, and tortoises. ["Friends," he said, "everything that is conditioned is impermanent, all phenomena are without self, and nirvāṇa is peace."][469] Having seen the truth, they [died and] went to a divine realm.[470]

Some monks in doubt asked the Lord Buddha, the remover of all doubts, "But what[471] deed did those monks who had been farmers do such that they first became farmers and then went forth as monks in the presence of the Blessed One, where by ridding themselves of all defilements, they directly experienced arhatship? And what deed did those gods that had been oxen do such that they were first reborn as oxen and then had a vision of truth?"

"Monks," the Blessed One said, "the deeds that they themselves have performed and accumulated have now come together, [and their conditions have matured. They remain before them like an oncoming flood and will certainly come to pass. Those deeds were performed and accumulated by them. Who else will experience their results? For those deeds that are performed and accumulated, monks, do not mature outside of oneself—neither in the element of earth nor in the element of water, in the element of fire or in the element of wind. Instead, those deeds that are performed and accumulated, both good and bad, mature in the aggregates, the elements, and the sense bases that are appropriated when one is reborn.

Actions never come to naught,
even after hundreds of millions of years.
When the right conditions gather and the time is right,][472]
then they will have their effect on embodied beings.

"Long ago, monks, in this present auspicious age, when people lived for twenty thousand years, there arose in the world a teacher named Kāśyapa,

[who was a tathāgata,
an arhat,
a perfectly awakened being,
perfect in knowledge and conduct,
a sugata,
a knower of the world,
an unsurpassed guide for those in need of training,
a teacher of gods and humans,
a buddha,
and a blessed one].[473]

"He stayed near the city of Vārāṇasī in the deer park at Ṛṣivadana (Mouth of Sages). Five hundred farmers went forth as monks in his order. There they never read or studied on their own, nor did they meditate. Instead, they stuffed themselves on food that was given out of faith, enjoyed themselves socializing, and passed their time in idleness.

"What do you think, monks? Those five hundred monks were none other than these five hundred farmers. The owner of the monastery[474] was none other than the householder for whom these farmers worked. Since the monks ate the food that was given out of faith, which belonged to the owner of the monastery, and since they never read or studied on their own and didn't even meditate but instead enjoyed themselves socializing and passed their time in idleness, because of that action, for five hundred births they became farmers working for this very owner of the monastery. Even in this lifetime they have become farmers who work for him. Since they went forth as monks in the order of the perfectly awakened Kāśyapa and followed the religious life, [465] they have now gone forth as monks in my order, where by ridding themselves of all defilements, they directly experienced arhatship.

"And those gods who had been oxen also went forth as monks in the order of the perfectly awakened Kāśyapa. There they violated lesser and minor precepts. Because of that action, they were reborn as oxen. Since they then cultivated faith in my presence, they were reborn among the gods. Since they had lived the religious life under the perfectly awakened Kāśyapa, they have now become gods and have had a vision of truth.

"And so, monks, the result of absolutely evil actions is absolutely evil, [the result of absolutely pure actions is absolutely pure, and the result of mixed actions is mixed. Therefore monks, because of this, you should reject absolutely evil actions and mixed ones as well] and strive [to perform only absolutely pure actions].[475] It is this, monks, that you should learn to do."

The Incident at Toyikā[476]

The Blessed One then addressed the venerable [Ānanda]:[477] "Come, Ānanda, let us go to Toyikā (Watering Hole)."

"Yes, Bhadanta," the venerable Ānanda replied, consenting to the Blessed One's request.

The Blessed One arrived at Toyikā, and in that place there was a brahman plowing his fields. The brahman saw the Lord Buddha,

who was adorned with the thirty-two marks of a great man
[whose body was radiant with the eighty minor marks,
who was adorned with a halo extending an arm's length,
whose brilliance was greater than a thousand suns,
and who, like a mountain of jewels that moved,][478]
was beautiful from every side.

Seeing him, the brahman reflected, "If I go to Lord Gautama and pay my respects, my work will suffer. If I don't go to him and pay my respects, my merit will suffer. Isn't there any skillful way such that neither my work nor my merit will suffer?" Then this thought occurred to him: "I will pay my respects standing right here. This way neither my work nor will my merit will suffer." Standing right there and still holding his cattle prod,[479] he paid his respects: "I pay my respects to the Lord Buddha."

The Blessed One then addressed the venerable Ānanda: "Ānanda, this brahman is making a mistake.[480] If he only had the proper knowledge and insight,[481] he would have known that in this place lies the undisturbed skeleton of the perfectly awakened Kāśyapa. Then he could have approached[482] and venerated me and, in this way, have venerated two perfectly awakened buddhas. How is that? In this place, Ānanda, lies the undisturbed skeleton of the perfectly awakened Kāśyapa."

Then the venerable Ānanda very quickly folded his upper garment into four as a seat and then said this to the Blessed One: [466] "May the Blessed One please sit down on this seat that I have specially prepared. In this way this bit of earth will be made use of by two perfectly awakened buddhas—previously by the perfectly awakened Kāśyapa and at present by the Blessed One."

The Blessed One sat down in that seat specially prepared for him. After sitting down, he addressed the monks: "Do you desire, monks, to see the undisturbed body of the perfectly awakened Kāśyapa?"

"Yes, Blessed One. It is the right time and the right occasion, Sugata, for the Blessed One to display the undisturbed body of the perfectly awakened Kāśyapa to the monks. Seeing it, the monks can cultivate faith in their hearts."

Then the Blessed One had a mundane thought.

Now it is a law of nature that any time a lord buddha has a mundane thought, all creatures, even tiny biting ants and the like, know that blessed one's thoughts with their minds.

The nāgas reflected, "What is the reason that the Blessed One has had a mundane thought? Because the Blessed One desires to see[483] the undisturbed body of the perfectly awakened Kāśyapa." Then they raised the undisturbed body of the perfectly awakened Kāśyapa.

The Blessed One then addressed the monks: "Imprint its image in your minds, monks, for it will disappear." And then it disappeared.

Practices of Faith at Toyikā

King Prasenajit heard that the Blessed One had raised the undisturbed body of the perfectly awakened Kāśyapa for the disciples to see. And upon hearing this, he became curious. So with the women of the palace as well as princes, ministers, military commanders, townspeople, and villagers, he set out to see it. Likewise Virūḍhaka, the householder Anāthapiṇḍada, the head officials Ṛṣidatta and Purāṇa, Viśākhā Mṛgāramātā, and many hundreds of thousands of other people set out to see it, some out of curiosity, others impelled by former roots of virtue. But in the meantime, it disappeared. That crowd of people heard that the body of the perfectly awakened lord Kāśyapa had disappeared. Hearing this, they felt miserable and dejected. "Our coming here has been in vain," they thought.

One of the lay disciples then began to circumambulate that place.

[467] And with his mind, he formed this thought: "How much merit will I get from respectfully walking around this place?"

Then the Blessed One, knowing with his mind the thoughts of that lay disciple and that large crowd of people, uttered this verse so that they wouldn't have any regrets:[484]

> Hundreds of thousands of golden coins or nuggets
> are not equal to the wise man, faithful in mind,
> who walks around shrines of a buddha.

One of the lay disciples then offered a lump of clay at this place and thus formed this thought: "The Blessed One has said how much merit is earned from walking around a shrine of a buddha. But how much merit will there be from offering a lump of clay?"

Then the Blessed One, knowing with his mind his thoughts as well, uttered this verse:

> Hundreds of thousands of gold pieces or nuggets
> are not equal to one, faithful in mind,
> who places a single lump of clay
> at a shrine of a buddha.

After hearing this, many hundreds of thousands of beings placed lumps of clay there as offerings. Others put loose flowers there and thus formed this thought: "The Blessed One has said how much merit is earned from respectfully walking around a shrine of a buddha and from offering a lump of clay. But how much merit will we get from offering loose flowers?"

Then the Blessed One, knowing their thoughts as well,[485] uttered this verse:

> Hundreds of thousands of bags of gold[486] or gold nuggets
> are not equal to one, faithful in mind,

who places heaps of loose flowers[487]
at shrines of a buddha.

Others festooned the area there with garlands and formed this thought: "The Blessed One has said how much merit is earned from offering loose flowers. But how much merit will we get from festooning the area with garlands?"

Then the Blessed One, knowing their thoughts as well,[488] uttered this verse:

Hundreds of thousands of carts of gold or gold nuggets [468]
are not equal to the wise man, faithful in mind,
who festoons with garlands
shrines of a buddha.

Others gave oil-lamp trees there and formed this thought: "The Blessed One has said how much merit is earned from festooning this area with garlands. But how much merit will we get from giving oil lamps?"

Then the Blessed One, knowing with his mind their thoughts as well, uttered this verse:

Hundreds of thousands of millions of gold pieces or nuggets
are not equal to the wise man, faithful in mind,
who makes a gift of oil lamps
at shrines of a buddha.

Others sprinkled perfume there and[489] formed this thought: "The Blessed One has said how much merit is earned from offering oil lamps. But how much merit will we get from sprinkling perfume?"

Then the Blessed One, knowing with his mind their thoughts as well, uttered this verse:

Hundreds of thousands of piles of gold or gold nuggets
are not equal to the wise man, faithful in mind,
who sprinkles perfume
at shrines of a buddha.

Others raised up flags and banners[490] there and formed this thought: "The Blessed One has said how much merit is earned from respectfully walking around a shrine of a buddha, from offering a lump of clay, from offering loose flowers, from festooning this area with garlands, from offering oil lamps, and from sprinkling the area with perfume. But how much merit will we get from raising up umbrellas, flags, and banners?

Then the Blessed One, knowing their thoughts as well,[491] uttered this verse:

Hundreds of thousands of mountains of gold
  equal in size to Mount Meru
are not equal to one, faithful in mind,
who raises umbrellas, flags, and banners
at shrines of a buddha.

This[492] is the tribute prescribed
for the immeasurable Tathāgata,
ocean-like in perfect awakening,
the unsurpassed caravan leader.

It occurred to them: "The Blessed One has said how much merit is earned from honoring with offerings a blessed one who has passed into final nirvāṇa. But how much merit will be earned in the case of one still living?" [469]

Then the Blessed One, knowing with his mind their thoughts as well, uttered this verse:

One may honor a buddha still living
as well as one passed into final nirvāṇa.
With one's mind equally faithful,
there is no difference in merit.

In this way buddhas are inconceivable
and the dharma of buddhas inconceivable as well.
For those who have faith in the inconceivable,[493]
the result is likewise inconceivable.[494]

It is not possible to understand the extent
of the virtues of those who are inconceivable,
of those who turn the unobstructed wheel of dharma[495]
of perfectly awakened buddhas.

Then the Blessed One gave a discourse on the dharma to that great crowd of people such that when they heard it, many hundreds of thousands of beings attained great distinction. Some set their minds on attaining awakening as a disciple and some on awakening as a solitary buddha; some obtained the [various levels of the] heat stage, the summit stage, and the tolerance stage, in accord with truth; some directly experienced the reward of the stream-enterer, some the reward of the once-returner, some the reward of the nonreturner, and some rid themselves of all defilements and thereby directly experienced arhatship. Almost the entire assembly became favorably inclined toward the Buddha, drawn toward the dharma, and well disposed toward the community.

And there in that place, faithful[496] brahmans and householders established a festival. In time it came to be known as the Toyikāmaha (Toyikā Festival).

So ends the [*Pañcakārṣakaśata-avadāna*],[497] the thirty-first chapter in the glorious *Divyāvadāna*.

32. *The Story of Rūpāvatī*

RŪPĀVATĪ-AVADĀNA[498]

A Discourse on Charity

THUS have I heard. At one time the Blessed One was staying in the city of Śrāvastī at the Jeta Grove in the park of Anāthapiṇḍada (Almsgiver to the Poor), together with a large community of monks, 1,250 in number. There the Blessed One was respected, honored, revered, and venerated by monks, nuns, male and female lay devotees, the king, royal ministers, various traders, ascetics, brahmans, wandering mendicants, townspeople, villagers, nāgas, yakṣas, antigods, heavenly birds, celestial musicians, kinnaras, and great snakes. [470] In addition, the Blessed One received an abundance of excellent provisions, both divine and human, of robes, begging bowls, bedding and seats, and medicines to cure the sick. And the Blessed One was unsullied by these, like a lotus by water.

At that time the Blessed One gained great and well-deserved fame through praises of his virtue. It was said:

The Blessed One is just like this—

> a tathāgata,
> an arhat,
> a perfectly awakened being,
> perfect in knowledge and conduct,

a sugata,
a knower of the world,
an unsurpassed guide for those in need of training,
a teacher of gods and humans,
a buddha,
and a blessed one.

> He himself has understood and directly experienced this [world][499] with its gods, [evil] Māra, and [lord] Brahmā, and the inhabitants of this world with their ascetics, brahmans, gods, and humans, and now he lives as a monk. He teaches the dharma that is excellent in the beginning, excellent in the middle, excellent in the end, and good in both meaning and letter. He makes perfectly clear the religious life that is complete, perfect, pure, and chaste.

Then the Blessed One addressed the monks: "And so, monks, if[500] beings were to know charity, the result of charity, and the consequence of offering charity as I know the result of charity and the consequence of offering charity,[501] then they would never eat the very last remaining morsel of food all by themselves without sharing it with others.[502] And the stingy thoughts that arise would not seize hold of their minds.[503] But monks, those beings who do not know the result of charity and the consequence of offering charity as I know the result of charity and the consequence of offering charity eat the very last remaining morsel of food[504] all by themselves, without giving it away or sharing it with others. And the stingy thoughts that arise do seize hold of their minds."

Some monks in doubt questioned the Lord Buddha, the remover of all doubts: "It is a wonder, Bhadanta, the extent to which beggars are now dear to the Blessed One."

"Monks, not only now, but also in the past, beggars were dear to me. Listen to this."

Rūpāvatī Offers Her Breasts

Long ago, monks, in a time gone by, in the outskirts of the North Country, [471] there was a capital city called Utpalāvatī (Blue Waterlily Place). It was thriving, prosperous, and safe,[505] with throngs of people. Then one day in the capital city of Utpalāvatī, a famine occurred—life was difficult, food was scarce, and it wasn't easy for people to keep on living seized with the cramps of hunger.

At that time in the capital city of Utpalāvatī there was a woman named Rūpāvatī (Beautiful).[506] She was beautiful, good-looking, and attractive, with an exceptionally lovely complexion.

One day, this woman Rūpāvatī[507] left her home and went out for a walk in the capital city of Utpalāvatī and entered a birthing room. At that time in the birthing room, a woman was giving birth. She bore a son who was beautiful,[508] good-looking, and attractive, with an exceptionally lovely complexion. This woman, pained and emaciated with hunger and ravenous at heart, grabbed the boy and wanted to eat his flesh, the flesh of her own son.[509]

When Rūpāvatī saw her, she said this: "Sister, what is this? What do you want to do?"

"Sister," she said, "I want to eat. I want to eat the flesh of my son."[510]

"Now sister," Rūpāvatī said, "isn't[511] there anything to be found in your home, some food or drink, something hard or soft to eat, or something to be licked up? The word *son* is precious in this world."

"No, sister, there is nothing to be found in my home. There isn't any food or drink or anything to be consumed, there isn't anything hard or soft or to be licked up. What is precious in this world is *life*."

"Now sister, wait a minute," Rūpāvatī said. "I'll go home and bring back some food just for you."

"Sister," she said, "there is something you should know. My womb has been destroyed. The earth has split open before me.[512] My heart is getting darker, and I've lost my bearings. No sooner will you walk out this door then the winds of life will leave me."

Then it occurred to Rūpāvatī, "If I take her son and go, this woman, pained and emaciated with hunger as she is, will die. But if I leave her son behind and go, she'll surely eat the boy. [472] What can I do so that both of them will survive?"

Then it occurred to her, "Even when one's intentions are without fault, many kinds of suffering are experienced here in saṃsāra. Repeatedly in the realms of hell, repeatedly in the animal realm, repeatedly in the world of Yama, [god of death,] and repeatedly in the world of humans, hands are cut off, feet are cut off, noses are cut off, ears and noses are cut off, and various body parts, large and small, are cut off. Many other kinds of suffering are experienced as well. What benefit is there in all this for me? Instead, I should generate in myself the strength, power, and courage[513] to satisfy this woman with my own flesh and blood and set this boy free."

"Sister," Rūpāvatī asked, "is there a knife in your home?"

"There is," the woman said.

"Very well. Show me where it is."

She showed her the place.

Rūpāvatī then took the sharp knife in hand, cut off both her breasts, and satisfied that woman with her own flesh and blood. And having satisfied the woman, she said this to her: "Sister, there is something you should know. I have now bought this boy with my own flesh and blood. I offer him back to you in trust, [but on this condition:] You are not to eat your son! Meanwhile I'll go home and bring back some food for you.'"

"Very well," she said, "but just for this one day, and no longer."

Then Rūpāvatī, with her blood flowing and streaming forth, went home. Rūpāvatī's husband saw Rūpāvatī coming from a distance, with her blood flowing and streaming forth, and upon seeing her, he said this to her: "Rūpāvatī, who disfigured you like this?"

She explained the situation in detail, and after doing so, she said this: "Dear husband, prepare some food for the woman."

"Dear wife," he said, "you prepare the food for her. I will perform a vow of truth: A wonderful and marvelous act such as this has never been seen or heard before! Dear wife, by this truth, this vow of truth, may both of your breasts reappear as they were before."

At the very moment[514] when that vow of truth was made, both of her breasts reappeared as they were before. [473]

Meanwhile it occurred to Śakra, lord of the gods, "This woman Rūpāvatī understands the importance of great sacrifices, and so she has performed a great sacrifice.[515] Oh no! I hope this woman doesn't cause me, Śakra, to fall from my home here.[516] I really should go and test her."

Then Śakra, lord of the gods, magically transformed himself into an eminent brahman. Taking up a golden staff and water pot, and cooling himself with a jeweled yak-tail fan with a gold handle, Śakra, lord of the gods, with the same ease that a strong man can flex and unflex his arm, disappeared from among the gods of Trāyastriṃśa (Thirty-Three) and reappeared in the capital Utpalāvatī.

While wandering for alms in the capital Utpalāvatī, Śakra, lord of the gods, approached the home of Rūpāvatī. Standing at her door, he called out for alms. Rūpāvatī took some almsfood and approached Śakra, who was in the guise of a brahman. Having approached, she offered him the almsfood. Then Śakra, lord of the gods, said this to Rūpāvatī: "Is it true, Rūpāvatī, that you sacrificed both of your breasts for the benefit of an infant boy?"

"It is true, noble brahman," she said.

"Rūpāvatī," he said to her, "while you were thinking, 'I shall sacrifice both of my breasts,' or as you were sacrificing them, or after you had sacrificed them, did any regrets come to mind?"

"No," she said. "As I was sacrificing both of my breasts, no regrets came to mind."

"Who in this world will believe you?" Śakra said.

"Very well then, brahman," Rūpāvatī said, "I will perform a vow of truth: Brahman,[517] while I was thinking, 'I shall sacrifice both of my breasts,' and as I was sacrificing them, and after I had sacrificed them, no notion to do otherwise came to mind and no regrets came to mind. Moreover, brahman,[518] this truth by which I sacrificed both of my breasts was for the benefit of an infant boy. It was not for royal power, not for personal pleasure, not for reaching heaven, not for becoming another Śakra, and not for the dominion of a wheel-turning king. It was for no other reason than that I may attain unsurpassed perfect awakening and so subdue the unsubdued, liberate the unliberated, console the unconsoled, and lead to final nirvāṇa those who have not reached final nirvāṇa. By this truth, this vow of truth, may my womanhood disappear and may manhood appear instead."[519] [474]

At that very moment, Rūpāvatī's female qualities disappeared, and male qualities appeared instead.

Śakra, lord of the gods, was pleased, excited, uplifted, delighted, and full of joy and pleasure. And right then, making use of his magical powers, he rose up into the sky and uttered this inspired utterance: "The female qualities of Rūpāvatī have disappeared and male qualities have appeared instead!"

And so the young woman Rūpāvatī came to be known as the young man Rūpāvata (Handsome).

Candraprabha Offers His Eyes

Now at one time in the capital city Utpalāvatī, a king passed away having no son. The learned chief ministers had this thought about the matter: "We need to appoint a king for the capital Utpalāvatī." It occurred to them, "There is no one more qualified than the young man Rūpāvata—he has performed meritorious deeds and virtuous actions. So they appointed the young man Rūpāvata as the king of the capital Utpalāvatī, and there he ruled for sixty years. And having ruled the kingdom according to dharma, he passed away.

After the dissolution of his body, he was reborn in the womb of the principal wife of a certain guildmaster and householder in that very capital Utpalāvatī. After a full eight or nine months, she gave birth to a boy who was beautiful, good-looking, and attractive, with an exceptionally lovely complexion. At the time of his birth, so much light emanated from his body that the light of the moon was eclipsed by his splendor.

Then a maidservant approached the guildmaster-householder and, having approached, said this to him: "Householder, you should know that a son has been born to you who is beautiful, good-looking, and attractive, with an exceptionally lovely complexion. At the time of his birth, so much light emanated from his body that the light of the moon was eclipsed by it."

The guildmaster-householder was pleased, excited, uplifted, and full of joy and pleasure. The very next morning he assembled those brahmans who could read signs, interpret omens, and divine the future, who were skilled in mantras controlling the earth and sky, and who knew the movements of the constellations and the planet Venus. To them, he showed his son and said, "Brahmans, you should know that my principal wife [475] gave birth to this boy who is beautiful, good-looking, and attractive, with an exceptionally lovely complexion. At the time of his birth, so much light emanated from his body that the light of the moon was eclipsed by it. Brahmans, look at the boy's features and give him a name."

Those brahmans who could read signs, interpret omens, and divine the future, who were skilled in mantras controlling the earth and sky, and who knew the movements of the constellations and the planet Venus, approached the boy. They looked him over and said, "This boy who has been born to you, householder, is beautiful, good-looking, and attractive, with an exceptionally lovely complexion. At the time of his birth, so much light emanated from his body that the light of the moon was eclipsed by it. Therefore let his name be Candraprabha (Moonlight)."

The guildmaster-householder fed those brahmans and saw them off, and then he presented the boy Candraprabha with four nurses—a lap nurse, a nurse maid, a wet nurse, and a playtime nurse.[520]

- A lap nurse is one who carries around a child on her lap and helps him to properly develop all parts of his body, large and small.
- A nursemaid is one who bathes a child and cleans the dirt from his clothes.
- A wet nurse is one who breastfeeds a child.
- A playtime nurse is one who knows how to get small[521] and young children alike to play with a variety of toys—heads, figurines, grotesque figures,[522] small baskets of kitchen implements,[523] service sets,[524] bamboo time-pieces,[525] . . . ,[526] elephants, horses, oxen, archers,[527] and medicine bags full of stalks, spoons, and grass placed before them.[528]

Candraprabha was raised and nourished by these four nurses, and he came to possess an abundance of glory and good fortune. When the boy Candraprabha was eight years old, his parents gave him a good bath, fully anointed him, and adorned him with all kinds of ornaments. Then, along with many other boys, he was sent off to learn how to write.

One day in the writing school, five hundred boys were studying how to write. The boy Candraprabha said this to those boys: "Hey friends,[529] we should all set our minds on attaining [476] unsurpassed perfect awakening."

"Candraprabha," they said, "what is a bodhisattva supposed to do?"

"He is to fulfill the six perfections," he said. "Which six?

The perfection of generosity,
the perfection of morality,
the perfection of tolerance,
the perfection of strength,
the perfection of meditation,
and the perfection of wisdom.

"That is why I give charity. I really should give charity even to those who have taken birth as animals."

Then he took a sharp knife, honey, and clarified butter and approached one of the large cremation grounds. He cut up his body with the knife, smeared it with honey and clarified butter, and abandoned himself there to be killed.

At that time in the large cremation ground there lived a bird named Uccaṅgama (High Flying).[530] He stood on Candraprabha's body, took hold of his right eye, pulled it out, and then let go of it. And then a second time and a third, that creature Uccaṅgama took hold of Candraprabha's right eye, pulled it out, and then let go of it.

Then Candraprabha said this to the bird Uccaṅgama: "Hey bird, what is this? You take hold of my eye, pull it out, and then let go of it?"

"There is nothing, Candraprabha, more dear to me than human eyes,"[531] he said. "Candraprabha, I think[532] you'll try to stop me."

"If a bird took hold of my eye a thousand times," Candraprabha said, "and he pulled it out and then let go of it again, I still wouldn't stop him."[533] After he spoke, a flock of birds gathered together and they turned Candraprabha into a fleshless pile of splintered bones. Thus he met his death.

Brahmaprabha Offers His Body

In that very capital Utpalāvatī, Candraprabha then took rebirth in the womb of the principal wife of an important brahman householder. After a full eight or nine months, she gave birth to a boy who was beautiful, good-looking, and attractive, with an exceptionally lovely complexion. At the time of his birth, so much light emanated from his body that the light of the Brahmā was eclipsed by it. So his parents gave him the name Brahmaprabha (Brahmā Light).

When the young brahman named Brahmaprabha was eight years old, he had learned all the brahmanical mantras by heart. When the young brahman Brahmaprabha became twelve years old, [477] he could instruct five hundred young brahmans[534] all by himself in the recitation of mantras. When the young brahman Brahmaprabha became sixteen years old, his parents said to him, "Brahmaprabha, we'll arrange for you to get married and settled down."

"Mother, Father," he said, "what's the use of my getting married and settling down?"

"What will you do then, Brahmaprabha?" they said.

"I want to undergo austerities and perform difficult deeds for the benefit of many beings," he said.

"Brahmaprabha," they said, "do as you see fit."[535]

The young brahman Brahmaprabha placed his head in veneration at his parents' feet, circumambulated them three times, left the capital Utpalāvātī, and approached a forest. At that time in the forest there lived two brahman seers. The two brahman seers saw the young brahman Brahmaprabha coming from a distance, and upon seeing him, they said this to him: "Come, Brahmaprabha. Welcome! You must be tired and exhausted. Why have you come to this forest?"

"I want to undergo austerities and perform difficult deeds for the benefit of all sentient beings," he said.

"Very well, then," they said. "As you wish. May you have success in all that you desire, and may your wishes be fulfilled."

Then the young brahman Brahmaprabha built a hut in a certain place, established a walkway for meditation, and underwent austerities for the benefit of sentient beings. One day, not far from Brahmaprabha's hut, there came to live a pregnant tigress. The young brahman Brahmaprabha saw her, and upon seeing her, he again approached the two brahman seers. Having approached the two brahman seers, he said this to them: "Seers, there is something you should know. Not far from my hut, a pregnant tigress has come to live. Who is willing to give her food?"

"We'll give her food," they said.

Then one day the tigress gave birth. Pained and emaciated with hunger, she wanted to eat her two cubs. She let one cub go and took the other, but she didn't eat him. The young brahman Brahmaprabha saw her, and upon seeing her, he approached the two brahman seers.[536] Having approached the two brahman seers, he said this: "Brahmans, there is something you should know. [478] That tigress gave birth, and now pained and emaciated with hunger, she wants to eat her two cubs. She let one go and took the other, but she didn't eat him. Who is willing to give her food?"

"We'll give her food," they said.

Then the two brahman seers approached the tigress. The tigress saw the two brahman seers coming from a distance, and upon seeing them, pained and emaciated with hunger as she was, she wanted to attack them.

Then it occurred to the two of them, "Who is willing to sacrifice one's life for one who has taken birth as an animal?" So right then, making use of their magical powers, they flew into the air.

The young brahman Brahmaprabha saw those two brahman seers, and upon seeing them, he said this to them: "Well now, brahmans. Both of you said that you would give food to the tiger. Brahmans, is this what truth is for the two of you, brahmans by birth?"

"Who is willing to sacrifice one's life for one who has taken birth as an animal?" they said.

"I am willing to sacrifice my life for one who has taken birth as an animal," the young brahman Brahmaprabha said. Then the young brahman Brahmaprabha approached the tigress and threw himself in front of her. Since the young brahman Brahmaprabha abided in the state of loving-kindness, the tigress wasn't able to attack him.[537]

Then it occurred to the young brahman Brahmaprabha, "This tigress can't eat my body while it's still alive." He looked here and there and then grabbed a very sharp sliver of bamboo[538] and made this vow of truth: "Pay attention to me! All those who live in this forest, even the eminent gods, nāgas, antigods, heavenly birds, kinnaras, and great snakes, should pay attention. I will make a sacrifice, a great sacrifice, a sacrifice superior to other sacrifices—that is, a complete sacrifice of my own throat. This complete sacrifice that I make is not for royal power, not for personal pleasure, not for becoming another Śakra, and not for the dominion of a wheel-turning king. It is for no other reason than that I may attain unsurpassed perfect awakening and so subdue the unsubdued, help to cross over those who have not crossed over, liberate the unliberated, console the unconsoled, and enable those to reach final nirvāṇa who have not reached final nirvāṇa. By this truth, this vow of truth, may my sacrifice not be in vain."[539] With that said, he slit his throat and threw himself down before the tigress.[540] [479]

As he was being mauled by the play of the tigress's claws
and his body was covered with goosebumps,
it looked[541] for a moment as if his wounded[542] chest
had the luminous nature of the moon
and sprouted fulsome rays of light.

As he joyfully[543] watched the tigress
madly seize his flesh and drink his blood,
his life-breath was disturbed
at the outset of the long journey ahead
and lingered for a moment, clutching at his throat.[544]

Monks, as soon as the young brahman Brahmaprabha sacrificed his throat, the billionfold world-system teetered, tottered, and tremored; quivered, quavered, and quaked; shifted, shuddered, and shook.

The east rose up and the west sank down.
The west rose up and the east sank down.
The south rose up and the north sank down.
The north rose up and the south sank down.
The middle rose up and the ends sank down.

The ends rose up and the middle sank down.
And the sun and the moon neither blazed, shined, nor illuminated.

Coda

"You may have [some doubt or uncertainty],[545] monks, as to the identity of the capital city called Utpalāvatī in the outskirts of the North Country at that time. Ponder no further. At that time and at that juncture what is now Puṣkalāvata (Abundance)[546] was the capital city called Utpalāvatī.[547]

"You may have some doubt or uncertainty, monks, as to the identity of the woman named Rūpāvatī in the capital city of Utpalāvatī at that time and at that juncture. Ponder no further. At that time and at that juncture I was the woman named Rūpāvatī.

"You may have some doubt or uncertainty, monks, as to the identity of the woman who gave birth in the birthing room at that time and at that juncture. Ponder no further. At that time and at that juncture the young lady Candraprabhā was the woman who gave birth in the birthing room.[548]

"You may have some doubt or uncertainty, monks, as to the identity of the infant boy at that time and at that juncture. Ponder no further. [480] At that time and at that juncture Prince Rāhula was the boy.

"You may have some doubt or uncertainty, monks, as to the identity of the boy named Candraprabha at that time and at that juncture. Ponder no further. At that time and at that juncture I myself was the boy named Candraprabha.

"You may have some doubt or uncertainty, monks, as to the identity of the five hundred boys at that time and at that juncture. Ponder no further. At that time and at that juncture these virtuous ones here now were those five hundred boys.

"You may have some doubt or uncertainty, monks, as to the identity of the bird named Uccaṅgama in that great cremation ground at that time and at that juncture. Ponder no further. At that time and at that juncture the monk Kauṇḍinya was the bird named Uccaṅgama.

"You may have some doubt or uncertainty, monks, as to the identity of the young brahman named Brahmaprabha at that time and at that juncture. Ponder no further. At that time and at that juncture I myself was the young brahman named Brahmaprabha.

"You may have some doubt or uncertainty, monks, as to the identity of the parents of the young brahman Brahmaprabha at that time and at that juncture. Ponder no further. At that time and at that juncture King Śuddhodana and [Queen] Māyādevī were the parents of the young brahman Brahmaprabha.

"You may have some doubt or uncertainty, monks, as to the identity of the forest at that time and at that juncture. [Ponder no further. At that time and at that juncture . . . was the forest.][549]

"You may have some doubt or uncertainty, monks, as to the identity of the two brahman seers at that time and at that juncture. Ponder no further. At that time and at that juncture the Bodhisattva Maitreya and the Buddha Suprabha (Radiant) were the two brahman seers in the forest.

"You may have some doubt or uncertainty, monks, as to the identity of the tigress at that time and at that juncture. Ponder no further. At that time and at that juncture the monk Kauṇḍinya was the [tigress].[550] [481]

"You may have some doubt or uncertainty, monks, as to the identity of the two tiger cubs at that time and at that juncture. Ponder no further. At that time and at that juncture the monk Ānanda and [Prince] Rāhula were the two tiger cubs.

"At that time, monks, I surpassed the bodhisattva Maitreya, who had set out forty ages ago, with a single sacrifice of my throat.[551] Hence, monks, in this way one should know the following:

"If all beings were to know the result of charity and the consequence of offering charity as I know the result of charity and the consequence of offering charity, then they would never eat the very last remaining morsel of food[552] all by themselves without giving it away or sharing it with others. And the stingy thoughts that arise would not seize hold of their minds. But monks, those beings who do not know the result of charity and the consequence of offering charity [as I know the result of charity and the consequence of offering charity][553] eat the very last remaining morsel of food[554] all by themselves without giving it away or sharing it with others.[555] And the stingy thoughts that arise do seize hold of their minds.

> He who doesn't see[556] what is put before him,[557]
> nor good and bad, nor services rendered,
> who doesn't see his duty to the wise
> nor to the noble community—
> he shall perish.
>
> But what is done, both good and bad,
> never perishes among the grateful.
>
> A good deed done well
> and an evil deed done maliciously
> will both inevitably mature
> and bear fruit."[558]

This was said by the Blessed One. With their minds uplifted, monks, nuns, male and female lay devotees, gods, nāgas, yakṣas, antigods, heavenly birds, kinnaras, great snakes, and the entire assembly rejoiced at the words of the Blessed One.

So ends the *Rūpāvatī-avadāna*, the thirty-second chapter in the glorious *Divyāvadāna*.

34. The Mahāyāna Sūtra on the Topic of Giving

DĀNĀDHIKARAṆA-MAHĀYĀNASŪTRA[559]

PRAISE to the Three Jewels!

Thus have I heard. At one time the Blessed One [482] was staying in the city of Śrāvastī at the Jeta Grove in the park of Anāthapiṇḍada (Almsgiver to the Poor), together with a large community of monks. There [the Blessed One][560] addressed the monks: "Monks, a wise person offers gifts in thirty-seven ways.[561]

1. At the right time he gives a gift that is approved by the Tathāgatha. He gives a gift that is appropriate, with the three bases fully purified.[562]
2. He gives a gift with respect to remove all faults and confusion.
3. He gives a gift with his own hand to acquire something worthwhile from a worthless body.
4. He gives a large gift,[563] which results in his enjoying the pleasures of a great sacrifice.
5. He gives a handsome gift, which results in his becoming attractive.[564]
6. He gives a fragrant gift, which results in his becoming fragrant.
7. He gives a tasty gift, which results in his obtaining a perfect sense of taste.
8. He gives a fine gift, which results in his obtaining fine pleasures.

9. He gives an extensive gift, which results in his obtaining extensive pleasures.
10. He gives a gift of food, which results in his being free from the cravings of hunger.[565]
11. He gives a gift of drink, which results in his being free from thirst in all lives to come.
12. He gives a gift of clothing, which results in his enjoying excellent clothing.
13. He gives a gift of shelter, which results in his having excellent summer chambers, penthouses, palaces, residences, floating mansions, gardens, and parks.
14. He gives a gift of a bed, which results in his enjoying himself in a well-to-do family.
15. He gives a gift of a vehicle, which results in his obtaining the [four] bases of success.
16. He gives a gift of medicine, which results in his attaining nirvāṇa that is free from old age, death, grief, and painful hindrances.
17. He gives a gift of dharma, which results[566] in his recollecting former lives.
18. He gives a gift of flowers, which results in his obtaining the flowers of the [seven] factors of awakening.
19. He gives a gift of a garland, which results in his being purified[567] from attachment, hate, and delusion.
20. He gives a gift of perfume, which results in his rebirth in pleasurable realms suffused with divine smells.
21. He gives a gift of incense, which results in the destruction of foul and bad-smelling odors.
22. He gives a gift of an umbrella, which results in his lordship and dominion in the dharma.
23. He gives a gift of a bell, which results in his having a beautiful voice.
24. He gives a gift of a musical instrument, [483] which results in his having a Brahmā-like voice.

25. He gives a gift of fine cloth, which results in his being crowned with fine cloth [as a diadem] and being consecrated by gods and humans.[568]

26–28. He gives a gift of bathing the shrines of the Tathāgatha and images of the Tathāgatha with fragrant water, which results in his having the thirty-two marks of a great man as well as the eighty minor marks.[569]

29. He gives a gift of a sūtra,[570] which results in his taking rebirth in acceptable families in all his births to come and instilling faith all around.

30. He gives a gift of the five essences,[571] which results in his having great strength in all his lives to come.

31. He gives a gift out of loving-kindness,[572] which results in the destruction of ill will.

32. He gives a gift out of compassion, which results in his obtaining great happiness.[573]

33. He gives a gift out of joy, which results in his obtaining joy and bliss at all times.[574]

34. He gives a gift out of equanimity, which results in the destruction of discontent.

35. He gives a gift that is diverse and variegated, which results in his obtaining a variety and multitude of diverse pleasures.

36. He gives a gift that is the complete sacrifice of all his wealth,[575] which results in his obtaining unsurpassed perfect awakening.

"In these thirty-seven ways, monks, a wise person gives a gift."

This was said by the Blessed One. With their minds uplifted, those monks rejoiced at the words of the Blessed One.

So ends the *Dānādhikaraṇa-mahāyānasūtra*, [the thirty-fourth chapter] in the glorious *Divyāvadāna*.

35. The Story of a Lonesome Fool

CŪḌĀPAKṢA-AVADĀNA[576]

Panthaka, Mahāpanthaka, and Their Paths to Arhatship

THE LORD BUDDHA was staying in the city of Śrāvastī at the Jeta Grove in the park of Anāthapiṇḍada (Almsgiver to the Poor).

Now in Śrāvastī there lived a certain brahman. He brought home a girl from an appropriate family as his wife, and with her he fooled around, enjoyed himself, and made love. Yet every child he had would die.

One day his wife became pregnant again. With cheek in hand, he sat lost in thought. Not far from him there lived an old midwife.[577] [484] She saw him and said, "Brahman, why do you sit there, with cheek in hand, lost in thought?"

"Every child I have dies," he said, "and now my wife has become pregnant again. She'll give birth to another child who will die as well."

"Call on me when it's time for your wife to give birth," she said.

When the time arrived for his wife to give birth, he called on the midwife, and she delivered the child.[578] A son was born. She bathed the boy, dressed him in white clothes, filled his mouth with fresh butter, and placed him in the young mother's hands.

"Hold this boy at the main crossroads [in the city]," she said to the young woman. "Tell whatever brahman or ascetic you see that this boy venerates the feet [of noble ones].[579] If he's still alive when the sun has set, take him and come back here. If he's dead, he should be left right there."[580]

So she took him, went to the main crossroads, and stood there.

Now it is the practice of non-Buddhist renunciants to get up at dawn and take ritual baths in sacred waters. The young woman, with respect and courtesy, venerated their feet and said, "This boy venerates the feet of noble ones."

"May he live long,[581] keep safe into old age, and fulfill the desires of his mother and father," they said.

Later in the morning some very senior monks got dressed, took their bowls and robes, and entered Śrāvastī for alms. The young woman, with respect and courtesy, venerated their feet and said, "This boy venerates the feet of noble ones."

"May he live very long, keep safe into old age, and fulfill the desires of his mother and father," the senior monks said.

In the morning the Blessed One also got dressed, took his bowl and robe, and entered Śrāvastī for alms. The young woman, with respect and courtesy, venerated his feet and said, "Blessed One, this boy venerates the Blessed One's feet."

"May he live long, keep safe into old age, and fulfill the desires of his mother and father," the Blessed One said.

In the evening twilight, she saw that her son was still alive. She took him and went back home.

"Is the boy alive?" they all asked her.

"He's alive," she said. [485]

"Where was he held?" they asked.

"On the main road."[582]

"What should the boy's name be?" they asked each other.

"The boy was held on the main road, so let the boy's name be Mahāpanthaka (Highwayman)."

As a boy, Mahāpanthaka was raised and nourished, and in time he grew up. When he grew up, he was entrusted to teachers to learn writing and then arithmetic, accounting, and matters relating to trademarks; correct behavior, laws of purity, and proper speech; the right ways to receive sacred ashes,[583] accumulate possessions,[584] and address others; the Ṛgveda, Yajurveda, Sāmaveda, and Atharvaveda; and lastly, how to sacrifice for himself and for others, teach and recite [the Vedas], and give and receive gifts.[585] The brahman Mahāpanthaka became devoted to these six duties,[586] and following his brahmanical duty,[587] he began to instruct a group of five hundred [young brahmans] in the recitation of the sacred syllable *oṃ*.

Now since the [elder] brahman was fooling around, enjoying himself, and making love with his wife, she became pregnant once again. When the time arrived for her to give birth, the brahman informed the midwife, and she delivered the child. A son was born. She bathed the boy, dressed him in white clothes, filled his mouth with fresh butter, and placed him in the young woman's hands.

"Hold this boy at the main crossroads," she said to the young woman. "Tell whatever brahman or ascetic you see that this boy venerates the feet of noble ones.[588] If he's still alive when the sun has set, take him and come back here. If he's dead, leave him there and come home."

The young woman, who was lazy by nature, took the boy and [instead of going to the main crossroads] stood on a small road.

Now it is the practice of non-Buddhist renunciants to get up at dawn and take ritual baths in sacred waters. The young woman, with respect and courtesy, venerated their feet and said, "Noble one, this boy venerates the feet of noble ones."

"May he live long, keep safe into old age, and fulfill the desires of his mother and father," they said.

In the evening twilight, she saw that he was still alive. She took him and went back home.

"Is the boy alive?" they asked her.

"He's alive," she said.

"Where did you hold him?" they asked.

"On such-and-such small road."

"What should the boy's name be?" they asked each other.

"The boy was held on a small road, so let the boy be given the name Panthaka (Bywayman)." [486]

As a boy, Panthaka was also raised and nourished, and in time he grew up. When he grew up, he was sent to a teacher to learn writing. [Trying to say the auspicious invocation *siddham*,] when he'd say *si*, he'd then forget *ddham*.[589]

So his teacher said to Panthaka's father, "Brahman, I have many boys to teach. I can't teach Panthaka. If a little is said to Mahāpanthaka, he grasps a lot. But by the time Panthaka has said *si*, he's already forgotten *ddham*!"[590]

"[Not][591] all brahmans become skilled in scripts and letters," Panthaka's father reflected. "Let him be a Vedic brahman in the oral tradition."

The [elder] brahman handed Panthaka over to a tutor for instruction in Vedic recitation. By the time *oṃ* was said to him, he would forget *bhuḥ*, and when *bhuḥ* was said, he would forget *oṃ*.[592]

"I have many young brahmans to instruct," the tutor said to the [elder] brahman. "I can't instruct Panthaka. By the time *oṃ* is said to him, he forgets *bhuḥ*! And when *bhuḥ* is said, he forgets *oṃ*!"

"Not all brahmans become masters of the Vedas," the [elder] brahman reflected. "He will be a brahman only by birth."

Wherever the [elder] brahman was invited as a guest, he would take his son Panthaka with him. Then one day the [elder] brahman fell sick. Though treated with medicines made from roots, stalks, leaves, and fruits, he continued to get worse.

"Son," he said to Mahāpanthaka, "after my death, no one will have to worry about you. But you must provide for Panthaka."

And with the words,

> All that is accumulated is lost in the end,
> what goes up comes down in the end,
> what comes together comes apart in the end,
> and what lives must die in the end.

. . . he died. They adorned his funeral bier with pieces of blue, yellow, red, and white cloth, and with great reverence[593] committed him to flames at the cremation grounds and cast off their grief.

After traveling through Kosala countryside, the venerable Śāriputra and Maudgalyāyana, each with five hundred followers, arrived in Śrāvastī. People in Śrāvastī heard that the venerable Śāriputra and Maudgalyāyana, after traveling through the Kosala countryside, each with five hundred followers, had now arrived in Śrāvastī. Hearing this, a crowd of people went out to see them. [487]

Now Mahāpanthaka was outside of Śrāvastī, at the base of a tree, instructing five hundred young brahmans in the recitation of brahmanical mantras. He saw that crowd of people leaving Śrāvastī.

"Friends, what is this?" he asked those young brahmans. "So many people are leaving the city."

"Instructor," they said to him, "Bhadantas Śāriputra and Maudgalyāyana, after traveling through the Kosala countryside, each with five hundred followers, have now arrived here in Śrāvastī. These people are going to see them."

"Are these two really worth seeing? They've left the highest caste to go forth as monks under the ascetic Gautama, who is of the second caste."

One young brahman there was a believer. "Instructor," he said, "don't speak like that. Those two are very powerful. If the instructor would listen to the dharma from these two,[594] he would certainly be pleased."

It was the practice of those young brahmans that when they had time off from their studies, they'd sometimes go to look around the city, sometimes take ritual baths in sacred waters, and sometimes collect firewood. One day all of them had time off from their studies, so they set out to collect firewood.

Meanwhile Mahāpanthaka went out for a walk. At the base of a tree,[595] he saw a lone monk. He approached him and said, "Monk, please take a moment and recite some words of the Buddha." The monk gave a detailed explanation of the tenfold path of virtuous actions. Filled with faith, Mahāpanthaka said, "Tell it to me once again in detail." Having done so, the monk departed.

One day the young brahmans once again had time off from their studies, so they set out to collect firewood. Mahāpanthaka again approached the monk. The monk gave a detailed explanation of the twelve links of interdependent arising, both forward and backward.

Filled with faith again, he said, "Monk, may I renounce, take ordination, and become a monk according to the dharma and monastic discipline that have been so well expressed. May I follow the religious life under the ascetic Gautama."

The monk reflected, "I will initiate him in the teachings. He will lift up the yoke of dharma." Then he said to him, "Brahman, do as I say."

"Monk, I am a renowned brahman," Mahāpanthaka said. "I can't take initiation right here. [488] Let's go into the countryside, and I'll take initiation there."

The monk brought him into the countryside, initiated and ordained him, and then said, "There are two activities of a monk—meditation and study. Which will you do?"

"I'll do both."

By day he deeply and diligently contemplated [the threefold collection of scripture known as] the Tripiṭaka, and by night he considered, evaluated, and contemplated it. Consequently, he rid himself of all defilements and directly experienced arhatship. Becoming an arhat,

> he was free from attachment in the three realms;
> he regarded clods of earth and gold as equal in value;
> he possessed equanimity toward the sky
>   and the palm of his hand;
> he didn't distinguish between being cut by a blade
>   and being anointed with sandalwood paste;
> the eggshell of his ignorance was broken by knowledge;

he obtained the special knowledges, superhuman faculties,
and analytic insights;
and he was averse to worldly attainments, temptations,
and honors.
He became worthy of respect, honor, and obeisance
from the gods, including Indra and Upendra.

When[596] Panthaka's wealth diminished, gave out, and was finally completely exhausted, it began to be difficult for him to make ends meet.

Meanwhile it occurred to [Mahā]panthaka,[597] "I have [obtained][598] all that I can obtain through listening. I really should go to Śrāvastī and pay my respects to the Blessed One." So the venerable Mahāpanthaka, along with five hundred followers, set out toward Śrāvastī. Traveling along, they eventually arrived in Śrāvastī. People in Śrāvastī heard that the noble Mahāpanthaka, along with five hundred followers, after traveling through the Kosala countryside, had now arrived in Śrāvastī. Hearing this, a crowd of people went [to see him].

Panthaka saw them and asked, "Friends, where are all these people going?"

"The Noble Mahāpanthaka, along with five hundred followers, after traveling through the Kosala countryside, has now arrived in Śrāvastī," they said. "All these people are going to see him."

Panthaka reflected, "He's not their brother or a relative. He's my brother! Why don't I go to see him?" So he went to see him as well.

When the noble Mahāpanthaka saw him, he asked, "Panthaka, how are you getting by?"

"It's difficult, but I'm getting by."

"Why don't you go forth as a monk?"

"I'm a fool, an absolute fool," he said. "I'm an idiot, a complete idiot.[599] Who will initiate me as a monk?"

Then the venerable Mahāpanthaka reflected, "Does he have any roots of virtue? Yes, he does. Then why isn't he fit to be a monk?"[600] So he said, "Come, I will initiate you as a monk." [489] He initiated and ordained him and then gave him instructions:

> One should not commit even the smallest sin
> in all the world in thought, word, or deed.
> One free from desires, mindful, and thoughtful
> does not experience the suffering that evil brings.

Even after the three months of the rainy season, Panthaka still couldn't learn the verse.[601] Others, even cowherds and cattle herders, heard it and memorized it.[602] With respect and courtesy, he would approach them and ask for help, and they would recite it for him.[603]

As a rule, the disciples of lord buddhas have two assemblies each year—one at the time of the full moon in the month of Āṣāḍha [in late June, early July], when the rainy season begins, and the other at the time of the full moon in the month of Kārtika [in late October, early November]. The senior disciples do likewise.

Those who assemble at the time of the full moon in the month of Āṣāḍha, when the rainy season begins, practice particular kinds of meditation and then pass the rainy season in various villages, towns, districts, and capitals. Those who assemble at the time of the full moon in the month of Kārtika ask about texts for study, ask questions about various topics,[604] and recite what they have learned.

The monks who were the students and pupils of the venerable Mahāpanthaka had passed the rainy season in the countryside, and on the full moon in the month of Kārtika, they approached the venerable Mahāpanthaka. Once there, some asked about texts for study, some asked questions about various topics, and some recited what they had learned. Those there who were fools, absolute fools, idiots, complete idiots, they served, waited upon, and paid their respects to the group of six monks. And so the venerable Panthaka served, waited upon, and paid his respects to the group of six monks.

"Venerable Panthaka, your fellow students ask the instructor about texts for study and subjects for inquiry," the group of six monks said to him. "You should go as well and ask your instructor about texts for study and ask questions about various topics."

"I haven't studied anything during the three months of the rainy season," Panthaka said. "I couldn't even learn a single verse. How can I ask for a text to study?"

"The Blessed One has surely said that those who aren't studying lack good sense," they said. "How can you master[605] a verse if you aren't studying? [490] Go and ask!"

He went and said, "Instructor, please give me a text to study."

The venerable Mahāpanthaka reflected, "Is this his own idea or did someone put him up to it?" He saw that someone had put him up to it. The venerable Mahāpanthaka reflected, "Will he learn from being inspired or learn from being chastised?" He saw that he would learn from being chastised. So he grabbed him by the neck and threw him out of the monastery. "You really are a fool, an absolute fool, an idiot, a complete idiot. What good will you ever do in this order?"

The venerable Panthaka began to cry. "Now I'm not a householder or a renunciant."

The Blessed One saw the venerable Panthaka outside the monastery wandering about.[606] Seeing him approach, the Blessed One said this: "Panthaka, why are you outside of the monastery crying? Why do you shed tears?"

"Bhadanta, my instructor threw me out. Now I'm not a householder or a renunciant."

"My child," the Blessed One said, "your instructor hasn't fulfilled the six perfections, performing many hundreds and thousands of difficult deeds over the course of three incalculable ages, so he doesn't comprehend the words coming from the best of sages. But I have fulfilled the six perfections, performing many hundreds and thousands of difficult deeds over the course of three incalculable ages, so I do comprehend them. Aren't you able to learn from the Tathāgatha?"

"Bhadanta, I am a fool, an absolute fool, an idiot, a complete idiot."

Then at that moment the Blessed One uttered a verse:

One ignorant because of his innocence[607]
is actually wise in this case.
But one ignorant and thinking himself wise
is rightly recognized as a fool.

It is impossible and inconceivable that lord buddhas would teach the dharma word by word. This is not possible.[608] Therefore the Blessed One addressed the venerable Ānanda: "Ānanda, teach Panthaka." So the venerable Ānanda began to teach him, but he wasn't able to do so.

The venerable Ānanda said this to the Blessed One: "Bhadanta, at this time I have to serve you, my teacher. I have to retain in my memory what I hear [491] and instruct groups of students. And I have to teach the dharma to those brahmans and householders who come to visit. I'm not able to teach Panthaka."

Then the Blessed One recited these two lines of verse to Panthaka:

I remove filth.
I remove impurity.[609]

Panthaka couldn't grasp these two lines of verse.

The Blessed One reflected, "His bad karma must be destroyed." And so the Blessed One addressed the venerable [Panthaka]:[610] "Panthaka, can you wipe clean the monks' sandals and shoes?"[611]

"Yes, of course, Bhadanta. I can do that."

"Go, wipe them clean."

He went to wipe clean the monks' sandals and shoes,[612] but the monks wouldn't give them to him.

"Give [him your sandals and shoes]," the Blessed One said. "His bad karma must be destroyed. I will give him two lines of verse to study. Please do that as well."[613]

One by one Panthaka wiped clean the monks' sandals and shoes,[614] and the monks repeated those two lines of verse for him to study. From studying on his own, he eventually memorized those two lines of verse.

Then one day, as night turned into dawn, the venerable Panthaka had this thought: "The Blessed One has said, 'I remove filth. I remove impurity.' But did the Blessed One say this with regard to filth on the inside or on the outside?" While thinking in this way, at that moment, three verses that he had never heard before presented themselves to him:

> Filth here is attachment, definitely not dirt.
> Filth in this case refers to attachment, not dirt.
> The wise remove this filth, but not
> those careless with the Sugata's teachings.
>
> Filth here is hate, definitely not dirt.
> Filth in this case refers to hate, not dirt.
> The wise remove this filth, but not
> those careless with the Sugata's teachings.
>
> Filth here is delusion, definitely not dirt.
> Filth in this case refers to delusion, not dirt. [492]
> The wise remove this filth, but not
> those careless with the Sugata's teachings.

After striving, struggling, and straining, Panthaka rid himself of all defilements and thereby directly experienced arhatship. Becoming an arhat,

> he was free from attachment in the three realms;
> he regarded clods of earth and gold as equal in value;
> he possessed equanimity toward the sky
> and the palm of his hand;

he didn't distinguish between being cut by a blade
and being anointed with sandalwood paste;
the eggshell [of his ignorance] was broken by knowledge;
he obtained the special knowledges, superhuman faculties,
and analytic insights;
and he was averse to worldly attainments, temptations,
and honors.
He became worthy of respect, honor, and obeisance
from the gods, including Indra and Upendra.

While Panthaka was sitting in meditation, Mahāpanthaka saw him. Now the knowledge and insight of arhats does not operate unless they focus their attention. Mahāpanthaka took Panthaka by the arm and said, "Come, first do your studies. You can meditate later."

Then the venerable Panthaka, who had rid himself of all defilements and thereby directly experienced arhatship, stretched out his arm like the trunk of an elephant. The venerable Mahāpanthaka looked and stared intently at Panthaka, who had turned away.[615]

"Venerable Panthaka, have you really amassed so many virtues?" he asked.

"Yes, I have."

The Venerable Panthaka Teaches Twelve Nuns

Even after the venerable Panthaka had rid himself of all defilements and thereby directly perceived arhatship, followers of other traditions were still rude, abusive, and disrespectful to him. [They would say], "The ascetic Gautama has said that 'My dharma is profound and is profound in implication, it is difficult to perceive and difficult to understand, it is beyond reason and beyond the scope of reason, it is subtle and only comprehensible to the wise and clever scholar.'[616] How deep can the dharma of someone be if his monastic community is now filled with fools, absolute fools, idiots, complete idiots, with Panthaka first and foremost!"[617]

The Blessed One reflected, "When there is a senior disciple who is great like Mount Sumeru, many people receive forgiveness.[618] Panthaka's virtues should be made known." And so the Blessed One addressed the venerable Ānanda: "Ānanda, go and inform Panthaka that he is to instruct the nuns."

"Yes, Bhadanta," the venerable Ānanda replied, consenting to the Blessed One's request, and then he approached the venerable Panthaka. Having approached, he said this to him: "Venerable Panthaka, the Teacher has said that you should instruct the nuns."

"What is the reason," the venerable Panthaka [reflected],[619] [493] "that the Blessed One bypasses the most senior monks and instead orders me to instruct the nuns? It's because my virtues are to be made known. I shall fulfill the Teacher's wish."

Some nuns arrived at the Jeta Grove as proxies for their monastic community, charged with offering their consent for the teachings.[620] "Who has the Blessed One appointed to instruct us?" they asked the monks.

"The venerable Panthaka," they said.

"Sisters," the nuns said to each other, "look at how women are insulted! And by someone who studied a single verse for three months and still couldn't memorize it! Nuns know the Tripiṭaka, can discourse on the dharma, and are gifted with eloquence that is inspired yet controlled. And yet he's going to instruct the nuns?"

They then returned to the assembly and were questioned by the other nuns.

"Sisters, who will come to instruct us?"

"The noble Panthaka," they said.

"Do you mean the noble Mahāpanthaka?"

"No, not him. The other one—the fool Panthaka."

A group of twelve nuns[621] heard this and were indignant. "Sisters, look at how women are insulted! And by someone who studied a single verse for three months and still couldn't memorize it! These nuns know the Tripiṭaka, can discourse on the dharma, and are gifted with eloquence that is inspired yet controlled. And yet he's going to instruct them?"

"Sisters," they said to each other, "six of us should arrange a lion throne adorned with vines measuring twelve hands in length. And six of us should enter Śrāvastī and make this announcement on the streets, roads, squares, and crossroads—'A great instructor of ours is coming [tomorrow]! [Remember!] Whoever among us hasn't seen the most subtle truths will have to pass a long time in saṃsāra!'[622] Now that barely educated bastard won't dare to instruct the nuns."[623]

So six of those women arranged a lion throne with vines measuring twelve hands in length, and six nuns entered Śrāvastī and made this announcement on the streets, roads, squares, and crossroads: "A great instructor of ours is coming [tomorrow]! [Remember!] Whoever among us hasn't seen the most subtle truths will have to pass a long time in saṃsāra!"

In the morning Panthaka got dressed, took his bowl and robe, and entered Śrāvastī for alms. [After wandering through Śrāvastī for alms,][624] he ate his meal,[625] and after eating, he returned from his alms-round. Then he put away his bowl and robe, washed his feet, and entered the monastery [494] to retreat into meditation. In the evening, the venerable Panthaka emerged from meditative seclusion,[626] took his outer robe, and set off [to instruct the nuns] with an attending monk following behind him.

Many hundreds of thousands of beings [went there as well],[627] some out of curiosity, others impelled by former roots of virtue. The people of the assembly saw the venerable Panthaka from a distance, and upon seeing him, they asked each other,[628] "Which of these two is here to instruct the nuns? The monk in front[629] or the monk following behind?"

"The monk in front,"[630] some of the people there said. [Recognizing Panthaka,] they began to express their indignation: "Look, friends.[631] These nuns have purposefully made fools out of us! How will someone who studied a single verse for three months and still couldn't memorize it instruct the nuns or recite[632] the dharma? We're leaving."

"Let's wait," others said. "If he'll teach the dharma, we'll listen. If he won't, we'll go." Having made this decision, the people of the assembly remained where they were.

The venerable Panthaka saw that a lion throne had been specially prepared, and upon seeing it, he reflected, "Was this prepared in good faith[633] or with the intent of doing harm?" He saw that it had been prepared with the intent of doing harm. So the venerable Panthaka stretched out his arm like the trunk of an elephant and put the lion throne back in its proper place.[634] Then he sat down on it. After he sat down, some people could see him and some couldn't see him. So, sitting there, the venerable Panthaka entered a state of meditative concentration such that when his mind was concentrated, he disappeared from his seat, rose up high in the sky in the eastern direction, [and appeared in the four bodily postures—that is to say, walking, standing, sitting, and lying down. Then he entered into the state of mastery over the element of fire. And when the venerable Panthaka had entered into the state of mastery over the element of fire, different kinds of light emerged from his body—they were blue, yellow, red, white, crimson, and the color of crystal. He displayed many other miracles as well. He made his lower body blaze in flames, and then a shower of cold water rained down from his upper body. What he displayed in the east, he then displayed in the south, and likewise in all four directions. After making use of his magical powers] and displaying these [four] miracles [in the four directions],[635] he withdrew those magical powers that he had activated and sat down in the seat specially prepared for him. After sitting down, the venerable Panthaka addressed those nuns: "Sisters, I studied a single verse for three months. Who has the strength and conviction[636] to listen to a single verse for seven days and nights and to parse its meaning literally and figuratively?"[637]

> One should not commit even the smallest sin
> in all the world in thought, word, or deed.

One free from desire, mindful, and thoughtful
does not experience the suffering that evil brings. [495]

The Blessed One has explained that one should avoid[638] all sins.[639]

During the time that it took the venerable Panthaka to analyze the meaning of the first half of the verse,[640] twelve thousand beings saw the [four noble] truths. Some directly experienced the reward of the stream-enterer, some the reward of the once-returner, some the reward of the nonreturner, and some went forth as monks and, by ridding themselves of all defilements, directly experienced arhatship. Some set their minds on attaining awakening as a disciple, some awakening as a solitary buddha, and some unsurpassed perfect awakening. Almost the entire assembly became favorably inclined toward the Buddha, drawn toward the dharma, and well disposed toward the community.

After the venerable Panthaka had instructed, incited, inspired, and delighted the people of the assembly with this discourse on the dharma, he got up from his seat and departed. Some monks saw him approaching and reflected, "Today the venerable Panthaka certainly won't have inspired faith in great numbers of people."[641] They couldn't bring themselves to ask the venerable Panthaka anything unpleasant face to face, so they asked his attending monk following behind him. "Venerable one, the venerable Panthaka didn't inspire faith in great numbers of people today, or did he?"

"There wasn't anyone that the venerable one didn't inspire with faith! The Blessed One turned the twelve-spoked wheel of dharma three times in Vārāṇasī at the deer park in Ṛṣivadana. Now the venerable Panthaka has set that wheel in motion once again. Although he didn't explain the meaning of a full verse, twelve thousand beings still saw the [four noble] truths."

Then the Blessed One addressed the monks: "Monks, among those monks who are my disciples, the foremost in skillfully transforming the minds of others is the monk Panthaka."

The monks questioned the Lord Buddha: "Look, Bhadanta. That group of twelve nuns was determined to ruin the venerable Panthaka, and yet they did him nothing but good."

"Yes, monks," the Blessed One said, "not only now, but also in the past. They were determined to ruin him, and yet they did him nothing but good. Listen to this."

The Blind Man and His Twelve Daughters-in-Law

Long ago, monks, in a certain market town, there lived a householder. He brought home a girl from an appropriate family as his wife, and with her he fooled around, enjoyed himself, and made love. From fooling around, enjoying himself [496], and making love, [a son was born].[642] Again and again he fooled around, enjoyed himself, and made love with her until twelve sons were born. Eventually he got them married and settled down. Then one day his wife died. The brahman, in his old age, [became blind].[643]

Now the blind man's daughters-in-law were ill behaved. When their husbands would go out, they'd have sex with other men. The brahman, though, was skillful in identifying sounds. He could differentiate between the sound of one of his sons and that of another man. When he heard the footsteps of another man, he'd start yelling at his daughters-in-law.

His daughters-in-law reflected, "This brahman is set on ruining us." So they gave him only coarse rice and a little whey.[644]

The brahman said to his sons, "These daughters-in-law of mine give me only coarse rice and a little whey."

So his sons said to their wives, "Why do you give our dear father only coarse rice and a little whey?"

"His merit is exhausted," they said. "If we put perfect grains of rice in a little pot[645] for him, they turn into coarse rice. And if we put curd in there, it turns into whey."

"How can this be?" they asked.

"We'll prove it to you," they said.

Then they conversed [among themselves]:[646] "Now we'll have to carry out what we promised." So they said to a potter, "Sir, can you make two pots, each having one mouth but with two compartments inside?"

"Yes, I can," he said. So he made two pots, each having one mouth but with two compartments inside. The daughters-in-law put coarse rice in one pot and whey in the other. Then, in front of their husbands, they put grains of rice in [the second compartment of] one pot and curd in [the second compartment of] the other. Then they prepared it.

"Now who should be fed[647] first," they asked, "our dear husbands' father or all of you?"

"Feed our father first," they said. Then, in front of their husbands, they took out coarse rice from one pot and served him, and then from the other pot they served him whey. Then in the same way, they took out excellent quality rice from the first pot and served their husbands, and then from the second pot they took out curd.

"Father," his sons said to him, "your merit is exhausted. [497] [When on your behalf] excellent quality grains of rice are placed in one pot and curds in another, they change into coarse rice and whey."

The brahman reflected, "I worked long and hard to collect what pleasures I have. What reason is there for my merit to be exhausted?"

When his daughters-in-law weren't looking, the brahman went into the kitchen, and searching around, groping with his hands, he found two pots, each having one mouth but with two parts inside. He hid them. When his sons returned, he showed them the pots. "Look, you say my merit is exhausted. Go and look! Only in our house are there pots with one mouth [and two parts inside]! My dear sons, other homes don't even have two pots, but we, unfortunate as we are, have two pots, each with [two parts inside and] a single mouth!"[648]

The brahman's sons then thrashed their wives. Bruised,[649] they reflected, "This brahman is set on ruining us. Let's kill him."

Then one day a snake-catcher came to town.

"Do you have a snake?" the daughters-in-law asked him.

"What kind of snake are you looking for, living or dead?" he asked.

"Dead," they said.

He reflected, "What will these women do with a dead snake? They must want to kill the old man."

As a rule[650] the poison of an angry snake flows in two places, the head and the tail. The snake-catcher made the snake angry, then cut off its head and tail and gave the women the middle part.[651] They prepared a kind of broth from it. Then they said to the brahman, "Father, would you like to drink some of this tasty broth?"[652]

The brahman reflected, "Would they really give me tasty broth? No doubt they'll give me something poisonous. I'll drink it anyway," he reflected. "Either way I'm going to die."

They gave him the tasty broth, and he drank it. The film over his eyes became suffused with tears.[653] He began to see. Then he collapsed and said, "I'm dying! I'm dying!"

"Don't drink so quickly," they said. Then they asked, "Father, will you drink some more?"[654]

"Yes, I'll drink some more," he said.

Again they gave him some of the tasty broth, and he drank that as well. The film over his eyes became suffused with more and more tears, [498] and he began to see more clearly.

Now his daughters-in-law began to behave just as they had behaved in the past, confident that he was blind. Then the brahman took his staff, got up, and said, "Do you think I still can't see? Well, now I can see!"

The daughters-in-law were ashamed and ran off.

"What do you think, monks? That brahman was none other than Panthaka at that time and at that juncture, and those twelve daughters-in-law of his were none other than these twelve nuns. Back then they were determined to ruin him but did him nothing but good. And now too they were determined to ruin him, but once again did him nothing but good."

The monks questioned the Lord Buddha: "Look, Bhadanta. The Blessed One inspired the venerable Panthaka with a small teaching,[655] delivered him from the hardships of saṃsāra, and established him in the unsurpassed supreme security that is nirvāṇa."

"Yes, monks," the Blessed One said, "not only now, but also in the past. I inspired him with a small teaching and established him in great lordship and dominion. Listen to this."

Mūṣikāhairaṇyaka and the Dead Mouse[656]

Long ago,[657] monks, in a certain market town, there lived a householder who was rich, wealthy, and prosperous. He brought home a girl from an appropriate family as his wife, and with her he fooled around, enjoyed himself, and made love. And so,[658] a son was born to him. He addressed his wife: "My dear, this son of ours will bring us into debt.[659] I'm going. I'll take my wares and set sail in the great ocean."

"Do as you wish," she said.

The householder reflected, "If I give her a lot of money she'll spend her time with other men." So he didn't give her any money at all.

Now the guildmaster who lived in the market town was a friend of the householder. The householder placed a lot of money in his hands and said, "If my wife [runs out of food and clothing],[660] please provide her with them." Then he took his goods and set sail in the great ocean. And right there, straightaway, he met with his death.

Meanwhile his wife, with her own hands and with the help of her relatives, [499] supported, protected, and nourished the boy.

"Mom," the boy asked his mother, "what kind of work did my father and forefathers do?"

She reflected, "If I tell him that they [were maritime merchants who] did their business on ships in the great ocean, no doubt he'll set sail in the great ocean as well. And right there, straightaway, he'll meet with his death." So she said, "It's been said[661] that your father and forefathers worked right here as merchants."

"Give me some money then," he said. "That way I can work as a merchant right here as well."

"Where is this money that I have?" she asked. "Somehow, with my own hands and with the help of my relatives, I've managed to support, protect, and nourish you. Where can I find such a huge amount of money? Still, the guildmaster was a friend of your father. Get some money from him and start this business of yours."

So the boy went to the guildmaster's home. One of his men told the boy to get lost,[662] once and then a second time. The man reprimanded him. Meanwhile a maidservant emerged from the guildmaster's house to throw away a pile of garbage with a dead mouse placed on top of it.[663]

The guildmaster[664] said to that man, "If one is a real man, he can pick himself up [and succeed] with just this dead mouse."

The boy heard this and reflected, "The guildmaster is a great man. He doesn't just say this or that. It must be true that one can pick oneself up [and succeed] with just a dead mouse." So he followed behind the girl, and after she threw out the garbage,[665] the boy took the dead mouse and went to the marketplace. There a merchant was playing with a cat. The boy showed the dead mouse to the cat, and when the cat saw it, he started jumping up after it.

"Give the dead mouse to the cat," the merchant said to the boy.

"Why should I give it away for nothing?[666] Pay me for it."

The merchant gave him two handfuls of beans.[667]

"If I eat them," the boy reflected, "then all my capital will be eaten up." So instead he roasted the beans in a frying pan[668] [500] and filled a pitcher[669] with cold water. Then he took those things, left town, and went to the place where lumbermen relax. There he waited. Then the lumbermen came.

"Uncles," he said to them, "put down your loads of wood. Relax for a while."

They set down their loads of wood, and he gave them each a little bit of beans and some cold water to drink.[670]

"Son,"[671] they said, "where are you going?"

"For wood."[672]

"Son, we got up and left early in the morning and we're just coming back now. Going this late, when do you think you'll get back?"[673] They each gave him a piece of wood.

Now the boy had a stock of wood.[674] He took it and went back to town. There he sold it, got some more beans and roasted them, filled a pot with water, and went back and waited in the same place. Just like before he divided up the beans among the lumbermen[675] and served them cold water.

"Son," they said to him, "every day take some beans and water, and come and wait right here. We'll bring a supply of wood for you." From then on, every day, the boy did just that.

"Uncles," he said to them, "don't take these loads of wood to the market. Put them in my house. That way I can pay you in a lump sum."[676] And so they put their loads of wood in his house.

Now one time there passed a week of rainy weather. The boy sold those loads of wood and made a lot of profit. [Nevertheless,] he reflected, "This wood business is a terrible business.[677] Even the sandalwood business is the same. I really should set up a sweet shop."[678] So he set up a sweet shop, and he conducted his business according to dharma. He made a lot of profit.[679] Then he reflected, "This sweet shop business is a terrible business. I really should set up a perfume shop." So he set up a perfume shop, [501] and he made a lot of profit.[680] Then he reflected, "This is also a terrible business. [I really should set up a goldsmith's shop. So he set up a goldsmith's shop, and he conducted his business according to dharma. He made a lot a of profit.][681] He surpassed all the other goldsmiths. And so he came to be known as Mūṣikāhairaṇyaka (Mouse Goldsmith).

Those goldsmiths said to each other, "Gentlemen, this Mūṣikāhairaṇyaka has surpassed all of us. Let's appeal to his vanity. We'll get him to set sail in the great ocean. Right there, straightaway, he'll meet with his death."

Standing not far from him they chatted among themselves: "Friends, to be sure, a man who once traveled on the back of an elephant may now travel by horseback, and one who traveled by horseback may now travel by palanquin, and one who traveled by palanquin may now travel on foot. And in just this way, Mūṣikāhairaṇyaka's fathers and forefathers [were once maritime merchants who] did their business on ships in the ocean, while Mūṣikāhairaṇyaka himself now struggles to make a living running a goldsmith's shop!"

Hearing this, Mūṣikāhairaṇyaka said, "What are you saying?"[682]

"Your father and forefathers [were maritime merchants who] did their business on ships," they said. "And now[683] you struggle to make a living running a goldsmith's shop."

He went home and asked his mother, "Mom, is it true that my father and forefathers [were maritime merchants who] did their business on ships in the great ocean?"

His mother reflected, "He must have heard something from someone. Well, it wouldn't be right if I deceived him by telling lies."

"Son, it's the truth."

"Give me permission," he said. "I too will set sail in the great ocean."

"Son, you're to stay right here," she said.

Again and again he told her that he was going. Finally, realizing that he was absolutely determined, she gave him permission. Then he had bells rung [in town] for the following proclamation: "Whoever among you is eager to set sail in the great ocean with Mūṣikāhairaṇyaka [as your caravan leader],[684] while being exempt from customs, transit, and freight fees, gather up goods for export across the great ocean." Five hundred traders then gathered up goods for export across the great ocean.

Then [the caravan leader][685] Mūṣikāhairaṇyaka performed auspicious rituals and benedictions for a safe journey, loaded his goods in carts, carriers, containers, and baskets and on camels, bulls, and donkeys, and then set out for the great ocean.[686] [502] Eventually he arrived at the shore of the great ocean.[687]

When the merchants saw the great ocean, they were afraid. They couldn't bring themselves to board the ship.

The caravan leader Mūṣikāhairaṇyaka said to the captain, "Tell us! Tell us,[688] my friend, of the glory of the great ocean as it really is!"

Then the captain proclaimed: "In the great ocean there are treasures such as these—jewels, pearls, beryl, and conch, quartz, coral, silver, and gold, emeralds, sapphires, red pearls, and right-spiraling conch shells. Whoever among you is eager to make himself happy with such treasures, and to delight his mother, father, wife, and children, servants, maids, workers, and laborers, friends, counselors, kinsmen, and relatives, and whoever wants, from time to time, to present to ascetics and brahmans gifts that guide one upward,[689] are a just reward for noble words, result in pleasure, and lead to heaven in the future, he should set sail in the ocean."

People desire wealth, so soon a crowd of people boarded. The ship couldn't take it.

"What can I say now so that they'll disembark?" the caravan leader reflected. "My friend," he said to the captain, "proclaim[690] for us the infamy[691] of the great ocean as it really is!"

"Listen, honorable merchants of Jambudvīpa (Black Plum Island)!" the captain proclaimed. "In the great ocean there are also great, great dangers—the danger of sea monsters like the Timi, the Timiṅgila, and the Timitimiṅgila, the danger of whirlpools, the danger of crocodiles, the danger of gharials,[692] and the danger of running into reefs. Thieves in black and white [clothes][693] may also come to steal your money.[694] They will completely and utterly destroy you. Whoever among you would give up his own dear life,[695] and give up his mother, father, wife, and children, servants, maids, workers, and laborers, friends, counselors, kinsmen, and relatives, he should set sail in the ocean."

Few men are brave. Many are cowards. A great many people disembarked, and the ship righted itself.

After the captain made this announcement three times, he released one of the ship's ropes, [503] then a second and a third.[696] And so the ship, urged on by powerful winds and well controlled by the great captain, set off like a great cloud.[697] And it met with favorable winds until it reached Ratnadvīpa (Treasure Island).

Then the captain made an announcement: "Listen, honorable

merchants of Jambudvīpa! There are glass jewels just like diamonds here in Ratnadvīpa. You should examine them carefully, one by one, as you collect them. Let's not have any regrets after you've arrived back in Jambudvīpa. And here in Ratnadvīpa there live demonesses known as *krońca* maidens. They'll sweet-talk a man in various ways, and right there, straightaway, he'll meet with his death. And there are also intoxicating fruits here in Ratnadvīpa. Whoever eats them will be in a stupor for seven nights. You mustn't eat them! And nonhumans live here in Ratnadvīpa as well. They'll put up with humans for seven days, but after seven days, they'll let loose a wind that will carry off a ship, regardless of whether one's work is finished."

After listening to this, the merchants remained attentive and on guard. They carefully examined the treasures one by one, and they filled their ship with them as one would with sesame seeds, rice, jujube berries, or horse gram. Then, with the help of favorable winds, they arrived back in Jambudvīpa. And it went on like this until they had successfully completed seven voyages. Then, at last, they returned home.

"Son," Mūṣikāhairaṇyaka's mother said to him, "you should get married here and settle down."

"First I have to pay off a debt,"[698] he said. "After that I'll get married."

"Son," she said to him, "neither your father nor your forefathers accrued any debt.[699] How did you get into debt?"

"Mother," he said, "this is something only I know." Then he had four mice prepared from four kinds of jewels. He filled a chest with gold, placed those four mice on the chest's four sides, and then went to the guildmaster's home.

Meanwhile the guildmaster was standing there praising none other than Mūṣikāhairaṇyaka: "Look, gentlemen. Mūṣikāhairaṇyaka is very powerful because of his merit. Whatever he takes, whether a blade of grass or a clump of dirt, it all turns into gold!"

While the guildmaster stood there chatting like this, the doorkeeper went to him and announced, [504] "Mūṣikāhairaṇyaka is standing at the door."

"Send him in," he said. "Or better yet, bring Mūṣikāhairaṇyaka to me."[700]

Mūṣikāhairaṇyaka entered and said, "This is your capital. This is your profit. Please accept them."

"I don't remember . . . Is it true that I gave you something?" the guildmaster said.

"I'll remind you," Mūṣikāhairaṇyaka said. So he reminded him.

"Whose son are you?" he asked.

"Such-and-such householder's."

"You are my friend's son," the guildmaster said. "It is I who have something to give to you! When your father was going [off to the great ocean], he placed [a lot of][701] money in my hands."

Then the guildmaster adorned his daughter with all kinds of ornaments and offered her to Mūṣikāhairaṇyaka as a wife.

"What do you think, monks? That guildmaster was none other than me at that time and at that juncture. Mūṣikāhairaṇyaka was none other than Panthaka at that time and at that juncture. Back then as well I inspired him with a small teaching[702] and established him in great lordship. And now too I inspired him with a small teaching,[703] delivered him from the hardships of saṃsāra, and established him in the unsurpassed supreme security that is nirvāṇa."

The monks asked the Lord Buddha, "Bhadanta, what deed did Panthaka do that resulted in his becoming a fool, an absolute fool, an idiot, a complete idiot?"

"Monks, the deeds that Panthaka himself has performed [and accumulated have now come together, and their conditions have matured. They remain before him like an oncoming flood and will certainly come to pass. Those deeds were performed and accumulated by Panthaka. Who else will experience their results?][704] For those deeds that are performed and accumulated, monks, do not mature outside of oneself—neither in the element of earth nor in the element of water, in the element of fire or in the element of wind. Instead, those [deeds that are performed and accumulated],[705] both good and bad, mature in the aggregates, elements, and sense bases that are appropriated when one is reborn.

> Actions never come to naught,
> even after hundreds of millions of years.
> When the right conditions gather and the time is right,
> then they will have their effect on embodied beings."

The Pork Dealer and Five Hundred Solitary Buddhas

Long ago, monks, when people lived for twenty thousand years, there arose in the world a teacher named Kāśyapa,

> who was a tathāgata,
> an arhat,
> a perfectly awakened being,
> perfect in knowledge and conduct,
> a sugata,
> a knower of the world,
> an unsurpassed guide for those in need of training,
> a teacher of gods and humans,
> a buddha,
> and a blessed one. [505]

He stayed near Vārāṇasī with a following of twenty thousand monks.[706] One monk there possessed the knowledge of the Tripiṭaka of Kāśyapa's teachings, but since he was stingy[707] he wouldn't teach even a single verse to anyone there.

Now at a later time,[708] in a certain market town, there was a pork dealer. Across from that market town on the other side of the river there was also another market town, and in that other market town a lunar holiday was being celebrated.

The pork dealer reflected, "If I slaughter some pigs and bring them to the other market town, there might not be anyone to buy the meat, and it will go bad. Instead, I'll take the pigs there while they're still alive.[709] Then I can slaughter them and bring them to wherever the buyers are."

He tied a large group of pigs together by their legs,[710] put them on board a boat, and set out. Those pigs began to shuffle about and made the boat flip over.[711] Right there, straightaway, the pigs met with their death.[712] As for the pork dealer, he was carried away by the current toward Vārāṇasī.

On the banks of that river there lived five hundred solitary buddhas. One of those solitary buddhas went to the river for water. He saw the pork dealer and reflected, "Is he dead or is he still alive?" He saw that he was still living, so he stretched out his arm like the trunk of an elephant and picked him up. Then he smoothed out the sand and there he placed him face down.[713] Water flowed out of the pork dealer's body.

In time the pork dealer got up. Seeing human footprints, he followed them until he saw those five hundred solitary buddhas. He began to serve them, providing them with leaves, flowers, fruits, and dental sticks. They gave him the leftover food from their bowls. And so he ate.

When[714] those solitary buddhas sat with their legs crossed and meditated, he would sit off to one side, cross his legs, and meditate as well. In this way he produced an unconscious state of mind[715] and was reborn among those divine beings who are unconscious.

"What do you think, monks? That monk who possessed the knowledge of the Tripiṭaka of the perfectly awakened Kāśyapa's teachings and who later became a pork dealer was none other than the monk Panthaka. Since he was stingy[716] and didn't teach a single verse to anyone, and since he butchered pigs, [he later passed away] from among the unconscious beings and was reborn here. As a result of that action, he became a fool, an absolute fool, an idiot, a complete idiot." [506]

The Venerable Panthaka and Jīvaka Kumārabhūta

When the venerable Panthaka went forth as a monk according to the dharma and monastic discipline that have been so well expressed, Jīvaka heard just that: "Panthaka has gone forth as a monk according to the dharma and monastic discipline that have been so well expressed." Then Jīvaka reflected, "If the Blessed One will come to Rājagṛha, I will feed the entire community of monks led by the Buddha but not Bhadanta Panthaka."[717]

Meanwhile the Blessed One, after staying in Śrāvastī as he long as he pleased, set out traveling toward Rājagṛha. Traveling along, he eventually arrived in Rājagṛha, and in Rājagṛha he stayed in the bamboo grove at Kalandakanivāpa (Squirrel Feeding Place).

Jīvaka Kumārabhūta (Forever Young) heard that the Blessed One, after traveling through the Magadha countryside, was now staying in the bamboo grove at Kalandakanivāpa. When he heard this, he approached the Blessed One and, having approached, placed his head in veneration at the Blessed One's feet and then sat down at a respectful distance. The Blessed One instructed, incited, inspired, and delighted Jīvaka Kumārabhūta, who was seated at a respectful distance, with a discourse on the dharma. After he instructed, incited, inspired, and delighted him in many ways with this discourse on the dharma, he became silent.

Jīvaka Kumārabhūta then got up from his seat, properly arranged his robe on one shoulder, bowed toward the Blessed One with his hands respectfully folded, and said this to him: "May the Blessed One, along with the community of monks, accept this invitation to eat at my home tomorrow."

Now lord buddhas are difficult to approach and their presence is difficult to bear, so Jīvaka Kumārabhūta wasn't able to say anything to the Blessed One about excluding Bhadanta Panthaka. [Nevertheless,][718] Jīvaka Kumārabhūta rejoiced and delighted in the words of the Blessed One,[719] left the Blessed One's presence, and approached the venerable Ānanda. Having approached, he placed his head in veneration at the venerable Ānanda's feet and then sat down at a respectful distance. Sitting down at a respectful distance, Jīvaka Kumārabhūta said this to the venerable Ānanda: "Please be informed, Bhadanta Ānanda, that I have invited the entire community of monks led by the Buddha to eat in my home tomorrow but not Bhadanta Panthaka."

"And so, Jīvaka, this will lead to an increase in your religious merit,"[720] the venerable Ānanda said.

Jīvaka Kumārabhūta rejoiced and delighted in the words of the venerable Ānanda, placed his head in veneration at the venerable Ānanda's feet, and then departed.

When the venerable Ānanda was sure that Jīvaka Kumārabhūta had departed, [507] he approached the venerable Panthaka. Having approached, he said this to him: "There is something you should know, venerable Panthaka. Jīvaka Kumārabhūta has invited the entire community of monks led by the Buddha to eat in his home tomorrow but not the venerable Panthaka."

"And so, Bhadanta Ānanda, this will lead to an increase in his religious merit," [the venerable Panthaka said].

That very night Jīvaka Kumārabhūta prepared hard and soft foods, both fresh and fine, and then at daybreak he got up, prepared the seats, and set out pitchers of water. Then he had a messenger inform the Blessed One that it was now the appropriate time: "It is time, Bhadanta. The food is ready. Now the Blessed One may do as the time permits."

Later in the morning the Blessed One got dressed, took his bowl and robe, and, leading the community of monks that surrounded him, approached Jīvaka Kumārabhūta's home. Having approached, he sat down in front of the community of monks in the seat specially prepared for him. After sitting down, the Blessed One addressed the venerable Ānanda: "Leave aside a place for Panthaka."[721]

Jīvaka Kumārabhūta took a golden water pitcher and stood in the area of the elders. The Blessed One wouldn't accept the stream of water [that he poured].[722]

"Why won't the Blessed One accept the stream of water [that I pour]?"[723] Jīvaka Kumārabhūta asked.

"The entire community of monks still hasn't assembled," the Blessed One said. "It isn't complete."[724]

"Blessed One, who hasn't come?" Jīvaka Kumārabhūta asked.

"The monk Panthaka,"[725] the Blessed One said.

"Blessed One," Jīvaka said, "I didn't invite him,"

"Jīvaka, didn't you invite the community of monks led by the Buddha?" the Blessed One asked.

"Yes, Blessed One, that is who I invited."

"Is Panthaka outside the community of monks?

"No, he isn't."[726]

"Then go and send for him," the Blessed One said to Jīvaka.

Jīvaka Kumārabhūta reflected, "I'll send for him out of deference to the Blessed One, but I won't serve him with respect."

He sent off a messenger: "Go and inform Bhadanta Panthaka."

Meanwhile the venerable Panthaka magically created thirteen hundred monks[727] and stood there among them. [508] The messenger went there and called out, "Panthaka!" Many monks replied. So the messenger returned to Jīvaka and said, "The bamboo grove at Kalandakanivāpa is filled with monks just as it was before."[728]

[Jīvaka Kumārabhūta told the Blessed One what had happened.][729]

"Go and say that whoever is the real Panthaka should come forward," the Blessed One said.

So the messenger went there and said, "Whoever is the real Panthaka should come forward."

Then the venerable Panthaka went to Jīvaka Kumārabhūta's house and sat down in his place.

Jīvaka Kumārabhūta began to serve the community of monks led by the Buddha. Then he served the venerable Panthaka but without respect.

The Blessed One reflected, "Since this senior disciple is great like Mount Sumeru, Jīvaka Kumārabhūta receives forgiveness. The venerable Panthaka's virtues should be made known." Therefore the Blessed One didn't pass his bowl to the venerable Ānanda.

As a rule the most senior monks' bowls are not to be taken [and filled with food] as long as there is no one to take the Blessed One's bowl [and fill it with food].[730]

The venerable Panthaka reflected, "Why are the bowls of the Blessed One and the most senior monks not being taken? It is because I am to make my virtues known here." Then the venerable Panthaka offered half his seat as a sign of respect, stretched out his arm like the trunk of an elephant, and took the Blessed One's bowl.

Now Jīvaka Kumārabhūta, who was standing in the area of the elders, saw this and reflected, "Who is this senior monk who makes use of his magical powers and displays a miracle?"[731] He went and followed the bowl until he eventually came to see the venerable Panthaka. When Jīvaka Kumārabhūta saw him, he fainted. Splashed with water, he regained his senses. Then he fell prostrate at the venerable Panthaka's feet, begged for forgiveness, and uttered these verses:

A shrine's virtues are eternal,
so too water infused with sandalwood.
The sweet smell of the lotus is eternal as well.
Pure liquid gold shines eternal, as does pure beryl.

The matchless anger in wicked people
is eternal like carvings in stone.
The joy in noble people is eternal,
and the forgiveness of arhats remains steadfast.

The venerable Panthaka said, "You are forgiven, Jīvaka."

The monks questioned the Lord Buddha: "Look, Bhadanta. When Jīvaka Kumārabhūta didn't know of the venerable Panthaka's virtues, [509] he was disrespectful, but when he knew of his virtues, he fell prostrate at his feet and begged for forgiveness."

"Yes, monks," the Blessed One said, "not only now, but also in the past. When he didn't know of his virtues, he was disrespectful, but when he knew of his virtues, he fell prostrate at his feet and begged for forgiveness. Listen to this."

The Thoroughbred Horse and the Potter

Long ago, monks, a caravan leader took five hundred horses from the North Country and came to the Middle Country to sell them.[732] Meanwhile a thoroughbred horse[733] had descended into the womb of one of his mares. From the very day that he descended, the caravan leader's horses no longer neighed.

The caravan leader reflected, "Have my horses fallen sick? Is that why they don't neigh?"

After some time, that mare gave birth. A colt was born. From that day on,[734] the horses were never quite normal again.[735]

The caravan leader reflected, "This colt that's been born must be an unlucky creature. It's his fault that my horses have taken sick." [With the other horses in tow,] he rode that mare of his each day, feeding her the appropriate foods mixed with fresh barley.[736]

Eventually the caravan leader arrived at a town called Pūjita (Worshipped) just as the rainy season began.[737] He reflected, "If I continue on, the horses' hooves will get wet and go bad,[738] and then the horses won't be fit for sale. I'll pass the rains right here." While he was passing the rains there,[739] some local residents who were craftsmen provided for him, offering him their goods. When it was time for the caravan leader to go, the craftsmen approached him, and he distributed various things among them.

Now there was one potter who lived there who had also provided for him, offering him his goods.

"Dear husband," his wife said to him, "the caravan leader is leaving. Go! Go there and ask him for something!"

So the potter brought a lump of clay to the caravan leader, who was already on his way out of town, and stood before him.[740] The caravan leader saw him and said to him, "My friend, you've come very late."

"Do you have anything to give me?"

"Everything is gone," he said. Now the caravan leader had misgivings about that colt, so he said, "Well, there is this one colt. [510] If you like him,[741] you can take him with you."

"That's just great," the potter said. "I'll make some pots, and he'll break them!" The colt began to lick the potter's feet with his tongue. The potter took a liking to the horse, so he took him and left.

"Did you get anything from the caravan leader?" his wife asked.

"Yes, I got something. This colt."

"That's just great. You'll make pots, and he'll break them!"

The colt began to lick her feet. She took a liking to him as well. Moving among the pots that were drying,[742] the colt didn't break a single one.

"Excellent," his wife said to him. "This colt moves about very knowingly."

One time the potter went to get some clay. The colt followed close behind him. When the potter had filled a sack with clay, the colt lowered his back. The potter then loaded the sack of clay on the colt's back, and the colt lead him back home.

"My dear, this is an excellent colt!" the potter said to his wife. "I'll never have to carry clay by myself again. I'll load it onto him out there, and you can unload it here." Then he offered the colt some chaff and straw.[743]

At that time in the city of Vārāṇasī, a king named Brahmadatta ruled a kingdom that was thriving, prosperous, and crowded with people.[744]

One day his thoroughbred horse died. Some neighboring vassal kings[745] heard that King Brahmadatta's thoroughbred horse had died.

"Either present us taxes and tributes," they ordered him, "or else as soon as you go to that park [you like] outside the city, we'll bind you around the neck and take you with us!"[746]

The king didn't present them with taxes and tributes, nor did he go out to the park.

Eventually the caravan leader arrived in the city of Vārāṇasī. King Brahmadatta heard that a caravan leader from the North Country had arrived in Vārāṇasī with horses for sale. He addressed his ministers: "Gentlemen, how long do I have to stay here in the city before I can return to the park. [511] Go and find a thoroughbred horse!"

The ministers went to the caravan leader and looked at his horses. "Gentlemen," they said to each other, "these horses could only have been trained by a thoroughbred,[747] but there's no thoroughbred horse here."

After examining the mare,[748] they conferred among themselves. "This mare gave birth to a thoroughbred horse, but he doesn't appear to be here." They then approached the caravan leader and asked, "Did you sell a horse or give one away to anyone?"

"I didn't sell any horse," he said, "but I did give away an unlucky colt to a potter in the town of Pūjitaka."[749]

Again they conferred among themselves. "Gentlemen, this caravan leader is a complete idiot! He's given away a lucky horse and comes here bringing nothing but unlucky ones!"

They went and asked the king's permission and then traveled to Pūjitaka. Once there they approached the potter and, having approached, asked, "What use do you have for this colt?"

"He carries clay for me," he said.

"We'll give you a donkey," they said. "You give us the colt."

"He's very good to me," he said.

"Then we'll give you a cart with four bulls."

"He's really very good to me," he said.

"If that's the case," they said, "then give it some thought, and we'll come back tomorrow." With these words, they departed.

Then the colt said, "Why don't you give me to them? Do you think I should carry clay and eat chaff and thorny straw?[750] I should carry a kṣatriya king who has been duly consecrated and eat roots smeared with honey off a golden plate! Since they say that I'm a colt, you should say, 'Are you embarrassed to say that he's a thoroughbred horse?' They'll come again[751] tomorrow and they'll tell you to name your price. You should say, 'Give me one hundred thousand gold pieces or else as much gold as the horse can pull with his right thigh.'"

The next day the ministers approached the potter and asked, "Friend, have you given it some thought?"

"I've given it some thought. Are you embarrassed to say that he's a thoroughbred horse?"

"He's an idiot," they said to each other. [512] "Does he even know whether or not this is a thoroughbred horse?[752] That caravan leader must have told him these things."

"Okay, let's say that he's a thoroughbred," they said. "Name your price."

"Either give me one hundred thousand gold pieces," he said, "or as much gold as the horse can pull with his right thigh."[753]

"He's strong," they reflected. "It's quite likely he can pull even more than that. Let's offer one hundred thousand gold pieces."

They went and informed King Brahmadatta that a thoroughbred horse was available for one hundred thousand gold pieces. The king, in turn, informed them that they should buy the thoroughbred horse for whatever the price.

So they bought him for one hundred thousand gold pieces. Then they brought him to Vārāṇasī and placed him in a stable.[754] He was given the most nutritious food,[755] but he wouldn't eat it.

"Have you brought back a thoroughbred horse that's sick?" the king asked.

"No, but let's examine him nonetheless."

Then the horse's groom uttered these verses:[756]

"Do you remember, swift horse, in the potter's stable[757]
when you lacked both food and water?[758]
You were merely a gaunt head,[759] skin, and bones,[760]
grazing on grass you had to crush with your teeth.

But that's not why you don't eat now, respected as you are.[761]
Don't stay here. Eat and lead a thousand vehicles![762]
This is a good stable for a thirsty horse.[763]
Why don't you eat? Tell me now. I've asked nicely."[764]

Though endowed with great speed, integrity, and fortitude,[765]
the horse became impatient and spoke to him angrily.[766]
Then the excellent horse cultivated thoughts of restraint,
and his mind was filled with loving-kindness for his groom.

"You are proud that an offering has been made
according to the rules,
but you have not followed them as I rightly deserve.[767] [513]
It is best if I die here quickly
if I am not approached as a sage.[768]

Even if a bad person insults you for a long time,[769]
if you are virtuous, dear sir, there is no insult.
But if a good person insults you for even a moment,
if you are virtuous, [dear sir,] this is an insult."[770]

The groom said to the king, "My lord, the proper procedures for him were not followed. That is why the horse won't accept the nutritious foods mixed with barley."

"What are the proper procedures that should be followed for him?"[771]

"For him, this is the protocol: Make the road look beautiful for two and a half leagues. Then a consecrated king with his fourfold army should come to meet him, and at the place where he stops, fine copper-colored cloth should be tied down.[772] The king's eldest son should hold a hundred-ribbed umbrella above the horse's head. The king's eldest daughter should shoo away flies with a golden fan encrusted with jewels. The king's principal queen should carry roots smeared with honey on a golden plate for him to eat. And the king's chief minister should clear away the horse's dung with a golden shovel."[773]

"Then he's really the king!" the king said. "I'm not the king."

"My lord," the groom said, "this protocol isn't to be followed for him all the time. However, it should be carried out for a week."

"The past cannot be done over," the king said, "but what remains to be done shall be done."

At the place [where he stopped],[774] fine copper-colored cloth was tied up. The king's eldest son held up a hundred-ribbed umbrella. The king's eldest daughter shooed away flies with a golden yak-tail fan encrusted with jewels. The king's principal queen carried roots smeared with honey on a golden plate for him to eat. The king's minister cleared away the horse's dung with a golden shovel.

> Bearing the very best smelling creams,
> the king, with the groom, propitiated the horse.
> And the principal queen, with sweet love in her heart,
> was presented to the most excellent horse.[775]

Since the king wanted to go to the parkland [outside the city],[776] the thoroughbred horse approached him and arched his back.

The king asked the groom, [514] "Is the king somehow causing him back pain?"

"No, the horse is thinking that the king will experience pain from mounting him," he said.

Then the horse bent down, and the king mounted him and set off. As the horse was going along, he came to some water, but he wouldn't cross it.

"Is he afraid?" the king asked the groom.

"No, your majesty, he isn't afraid. He's thinking that he must not splash the king with water from his tail."

So his tail was put in a golden tube.[777] Only then did he enter the water.

Eventually the king arrived at the park, and there he remained without concern.

The neighboring vassal kings heard that King Brahmadatta had gone to the park, so they entered Vārāṇasī and closed the gates to the city. When King Brahmadatta heard that the vassal kings had barred the gates to the city, he mounted the thoroughbred horse.

Now in between Vārāṇasī and the park there was a lotus pond called Brahmāvatī (Presided Over by Brahmā) that was blanketed with blue, red, and white waterlilies. Gliding over those lotuses, the thoroughbred horse entered Vārāṇasī. The king was pleased and said to his ministers, "Gentlemen, what should be done for one who has given life back[778] to a kṣatriya king who has been duly consecrated?"

"My lord, he should be given half of the kingdom."

"He's an animal," the king said. "What use would he have with half a kingdom? Instead, on his behalf, for a week offerings are to be made, meritorious deeds are to be performed, and an unscheduled lunar festival is to be celebrated." And so for a week the ministers began to make offerings and perform meritorious deeds. And throughout the week they administered a lunar festival, even though it wasn't the appropriate time for one.

The caravan leader asked some men, "Gentlemen, why is there a lunar festival going on now when one isn't scheduled?"

"There's a town called Pūjita," they said, "and a thoroughbred horse was purchased from a potter there for one hundred thousand gold pieces and then brought here. The horse has given the king his life back. It's on his behalf, for a week, that they've now begun to make offerings, perform meritorious actions, and celebrate a lunar festival, even though it isn't the appropriate time for one."

The caravan leader reflected, "Could the colt that I gave up be this thoroughbred horse? I'll go and see." So he went to the thoroughbred horse, and the horse said to him, "My friend, what did you get for those horses of yours? [515] I got the potter one hundred thousand gold pieces!"

The caravan leader fainted and fell to the ground. Splashed with water, he regained his senses, and then he fell before the thoroughbred horse and begged for forgiveness.

"What do you think, monks? That caravan leader was none other than Jīvaka at that time and at that juncture. That thoroughbred horse was none other than Panthaka at that time and at that juncture. Back then as well when Jīvaka didn't know of Panthaka's virtues, he was disrespectful to him, but when he knew of his virtues, he fell prostrate at his feet and begged for forgiveness. Now too when he didn't know of his virtues, he was disrespectful, but when he knew of his virtues, he fell prostrate at his feet and begged for forgiveness."

So ends the *Cūḍāpakṣa-avadāna*, the thirty-fifth chapter in the glorious *Divyāvadāna*.

36. The Story of Mākandika

MĀKANDIKA-AVADĀNA[779]

Mākandika, Anupamā, and the Marriage Plot

THE LORD BUDDHA, after traveling through the Kuru countryside, arrived at the town of Kalmāṣadamya (Spotted Bullock).

At that time in Kalmāṣadamya there lived a wandering mendicant named Mākandika,[780] who had a wife named Sākali.[781] To him, a daughter was born who was beautiful, good-looking, and attractive, and sound in all parts of her body. Her limbs were fine, very fine. She was beyond comparison. For three weeks—that is, twenty-one days—the occasion of her birth was celebrated in full, and at the conclusion of the celebration,[782] a name was selected for her.

"What should this girl's name be?"

"This girl is beautiful, attractive, and pleasing," said Mākandika's relatives, "and sound in all parts of her body. Her limbs are fine, very fine. She is beyond comparison. Let the girl's name be Anupamā (Incomparable)." And so she was given the name Anupamā.

As she was raised and nourished, Mākandika reflected, "I won't give this girl in marriage to anyone because of his high standing, nor because of his wealth or learning. Instead, I'll give her to whatever man is as beautiful or more beautiful than she is." [516]

Meanwhile the Blessed One, having traveled through the Kuru countryside, arrived at Kalmāṣadamya, and once there he settled down in a Kuru village.

In the morning, the Blessed One got dressed, took his bowl and robe, and entered Kalmāṣadamya for alms. After wandering through Kalmāṣadamya for alms, he ate his meal, and after eating, he returned from his almsround. He then put away his bowl and robe, washed his feet, and sat at the base of a tree, crossing his legs so that he was curled up like the winding coil of a sleeping snake king.

At that time the mendicant Mākandika had gone out to get flowers and firewood. From far away the mendicant Mākandika saw the Blessed One sitting at the base of a tree, his legs crossed so that he was curled up like the winding coil of a sleeping snake king.

He was attractive,
he was handsome,
his mind and senses were calmed,
he possessed the highest mental tranquility,
and he shined with splendor
like a sacrificial pillar made of gold.

Seeing him, Mākandika was pleased and delighted, and he reflected, "This ascetic is attractive and handsome, and he would captivate anyone. A suitable husband is difficult to find for any woman, but how much more so in the case of Anupamā. I have found a son-in-law!"

Mākandika approached his home and, having approached, said to his wife, "Let me tell you this, my dear. I have found a husband for our daughter! Adorn her! I will give Anupamā to him in marriage."

"To whom will you give her?" she asked.

"To the ascetic Gautama," he said.

"Let's go and see him," she said.

So Mākandika went with her. Sākali saw him from a distance, and as she approached, a memory occurred to her. She uttered this verse:

Wise one, I saw this great seer
wandering for alms in Kalmāṣadamya.
As he passes, the earth lights up for him
with the splendor of jewels[783] and remains flat.[784]

A husband like this won't accept a maiden.[785]
Turn back! Let's go home.

Then he uttered a verse: [517]

Inauspicious Sākalikā! At this auspicious time,
you speak inauspicious words.[786]
If he is quickly made to stray,[787]
he'll again indulge in sense pleasures.

Sākalikā adorned Anupamā in fine clothes and jewelry and then set out.

Meanwhile the Blessed One had moved from that part of the forest to another. The mendicant Mākandika saw the Blessed One laying out grass for a bed, and seeing this, he addressed his wife: "Let me tell you this, my dear. This bed of grass is for your daughter!"

She uttered this verse:

An impassioned man's bed is in disarray.
A hateful man's bed is forcibly beaten down.
A deluded man's bed is arranged backward.[788]
But this bed has been used by one free from attachment.

A husband like this won't accept a maiden.
Turn back! Let's go home.

[To which Mākandika replied:]

Inauspicious Sākalikā! At this auspicious time,
you speak inauspicious words.
If he is quickly made to stray,
he'll again indulge in sense pleasures.

The mendicant Mākandika saw the footprints of the Blessed One, and seeing them, he said to his wife, "These are the footprints, my dear, of your future son-in-law!"

She uttered this verse:

An impassioned man's footprint is lightly cast.
A hateful man's footprint is deeply pressed.
A deluded man's footprint is splayed out.
But a footprint like this belongs to one free from attachment.

A husband like this won't accept a maiden.
Turn back! Let's go home.

[To which Mākandika replied:]

Inauspicious Sākalikā! [At this auspicious time,
you speak inauspicious words.
If he is quickly made to stray,
he'll again indulge in sense pleasures].[789]

Then the Blessed One spoke aloud. The mendicant Mākandika listened and heard[790] that it was the Blessed One speaking aloud. Hearing this, he addressed his wife: "This, my dear, is your future son-in-law speaking aloud!"

Then she uttered this verse: [518]

An impassioned man has a faltering voice.
A hateful man has a harsh voice.

A deluded man has an agitated voice.
But this man is a buddha, with a thundering
  Brahmā-like voice.[791]

A husband like this won't accept a maiden.
Turn back! Let's go home.

[To which he replied:]

Inauspicious Sākalikā! [At this auspicious time,
you speak inauspicious words.
If he is quickly made to stray,
he'll again indulge in sense pleasures].[792]

The Blessed One observed the mendicant Mākandika from a distance. The mendicant Mākandika saw the Blessed One observing him, and seeing this, he addressed his wife: "This, my dear, is your future son-in-law looking at me!"

She uttered this verse:

An impassioned man has a fickle gaze.
A hateful man sees as does a snake with deadly venom.
A deluded man looks out as though into dense darkness.
But the man who is free from attachment, brahman,
looks ahead with eyes downcast.[793]

A husband like this won't accept a maiden.
Turn back! Let's go home.

[To which Mākandika replied:]

Inauspicious Sākalikā! [At this auspicious time,
you speak inauspicious words.

If he is quickly made to stray,
he'll again indulge in sense pleasures].[794]

The Blessed One began doing walking meditation. The mendicant Mākandika saw the Blessed One doing walking meditation, and upon seeing him, he addressed his wife: "This is your future son-in-law doing walking meditation!"

She uttered this verse:

Both his eyes and his gaze,
when he walks and when he stands,[795]
are still like a lotus in calm water,
each eye resplendent on his distinguished face.

A husband like this won't accept a maiden.
Turn back! Let's go home.

[To which Mākandika replied:]

Inauspicious Sākalikā! At this auspicious time,
you speak inauspicious words. [519]
If he is quickly made to stray,
he'll again indulge in sense pleasures.

Vaśiṣṭha, Uśīra, and Maunalāyana[796]
were deluded by a desire for offspring.
This law of the sages is truly eternal,
and this eternal law produces offspring.[797]

Then the mendicant Mākandika approached the Blessed One and, having approached, said this to him:

May the Blessed One behold my virtuous daughter,
a shapely and well-adorned young woman.
I offer this amorous girl to you.
With her behave like a man of virtue,
like the moon in the sky with his consort Rohiṇī.[798]

The Blessed One reflected, "If I address Anupamā with kind words, given the situation, she'll end up dying in a sweat of passion. Instead, I'll speak to her with harsh words." With this in mind, he uttered this verse:

Brahman, even when I saw Māra's daughters,
I felt neither craving nor passion[799]—
I have no desire at all for sensual pleasures.
Therefore I can't bring myself to touch this girl,
filled as she is with piss and shit,
not even with my foot.[800]

Then Mākandika uttered this verse:

Is it that you see this daughter of mine
as defective, or without beauty and virtue,
that you have no desire for this beautiful girl,
like a sensualist for the solitary?[801]

And then the Blessed One uttered these verses:

A deluded man who desires sense objects,
would long for your daughter, brahman,
Such a deluded man, not free from passion,
would long for a lovely girl
likewise attached[802] to sense objects. [520]

But I am a buddha, best of sages, fully active,[803]
who has obtained awakening, auspicious and unsurpassed.
Just as a lotus is not defiled by drops of water,
so I live in the world, completely undefiled.

And just as a blue waterlilly in muddy water
is in no way defiled by mud,[804]
in just this way, brahman, I live in the world,
totally separate[805] from sense pleasures.

In response, Anupamā, whom the Blessed One had described using the words *piss* and *shit*, became joyless and depressed. The passion that possessed her was gone, and [self-]loathing came to possess her instead. She felt heaviness in her bones, and her eyes glazed over.[806]

At that time a certain old monk[807] was standing behind the Blessed One, and the old monk said this to him:

You who see all, accept this girl then offer her to me.
Then she will be in my charge,[808] Blessed One.
Since I am lustful, wise one, let me enjoy
this ornamented beauty as I please.

Thus addressed, the Blessed One said this to the old monk: "Go away, foolish man! Don't remain before me!"

Enraged, [the old monk] uttered this verse:

This bowl of yours, this robe and staff
and water pot—may they desert you![809]
And you can care for the discipline yourself,
like a nursemaid for a child on her lap.

Having spoken thus,[810] the old monk rejected the discipline, and thinking "This man is certainly not noble," he approached the mendicant Mākandika. Having approached, he said this to him: "Offer Anupamā to me."

Incensed, Mākandika said, "Old man [521], I wouldn't give her to you even to look at, much less to touch."

After the mendicant Mākandika spoke these words,[811] the old man became so angry at him that he coughed up hot blood. Then he died and was reborn in the realms of hell.

Some monks in doubt questioned the Lord Buddha, the remover of all doubts: "Look, Bhadanta. Anupamā was offered in marriage,[812] and yet the Blessed One did not accept her."

"Yes, monks," the Blessed One said, "not only now, but also in the past. She was offered in marriage, and yet I did not accept her. Listen to this."

The Blacksmith and the Expert Craftsman

Long ago, monks, in a certain market town there lived a blacksmith. He brought home a girl from an appropriate family as his wife, [and with her he fooled around, enjoyed himself, and made love. After some time, from fooling around, enjoying himself, and making love, his wife became pregnant. After eight or nine months, she gave birth][813] to a daughter who was beautiful, good-looking, and attractive. Raised and nourished, in time she grew up. The blacksmith reflected, "I won't give my daughter in marriage to anyone because of his high standing nor because of his beauty or wealth. I'll only give her in marriage to the man who is my equal or my better as a craftsman."

Meanwhile a young man begging for alms entered the blacksmith's home. The girl brought alms out to him. When the young man saw her, he said, "Young woman, have you been given in marriage to anyone or not?"

"At the time when I was born," she said, "my father made a resolution[814] that makes it difficult for him to give me in marriage to anyone."

"What did your father say?"

"That he would only give me in marriage to the man who was his equal or better as a craftsman."

"What craft does your father know?"

"He makes needles that float on water."

The young man reflected, "Even though I don't desire the girl, her father's pride should be destroyed."

Now the young man was an expert in many kinds of arts and crafts. So he borrowed some blacksmith's tools,[815] and elsewhere in a workshop he fashioned very fine needles that floated on water. He then fashioned one large needle into which seven needles could fit and float with it. After making all these needles, he returned to the blacksmith's home and called out, "Needles! Needles!" The blacksmith's daughter saw him and uttered this verse [522]:

> You must be mad, reckless, or with no sense.
> You come to sell needles at a blacksmith's house!

Then the young man uttered these verses:

> I'm not mad, reckless, or with no sense,
> but to topple your father's pride I exhibit my craft.
>
> If your father were to know the extent of my skill,
> he'd give you to me, and great[816] wealth besides.

"What craft do you know?" she asked.

"I can make a needle that floats on water."

She informed her mother, "Mom, a craftsman has come."

"Send him in," she said. The girl sent him in.

"What craft do you know?" the blacksmith's wife asked. He explained. She informed her husband, "Dear husband, this boy is a craftsman. He knows such-and-such a craft."

"If that's the case, bring some water," he said. "Then I'll see."

She filled a pot with water and placed it before him. The young man threw in a needle. It began to float. And so too did a second and a third needle. Then he threw in the large needle. It began to float as well. He then inserted one of the needles into the large needle. It continued to float, just as before. Then he inserted a second needle, a third, and so on until he had placed seven needles into the large needle. Just as before, it continued to float.

The blacksmith reflected, "He is a better craftsman than me! I'll offer him my daughter in marriage." With this in mind, he adorned the young girl with all kinds of ornaments, then took her with his left hand and with his right hand picked up a small golden pitcher. He then stood in front of the young brahman and said, "Young man, I offer this daughter of mine to you as a wife."

"I don't desire her," the young man said. "I desire only that the pride you have should be destroyed. This is why I have displayed my craft."

The Blessed One said, "What do you think, monks? The young man was none other than me at that time and at that juncture. The blacksmith was none other than Mākandika at that time and at that juncture.[817] The blacksmith's wife was none other than Mākandika's wife at that time and at that juncture. [523] And the blacksmith's daughter was none other than Anupamā at that time and at that juncture. Then too she was offered in marriage, but I did not accept her. Now again she was offered in marriage, and yet again I did not accept her.

Once again some monks in doubt questioned the Lord Buddha, the remover of all doubts: "Look, Bhadanta. That old man made improper advances toward Anupamā and then he met with his death."[818]

"Yes, monks," the Blessed One said, "not only now, but also in the past. He made improper advances toward Anupamā, and then he met with his death, as did his wives. Listen to this."

Siṃhala and the Demon

Long ago, monks, in the city of Siṃhakalpā (Leonine) a king named Siṃhakeśarin (Lion Mane) ruled a kingdom that was thriving, prosperous, and safe, with plenty of food and throngs of people, [that was free from quarrel and strife, with no hustle and bustle, thieves, or diseases, that was rich in rice, sugarcane, cattle, and buffalo. He was a just and virtuous king, and][819] he ruled according to dharma.

At that time in Siṃhakalpā there lived a caravan leader named Siṃhaka (Little Lion) who was rich, wealthy, and prosperous, with vast and extensive holdings, [and who had amassed a wealth like the god Vaiśravaṇa. Truly, he rivaled Vaiśravaṇa in wealth.

The caravan leader Siṃhaka] brought home a girl [from an appropriate family as his wife.][820] She became pregnant, and she heard no unkind words until the fetus matured.[821] After eight or nine months, she gave birth. A boy was born who was beautiful, good-looking, and attractive, radiant with a golden complexion, who had a parasol-shaped head, lengthy arms, a broad forehead, a sonorous voice,[822] joined eyebrows, a prominent nose, and who was sound in all parts of his body.

[Then his relatives came together and assembled.][823] For three weeks—that is, twenty-one days—they celebrated the occasion of his birth in full, and then they selected a name for him.[824]

"What should this boy's name be?"

"This boy is the son of the caravan leader Siṃhaka,"[825] his relatives said. "So let the boy's name be Siṃhala (Related to Siṃha)." And so he was given the name Siṃhala.

The boy Siṃhala was given over to eight nurses—[two shoulder nurses, two nursemaids, two wet nurses, and two playtime nurses. Raised by these eight nurses, who nourished him with milk, yogurt, fresh butter, clarified butter, buttercream, and other special provisions that were very pure, he grew quickly like a lotus in a lake.

When he grew up, he was entrusted to teachers to learn writing and then arithmetic, accounting, matters relating to trademarks, and to debts, deposits, and trusts, the science of building-sites, the science of cloth, the science of wood, the science of jewels, the science of elephants, the science of horses, the science of young men, and the science of young women.][826] In each of the eight sciences, he became learned and well versed, capable of explaining and expounding upon them.

On Siṃhala's behalf, his father had three residences built—one for the cold season, one for the hot season, and one for the rainy season; and he had women's quarters established—senior, intermediate, and junior.

One day Siṃhala said to his father, "Dad, give me permission to set sail in the great ocean."

"Son," he said, "so vast is my wealth that even if [524] you made use of my jewels as you would sesame seeds, rice, lentils, and so on, even then my riches wouldn't diminish, give out, or be completely exhausted. So, for as long as I live, fool around, enjoy yourself, and make love! After I die, you can acquire your own wealth."

Again and again Siṃhala said, "Dad, give me permission to set sail in the great ocean."

Realizing that his son was absolutely determined, he said, "Son, do as you wish, but you'll have to withstand fear and dread." Then he had bells rung in the capital Siṃhakalpā for the following proclamation: "Listen, respected citizens of Siṃhakalpā and merchants visiting from other countries! The caravan leader Siṃhala will set sail in the great ocean. Whoever among you is eager to set sail in the great ocean with Siṃhala as your caravan leader, all the while exempt from customs and freight fees, gather up your goods for export across the great ocean." Five hundred merchants then gathered up their goods for export across the great ocean.

Siṃhala said farewell to his mother and father, his servants, his friends, relations, and relatives, and at an opportune day, date, and time he performed auspicious rituals and benedictions for a safe journey. Then he loaded[827] many goods for export across the ocean in carts, carriers, baskets, and containers, and on camels, bulls, and donkeys, and with his attendants and the five hundred merchants, he set out. After passing through marketplaces, hamlets, villages, districts, and capitals, one after another, and seeing various trading centers, he arrived at the seashore.

Here the full *Demon Sūtra* (*Rākṣasī-sūtra*) is to be told in its entirety.[828]

. . . All the merchants fell from Bālāha, the king of horses, and were eaten by the demons. Only Siṃhala managed to return to Jambudvīpa (Black Plum Island) safe and sound.

Siṃhala's wife, who was also a demon, was addressed by the other demons: "Sister, each of us has eaten her own husband, yet you let your husband escape. It would be best if you brought him to us. If not, we'll eat you."

Frightened, she said, "If you insist,[829] bear with me and I'll bring him to you.

"Very well then," they said. "Do as you say."

The demon who was Siṃhala's wife magically transformed herself so that she had a terrifying appearance and then traveled at great speed and appeared before the caravan leader Siṃhala. The caravan leader Siṃhala [525] unsheathed his sword, and she became frightened and ran away.

Meanwhile a caravan arrived from the Middle Country. That demon [took on human form,] fell prostrate at the caravan leader's feet, and [telling a lie] said, "Caravan leader, I am the daughter of the king of Tāmradvīpa (Copper Island). He gave me to the caravan leader Siṃhala as a wife. While he was sailing across the great ocean, his ship was destroyed by a kind of fish—a *makara* monster. As a result he decided that I was inauspicious, and he abandoned me. Please make him take me back as his wife."

"I'll make him forgive you and take you back."

The caravan leader approached Siṃhala. After standing there for a while making small talk, he then said, "Friend, you married this princess. Don't abandon her unjustly. Forgive her!"

"Friend, she isn't a princess," he said. "She is a demon from Tāmradvīpa."

"Then how did she get here?"

Siṃhala explained what had happened.

The caravan leader remained silent.

In due course the caravan leader Siṃhala arrived back home.

The demon assumed the form of a very lovely woman, young and exceedingly beautiful, and magically created a son with a handsome appearance who looked just like Siṃhala. She then took this son and arrived at the capital Siṃhakalpā. Once there she waited by the door to the caravan leader Siṃhala's home. A crowd of people recognized the boy by his face and whom it resembled.

"Friends," they said, "it's clear—this boy must the son of the caravan leader Siṃhala."

"Gentlemen, you've recognized him!" the demon said. "Indeed this is his son."

"Sister, where have you come from?" they asked. "And whose daughter are you?"

"Gentlemen, I am the daughter of the king of Tāmradvīpa," she said. "I was given to the caravan leader Siṃhala as a wife. While the caravan leader was sailing across the great ocean, his ship was destroyed by a fish of some kind. As a result he decided that I was inauspicious, and he abandoned me unjustly. Somehow I managed to make it here. I also have a small child.[830] Please make the caravan leader Siṃhala forgive me!"

The people informed Siṃhala's mother and father, who said to him, "Son, don't [abandon][831] this princess. She is helpless and has a small child.[832] Forgive her."

"Father, she isn't a princess," he said. "She is a demon who has come here from Tāmradvīpa."

"Son," his parents said, "all women are demons! Forgive her."

"Father, if you and Mother approve of her, then you can take care of her at home. [526] I'll go elsewhere."

"Son," they said, "we'd take very good care of her but only for your sake. If you don't approve of her, what do we want with her? We won't take care of her." So Siṃhala's parents sent her away.

She then went to King Siṃhakeśarin, whose ministers informed him, "My lord, a very beautiful young woman stands at the palace gate."

"Send her in," said the king. "I'll see her."

The ministers sent her in, and she captivated everyone's senses. When the king saw her, he was overcome with passion. After addressing her courteously with words of welcome, he said, "Where did you come from? How did you get here? And to whom do you belong?"

She fell prostrate at the king's feet and said, "My lord, I am the daughter of the king of Tāmradvīpa. I was given to the caravan leader Siṃhala as a wife. While he was sailing across the great ocean, his ship was destroyed by a fish of some kind—a *makara* monster. Hearing[833] that I was inauspicious, he abandoned me unjustly. Somehow I managed to make it here. I also have a small child.[834] My lord, please make the caravan leader Siṃhala forgive me!"

The king consoled her and then ordered his ministers: "Gentlemen, go and summon the caravan leader Siṃhala." They summoned him.

"Siṃhala," the king said, "take care of this princess. Forgive her."

"My lord, she isn't a princess," he said. "She is a demon who has come here from Tāmradvīpa."

"Caravan leader, all women are demons!" the king said. "Forgive her. Or, if you don't approve of her, give her to me."

"My lord, she is a demon!" the caravan leader said. "I won't give her to you nor will I choose her as a wife." The king nevertheless invited her into the royal women's quarters. He had fallen under her spell.

One day she gave a sleeping potion[835] to the king and the palace women. Then she went back to the demons of Tāmradvīpa and said, "Sisters, what use to you is the caravan leader Siṃhala? I've given a sleeping potion to King Siṃhakeśarin and the palace women. Come! Let's eat them."

The demons assumed their true and absolutely terrifying forms, with deformed hands, feet, and noses, and then at night came to Siṃhakalpā. There they ate the king and all the palace women and attendants.

When dawn broke, the palace gates didn't open. Carrion-eating birds began to circle over the palace. Ministers, soldiers, townspeople, and villagers stood at the palace gates. [527] Word spread all around the capital Siṃhakalpā: "The palace gates haven't opened! Carrion-eating birds are circling over the palace! Ministers, soldiers, townsmen, and villagers are standing at the palace gates!"

When the caravan leader Siṃhala heard this, he quickly took his sword and went to the palace.

"Friends, brace yourselves,"[836] he said. "That demon has eaten the king."

"What do we do now?" the ministers asked.

"Bring a ladder," he said. "I'll take a look."

They brought a ladder, and the caravan leader Siṃhala took his sword and climbed up. The demons were frightened of him and fled, some taking with them [human][837] hands and feet, others taking heads. Then the caravan leader Siṃhala opened the gates to the palace, and the ministers had the palace cleaned up.

Townspeople, ministers, and villagers gathered together and said, "Friends, the king, along with the palace women and royal attendants, has been eaten by demons. The king has no son. So who should we consecrate as the new king?"

"One who is virtuous and wise," some said.

"Who besides the caravan leader Siṃhala is virtuous and wise?" others said. "Let's consecrate the caravan leader Siṃhala as king."

"Yes! Let's do so."

So they said to the caravan leader Siṃhala, "Caravan leader, please accept the throne and be our king."

"I make my living working as a merchant," he said. "What's the use of me being king?"

"Caravan leader," they said, "no one else can govern the kingdom. Please accept."

"I'll accept on one condition—you must follow my orders."

"Please accept. We'll follow your orders. Good luck to you!"[838] The people then beautified the city, and with great honor consecrated the caravan leader Siṃhala as king.

Siṃhala invited[839] teachers of various sciences from other countries, and from them he learned a great deal, studying archery from master archers and the like.

"Gentlemen," he ordered his ministers, "prepare the four branches of the military! Let's go! Let's drive the demons out of Tāmradvīpa!"

The ministers readied the four branches of the military. King Siṃhala loaded onto boats the very best elephants, horses, chariots, and men from the four branches of the military and then set out for Tāmradvīpa. In due course they arrived at the shores of Tāmradvīpa. [528]

The flag that signals disaster[840] for the demons began to flutter. The demons began to talk among themselves: "Friends, the flag that signals disaster[841] is fluttering. The people of Jambudvīpa must have come, eager for battle. Let's find out."

The demons went to the seashore and saw that many hundreds of ships had reached the shore.[842] Seeing this, they attacked with half their forces. Soon they were overpowered by the expert opposition and were slaughtered by the master archers. The surviving demons fell prostrate at King Siṃhala's feet and said, "My lord, forgive us!"

"I will forgive you," he said, "on one condition—you must relinquish control of the city,[843] go someplace else, and never commit an offense against anyone in my dominion."

"My lord," they said, "we'll do as you say."

"Good."

The demons relinquished control of the city and went elsewhere to live. Since King Siṃhala settled the area, it came to be known as Siṃhaladvīpa (Siṃhala's Island).[844]

"What do you think, monks? Siṃhala was none other than me at that time and at that juncture. King Siṃhakeśarin was none other than the old monk at that time and at that juncture. And the demon was none other than Anupamā at that time and at that juncture. Even then, the old man, because of his improper conduct toward Anupamā, met with his death. And now too, because of his improper conduct toward Anupamā, the old man has met with his death once again."

Jealous Anupamā and Faithful Śyāmāvatī

The mendicant Mākandika took Anupamā and went to Kauśāmbī, where he settled in a certain park. The man guarding the park informed King Udayana, king of the Vatsas, "Your majesty, a woman that is beautiful, good-looking, and attractive is staying in the park. She is suitable for my lord."

Hearing this, the king went to the park, and when he saw her, his senses were captivated. From the very moment he saw her, his heart was lost to her.

"To whom does this girl belong?" he asked the mendicant Mākandika.

"My lord," he said, "she is my daughter. My lord, she is no one else's."[845]

"Why not give her to me?"

"My lord, let her be given to the king."

"Excellent!" [529]

The great king had many wives.[846] Mākandika's daughter became another and moved into the Puṣpadanta Palace.[847] She was given an amount equal to the Puṣpadanta Palace[848] as well as five hundred attendants and a daily allowance of five hundred *kārṣāpaṇa* coins for fragrances and garlands. The mendicant Mākandika was appointed a chief minister. At that time King Udayana had three chief ministers: Yogāndharāyaṇa, Ghoṣila, and Mākandika.

One time a man approached King Udayana.

"Who are you?" the king asked.

"My lord, I am a bearer of good news," he said.

"Gentlemen," the king ordered his ministers, "offer a job to this bearer of good news." So the ministers gave him a job.

Later another man approached.

"Who are you?" the king asked him.

"My lord, I am a bearer of bad news," he said.

"Gentlemen," the king ordered his ministers, "offer a job to this bearer of bad news as well."

"My lord should never listen to bad news," they said.

"Gentlemen," the king said, "the duties of a king are vast. Offer him the job." So the ministers gave him a job as well.

One time King Udayana, Anupamā, and Śyāmāvatī (Dusky) [one of the king's other wives] were together in the same place. Then the king sneezed.

"Praise to the Buddha!" Śyāmāvatī said.

"Praise to my lord!" Anupamā said. And then she added, "Your majesty, Śyāmāvatī eats food that belongs to my lord, yet she praises the ascetic Gautama."

"Anupamā, don't take it that way,"[849] he said. "Śyāmāvatī is a lay disciple of the Buddha. Of course she offers praise to the ascetic Gautama."

Anupamā remained silent.

Then she said to her maidservant, "Girl, when my lord, Śyāmāvatī, and I are in private, throw a brass bowl down the stairs."

"As you wish."

And so, when the three of them were in private, the maidservant threw a brass bowl down the stairs.

"Praise to the Buddha!" Śyāmāvatī said.

"Praise to my lord!" Anupamā said. Then she added, "Śyāmāvatī eats food that belongs to my lord, yet she praises the ascetic Gautama."

"Anupamā," the king said, "don't make a fuss about this. She is a lay disciple of the Buddha. No offense has been committed here."

Now King Udayana would eat with[850] Śyāmāvatī one day and with

Anupamā the next day. Anupamā[851] ordered the royal bird-catcher: "On those days when it is Śyāmāvatī's turn to eat with the king, [530] bring him live partridges." And so the bird-catcher brought the king live partridges.

"Deliver them to Anupamā," the king said.

Anupamā heard this and said, "My lord, it's not my turn. It's Śyāmāvatī's turn."

"Friend," the king said, "go and deliver these to Śyāmāvatī."

The bird-catcher brought them to Śyāmāvatī. "Prepare these for my lord."

"What am I, a butcher of birds?" she asked. "It isn't permissible for me to kill living beings. Go away!"

The bird-catcher went and informed the king, "My lord, Śyāmāvatī said, 'What am I, a butcher of birds? It isn't permissible for me to kill living beings. Go away!'"

Anupamā heard this and said, "My lord, if she were told to prepare them for the ascetic Gautama, she and her attendants would prepare them immediately."

"Perhaps this is so," the king reflected. He spoke to the bird-catcher: "Friend, go and say this to Śyāmāvatī: 'Prepare them for the Blessed One.'"

The bird-catcher set out, and then in secret Anupamā said to him, "First kill the birds and then bring them to her." So the bird-catcher killed the birds and then brought them to Śyāmāvatī. He told her, "My lord said to prepare these for the Blessed One." So Śyāmāvatī and her attendants began to prepare them. The bird-catcher went and informed the king, "My lord, Śyāmāvatī and her attendants are preparing the birds."

Anupama said, "Did my lord hear that? If it isn't permissible for her to kill living beings, then it isn't permissible for her to do so on behalf of the ascetic Gautama, nor is it permissible for her to do so on behalf of my lord. But if it is permissible for her to do so on behalf of the ascetic Gautama, how is it that she thinks that it isn't permissible on behalf of my lord?"[852]

The king was enraged. He drew his bow and set out.

The world is made up of friends, enemies, and those in between.

One of Śyāmāvatī's attendants informed her, "My lord is absolutely furious. He has drawn his bow and is coming here! Beg him for forgiveness!"

Śyāmāvatī addressed her retinue:[853] "Sisters, you must all enter into a state of loving-kindness." So they all entered into a state of loving-kindness.

Then the king arrived, drew his bowstring to his ear, and shot an arrow. In midflight it fell to the ground. He shot a second arrow. It reversed direction and fell near the king. As he prepared to shoot a third arrow, Śyāmāvatī said, "My lord, don't shoot. Don't think that with all your power you can do everything."[854]

Becoming subdued, the king said, "Are you a goddess, a nāga, a yakṣa?[855] Or are you a celestial musician, a kinnara woman, or a great snake?

"No," she said.

"Then what are you?"

"A disciple of the Blessed One; a nonreturner. I have directly experienced the reward of the nonreturner in the presence of the Blessed One. And these five hundred women have seen the [four noble] truths."

The king was filled with faith and said, "I grant you a wish." [531]

"If my lord has faith," she said, "then when his majesty enters the women's quarters, may he hold himself in accordance with the dharma in my presence."[856]

"Very well," the king said. "It will be done."

The king [would take pleasure fooling around, enjoying himself, and making love] with Anupamā,[857] and in Śyāmāvatī's presence, he would follow the dharma and cultivate faith.[858] And when the king received fresh grains, fresh fruits, and the first pickings of a new harvest,[859] he would offer them first to Śyāmāvatī.

Now women are naturally jealous. So Anupamā reflected, "The king enjoys making love with me, but he makes offerings to Śyāmāvatī of fresh grains, fresh fruits, and the first pickings of a new harvest. I must devise a plan to have her killed!" And so Anupamā became obsessed with finding some way that Śyāmāvatī was vulnerable so that she could have her killed.

Now the king had a certain village chief [in his kingdom] who started a rebellion against him, so he sent in a division of the army. It returned beaten and defeated. So too did a second division and a third.

"My lord's power grows weaker," the king's ministers said. "The village chief's power increases. If my lord doesn't lead the battle himself, it's very likely that the village chief will become impossible to subdue."

Then the king had bells rung in Kauśāmbī for the following proclamation: "Everyone who lives by the sword in my dominion must join me in battle."

In preparation for his departure, the king addressed Yogāndharāyaṇa: "You stay here."

Yogāndharāyaṇa wouldn't consent. "I'm going with my lord!"[860] he said.

Then the king addressed Ghoṣila, and Ghoṣila said the same thing.

So the king had Mākandika stay behind and put him in charge, and he told him, "Please take good care of Śyāmāvatī."[861]

Even as the king prepared to depart, Mākandika followed him around, and the king repeated the same instructions. Though Mākandika was being kept from joining the battle, he nonetheless complied.

Mākandika then approached Anupamā.

"Father," she asked, "who has my lord put in charge here?"

"Me."

"Excellent!" she reflected. "I can take revenge with your help." With this in mind, she said, "Don't you know[862] who Śyāmāvatī is to me?"

"My daughter, I know that she is your co-wife."

"Father, that is true. And don't you know[863] which emotion is the most troubling?"

"My daughter, I know about envy and stinginess."[864]

"Father, if that's the case, have Śyāmāvatī killed."

"Do you think I'm that two-faced?" he asked. "Three times the king ordered me to take good care of Śyāmāvatī. [532] Her name shouldn't even be uttered!"[865]

"Father," Anupamā said, "are you that much of a fool? Is there any father so averse to his daughter's welfare that he feels more love for her co-wife? Have her killed! Then everything will be okay. If not, I'll put you back in the position you were in before."

Fearful, Mākandika reflected, "Kings fall under the power of women. Perhaps that's the case now." With this in mind, he said, "Daughter, I can't have her killed just like that! I'll devise a plan."[866]

"Very well," she said. "Do as you say."

Mākandika went to Śyāmāvatī and said, "My queen, is there anything I can do for you?"

"No, Mākandika, there's nothing you can do for me. These girls, however, study the word of the Buddha at night by lamplight. For this they need birchbark, ink, and reed pens as well as oil and wicks."[867]

"Very well, my queen," he said. "I will procure them." He procured them in great quantities then had them delivered and piled up at the gatehouse to the women's quarters [of the Puṣpadanta Palace].

"Mākandika," Śyāmāvatī said, "that's quite enough."

"My queen," Mākandika said, "I'll have all this brought inside. Then it won't be necessary to make repeated deliveries."[868]

Mākandika then set fire to the last pile of birchbark and brought in some grass. He kindled the flames and set the gatehouse on fire.

A crowd of people from Kauśāmbī rushed to put out the flames. Mākandika drew his sword and began to drive back the crowd.

"Stand back! Who are you to see the king's women!"[869]

A master mechanic[870] from Kauśāmbī said, "I'll use a special device to move this burning gatehouse someplace else."

But Mākandika spoke to him just as he had to the crowd, and the man fled.

Then Śyāmāvatī, using her magical powers, flew up into the air and said, "Sisters, the deeds that we ourselves have performed and accumulated have now come together, and their conditions have matured. They remain before us like an oncoming flood and will certainly come to pass. Those deeds were performed and accumulated by us alone. Who else will experience their results? As the Blessed One said,

> Not in the sky or in mid-ocean
> or by entering a mountain cave
> is there a place on earth to be found
> where one isn't overpowered by karma.[871] [533]

"Therefore you should stay focused on karma." And with that said, she uttered a verse:

> I saw the Blessed One,
> who is like a bulwark,
> and came to know the [four noble] truths
> and follow the teachings of the Buddha.

Led by Śyāmāvatī, those women flew into the air and then, like moths, cast themselves into the fire. And so, right there, those five hundred women, led by Śyāmāvatī, were consumed by the blaze. Kubjottarā (Hunchback), [Śyāmāvatī's maidservant], escaped through a water drain.[872]

Mākandika had the bodies of those five hundred women dumped at the cremation ground, and he had the palace cleaned up, inside and out. He also had a crowd of weeping people, both residents of Kauśāmbī and visitors from other countries, chased away.

The next morning a large group of monks got dressed, took their bowls and robes, and entered Kauśāmbī for alms. That large group of monks heard that in the city of Kauśāmbī, while Udayana, king of the Vatsas, had gone to the countryside, the women's quarters of his palace were consumed in a fire, as were five hundred women led by Śyāmāvatī.[873] Hearing this, they continued their almsround in Kauśāmbī, and when they were finished, they returned and approached the Blessed One.[874]

"Bhadanta," they said, "while wandering for alms in Kauśāmbī, we monks, who are many in number, heard that the women's quarters in the palace of Udayana, king of the Vatsas, were consumed in a fire[875] and that five hundred women led by Śyāmāvatī were consumed in the fire as well."

"Monks," the Blessed One said, "great is the demerit that this deluded man has earned. As a result, while Udayana, king of the Vatsas, had gone to the countryside, the women's quarters of his palace were consumed in a fire, as were five hundred women led by Śyāmāvatī. Monks, although this deluded man generated great demerit, those women did not suffer a bad rebirth. All those who died were pure individuals. Why is that?

"There were, in the women's quarters, women who had rid themselves of the five bonds to the lower realms of existence and have thus become spontaneously reborn [in a final existence], where they will attain final nirvāṇa. They are now nonreturners, destined not to return to this world again. Like this were the women in the women's quarters.

"There were, in the women's quarters, women who had rid themselves of the three bonds to existence as well as attachment, hate, and delusion[876] [534] and, having died, have now become once-returners. They will return to this world only once before putting an end to suffering. Like this were the women in the women's quarters.

"There were, in the women's quarters, women who had rid themselves of the three bonds to existence and have thus become stream-enterers, destined never to suffer a karmic downfall and devoted to constant meditation.[877] Their seventh existence will be their last, for after being reborn and cycling through saṃsāra as gods and humans seven times, they will put an end to suffering. Like this were the women in the women's quarters.

"There were, in the women's quarters, women who even at the cost of their own lives never transgressed the discipline. Like this were the women in the women's quarters.

"There were, in the women's quarters, women who died with faith in their hearts for me[878] and, after the dissolution of their bodies, have now been reborn in a favorable existence among the gods in a heavenly realm. Like this were the women in the women's quarters.

"Come,[879] monks, [let us behold] the bodies of the five hundred women who were led by Śyāmāvatī."

"Yes, Bhadanta," the monks replied, consenting to the Blessed One's request.

Then the Blessed One, together with that large group of monks, approached the [charred] bodies of those five hundred women. Having approached, the Buddha addressed the monks: "Monks, it is these five hundred bodies that made Udayana, king of the Vatsas, impassioned, attached, and lustful, that made him enslaved, infatuated, enthralled, and entranced. But a wise person would never touch them, not even with his foot."

And he uttered this verse:

> This world, which fosters delusion,
> appears as if magnificent.
> Fools, bound by attachment
> and enveloped in darkness,
> see the unreal as real, but
> in what they see there is nothing.

And then he said, "So then, monks, this is to be learned: 'We won't even have bad thoughts toward a burned stump, let alone a body with sensory consciousness.'[880] It is this, monks, that you should learn to do."

Now the citizens of Kauśāmbī gathered together and began to talk among themselves. "Friends, such a terrible misfortune has befallen the king! Who among us will inform the king of this?"

Some of them said, "Whoever is the bearer of bad news should inform him. Let's send for him."

"Yes, let's do it," others said. [535] So they summoned him and said, "Notify my lord of all the bad things that have occurred."

"Pay me my wages. Isn't the bearer of bad news to be paid? Well, now is the time.[881] Otherwise, you can notify him yourselves."

"But it's for this very reason that you've been given a job," they said. "It's your duty! Notify him."[882]

"I'll notify him on one condition—you must do as I say."

"Tell us! We'll do it."

"The king is to be notified in the following way: Provide me with five hundred male elephants, five hundred female elephants, five hundred stallions, five hundred mares, five hundred boys, five hundred girls, and one hundred thousand gold coins. Then, on a canvas, draw the town of Kauśāmbī and the Puṣpadanta Palace, showing the birchbark, ink, reed pens, oil, and wicks,[883] as well as Mākandika setting fire to the last pile of birchbark. And show the gatehouse catching fire, the people of Kauśāmbī rushing to put it out, and Mākandika drawing his sword and driving them back. And show the master mechanic coming and saying, 'I'll move this burning gatehouse someplace else,' and then Mākandika driving him back as well. And show the five hundred women led by Śyāmāvatī flying into the air and then casting themselves into the fire."

"Yes, we'll do it," they said.

So they presented him with five hundred male elephants, five hundred female elephants, five hundred stallions, five hundred mares, five hundred boys, five hundred girls, and one hundred thousand gold coins. And, on a canvas, they drew the town of Kauśāmbī and the

Puṣpadanta Palace, showing birchbark, ink, reed pens, oil, and wicks,[884] as well as Mākandika setting fire to the last pile of birchbark. And it showed the gatehouse catching fire, the people of Kauśāmbī rushing to put it out, and Mākandika drawing his sword and driving them back. And it showed the master mechanic coming and saying, "I'll move this burning gatehouse someplace else," and then Mākandika driving him back as well. And it showed the five hundred women led by Śyāmāvatī flying into the air and casting themselves into the fire. All of this was drawn on that canvas.

Then the bearer of bad news sent a letter to the king's ministers that said, "Such a terrible misfortune has befallen the king! I will notify him in a skillful way. [536] You must provide assistance." After writing that letter to them,[885] the bearer of bad news, accompanied by the four branches of the military, went to a certain district and waited.

Then he sent a letter to [King][886] Udayana saying, "My lord, I am king in this district. My son has been carried off[887] by Death. I shall therefore do battle against him. If you can defeat him in battle, that would be good. If not, I'll pay Death a ransom of five hundred male elephants, five hundred female elephants, five hundred stallions, five hundred mares, five hundred boys, five hundred girls, plus one hundred thousand gold coins to recover my son."

Meanwhile the powerful village chief would not surrender to King Udayana.

[After reading the letter,] the king said to his ministers, "Gentlemen, can this king be such a fool? Is there anyone carried away by death that can be brought back? What's done is done."[888]

Then King Udayana wrote back to him saying, "A village chief named such-and-such will not surrender to me. First offer us your help, and then I'll help you." The king's ministers sent off the letter, and as soon as the bearer of bad news heard what it said, he came and set up camp not far from the village chief.

The village chief heard about this and reflected, "I'm already surrounded in ten directions by one king, and now there is a second.[889]

I'll give up my homeland again but not my life." He placed his sword in supplication against his neck,[890] went out, and fell prostrate at King Udayana's feet. King Udayana appointed him as a tribute-paying vassal.

Now that bearer of bad news, in the guise of a king, went before King Udayana and said, "My lord, my son has been carried off by Death. Please help me. I shall do battle against him. If you can defeat him in battle, that would be good. If not, to recover my son, I'll pay Death a ransom of five hundred male elephants, five hundred female elephants, five hundred stallions, five hundred mares, five hundred boys, five hundred girls, plus one hundred thousand gold coins."

"Dear friend, you're a fool!" King Udayana said. "Is there anyone who can be brought back from death?"

"My lord, no one can," he said. "And since this is so, look at this canvas."[891] He then spread it out.

The king examined the canvas, and looking[892] as if pierced in the vitals, [537] he said, "What?" Then he said, "Friend, are you saying that five hundred women led by Śyāmāvatī were consumed in a fire?"

The bearer of bad news took off his royal insignia and crown and uttered this verse:

> I'm no king, nor the son of a king,
> but a servant, my lord, living at your feet.
> I have come here, prostrate before you,
> to deliver very bad news.

The king examined the canvas closely and thought to himself, "This is the city of Kauśāmbī, this is the palace, this is Mākandika using birchbark and so on to set fire to the Puṣpadanta Palace, and this is five hundred women led by Śyāmāvatī being consumed in the fire after flying into the air and casting themselves into the flames." Having thought this over, he said, "Friend, are you saying that Śyāmāvatī has been consumed in a fire?"

"My lord, I'm not saying so. It's my lord himself who says so."

"Friend, you've informed me in a skillful way. Otherwise, I would have decapitated you with my sword and tossed your head to the ground." With that said, King Udayana fainted and fell to the ground.

Splashed with water, the king regained his senses and said, "Gentlemen, prepare the four branches of the military for battle! Let's go to Kauśāmbī." The ministers prepared the four branches of the military for battle. The king set out for Kauśāmbī and arrived there in due course. He heard all the details from the townspeople and became enraged. The townspeople tried to console him.

Then the king ordered Yogāndharāyaṇa, "Go! Put Mākandika along with Anupamā in the torture chamber and torture them!" But Yogāndharāyaṇa secretly secured[893] them in an underground chamber. After seven days the king's grief departed—he was free from grief.[894]

"Yogāndharāyaṇa," the king said, "where is Anupamā?"

Yogāndharāyaṇa reminded him of his previous order.[895]

"Good," the king said. "Mākandika killed Śyāmāvatī, and you killed Anupamā. So now I should go forth as a monk."[896]

"My lord," Yogāndharāyaṇa said, "it is for this very reason that I secured her in an underground chamber. I'll see if she is still alive."

Yogāndharāyaṇa brought her from the underground chamber. She seemed untroubled, and she had a fresh appearance.

When the king saw her, he reflected: "She looks fresh. [538] She hasn't been without food! She must have been having sex with another man!" With this in mind, he said, "Anupamā, have you had sex with another man?"

"Heaven forbid! I would never do that."

"How would I know?"

"Do you have faith in the Blessed One?"

"I have faith in Gautama."

"Before he was the ascetic Gautama. Now he is the Blessed One."

"What will I say to the Blessed One about Anupamā's fresh appearance?[897] What will I say to him about Śyāmāvatī?"[898] With this in mind, the king approached the Blessed One and, having approached, placed his head in veneration at the Blessed One's feet and then sat down at a respectful distance. Udayana, king of the Vatsas, then said this to the Blessed One: "Bhadanta, what deed did those five hundred women led by Śyāmāvatī do that resulted in their being consumed in a fire? And how did Kubjottarā manage to escape through a water drain?"[899]

"Great king," the Blessed One replied, "the deeds that they themselves have performed and accumulated have now come together, and their conditions have matured. [They remain before them like an oncoming flood and will certainly come to pass. Those deeds were performed and accumulated by them. Who else will experience their results? For those deeds that are performed and accumulated, your majesty, do not mature outside of oneself—neither in the element of earth nor in the element of water, in the element of fire or in the element of wind. Instead, those deeds that are performed and accumulated, both good and bad, mature in the aggregates, elements, and sense bases that are appropriated when one is reborn.

Actions never come to naught,
even after hundreds of millions of years.
When the right conditions gather and the time is right,][900]
then they will have their effect on embodied beings."

King Brahmadatta, the Palace Women, and the Solitary Buddha

Long ago, your majesty, in a time gone by, in the city of Vārāṇasī, a king named Brahmadatta ruled a kingdom that was thriving, prosperous, and safe, with plenty of food and throngs of people, [that was free from quarrel and strife, with no hustle and bustle, thieves, or diseases, that was rich in rice, sugarcane, cattle, and buffalo. He was a just and virtuous king,][901] and he ruled according to dharma.

When no buddhas are born, solitary buddhas can arise in the world. They have compassion for the poor and neglected, they live in remote areas, and they alone are worthy of people's offerings.

At that time a certain solitary buddha, after wandering through the countryside, arrived in Vārāṇasī. He settled in a hut in a certain park.

Meanwhile King Brahmadatta, together with the palace women and his attendants, went out to that same park. After bathing in a lotus pond used for playing, the palace women caught a chill. Then the chief queen addressed her maidservant: "Girl, we're really suffering from the cold. Go and set fire to that hut."

The maidservant lit a torch and went to the hut, where she saw that solitary buddha. She informed the queen, "My lady, a renunciant is staying in that hut."

"Never mind the renunciant," she said. "Set the hut on fire!" But the maidservant wouldn't do it. At that, the queen became angry and did it herself. The solitary buddha [simply] walked away.

All of the palace women expressed their approval: "My lady, it's good that you made a fire. Now we're all warm." [539]

The solitary buddha reflected, "These poor women are [spiritually] beaten and battered. Let them not be beaten down even further. I'll do them a favor." Out of compassion for them, he flew up into the air and began to perform the miraculous deeds of causing [fire and][902] heat, making rain and lightning.

Magic quickly wins over ordinary people. Like a tree cut down at the roots, the women fell prostrate at his feet and begged for forgiveness: "Come down! Come down, O you who are so righteous and worthy of offerings! Offer us a helping hand, for we are mired in the mud of desire."

Out of compassion for them, the solitary buddha came down. The women[903] made offerings to him and then made a fervent aspiration: "Although we have committed a terrible offense against one so righteous and worthy of offerings, may we not suffer the consequence of that deed. Since we have made offerings, by this root of virtue may we attain such virtues so that we may please a teacher even more distinguished than this one."

"What do you think, your majesty? King Brahmadatta's chief queen was none other than Śyāmāvatī at that time and at that juncture. Those five hundred women [led by the chief queen] were none other than these five hundred women [led by Śyāmāvatī] at that time and at that juncture. And the maidservant was none other than Kubjottarā at that time and at that juncture. Since those women expressed their approval when the solitary buddha's hut was burned, as a result of that action, they burned in various hells for many years. Even now, after seeing the [four noble] truths, they were consumed by fire, although Kubjottarā escaped through a water drain.[904] Since those women made a fervent aspiration, they came to see the [four noble] truths in my presence.

"And so, your majesty, the result of absolutely evil actions [is absolutely evil, the result of absolutely pure actions is absolutely pure, and the result of mixed actions is mixed. Therefore monks, because of this, you should reject absolutely evil actions and mixed ones as well] and strive to perform [only absolutely pure actions].[905] It is this, your royal majesty, that you should learn to do."

Then Udayana, king of the Vatsas, rejoiced and delighted in the words of the Blessed One, placed his head in veneration at the Blessed One's feet, and then left the Blessed One's presence.

Some monks in doubt asked the Lord Buddha, the remover of all doubts, "What deed, Bhadanta, did Kubjottarā do that resulted in her becoming a hunchback?"

"Monks," the Blessed One said, "the deeds that Kubjottarā herself has performed and accumulated [have now come together, and their conditions have matured. They remain before her like an oncoming flood and will certainly come to pass. Those deeds were performed and accumulated by Kubjottarā. Who else will experience their results?

For those deeds that are performed and accumulated, monks, do not mature outside of oneself—neither in the element of earth nor in the element of water, in the element of fire or in the element of wind. Instead, those deeds that are performed and accumulated, both good and bad, mature in the aggregates, the elements, and the sense bases that are appropriated when one is reborn.

> Actions never come to naught,
> even after hundreds of millions of years.
> When the right conditions gather and the time is right,][906]
> then they will have their effect on embodied beings." [540]

The Householder Sandhāna, His Daughter, and the Solitary Buddhas

Long ago, monks, in the city of Vārāṇasī, a king named Brahmadatta ruled a kingdom [that was thriving, prosperous, and safe, with plenty of food and throngs of people, that was free from quarrel and strife, with no hustle and bustle, thieves, or diseases, that was rich in rice, sugarcane, cattle, and buffalo. He was a just and virtuous king,][907] and he ruled according to dharma. Then soothsayers predicted that there would be a drought for twelve years. The king had bells rung in Vārāṇasī for the following proclamation: "Whoever has enough food for twelve years should stay. Whoever doesn't should go elsewhere and return after the proper time has passed."

At that time in Vārāṇasī there lived a householder named Sandhāna (Mediator),[908] who was rich, wealthy, and prosperous, [with vast and extensive holdings, who had amassed a wealth like the god Vaiśravaṇa.][909] Truly, he rivaled Vaiśravaṇa in wealth. He summoned the officer in charge of his granaries and said, "Friend, will there be enough food for me and my family for twelve years?"

"Yes, sir, there will be," he said.

When no buddhas are born, solitary buddhas can arise in the world. [They have compassion for the poor and neglected, they live in remote areas, and they alone are worthy of people's offerings.

Meanwhile five hundred solitary buddhas, after wandering through the countryside, arrived in Vārāṇasī. They approached the householder Sandhāna and asked, "Householder, can you provide five hundred monks with food for twelve years?"

"I'll ask the granary officer and inform you," he said. So he summoned his granary officer and said, "Friend, is there enough food for me and my family and these five hundred renunciants to last twelve years?"

"Yes sir, there is," he said.

The householder Sandhāna then addressed the five hundred solitary buddhas: "Gentlemen, all of you please come, and we will provide you with food."

The five hundred solitary buddhas took up residence there.

By that time another five hundred solitary buddhas, after wandering through the countryside, arrived in Vārāṇasī. They also approached the householder Sandhāna and asked, "Householder, can you provide five hundred monks with food for twelve years?"

"I'll ask the granary officer and let you know," he said. So he summoned his granary officer and said,][910] "Friend, is there enough food for me and my family and these five hundred renunciants to last twelve years?"[911]

"Yes, sir, there is," he said.

So the householder promised the solitary buddhas that he would provide them with food. He had an alms house built,[912] [and he appointed servers and ushers.][913] Every day those one thousand solitary buddhas would eat there.

Then one of the solitary buddhas became sick, and one day he didn't come for alms.

"Father," Sandhāna's daughter said to him, "one of the renunciants didn't come today."

"My daughter," he said, "which one?"

Hunching her back, she said, "Father, he's like this."

Since she mocked a solitary buddha, as a result of that action, she became a hunchback.

Once again those monks asked the Lord Buddha, "What deed, Bhadanta, did Kubjottarā do that resulted in her becoming learned in the teachings?"

"At that time and at that juncture," the Blessed One said,[914] "there was an elder in the community of solitary buddhas who suffered from an excess of the wind humor. When he ate, his bowl would shake.

"Sandhāna's daughter took off the bangles from her hand and said to that solitary buddha, 'Noble one, steady your bowl with these.'[915]

"He placed his bowl on them, and it held firm.[916]

"Falling prostrate at his feet, she made this fervent aspiration: 'Just as this bowl holds firm, may the dharma teachings that enter my mental continuum remain firmly in place.' [541] Since she made a fervent aspiration, as a result of that action, she became learned in the teachings."

Again those monks questioned the Lord Buddha: "What deed, Bhadanta, did Kubjottarā do that resulted in her becoming a slave?"

"Monks," the Blessed One said,[917] "because she was intoxicated with the power of authority, she addressed one of her attendants with the word *slave*. As a result of that action, she became a slave."

Again those monks questioned the Lord Buddha: "What deed, Bhadanta, did Anupamā do that resulted in[918] her being shut in an underground chamber without food and yet emerging [seven days later][919] with a fresh appearance?"

"Monks," the Blessed One said, "the deeds that Anupamā herself has performed and accumulated [have now come together, and their conditions have matured. They remain before her like an oncoming flood and will certainly come to pass. Those deeds were performed and accumulated by Anupamā. Who else will experience their results? For those deeds that are performed and accumulated, monks, do not mature outside of oneself—neither in the element of earth nor in the element of water, in the element of fire or in the element of wind. Instead, those deeds that are performed and accumulated, both good and bad, mature in the aggregates, the elements, and the sense bases that are appropriated when one is reborn.

Actions never come to naught,
even after hundreds of millions of years.
When the right conditions gather and the time is right,][920]
then they will have their effect on embodied beings."

Śrīmatī and Śāriputra Cross Thresholds

Long ago, monks, in a certain market town, there lived two girls who were close friends, a kṣatriya girl and a brahman girl.

When no buddhas are born, solitary buddhas can arise in the world. They have compassion for the poor and neglected, they live in remote areas, and they alone are worthy of people's offerings.

At that time a certain solitary buddha was passing the night in a certain quiet place. The next day, in the morning, the solitary buddha got dressed and went out for alms.[921] Seeing him, the two girls were filled with faith, and they offered him a bowl full of fine foods. As a result of that action, one of them was reborn as Anupamā and the other as the daughter of the householder Ghoṣila (Renowned). She was an extremely beautiful girl named Śrīmatī (Glorious).

One time the king saw Śrīmatī and asked, "Whose daughter is that?"

"The householder Ghoṣila's," his ministers said.

Then the king summoned the householder Ghoṣila and said, "Householder, is this girl your daughter?"

"Yes she is, my lord," he said.

"Is there a reason she can't be given to me [in marriage]? Please give her to me."

"Yes, my lord, she shall be given to you," he said.

So the householder Ghoṣila gave [his daughter in marriage to the king]. Udayana, king of the Vatsas, brought her into the women's quarters of the palace and married her with great ceremony.

After some time Śrīmatī said to the king, "My lord, I long to see the monks."

"You may long for this, but monks are [not][922] allowed to enter the palace," the king said.

"My lord, I've truly been put in prison.[923] In any case, if I don't get to see the monks, starting today I won't eat and I won't drink." And so she began to fast. [542]

The king spoke with the householder Ghoṣila: "Householder, have you no concern for your daughter?"

"My lord, what are you saying?"

"She has begun a fast."

"Why?"

"She longs to see the monks. Therefore[924] you should cut a doorway from your side [of the courtyard], invite the community of monks for a meal in the courtyard,[925] then prepare food in your home and feed them."

Now the homes of the king and Ghoṣila shared a common boundary wall. The householder Ghoṣila cut a doorway into it. He then had the grounds prepared[926] and approached the Blessed One. Having approached, he placed his head in veneration at the Blessed One's feet and then sat down at a respectful distance. The Blessed One instructed, incited, inspired, and delighted the householder Ghoṣila, who was seated at a respectful distance, with a discourse on the dharma. After he instructed, incited, inspired, and delighted him in many ways with this discourse on the dharma, he became silent.

The householder Ghoṣila then got up from his seat, bowed toward the Buddha with his hands respectfully folded, and said this to him:

"May the Blessed One, along with the community of monks, accept this invitation of mine to eat at my home tomorrow."

[The Blessed One accepted the householder Ghoṣila's invitation with his silence. Then the householder Ghoṣila, realizing that by his silence the Blessed One had accepted his invitation, placed his head in veneration at the Blessed One's feet and then left the Blessed One's presence.

That very night the householder Ghoṣila prepared hard and soft foods, both fresh and fine, and then at daybreak he got up, prepared the seats, and set out pitchers of water.][927] Then he had a messenger inform the Blessed One that it was now the appropriate time: "It is time, Bhadanta. The food is ready. Now the Blessed One may do as the time permits."

The Blessed One, however, refrained from partaking of that gift.[928] So the community of monks set out with Śāriputra leading the way.

There are five reasons why lord buddhas abstain from partaking of gifts of almsfood that have been prepared.[929]

"Venerable ones," [Śāriputra said to the monks,] "orders from four types of people are not to be refused:

> a perfectly awakened tathāgatha arhat,
> an arhat monk who has destroyed the corruptions,
> a monastic official,[930]
> and a kṣatriya king who has been duly consecrated."

Śāriputra then established himself in a state of mindfulness and thought, "Let us enter."[931]

Śāriputra entered [the courtyard of the householder Ghoṣila] and sat down in front of the community of monks in the seat specially prepared for him. When Queen Śrīmatī was sure that the community of monks led by Śāriputra was comfortably seated, [she served and indulged them, with her own hands, with hard and soft foods, both fresh and fine. When she had served and indulged them, with her own hands, with many courses of hard and soft foods, both fresh and fine, and was sure that the venerable Śāriputra had finished eating, washed his hands, and set aside his bowl,][932] she then sat down in front of Śāriputra, taking a lower seat, to listen to the dharma.

Then the venerable Śāriputra instructed, incited, inspired, and delighted Queen Śrīmatī with a discourse on the dharma. But she didn't reach sight of the [four noble] truths. Then the venerable Śāriputra reflected, [543] "Does she have any roots of virtue or not?"[933] He saw that she did. "Are they connected with someone?" He saw that [they were connected] with himself.

While he was teaching and discussing the dharma, the sun began to set. The monks got up from their seats and departed. The venerable Śāriputra reflected, "Even though the Blessed One has not given his permission [for me to remain here], it is quite likely that, considering the situation,[934] he would give his permission." And so he remained right where he was, with the intention of obtaining a new disciple.

Then the venerable Śāriputra, knowing her inclinations, propensities, makeup, and nature, gave a discourse on the dharma such that when Śrīmatī heard it, [with her thunderbolt of knowledge she broke though] that mountain, which is the false view of individuality that arises with its twenty peaks of incorrect views, [and directly experienced the reward of the stream-enterer. Having seen the truth, three times she uttered this inspired utterance:

What the Blessed One has done for the likes of me, Bhadanta,
  neither my mother nor my father have done,
  nor any dear one,
  nor any kinsmen or relatives,
  nor any king,
  nor any deities or deceased ancestors,
  nor ascetics or brahmans.
Oceans of blood and tears have dried up!
Mountains of bones have been scaled!

The doors to the lower realms of existence have been closed!
The doors to heaven and liberation have been opened!
We have been established among gods and humans!

And then she said,

Because of your power,
closed is the truly terrifying path
to the lower realms of existence,
defiled as it is by many sins.
Open is the realm of heaven,
which is filled with merit.
I have found the path to nirvāṇa!

From taking refuge in you,
today I have obtained
freedom from sin and
a pure and fully purified vision.
I have attained that beloved state
so beloved to the noble ones
and crossed to the far shore
of the sea of suffering.

O you who are honored in this world
by demons, humans, and gods
and freed from birth,
old age, sickness, and death,
even in a thousand lives,
seeing you is extremely rare.
O sage, seeing you today
brings great results!

> I have crossed over, Bhadanta! I have crossed over! And so, I take refuge in the Lord Buddha, in the dharma, and in the community of monks. Hereafter, and for as long as I live and breathe,][935] consider me a faithful disciple who has taken the three refuges.

Then the venerable Śāriputra, having established Śrīmatī in the [four noble] truths, departed and approached the Blessed One. Having approached, he placed his head in veneration at the Blessed One's feet and then sat down at a respectful distance. Sitting at a respectful distance,[936] the venerable Śāriputra explained the situation to the Blessed One in detail.

"Excellent, Śāriputra! Excellent! [In fact,[937]] orders from seven types of people are not to be refused:

> a perfectly awakened tathāgatha arhat,
> an arhat monk who has destroyed the corruptions,
> a kṣatriya king who has been duly consecrated,
> an elder of the monastic community,
> a monastic official,
> a teacher,
> and an instructor."

Then the Blessed One, with the desire to establish a rule, offered praise—and so on as it has been said before, up until—the previous regulation.[938] "And this regulation," [he said,] "is established as a rule.[939] In this way my disciples should offer instruction in the precepts of the monastic discipline:

> Whatever monk—when night has not yet departed, dawn not yet arisen, and treasures or those considered as treasures not put away—crosses the threshold or [comes] near the threshold of a kṣatriya king who has been duly consecrated

commits a serious offense, except if there is a valid reason [as in the case of Śāriputra]."[940]

Commentary:

- By "whatever monk" is meant "Udāyin, or someone of the same [virtuous] character."
- By "when night has not yet departed" is meant "before daybreak."
- By "not yet arisen" is meant "not yet appeared."[941]
- By "dawn" is meant "[the successive stages of] dawn: twilight blue dawn, yellow dawn, red dawn." In this sense, "twilight blue dawn" is characterized by twilight blue light; "yellow dawn" is characterized by yellow light; and "red dawn" is characterized by red light. But here "red dawn" is intended.
- Regarding "treasures," the treasures indicated are gems, pearls, beryl, [conch, quartz, and coral, silver and gold, emeralds, sapphires, red pearls,][942] and right-spiraling conch shells. [544]
- Regarding "or those things considered as treasures"—those things considered as treasures means all weapons used in battle and all musical instruments used by celestial musicians.
- Regarding "a kṣatriya king who has been duly consecrated,"[943] even a woman consecrated on the throne in accordance with the royal coronation ceremony is [to be considered] a kṣatriya king who has been duly consecrated. Even a kṣatriya, brahman, vaiśya, or śūdra, if consecrated in accordance with a royal coronation ceremony, is [to be considered] "a kṣatriya king who has been duly consecrated."
- By "threshold" is meant three different thresholds: the threshold to a city, the threshold to a palace, and the threshold to a women's quarters.
- By "or near the threshold" is meant "in the vicinity of it."
- By "crosses" is meant "goes beyond."

- By "except if there is a valid reason" means "excluding a valid reason."
- By "serious offense" is meant [a deed whose karmic consequences] burn, cook, [and cause the downfall of beings into the lower realms—those of hell beings, animals, and hungry ghosts. And as long as the offense is not confessed, it obscures virtuous dharmas. Therefore it is said to be a "serious offense."][944]

Considering this, how does an offense occur?

If a monk, thinking it is after daybreak, crosses the threshold to a city before daybreak, he commits a minor offense.
If he is in doubt that it is before daybreak,
he commits a minor offense.
If it is after daybreak but he thinks that it is before daybreak,
he commits a minor offense.
If he is in doubt that it is after daybreak,
he commits a minor offense.

If a monk, thinking it is after daybreak,[945] crosses the threshold to a women's quarters before daybreak, he commits a serious offense.
[If he is in doubt that it is before daybreak,
he commits a serious offense.][946]
If it is after daybreak but he thinks that it is before daybreak,
he commits a minor offense.
If he is in doubt that it is after daybreak,
he commits a minor offense.

There is no offense, however, when the king calls out, "Queens! Princes! Ministers! One or another of the eight dangers has appeared!" That is, the danger of kings, robbers, humans, nonhumans, wild animals, fire, water, [and serpents].[947] For the first [monk] ever to do it—and so on as before—there is no offense.[948]

So ends the *Mākandika-avadāna*, [the thirty-sixth chapter] in the glorious *Divyāvadāna*.

37. *The Story of Rudrāyaṇa*

RUDRĀYAṆA-AVADĀNA[949]

King Rudrāyaṇa, King Bimbisāra, and the Gift of a Buddha Image

THE LORD BUDDHA was residing in Rājagṛha in the bamboo grove at Kalandakanivāpa (Squirrel Feeding Place).

Once there were two great cities, Pāṭaliputra and Roruka.[950] When Pāṭaliputra would prosper, Roruka would fall on hard times.[951]

In the great city of Roruka, [545] a king named Rudrāyaṇa ruled a kingdom that was thriving, prosperous, and safe, with plenty of food and throngs of people, and where the trees were always full of flowers and fruit. There the [rain] god would offer showers of rain in just the right amount at the appropriate times, and the harvest was exceedingly rich. His [favorite] queen was named Candraprabhā (Moon Glow); his son, the prince Śikhaṇḍin (Topknot); and his chief ministers, Hiru (Modest) and Bhiru (Pious).[952]

In Rājagṛha, King Bimbisāra (Precious as Gold) likewise ruled a kingdom that was thriving, prosperous, and safe, with plenty of food and throngs of people. His principal queen was named Vaidehī (Resident of Videha);[953] his son, the prince Ajātaśatru (Without Enemies); and his chief minister, the great minister from Magadha, the brahman Varṣakāra (Controlling).[954] There the trees were always full of flowers and fruit, the [rain] god would offer showers of rain in just the right amount at the appropriate times, and the harvest was exceedingly rich.

One day some merchants from Rājagṛha brought their goods to Roruka.

King Rudrāyaṇa, surrounded by his cabinet of ministers, addressed them:[955] "Gentlemen, does any other king have such lands that are thriving, prosperous, and safe, with plenty of food and throngs of people, where the trees are always full of flowers and fruit, where the [rain] god offers showers of rain in just the right amount at the appropriate times, and where the harvest is also exceedingly rich?"

"My lord," the merchants said, "there is the city of Rājagṛha in the lands to the east. There King Bimbisāra rules a kingdom that is thriving, prosperous, and safe, with plenty of food and throngs of people, where the trees are always full of flowers and fruit, where the [rain] god offers showers of rain in just the right amount at the appropriate times, and where there is an exceedingly rich harvest."

As soon as King Rudrāyaṇa heard this, he felt a fondness for King Bimbisāra [and wished to win him over]. He addressed his ministers: "Gentlemen, what is difficult for this king to obtain?"

"My lord, you own jewels, that king owns fine clothing. For him, jewels are rare."

So King Rudrāyaṇa filled a basket with jewels and sent it to him as a gift along with a letter. "Dear friend," it said, "you are my unseen ally. If there is anything you need done in the city of Roruka, you should write to me. I can get you anything."

The ministers took the gift and set out for Rājagṛha, and in due course they arrived there. They presented King Bimbisāra with the basket of jewels as well as the letter. [546] King Bimbisāra read out the letter and then addressed his ministers: "Gentlemen, what is difficult for that king to obtain?"

"My lord," the ministers said, "you own fine clothing, that king owns jewels. For him, fine clothing is rare."

So King Bimbisāra filled a basket with clothing that was precious and sent it to him as gift along with a letter. "Dear friend," it said, "you are my unseen ally. If there is anything you need in Rājagṛha, you should write to me. I can [likewise] get you anything."

The ministers took the gift and set out for Roruka, and in due course they arrived there. They presented King Rudrāyaṇa with the basket of garments as well as the letter.[956]

One day,[957] while King Rudrāyaṇa was surrounded by his cabinet of ministers, he addressed them: "Gentlemen, what[958] is that king's height and build?"

"Just like my lord's," they said. "But [in battle] that king is the first to attack."

"So how is it that he does battle with neighboring kings?" [King Rudrāyaṇa reflected].[959]

Now King Rudrāyaṇa had jeweled [body] armor that was endowed with five special qualities—it would remain cool when touched with heat and warm when touched with cold, it was difficult to cut, it was difficult to pierce, it would ward off poison, and it was naturally luminous. King Rudrāyaṇa sent King Bimbisāra this jeweled armor as a gift along with a letter. "Dear friend," it said, "I have sent this jeweled armor to you as a gift. It is endowed with five special qualities—it remains cool when touched with heat and warm when touched with cold, it is difficult to cut, it is difficult to pierce, it wards off poison, and it is naturally luminous. Please don't give it to anyone else."

A messenger took that jeweled armor and the letter and set off for Rājagṛha, and in due course he arrived there. He gave King Bimbisāra the jeweled armor as well as the letter. When King Bimbisāra saw the jeweled armor, he was stunned. He summoned some jewel experts.

"Figure out the value of this jeweled armor," he said.

"My lord," they said, "each and every jewel here is priceless."

As a rule, each and every one of those things whose value cannot be calculated must be worth millions.[960]

King Bimbisāra was distressed and said, "What should I offer him as a gift in return?" Then he reflected, "There is the Lord Buddha. His knowledge is unsurpassed, and he has power over a king, even one who gives away everything. I'll go and ask him."[961]

So King Bimbisāra took the jeweled armor and approached the Lord Buddha. [547] Having approached, he placed his head in veneration at the Blessed One's feet and then sat down at a respectful distance. Then King Bimbisāra said this to the Blessed One: "Bhadanta, in the city of Roruka lives a king named Rudrāyaṇa. He is my unseen ally. As a gift he sent me this jeweled armor that is endowed with five special qualities. What gift should I send him in return?"

"Have an image of the Taghāgata inscribed on a piece of cloth and send it to him as a gift," the Blessed One said.

King Bimbisāra summoned some painters and said, "Paint an image of the Tathāgata on a piece of cloth."

Lord buddhas, however, are imposing,[962] and the painters couldn't apprehend the Blessed One's appearance.[963]

"If my lord would feed the Blessed One in his home," they said, "then we can[964] apprehend the Blessed One's appearance."

King Bimbisāra invited the Blessed One to his home for a meal and fed him.

Now lord buddhas are sights one never tires of seeing. The painters remained staring at whatever part of the Blessed One they happened to look at, and they just couldn't get enough.[965] They couldn't apprehend the Blessed One's [full] appearance.

"Your majesty," the Blessed One said, "these painters will just exhaust themselves. They can't apprehend the appearance of the Tathāgatha. Instead, bring a piece of cloth here."

The king brought a piece of cloth. The Blessed One cast his shadow on it and said [to the painters], "Now fill it in with various colors. And underneath the image write the [vows for] taking refuge and the precepts. Then depict the twelve links of interdependent arising, both forward and backward. And then write these two verses:

Strive! Go forth!
Apply yourselves to the teachings of the Buddha!
Destroy the army of death
as an elephant would a house of reeds.

Whoever diligently follows
this dharma and monastic discipline
will abandon the endless cycle of rebirth
and put an end to suffering.

If King Rudrāyaṇa says, 'What is this?' you should reply:

This is who you go to for protection.[966]
This is the precepts.
This is the cycle of being in the world.[967]
This is the encouragement.[968]

The painters drew everything as they were instructed.

"Your majesty," the Blessed One said to King Bimbisāra, "offer this in writing to Rudrāyaṇa: 'Dear friend, I have sent you a gift unsurpassed in the three worlds. [548] On its behalf, beautify the road [into the city] for two and half leagues. Then, together with your fourfold army, personally go out and receive it. You should then place it in a large open space, honor it with great ceremony, and unveil it. Doing so, you will gain great merit."

King Bimbisāra wrote the letter as he was instructed and sent it off. When the letter was presented to King Rudrāyaṇa, he had it read it out loud and was enraged.[969]

"Gentlemen," he said to his ministers, "what sort of gift has he sent to me that I should honor it in this way? Prepare the four branches of the military for battle! I will crush his kingdom."

"My lord," his ministers said, "that king, it is heard, is a great being.

He certainly wouldn't send just anything as a return gift.[970] Let's proceed accordingly.[971] If my lord is not fully satisfied, we'll know what to do."

"Do as you wish."

The king beautified the road [into the city] for two and a half leagues. Then, together with his fourfold army, he personally went out and received the gift and ushered it in. He then placed it in a large open space, honored it with great ceremony, and unveiled it.

Merchants from the Middle Country, who had brought their goods to the city, saw the image of the Buddha and cried out in one voice: "Praise to the Buddha!" Hearing this cry of "Buddha" for the first time, the king felt goosebumps all over.

"Gentlemen," he said, "who is this person named Buddha?"

"My lord," they said, "he was born a prince of the Śākyas on the slopes of the Himālayas, on the banks of Bhāgīrathī River, not far from the hermitage of the seer Kapila. And it was foretold by brahmans, astrologers, and soothsayers:[972]

> If he will cling to his home as a householder, then he will be a wheel-turning king, a victor with a fourfold army,[973] a just and virtuous ruler, and a possessor of the seven treasures. These seven treasures of his will have the form of the most-treasured wheel, the most-treasured elephant, the most-treasured horse, the most-treasured jewel, the most-treasured woman, the most-treasured householder, and the most-treasured counselor. And he will have a full one thousand sons who are brave, heroic, in excellent physical condition, and who destroy enemy armies. He will conquer the sea-bound earth without violence and without weapons [549] and then rule there justly and peacefully,[974] so that it will be entirely fertile, without enemies, and without oppression. But if he shaves off his hair and beard, puts on ochre robes, and with right belief, goes forth from home

> to homelessness, he will be a tathāgata, an arhat, a perfectly awakened one, acclaimed in the world.

"He is the one named Buddha. And this is his image."

"What is this?" asked the king.

"Who you go to for protection."

"What is this?"

"The precepts."

"What is this?"

"How the world comes into being and passes away."[975]

"What is this?"

"The encouragement."[976]

The king clearly grasped interdependent arising, both forward and backward.

At dawn the next day, King Rudrāyaṇa, surrounded by his ministers, put aside[977] all his work and all his duties. He then sat down, crossing his legs and holding his body upright, and made his mindfulness fully present. He carefully examined, both forward and backward, the twelve links of interdependent arising—namely, when this is, that is. From the arising of this comes the arising of that—namely, with ignorance as a condition, formations come to be . . . from their arising to their cessation.[978] Carefully examining, both forward and backward, those twelve links of interdependent arising, with his thunderbolt of knowledge he broke through that mountain, which is the false view of individuality that arises with its twenty peaks of incorrect views, and directly experienced the reward of the stream-enterer. Having seen the truth, he recited this verse:

> The Buddha, jewel of the earth,[979]
> has purified my eye of knowledge!
> Praise to him, the excellent doctor,
> whose medicine is like this!

Then King Rudrāyaṇa sent this message to King Bimbisāra: "Dear friend, thanks to you, I have lifted up my feet from the realms of hell beings, animals, and hungry ghosts! I have been established among gods and humans! Oceans of blood and tears have dried up! Mountains of bones have been scaled! With the thunderbolt of knowledge I have broken through that mountain, which is the false view of individuality that has accumulated since time immemorial, and directly experienced the reward of the stream-enterer. I want to see a monk! Please send a monk."

King Bimbisāra approached the Blessed One and, having approached, placed his head in veneration at the Blessed One's feet and then sat down at a respectful distance. Sitting down at a respectful distance, he said this to the Blessed One: "Bhadanta, King Rudrāyaṇa has seen the [four noble] truths. He has sent me a message that he wants to see a monk."

The Blessed One reflected, [550] "Which monk should train King Rudrāyaṇa, his retinue, and the residents of Roruka? The monk Kātyāyana."

Then the Blessed One addressed the venerable Mahākātyāyana: "Kātyāyana, turn your attention to King Rudrāyaṇa in the city of Roruka, his retinue, and the residents of Roruka."

The venerable Mahākātyāyana consented to the Blessed One's request. Then he placed his head in veneration at the Blessed One's feet and left the Blessed One's presence.

The very next morning the venerable Mahākātyāyana got dressed, took his bowl and robe, and entered Rājagṛha for alms. After wandering through Rājagṛha for alms, he ate his meal, and after eating, he returned from his almsround.[980] He then put away the bedding that he had used,[981] collected his bowl and robe, and with five hundred followers set off toward Roruka.

King Bimbisāra sent a letter to King Rudrāyaṇa: "Dear friend, I have sent to you a monk, a great disciple who is like the Teacher. On his behalf, beautify the road [into the city] for two and half leagues and beautify the city as well. Then, together with your fourfold army, personally go out and receive him. You should also commission five hundred monastic dwellings; give out[982] five hundred chairs, seats, cushions, woolen blankets,[983] pillows, and shawls; and distribute five hundred meals. Doing so, you will gain great merit."[984]

King Rudrāyaṇa beautified the road for two and a half leagues and beautified the city as well.[985] Then he personally went out to receive the venerable Mahākātyāyana, along with many hundreds and thousands of followers,[986] and with great honor ushered him into the city of Roruka. He also commissioned five hundred monastic dwellings outside of the city; gave out five hundred chairs, seats, cushions, woolen blankets, pillows, and shawls; distributed five hundred meals; and had a seat specially prepared for the venerable Mahākātyāyana in a wide-open tract of land.

The venerable Mahākātyāyana sat down in front of the community of monks in that seat specially prepared for him. Many hundreds and thousands of beings gathered around, some out of curiosity, others impelled by former roots of virtue.

Then the venerable Mahākātyāyana, knowing the inclinations, propensities, makeup, and nature of that assembly, gave them a discourse on the dharma such that when they heard it, many hundreds and thousands of beings attained great distinction. [551] Some directly experienced the reward of the stream-enterer;[987] some the reward of the nonreturner; and some went forth as monks and, by ridding themselves of all defilements, directly experienced arhatship. Some set their minds on attaining awakening as a disciple, some awakening as a solitary buddha, and some unsurpassed perfect awakening. Almost the entire assembly was affected and became favorably inclined toward the Buddha, drawn toward the dharma, and well disposed toward the community.

Rudrāyaṇa, Candraprabhā, and Śikhaṇḍin

In the city of Roruka lived two householders, Tiṣya and Puṣya. They approached the venerable Mahākātyāyana and, having approached, placed their heads in veneration at the venerable Mahākātyāyana's feet and then sat down at a respectful distance. Then they said this to him: "Noble Mahākātyāyana, may we renounce, take ordination, and become monks according to the dharma and the monastic discipline that have been so well expressed. Noble Mahākātyāyana, may we follow the religious life in your presence."[988]

And so the venerable Mahākātyāyana initiated and ordained them and offered them instruction. After striving, struggling, and straining, they came to understand that ever-turning five-spoked wheel of saṃsāra; they dealt a final blow to rebirth with all its conditioning factors,[989] since such things are subject to decay and decline, scattering and destruction; and by ridding themselves of all defilements, they directly experienced arhatship. Becoming arhats,

they were free from attachment in the three realms;
they regarded clods of earth and gold as equal in value;
they possessed equanimity toward the sky
  and the palms of their hands;
they didn't distinguish between being cut by a blade
  and being anointed with sandalwood paste;
the eggshell [of their ignorance] was broken by knowledge;
they obtained the special knowledges, superhuman faculties,
  and analytic insights;
and they were averse to worldly attainments, temptations,
  and honors.
They became worthy of respect, honor, and obeisance
  from the gods, including Indra and Upendra.

Then they performed the miraculous deeds of causing fire and heat, making rain and lightning, and then passed into the realm of remainderless nirvāṇa. Their relatives performed funeral ceremonies for their bodies and constructed two stūpas, one for Tiṣya, the other for Puṣya.

Every day King Rudrāyaṇa would listen to the dharma from the venerable Mahākātyāyana and announce to the women of the palace, "The dharma that the noble Mahākātyāyana teaches is so sweet. What he propounds[990] is sweet like honey!"

"The appearance of the Buddha has been benefical for my lord," they said [one day].

"How is that?"

"For you can listen to the dharma."

"If that's the case, why don't you listen as well?" [552]

"My lord, we are modest. How can we go there to listen to the dharma? But if the noble Mahākātyāyana would come here and teach the dharma, then we could listen as well."

King Rudrāyaṇa spoke to the venerable Mahākātyāyana: "Noble one, the women of my palace want to listen to the dharma."[991]

"Your majesty," he said, "monks are not permitted to enter women's quarters and teach the dharma. Entering women's quarters has been prohibited by the Blessed One."

"Noble one, in that case who teaches the dharma to palace women?"

"Your majesty, it is the nuns."

So King Rudrāyaṇa sent a letter to King Bimbisāra: "Dear friend, the women of my palace want to listen to the dharma. Please send a nun."

King Bimbisāra read out the letter and then approached the Blessed One. Having approached, he placed his head in veneration at the Blessed One's feet and then sat down at a respectful distance. Sitting down at a respectful distance, King Bimbisāra said this to the Blessed One: "Blessed One, King Rudrāyaṇa sent a letter saying, 'The women of my palace want to hear the dharma. Please send a nun.' How is it best to proceed in this case?"

The Blessed One reflected, "Which nun should train the women of King Rudrāyaṇa's palace[992] as well as the female residents of Roruka?" He saw that it was the nun Śailā.

So the Blessed One addressed the nun Śailā: "Śailā, turn your attention to the women of King Rudrāyaṇa's palace in the city of Roruka as well as the female residents of Roruka."

"Yes, Bhadanta," the nun Śailā replied, consenting to the Blessed One's request. Then she placed her head in veneration at the Blessed One's feet and departed from the Blessed One's presence.

The very next morning, the nun Śailā got dressed, took her bowl and robe, [and entered] Rājagṛha for alms. After wandering through [Rājagṛha for alms,][993] she ate her meal, and after eating, she returned from her almsround.[994] She then put away the bedding and seat that she had used,[995] collected her bowl and robe, and with five hundred followers set off toward the city of Roruka.

King Bimbisāra sent a letter to King Rudrāyaṇa: "Dear friend, I have sent to you a great disciple who is like the Teacher[996] accompanied by five hundred followers. On her behalf, beautify the road [into the city] for two and half leagues and beautify the city as well. Then, together with your fourfold army, personally go out and receive her. [553] You should also commission five hundred monastic dwellings within the city; give out five hundred chairs and seats as well as five hundred cushions, woolen blankets,[997] pillows, and shawls; and distribute five hundred meals. Doing so, you will gain [great][998] merit."

King Rudrāyaṇa read out the letter, and with feelings of joy he beautified the road [into the city] for two and half leagues and [beautified the city as well].[999] Then he personally went out to receive her, along with many [hundreds and][1000] thousands of followers, and with great honor ushered her into the city of Roruka. He also commissioned five hundred monastic dwellings within the city; gave out five hundred chairs, seats, cushions, woolen blankets, pillows, and shawls; and distributed five hundred meals.

Every day the nun Śailā entered the women's quarters of King Rudrāyaṇa's palace and taught the dharma.

Now King Rudrāyaṇa was an expert veena player and Queen Candraprabhā an expert dancer. One day King Rudrāyaṇa was playing the veena, and Queen Candraprabhā was dancing, and while she was dancing, the king saw a sign indicating her impending death. Looking at her closely, up and down, he reflected, "After a week she will die." The veena slipped from his hand and fell to the ground.

"My lord," Queen Candraprabhā said, "I hope I'm not dancing badly."[1001]

"Queen, you aren't dancing badly. It's just that, as you were dancing, I saw a sign indicating your impending death. After seven days you will die."

Queen Candraprabhā fell prostrate at the king's feet and said, "My lord, if that is so, since I have already served my lord, if my lord permits, I shall go forth as a nun."

"Candraprabhā," the king said, "I give you my permission on one condition. If you go forth as a nun and, by ridding yourself of all defilements, directly experience arhatship, this itself will be an end to your suffering. But if you die with some bonds to existence still remaining and are reborn among the gods, being a god you should show yourself to me."

"Yes, my lord," she said. "As you wish."

King Rudrāyaṇa handed her over to the nun Śāilā: "Noble one, Queen Candraprabhā[1002] wants to renounce, take ordination, and become a nun according to the dharma and monasic discipline that have been so well expressed. Please initiate and ordain her." [554]

"As you wish," said the nun Śailā. "I will initiate her." So the nun Śailā initiated and ordained Queen Candraprabhā. Then, after focusing her attention,[1003] she offered this instruction: "Cultivate a consciousness of death."

Queen Candraprabhā began to cultivate a consciousness of death, and on the seventh day, she died and was reborn among the gods of Cāturmahārājika (Four Groups of the Great Kings).

It is a law of nature that three thoughts arise in divinely born sons and daughters who have recently taken rebirth—"From where did I die and pass away? Where have I been reborn? As a result of what deed?"

The goddess Candraprabhā reflected, "From where did I die and pass away? From among humans. Where have I been reborn? Among the Cāturmahārājika gods. As a result of what deed? Following the religious life in the Blessed One's order." Then it occurred to her, "It wouldn't be right for me to wait until my time here [in heaven] is finished[1004] before I went to see the Blessed One. I really should go to see the Blessed One even before my time here is done."

That very night the divinely born Candraprabhā put on earrings that were flawless and dangling[1005] and adorned her body with strings and necklaces of pearls. Then she filled her arms[1006] with divine blue[1007] and white waterlilies, white lotuses, and coral-tree flowers,[1008] and illuminating the entire bamboo grove in Kalandakanivāpa[1009] with a great blaze of light, showered the Blessed One with flowers and then sat down in front of him to listen to the dharma.

Then the Blessed One, knowing her inclinations, propensities, makeup, and nature, gave her a discourse on the dharma that elucidated the four noble truths. When the divinely born Candraprabhā heard this, with her thunderbolt of knowledge she broke through that mountain, which is the false view of individuality that arises with its twenty peaks of incorrect views, and directly experienced the reward of the stream-enterer. Having seen the truth, three times she uttered this inspired utterance:

> What the Blessed One has done for the likes of me, Bhadanta,
> neither my mother nor my father have done,
> nor any king,
> nor any deities or dear ones,
> nor any kinsmen, relatives, or deceased ancestors,
> nor ascetics or brahmans.
> Oceans of blood and tears have dried up!
> Mountains of bones have been scaled!
> The doors to the lower realms of existence have been closed!
> The doors to heaven and liberation have been opened!
> [I][1010] have been established among gods and humans!

And she said,

Because of your power,
closed is the truly terrifying path
to the lower realms of existence,
bound up as it is with suffering.[1011] [555]
Open is the realm of heaven,
which is filled with merit.[1012]
I have found the path to nirvāṇa!

From taking refuge in you,
today I have obtained
freedom from sin and a
pure and fully purified vision.
I have attained that beloved state
so beloved to the noble ones
and crossed to the far shore[1013]
of the sea of suffering.

O you who are honored in this world
by demons, humans, and gods,
and freed from birth,
old age, sickness, and death,
even in a thousand lives
seeing you is very rare.
O Sage, seeing you today
brings great results!

Then she bowed down,
her necklaces of pearls drooping,
venerated his two feet,
and was filled with joy.
Respectfully circumambulating[1014]

the Conqueror of the Enemy,[1015]
she faced the realm of the gods
and went off to heaven.

Then the divinely born Candraprabhā, like a merchant with fortune found, like a farmer with a rich harvest,[1016] like a warrior victorious in battle, and like a patient released from every illness, by the very same power that enabled her to come before the Blessed One, set off for her home in heaven.[1017] Then it occurred to her, "I promised King Rudrāyaṇa that I would show myself to him."

And so the divinely born Candraprabhā approached King Rudrāyaṇa. At that time King Rudrāyaṇa was asleep all by himself on the top floor of his palace. Candraprabhā created a great blaze of light, snapped her fingers, and woke up the king.

Disoriented, his eyes still stuck in sleep, and not thinking clearly,[1018] he said, "Who are you?"

"I am Candraprabhā," she said.

"Come here," the king said. "Let's make love."

"My lord," she said, "I have died and passed away [from this realm] and been reborn among the Cāturmahārājika gods. If you want to have sex with me, then go forth as a monk in the presence of the Blessed One. If, as it happens, you rid yourself of all defilements and thereby directly experience arhatship in this lifetime,[1019] this itself will be an end to your suffering. If you die with some bonds to existence still remaining, you will be reborn among the Cāturmahārājika gods. There you can have sex with me." With that said, she vanished on the spot.

King Rudrāyaṇa spent the whole night thinking about renouncing, [556] then early the next morning he got up and addressed his ministers: "Look here gentlemen. Where does Queen Candraprabhā reside?"

"My lord," they said. "She has died."

King Rudrāyaṇa reflected, "It wouldn't be appropriate, now that I've been urged by a deity to renounce, to remain a householder, clinging to my home, hoarding wealth and enjoying sensual pleasure.[1020] I really should consecrate Prince Śikhaṇḍin as king, shave off my hair and beard, put on ochre robes, and with right belief, go forth from home to homelessness."

He sent a messenger to summon his two chief ministers, Hiru and Bhiru. "Gentlemen," he said, "inasmuch as Prince Śikhaṇḍin is my son, he is yours as well. You two should keep him from doing wrong and guide him toward what is right. I will go forth as a monk according to the dharma and monastic discipline that have been so well expressed."

The two of them stood there choked up with tears.

"Son," he said to Prince Śikhaṇḍin, "just as you would listen to my words and mind what I say to do, you should listen to the words of the chief ministers Hiru and Bhiru and mind what they say to do. I am going forth as a monk according to the dharma and monastic discipline that have been so well expressed."

Hearing this, he too was choked up with tears.

Then King Rudrāyaṇa had the bells rung in the city of Roruka for the following proclamation: "Residents of Roruka and visitors from other countries, please listen! I am going to shave off my hair and beard, put on ochre robes, and with right belief, go forth from home to homelessness. If I have caused anyone the slightest harm while ruling the kingdom, please forgive me."[1021]

The townspeople and villagers were very devoted to the king, and when they heard this, all of the residents of Roruka as well as those visiting from other countries were choked up with tears. Then King Rudrāyaṇa installed Prince Śikhaṇḍin as king, took leave of his relatives, made offerings and performed meritorious deeds for ascetics and brahmans, for the destitute and for beggars, and with only a single man as an attendant, [set off][1022] toward Rajagṛha.

Śikhaṇḍin, who was now king, along with the palace women,[1023] ministers, townspeople, and villagers, as well as those visiting from other countries, gathered close behind Rudrāyaṇa. Followed by these many hundreds and thousands of beings, Rudrāyaṇa walked out of the city of Roruka and stood for a moment in a park that was adorned with various thickets of trees, [557] filled with various flowers and ponds, and that resounded with the calls of geese, herons, peacocks, parrots, mynahs, cuckoos, and peacock pheasants. Then he looked at the city of Roruka and addressed King Śikhaṇḍin: "Son, I have ruled according to dharma. That is why these hundreds and thousands of beings have followed behind me. You too should rule according to dharma."

Having comforted that crowd of people, he said, "Friends, this is who I have appointed as your king. Turn back and live happily!" And with that said, he set off.

King Śikhaṇḍin, accompanied by the palace women, princes, ministers, townspeople, and villagers, gazed for a few moments with tear-filled eyes and then turned back and returned to the city of Roruka.

In due course King Rudrāyaṇa arrived in the city of Rājagṛha. Standing in the park [outside of town,] he addressed his servant: "Go, my friend. Go and inform King Bimbisāra that one named Rudrāyaṇa is staying in the park."

His servant went and informed King Bimbisāra, "My lord, King Rudrāyaṇa is staying in the park."

When the king heard this, he immediately got up and addressed his men:[1024] "Gentlemen, a king with a great army has arrived here unannounced. Why didn't any of you know this?"

"My lord," they said,[1025] "where is this army of his? He has come by himself."

King Bimbisāra reflected, "It wouldn't be right for me to simply usher in a duly consecrated kṣatriya king. I should usher him in with great honor." With this in mind, he beautified the road and the city and went out to meet him with his fourfold army. King Bimbisāra embraced him, had him seated on the back of an elephant, and led him into the great city of Rājagṛha. There he was bathed in water infused with various scents, adorned with clothes, scents, garlands, and creams worthy of a king, and then fed.

When Rudrāyaṇa had recovered from the fatigue of his travels, King Bimbisāra said, "Dear friend, you have abandoned a vast kingdom, with its palace women, princes and ministers, townspeople and villagers. What's your purpose in coming here? I hope it's not that a neighboring king has overthrown your kingdom. Have you been attacked by a prince or by someone under the influence of an evil minister who rejoices at the thought of kingship?"

"Dear friend,"[1026] he said, "I want to renounce, take ordination, and become a monk according to the dharma and monastic discipline that have been so well expressed."

Hearing this, King Bimbisāra was overjoyed. [558] He puffed up his chest,[1027] extended his right arm, and uttered this inspired utterance:

> Oh Buddha!
> Oh dharma!
> Oh community!
> Oh the clearly expressed dharma!
> Even today there are men such as you who abandon vast kingdoms, vast numbers of palace women, vast numbers of kinsmen and relatives, and vast treasuries and granaries, and wish[1028] to renounce, take ordination, and become monks according to the dharma and monastic discipline that have been so well expressed.

With that said, he brought King Rudrāyaṇa before the Blessed One.

At that time the Blessed One was seated in front of an assembly of many hundreds of monks,[1029] and he was teaching the dharma. The Blessed One saw the king of Magadha, Śreṇya Bimbisāra, from a distance, and upon seeing him, he addressed the monks: "That, monks, is King Bimbisāra, and he is coming with a gift! For a tathāgata, there is no gift that compares with the gift of a new disciple." With that said, he fell silent.

King Bimbisāra placed his head in veneration at the Blessed One's feet and then sat down at a respectful distance. Sitting down at a respectful distance, King Bimbisāra said this to the Blessed One: "Bhadanta, this is King Rudrāyaṇa. He wants to renounce, take ordination, and become a monk according to the dharma and monastic discipline that have been so well expressed. May the Blessed One, out of compassion for him, initiate and ordain him."

Then the Blessed One addressed him, uttering the "Come, O monk" formula for ordination: "Come, O monk! Follow the religious life!" As soon as the Blessed One finished speaking, there Rudrāyaṇa stood—head shaved, garbed in monastic robes, bowl and water pot in hand,[1030] and with the disciplined deportment of a monk who had been ordained for one hundred years.

"Come," the Tathāgata said to him.
With head shaved and a body wrapped in robes,
he instantly attained tranquility of the senses,
and so he remained by the will of the Buddha.[1031]

The next morning the venerable Rudrāyaṇa got dressed, took his bowl and robe, and entered Rājagṛha for alms. A large crowd of people saw him, and word spread throughout the city—"King Rudrāyaṇa has been initiated by the Blessed One, and he has entered Rājagṛha begging for alms!"

Hearing this, many hundreds and thousands of beings gathered around him. Even young women cloistered in their homes stood by various windows, vents shaped like bulls' eyes, and railings and began to peer out. The ministers informed King Bimbisāra, "My lord, King Rudrāyaṇa has entered Rājagṛha for alms, [559] and many hundreds and thousands of people have surrounded him."

Hearing this, King Bimbisāra approached the monk Rudrāyaṇa and, having approached, said this to him:

You enjoyed thousands of villages
and Roruka as well, O lord of men.
Now desiring alms that are cast off—
aren't you tormented?

You enjoyed eating from large bowls[1032]
of either gold or silver.[1033]
Now eating from a clay bowl—
aren't you tormented?

You enjoyed excellent rice
and meat with sauce.[1034]
Now eating dried-up rice gruel—
aren't you tormented?

You abandoned silk, cotton, and linen
from Koṭumbara and Vārāṇasī.
Now wearing old rags—
aren't you tormented?

You slept in a penthouse
with doors closed and bolted.[1035]
Now sitting at the roots of trees—
aren't you tormented?

You rested on a bed
that was soft like cotton.
Now sleeping on a bed of grass—
aren't you tormented?

You had a worthy and cherished wife
who was obedient and spoke sweetly.

And you left her crying—
aren't you tormented?

The backs of elephants were your vehicles,
as were horses and chariots.
Now you roam about on the ground on foot—
aren't you tormented?

You abandoned a treasury and storerooms
as well as great riches.
Now you possess nothing—
aren't you tormented?

Rudrāyaṇa said,

Poverty subdues a man,
even if he is indomitable,
for he must beg for his food.
Even the ox is tamed by the yoke.[1036]

King Bimbisāra said,

Are you upset, King?
Why speak as if you're destitute?
I'll give you half of my kingdom.
Enjoy your fill of pleasure![1037]

Are you upset, King?
Why speak as if you're destitute?
I will offer you the finest pleasures,
whatever it is that your heart desires. [560]

Rudrāyaṇa said,

King, destitute is one in this world
not in contact with the Buddha's dharmic form.[1038]
My lord, for one without aspirations on the triple path[1039]
the permanant state of nirvāṇa is surely secured.[1040]

But a king[1041] attached to what is unjust
on account of his aversion to dharma
is destitute, O King. Let this be known.
He will wander from darkness to darkness.

Listen to me, your majesty.
I will teach you the nature of dharma.
After hearing the dharma, if you understand it,
you will be pleased.[1042]

The body is without virtue
yet has one very great virtue.
Just as you fashion it,
so it will take shape.

One hundred years are said
to be the life span of a man.[1043]
What fun and pleasure is there
in children, wives, and money?[1044]

The work of a wife is said
to instill enmity in the son.[1045]
Thieves[1046] long for wealth.
King, I am free from bondage.

Medicines offer no protection,
nor do wealth or relatives.
Scientific learning, strength, and heroism
offer no protection from death.

Even powerful gods in this world,
living long lives in high places,
when their lives are finished will pass away—
who here[1047] is freed from bodily destruction?

Even the powerful rulers of kingdoms,
the Vṛṣṇis and Andhakas, the Kurus and Pāṇḍavas,[1048]
wealthy and burning with fame,[1049]
are not able to avoid death.[1050]

Not by restraint nor asceticism, O King,
not by an act of heroism and valor
nor massive wealth or vast riches[1051]
is one ever able to be released from death. [561]

Not in the sky or in mid-ocean
or by entering a mountain cave
is there a place on earth to be found[1052]
where one is not overpowered by death.[1053]

Not in the sky or in mid-ocean
or by entering a mountain cave
is there a place on earth to be found
where one is not overpowered by karma.

What pleasure is there in seeing
bones pigeon-gray in color

cast off and discarded
in the ten directions?[1054]

What pleasure is there in seeing
skulls the color of conch shells
discarded[1055] like gourds
in the autumn [wind]?[1056]

You shield it in the heat
and cover it in the cold.
But still, King, death will destroy
the self that is dear to you.

Under the influence of death,[1057]
one eats, dresses, and makes offerings.
All this is known as what is his;
the rest inevitably goes away.[1058]

A person accumulates true wealth,
which cannot be shared with others[1059]
and cannot be stolen by thieves,
through gifts and other good deeds.

Sickness, old age, and death will soon drag you off,
as a tiger would a deer he has slain.
Your friends can't cure the disease,
nor can all your kinsmen gathered together.

Left over from his earnings are
goods, grain, silver, and gold.[1060]
And contriving to claim this inheritance
are his sons, wives, and dependents.

If one's father dies with debt
his beloved sons won't [light] his funeral pyre.[1061]
They won't cry at his death with faces teary
nor say, "This is my father! What am I to do?"[1062] [562]

But if they think him rich,[1063] with disheveled hair
and faces teary, they do cry, "It's my father!"
They bring the flame before him and say,
"Oh! Would that he had lived forever!

Bearing his corpse wrapped in a shroud,
they take the flame and light his pyre.[1064]
While his relatives weep, he burns
with just a single cloth,
leaving behind worldly pleasure.[1065]

When he is born, he is born alone,
and when he dies, he dies alone.
Alone one suffers in this world,
for no being has a companion
while cycling through saṃsāra.

Seeing all this, good people
go forth and are no longer confined.
Those who forsake all contact with others
will never again bed down in a womb.

With each answer, King Bimbisāra was refuted by the eloquent monk Rudrāyaṇa. King Bimbisāra, at a loss for words, left silently.

Now for a while King Śikhaṇḍin managed to rule his kingdom justly, but then he began to rule unjustly.

"My lord," Hiru and Bhiru said, "rule the kingdom justly, not unjustly. Why is that? My lord, people are like trees that produce flowers and fruit. In the same way, my lord, that flower-bearing and fruit-bearing trees are carefully protected at the appropriate times so that when the time is right they always produce flowers and fruit, people who are protected will, when the time is right, always offer taxes and tributes."

The king was persuaded by his chief ministers, but after ruling the kingdom justly for a while, he once again began to rule unjustly. His chief ministers spoke to him three times about this, but the king's craving was spreading. Even though he was admonished, he kept backsliding.[1066] Infuriated, the king addressed his ministers: "Gentlemen, what sort of punishment is appropriate for someone who, three times, rejects the command of a kṣatriya king who has been duly consecrated?"

Some evil ministers among them said, "My lord, what more is there to know? His punishment is death." And they uttered these verses: [563]

> In the case of an evil minister,
> a loose tooth, or a [foul][1067] meal,
> the only pleasure to be found
> is in its removal.
>
> He who won't put to death a minister,
> even though intelligent, wise, a skilled disciplinarian,
> and in charge of the treasury and army,
> will himself be killed.

"Gentlemen," King Śikhaṇḍin said, "these two ministers were appointed by my father. I won't have them killed. But they should stay out of my sight." So the two of them were denied access to the king. Two other ministers, both of whom were evil, were appointed in their place.

"My lord," the two evil ministers said, "unless they are broken,[1068] shredded, heated, and crushed, sesame seeds don't yield sesame oil.[1069] Lord of men, like this are your subjects."

"What[1070] is done by these two ministers is final and not to be questioned," the king said. The two ministers then began to oppress the people.

Meanwhile a certain merchant who had brought his goods from the city of Roruka arrived in Rājagṛha. The venerable Rudrāyaṇa saw him and said,

> I hope Śikhaṇḍin is in Roruka,
> fit and healthy with his retinue,
> that he rules his kingdom justly
> and no enemy gives him trouble.

And the merchant said,

> It is true—Śikhaṇḍin is in Roruku,
> fit and healthy with his retinue,
> and no enemy gives him trouble.
> But he always rules unjustly.

The venerable Rudrāyaṇa began to question him. "Who is the chief minister? Under whose influence does Śikhaṇḍin oppress his subjects?"[1071]

"My lord," he said, "the ministers Hiru and Bhiru have been denied access to the king. Two other ministers, both of whom are evil, have been appointed in their place. It is under their influence that Śikhaṇḍin oppresses the people."

"Go, my friend," Rudrāyaṇa said, "console the residents of Roruka. I will go there on an alms tour.[1072] [564] I will keep Śikhaṇḍin from doing wrong and guide him toward what is right."

The merchant then disposed of his goods, took up new goods in turn, and set out. In due course, he arrived in Roruka, and he secretly informed his relatives, "Friends, I brought my goods to Rājagṛha, and there I saw the old king. He said, 'I will go to Roruka for an alms tour. I will keep Śikhaṇḍin from doing wrong and guide him toward what is right so that he won't oppress the people.'"

His relatives informed others, who in turn also informed others. In this way, from ear to ear, word also reached the ears of the two evil ministers. They reflected, "If the old king comes, he'll certainly reestablish Hiru and Bhiru as the chief ministers and make trouble for us. A plan needs to be devised so that the old king is killed while he is on his way here." So the two ministers informed King Śikhaṇḍin, "My lord, it is heard that the old king is coming."

"But he has gone forth as a monk," the king said. "What's his purpose in coming here?"

"My lord," they said, "how will one who has ruled even a single day ever be happy without a kingdom? He wants to rule this kingdom again!"

"If he becomes king," Śikhaṇḍin said, "then I'll be a prince as I was before. What's the objection?"[1073]

"My lord," they said, "this wouldn't be proper. How can someone who is now greeted respectfully by princes, ministers, townspeople, and villagers with thousands of folded hands, and who has ruled a kingdom, once again live the life of a prince? Better to leave the country than to live a prince's life. A man who once traveled on the back of an elephant may now travel by horseback, and one who traveled by horseback may now travel by palanquin, and one who traveled by palanquin may now travel on foot. In this way, one who once ruled a kingdom may now resume the life of a prince."

Having fallen prey to their deception, he said, "What's right then? How should I proceed?"

"My lord," they said, "he should be killed. If he isn't killed, he'll inevitably fall under the influence of evil ministers and kill my lord."

Thus addressed, he stood silent for a moment, his face full of sadness and pity, his heart overcome with tears, and he spoke with drawn-out words full of compassion and torment: [565] "Gentlemen, how can I kill my father?"

And the two ministers said, "Hasn't my lord heard?

Whether he be your father or brother,
or a son come forth from your body,
you should act against those who oppose you
and work to expand your lands.[1074]

And it is said,

One may have a thousand sons
who have boarded a single boat,
but if one among them is an enemy,
for his sake they should all be drowned.

And elsewhere it has been said,

One should sacrifice one person for the sake of the family,
one family for the sake of the village,
one village for the sake of the province,
but for one's own sake, one should sacrifice the earth.[1075]

"My lord, nothing should torment you.[1076] He deserves death and should be killed. If my lord delays now, those[1077] princes, ministers, townspeople, and villagers that are devoted to my lord will surely get upset and make trouble."

There is no evil act that a person who indulges the passions won't commit.

"Do as you must."

Pleased, satisfied, and delighted, the two evil ministers tried to incite some assassins: "Friends, go and kill the old king! We'll share the spoils with you."

The townspeople and villagers were very devoted to the old king, and no one could bring himself to kill him. Though the two ministers enticed them with silver, gold,[1078] gifts of villages, and so on, they still wouldn't do it. Incensed, the two ministers commanded the guards to the prison: "Men, go and lock up those people in prison, along with their children and wives and their friends, relations, and relatives."

When the people heard this they were afraid, so they consented and said, "My lord, don't be angry. We are your obedient servants. We'll go." So they set out with sharp daggers concealed under their arms.

After the three months of the rainy season, the venerable Rudrāyaṇa, with his robes fixed and readied, took his bowl and robe and approached the Blessed One. Having approached, he placed his head in veneration at the Blessed One's feet and then said this to him: "Bhadanta, I want to travel to the city of Roruka."

"Go Rudrāyaṇa," the Blessed One said. "And keep in mind the fact that your karma is of your own making."

The venerable Rudrāyaṇa then placed his head in veneration at the Blessed One's feet and left the Blessed One's presence. [566]

The very next morning the venerable Rudrāyaṇa got dressed, took his bowl and robe, and entered Rājagṛha for alms. After wandering through Rājagṛha for alms, he ate his meal, and after eating, he returned from his almsround. He then put away the bedding and seat that he had used, collected his bowl and robe, and then was impelled by the force of his karma:

> Karma drags one far away,
> and it drags one from afar.

It drags a creature to that place
where his karma will mature.

And so the venerable Rudrāyaṇa set out for Roruka. While traveling along, as he gradually made his way there, he entered a market town for alms. After wandering about for alms, he left town and then encountered those assassins. The assassins saw him, and he recognized them. The venerable Rudrāyaṇa then spent a day and a night with those men in the same park.

And then he asked them,

I hope Śikhaṇḍin is in Roruku,
fit and healthy with his retinue,
that he rules his kingdom justly
and no enemy gives him trouble.

"My lord," they said,

It is true—Śikhaṇḍin is in Roruku,
fit and healthy with his retinue,
and no enemy gives him trouble.
But he always rules unjustly.

Best of men, you did what was befitting to you,
marking the defeat of [karma by] a noble one.[1079]
But what is befitting to him,
soon you will know, gentle one.[1080]

"Gentlemen," the venerable Rudrāyaṇa said, "isn't Śikhaṇḍin pleased that I'm going there?"

"My lord," they said, "he isn't pleased."

"Gentlemen," he said, "if that's the case, I won't go. I'll turn back."

Then they uttered this verse:

Where will you go, hero among men?
Your son is not pleased that you're alive.
Unfortunate are we, employed by the king,
who have come here to kill you.

The venerable Rudrāyaṇa said, "Gentlemen, are you men my assassins?"

"Yes, my lord. We are assassins."

He reflected, "The Blessed One said, 'Rudrāyaṇa, keep in mind the fact that your karma is of your own making.' [567] This is what he meant by that. Existence is so altogether fleeting." With this understanding, he said to them, "Gentlemen, I have yet to achieve the goal for which I went forth as a monk. Wait a moment while I fulfill that duty that is encumbent upon me."[1081]

They conversed among themselves and then said, "My lord, do as you must."

Then the venerable Rudrāyaṇa sat at the base of a tree, crossing his legs so that he was curled up like the winding coil of a sleeping snake king, and remained in this peaceful posture.

The Blessed One has said that there are five benefits in having great learning. Such a person is

well versed in the aggregrates,
well versed in the elements,
well versed in the sense bases,
well versed in interdependent arising,
and not dependent on another for instruction or admonition.[1082]

Having gathered his strength, the venerable Rudrāyaṇa came to understand that ever-turning five-spoked wheel of saṃsāra; he dealt a final blow to rebirth in all realms of saṃsāra, since they are subject to decay and decline, scattering and destruction; and by ridding himself of all defilements, he directly experienced arhatship. Becoming an arhat,

he was free from attachment in the three realms;
he regarded clods of earth and gold as equal in value;
he possessed equanimity toward the sky
and the palm of his hand;
he didn't distinguish between being cut by a blade
and being anointed with sandalwood paste;
the eggshell [of his ignorance] was broken by knowledge;
he obtained the special knowledges, superhuman faculties,
and analytic insights;
and he was averse to worldly attainments, temptations,
and honors.
He became worthy of respect, honor, and obeisance
from the gods, including Indra and Upendra.

Having obtained arhatship, the venerable Rudrāyaṇa experienced liberation, pleasure, and joy, at which time he uttered this verse:

Though free from yokes and bonds,
torments and obstacles,
even now the monk Rudrāyaṇa
is not free from the dharma of kings.

With that said, he said to the assassins, "My friends, that which I should achieve I have achieved. Now it is your turn to fulfill the purpose for which you have come here."

"My lord," they said, "what should we say if King Śikhaṇḍin asks us, 'What did the old king pronounce at the time of his death?'"

"My friends, it should be said:

You have earned much demerit
from killing your father for a kingdom.
I will attain final nirvāṇa.
You will go to the Avīci hell.

"And this too should be said: 'You have committed two deadly sins at once—you have killed your father as well as an arhat monk who had destroyed the corruptions. You will pass a long time in the great hell known as Avīci (Ceaseless Torture). Confess your sin as sin![1083] Maybe then this karma will diminish, give out, and be completely exhausted.'" [568]

Then the venerable Rudrāyaṇa reflected, "I should make use of my magical powers and leave so that this living being[1084] [who plans to kill me] won't end up in hell." But when he began to make use of his magical powers to escape, karma ruined his plan.[1085] Not even an inkling of magical powers appeared to him, let alone magical powers themselves.[1086] Then one of those men, who was cruel at heart and who had abandoned any concern for the next world, withdrew a dagger from under his arm, cut off the venerable Rudrāyaṇa's head, and tossed it to the ground.

Then the Blessed One displayed his smile.

The Buddha's Smile and a Rain of Dirt

Now it is a law of nature that whenever lord buddhas manifest their smiles, rays of blue, yellow, red, and white light emerge from their mouths, some going downward and some going upward. Those that go downward enter the various hells[1087]—Sañjīva (Reviving), Kālasūtra (Black Thread), Saṃghāta (Crushing), Raurava (Shrieking), Mahāraurava (Loud Shrieking), Tapana (Heat), Pratāpana (Extreme Heat), Avīci (Ceaseless Torture), Arbuda (Blistering), Nirarbuda (Blisters Bursting), Aṭaṭa (Chattering Teeth), Hahava (Ugh!), Huhuva (Brrr!), Utpala (Blue Waterlily), Padma (Lotus), and Mahāpadma (Great Lotus). Becoming cold, they descend into the hot hells, and becoming hot, they descend into the cold hells. In this way, those rays of light alleviate the particular torments of those beings who dwell in these various hells. And so they think, "Friends, have we died and passed away from this place? Have we been reborn somewhere else?"

Then, in order to engender their faith, the Blessed One manifests a magical image of himself. Seeing this magical image, they think, "Friends, we haven't died and passed away from this place, nor have we been born someplace else. Instead, it's this person who we've never seen before; it's by his power that our particular torments are alleviated." Cultivating faith in their hearts toward this magical image, they then cast off that karma still to be suffered in these hells and take rebirth among gods and humans, where they become vessels for the [four noble] truths.

Those rays of light that go upward enter the various divine realms[1088]—Cāturmahārājika (Four Groups of the Great Kings), Trāyatriṃśa (Thirty-Three), Yāma (Free from Conflict), Tuṣita (Content), Nirmāṇarati (Delighting in Creation), Paranirmitavaśavartin (Masters of Others' Creations), Brahmakāyika (Brahmā's Assembly), Brahmapurohita (Brahmā's Priests), Brahmapārṣadya (Brahmā's Retinue),[1089] Mahābrahmaṇa (Great Brahmā), Parīttābha (Limited Splendor), Apramāṇābha (Immeasurable Splendor), Ābhāsvara (Radiant), Parīttaśubha (Limited Beauty), Apramāṇaśubha (Immeasurable Beauty), Śubhakṛtsna (Complete Beauty), Anabhraka (Unclouded), Puṇyaprasava (Merit Born), Bṛhatphala (Great Result), Abṛha (Not Great), Atapa (Serene), Sudṛśa (Clear Sighted), Sudarśa (Good-Looking), and finally Akaniṣṭha (Supreme). There they proclaim the truth of impermanence, suffering, emptiness, and no-self. And they utter these two verses: [569]

Strive! Go forth!
Apply yourselves to the teachings of the Buddha!
Destroy the army of death
as an elephant would a house of reeds.

Whoever diligently follows
this dharma and monastic discipline

will abandon the endless cycle of rebirth
and put an end to suffering.

Then those rays of light, having circulated through the billionfold world-system, come together directly behind the Blessed One.

If the Blessed One wants to reveal the past,
they vanish into the Blessed One from behind.
If he wants to predict the future,
they vanish into him from the front.[1090]
If he wants to predict a rebirth in hell,
they vanish into the sole of a foot.
If he wants to predict a rebirth as an animal,
they vanish into a heel.
If he wants to predict a rebirth as a hungry ghost,
they vanish into a big toe.
If he wants to predict a rebirth as a human,
they vanish into his knees.
If he wants to predict a reign of an armed wheel-turning king,
they vanish into his left palm.
If he wants to predict a reign of a wheel-turning king,
they vanish into his right palm.
If he wants to predict a rebirth as a god,
they enter his navel.
If he wants to predict an awakening as a disciple,
they vanish into his mouth.
If he wants to predict an awakening as a solitary buddha,
they vanish into the circle of hair between his eyebrows.
If he wants to predict unsurpassed perfect awakening,
they vanish into his *uṣṇīṣa*.

In this case, those rays of light circumambulated the Blessed One three times and then vanished into the sole of one of the Blessed One's feet.

The venerable Ānanda then respectfully cupped his hands together and addressed the Blessed One:

A bundle of diverse light rays,
variegated with a thousand colors,
comes forth from your mouth.
They illuminate every direction,
as though the sun were rising.

And then he uttered these verses:

Without pride, free from grief and passion,
buddhas are the cause of greatness in the world.
Not without reason do victors, defeaters of the enemy,
display a smile, white like the conch or lotus root.

O you who are resolute, an ascetic, and an excellent victor,[1091]
you know at once with your mind the desires of your listeners.
Destroy their doubts that have arisen, O best of sages,
with words excellent, enduring, and virtuous.

Masters, awakened ones,
those with the patience of an ocean or great mountain,
do not display a smile without reason.
Masses of people yearn to hear why it is
that resolute ones display a smile.

"It is so, Ānanda," the Blessed One said. "It is so. [570] Perfectly awakened tathāgatha arhats do not manifest a smile, Ānanda, without proper cause and reason. However, Ānanda,

Though free from yokes and bonds,
torments and obstacles,
still the monk Rudrāyaṇa
has been deprived of life.[1092]

"Ānanda, Rudrāyaṇa has obtained arhatship and been deprived of life."

Hearing this, the venerable Ānanda stood there, choked up with tears.[1093]

Meanwhile those assassins took the venerable Rudrāyaṇa's bowl, robe, and staff and went to Roruka where they informed the two evil ministers, "The old king has been killed." Hearing this, they were pleased and delighted and approached King Śikhaṇḍin.

"My lord," they said, "Congratulations! Now my lord's kingdom is without enemies!"

"How is that?"

"The enemy of my lord has been killed."

"What enemy?"

"The old king, my lord."

"How do you know that he was killed?"

Those assassins were then brought before him.

"My lord, these assassins are the ones who killed him."

"Gentlemen," King Śikhaṇḍin asked them, "how big was the old king's army?"

"My lord, where was this army of his? Here is his bowl, robe, and staff."

King Śikhaṇḍin fainted and fell to the ground. Splashed with water, the king regained his senses and said, "Gentlemen, what did the old king pronounce at the time of his death?"

"My lord, as the old king breathed his last,[1094] he said,

You have earned much demerit
from killing your father for a kingdom.

I will attain final nirvāṇa.
You will go to the Avīci hell.

"And this too should be said: 'You have committed two deadly sins at once—you have killed your father as well as an arhat monk who had destroyed the corruptions. You will pass a long time in the great hell known as Avīci. Confess your sin as sin! Maybe then this karma will diminish, give out, and be completely exhausted.'"

Struck by the arrow of grief,[1095] the king began to wilt like a reed plucked while still green [and immature].[1096] He summoned Hiru and Bhiru, his former chief ministers, and said, "Gentlemen, why didn't you stop me from commiting such a terrible deed?"

They said, "We were kept out of my lord's sight. How could we stop you?" [571]

The king then put the two evil ministers out of his sight, and Hiru and Bhiru were reestablished as chief ministers.

Now the two evil ministers secretly made two holes, one in the stūpa for Tiṣya and the other in the stūpa for Puṣya, and placed a kitten in each. Every day they trained the two kittens by giving them bits of meat: "Hey Tiṣya! Hey Puṣya! By this truth, this vow of truth, having deceived the people with your magical power and ruined[1097] offerings made in good faith, you were reborn in this lesser and lower existence as cats. By this truth, this vow of truth, accept these bits of meat,[1098] circumambulate your stūpa, and enter your hole."

When the two kittens had become well trained, those two evil ministers said to the [now principal] queen of [the deceased] King Rudrāyaṇa,[1099] "Your highness, your son has become lean and weak, wearied and emaciated. How can you ignore this?"

"What should I do?" she said. "It was you two who made him commit such a terrible deed."

"Your highness," they said, "when the bucket has fallen, do you want to toss in the rope as well?"

"Very well," she said. "Now with regard to killing his father, I can clear his mind about that.[1100] But who can clear his mind about killing an arhat?"

"Your highness," they said, "we can clear his mind about killing an arhat."

"If that's the case," she said, "it would be excellent."

The queen went to the king and said, "Son, why are you so pale, lean, and weak, wearied and emaciated?"

"Mother," he said, "so you're asking me as well—'Why are you so pale, lean, and weak, wearied and emaciated?' Why shouldn't I be pale, lean, and weak, wearied and emaciated? Under the influence of evil ministers, I committed two deadly sins at once—I killed my father as well as an arhat monk who had destroyed the corruptions. I will pass a long time in the great hell known as Avīci."

"Son," she said, "guarantee my safety and I will tell you the truth."

"Your safety is guaranteed," he said.

"My son," she said, "in truth,[1101] the king wasn't your father. When I was fertile, I made love with another man. Then you were born."

King Śikhaṇḍin reflected, "I haven't killed my father!" With this in mind, he said, "Mother, if that's the case, then I didn't kill my father. But there was still the killing of an arhat. How does one get out of that?" [572]

"Son," she said, "you should consult those who are masters of knowledge. They'll bring you closure."[1102] With that said, she departed.

The queen summoned the two evil ministers and said, "I have cleared his mind about killing his father. Now you two should clear his mind about killing an arhat."

Meanwhile King Śikhaṇḍin ordered his ministers, "Assemble all the ministers and those who are masters of knowledge."

So they assembled all the ministers and those who were masters of knowledge. The two evil ministers assembled together with them. All those people who were in the king's service began to speak congenially.[1103]

"My lord," some of them there said, "who saw him attaining arhatship?"

"My lord," others said, "arhats are like omniscient beings and can fly through the air!"

Then the evil ministers said, "My lord, why do you grieve about this?"

"You ask why I grieve about this?" the king said. "You were the ones who made me kill an arhat!"

"My lord, there are no arhats, so how can there be the killing of arhats?"

"I saw the arhats Tiṣya and Puṣya before my eyes!" the king said. "They performed miraculous deeds of causing fire and heat, making rain and lightning, and have now passed into the realm of remainderless nirvāṇa. And yet you two say, 'There are no arhats, so how can there be the killing of arhats?'"

The evil ministers said, "We will prove to my lord that they deceived the people with their magic, ruined offerings made to them in good faith, and were reborn in a lesser and lower existence as cats. Even to this day they each live in their own stūpa."

"Gentlemen," the king addressed the ministers, "if that's the case, then come. Let's go and see whether this is true."

Word spread throughout the city of Roruka. All the people living in the countryside also came out to see [whether it was true].[1104] Then the two evil ministers said, "Hey Tiṣya! Hey Puṣya! By this truth, this vow of truth, having deceived the people with your magical power and ruined offerings made in good faith, you were reborn in this lesser and lower existence as cats and now each of you lives in your own stūpa. By this truth, this vow of truth, each of you take these bits of meat, circumabulate your stūpa, and enter your hole."

Thus addressed, those two cats came out of their stūpas, and many hundreds and thousands of beings saw them. [573] Then the two cats took those bits of meat, circumambulated their respective stupas, and entered their respective holes.

"Did my lord see that?" the two evil ministers asked.

"I saw it," the king said.

"My lord, there are no arhats in this world. It's only people's empty talk."

The king's view that there were arhats in the world immediately disappeared. Those who were nonbelievers developed a false view. Those who stood between nonbelief and belief had doubt. And those who were believers were stunned,[1105] dejected, and suspicious.[1106]

King Śikhaṇḍin reflected, "If there are no arhats in the world, why should I give alms to the noble Mahākātyāyana[1107] and the five hundred members of his retinue, and to the nun Śailā and the five hundred members of her retinue?" So he stopped giving alms to the monks and nuns, and the monks and nuns left Roruka. But the venerable Mahākātyāyana and the nun Śailā stayed there in accordance with the rules of the monastic discipline.[1108]

After some time, King Śikhaṇḍin left the city of Roruka just as the venerable Mahākātyāyana was entering it for alms. The venerable Mahākātyāyana saw the king and then stepped off to one side and waited. "May he not refute his faith!" he thought.

King Śikhaṇḍin saw him standing off to one side, and upon seeing him, he said, "Gentlemen, why does the noble Mahākātyāyana, having seen me, step off to one side and wait?"

Following behind the king were the chief ministers Hiru and Bhiru. "My lord," they said, "the noble Mahākātyāyana must be thinking that the lord proceeds after performing auspicious rituals and benedictions for a safe journey; that he shouldn't experience a loss of faith; and that since the work of dyeing [robes] is difficult,[1109] the lord shouldn't splatter[1110] his robes with dirt."[1111]

The king stood silently.

The venerable Mahākātyāyana then continued wandering for alms in the city of Roruka. Just as he was leaving, King Śikhaṇḍin was entering. Just as before, the venerable Mahākātyāyana stepped off to one side.

"Gentlemen," King Śikhaṇḍin said, "when the noble Mahākātyāyana saw me before, he stepped off to one side and waited, and now [he does the same]. What is the reason for this?"

Following behind the king were the two evil ministers. "My lord," they said, "Mahākātyāyana said, [574] 'Let me not go forth [soiled] with the dirt of this father-killer!'"[1112]

Being indiscriminate, the king became furious when he heard this. "Gentlemen," he said, "whoever holds me dear should throw a handful of dirt on that shaven-headed ascetic!"

All of the people there threw a handful of dirt. Since the king had a great army, and each and every person threw a single handful of dirt on the venerable Mahākātyāyana, a huge pile of dirt was amassed on top of him.[1113] The venerable Mahākātyāyana, however, had magically created a hut of leaves for himself where he remained. The cowherds and shepherds saw that the venerable Mahākātyāyana was buried and, being alert,[1114] gathered around him. The chief ministers Hiru and Bhiru, who had been lagging behind the king, then arrived there.

"Gentlemen," they asked, "what is this?"

"This evil king who killed his father," they said, "has buried the noble Mahākātyāyana, who does no wrong and causes no harm,[1115] under a pile of dirt."

With lumps in their throats and faces streaked with tears, the two of them, along with the cowherders and shepherds, began to remove the dirt. Then the venerable Mahākātyāyana emerged. Hiru and Bhiru fell prostrate at his feet and asked, "Noble sir, what is this?"

"What else could have happened?"[1116] he said.

"Noble one," the two of them said, "Śikhaṇḍin has perpetrated this deed upon Mahākātyāyana[1117] with the help of the people. What will come of this?"[1118]

"Seven days from now the city of Roruka will be buried under a pile of dirt."

"Noble one, what will be the sequence of events?"

"Venerable ones, on the first day a great wind will come that will clear the city of Roruka of stones, pebbles, and gravel. On the second day, a rain of flowers will fall. On the third, a rain of fine clothes. On the fourth, a rain of silver.[1119] On the fifth, a rain of gold. Then all those who live in the vicinity of Roruka who performed this collective deed will enter the city. After they enter, on the sixth day, a rain of diamonds will fall. And on the seventh day, there will be a rain of dirt."

"Noble one," the two chief ministers said, "are we to share in this karma?"

"My friends, you two won't share in this karma."

"Noble one, if that's the case, how can we get out of the city?"

"You should dig an underground channel from your home to the river and keep a boat stored near your house," he said. [575] "When the rain of diamonds falls, fill the boat with them and escape."

The two chief ministers fell prostrate at his feet and then entered Roruka. They went before the king and said, "Has my lord done anything to the noble Mahākātyāyana? Why was he buried under a pile of dirt?"[1120]

"Gentlemen," the king said, "is he alive?"

"He is alive, my lord."

"What does he say?"

"My lord, this is what he says—'Seven days from now the city of Roruka will be buried under a pile of dirt.'"

"What does he say will be the sequence of events?"[1121]

"My lord, this is what he says:

> On the first day a great wind will come that will clear the city of Roruka of stones, pebbles, and gravel. On the second day, a rain of flowers will fall. On the third day, a rain of fine clothes. On the fourth, a rain of silver. On the fifth, a rain of gold. Then all those who live in the vicinity of Roruka who performed this collective deed will enter the city. After they enter, on the sixth day, a rain of diamonds will fall. And on the seventh day, there will be a rain of dirt."[1122]

The two evil ministers said, "What else would someone say who no longer receives alms and was buried under a rain of dirt? Or perhaps he is saying that this evil deed comes from the lord himself!"[1123]

"That may be so," King Śikhaṇḍin reflected.

The chief ministers Hiru and Bhiru both made faces, wrung their hands in despair, and departed.

Now poor Hiru had a boy, a son named Śyāmāka (Dark One), and poor Bhiru had a daughter, a girl named Śyāmāvatī (Dusky). Hiru presented the boy Śyāmāka to the venerable Mahākātyāyana and said, "Noble one, if he has any roots of virtue, then initiate him. If not, let him be your personal attendant."

Bhiru likewise presented his daughter Śyāmāvatī to the nun Śailā and said, "Noble one, if she has any roots of virtue, then initiate her. If not, in Kauśāmbī there is a householder named Ghoṣila (Renowned) who is a friend of mine. [576] Hand her over to him."

The nun Śailā agreed. She then took Śyāmāvatī and, making use of her magical powers, left Roruka. In Kauśāmbī, she gave her to the householder Ghoṣila[1124] and explained the situation as she had been instructed.

The venerable Mahākātyāyana, however, stayed right where he was. The chief ministers Hiru and Bhiru dug an underground channel between their homes and the river and placed a boat nearby. Then, one day, a great wind came that cleared the city of Roruka of stones, pebbles, and gravel. On the second day, a rain of flowers fell.

"My lord," the two evil ministers said, "it is heard that on behalf of King Māndhātā a rain of gold fell for seven days.[1125] This rain of flowers has fallen for my lord. Soon a rain of fine clothes will fall."

On the third day a rain of fine clothes fell.

"This rain of fine clothes has fallen for my lord," the two evil ministers said. "Soon a rain of silver will fall."

On the fourth day a rain of silver fell.

"This rain of silver has fallen for my lord," the two evil ministers said. "Soon a rain of gold will fall."

On the fifth day a rain of gold fell.

"This rain of gold has fallen for my lord," the two evil ministers said. "Soon a rain of diamonds will fall."

Then[1126] those who lived in the vicinity of Roruka who had performed that collective deed entered the city of Roruka. After they entered, on the sixth day, a rain of diamonds fell. The chief ministers Hiru and Bhiru filled their boat with them and fled.

In one region, Hiru[1127] founded a city name Hirukam. It came to be known as Hirukam.[1128] In another region, Bhiru founded a city called Bhiruka. It came to be known as Bhirukaccha.[1129]

On the seventh day, a rain of dirt began to fall. Nonhumans blocked the gates to the city.[1130]

"Noble one," Śyāmāka said, "what is all this noise and commotion?"

"Son," the venerable Mahākātyāyana said, "hold a brass bowl out the window and then retrieve it."[1131]

So he held a brass bowl[1132] out the window and then retrieved it. It was filled up halfway with dirt.[1133] [577]

The venerable Mahākātyāyana reflected, "There is still some room left."[1134] A short while later he held it out again; it was heaped full.[1135] Then he reflected, "Now there's no room left.[1136] It's time to go."

Then the guardian deity of Roruka approached the venerable Mahākātyāyana and, having approached, venerated his feet and said, "Noble one, I will come with you. I will serve the noble one." The venerable Mahākātyāyana consented.

"Son," the venerable Mahākātyāyana said to Śyāmāka, "take hold of the edge of my robe. Let's go."

Śyāmāka took hold of the edge of his robe, and then making use of his magical powers, the venerable Mahākātyāyana set off up into the sky with Śyāmāka in tow. The guardian deity of Roruka, making use of her own magical powers, followed close behind them. Soon the city of Roruka was buried under a pile of dirt.

In due course they arrived at a market town called Khara,[1137] and there they stayed in a granary.[1138] The venerable Mahākātyāyana left

Śyāmāka at the granary and entered the town for alms.[1139] As a result of the divine power of the deity [from Roruka], the grain in the granary began to increase. A man staying there saw Śyāmāka, then approached him and said, "Boy, as a result of your power, the grain in this granary is increasing!"

"It isn't a result of my power that the grain in this granary is increasing," Śyāmāka said. "It's because the guardian deity of Roruka has come here and now stays in this place. It's because of her power that the grain in the granary increases."

The man approached the deity, fell prostrate at her feet, and said, "Deity, I'm going to my village. Hold on to this lock and key[1140] until I return. Don't give them to anyone except me." The deity accepted them.[1141]

The man went into town, gathered together the town's residents, and said, "Friends, the guardian deity from Roruka has come here and now stays in the granary. As a result of her power, the grain at the granary increases. I have placed in her hands a lock and key and [said],[1142] 'Deity, I'm going to my village. Hold on to this lock and key until I return. Don't give them to anyone except me.' I now have a deal for all of you: [578] If you appoint my son as guildmaster, I'll commit suicide. Then the deity will never leave town, your life's pleasures will increase, and all disasters will be averted."

The town's residents appointed the man's son as guildmaster, and the man committed suicide. The town's residents then made[1143] the entire town beautiful with scents and flowers, as well as with umbrellas, flags, and banners, and then took an offering and approached the deity. Having approached, [the new guildmaster] fell prostrate at her feet and said, "Deity, please settle down here.[1144] Please stay!"

"There is no place for me here. I am the personal attendant of the noble Mahākātyāyana."

"Deity," the venerable Mahākātyāyana said,[1145] "focus your attention on the person from whom you received the lock and key." She began to focus her attention and saw that that person had died.

"Gentlemen," she said to the town's residents, "I will stay on one condition—construct an altar for the noble one just as you did for me."[1146]

They agreed. The town's residents constructed an altar for the noble Mahākātyāyana just as they had for the deity. Then the deity took the lamp that had been set out for her in town and placed it on the altar for the venerable Mahākātyāyana.[1147] A man standing on a protective wall[1148] saw her take the lamp and go by. He reflected, "This deity that goes by must be the noble Mahākātyāyana's mistress."

The deity read the man's mind and was furious. "The residents of this market town entertain evil thoughts. They slander the noble Mahākātyāyana, who is virtuous[1149] and who is never satisfied with the merit he has earned."

The deity then[1150] spread a plague in that market town, and many people died. As the dead were being brought out on all sorts of funeral biers, they began to get tangled together.[1151] The town's residents summoned soothsayers and asked, "What is this?"

"It's the wrath of the deity," the soothsayers said.

The town's residents began to beg the deity for forgiveness.

"You dishonor the noble Mahākātyāyana, who is virtuous," the deity said.

"Forgive us, deity," they said. "No one will dishonor him again."

"I will forgive you on one condition," she said. "Honor the noble Mahākātyāyana just as you honored me."[1152] [579]

"Forgive us, deity," they said. "We'll act in a more respectful manner."

The deity forgave them,[1153] and they in turn honored the venerable Mahākātyāyana in a more respectful manner.

After passing the rainy season there, the venerable Mahākātyāyana took Śyāmāka, bid farewell to the deity, and prepared to set off.

"Noble one," the deity said, "give me some token so that I can stay here and still serve you."

He gave her that brass bowl.[1154] The deity put it down[1155] and right there established a stūpa and initiated a festival. It came to be known as

Kāṃśimaha (Brass Bowl Festival).[1156] Even today monks who venerate shrines venerate it.

Śyāmāka clung to the edge of the venerable Mahākātyāyana's robe, and as he was hanging there, cowherders and cattleherders saw him. "Someone is hanging! Someone is hanging!" they shouted. And so the people in that place came to be known as the Lambakapāla (Hanging Herders).[1157]

Then the venerable Mahākātyāyana arrived at another market town. Leaving Śyāmāka at the base of a tree, he entered the town for alms. In that market town, the king had died without a son, so the townspeople and villagers had gathered together.

"Gentlemen," they said, "who should we anoint as king?"

Some of the people there said, "One who is very powerful because of his merit."

Others said, "How is such a person identified?"

"Appoint examiners," some others said.

So they appointed examiners, who began to travel around and about.[1158] They saw someone taking a nap under a tree. As they contemplated his appearance, they saw that the shadows of the other trees were leaning eastward and prone eastward, but the shadow of that particular tree never left Śyāmāka's body. Seeing this, they began to speak among themselves: "Gentlemen, this being is very powerful because of his merit. We should anoint him [as king]."

They woke him and said to him, "Boy, accept the throne!"

"I'm not interested in being a king," he said. "I am the personal attendent of the noble Mahākātyāyana."

The venerable Mahākātyāyana heard this and then began to focus his attention [580]—"Does the boy possess the karma for becoming a king or not?" He saw that he did. So he said, "Son, accept the throne. But you must rule according to dharma."

Śyāmāka accepted the throne, and they anointed him as king. Since the boy Śyāmāka ruled there, it came to be known as Śyāmākarājya (Kingdom of Śyāmāka).

The venerable Mahākātyāyana then arrived in Vokkāṇa.[1159] The venerable Mahākātyāyana's mother had been reborn in Vokkāṇa, and when she saw the venerable Mahākātyāyana, she said, "Oh! After a long time I get to see my dear son.[1160] After such a long time I get to see him." Then a stream of milk began to flow from her breasts.

"Mother, mother," the venerable Mahākātyāyana consoled her.

Then she offered food to the venerable Mahākātyāyana.

Knowing her inclinations, propensities, makeup, and nature, he then gave her a discourse on the dharma that elucidated the four noble truths.[1161] When she heard this, with her thunderbolt of knowledge she broke through that mountain, which is the false view of individuality that arises with its twenty peaks of incorrect views, and directly experienced the reward of the stream-enterer. Having seen the truth, three times she uttered this inspired utterance:

What the Blessed One has done for the likes of me, Bhadanta,
  neither my mother nor my father have done,
  nor any king,
  nor deities or dear ones,
  nor any of my kinsmen or relatives,
  nor deceased ancestors,
  nor ascetics or brahmans.
Oceans of blood and tears have dried up!
Mountains of bones have been scaled!
The doors to the lower realms of existence have been closed!
The doors to heaven and liberation have been opened!
I have been established among gods and humans!

And she said,

A good son should perform
an incredible deed for his mother,[1162]
and you have done that for me,
focusing my mind on liberation.

You lifted me out of the lower realms of existence
and established me in heaven and liberation.
Well done, my son! With great effort,[1163]
you have accomplished an incredible deed.

The venerable Mahākātyāyana then established that good daughter[1164] in the [four noble] truths and said, "Mother, farewell. I'm going now."

"Son," she said, "if that's the case, give me something[1165] so that I can stay here and still offer worship."

He gave her his staff. [581] She constructed a stūpa and in it mounted that [staff].[1166] And so it came to be known as the Staff Stūpa. Even today monks who venerate shrines venerate it.

The venerable Mahākātyāyana, wanting to travel to the Middle Country, arrived in Sindhu. That [guardian] deity living in the North Country said this to the venerable Mahākātyāyana: "Noble one, give me some token so that I can stay here and still offer worship."

He reflected, "The Blessed One has said that shoes[1167] are not to be worn in the Middle Country. I'll offer them to her."[1168] So he gave his shoes to her.[1169] She built two altars, placing them inside. The site came to be known as Pūleśvara (Lord of Shoes).[1170]

In due course the venerable Mahākātyāyana arrived in Śrāvastī. Seeing him, the monks said, "Welcome! Welcome, venerable one! Did your travels go well?"

"Venerable ones," he said, "in some measure they were pleasant and in some measure unpleasant."

"What was pleasant and what was unpleasant?" the monks asked.

"The service I did for sentient beings—that was pleasant," he said. "King Śikhaṇḍin and the residents of Roruka[1171] burying me under a pile of dirt, and the chief ministers Hiru and Bhiru barely escaping—that was unpleasant."

Then some petty[1172] monks there said with scorn, "That father-killer murdered the venerable Rudrāyaṇa, who had attained arhatship and who did no wrong and caused no harm.[1173] This is only the flower for him. The fruit will be something else entirely."

Some monks in doubt asked the Lord Buddha, the remover of all doubts, "Bhadanta, what deed did the venerable Rudrāyaṇa do so that he was born in a family that was rich, wealthy, and prosperous; went forth as a monk in the Blessed One's order where, by ridding himself of all defilements, he directly experienced arhatship; and having obtained arhatship was then killed by a sword?"

The Blessed One said, "The deeds that the monk Rudrāyaṇa[1174] has performed and accumulated have now come together, and their conditions have matured. They remain before him like an oncoming flood and will certainly come to pass. Those deeds were performed and accumulated by Rudrāyaṇa. Who else will experience their results? [582] For those deeds that are performed and accumulated, monks, do not mature outside of oneself—neither in the element of earth nor in the element of water, in the element of fire or in the element of wind. Instead, those deeds that are performed and accumulated, both good and bad, mature in the aggregates, the elements, and the sense bases that are appropriated when one is reborn.

> Actions never come to naught,
> even after hundreds of millions of years.
> When the right conditions gather and the time is right,
> then they will have their effect on embodied beings.

The Hunter and the Deer Park

Previously, monks, in a time gone by—when no lord buddhas are born, solitary buddhas can arise in the world.[1175] They have compassion for the poor and neglected, they live in remote areas, they are [solitary] like the rhinoceros, and they alone are worthy of people's offerings.

Now in a certain market town there lived a hunter. And not far from that town was a pond that was a refuge for many deer. Every day the hunter would [go there and] set many traps and bait snares for the decimation, destruction, and death of many deer. Those traps and baited snares of his never failed.

Meanwhile a solitary buddha, after traveling through the countryside, arrived at that market town and stayed in a temple there for a day and night.[1176] In the morning, he got dressed, took his bowl and robe,[1177] and entered the market town for alms. After wandering for alms, he reflected, "During the day the temple is crowded. I'll eat my alms and pass my time outside of town in a peaceful place." He left town, and as he approached the pond, he thought, "This is a peaceful place—yes, this is a peaceful place."

Having approached the pond, he placed his bowl and strainer[1178] off to one side, washed his feet, rinsed his hands, strained water, gathered dried leaves, and sat down. When he finished his meal, he rinsed his hands, mouth, and bowl,[1179] placed his bowl and strainer back in their proper place, washed his feet, sat down at the base of a tree, and crossing his legs so that he was curled up like the winding coil of a sleeping snake king, remained in this peaceful posture.

On that day, because of the smell of a human, not even a single deer was captured. The hunter got up at dawn and approached the pond. He checked his traps and baited snares,[1180] but he didn't see even a single deer. [583] It occurred to him, "Those traps and baited snares of mine always catch something. Why is it that today not even a single deer was caught?" So he began to search all around the pond. He saw human footprints, and he followed those tracks until he saw that solitary buddha sitting in a peaceful posture. He reflected, "Peaceful beings who have gone forth as monks enjoy themselves in places like this. If I don't destroy him today, he'll surely destroy my livelihood. Certainly he must be killed."

Then the hunter, who was cruel at heart and who had abandoned any concern for the next world, drew to his ear his bow, which was the size of an elephant's trunk,[1181] and then struck the solitary buddha in a vital point with a poisoned arrow. That great being, the solitary buddha, reflected, "Let this poor hunter not be forever beaten and battered. I'll give him a helping hand." So like a royal goose with outstretched wings, he flew high into the sky and began to perform the miraculous deeds of causing fire and heat, making rain and lightning.

Magic quickly wins over the ordinary person. Like a tree cut down at the roots, the hunter fell prostrate at the solitary buddha's feet and said, "Come down! Come down, O you who are so righteous and worthy of offerings! Offer me a helping hand, for I am mired in the mud of defilement!"

Out of compassion for the hunter, the solitary buddha descended. Then he extracted the arrow from his body and applied a poultice.

"Noble one," the hunter said, "let us go to my home. Whatever little bit of gold there is to give away, I'll make sure it reaches you."[1182]

Then the solitary buddha reflected, "Whatever I was to achieve with this foul body [has been achieved].[1183] Now it is time that I pass into that peaceful realm of remainderless nirvāṇa." Right in front of the hunter, the solitary buddha again ascended into the sky, displayed various miracles, and then passed into the realm of remainderless nirvāṇa.

That hunter was wealthy, so he built a funeral pyre with all kinds of scented woods, set fire to it, and later extinguished it with milk. The hunter then placed the solitary buddha's bones in a new pot[1184] and established a stūpa for his remains.[1185] Umbrellas, flags, and banners were raised there, and then the hunter honored it with offerings of perfume, garlands, and incense, fell prostrate before it, and made this fervent aspiration: "Although I have committed a terrible offense against one so righteous and worthy of offerings, may I not suffer from this deed. And since I have also performed a good deed, by this root of virtue may I be reborn in a family that is rich, wealthy, and prosperous, [584] and may I obtain such virtues so that I may please and not displease a teacher even more distinguished than this one!"

"Monks, what do you think? The hunter at that time and at that juncture was none other than the monk Rudrāyaṇa. Since he struck a solitary buddha in a vital point with a poisoned arrow, as a result of that action, he burned in hell for many hundreds of years, many thousands of years, and because of the karma remaining from that act, five hundred times he has been reborn as a deer at this very pond and then struck in a vital point with a poisoned arrow.[1186] Even today, after obtaining arhatship, he died by the sword."

Once again some monks in doubt asked the Lord Buddha, the remover of all doubts, "Bhadanta, what deed did Śīkhaṇḍin, the residents of Roruka, and the venerable Mahākātyāyana do so that they were buried under piles of dirt, while the chief ministers Hiru and Bhiru escaped?"

"Monks," the Blessed One said, "the deeds that they themselves performed and accumulated have now come together, and their conditions have matured. They remain before them like an oncoming flood and will certainly come to pass. Those deeds were performed and accumulated by them. Who else will experience their results? For those deeds that are performed and accumulated, monks, do not mature outside of oneself—neither in the element of earth nor in the element of water, in the element of fire or in the element of wind. Instead, those deeds that are done, both good and bad, mature in the aggregates, the elements, and the sense bases that are appropriated when one is reborn.

> Actions never come to naught,
> even after hundreds of millions of years.

When the right conditions gather and the time is right,
then they will have their effect on embodied beings."

A Girl Throws Garbage on a Solitary Buddha

Monks, previously, in yet another market town, there lived a householder. He brought home a girl from an appropriate family as his wife, and with her he fooled around, enjoyed himself, and made love. From fooling around, enjoying himself, and making love, a son was born. Then, from once again fooling around, enjoying himself, and making love, a daughter was born.[1187] When daughters were born in that town, suitors would eventually come to them with proposals of marriage. [585] But no one came for her.

When no buddhas are born, solitary buddhas can arise in the world. They have compassion for the poor and neglected, they live in remote areas, and they alone are worthy of people's offerings.

Meanwhile a solitary buddha, after traveling through the countryside, arrived in that market town. The girl, who was cleaning her house, threw her garbage over the railing. It fell on the head of that solitary buddha as he was wandering for alms.

That girl saw the garbage fall on the solitary buddha's head, but she felt no regret. By chance,[1188] on that very day a suitor came for her.

"What did you do today so that a suitor came for you?"[1189] her brother asked.

"I threw some garbage on that solitary buddha," she explained.

Her brother smiled.

Then that girl informed another girl,[1190] and she informed yet another.[1191] And so this heretical belief arose in people's minds: "When suitors approach a young woman for marriage, she should throw garbage on that solitary buddha."

All solitary buddhas, great beings that they are, recoil from dishonor. And so that solitary buddha left town. Then the young women in town began to throw garbage on top of seers who possessed the five superhuman faculties. They left town as well. Then they began to throw garbage on top of their parents.

In that market town there lived two virtuous[1192] householders. "Friends," they said,[1193] "this is a false dharma that is spreading.[1194] It must be stopped!" Once admonished by those two householders, young women in town stopped their dishonorable ways.

"What do you think, monks? That girl who threw garbage on a solitary buddha was none other than Śikhaṇḍin. The residents of that market town were none other than the residents of Roruka. Since they propagated a heretical belief about solitary buddhas,[1195] as a result of that action, they were buried under a pile of dirt. The two householders who stopped them were none other than the chief ministers Hiru and Bhiru.[1196] As a result of that action, they escaped. That girl's brother who smiled was none other than the monk Kātyāyana. Since he smiled, as a result of that action, he was buried under a pile of dirt. Had he not smiled, he wouldn't have been buried under a pile of dirt.[1197] [586] If he had developed a heretical view, then when the monk Kātyāyana was buried under a pile of dirt, he would have straightaway met with his death.

"And so, monks, the result of absolutely evil actions is absolutely evil, the result of absolutely pure actions is absolutely pure, and the result of mixed actions is mixed. Therefore monks, because of this, you should reject absolutely evil actions and mixed ones as well and strive to perform only absolutely pure actions. It is this, monks, that you should learn to do."

The monks rejoiced at the words of the Blessed One.

So ends the *Rudrāyana-avadāna*, the concluding chapter in the glorious *Divyāvadāna*.

Appendix

The Cosmos According to the *Divyāvadāna*

Buddhist cosmology normally divides life within saṃsāra into three realms—the desire realm, the form realm, and the formless realm. The *Divyāvadāna* mentions the various existences and heavens in the desire realm as well as the seventeen heavens in the form realm, but it doesn't mention the four spheres in the formless realm, which are populated by a class of gods with minds but no physical bodies.

These three realms are inhabited by five types of beings: gods, humans, hungry ghosts, animals, and hell beings. Other Buddhist cosmologies include a realm of antigods (*asuras*) between those of humans and hungry ghosts. The *Divyāvadāna* mentions the antigods and Vemacitrin, one of their chiefs, but they do not seem to inhabit their own level of existence.

Other materials also describe a correspondence between psychology and cosmology, such that one's state of mind corresponds to one's level of existence. For example, beings in the desire realm *(kāmadhātu)* tend to have thoughts within the sphere of desire *(kāmāvacara)*, and beings that attain high levels of meditative awareness psychically visit, as it were, the levels of existence of higher classes of beings. The *Divyāvadāna*, however, does not discuss this connection.

The chart that follows presents the various types of beings, the realms and levels of existence that they inhabit, and their average lifespans.[1198] Please read it as two long columns.

TYPE OF BEING	LIFESPAN	
Gods *(deva)*		FORMLESS REALM *arūpadhātu*
Naivasañjñānāsañjñāyatana (Sphere of Neither Consciousness nor Unconsciousness)	84,000 eons	
Ākiñcanyāyatana (Sphere of Nothingness)	60,000 eons	
Vijñānānantyāyatana (Sphere of Infinite Consciousness)	40,000 eons	
Ākāśānantyāyatana (Sphere of Infinite Space)	20,000 eons	
Gods *(deva)*		FORM REALM *rūpadhātu*
Akaniṣṭha (Supreme)[1199]	16,000 eons	
Sudarśa (Clear Sighted)	8,000 eons	
Sudṛśa (Good-Looking)	4,000 eons	
Atapa (Serene)	2,000 eons	
Abṛha (Not Great)	1,000 eons	
Bṛhatphala (Great Result)	500 eons	
Puṇyaprasava (Merit Born)	250 eons	
Anabhraka (Unclouded)	125 eons	
Śubhakṛtsna (Complete Beauty)	64 eons	
Apramāṇaśubha (Immeasurable Beauty)	32 eons	
Parīttaśubha (Limited Beauty)	16 eons	
Ābhāsvara (Radiant)	8 eons	
Apramāṇābha (Immeasurable Splendor)	4 eons	
Parīttābha (Limited Splendor)	2 eons	
Mahābrahmaṇa (Great Brahmā)	1 eon	
Brahmapurohita (Brahmā's Priests)	1/2 eon	
Brahmakāyika (Brahmā's Assembly)	1/3 eon	

Human Beings *(manuṣya)*	variable	DESIRE REALM *kāmadhātu*
FOUR CONTINENTS *(caturdvīpa)*		
Jambudvīpa (Black Plum Island) in the south		
Pūrvavideha (Eastern Videha) in the east		
Aparagodānīya (Western Godānīya) in the west		
Uttarakuru (Northern Kuru) in the north		
Hungry Ghosts *(preta)*	unspecified	
Animals *(tiryagyoni)*	unspecified	
Hell Beings *(naraka)*	unspecified	
COLD HELLS		
Arbuda (Blistering)[1201]		
Nirarbuda (Blisters Bursting)		
Aṭaṭa (Chattering Teeth)		
Hahava (Ugh!)		
Huhuva (Brrr!)		
Utpala (Blue Lotus)[1202]		
Padma (Lotus)		
Mahāpadma (Great Lotus)		
HOT HELLS		
Sañjīva (Reviving)		
Kālasūtra (Black Thread)		
Saṅghāta (Crushing)		
Raurava (Shrieking)		
Mahāraurava (Loud Shrieking)		
Tapana (Heat)		
Pratāpana (Extreme Heat)		
Avīci (Ceaseless Torture)		

DESIRE REALM
kāmadhātu

Gods *(deva)*

SIX HEAVENS

Paranirmitavaśavartin (Masters of Others' Creations)	9,219,000,000 years
Nirmāṇarati (Delighting in Creation)	2,304,000,000 years
Tuṣita (Content)	576,000,000 years
Yāma (Free from Conflict)	144,000,000 years
Trāyastriṃśa (Thirty-Three) home to Śakra, lord of the gods	36,000,000 years[1200]
Cāturmahārājika (Four Groups of the Great Kings)	9,000 years

Four Great Kings

- Kubera = Vaiśravaṇa = Dhanada (Bestower of Wealth)
  guardian of the north and lord of the yakṣas
- Dhṛtarāṣṭra (One Whose Kingdom Is Secure)
  guardian of the east and lord of celestial musicians
- Virūḍhaka (Sprouted)
  guardian of the south and lord of the *kumbhāṇḍa*s
- Virūpākṣa (Ugly Eyes)
  guardian of the west and lord of the nāgas

Sadāmatta Gods (Ever-Intoxicated)

Mālādhāra (Bearing Garlands)

Karoṭapāṇi (Bowl-in-Hand)

Notes

1 As an example, see the ways that Dölpa, Gampopa, and Sakya Paṇḍita (2015: 115, 169, 228, 407, 417), great Tibetan scholars from the twelfth and thirteenth centuries, integrate into their expositions of Buddhist practice various stories that are preserved in the *Divyāvadāna*—although they likely knew these stories from their versions in the *Mūlasarvāstivāda-vinaya*.

2 See too Maria Heim's (2014: 181–216) exploration of how Buddhaghosa, the great fifth-century commentator, understands Buddhist stories and "their capacity to produce affective experience." As Heim (2014: 214) explains, "Stories reflect on action in particular ways and value a particularism that does not necessarily lead to universals or to grand theory. They are open in important ways to multiple interpretations, and they place value on the *process* of puzzling through the opacity of human action."

3 See, for example, Mukhopadhyaya 1954, Sharma 1992, and Miyazaki, Nagashima, Tamai, and Liqun 2015. See too DS 4.

4 See too Klaus 1983: 5–22.

5 Cowell and Neil (Divy vi) explain that "all these mss., except F, are thus only modern copies, made with more or less care from one original, which is now in the possession of Pandit Indrānand of Patan, Nepal," and which, they note, Cecil Bendall examined and dated to the seventeenth century. The manuscript tradition, however, may not be so singular. Jonathan Silk (2008c: 67) quotes an email from Hengo Harimoto, who identifies this ur-manuscript as one filmed by the Nepal-German Manuscript Preservation Project: "This manuscript (NGMPP reel A 123/6, National Archives Kathmandu acc. no. 3/295) is most likely the one once seen by Bendall . . . Having said that, I am very skeptical that this manuscript was the source of all the other mss. Cowell and Neil used." Still, the manuscripts of the *Divyāvadāna* appear to be quite uniform. As Silk (2008a: 138) writes of his experience reediting the *Dharmaruci-avadāna*, "I have spot-checked one Kyoto University manuscript (Goshima and Noguchi 1983: no. 49), and slightly more carefully one Tokyo University manuscript (Matsunami 1965: no. 187). Unfortunately, both are of almost no help in correcting the edition, and there is little point to recording their errors." For more on the *Divyāvadāna*'s manuscript history, see DS 8–15. See too Formigatti 2016.

6 For more on the hazards of this practice, see Silk 2008c. See too Pollock 2011. Often, however, there isn't that much to change. As Silk (2008c: 66n 25) goes on to observe:

"In my study of a portion of the *Dharmarucy-avadāna*, for which I was able to compare the Nepalese tradition recorded in the 1886 edition of Cowell and Neil with the text found in centuries earlier Gilgit manuscripts, I discovered less variation between the traditions than I expected, although Cowell and Neil's text can be corrected in numerous instances." Even Satoshi Hiraoka (HA, HC, HD), who has compared the stories in the *Divyāvadāna* with other Sanskrit sources, as well as Tibetan and Chinese translations and so on, suggests only a minimum of emendations.

7 To gain some sense of the difficulty of comparing the two texts, see Vogel and Wille's (GM-Saṅgh 291–93) translation of the final portion of the Sanskrit version of the *Saṅgharakṣita-avadāna* that is preserved in the *Mūlasarvāstivāda-vinaya*. Note the numerous discrepancies in the footnotes between the Sanskrit and Tibetan versions of the text, and compare their translation to my translation of the corresponding section in the *Divyāvadāna* (Divy 343–44).

8 For a revised edition of part of the text (Divy 254.3–262.6), see Silk 2008a: 138–45. For translations, see Zimmer 1925: 1–79 and Hiraoka 2007: i, 424–69. For partial translations, see Silk 2008a: 145–52 and Strong 2002: 19–23 (Divy 246.5–253.27). For an erudite study of the story, see Silk 2009. For Sanskrit parallels, see GBM 1354.4–1358.8 [cf. Divy 254.4–262.6] and GBM 1474.1–1483.8 [cf. Divy 254.4–260.11]—cf. Silk 2008a: 178–83; *Mahāvastu* i, 231.17–243.11 [cf. Divy 246.5–254.2] and 243.12–248.4 [cf. Divy 254.3–261.24, 228.22–233.16, and 234.4–241.16]; and *Avadānakalpalatā* no. 89 (Silk 2008a: 153–70; Rani 2005: 82–84 and woodcut L-10; Tucci 1949: ii, 521 and plate 125). For an interesting Jain reworking, see Lefeber 1995: 427–29. There is no corresponding Tibetan text. For more, see Lamotte 1944: i, 409–15; Hiraoka 2007: i, 460; HC 61; and Grey 2000: 85–87.

9 Divy 229.3–4, *bhūtaṃ varṇam*. Hiraoka (HA 12; HC 61) suggests *yathābhūtaṃ varṇam*. Cf. Divy 502.4.

10 Following Speyer (1902: 358), read *bhūtaṃ avarṇam*. Divy 229.19, *bhūtaṃ varṇam*. Hiraoka (HA 12; HC 61) suggests *yathābhūtaṃ avarṇam*. A parallel passage occurs on Divy 502.16, and the corresponding Tibetan (P 1032 *ñe* 74a6; D 3 *ja* 78a4) suggests the same emendation.

11 Divy 229.26, *vyavasthitaḥ*. Hiraoka (HA 12; HC 61) suggests *vyavasitaḥ*. That is, "has decided." Cf. Divy 229.15.

12 Divy 230.12, *āpadyante*. To agree with *puruṣam*, one might expect *āpadyate*, and Vaidya (Divy-V 142.29) emends accordingly. Nevertheless, one also finds *āpadyante* in a parallel passage at Divy 503.10. Buddhist Hybrid Sanskrit materials commonly use the plural for a subject in the singular. Cf. Edgerton 1993: i, 38, §5.1.

13 Following Hiraoka (HA 12; HC 62), read *anukūlena*. Divy 230.21, *anukūlam*. Cf. Divy 502.17, which in a parallel passage reads *anuguṇena*.

14 Divy 230.24, *dvistriyojana-*. Hiraoka (HA 12; HC 62) suggests *dvitriyāvatsapta-*.

15 Following Speyer (1902: 123) and Hiraoka (HA 12; HC 62), read *-oparimaṃ dakaskandham*. Divy 231.1, *-oparimandakaskandham*. I follow Speyer in reading *daka* in the sense of *udaka*.

16 The cover of this book features a photograph of a sculpted medallion (circa second century BCE) from the Buddhist stūpa at Bharhut in central India. The sea monster Timitimiṅgila is shown attacking a boat carrying Vasuguta and his two companions. The top of the medallion shows them rowing home after their escape. The medallion

bears two inscriptions: "Vasuguta being rescued by the Great Lord from the belly of Timitimiṅgila" and "This rail bar is the gift of Vijitaka." The medallion is currently housed at the Bharat Kala Bhavan in Varanasi. Thanks to John C. and Susan L. Huntington, and also Ajay Kumar Singh, director of Bharat Kala Bhavan. A special thanks to Monika Zin and Jutta Jain-Neubauer for all their help in securing a new photograph of the medallion. Cf. Chandra 1977: plate IV. For a line drawing, see Cunningham 1879: plate xxxiv, no. 2. For more on the accompanying inscription, see Visvanathan 2009: 127–128 and Sircar 1961–62: 207–208. For an instance of Timitimiṅgila's appearance in Jain materials, see Lefeber 1995: 428.

17 Divy 231.11, *te*. Speyer (1902: 123) and Hiraoka (HA 12; HC 62) suggest *teṣām*.

18 Divy 231.23, *mucyemaḥ*. Vaidya (Divy-V 143.24) emends to *mucyema*, the more standard form of the optative.

19 Following Cowell and Neil's query (Divy 233n1), read *vahane*. Divy 233.4, *vahanam*.

20 Divy 233.12, *bhagavato 'ntike*. In the *Divyāvadāna*, the term *antike* generally means "in the presence of," although sometimes it means "with regard to" or, more figuratively, "under" (cf. Rotman 2009: 254n46). The text is very concerned with issues of presence, for being near great fields of merit such as the Buddha is very beneficial to one's spiritual progress (cf. Rotman 2009: 113–28). I translate this idiom according to context.

21 Divy 233.23, *tadrūpo guṇagaṇo 'dhigataḥ*. Hiraoka (HA 12; HC 62) suggests omitting *tadrūpo*. I agree with Silk (2008b: 51n51), who observes that "the term *guṇagaṇo* is not altogether clear, but it seems to me that Edgerton 1953 s.v. is wrong to define it as 'reckoning, counting, calculation of virtues.'" The phrase seems to indicate that the person in question has not obtained any great collection of virtues and, hence, has not achieved significant spiritual progress. The same stock phrase also occurs in the *Avadānaśataka* (e.g., ii, 51.5).

22 Following Speyer (1902: 123) and Hiraoka (HA 12; HC 62), read *etāny eva tāni*. Divy 234.3, "just that many are" (*etāvanty etāni*).

23 Following Speyer (1902: 124), Vaidya (Divy-V 145.11), and Hiraoka (HA 12; HC 62), omit *ca*. Divy 234.17, *ca*.

24 Following Speyer (1902: 124) and Hiraoka (HA 12; HC 62), read *tadaiva*. Divy 234.18, *tadeva*.

25 Following Speyer (1902: 124) and Hiraoka (HA 12; HC 62), read *abhyavahṛtya*. Divy 234.25, *avahṛtya*.

26 Divy 235.4–5, *brāhmaṇyā nendriyāṇām*. Vaidya (Divy-V 145.22) emends to *brāhmaṇyās te indriyāṇām*.

27 Divy 235.8–9, *garbhalambhasamakālam eva sa evaṃvidha upakramaḥ kṛtaḥ*. Edgerton (BHSD) suggests reading *upakrama* here as "violence, doing violence to, attack (by violence)." One might therefore translate this passage as "This type of violent attack began when the fetus first formed." The term *upakrama* also occurred previously (Divy 235.3, 235.4), and there I translated it as "treatment." Cf. Divy 247.24 and 254.24–25. Likewise puzzling here is the use of *kṛtaḥ*.

28 Following Speyer (1902: 124) and Hiraoka (HA 12; HC 62), read *bhūtagrahāveśābādhākāra*. Divy 235.11, *bhūtagrahāveśo bādhākāra*.

29 Following Speyer (1902: 124), Vaidya (Divy-V 145.32), and Hiraoka (HA 12; HC 62), read *-svajana-*. Divy 235.19, *-sajana-*. Cf. Divy 234.24.

30 Divy 235.27, *dharmaśravaṇakathām*. Hiraoka (HA 12; HC 62) suggests *dharmakathām*.

31 For more on this passage, see DS 24–25.

32 For thoughts on Dharmaruci and the Buddhist sect known as the Dhammarucikas, see Silk 2013.

33 Following Speyer (1902: 124), Vaidya (Divy-V 146.9–10), and Hiraoka (HA 12; HC 62), read *āhārakṛtyaṃ kuru*. Divy 236.6, *āhāraṃ kṛtyaṃ kuru*.

34 Following Cowell and Neil's query (Divy 237n1), read *saṃlakṣitam*. Divy 237.1, *saṃlakṣitaḥ*.

35 Divy 237.21, *sārdham sarvarūpaiḥ*. The term *sarvarūpa* appears to be nearly synonymous with *garbharūpa* (Divy 238.24), *gṛhajana* (Divy 238.26), and *svagarbharūpa* (Divy 249.28).

36 Read *nīlavāsasaiḥ*. Divy 238.23, "of the Dark Clothed One" (*nīlavāsasaḥ*). Cowell and Neil (Divy 707) and Edgerton (BHSD, s.v. *nīlavāsas*) suggest that the "dark-clothed one" could be an epithet of Kubera, who is lord of the yakṣas. Cf. Divy 221.1 and 229.25.

37 Divy 240.3, *asthiśakala*. Although I previously translated this term as "skeleton" (Divy 239.29), here that translation seems too specific to capture Dharmaruci's incredulity. In what follows, however, when the Buddha uses the same term (Divy 240.11) to tell Dharmaruci that this object is, in fact, a "skeleton," Dharmaruci is shocked.

38 Following Hiraoka (HA 12; HC 62), read *vyaktiṃ nopalabdham*. Divy 240.4–5, *vyaktiṃ copalabdham*. Perhaps, "Then he did manage to get a clear sense of its size," although this doesn't make sense in context.

39 Divy 240.13–14, *tṛpyasva dharmaruce bhavebhyas tṛpyasva bhavopakaraṇebhyaḥ*. The Buddha had previously declared that Dharmaruci, owing to the donor's gift of a cartload of food, was finally "satisfied" (*tṛptaḥ* | Divy 239.20). Now the Buddha asks him to be satisfied with existence. For a similar sentiment, see Divy 177.19–21.

40 Following Vaidya (Divy-V 148.28) and Hiraoka (HA 12; HC 62), read *atīva saṃvignaḥ*. Divy 240.16, *atīvasaṃvignaḥ*.

41 For more on this stereotypical description of arhats, see DS 397n163.

42 Following Divy 97.26, 180.26, etc., Vaidya (Divy-V 249.1), and Hiraoka (HA 12; HC 62), read *vidyā-*. Divy 240.24, *avidyā-*.

43 Divy 242.6–7, *baṇikśreṣṭhī*. Ivo Fišer (1954) examines the role of the *seṭṭhi* (Skt. *śreṣṭhin*) in the Pāli Jākatas and concludes that "guildmaster" is an incorrect translation in that context, for the *seṭṭhi* is a wealthy trader, and sometimes banker and bankroller, but not the head of a guild. Fišer (1954: 265) also concludes that "it would be much safer not to translate the term *seṭṭhi* at all." In the *Divyāvadāna*, however, I think "guildmaster" is an appropriate rendering for the term, as it refers to an appointed position.

44 Divy 242.8, *ṣaṣṭim*. Hiraoka (HA 12; HC 62) suggests its omission.

45 Following Speyer (1902: 124), read *pratyāgataprāṇajīvita*. Divy 242.27, *pratyāgataprāṇo jīvita*.

46 Vaidya (Divy-V 243.1) omits *tac chāsanam antarhitaṃ kṣemaṅkarasya* (Divy 243.1).

47 Divy 243.2, *caityam alpeśākhyam*. While this could be translated more literally as "a weak shrine," I follow Edgerton's (BHSD) understanding of *alpeśākhya* as "insignificant, petty." In what follows (Divy 243.8–9), the shrine is made to be *maheśākhyatara*,

which I translate as "even more special," but which could be read more literally as "even more powerful." Although I argue for this latter understanding of *maheśākhya* elsewhere (Rotman 2009: 224n32, 225n33), here the emphasis seems to be on appearance, not strength. Could the guildmaster's renovations really make the Buddha Kṣemaṅkara's shrine "more powerful"? Cf. Divy 258.16.

48 This passage has received a lot of scholarly attention, for it offers a detailed description of an early Buddhist stūpa in India. See, for example, La Vallée Poussin 1937; Weller 1953; Alsdorf 1955; Kuiper 1959; M. Bénisti 1960: 74–77; Roth 1980; Roth 1985: 183–96; Schopen 1997: 50n61, 82n10; Rhie 1999: i, 254, 279–80; and von Hinüber 2016. For a conjectural sketch of the stūpa here described, see Rhie 1999: ii, fig. 4.4i. Roth (1985: 185–86) offers this translation: "After that they began to construct four flights of stairs on precisely all four sides of the stūpa, each with a so-called 'neck-onset,' according to the order (of the structural components). The first platform, then the second, according to the order (of the structural components), then the third platform (were constructed), up to the 'egg-dome,' according to the order (of the structural components); and the 'egg-dome' thus constituted was laid out in a comprehensive manner (at the point) where the pole-mast had already been placed inside. After this, a cuboid addition was contructed above the completely new 'egg dome,' according to the order (of the structural componenets), the mast was erected and the great treasure-jewel was placed upon the rain basin (at the pinnacle)."

49 Divy 244.8, *pratikaṇṭhukayā* (ms. D, *pratikaṇṭhakayā*). This is obscure. Edgerton (BHSD) translates it as "singly, severally, one by one," but it is likely an architectural term. Agrawala (1966: 74) takes it to mean "the space between the actual *stūpa* and the railing," and Von Hinüber (2016: 37) explains it as "the 'counter-wall' or periphery, the outer part of the *vedikā* out of which the drum and the dome rise." My translation builds on von Hinüber's explanation. A special thanks to Marylin Rhie (personal communication) for her insights into this passage and the mechanics of early Indian stūpa renovation. She concludes that the renovation refers to a "Gandhāran-style stūpa of around the third to fourth century CE."

50 Divy 244.10–12, *tathāvidhaṃ ca bhūpasyāṇḍaṃ kṛtaṃ yatra sā yūpayaṣṭir* (following ms. D; mss. AC, *sāyupaṣṭir*; ms. B, *sāpayaṣṭir*) *abhyantare* (mss., *abhyantara*) *pratipāditā*. Following Roth (1985: 186) and von Hinüber (2016: 37n36), read *bhūyasyāṇḍam* for *bhūpasyāṇḍam*. Alsdorf (1955: 15), Vaidya (Divy–V 151.2), and Hiraoka (HA 12; HC 62), following Cowell and Neil's query (Divy 244n2), read *stūpasyāṇḍam*. Accordingly, M. Bénisti (1960: 76) offers this translation: "Le dôme du *stūpa* (*stūpasyāṇḍa*) fut fait de telle sorte que le poteau du *stūpa* (*stūpayaṣṭi* [for *yūpayaṣṭi*]) se trouva placé (*pratipāditā*) à l'intérieur." I agree with Roth (1985: 189), however, that there is "no good reason" to emend *yūpayaṣṭi* to *stūpayaṣṭi*—although La Vallée Poussin (1937: 281) proposed it as well—even though the precise meaning of *yūpayaṣṭi* is unclear. It is either a "post" (i.e., a de facto synonym for *yaṣṭi*, which appears in the following sentence) or a "shaft for a post," into which the post will then be erected. Alsdorf (1955: 15) provides this translation: "Und die Kuppel des Stūpas [read *stūpasya*] wurde so gemacht, dass darin die Yūpayaṣṭi ins Innere eingelassen war." Rhie (1999: i, 254) describes this as "the egg-like dome into which the shaft for a pole is to be sunk."

51 Divy 242.12, *atinavāṇḍasya*. Alsdorf (1955: 13) and von Hinüber (2016: 37n36)

emend to *abhinavāṇḍasya*. As von Hinüber (2016: 37n36) notes, this reading in conjunction with the term *bhūyasyāṇḍam* in the previous sentence "clearly shows, as rightly emphasized by L. Alsdorf, that the dome was enlarged as well."

52 Divy 244.22, *utpalaṃ padmaṃ kumudaṃ puṇḍarīkaṃ*. I follow Rau (1954) and Hanneder (2002, 2007) in translating these terms.

53 These appear to be different varieties of jasmine, for the most part. For more, see the Pandanus Database of Indian Plants at http://iu.ff.cuni.cz/pandanus/database/. And for more about this idyllic vision of beautiful and fragrant flowers, see Ali 2003 and Schopen 2006.

54 Divy 244.25–26, *sarvartukālikāḥ puṣpaphalāḥ stūpapūjārtham*. The term *vṛkṣa* ("tree") seems to be implied. Cf. Divy 62.9, 62.13, 127.5–6, etc. Otherwise, "Flowers and fruits remained year round to honor the stūpa."

55 Read *sthāvarā vṛttiḥ prajñaptā*. Divy 244.26, *sthāvarāvṛttiprajñaptāḥ*. Another possibility would be to emend the text to *sthāvarā vṛtiḥ prajñaptā*. That is, "a permanent boundary hedge was established."

56 Following Vaidya (Divy-V 151.12) and Hiraoka (HA 12; HC 62), read *stūpadāsā dattāḥ*. Divy 244.26, *stūpadāsadattāḥ* (mss., *stūpadāsādattā*).

57 Bodhisattvas are said to perfect the various virtues—in other words, fulfill the various perfections—during three incalculable time periods (*asaṅkhyeya*) of a great age (*mahākalpa*) (Kloetzli 1997: 85). Cf. Dayal 1932: 76–79.

58 Divy 245.24, *smṛtiṃ pratilabhethāḥ*. Cf. Divy 261.22.

59 Divy 245.27, *sugataḥ*. Hiraoka (HA 12; HC 63) suggests *jagataḥ*. That is, "in the world." Cf. Divy 252.14. At Divy 227.4, the corresponding Tibetan (1030 *ge* 170a3; 1 *kha* 181b4) suggests the same emendation. Cf. Divy 228.1.

60 Following Divy 54.13, 141.17, etc. and Hiraoka (HA 12; HC 63), read *vidyācaraṇasampannaḥ*. Divy 246.5, *vidyācaraṇasamyaksaṃbuddaḥ*.

61 Divy 246.12, *sābhisaṃskāreṇa*. Here and in what follows (Divy 246.15, 248.10, etc.), the term *sābhisaṃskāreṇa* seems to mean "following the proper formalities." Elsewhere in this story (Divy 250.20, 250.24) and in the rest of the text, however, the term refers to a quality of mind that yields great karmic results. In "The Story of a Woman Dependent on a City for Alms," a beggar woman cultivates "a great resolution of mind" (*mahatā cittābhisaṃskāreṇa* | Divy 90.26), and as such her offering of an oil lamp to the Buddha produces for her amazing results. And in "The Miracle Sūtra," the Buddha, "with a resolute [mind]" (*sābhisaṃskāreṇa* | Divy 158.5) puts his foot down on the ground, and as a result the whole world-system begins to shake. Edgerton (BHSD) translates the term as "with proper preparation of mind; with fixed, determined mentality."

62 Divy 246.13, *sāmantarājan*. Here I take *sāmanta* in the sense of "neighboring," although elsewhere it seems to mean "vassal" (Divy 328.27–28).

63 Vaidya (Divy-V 152.24) omits *prāsādikāv abhirūpau | tau ca gatvā tatra yajñe brāhmaṇapaṅktiṣu prajñapteṣv āsaneṣu* (Divy 247.7–8).

64 This is one of the magical powers (Skt., *ṛddhi*; Pāli, *iddhi*) frequently enumerated in Pāli literature (e.g., *Dīgha-nikāya* i, 78).

65 Divy 248.24, *nīlotpalapadma*. Previously the girl asked for some *nīlotpala* (Divy 248.21), and later what appear as a result of her merit are *nīlapadma* (Divy 248.25). Usually *utpala* and *padma* refer to different kinds of flowers, as in the common expres-

sion "blue, red, and white waterlilies" (*utpalapadmakumuda-* | Divy 186.3, 221.11, etc.). In the *Divyāvadāna*, *padma* seems to be a generic term that encompasses both "lotus" and "waterlily." Santona Basu (2002: 93) makes much the same claim for the use of *paduma*—the Pāli term for *padma*—in the Pāli canon.

66 Note that the waterlilies appear as a result of Sumati's merit, and not, as we might expect here, the girl's merit.

67 Following Speyer (1902: 125) and Hiraoka (HA 13; HC 63), read *praveśitāni*. Divy 249.4, *praveśakāni*.

68 Following Cowell and Neil's query (Divy 249n3) and Hiraoka (HA 13; HC 63), read *mām api*. Divy 249.25, *mamāpi*.

69 The text is silent about Sumati's response to the girl's demand. He accepts the flowers from her, but he is never shown making the fervent aspiration she requested.

70 Following Vaidya (Divy-V 154.26) and Divy 250.24, read *sābhisaṃskāreṇa*, although *sābhisaṃskāram* is also possible. Divy 250.20, *sābhisamskāra*. Cf. Divy 158.5, *bhagavatā sābhisaṃskāreṇa pṛthivyāṃ padau nyastau*; Divy 364.26, *bhagavatā sābhisaṃskāraṃ nagaradvāre padaṃ pratiṣṭhāpitam*.

71 This scene is found in Gandhāran stone sculpture, both in reliefs and in large, independent statues. See, for example, Kurita 2003: i, figs. 6, 7, 9, and 11. My thanks to Marilyn Rhie for these references.

72 Following Speyer (1902: 125) and Hiraoka (HA 13; HC 63), read *jaṭāḥ saṃstīrya*. Divy 252.2, *jaṭāṃ* (mss., *jaṭā*) *saṃtīrya*.

73 Divy 252.3–4, *yadi buddho bhaviṣyāmi bodhāya budhabodhana* | *ākramiṣyasi me padbhyāṃ jaṭāṃ janmajarāntakām*. One might also translate the verse in a different order to capture a more tempered sentiment: "If, with your feet, you will tread on my matted hair, | which will bring an end to birth and old age, | I will become a buddha, O awakener to wisdom, | for the sake of awakening others." There also could be a pun here. The verse might be read, "If, with your words, you will solve the tangle of desires that leads to rebirth and old age . . ." Hiraoka (HA 13; HC 63) suggests the vocative *janmajarāntaka* for *janmajarāntakām* to avoid having to read this compound as an adjectival phrase modifying *jaṭāṃ*.

74 Following Cowell and Neil's restoration (Divy 252.12; cf. Divy 252n7), *nṛbhavād dhi mukto* [*mukto*]. Speyer (1902: 125) suggests *nṛbhavādhimukto* [*yukto*]. Perhaps, "bound to human existence." Hiraoka (HA 13; HC 63) concurs.

75 Divy 253.26 (omitted). Part of the text has been lost.

76 Jonathan Silk (2008a) has critically reedited the following section of the story (Divy 254.3–262.6), making use of two fragmentary Gilgit manuscripts: Gilgit folios 1474–83 (= G1) and folios 1354–58 (= G2). My thanks to him for his excellent work, which I rely on in what follows.

77 Following the Tibetan (*Mahāvyutpatti* 91), *'khor ba 'jig*. In Pāli, *Kakusandha*. Perhaps, "Living (= *saṃsthā*?) in the Mountains."

78 Conjecure based on Divy 54.14–15, 141.19–20, etc., and on parallels noted by Speyer (1902: 125). Cf. *Avadānaśataka* i, 285.17–286.2, and ii, 29.7–9. Silk (2008a: 145n73) and Hiraoka (2007: i, 466n67) concur.

79 Divy 254.7–8, *sa ca kalatrasahāyaḥ*. The cliché generally reads *sa tayā sārdhaṃ* | Divy 1.5–6, 24.13, 87.14, etc.

80 Following G2 (Silk 2008a: 139n5), Silk (2008a: 139.8), and Hiraoka (HA 13; HC

63), read *baṇig dharmaṇā*. Speyer (1902: 125–26) emends to *baṇig dharmeṇa*. Divy 254.12 and G1, *baṇig dharmāṇām*.

81 Following Gilgit mss. (Silk 2008a: 139n6), Speyer (1902: 126), and Hiraoka (HA 13; HC 63), read *baṇiglobhenāvṛtaḥ*. Divy 254.12, *baṇiglokenāvṛtaḥ* (mss. BCD, *baṇiklokanāvṛtaḥ*; ms. A, *baṇiglobhakenāvṛtaḥ*). Silk (2008a: 139.9) reads *vaṇig lobhenāvṛtaḥ*.

82 Divy 254.13, *ciram*. Silk (2008a: 139.10) and Hiraoka (HA 13; HC 63), following G1 and G2 (Silk 2008a: 139n7), read *ciraṃ pravṛttir*. Silk (2008a: 145) offers this translation: "And for an exceedingly long time no tidings came from him."

83 Divy 254.16, *kulārthāgatam*. Silk (2008a: 139.12) and Hiraoka (HA 13; HC 63), following G1 and G2 (Silk 2008a: 139n9), read *kulānvāgatam*.

84 Following Gilgit mss., the Tokyo and Kyoto University mss. of the Divy (Silk 2008a: 139n11), Silk (2008a: 139.17), and Hiraoka (HA 13; HC 63), read *rāgavinodakam*. Divy 254.21, *rogavinodakam*.

85 Divy 254.22, *vṛddhayuvatī*. The term is peculiar, for it is a compound of opposites—"old woman–young woman" or even "old maid," although that term has very different connotations. The woman in question is clearly a kind of madam or procuress. For more on the term, see Silk 2008a: 177–78. In what follows, the woman is mostly referred to as "an old woman" (*vṛddhā* | Divy 254.23, 254.25, 255.1, etc.). Cf. 483.25–484.1.

86 Divy 254.26, *vijñāpyam*. Hiraoka (HA 13; HC 63), following GBM 1475.2, suggests *me vijñaptim*.

87 Divy 255.5, *evaṃvidhopakramayuktaḥ*. Here I take *upakrama* in the sense of "plan," although Silk (2008a: 146n82) reads it in the sense of "sexual approach." He offers this translation: "If there's no other man suitable for such an approach . . ."

88 Divy 255.6, *bhavati*. Silk (2008a: 139.26) and Hiraoka (HA 13; HC 63), following G1 and G2 (Silk 2008a: 139n14), read *bhavatu*.

89 Following G1, G2 (Silk 2008a: 140n16), Silk (2008a: 139.31–140.1), and Hiraoka (HA 13; HC 63), read *kiṃ pratiṣṭhito 'sy atha na*. Divy 255.13, *kiṃ pratiṣṭhito 'syārthena*. Perhaps, "Why are you only concerned with money?"

90 Here the madam is tempting the boy with a younger version of herself. She is "old-young" (*vṛddhayuvatī*), and the potential lover she describes is "young-young" (*taruṇayuvatī* | Divy 255.14.15). In what follows, I translate the latter simply as "young girl." The term *yuvatī* seems to have a sexual connotation—something like "in her prime."

91 Following G2 (Silk 2008a: 140n18), Silk (2008a: 140.7), and Hiraoka (HA 13; HC 63), read *maṃnimitte*. Silk (2008a: 146) offers this translation: "Mother, did you say something to that young woman about me?" Divy 255.21, *saṃnimitte*. Cowell and Neil (Divy 255n6) query *tan nimmite*. Cf. 255.22. Perhaps, "What have you said to the young girl about this matter?"

92 Following G1 (Silk 2008a: 140n19), Silk (2008a: 140.8), and Hiraoka (HA 13; HC 63), read *tvannimittam*. Divy 255.22, *tannimittam*.

93 Following Vaidya (Divy-V 158.1) and Hiraoka (HA 13; HC 63), read *nimitte na*. Divy 255.22, *nimittena*. Silk (2008a: 140.9, 147) reads likewise and offers this translation: ". . . and she agreed thanks to my suggestion."

94 Divy 255.24, *na ca śarīram āvṛtaṃ kariṣyati*. The meaning here is obscure, for *āvṛtaṃ*

is peculiar. G1 (Silk 2008a: 147n90) reads *āvṛtta*, but that too is peculiar. Silk (2008a: 147) offers this translation: "She won't reveal her body." Cf. DS 424n500 for a discussion of *saṃvṛtaḥ*.

95 Divy 255.24, *vānveṣaṇe*. Silk (2008a: 140.10, 147n91) and Hiraoka (HC 13; HC 63–64) suggest *vācānveṣaṇe*.

96 Divy 256.1, *icchāpitaḥ sa vo 'yaṃ dārakaḥ*. One could also take this to mean "I have stirred up desire in this boy of yours."

97 Following Silk (2008a: 140.19–20) and Hiraoka (HA 13; HC 64), read *niśi kāle apratyabhijñātarūpe kāle*. Divy 256.7, *niśi kālam apratyabhijñātaṃ rūpe kāle*. Cowell and Neil (Divy 707) offer a literal but puzzling translation: "He did not notice black in the darkness, she came to him in a black dress." G1 and G2 (Silk 2008a: 140n25), *niśi kālam apratyabhijñātarūpe kāle*. Speyer (1902: 126) suggests *niśi vikāle apratyabhijñātarūpe kale*. Another possible emendation would be *niśi kālam apratyabhijñātam arūpe kāle*. That is, "He didn't realize the night had approached, and at that time when forms are indistinct . . ."

98 Divy 256.9–10, *avyaktiṃ vibhāvyamāne*. Hiraoka (HA 13; HC 64), following GBM 1477.3, emends to *abhāvyamāne*. Cf. Hiraoka 2007: i, 467–468n84.

99 Divy 256.21, *vartamānena ratikrīḍākrameṇa*. Silk (2008a: 140.27) and Hiraoka (HA 13; HC 64), following G1 (Silk 2008a: 140n26), read *vartamāne ratikrīḍākrame*.

100 Following G1, G2 (Silk 2008a: 140n27), Silk (2008a: 140.30), and Hiraoka (HA 13; HC 64), read *ratikrīḍām anubhaveyam*. Divy 256.21, *ratikrīḍā bhavema*. Speyer (1902: 126) suggests *ratikrīḍām anubhavema*. Vaidya (Divy-V 158.18–19) emends to *ratikrīḍā bhavet*.

101 Vaidya (Divy-V 158.19) omits *tathaiva* (Divy 256.22).

102 Following Edgerton (BHSD, s.v. *pontī*), Silk (2008a: 141.4), and Hiraoka (HA 13; HC 64), read *upariprāvaraṇapontīm*. Divy 256.26, *upariprāvaraṇapotrīm* (ex conj.; ms. A, *-yāntīm*; ms. B, *-yontim*; mss. CD, *-yontīm*).

103 Following Vaidya's emendation (Divy-V 158.30), read *kariṣyāmi*. Divy 257.11, *smariṣyāmi*. Silk (2008a: 141.15, 148) reads likewise and offers this translation: "How shall I not be mindful of my depression, or my bewilderment?" G2 (Silk 2008a: 141n31), *gamiṣyāmi*.

104 Following G1 (Silk 2008a: 141n32), Silk (2008a: 141.17), and Hiraoka (HA 13; HC 64), read *manaḥśokam*. Divy 257.12, *manaḥśūkam*.

105 Divy 257.15, *evaṃ eva mātṛgrāmaḥ*. Perhaps, "Women are just the same." Silk (2008a: 148) offers this translation: "it is rather the female sex [which is the agent of the fault]."

106 Divy 257.20–21, *anunayavacanaiḥ*. Edgerton (BHSD) translates this as "with words of (impure sexual) love." Cf. Divy 519.11, where the corresponding Tibetan (D 3 *ña* 172b1) takes the same expression to mean "words of passion" (*rjes su chags ba'i tshig* = Skt., <*anurāgavacanam*>). Silk (2008a: 148) translates this as "conciliatory words." See also Divy 258.4, *anuvṛttivacanaiḥ*.

107 Divy 258.1, *āgamiṣyatīti*. Silk (2008a: 141.31) and Hiraoka (HA 13; HC 64), following G1 and G2 (Silk 2008a: 141n37), read *āgamiṣyāmīti*.

108 Following Vaidya (Divy-V 159.14), Silk (2008a: 142.4), and Hiraoka (HA 13; HC 64), read *karmākaraṇīyam*. Divy 258.6, *karma karaṇīyam*.

109 Following G1, G2 (Silk 2008a: 177), Silk (2008a: 142.16), and Hiraoka (HA 13; HC 64), read *ekaphelāyām*. Silk (2008a: 149) offers this translation: "Later while eating

together with his father atop a cargo crate . . ." Silk (2008a: 176–77) also provides a detailed discussion of the term. Cf. Divy 503.24, *suvarṇasya phelāṃ pūrayitvā*. Divy 258.20, *ekaphalāyām*.

110 Divy 258.27, *hiraṇyasuvarṇam*. Sometimes this compound appears to be a *dvandva*, and I translate it as "gold and golden things," "gold and valuables," or even "silver and gold." Cf. Divy 575.11. Also possible is "gold nuggets and coins" or "gold and bullion." Elsewhere the compound seems to refer to one thing (i.e., "golden valuables"), like *maggapatha* in Middle Indic (literally, "path-path"). In Hindi, such reduplicative compounds are common. There are rhyming ones meaning "X and the like"—for example, "tea and drinks" (*cāy vāy*) and "food and snacks" (*khāna vāna*). There are also translation compounds—terms with similar meanings in different dialects or registers conjoined for a sense of expansiveness. Most common are *śādī-vivāh* for "wedding" (literally, "wedding-wedding") or *rīti-rivāj* for "custom." Although translation compounds are unattested by Pāṇini, there are numerous redundant compounds, if not translation compounds, in Pāli and Buddhist Sanskrit (Dhadphale 1980).

111 Divy 258.28, *tasya ca gatasya*. Silk (2008a: 142.23) and Hiraoka (HA 13; HC 64), following G1 (Silk 2008a: 142n51), read *tasya cāgatasya*.

112 Divy 259.14, *sa vicintya*. Silk (2008a: 143.7), following G1 and G2 (Silk 2008a: 143n55), reads *sa ciraṃ vicintya*.

113 In what follows, however, they wait until he is finished eating before they kill him.

114 Divy 259.23–24, *antargṛhaviśrabdhacārakramam*. Silk (2008a: 143n58; cf. 183, folio 1357.2) reads *arhantaṃ viśvastacārakramam*. As Silk (2008a: 151n105) notes, the syntax of this sentence is peculiar.

115 The "boy" (*dāraka*) has now become a "man" (*puruṣa*).

116 As Silk (2008a: 152n111) rightly observes, "To prevent futher trouble he [i.e., the bodhisattva] seems willing to 'ordain' Dharmaruci, but the Buddhist practice appropriate for the latter [i.e., concentration on the three refuges] is the most basic and introductory available. It is important to note that in refusing to teach Dharmaruci the rules of training [i.e., the precepts], he is in fact denying him access to the monastic state, and thus not ordaining him at all."

117 Divy 261.22, *smṛtaṃ pratilabethāḥ*. Or perhaps, "you will regain your memory." Cf. Divy 245.24.

118 For translations, see Zimmer 1925: 105–74 and Hiraoka 2007: i, 470–518. For Sanskrit parallels, see GBM 1484–85 [only a single folio extant]; Gāndhārī manuscript fragments, and their translation, in Baums 2002 and 2016 [cf. Divy 268.15–269.29, 270.1–271.7, and 280.27–281.21]; *Mahāvastu* ii, 271.1–276.15 [cf. Divy 282.19–289.9]; *Avadanakalpalata* no. 9 (Rani 2005: 20–21 and woodcut R-7; Tucci 1949: ii, 452 and plate 104). The corresponding Tibetan can be found at P 1035 *de* 10b2–28b1 and D 6 *tha* 12a3–31a4, although I only refer to the Derge in what follows. For more, see Hiraoka 2007: i, 502; HC 64; and Grey 2000: 136–37.

119 Divy 262.20, *divyamānuṣīm*. This compound is generally understood as a *dvandva* (i.e., "divine and human"), but the meaning here seems to be "human yet of a divine nature." Cf. DS 429n577. Baums (2002: 297) translates it as "semi-divine."

120 Divy 263.8–9, *sa bhūriko gaṇitre kṛtāvī śvetavarṇāṃ gṛhītvā gaṇayitum ārabdhaḥ*. Edgerton (BHSD) recognizes that this passage is obscure but takes *gaṇitra* as "(astrological) calculation" and *śvetavarṇā* as "chalk." Cowell and Neil (Divy 679, 692) sug-

gest "astrologer's instrument" for both terms. Cf. Zimmer 1925: 107. For *śvetavarṇā*, the Tibetan (12b5) reads *rdo rgyus kha dog dkar ba*.

121 Following Speyer (1902: 127), the Tibetan (12b6), and Hiraoka (HA 13; HC 64), read *-abhiprasatsyati*. Divy 263.13, *-abhipraśaṃsyati* (mss., *-abhiprasaṃśyati*).

122 Following Vaidya (Divy-V 162.24), read *agrajyotir*. Divy 263.19, *agrejyotir*. Hiraoka (HA 13; HC 64), following the Tibetan (13a1) and the Chinese, suggests *agner dyotir*.

123 Following Divy 270.2 and Hiraoka (HA 13; HC 65), read *samāttaśikṣaḥ*. Divy 263.29–30, *śamānuśikṣāḥ*. Cf. Edgerton (BHSD, s.vv. *samātta, samādatta*) and Baums 2002: 295n2.

124 For more on this line, see Edgerton (BHSD, s.v. *upasaṃkrama*). Cf. Divy 272.16–17.

125 Following Vaidya (Divy-V 163.18), add *catur*. Divy 264.29 (omitted).

126 Divy 265.2, *asaṃhatavihārīṇām* (ms. B, *asaṃbhavavihārisa*). Cf. Divy 95.19, *saṃghātavihāriṇām*. Hiraoka (HA 13; HC 65) suggests its omission. As he explains (HC 65), this compound "does not mention any number even though the standard cliché is supposed to modify the Buddha with numerical phrases. Tib. *drug la rtag tu ngas pa* (14a1) mentions the number 'six' but it is unclear to what this 'six' exactly refers."

127 Following Hiraoka (HA 13; HC 65), read *narakān*. Divy 265.21, *narakam*.

128 Following Divy 68.2 and 138.9–10, add *ye śītanarakās teṣūṣṇībhūtvā nipatanti*. Divy 265.22 (omitted).

129 Divy 68.6 adds *darśanam*.

130 Divy 266.3, *devān*. Understand as *devanikāyān*.

131 Here other instances of this formulaic passage (e.g., Divy 68.16, 138.23, 568.28) add "Abṛha (Not Great)" (*abṛhān*). Divy 266.7 (omitted).

132 Following Vaidya (Divy-V 164.28) and Aśokāv 33.21, read *dhīra buddhyā*. Divy 266.25, *dhīrabuddhyā*. And following Vaidya (Divy-V 164.29), Hiraoka (HA 13; HC 65) and Aśokāv 33.21, read *śramaṇa jinendra*. Divy 266.25–26, *śramaṇajinendra*.

133 Read *ādhvagagaṇa*. Hiraoka (HA 13; HC 65) concurs. Cf. DS 426n527. Divy 267.21–22, *ādhvagaṇa* (mss., *andhagaṇa*).

134 Other instances of this passage (e.g., Divy 126.7–8, 148.18–19, 182.12–13) here include "like the great king Virūpākṣa surrounded by a group of nāgas" (*virūpākṣa iva nāgagaṇaparivṛtaḥ*). Divy 267.26 (omitted).

135 For a list of these eighteen benefits, see Divy 92.15–93.2; trans. in DS 179.

136 The Schøyen Collection contains eleven fragments of the *Jyotiṣka-avadāna*. Stefan Baums (2002, 2016) has examined these fragments and their corresponding passages in the *Divyāvadāna* and the Tibetan. Based on these sources, he offers a reconstruction of the Sanskrit text. My thanks to him for his helpful suggestions.

137 Divy 268.19–20, *mā haiva bhagavatā bhāṣitaṃ vitathaṃ syād iti*. This sentence can also be read as more of an assertion. Perhaps, "Never could it be that the Blessed One would speak falsely!" or, following Baums (2002: 297), "But what is said by the Blessed One may not be false!" Considering, however, that the speaker here is a brahman boy *not* immersed in faith, I read this as a bit of a question, not just an assertion of the Buddha's infallibility. Cf. Divy 272.3–4, 272.9–10, 272.15–16.

138 Divy 268.25, *gacchāmaḥ*. The Schøyen fragments (Baums 2016: 346) read *gacchāvaḥ*.

As Baums notes, "Curiously, within the same line of our manuscript this dual form is followed by plural *gacchāmo*."

139 Divy 268.28, *gāthām*. The Schøyen fragments (Baums 2016: 346) read *gāthe*. Here too, Baums notes, we find "the dual *gāthe* in place of the *Divyāvadāna*'s apparent singular (or possibly plural) *gāthāṃ* (the Tibetan has simple *tshigs su bcad pa*). Both cases may represent an incomplete attempt at greater grammatical precision on the part of our manuscript's scribe."

140 Divy 269.3, *nadasyate*. The Schøyen fragments (Baums 2002: 292) and Hiraoka (HA 13; HC 65) read *nadiṣyate*.

141 Divy 269.5–6, *himapaṅkaśītalāh*. Baums (2016: 349) translates this as "cool like an ointment made of snow."

142 Divy 269.17, *-kumārāmātya-*. Agrawala (1966: 70) argues that this expression should be taken as a single term, meaning something like "chief ministers," as per its meaning in Gupta inscriptions ("a personal title conferred on the highest dignitary by the king like a minister, a commander, a member of the royal household"). I take it as two terms, "princes and ministers," as does Baums (2002: 297n12).

143 Following the Schøyen fragments (Baums 2002: 295), the Tibetan (Baums 2002: 300), Divy 269.30, and Hiraoka (HA 13; HC 65), read *sattvaḥ*. Divy 269.29, *bodhisattvaḥ*.

144 Following mss. ABD (Divy 270n1), Baums (2002: 295n2, 298n14), and Hiraoka (HA 13; HC 65), read *samāttaśikṣāḥ*. Baums (2002: 298) translates this as "we have undertaken vows." Divy 270.2, *śamāttaśikṣāḥ* (mss. ABD, *samātta-*; ms. C, *śamātta-*).

145 A pericarp is the part of the flower that surrounds the seeds and develops from the ovary wall, suggesting that the lotus is "giving birth" to the boy. For more on lotus births, see Basu 1968.

146 Following the Schøyen fragments (Baums 2002: 295) and Hiraoka (HA 14; HC 65), read *nihatamadamānaprabhāvāḥ*. Divy 270.7–8, *nipātamadamānā na ca prabhāvāḥ*. Speyer (1902: 127–28) suggests *viyātamadamānā hataprabhāvāḥ pravṛttāḥ*. Vaidya (Divy-V 167.5) suggests *naṣṭaprabhāvāḥ*. Cf. Divy 126.17–18, *bhagnaprabhāvāḥ*.

147 Divy 270.11, *sarveṇa sarvaṃ na bhaviṣyasīti*. Similar idioms occur throughout the text: "They will completely deprive you of life" (*sarveṇa sarvaṃ jīvitād vyaparopayanti* | Divy 39.1–2), "They will completely and utterly destroy you" (*sarveṇa sarvaṃ jīvitād vyaparopayiṣyanti* | Divy 39.3–4, 502.21), "Don't think that with all your power you can do everything" (*mā sarveṇa sarvaṃ bhaviṣyati* | Divy 530.26), etc. Baums (2002: 298) offers this translation for the present passage: "you will completely and totally cease to exist."

148 Divy 270.11–12, *sa na pratigṛhnāti*. The verbal form here indicates that the boy is a kind of offering, available because of the Buddha's special powers, and Subhadra is refusing to accept it.

149 Divy 270.16, *pratigṛhnataḥ*. The Schøyen fragments (Baums 2002: 295) and Hiraoka (HA 14; HC 65) read *pragṛhṇataḥ*, which correctly fits the meter.

150 Following the Schøyen fragments (Baums 2002: 295), add *bhagavān*. Divy 270.20 (omitted).

151 Divy 270.28–29, *yady evaṃ gṛhaṃ praveśayasi niyatam te gṛham utsādayan* (mss., *utsādaṃ*) *bhaviṣyasi*. The Schøyen fragments (Baums 2002: 296) read *uddāyādaṃ bhavati*. Baums (2002: 298) offers this translation: "inevitably your house becomes

heirless." Or, as Baums (2002: 298n16) notes, "read *uddāhayan* and translate 'inevitably he will cause your house to burn down' on the evidence of the Tibetan [*tshig bar*]?" Speyer (1902: 128) and Hiraoka (HA 14; HC 65) suggest *utsādaṃ gamiṣyati*. That is, "your house will go to ruin." Vaidya (Divy-V 157.20–21) emends to *yady evaṃ gṛham praveśayasi nīyatām | te gṛham utsādayad bhaviṣyasi*.

152 There are a number of sculptures from early Gandhāra that feature Jyotiṣka's fiery birth. For more on these representations, see Rotman 2009: 275–76n33.

153 Following the Schøyen fragments (Baums 2002: 296), Speyer (1902: 128), Vaidya (Divy-V 167.24), and Hiraoka (HA 14; HC 65), read *bhavatu*. Divy 271.6, *bhavati*.

154 There are interesting similarities between Jyotiṣka and Jīvaka. Jyotiṣka was retrieved from a pyre and then reared by King Bimbisāra. Jīvaka was retrieved from a trash heap, where he'd been abandoned as a child, and then reared by King Bimbisāra's son Prince Abhaya (DPPN, s.v. *Jīvaka Komārabhacca*). Elsewhere it is said that Prince Abhaya was Jīvaka's natural father (DPPN, s.v. *Abhaya*), making King Bimbisāra Jīvaka's natural grandfather, not just his adopted one.

155 Following Speyer (1902: 128), Vaidya (Divy 167.24), and Hiraoka (HA 14; HC 65–66), read *tathopakrāntā*. Divy 272.16–17, *tathā tathāpakrāntā* (ms. A, *tathā prakrāntā*; ms. B, *tathā 'prakrāntā*; ms. C, *tathā 'prakāntā*; ms. D, *tathā prakrāntau*) *yathā kālagatā*. Edgerton (BHSD, s.v. *apakrānta*) follows ms. A and translates this as "treated," "behaved towards." Cf. Divy 264.12–13, *tathoprakrāntā yathā kālagatā*.

156 Vaidya (Divy-V 168.23) omits Divy 272.18–22.

157 Following Speyer (1902: 128), Vaidya (Divy 167.24), and Hiraoka (HA 14; HC 66), read *tathopakrāntā*. Divy 272.21, *tathā tathāpakrāntā* (*sic* mss. ACD; ms. B, *tathā 'prakrāntā*) *yathā kālagatā*.

158 Divy 272.24, *salokānāṃ pātayāmaḥ*. Cf. Divy 273.2, 273.11, *saṃkāraṃ pātayāmaḥ*. Vaidya (Divy-V 168.25) reads *salokānāṃ* [*sālohitānāṃ?*] *saṃkāraṃ pātayāmaḥ*. Edgerton (BHSD) explains *saṃkāra* as "impurity in the sense of pariahhood, outcaste state, expulsion from caste."

159 Here (Divy 273.5), and in what follows, Jyotiṣka is referred to as a *kumāra*, which can mean both "boy" and "prince." Since Jyotiṣka was raised in the palace, he is like a prince. Even when he was first born, the Buddha refers to him as a "little *kumāra*" (*kūmāraka* | Divy 271.13). Later in the story, however, he assumes control of his familial house and is referred to as a "householder" (*gṛhapati* | Divy 274.21), not a king. Nevertheless, his home is still a palace, and it does possess a "lion throne" (*siṃhāsana* | Divy 279.14). Jyotiṣka's ambiguous status is most apparent in his interactions with Ajātaśatru, King Bimbisāra's true son and heir. Both are called *kumāra*. I translate the former as "the boy Jyotiṣka" and the latter as "Prince Ajātaśatru," although this misses the playfulness of the original.

160 Cf. Divy 58.28–59.1, 100.14–15.

161 Following Vaidya (Divy 169.26) and Edgerton (BHSD, s.v. *upanirbaddha*), read *upanibaddham*. Divy 274.14, *upanirbaddham*. For more on such editorial insertions and their implications, see Schopen 2000: 187nXIII.7.

162 Divy 274.22–23, *viṣṭhayā vā śiṭayā vā karkaṭakena vā*. I follow Cowell and Neil's (Divy 690) understanding of *viṣṭhā*, although the term is unclear. "All that is clear," as Edgerton (BHSD) observes, "is that it is some means of catching and holding." Edgerton also suggests that it might be the equivalent of A[rdha]M[ā]g[adhī], *ciṭṭhā* and

Skt., *ceṣṭā*; hence, "with movements (of the hands, etc.)." Edgerton (BHSD) takes *śiṭā* as "rope." Cf. Divy 113.16, 281.2. Vaidya (Divy 170.1) emends to *śītayā*. Perhaps it is related to Hindi *sīḍhī*. For more on these terms, see Hiraoka 2007: i, 509n83.

163 Divy 274.25, *tīrthyasparśanaṃ gacchanti*. Here the text explains that "non-Buddhist renunciants" (*tīrthya*), which I sometimes translate as "heretics," are so called because they "touch" or "come into physical contact with" (*sparśana*) various *tīrtha*s—"descents into rivers or sacred bodies of water," "holy places," "shrines." Cf. Divy 484.14–15. See also Divy-V 404.20, v. 824, *tīrthavṛkṣeṣu*.

164 Cf. Divy 150.11, which reads "sins exposed" (*vivṛtapāpaiḥ*) for "sins cleansed" (*dhūtapāpaiḥ*).

165 Although there are numerous characters named Kāśyapa (Pāli, Kassapa) in Buddhist literature, Daśabala Kāśyapa (Pāli, Kassapa Dasabala) is a name generally used to designate the twenty-fourth buddha—the third of the present auspicious age—and only one of seven buddhas mentioned in the texts of the Pāli canon (e.g., *Dīgha-nikāya* ii, 2). The Buddha Daśabala Kāśyapa also figures in a number of stories in the *Divyāvadāna* (Divy 22–24, 342–43, 346–48). Here, however, it is a monk—not a buddha—that is given the name Daśabala Kāśyapa. If he did possess the ten powers (*daśabala*) that his name indicates, he would, by definition, be a buddha.

166 Divy 275.9, *āhūyati*. Vaidya (Divy-V 170.11) emends to *āhvayati*.

167 Cf. Divy 44.16–18.

168 Divy 275.20, *abhramayam*. The term *abhra* often means "cloud," but here the meaning is less certain. The Tibetan (21b3) reads "wooden" (*shing las byas pa*).

169 Following Vaidya (Divy-V 170.22), read *api tv adhīṣṭāni*. Divy 275. 24, *api tv adhiṣṭhāni*. Cowell and Neil (Divy 275n5) query *adhiṣṭhāne* or *adhīṣṭāni*.

170 Divy 275.28, *vyāḍayakṣa*. One might also take it to mean "fierce yakṣas." As Edgerton (BHSD) notes, "this compound is not otherwise recorded."

171 Divy 276.3, *dāpiyitavyam* (mss., *dāpitavyam*). Cowell and Neil (Divy 276n1) query *dāpitavyaḥ*. Vaidya (Divy-V 170. 27) suggests *dāpayiṣyati*.

172 Here (Divy 277.14) the text reads "the boy Jyotiṣka" (*jyotiṣkaś ca kumāraḥ*), but by now Jyotiṣka has grown up and become a householder. Presumably Jyotiṣka was visiting the palace to see his surrogate father, King Bimbisāra. Perhaps the text imagines him as a kind of prince (*kumāra*). See too note 159.

173 This incident is recounted in "The Story of Māndhātā" (Divy 213.21ff.; trans. in DS 351ff.).

174 Following Speyer (1902: 128), the Tibetan (23a7), and Hiraoka (HA 14; HC 66), read *vismitya*. Divy 278.22, "having forgotten" (*vismṛtya*).

175 Read *gacchāmaḥ*. Divy 278.28, "Go" (*gaccha*).

176 Other such incidents where a palace floor is mistaken for water can be found in the *Mahābhārata* (Ādi-Parvan, book 2.46) and also in the Qur'an (27.44), as noted by Cowell and Neil (Divy 707). See too Schiefner 1893: 360–61. For some observations on these parallels, see Grierson 1913.

177 Following 279.7, read *dṛśyante*. Divy 279.12, *paśyanti*.

178 According to Buddhaghosa, "An Enemy Before Birth." Cf. DPPN, s.v. *Ajātasattu*.

179 For another instance of brothers dividing up their possessions, see Divy 29.18ff.; trans. in DS 78ff.

180 Following Speyer (1902: 128), Vaidya (Divy-V 173.29), and Hiraoka (HA 14; HC 66), read *na śakitaṃ*. Divy 280.29, *na śaṅkitaṃ*.

181 Following the Schøyen fragments (Baums 2002: 296) and Hiraoka (HA 14; HC 66), read *anyam*. Divy 280.30, *anyad*.

182 Hiraoka (HA 14; HC 66), "for consistency with the form from a previous example," i.e., Divy 37.1–2 (HA 40), reads *-karaka-*. Divy 281.24, *-kara-*. But see Divy 48.21, 159.9, 281.24, etc. For more on this difference, see Edgerton (BHSD, s.vv. *kara*, *karaka*).

183 Following Vaidya's emendation (Divy-V 174.19), read *upasthitaḥ*. Divy 281.27–28, *nopasthitaḥ*. Cf. Divy 48.24 and 159.12, *naiva sthitā*, which Vaidya (Divy-V 29.32 and 98.22) emends to *evaṃ sthitā*, and Divy 342.2, *nopasthitā*, which Vaidya (Divy-V 211.23) also emends to *evaṃ sthitā*. Hiraoka (HA 14; HC 66) suggests "clothed" (*nepatthitaḥ*). Edgerton (BHSD, s.v. *nepatthita*) maintains that "some such form (possibly with Prakritic v for p) must be read in Divy 48.24, 49.16, 159.12, 342.4, 463.26, 558.22 . . . in all these the mss. (followed by the edd.) are corrupt . . ." Nobel (1955: i, 72n3) argues likewise.

184 Following Divy 54.2, 131.7, 141.4, etc., and Hiraoka (HA 14; HC 66), read *labdhasaṃbhārāṇi*. Divy 282.11, *labdhasaṃhārāṇi*. Cf. DS 413n356.

185 Cf. *Anaṅgaṇa Sutta* in the *Majjhima-nikāya* (i, 24–32).

186 Following Divy 283.6, add *traimāsīm*. Divy 283.27 (omitted).

187 Following Divy 64.26, 66.5, 81.12, add *āsanāni prajñapya*. Divy 284.27 (omitted).

188 Following Divy 65.9, 81.23, 97.9, etc., and Hiraoka (HA 14; HC 66), read *apanītapātram*. Divy 285.9, *apanīya pātram*. Cf. Divy 53.13, which reads *apanītapātram*, but all the mss. (Divy 53n1) read *apanīya pātram*.

189 Divy 285.14–15, *eṣa eva grantho vistareṇa kartavyaḥ*. Unlike the expression "and so on as before" (*pūrvavad yāvat*), this is not instructions to fill in the missing words of a stock expression but rather looser directions to the reader/reciter to recast the previous events for King Bandhumān.

190 Ordinary "wood" (*kāṣṭha*) is used as firewood; various kinds of "fragrant wood" (*gandhakāṣṭha*), such as sandalwood and agarwood, are not. Fragrant woods are expensive and often used ritually, such as for building funeral pyres (e.g., Divy 327.24, 350.18–19).

191 Divy 285.25–26, *sugandhatailena ca vastrāṇi tīmayitvā khādyakāny ullāḍayitum*. Cowell and Neil (Divy 285n4) query *ulloḍayitum*, and in their index (Divy 676) suggest "cook." The Tibetan (28b2) also reads "cook" (*btso ba*). Edgerton (BHSD, s.v. *tīmayati*), citing this passage, suggests "makes wet, sprinkles."

192 Following Divy 288.15–16, read *maṇḍalavāṭaḥ*. Divy 286.15, *maṇḍavāṭaḥ*. Zimmer (1925: 165) understands it to be a "round pavilion." The term might also refer to a circular hedged-in garden. Cf. Edgerton (BHSD, s.v. *maṇḍalamāḍa*).

193 Śakra can see what is below him, in a cosmological sense, but not what is above him. Cf. DS 421n450.

194 Following Divy 287.4, the Tibetan (30b1), and Hiraoka (HA 14; HC 66), add *paśya*. Divy 288.21 (omitted).

195 Divy 288.27, *dṛṣṭasatyaḥ*. The text doesn't specify when King Bandhumān had come to this vision of truth, which is unusual, for the text is usually specific and detailed about such moments of awakening (Divy 47.9–18, 52.22–53.10, 75.25–76.1). One

who has seen the truth, according to the text, has understood the four noble truths and attained one of the stages of religious development culminating in arhatship. In what follows (Divy 289.11–14), the Buddha explains that the householder Anaṅgaṇa, as a result of his act of harsh speech toward the king, will burn on a funeral pyre with his mother five hundred times. The severity of this karmic penance is likely due to the fact that King Bandhumān had achieved a high level of spiritual distinction, and so the householder Anaṅgaṇa's sin was directed toward a great field of merit—a king *and* a realized being simultaneously.

196 Divy 288.27–28, *tasyāntike tvayā kharavākkarma niścāritam*. Usually I translate an object in the genetive + *antike* quite literally as "in the presence of that object," but here the use is more figurative. The householder Anaṅgaṇa spoke harshly *toward* King Bandhumān, but not *in his presence*. Cf. Divy 313.2–3, 313.27.

197 For translations, see Burnouf 1844: 90–98 and 2010: 130–37; Zimmer 1925: 85–101; and Hiraoka 2007: i, 519–36. For Sanskrit parallels, see *Avadānakalpalatā* no. 42 (Rani 2005: 49 and woodcut R-13; Tucci 1949: ii, 481 and plate 113). The corresponding Tibetan can be found at P 1019 *ke* 52b5–57b8 and D 350 *aḥ* 50a5–55b7. For more, see Hiraoka 2007: i, 528; HC 66; and Grey 2000: 153.

198 For a Pāli version of this passage, see the *Itivuttaka* (18–19).

199 Divy 290.25, *tiṣṭhet*. Cf. Divy 470.18, *tiṣṭheyuḥ*; Divy 470.24 and 481.15, *tiṣṭhati*.

200 Following Vaidya (Divy-V 180.23), read *prabhūtasattvasvāpateyaḥ*. This can mean either that "his subjects were affluent" or that "he was affluent with many subjects." Divy 291.8, *prabhūta sattvasvāpateyaḥ* (mss. ABC, *satta-*). Hiraoka (HA 14; HC 66), following the Tibetan (53b1; 51a3), suggests *prabhūtasvāpateyaḥ*. Also possible is that *satta* is an error for *santa*. Cf. Divy 286.3, *santaḥsvāpateyam*; Divy 439.30, *sarvasantaṃ svāpateyam*.

201 Divy 291.27–28, *adyāgreṇa vo grāmaṇyaḥ sarvabaṇijo 'śulkān agulmān muñcāmi*. More literally, "From now on, officers, I exempt all of your merchants . . ." Perhaps take *vo* as accusative, or leave it out.

202 Following the Tibetan (54a1; 51b5), Vaidya (Divy-V 181.5), Hiraoka (HA 14; HC 66), and the Chinese, read *anenopāyena*. Divy 292.1, "in many ways" (*anekopāyena*). Also possible is that the king is said to rule "following many strategems" and not simply "according to dharma" (Divy 291.22) as he did before. I understand the famine to occur as a result of the king's policy, and so too the rains of food that will eventually fall to break the famine. Burnouf (2010: 132; cf. 1844: 92), however, offers this translation: "He governed in this way for many years, when one day there appeared a baleful constellation which announced that the god India would refuse to give rain for twelve years."

203 Following Vaidya (Divy-V 181.22) and Hiraoka (HA 14; HC 66), read *upasaṃkrāntāḥ*. Divy 292.29, *upasaṃkrāntaḥ*.

204 Divy 293.4, *yasyedānīṃ devaḥ kālam manyate*. This polite turn of phrase is often directed toward the Buddha, especially at those times when he is being told that his food is ready. I usually translate it as "Now my lord may do as the time permits."

205 Divy 293.16, *mānikā*. According to Puri (1965: 114), "nearly eight ounces."

206 Following the Tibetan (55a4; 53a1) and Hiraoka (HA 14; HC 66), read *evaṃ kariṣyatīti*. Divy 293.24, *kālaṃ kariṣyatīti*.

207 Hiraoka (HA 14; HC 66), following the Tibetan (55a5; 53a1), inserts *apitṛjñaiḥ*. That is, "nor honor their fathers."

208 This is a module found with some frequency in Āgama-Nikāya texts. See, for example, *Mahāsūtra* 4 §12.3 (Skilling 1994: ii, 389–90).

209 Following the Tibetan (55b1; 53a6) and Hiraoka (HA 14; HC 66), read *yathāpratyayaṃ prāptān dharmān avalokya*. Divy 294.11, *yathāprāptān dharmān avalokya*. Perhaps, "observing phenomena as they came to his attention," but this doesn't connect with the verse that follows. Vaidya (Divy-V 182.13) drops *dharmān*. Burnouf (2010: 133; cf. 1844: 94) offers this translation: "having contemplated the laws that he had just attained."

210 Divy 294.15, *khaḍgaviṣāṇakalpaḥ*. For more on this disputed term, which can also mean "like the horn of a rhinoceros" and which is commonly understood as a metaphor for the solitary buddha, see Salomon 2000: 10–14. For a parallel verse in the Pāli materials, see *Suttanipāta*, v. 36. Bhikkhu Bodhi (2017: 162) offers this translation: "For one who has formed bonds, there is affection; following on affection, this suffering arises. Discerning the danger born of affection, one should live alone like a rhinoceros horn" (*saṃsaggajātassa bhavanti snehā snehanvayaṃ dūkkhamidaṃ pahoti | ādīnavaṃ snehajaṃ pekkhamāno eko care khaggavisāṇakappo*). Cf. Norman 1984: 5.

211 Divy 296.3, *yathādhautena*. Egderton (BHSD) takes this to mean "with begging-bowl just as cleaned, i.e., not having received any almsfood." Rhys Davids and Stede (PTSD, s.v. *yathādhota*) similarly understand the Pāli equivalent: "as if it were washed (so to speak), clean, unsoiled." Also possible, however, is that this could mean "as though unwashed," for if one receives no food, then one has no reason to wash one's bowl.

212 Following Cowell and Neil's query (Divy 296n6), read *krīḍitā ramitāḥ*. Divy 296.21, *krīḍatā ramatā*. This is a strange locution. These two words are often coupled with a form of *paricārayati* to indicate sexual activity.

213 Soft foods (*bhojana*) are similarly defined in the Pāli materials. See Upasak 1975, s.v. *bhojana*.

214 Vaidya (Divy-V 184.11) omits *saptāhaṃ tailavarṣam pravarṣanti* (Divy 297.21–22).

215 For a translation, see Hiraoka 2007: i, 537–72. For Sanskrit parallels, see Sanskrit fragments from Turfan (Sander and Waldschmidt 1985: nos. 1330 and 1524) and GBM 1486–1487.4 (end of the story). The corresponding Tibetan can be found at P 1032 *ñe* 106a7–113b6 and D 3 *ja* 113b3–122b1. For more, see Hiraoka 2007: i, 557, and HC 67. See too Jean Przyluski's (1920: 314–19) translation of the first part of this story (= Divy 298.24–301.4) from the Chinese version of the *Mūlasarvāstivāda-vinaya*.

216 Divy 299.2–3, *tiraścām anyonyabhakṣaṇādīni*. Cf. Aśokāv 60.10–11, *tiryakṣvanyonyabhakṣaṇaparitrāsaduḥkham*. Strong (1989: 225) translates this as "among the animals, the suffering coming from the fear of eating one another."

217 Divy 299.6, *sārdhaṃvihārī*. Here the term could mean "student," "classmate," or "co-resident in the monastery," although it is the first of these meanings that seems to prevail in the *Divyāvadāna*. On Divy 18.27, it refers to the "students" of the venerable Mahākātyāyana, for they address him as "instructor" (*upādhyāyaḥ* | Divy 19.2–3). On Divy 345.10, it refers to a novice who was the "student" of an arhat. These students "lived with" their teachers, as the term literally means, for together they were

co-residents in the same monastery or, at least, monastic order. The term is often paired with *antevāsin* (e.g., Divy 18.17, 299.6, 489.16), with which it is a near synonym; the latter refers to a student who "lives near" his teacher. Edgerton explains the term as follows: "*a co-resident monk*, regularly however applied to those who are undergoing training, virtually *(fellow-)pupil*." Rhys Davids and Stede (PTSD, s.v. *saddhivihārika*) take the Pāli equivalent to mean "co-resident, fellow-bhikkhu; pupil." Bodhi (2000: 1193; *Saṃyutta-nikāya* iv, 103) translates it as "co-resident [monk]."

218 Divy 299.11, *avavāditaḥ* (ms. A, *avabodhitāḥ*; ms. C, omitted; ms. D, *avavoditaḥ*). Vaidya (Divy-V 185.10–11) likewise reads *avavāditaḥ*. Speyer (1902: 128–29) and Hiraoka (HA 14; HC 67) suggest *avoditāḥ*, the past passive participle of *ava* √*vad*, which also occurs at Divy 300.2, with no manuscript variants. Contra Hiraoka, Edgerton (BHSD, s.v. *avoditāḥ*) suggests emending *avoditāḥ* in both cases: "possibly *ovaditāḥ* or *ovāditāḥ*, if not *avavad[itāḥ]* or *avavād[itaḥ]*."

219 Vaidya (Divy-V 185.13) omits this question (Divy 299.16–17).

220 Divy 300.8, *dvārakoṣṭhake*. Although I translate this term as "gateway" when it refers to a part of a home (Divy 17.12) or a stūpa (Divy 244.17) and "doorway" when it refers to a part of the women's quarters (Divy 532.12–13, 532.16, 532.20), Gregory Schopen (2000: 173–75nVIII.20) argues convincingly that *dvārakoṣṭhaka*, when referring to a part of a monastery, refers to an "entrance hall." It is akin to the foyer of a building or the narthex of a church.

221 For more on this story and its description of the wheel of existence, see Przyluski 1920: 316–17 and Teiser 2006: 67–72, 77–79.

222 One could also translate this as "After three weeks—that is, on the twenty-first day..." The Tibetan concurs.

223 Hiraoka (HA 14; HC 67) suggests *ṛṇadharaḥ*. Divy 301.10, *ṛṇaharaḥ*. As Edgerton (BHSD, s.v. *ṛṇadhara*) explains: "The situation suggests *ṛṇadhara*, debt-establisher, and *dhanahara*, remover of wealth; i.e., a financial liability... But (a) *ṛṇahara* rather than *ṛṇadhara* (or else *ṛṇahāraka*) is read every time but once (h M[iddle] Indic for dh?); and (b) in Divy 5.12 *mahāsamudram avatareyaṃ dhanahārikaḥ*, the latter means to get wealth." Cf. DS 422n463. See too Schopen 2014: 616.

224 Divy 302.3, *kuṭkuñcakā*. Edgerton (BHSD, s.vv. *kuṭukuñcaka*, *kuṭa-*, *kuṭku-*) suggests "niggardly." Agrawala (1966: 70) offers this gloss: "such persons as make their faces wry and needlessly find fault with others."

225 Read *karmāṇi*. Divy 302.4, "suffering" (*duḥkhāni*).

226 According to Edgerton (BHSD, s.v. *anuśaṃsa*), "Pāli lists five (PTSD; other lists occur), and five are often mentioned in BHS, but they are different for different works of merit, and other numbers (as 10, 18) also occur; I have not found the PTSD list in BHS." For a translation of a corresponding passage in Tibetan, see Vogel and Wille (GM-Saṅgh 286–87). See too *Dīgha-nikāya* ii, 86.

227 Divy 302.26–27, *nayena kāmaṅgamaḥ* (ms. C, *kāmagamaḥ*). Speyer (1902: 129) and Hiraoka (HA 14; HC 67) suggest *nayenakāmaṅgamaḥ*. That is, "not allowed to go where one likes." Edgerton (BHSD) offers this explanation of *kāmaṃgama*: "going according to the desire of (of someone else, sc. a master); a servant."

228 Divy 303.3, *anuprāpnuvataḥ*. Speyer (1902: 129) and Hiraoka (HA 14; HC 67) suggest *ananuprāpnuvataḥ*. I read the text as is in the sense of "in the process of obtaining." Vogel and Wille (GM-Saṅgh 287) offer this translation: "For me, who (may)

attain truly supreme salvation (or) nirvāṇa, (even if) being guilty of a sin, there will (still) be rebirth among the gods."

229 Following mss. BD (Divy 303n3) and Divy 499.9, read *āyāpitaḥ*. Divy 303.28, *āpyāyitaḥ* (mss. AC, *āyāyitaḥ*). See BHSD, s.vv. *āyāpita, āpyāyaka.*

230 Following Vaidya (Divy-V 188.6), read *sphaṭitaparuṣā*. Divy 304.7, *sphaṭitapuruṣā*. Perhaps, "weather-beaten men." Hiraoka (HA 14; HC 67), following the Tibetan (109a5; 117a2), reads *bhṛtakapuruṣā*. That is, "day laborers."

231 Divy 304.26, *lokākhyāyikāyām*. Edgerton (BHSD) explains this and *lokākhyānakathā*, which appears on the following line (Divy 304.27), as "story-telling about the world"—"certainly not philosophical discussion about (the creation, etc., of) the world, which is the scholastic interpretation of Pāli *lokakkhāyikā*." Cf. Divy 109.27–28; trans. in DS 203. See also DS 425n509 on the difference between *ākhyāyikā* and *kathā*.

232 Following Edgerton (BHSD, s.v. *atisvāra*) and Hiraoka (HA 14; HC 67), read *atitvareṇa*. Divy 304.28, *atisvāreṇa*.

233 Divy 305.7, *prasannādhikāraṃ karomi*. Edgerton (BHSD, s.v. *adhikāra*) suggests this expression means "service tendered by one who is kindly disposed, i. e., service of friendship." Schopen (1996: 99) offers this translation: "Son, I am not giving two days' wages, but I, being grateful, am giving a token of my gratitude." For more on this idea of the "duty of one who has faith," see Rotman 2009: 76–82.

234 Divy 306.23, *sukumārī*. Earlier in this story, the boy is described as "young and frail" (*sukumāraḥ* | Divy 303.30), first by his mother and then by the householder who employs him. Now "cow dung" is similarly described. It is, like the boy, "fresh" and "thin," if not "delicate."

235 Divy 307.1, *nandopananda bhṛtakapuruṣaḥ*. Edgerton (BHSD, s.v. *nandopananda*) reads it as a compound: "he is a serving-man of Nanda and Upananda."

236 Divy 307.2, *kulopakagṛheṣu*. As Edgerton (BHSD, s.v. *upaka*) explains, "*kulopaka* (= Pāli, *kulūpaka*) lit. *belonging to a family*, = *family associate*, said of a monk who is regularly supported by a certain family . . . also, by extension, said of the houses visited by such monks."

237 Divy 307.2, *purobhaktakām*. The Tibetan (110b8; 119a2) reads *khye'u tshus*. These monks are having an early meal (i.e., a pre-meal snack), which is against monastic regulations. Monks are normally enjoined to eat only a single meal of almsfood a day. See, for example, Pāyantika no. 32 of the *Prātimokṣa-sūtra* of the Mūlasarvāstivādins. See too Prebish 1996: 79 and Wijayaratna 1990: 68–69.

238 Read *aryāḥ*. Divy 307.3, "noble one" (*ārya*).

239 Following Divy 307.22, add *gṛhe*. Divy 307.25 (omitted).

240 Here I take "in just the same way" (*evam eva* | Divy 308.3) to mean that the boy gives the food to the merchants as a gift; that he feeds them with his own hands; and that the feeding takes place in the home of the householder who formerly employed him.

241 Divy 308.12, *tad ayaṃ paṭakaḥ prajñaptaḥ*. The term *prajñapta* is generally used to describe the Buddha's seat, which is "specially prepared" (i.e., properly laid out).

242 Divy 309.8 *puṇyamaheśākhya iti*. For more on this expression, see Rotman 2009: 48. See too note 47.

243 Divy 309.20, *manuṣyakā*. Hiraoka (HA 14; HC 67), following the Tibetan (112b1; 120b6), suggests *amanuṣyakā*.

244 Divy 309.25–26, *prabhūtaṃ svāpateyam*. Hiraoka (HA 14; HC 67) suggests *prabhūtasvāpateyam*, so the compound can be taken as a *bahuvrīhi*.

245 Following Divy 71.27 and 75.27–28, read *atikrānto 'haṃ bhadantātikrāntaḥ*. Divy 311.5–6, *abhikrānto 'haṃ bhadantābhikrāntaḥ*. There seems to be some slippage between *atikrāntaḥ* and *abhikrāntaḥ*. At Divy 71.27, mss. ABC (Divy 71n8) read *abhi-*, and at Divy 75.27–28, all the mss. (Divy 75n3) read *abhi-*. The editors emend to *ati-* in both cases, although not at Divy 311.5. Here mss. AB (Divy 311n1) read *abhikānto*, which suggests a different reading. Since the Pāli equivalent of both the Sanskrit terms *abhikrānta* and *abhikānta* is *abhikkantam*, perhaps the expression *abhikrāntam aham* is a hyper-Sanskritization meaning "I am very fine" and not "I have crossed over." Edgerton (BHSD, s.v. *abhikrānta*) suggests *atikrāntābhikrāntaḥ*, which he translates as "having passed over the approach (to the religious goal)." Hiraoka (HA 14; HC 67), following Edgerton, suggests *bhadantāham atikrāntābhikrānta*. Cf. DS 410n321.

246 Following Divy 80.18–20, 85.1–3, 89.9–11, and Hiraoka (HA 14; HC 67), add *saṃdarśayati samādāpayati samuttejayati saṃpraharṣayati | anekaparyāyeṇa dharmyayā kathayā*. Divy 311.9 (omitted).

247 Following Hiraoka (HA 14; HC 67–68), read *prāntaśayanāsanasevī tena*. Divy 312.8–9, *prāntaśayanāsanasevinas te na*. Although *prāntaśayanāsanasevī* doesn't occur elsewhere in the *Divyāvadāna*, it does occur in the *Avadānaśataka* (i, 108.18, 113.8, etc.). There is no corresponding Tibetan to the term in question.

248 Divy 313.4, *kṣataḥ*. Vaidya (Divy-V 193.20) emends to *kṣamaḥ*. That is, "forgiving."

249 Following Speyer (1902: 130) and Hiraoka (HA 15; HC 68), read *dvitīya āgacchati*. Divy 313.8, *dvitīyam āgacchati*.

250 Following Speyer (1902: 130), Vaidya (Divy-V 193.28), and Hiraoka (HA 15; HC 68), read *sa mūlanikṛttaḥ*. Divy 313.15, *samūlanikṛttaḥ* (mss., *mūlanikṛnta*).

251 Following Speyer (1902: 130), Vaidya (Divy-V 193.28), and Hiraoka (HA 15; HC 68), read *saputraḥ*. Divy 313.16, *sa putraḥ*.

252 Since the solitary buddha is floating in the sky, the householder and his son don't exactly fall at his feet. The idiom, however, has been reified and is used even when it doesn't quite fit. See too DS 436n671.

253 Divy 313.17, *sadbhūtadakṣiṇīya*. Speyer (1902: 130) and Hiraoka (HA 15; HC 68) suggest *sadbhūta dakṣiṇīya*.

254 Here (Divy 314.8–9) the text reads *iyaṃ tāvad utpattir na tāvad buddho bhagavān śrāvakāṇāṃ vinaye śikṣāpadam*. This appears to be corrupt so I have left it out.

255 This avadāna, unlike the others in this volume, is glossed as a *prakaraṇa*, which can designate a work of fiction, like a drama or a play, as well as a treatise or investigation. It isn't clear how to understand the term here.

256 Ms. D (Divy 314n1) reads "So ends the twenty-first chapter in the *Divyāvadāna*, that of Sahasodgata in the glorious *Divyāvadāna*" (*iti śrīdivyāvadāne sahasodgatasya divyāvadāne ekaviṃśatimaḥ*).

257 For translations, see Ohnuma 2004a and Hiraoka 2007: i, 573–607. For Sanskrit parallels, see GBM 1487.4–1507.3; *Mahajjātakamālā* no. 48; Haribhaṭṭa's *Jātakamālā* no. 5 (Hahn 1992: 44–50); and *Avadānakalpalatā* no. 5 (Rothenberg 1990; Rani 2005: 16 and woodcut R-2; Tucci 1949: ii, 444 and plate 102). The corresponding

Tibetan can be found at P 1017 *ke* 24a4–33b2 and D 348 *aḥ* 22a4–31b3. See too Frye 1981: 105–14. For more, see Hiraoka 2007: i, 588; HC 68; and Grey 2000: 52–53.

Jens-Uwe Hartmann (1977) edited and translated into German the version of this story preserved in the *Gilgit Buddhist Manuscripts.* He also compared that version of the story with the one preserved in the *Divyāvadāna* and compiled a list of alternate readings and textual emendations (1980). My thanks to him for sharing his work and his insights. The symbols he uses are as follows: ( ) *akṣaras* that are either damaged or whose reading is uncertain; [ ] gap in the text; { } *akṣara* or letter that is to be omitted; < > restored without text gap.

258 Divy 314.16–17, *na tv eva pitṛmaraṇam āgamitavantau* (mss., *ārāgitavantau*). Edgerton (BHSD, s.v. *ārāgayati*) offers this translation: "(they entered nirvāṇa, or died,) *but did not attain* (wait for) *their father's death* (i.e., they predeceased him)." Then he notes, "acc[ording] to ed[itors] in [Divy] 314.23 and 315.3 mss. have *āgamitavantau, waited for*, which is the essential meaning in any case, but prob[ably] a lect[io] fac[ilior]." Hiraoka (2007: i, 588–89n3), following the Tibetan (24a6–7; 22a6–7) and the Chinese, understands *pitṛ* to refer to the Buddha, although he notes that this is a peculiar usage. Nevertheless, followers of the Buddha are his proverbial sons, as with the term *śākyapūtriya.* Ohnuma (2004a: 144) understands *pitṛ* to mean *pitṛloka* and offers this translation: ". . . were liberated in the sphere of nirvāṇa-without-remainder before they could die the normal death that leads to the realm of ancestors?"

259 Following Speyer (1902: 340), Vaidya (Divy-V 195.15), the Tibetan (24b4; 22b5), and Hiraoka (HA 15; HC 68), read *suvibhaktā*. Divy 315.8, *savibhaktā.*

260 Divy 315.8, *uccaistoraṇa-*. Hiraoka (HA 15; HC 68) reads *uccatoraṇa-*, taking *ucca* as an adjective. GBM 1488.3 (Hartmann 1977: 23), *udviddha-*.

261 These homes of wealthy merchants are not only placed first, but they appear to be in a separate class from everyone else's homes, even those of kings. For more on the elevated status of merchants in early Indian Buddhism, see Rotman (in progress).

262 Read *āvasāḥ*. Divy 315.11, *āvasaḥ*.

263 Divy 315.11, *nītimaulidharāṇām.* GBM 1488.4 (Hartmann 1980: 258), *nītindharāṇām*. Perhaps, "law-abiding citizens." Cf. Divy 317.16.

264 Read *sarvakālikakusumagandhā*. Divy 315.13–14, *sarvakālikāś ca kusumagandhā.* Cf. GBM 1488.5 (Hartmann 1977: 24), *kusumagandhāś ca sarvākālikā* [read *sarva-*] *īdṛśā gandhā.*

265 Divy 315.17, *-ardhacandra-*. These objects are, quite literally, "crescent shaped," but it is unclear whether they are windows, decorations, or even corridors.

266 Following Cowell and Neil's query (Divy 315n3), read *puṇḍarīkātisurabhi-*. Speyer (1902: 340) and Hiraoka (HA 15; HC 68) suggest *puṇḍarīkādisurabhi-*. Divy 315.18, *puṇḍarīkāni surabhi-*.

267 Following Cowell and Neil's query (Divy 315n3), Speyer (1902: 340), and Hiraoka (HA 15; HC 68), read *parimaṇḍitā 'tisvādu-*. Divy 315.18, *parimaṇḍitāṇi svādu-*.

268 Following Hiraoka (HA 15; HC 68) and GBM 1488.8 (Hartmann 1977: 24), omit *sūtra-*. Divy 315.20, *tamālasūtra-*. Likely emend to *tamālapatra.*

269 Following Vaidya (Divy-V 195.24) and Hiraoka (HA 15; HC 68), read *-saṃchannā kalaviṅka-*. Divy 315.21–22, *-saṃchannakalaviṅka-*.

270 Following Divy 325.8, 15, 18, etc. and Hiraoka (HA 15; HC 68), read *maṇiratnagarbham.* Divy 315.23–24, "Containing a Jewel" (*maṇigarbham*). Perhaps this park is

where King Candraprabha, as a wheel-turning king and a possessor of the seven treasures, keeps his most-treasured jewel. Cf. Divy 60.16–18.

271 For more on birds in Sanskrit literature, see Linke 1997.

272 Following GBM 1489.3 (Hartmann 1980: 259) and Hiraoka (HA 15; HC 68), read *svayamprabhaḥ*. Divy 316.2, "a self-made man" (*svayamprabhuḥ*).

273 Following GBM 1490.1 (Hartmann 1980: 259) and Hiraoka (HA 15; HC 68–69), read *suvarṇabheryaḥ saṃtāḍya.* Divy 316.18, *suvarṇabhery asaṃtāḍya.* Cowell and Neil (Divy 316n4) query *suvarṇabherīḥ saṃtāḍya*, which Vaidya (Divy-V 196.7–8) follows.

274 Following Vaidya (Divy-V 196.9), read *śayanāsanāpāśraya-*. Divy 316.20, *śayanāsanam apāśraya.*

275 Hiraoka (HA 15; HC 69), following the precedent of the preceding phrase and the Tibetan (25b5, 23b7), adds "powder" (*cūrṇa*). GBM 1490.4 (Hartmann 1977: 25) concurs. Divy 316.22 (omitted).

276 Divy 316.22–23, *kāmadohinyaḥ*. GBM 1490.4 (Hartmann 1977: 25), *kamadohinyaḥ* [read *kāma-*]. The Tibetan (25b5; 23b7) reads *khar po'i bzho snod rnams.* Hiraoka (HA 15; HC 69) suggests *kaṃsa-*. Perhaps, "with their own brass pails filled with milk." Cf. Edgerton (BHSD, s.v. *kaṃsadoha*).

277 On the terminology of silk in India, see Liu 1996: 50–56.

278 Divy 316.26–27, *-dukūlamayaśobhanavastrāṇy* (ex conj.; ms. A, *-dukūlasmyaśobhanavastrāṅgaparāntaka-*; mss. BD, *-dukūlasmyaṅgāparāntaka-*; ms. C, *dukūlaśobhanavastrāsmyaṅgāparāntaka-*) *aparāntakaphalakaharyaṇīkambala-*. GBM 1490.6 (Hartmann 1977: 25), *-dugūlaśṛṅgaparāntaka{ṃ} haryaṇīyaka{ṃ} (kamba)la-*. Following Cowell and Neil's conjecture, the first half of the compound is clear (*-dukūlamayaśobhanavastrāṇy-*), but the latter half of the compound is problematic (*-aparāntakaphalakaharyaṇīkambala-*). First, the reading *aṅgāparāntaka* (mss. BCD) is perhaps akin to the term *aśmāparāntaka* that occurs throughout the *Koṭikarṇa-avadāna* (DS 392b85). That compound is a conjunct of two place names (i.e., Aśma and Aparānta), and perhaps it is the same here, although this pairing would be odd as Aṅga was a country in what is now Bengal and Aparāntaka a country in what is now the northern Konkan area of western India. The Tibetan (25b6; 24a2) reads *mri gā pā na*. Cf. Hiraoka 2007: i, 592n62. The term *phalaka* is also ambiguous. While I understand it to mean "bark," Upreti (1995: 47) writes of "finely polished skin sheets from Aparāntaka (*aparāntaka phalaka*)"—likely because on Divy 19.19–21 different kinds of skins (*carma*) used in the regions of Aśmāparānta are mentioned. Cf. Edgerton (BHSD, s.vv. *phala*, *phalaka*) and Hiraoka 2007: i, 592n63. In addition, there is the unattested *haryaṇī*. M. G. Dhadphale (personal communication) suggests this etymology: *aṇi* means "needle" and *hari* comes from √*aḍ* meaning "to plow." In other words, "plow-shaped needles," which would have been used to crochet fabric. The Tibetan (25b7; 24a2) reads *bag le pa*. The *Mahāvyutpatti* (5871) equates this with Skt., *vakkali*, which Edgerton (BHSD) explains as "a kind of textile material." This may have some connection with the Marathi word *vākaḷ*, a kind of quilt or blanket.

279 Divy 317.13, *harṣakaṭa-*. Agrawala (1966: 69) thinks it is the equivalent of *dolāvalaya* and means "loose bracelet." Edgerton (BHSD) cites *harṣa* as "necklace" and *kaṭa* as "bracelet."

280 Divy 317.23, *-tāla-*. This is obscure, although the instrument in question was probably used, like a metronome, for "keeping rhythm" or "beating time" (*tāla*).

281 Following Divy 320.12–13, the Tibetan (26b2; 24b6), GBM 1492.3 (Hartmann 1977: 27), and Hiraoka (HA 15; HC 69), add *rājñaḥ*. Divy 317.29 (omitted).

282 Following Cowell and Neil's query (Divy 317n5), Divy 320.14, and Hiraoka (HA 15; HC 69), read *valgur manojñaśabdaḥ*. Divy 317.30, *varṇamanojñaśabdaḥ*. Perhaps, "praiseworthy and pleasing sounds."

283 Divy 318.6, *dvāśaptatir ayutakoṭiśatāni*. The term *ayuta*, as Edgerton (BHSD) notes, means "10,000" in standard Sanskrit, but "oftener = 100 koṭis or 1,000,000,000." Hence, *dvāśaptati* (72) x *ayuta* (1,000,000,000) x *koṭi* (10,000,000) x *śata* (100) = 72,000,000,000,000,000,000. The Tibetan (26b4; 24b7–25a1) concurs. More colloquially, and perhaps even more in the spirit of the original, one might say "seventy-two gazillion."

284 Following Divy 318.26–27 and Hiraoka (HA 15; HC 69), read *varṇākṛtiliṅgasaṃsthānam*. Divy 318.7–8, *varṇākṛtiliṅgasthairyam*. Perhaps, "complexion, form, and inherent characteristics."

285 Divy 318.19–20, *rājaparikarṣakau rājaparipālakau*. GBM 1493.4 (Hartmann 1977: 29), *rājaparikarṣakau rājyaparipālakau*. That is, "managers of the king and protectors of the kingdom."

286 Divy 319.3, *sarvaparityāge*. GBM 1494.1 (Hartmann 1977: 29), *sarvaparityāgī*.

287 Divy 319.6, *koṣakoṣṭhāgāram*. Usually I translate this as "treasuries and granaries" or just "granaries." Cf. DS 428n557.

288 Divy 319.11 and GBM 1494.5 (Hartmann 1977: 29), *potaḥ*. The Tibetan (27b1; 25b5), however, reads "head."

289 Divy 319.11, *kulasthaḥ*. Or perhaps, "who was a member of King Candraprabha's family." Both readings are possible, and both readings make sense within the context of the story.

290 Following Divy 391.5–6, 475.5, and Hiraoka (HA 15; HC 69), read *vipañcikāḥ*. Divy 319.14, *vipaścikāḥ* (mss., *vipañci-*). GBM 1494.6 (Hartmann 1977: 29), *vipañcanakāḥ*. Cf. Edgerton (BHSD, s.v. *vipañcika*).

291 Following Cowell and Neil's query (Divy 319n3), Divy 319.19, GBM 1494.6 (Hartmann 1980: 259), and Hiraoka (HA 15; HC 69), read *nirdeśam*. Divy 319.15, *nirdośam*. Perhaps, "nullify its evil effects."

292 Read *vipañcikaiḥ*. Divy 319.16, *vipaścikaiḥ*. See note 290.

293 Following Vaidya (Divy-V 198.7), Hartmann (1980: 259), and Hiraoka (HA 15; HC 69), read *svapnopamaiḥ*. Divy 320.4, *svapnomapaiḥ*. GBM 1495.6 (Hartmann 1980: 259) reads "dreams" (*svapanaiḥ*).

294 Vaidya (Divy-V 198.11) omits Divy 320.10–12.

295 Following the Tibetan (28a4; 26a7), Divy 317.28–29, GBM 1495.8–1496.1 (Hartmann 1977: 31), and Hiraoka (HA 15; HC 69), read *tālavaṃśanirghoṣaḥ*. Divy 320.12, *tāsām eva śabdanirghoṣaḥ*.

296 Following Divy 318.2–3, GBM 1496.2 (Hartmann 1980: 259), and Hiraoka (HA 15; HC 69), read *abhyantaraṃ devapuraṃ nṛttagītavāditaśabdena nirnāditam* (GBM, *nināditam*). Divy 320.16, *anyataraṃ devapuraṃ nṛttagītavāditam*.

297 His name can mean both "Having Cruelty in His Eyes" and "Possessing a Rosary of

Rudrākṣa Beads." That at least the former meaning is possible is affirmed later (Divy 322.22) when the brahman is referred to as "cruel-minded" (*raudracitta*).

298 The following verses in the *Divyāvadāna* (Divy 321.9–27) correspond in interesting and significant ways with their counterparts in the *Gilgit Buddhist Manuscripts* (GBM 1497.2–7). Hartmann (1980: 259–62) offers text and translation for these verses:

The Kinnara crowds are weeping, and so are the forest deities;
"fie, fie" make the immortals staying in heaven.
The moon does not beam and the one of thousand rays (the sun)
is not shining;
here not even the sound of instruments can be heard
anymore. (1)

rudaṃti kinnaragaṇā vanadevatāś ca
dhigdhiḥ karoti {//} *amarā gagane sthitāś ca* |
candro na bhāti na vibhāti sahasraraśmir
naivādya vāditaravo 'pi niśāmyate 'tra ||

Those clumps of trees bearing fruits and blossoms
fall to the ground as well, unmoved by the wind.
Clearly this noise is heard which resembles a too dreadful one.
A tremendous misery will become evident in the city. (2)

ete 'pi pādapagaṇāḥ phalapuṣpanaddhā
bhūmau patanti anilena anīri[*tā*]*(ni)* |
saṃ(śrū)yate dhvanir iyaṃ ca yathātibhīmo
vyaktaṃ bhaviṣyati pure vyasanaṃ sughoraṃ ||

Therefore all the townspeople bear
this conglomerated misery in their mind;
moaning they beat their breasts with their hands,
a speechlessness unparalleled holds back the words. (3)

tatkāraṇena puravāsijanāḥ[a] *samagrāḥ*
saṃpiṇḍitaṃ manasi duḥkha[*m idaṃ vahanti*] |
utkrośatām[b] *urasi*[c] *baddhakṛtāgrahastaiḥ*
vaisvaryam apratisamaṃ niruṇaddhi vācaṃ ||

[a]Ms., puna-.
[b]Following Divy 321.21. Ms., *ukrośatām*
[c]Following the Tibetan (28b8; 27a3). Ms., *anasi.*

Women with moonlike faces weep,
and all citizens cry bitterly.
The clouds resound without having water,
and the ponds are nearly dried up. (4)

candrānanāś ca prarudanti nāryaḥ
paurāś ca sarve karuṇaṃ ru[danti |
ete payo]dā ninadaṃty atoyā
jalāśayāḥ śoṣam upāgatāś ca ||

Fires burn hills and forest innumerably;
in the great confusion people weep in every house.
The earth is shaking like a ship on the water moved by the wind,
and rough winds mixed with dust are blowing. (5)

śailāṃ vanāni ca dahaṃti bhṛṣaṃ [bhṛśaṃ?] hutāśā{ḥ}
adhyākulāḥ pratigṛhaṃ manujā rudaṃti |
bhūr naur i[vāmbhasi cacā]la samīraṇāstā{ḥ}
vātāḥ pravanti ca kharā{ḥ} rajasā vimiśrāḥ ||

Now the unfavourable signs are numerous;
therefore we had better move from here to a favourable region. (6)

aśivāni nimittāni pracurāṇi hi sāṃpratam |
kṣemāṃ diśam ato 'smākam ito gaṃtuṃ kṣamaṃ bhave[t ||]

299 Divy 321.10, *vanadevatāś ca dhikkāram utsṛjanti.* GBM 1497.2–3, *karoti.* To fit the number and meter, Hartmann (1980: 260) suggests *karonti.* Hiraoka (HA 15; HC 69–70) concurs. Speyer (1902: 340–41) suggests the metrically appropriate *vanadevatā . . . utsṛjati.*

300 Divy 321.10–11, *devagaṇā api tasthuḥ.* Perhaps, "Hordes of kinnaras and forest deities cry and call out in distress; the assemblies of the gods are likewise startled." Speyer (1902: 340–41) suggests "shed tears" (*api sāśruḥ*). Vaidya (Divy-V 198.30) emends this to "are unsettled" (*na sthuḥ*). Hiraoka (HA 15; HC 70), following GBM 1497.2–3 and the Tibetan (28b5–6; 27a1), suggests *amarā gagane sthitāś ca.*

301 Divy 321.11–12, *naiva vādyavāditaravaḥ.* Hartmann (1980: 260) and Hiraoka (HA 15; HC 70), following GBM 1497.2–3 and the Tibetan (28b6; 27a1), suggest *naivādya vāditaravaḥ.* Speyer (1902: 341) suggests *ke* for *naiva* to correct the meter.

302 Divy 321.13, *pavanair api cālitāni.* Perhaps emend to *cālitāś ca.* Speyer (1902: 341) suggests *cālitā na.* Hartmann (1980: 260) and Hiraoka (HA 15; HC 70), following GBM 1497.3–4 and the Tibetan (28b6; 27a2), suggest *anilena anīritāni.*

303 Divy 321.14, *mahāntam.* Cowell and Neil (Divy 321n3) note "Sic mss.," for the gender is incorrect. Perhaps emend to *mahat ca.* Hartmann (1980: 260) and Hiraoka (HA 15; HC 70), following GBM 1497.3–4 and the Tibetan (28b7; 27a2), suggest *sughoraṃ.*

304 Following Speyer (1902: 341), GBM 1497.2, and Hiraoka (HA 15; HC 70), read *vyaktam.* Divy 321.14, *vyaktaḥ.*

305 Following Speyer (1902: 341) and Hiraoka (HA 15; HC 70), read *-kaṇṭhānanāḥ.* Divy 321.16, *kaṇṭhānanā.*

306 Divy 321.14–18. Not found in GBM or in the Tibetan. As Hartmann (1980: 260)

notes, "Mention of the name Bhadraśilā already hints at the possibility of a later insertion."

307 Divy 321.19, *kiṃ kāraṇam*. Hartmann (1980: 260) and Hiraoka (HA 15; HC 70), following GBM 1497.4 and the Tibetan (28b7; 27a2), read *tatkāraṇena*.

308 Following Vaidya (Divy-V 199.10), the Tibetan (28b7; 27a3), Hartmann (1980: 260), and Hiraoka (HA 15; HC 70), read *vahanti*. Divy 321.20, *vadanti*. Perhaps, following Ohnuma (2004a: 151), "But why do all of the people living in the city speak of their collective sadness only in their minds?"

309 Divy 321.21, *ardhakṛtāgrahastaiḥ*. Hartmann (1980: 261) and Hiraoka (HA 15; HC 70), following the *Mahajjātakamālā* (Hartmann 1980: 261), suggest *ūrdhvakṛtāgrahastaiḥ*. Perhaps "with raised hands" or "with outstretched hands." GBM 1497.5, *baddhakṛtāgrahastaiḥ*. Another possibility is *arthakṛtāgrahastaiḥ*, or even *arthakṛte 'grahastaiḥ*.

310 Divy 321.21, *aiśvaryam*. The *Mahajjātakamālā* (Hartmann 1980: 261) reads *vākyam*, and Hiraoka (HA 15; HC 70) reads likewise. Hartmann (1980: 261), following GBM 1497.5, prefers *vaisvaryam*.

311 Following Cowell and Neil's query (Divy 321n6), read *śoṣam amī vrajanti*. Divy 321.23, "filled with grief" (*śokam amī vrajanti*). Hartmann (1980: 261) and Hiraoka (HA 16; HC 70), following GBM 1497.5–6 and the Tibetan (29a1; 27a4), suggest *śoṣam upāgataś ca*. Lines c and d of verse 4 along with lines c and d of verse 5 in the GBM form lines a, b, c, and d of verse 5 in both the *Divyāvadāna* and the *Mahajjātakamālā*. Lines a and b of verses 5 and 6 in the GBM are not found in these other texts.

312 Divy 321.24, *bhuvor ivāmbhasi ca vālasamīraṇāstā* (ms. D, *vavālahamī-*). This line loses the Vasantatilaka meter. Hartmann (1980: 261) and Hiraoka (HA 16; HC 70), following GBM 1497.6–7, read *bhūr naur ivāmbhasi cacāla samīraṇāstāḥ*. Hartmann (1980: 261) supplies *cacāla* on the basis of the Tibetan (29a1–2; 27a4–5). One could also emend to *bālasamīraṇās te*. The *Mahajjātakamālā* (Hartmann 1980: 261) preserves the following reading in the Triṣṭubh meter: "the earth with ponds and mountains is shaking" (*bhūś cāpi sābdhiś calate saśailā*).

313 Following GBM 1497.7, the Tibetan (29a2; 27a5), Hartmann (1980: 261), and Hiraoka (HA 16; HC 70), read *pracurāṇi*. Divy 321.26, *pravarāṇi*. Speyer (1902: 341) suggests *pravartante*.

314 Divy 321.26, *kṣemaḥ*. Speyer (1902: 341), Hartmann (1980: 261), and Hiraoka (HA 16; HC 70) suggest *kṣamaṃ*. GBM 1497.7 and the Tibetan (29a2; 27a5) also preserve this reading, but the *Mahajjātakamālā* (Hartmann 1980: 261) preserves *kṣemaḥ*.

315 Following GBM 1498.8, Hartmann (1980: 262), and Hiraoka (HA 16; HC 70–71), read *chetsyasīti*. Vaidya (Divy-V 200.2) reads *chetsyasi*. Divy 322.22, *chetsyati*. This form of the verb, as Hartmann (1980: 262) observes, was likely created by the *akṣara -sī-* being dropped, intentionally or otherwise.

316 Divy 323.20, *kiṃ idānīṃ prāptakālam iti*. GBM 1500.1 (Hartmann 1980: 262), *(ki) m idānīṃ prāptakāla iti*. Perhaps, "Is his time really up now?" or "Is it now really time for his death?"

317 Following GBM 1500.3, the Tibetan (30a6; 28a7), Hartmann (1980: 262), Hiraoka (HA 16; HC 71), and Divy 284.15, read *dūtena prakrośya*. Divy 323.22, "called out from a distance" (*dūreṇa prakrośya*).

318 Following GBM 1500.4, add *brāhmaṇa*. Divy 323.23 (omitted).

319 Divy 323.30–31, *paramatyāgaprativiśiṣṭam tyāgaṃ parityaktukāmaḥ*. GBM 1500.7 (Hartmann 1980: 262), *sarvaparityā(gī) prativiśiṣṭaṃ tyāgaṃ parityaktukāmaḥ*. Perhaps, "who sacrificed everything and who wanted to make a sacrifice that would be greatly distinguished." The Tibetan (30b1; 28b3) concurs. Hiraoka (HA 16; HC 71) reads likewise.

320 Following Speyer (1902: 341) and Hiraoka (HA 16; HC 71), read *yācyatām*. Divy 324.1, *yacchatāṃ*. Perhaps, "Since I'm giving away [everything]." Cowell and Neil (Divy 324n1) query "it is said" (*ucyatām*). There is no corresponding word in GBM or in the Tibetan.

321 Following Hartmann (1980: 263), read *śubhabodhisattva sarvajñatām*. Speyer (1902: 342) and Hiraoka (HA 16; HC 71) read *śubha bodhisattva sarvajñatām*. Divy 324.4–5, *śubhabuddhisattvasarvajñatām*.

322 Following Speyer (1902: 342), read *mahākaruṇāgracetaḥ*. Divy 324.5–6, *mahākāruṇāgracetā*. Hiraoka (HA 16; HC 71), following GBM 1501.2 and the Tibetan (30b3; 28b5), reads *mahākaruṇātmacetaḥ*. That is, "possessing a mind that has great compassion at its core."

323 Following Speyer (1902: 342), Vaidya (Divy-V 200.32), and Hiraoka (HA 16; HC 71), read *bhavādya*. Divy 324.6, *bhavādyaḥ*. Hartmann (1980: 263–64) offers text and translation for the corresponding verse at GBM 1501.1–2:

You stand firm in the flawless Dharma, shining bodhisattva,
with all your heart desiring omniscience, saint.
Leave me your head, being of great compassion;
because the good beings are ones who take delight in giving away
everything. (7)

dharme sthito 'si vimale subhabuddhisatva[a]
sarvajñātām abhilaṣaṃ hṛdayena sādho |
mahyaṃ śiraḥ sṛja mahākaruṇātmacetaḥ
sarvasvadānaniratā hi bhavaṃti satvāḥ ||

[a]Following Divy 324.4 and the Tibetan (30b3). Ms., subhabuddhisatvaḥ.

324 Divy 324.11, *kharpam*. This seems to be a form of *kharparam* ("skull"), which is found in ms. D (Divy 324n2), modified to fit the meter. GBM 1501.1–4 (Hartmann 1980: 263–65), *śīrṣam*. Speyer (1902: 342) and Hiraoka (HA 16; HC 71) suggest likewise.

325 The *Gilgit Buddhist Manuscripts* (GBM 1501.1–4) preserves a quite different reading for this verse, and it also contains an additional verse (verse 9) that is not found in the *Divyāvadāna*. Hartmann (1980: 263–65) offers the verses with translations:

I am the only son of my father;
yet, take this head of mine!
Your thoughts are fruitbearing;
may I attain enlightenment by giving away the head! (8)

pitur hy ahaṃ yady api caikaputras
tathāpi me śīrṣam idaṃ gṛhāṇa |
tvacccintitānāṃ saphalatvam asti
śiraḥpradānād dhi labheya bodhiṃ ||

I will fulfill your wish; nothing else can be done with this head of mine
consisting of brain, blood, and fat.
If there is, however, a wish for my head caused by your egocentricity,
well then, receive it; my sacrifice shall be fruitbearing. (9)

kāmaṃ kariṣyami na kṛtyam anena kiṃci<d>
mastiṣkaśoṇitavasāśirasā mama tvaṃ |
(yady arthi)tā tu śirasā tava māmakena
hanta pratīccha saphalo 'stu mamātisargaḥ ||

326 Following GBM 1501.6, the Tibetan (30b7; 29a1), Hartmann (1980: 265), and Hiraoka (HA 16; HC 71), read *mauliḥ śiraḥsthaḥ patitaḥ*. Divy 324.15, *maulaya iti śirasaḥ patitāḥ*.

327 Divy 324.22–23, *dhanyās te puruṣa deva ya evam atyadbhutarūpadarśanaṃ vā* [read *vaḥ*] *drakṣyantīti*. GBM 1502.1 (Hartmann 1980: 265), *dhanyās te puruṣā loke ye devaṃ puna[r] drakṣyaṃtīti*, which Hartmann translates as "Lucky are those people in the world who will see His Majesty again!" The Tibetan (31a1; 29a3) reads likewise.

328 In the *Gilgit Buddhist Manuscripts* (GBM 1502.7–1503.1), the first mention of these trees comes at the end of a description of the flora in the Maṇiratnagarbha Park. The Tibetan (31a6–8; 29a7–b2) preserves the same, but it mentions only a *campaka* tree, and instead of a red amaranth tree, it speaks of "elevation" (*stegs bu*). Cf. Hartmann 1980: 265. This passage, however, does not occur in the *Divyāvadāna* (Divy 325.7); the first mention of the trees comes here (Divy 325.23–24). In the corresponding passage, GBM 1503.7 mentions only a *campaka* tree, the more important of the two trees for the narrative.

329 Divy 326.9, *eṣa eva devate sapṛṣṭhībhūto* (*sic* mss.) *maitrīyo* (mss. ABC, *maitrīyaḥ yaḥ*; ms. D, *maitrīyaḥ syād*) . . . Contra Edgerton (BHSD, s.v. *pṛṣṭhībhavati*), who takes *sapṛṣṭhībhūtaḥ* here to mean "(made) averse, turned away (from wordly things)," I follow Hartmann (1980: 265–66), who understands it to mean "outrun, surpassed." Cf. Divy 481.4–5. GBM 1504.4ff. (Hartmann 1980: 265–66), *eṣa eva devate sa pradeśo yatra mayā vyāghryā ātmānaṃ* (ms., *vyāghryātmānaṃ*) *parityajya catvāriṃśatka[lpasaṃ]prasthito maitreyo bodhisatva{ḥ} ekena śirasaḥ* (ms., *śirasā*) *parityāgena avapṛṣṭhīkṛtaḥ*, which Hartmann translates as "This is the very spot, deity, where I sacrificed myself for the tigress and where I, on account of one single giving up of the head, left behind the Bodhisattva Maitreya who had set out forty kalpas ago." Hiraoka (HA 16; HC 71), following GBM and the Tibetan (32a2–3; 30a3–4), reads *sa pradeśo yatra mayā*.

330 Following GBM 1504.7 (Hartmann 1980: 266), the Tibetan (32a5; 30a5), and Hiraoka (HA 16; HC 71), read *atityāgam*. Divy 326.16, *asmin tyāgam*. Cowell and Neil (Divy 326n5) query *tyāge*.

331 Divy 326.17, *yena cāhaṃ satyena svaśiraḥ parityajāmi*. GBM 1504.7 (Hartmann 1977: 41–42), *na cāhaṃ śiraḥ parityajāmi*. Cf. the Tibetan (31b6; 29b7).

332 Divy 326.19, *cakravartivijayāya*. Hiraoka (HA 16; HC 71), following GBM 1504.7 (Hartmann 1980: 266) and the Tibetan (32a6; 30a6), reads *cakravarttiviśayārthāya*. That is, "for the dominion of a wheel-turning king." Cf. Divy 473.24–25 and 478.25–26.

333 Divy 326.24, *sarṣapaphalapramāṇadhātavaḥ*. GBM 1505.2 (Hartmann 1977: 42), *sarṣapaphalamātrādhātavaḥ*.

334 Following GBM 1505.3 (Hartmann 1980: 266), the Tibetan (32b1; 30b2), and Hiraoka (HA 16; HC 71), read *śrāntakāyā*. Divy 326.26, *śāntakāyā*, which Ohnuma (2004a: 156) translates as "with pure bodies." Cf. Divy 326.27, *viśrāntā*.

335 Divy 326.27, *dhātuparam*. Hiraoka (HA 16; HC 72), following GBM 1505.3 (Hartmann 1980: 266) and the Tibetan (32b2; 30b2), reads *dhātudharam*. That is, "reliquary."

336 Divy 327.5, *praṇītatvāt*. One might expect *praṇīte*. The Tibetan (32b5; 30b5) reads *phul du byung ba'i*. See too Divy 14.18, 98.21, etc.

337 Following GBM 1505.8 (Hartmann 1980: 266), the Tibetan (32b6; 30b5), Hiraoka (HA 16; HC 72), and Divy 158.8–9, read *vyathitaḥ pravyathitaḥ saṃpravyathitaḥ*. Divy 327.9, *vyadhitaḥ pravyadhitaḥ saṃpravyadhitaḥ*.

338 Divy 327.14, *śirograhāya*. Read as a defective gerund for *śiro gṛhītvā*. GBM 1506.2 (Hartmann 1977: 43), *śiro gṛhāya*.

339 Divy 327.24–25, *dhmāpitāni* (ms. C, *dhmāpitātāni*; ms. D *-tāni tāni*). GBM 1506.6 (Hartmann 1977: 43), *dhyāpitaḥ* [read *dhmāpitaḥ*]. Cf. Divy 583.24–25.

340 Divy 328.11–12, *eṣa eva sa tena kālena tena samayena devadatto babhūva*. More literally, "Because at that time and at that juncture he was none other than Devadatta." Based on the other identifications in this passage, this sentence appears to be incomplete, with the identification reversed. I correct accordingly.

341 This is made more explicit in the *Gilgit Buddhist Manuscripts* (GBM 1507.5–6; Hartmann 1977: 44): "Back then too without witnessing my death, they died without waiting for the death of their [spiritual] father. And now as well, without witnessing my final nirvāṇa, they have passed into final nirvāṇa without waiting for the death of their [spiritual] father" (*tadāpy etau mama maraṇaṃ apaśyantau tatprathamata* [read *thamataḥ*] (*kā*)*laṃ kṛtavantau na ca pitṛmaraṇam āgamitavantau* | *etarhy api mama* [*parini*]*rvāṇam apaśyantau tatprathamataḥ parinirvṛtau na ca pitṛmara*(*ṇam ā*)*gamita*(*vantau*)). Divy 328.17, *pitṛmaraṇam ārāgitavantau*. Cowell and Neil (Divy 328n1) query *āgamitavantau*. Cf. Divy 314.17 and 314.23.

342 As Cowell and Neil (Divy 328) note, "Here the mss. gives the following fragment."

343 Read *-rājyādiḥ rāja-*. Divy 328.22–23, *-rājyādayo rāja-*. Alternatively, this compound could be joined with the compound that follows.

344 Divy 328.25, *-itara-*. More literally, "other than."

345 These seem to be a version of the eight types of suffering as found, for example, in the *Dhammacakkappavattana Sutta* (*Saṃyutta-nikāya* v, 420): birth; aging; sickness; death; sorrow, lamentation, pain, grief, and despair; union with the unpleasant; separation from the pleasant; and not getting what one desires.

346 For translations, see Burnouf 1844: 313–35, 2010: 310–26 and Hiraoka 2007: ii, 1–50 (stories 23–25). For a partial translation, see Vogel 1926: 187–89. For a translation

of the preamble to the text, see Ware 1938. For Sanskrit parallels, see Gāndhārī manuscript fragments, and their translation, in Lenz and Neelis (forthcoming) [cf. Divy 335]; GM-Saṅgh 254/43r1–265/47v10–48r1 [MSV iv, 27.1–46.15]—translated in GM-Saṅgh 267–93; and Lévi 1932: 18–19 [cf. Divy 336.22–339.5]; a Sanskrit fragment from Turfan (Sander and Waldschmidt 1985: no. 1030); *Śikṣāsamuccaya* 57.11–59.6 [cf. Divy 342.13–343.23]; and *Avadānakalpalatā* no. 67 (Rani 2005: 68–69 and woodcut L-5; Tucci 1949: ii, 506 and plate 120). The corresponding Tibetan can be found at P 1030 *khe* 99a3–114b1 and D 1 *ka* 100a1–116a2 [cf. Eimer 1983]. For more, see Hiraoka 2007: ii, 23; HD 36; and Grey 2000: 345.

347 For summaries of the story, see Mitra 1981: 64–65 and Panglung 1981: 8–9.

348 Although a version of chapters 23–25 of the *Divyāvadāna* appears in the *Mūlasarvāstivāda-vinaya*, the text of the narrative found in Nalinaksha Dutt's edition of the text (MSV iv, 27–51, 52–72), as well as in S. Bagchi's (1967–70: ii, 86.13–99.7, 99.8–109.8), is not from the manuscript finds in Gilgit, as is the rest of the text. It is, in fact, a reconstruction based on the *Divyāvadāna* itself. Folios 43–49, which correspond to Divy 335.7–388.3, were, as Vogel and Wille (GM-Saṅgh 247) explain, entrusted "for inspection to Sir. A. Stein and committed by him to L. D. Barnett, the librarian of the British Museum, who in turn forwarded them for treatment to S. Lévi. After the latter's publication in 1932 of folios 49v3 to 55v10 [*Journal Asiatique* 220: 26ff.], they remained untraceable until 1949 when, along with some photographs of the Stein Collection, they were delivered anew to the British Museum and deposited there under the shelf-mark Or. 11878A. Since the leaves were not available when he was preparing his edition of the Vinayavastu, N. Dutt resorted by way of a stopgap to reprinting—with some changes and transpositions—the abridged *Divyāvadāna* parallel and Lévi's specimen respectively; so did, relying on him, S. Bagchi. After Raghu Vira had obtained a microfilm of them as early as the mid-1950s, they were ultimately included in then ten-volume facsimile reproduction of the New Delhi Collection [GBM 6, nos. 686–707]." V. Näther published an edition and German translation of the missing text in 1975; Vogel and Wille published a revised edition of the text and an English translation in 1996. Nevertheless, as Vogel and Wille (GM-Saṅgh 248) note, "The whole former part of the *Nāgakumārāvadāna* and roughly the first quarter of the *Saṃgharakṣitāvadāna* have been lost in the original Sanskrit."

349 Helmut Eimer (1983) has critically edited from the Tibetan the Pravrajyāvastu portion of the *Mūlasarvāstivāda-vinaya*, which contains versions of the *Nāgakumāra-avadāna* (1983: 247.17–260.22, 302.1–306.25) and the *Saṅgharakṣita-avadāna* (1983: 260.23–301.27). Ware (1938) has edited and translated into English the first part of the *Nāgakumāra-avadāna*, from both Tibetan and Chinese.

350 See Dutt's comments at the bottom of MSV iv, 46. According to Vogel and Wille (GM-Saṅgh 248), "Owing to a mistake by its compiler, the *Divyāvadāna* also gives the final portion of the tale of the present relative to the *Nāgakumārāvadāna*, which is hardly comprehensible by itself . . ." In fact, at the end of that story, as Cowell and Neil (Divy 346n8) observe, "all the mss. add here 23 (for 24?)," indicating some discrepancy in ordering.

351 Following the Tibetan (Eimer 1983: ii, 259.8–12), *de nas rgya mtsho chen po'i klu de dag bram ze dang khyim bdag gi cha lugs kyis mngon du lhags pa dang | des de dag la chos ston to | de dag gis de las chos thos nas dge slong glo bur du 'ongs pa dang | 'gro bar*

chas pa rnams la yo byad thams cad kyis bstabs pa dang | drug sde dag gis smras pa | dga' bo nye dga'...

For a full translation of the frame story that precedes the story of Saṅgharakṣita, see Ware 1938: 65–67. For a translation of the opening passage of this story in the *Divyāvadāna*, see Divy 707–8. With the help of a translation from the Tibetan by Léon Feer, Cowell and Neil (Divy 707) try to make sense of the manuscripts that "are all alike sadly corrupt."

352 Divy 329.1, *mahallena*. The term *mahalla* (or *mahallaka*) often refers to one who has renounced late in life and has little scholastic training (Ray 1994: 207n18; Durt 1980). In this case, the referent is a nāga who has taken the form of an old monk in order to teach other nāgas who have taken the form of brahmans and householders. Vogel and Wille (GM-Saṅgh 267) translate the term as "senior." Also possible is "old man."

353 Divy 329.1, *khustikayā*. The term is obscure. Elsewhere in the *Divyāvadāna*, it means "bald," in reference to someone's head (Divy 426.28), and "worn out," in reference to clothes (Divy 173.3). Here, explains Edgerton (BHSD, s.v. *khusta*), it describes "a religious text, in a deprecatory sense, app. poor, unsatisfactory, perh. lit. old, worn-out, stale, out-of-date." One could also take it to mean "defective," "imperfect," or "abridged." Cowell and Neil (Divy 707n3) wonder, "Is it not an equivalent for the Pāli *khuddaka* in the *Khuddaka-nikāya*?" Vogel and Wille (GM-Saṅgh 267) translate it adverbially as "poorly."

354 Divy 329.3, *yuktamuktapratibhānāḥ*. Cowell and Neil (Divy 707) offer this translation: "having minds fixed and liberated." Lojda (2009: 90n40) suggests "gifted with suitable and uninhibited courage (in speech)." The Tibetan (Eimer 1983: ii, 259.15–16) reads *rigs pa dang grol ba'i spobs ma can*, which Ware (1938: 65) translates as "are only bold for what is proper and pertaining to salvation." Versions of this expression occur in a variety of sources; for more, see Hiraoka 2007: ii, 24n2.

355 Following Cowell and Neil's query (Divy 329n4) and Hiraoka (HA 16; HD 36), read *adhyeṣayati*. Divy 329.3, *adhyeṣayasi*.

356 Divy 329.18, *nirmitaḥ*. In Buddhist art, to quote J. Ph. Vogel (1926: 37), "the nāga is sometimes [shown] as a mere animal, sometimes as a human creature, but generally human and animal properties are strangely blended." Nāgas straddle the realms of human and serpent and at times can appear as one, the other, or both.

357 Previously the group of six monks criticized the nāga-cum-old-man for using a faulty version of the *Gradual Sayings*. Now the Buddha explains that his version of the *Gradual Sayings* was indeed the right one. Once again, the group of six monks show themselves to be deficient with regard to the dharma, if not defiant.

358 Read *kathayati*. Divy 329.21, "reflected" (*saṃlakṣayati*).

359 Divy 330.1–2, *anāpattayas* (mss., *anāpattis*) *tanmukhikayā nirgatā bhavanti*. This is obscure. Edgerton (BHSD, s.vv. *anāpatti*, *tanmukhikayā*) suggests reading *anāpattis* with the manuscript and taking the instrumental *tanmukhikayā* adverbially as "for this reason" or "by that means." One might then emend *bhavanti* to *bhavati* and interpret as "The absence of an offense disappears by that reason." Or even, "His innocence disappears as soon as he opens his mouth." Cowell and Neil (Divy 708) suggest, "Through this consideration, they (*ṣaḍvargikas* [i.e., group of six monks]?) go forth

innocent." The Tibetan (Eimer 1983: ii, 260.21–22; cf. 99b4; 100b2) reads *de'i ngor mgron du bos pa la ni ltung ba med do*, which Ware (1938: 67) translates as "In this connection, for a guest there is no sin." Vogel and Wille (GM-Saṅgh 268) translate the same as "For him who has been invited to an entertainment in his presence there is no wrong." The most difficult problem here is making sense of *tanmukhikayā*. Instead of reading the term as an adverb, I follow the Tibetan—and Vogel and Wille's understanding of it—and take *de'i ngor* to mean "in his presence." Likewise, I take *mgron du bos pa* as an interpretive gloss of the suffix *-ika*, in the sense of "being invited to an event." Hence, I translate the term as "[monks] invited into his presence [for a teaching of the dharma]." One might then emend *tanmukhikayā* to the more standard *tanmukhikā*, recognizing the former as a scribal error—a kind of reflex addition in response to the preceding *anāpattayas*. Then again, it may simply be a Buddhist Hybrid Sanskrit form. My sense of the overall meaning here is that a person who teaches without being requested to do so commits an offense but monks attending such a teaching remain innocent. My thanks to Johannes Schneider for his help with this passage.

360 Hiraoka (HA 16; HD36) suggests omitting this sentence. "Otherwise," he explains, "the wife would become pregnant twice in a row without any delivery" (HD 36).

361 Divy 330.12–13, *kim asmākaṃ kāśadhānād vā kuśadhānād vā paścācchramaṇā bhavanti*. The meaning of *dhāna* here is unclear. Perhaps, "are attending disciples born to us from *kāśa* grass or *kuśa* grass?" Cowell and Neil (Divy 330n3) suggest that "probably the word is really the Pāli *thāna* [= Skt. *sthāna*; Eng., place] in both places." Based on the Tibetan (99b8; 100b6), which reads *rtsva ka sha'i byings sam | ku sha'i byings nas*, Hiraoka (HA 16; HD36) suggests *kāśadhātor vā kuśadhātor*. As Hiraoka (HD 36) explains, "the word in question is *byings* (a secondary form of *dbyings*) which is supposed to correspond to Skt. *dhātu*. *Dhātu* fits fine in the context because it means 'element/substance,' although in form the word is not close to the readings of the manuscripts." Vogel and Wille (GM-Saṅgh 268) offer this translation of the Tibetan: "Why does it happen that a mendicant walking behind me stems from the Kāśa-grass region or the Kuśa-grass region [i.e., from Yama's realm]." Another possibility is that it should be understood in the sense of *adhāna* or "placing." That is, "Do you think that attending disciples are produced just by placing *kāśa* grass or placing *kuśa* grass before us?" This might explain Amy Langenberg's (2013: 265) translation of the sentence: "do you think our monastic attendants come from spreading *kāśa* grass or *kuśa* grass?" Also possible is that the word in question is connected to *vidhāna*, which occurs in the following sentence (Divy 330.14). Regardless, the point of this sentence seems to be that brahmanical offerings are not enough; they may fuel a fire but they are not a replacement for the offering of a disciple. Disciples, as it were, don't simply grow on trees. For more on *kāśa* and *kuśa* grass, which appear together frequently, see Gonda 1985: 29–51, 133–34.

362 Following Divy 2.25, 24.16, etc., add *atyayāt*. Divy 330.18 (omitted).

363 Vaidya (Divy-V 205.6) omits Divy 331.6.

364 Divy 332.2, *bhayabhairava-*. The Pāli equivalent is well known, as the *Bhayabherava Sutta* appears in the *Majjhima-nikāya* (i, 16–24). Ñāṇamoli and Bodhi (1995: 102) likewise translate the compound as "fear and dread."

365 Following Divy 5.11–12 and Hiraoka (HA 16; HD 36), read *sāmudraṃ yānapātram*. Divy 332.8, *samudrayānapātram* (mss., *samudraṃ*).

366 Divy 333.3, *nāgabhavanam*. Here *bhavanam* seems to refer not to a building or a palace but to a domain—i.e., the world of nāgas. I translate accordingly throughout the story.

367 Divy 333.8, *vinipatitaśarīrāḥ*. Cf. DS 414n363.

368 The text (Divy 333.12) simply says, "he said" (*sa kathayati*). What follows in the story, however, makes it clear that the speaker is a fourth nāga—the very same being who had appeared, like a phantom, as an old monk at the beginning of the story. Cf. Burnouf 2010: 313n165, 1844: 317n3. And as the Buddha previously attested, he knows the *Gradual Sayings* well. In the Tibetan (102b2; 104a1), the fourth nāga is also the one who encourages the three young nāgas to study in the first place.

369 Divy 333.14–15, *uddeśaṃ gṛhnāti*. Vaidya (Divy-V 206.20) emends to *gṛhṇāti*. Vogel and Wille (GM-Saṅgh 271) translate this expression here and in what follows as "gave an exposition."

370 Divy 333.17–18, *dantakāṣṭhaṃ visarjaya*. For more on dental sticks, see Ch'en 1945–47: 291n186.

371 Divy 333.18, *bhagavato maṇḍalakam āmārjaya*. As Handurukande (1982: 146n11) remarks, "a maṇḍalaka is a circular spot marked out and ceremonially prepared for a sacred rite." For more on this passage and the perfumed chambers, see Strong 1977: 400–404.

372 Here the text (Divy 333.20) uses the pronoun "he" (*sa*), which I'm assuming refers to the fourth nāga.

373 Divy 334.16, *śiloccayo 'śecanakā darśanena buddhaś ca bhagavatāṃ vara*. Hiraoka (HA 16; HD 36), following Speyer (1902: 342–43), reads *śiloccayaḥ darśanenāsecanakā buddhaś ca jagatāṃ varaḥ*.

374 Read *kutrāryasaṃgharakṣitaḥ*. The Tibetan (103b1; 104b3) concurs. Divy 334.20, "Where is that Saṅgharakṣita?" (*kutrāyaṃ saṃgharakṣitaḥ*).

375 Divy 335.2, *udgataṃ* (mss., *udgata*) *mañcapīṭha-*. Cf. Schopen 2006: 502 for the way that this translation conforms "to what has been found at a number of actual monasteries in India" and how these benches allow for monastics to engage with the beauty of their surroundings.

376 Cf. GM-Saṅgh 254/43r2; 255/43v1; 256/43v10, *yāvat teṣāṃ bhojanakālo jātaḥ gaṇḍir ākoṭitā*.

377 Divy 335.14, *yathāgatya*. GM-Saṅgh 254/43r2, *yathāgantryā*. The idea here is that they entered according to seniority, which is also their seating order, and that they sat down in that order as they arrived. See also GM-Saṅgh 274n9.

378 Divy 335.15, *ayomudgarāḥ* (mss., *ayomudgalāḥ*) *prādurbhātāḥ*. GM-Saṅgh 254/43r3, *teṣāṃ svāni śāstrāṇy* [read *pātrāṇy*] *ayomudgarāṇi prādurbhūtāni*.

379 Following GM-Saṅgh 254/43r5, read *tair asmābhiḥ*. Divy 335.24, *taiḥ asmākam*.

380 Divy 335.25, *pratyekanarakeṣu*. The meaning of this expression is unclear. In the *Divyāvadāna*, the term seems to mean "personal hell"—a hell realm of particular design for particular individuals. According to Edgerton's extensive note (BHSD), this hell realm "seems clearly to be a place of less severe punishment than a (*mahā–*, or regular) [hell realm]." The *Mahāvyutpatti* (4944) explains this as *nyi tshe ba'i*, perhaps in the sense of "epheremal." Accordingly, Burnouf (2010: 315; cf. 1844: 320) takes it

to mean "a hell that changes each day." According to a nineteenth-century Tibetan commentator (Kon-sprul Blo-gros-mtha'-yas 1995: 114), "on each of the four sides of each of the eight [hot] hells are the four neighboring hells [*pratyekanaraka*]: [1] Pit of Live Embers [*kukūla*], [2] Swamp of Filth [*kuṇapa*], [3] Road of Razor Blades [*kṣuramārga*], [Forest with] Leaves Like Swords [*asipattravana*], Forest of Iron Spikes [*ayaḥśālmalīvana*], and [4] River Without Ford [*nadīvaitaraṇī*]."

381 Following GM-Saṅgh 254/43r6 and Hiraoka (HA 16; HD 37), add *bhadanta*. Divy 335.27 (omitted).

382 Following Divy 335.6–8 and Hiraoka (HA 16; HD 37), read *yāvat paśyati śobhanāṃ śayanāsanaprajñaptiṃ kṛtāṃ praṇītaṃ cāhāraṃ upahṛtam*. Divy 336.8–9, *yāvat paśyati śobhanāṃ śayanāsanaprajñaptiṃ kṛtvā* (*sic* mss. but cf. supra) *praṇītaṃ cāhāraṃ samanvāhṛtya*. For more on *samanvāharati* and its technical meanings, see Edgerton (BHSD) and DS 408n304.

383 Divy 336.10, *tena dṛṣṭādīnavena bhuktam*. Cf. GM-Saṅgh 255/43r10–v1, *sa kathaya(t)i saṃghamdhye eva bhokṣyāmīti | te kathayanti bhadan[t]a saṃ(gharakṣita) mārgaparikhinnas tvaṃ idānīm eva bhuṃkṣva ādīnavo 'tra bhaviṣyatīti*.

384 Divy 336.19, *nābhiśraddadhāsyanti*. Cf. Divy 335.21 and 337.15–16, *nābhiśraddadhāsyasi*.

385 Divy 336.23, *anāryaparigṛhītaiḥ*. Hiraoka (HA 16; HD 37), following GM-Saṅgh 255/43v4, the Tibetan (105a8; 106b3), and the Chinese, reads *mātsarya-*. That is, "stinginess."

386 Following Divy 336.2 and 338.5, read *śramaṇāḥ kāśyapīyāḥ*. Divy 337.5, "brahman followers of the Buddha Kāśyapa" (*brāhmaṇāḥ kāśyapīyāḥ*). GM-Saṅgh 255/43v6 reads *śramaṇāḥ śākyaputrīyā iti*—perhaps a scribal error based on GM-Saṅgh 256/44r8—which the editors (GM-Saṅgh 255n9) suggest emending to *śramaṇāḥ kāśyapīyā iti*, the reading preserved in the corresponding Tibetan (Eimer 1983: ii, 275.17) and at GM-Saṅgh 254/43r7. GM-Saṅgh 256/44r6 likewise reads *śramaṇāḥ śākyaputrīyā iti*, and again the editors (GM-Saṅgh 256n11) suggest emending to *śramaṇāḥ kāśyapīyā iti*, which corresponds with the Tibetan (Eimer 1983: ii, 278.6). See too GM-Saṅgh 274n15 and 276n34. Worthy of note here is that the disciples of the Buddha Kaśyapa are not said to be brahmans. Furthermore, I follow Edgerton (BHSD) and take *kāśyapīya* here to mean "followers or disciples of the Buddha Kāśyapa" and not "members of the Kāśyapīya sect." My thanks to Peter Skilling (personal communication) for his help with this passage.

387 Following Divy 336.5–10. Divy 337.7, "and so on as before" (*purvavat yāvat*).

388 Divy 337.21–22, *ayam api eko 'smākaṃ dakṣiṇāṃ śodhayiṣyati*. The meaning of the verb *śodhayiṣyati* is unclear, and hence this sentence is open to different interpretations. Burnouf (2010: 317; cf. 1844: 322) translates it as follows: "he will be sufficient on his own to attract alms for us." Vogel and Wille (GM-Saṅgh 277) offer this translation for the nearly identical corresponding passage from the Gilgit manuscripts: "(For) he alone will get an expiatory gift for us" (*ayam eko 'asmākaṃ dakṣiṇāṃ śodhayiṣyatīti* | GM-Saṅgh 256/44r3). Paul Harrison (personal communication) understands it to mean "All on his own he will purify the offerings given to us." The virtuous monk, in other words, will generate merit for the donor as only a worthy recipient can do; as such, the monks will get more offerings.

389 Divy 337.22, *anisaṅgena*. Cowell and Neil (Divy 337n8) query *aniṣaṅgena*.

GM-Saṅgh 256/44r3 reads *anuṣaṅgenga*, which is better still. The Tibetan (106b8; 107b4) reads *de'i zhar gyis*.

390 Following Hiraoka (HA 16; HD 37), read *dattaḥ*. Divy 337.25, *dagdhaḥ* (mss., *dagdhaṃ*).

391 Following Hiraoka (HA 16; HD 37), read *taṭṭvākārān*. Divy 338.8, "benches" (*khaṭvākārān*). Likewise, GM-Saṅgh 256/44r7 reads *khaṭvākārān*, but Vogel and Wille (GM-Saṅgh 256n11) emend to *taṭṭvākārān*. Cf. Edgerton (BHSD, s.vv. *khaṭu*, *taṭṭu*). See also Divy 343.1–5, which explains the logic of this reading.

392 Following GM-Saṅgh 256/44r7, the Tibetan (106b5; 108a2), and Hiraoka (HA 16–17; HD 37), add *madhye cchinnāṃs tantunā dhāryamāṇāṃ gacchantaḥ*. A similar expression also occurs at Divy 342.11–12. Divy 338.9 (omitted).

393 Following Speyer (1902: 343) and Hiraoka (HA 17; HD 37), read *sa śukladharmaḥ*. Divy 338.17, *saśukladharmaḥ*. GM-Saṅgh 257/44r9 reads *saśukaḥ*. Vogel and Wille (GM-Saṅgh 257n13) emend this to *saśukladharmaḥ*, explicitly following the reading in the *Divyāvadāna* contra Speyer (GM-Saṅgh 278n52). They translate the term as "well-conducted" (GM-Saṅgh 278).

394 GM-Saṅgh 257/44r9–4r10 reads *tatraiko ṛṣir janapadacārikāṃ gataḥ tasya santikā kuṭikā ayuṣmate saṃgharakṣitāya dattā*, which Vogel and Wille (GM-Saṅgh 279) translate as "Thereupon (the) one seer went to the countryside (and) gave his own hut to the reverend Saṃgharakṣita."

395 Following GM-Saṅgh 257/44r10, read *bhavantaḥ*. Divy 338.25, *bhadanta*.

396 Following GM-Saṅgh 257/44r10, the Tibetan (107a2; 180a7), and Hiraoka (HA 17; HD 37), read *śucyupacārā ete*. Vogel and Wille (GM-Saṅgh 279) offer this translation: "Sirs, these mendicants of Śākyaputra perform holy actions." Divy 338.25, *sucy api mārjanty ete* (ex conj.; ms. A, *śucyam api vārāpyete*; ms. B, *śucyam api cārapyate*; ms. C, *śucyam api cārāpyete*; ms. D, *śunyam api cārāpyete*). Perhaps, "cleanse what is already clean." This is Cowell and Neil's conjecture (Divy 338n6), for as they note, "the mss. are all corrupt."

397 Divy 339.5, *sukhitā tvam*. Although the words here are clear, the tone is not. Burnouf (2010: 318; cf. 1844: 324) offers this translation: "You are happy." Vogel and Wille (GM-Saṅgh 279) translate this as "You [should be] happy!" While this could be construed as a greeting—"May you be happy!"—my sense is that he is telling her that she has it easy while he is living under a strict set of conditions.

398 Following GM-Saṅgh 257/44v5, the Tibetan (107a8; 108b6), and Hiraoka (HA 17; HD 37), read *brāhmaṇapratisaṃyuktā gathā bhāṣitavyā iti*. Divy 339.21, *brāhmaṇapratisaṃyuktaṃ bhāsayāmīti*. The mss. (Divy 339n1), however, read *brāhmaṇapratisaṃyuktā*, hinting at the proposed emendation.

399 These are the first two verses in the "Chapter on Brahmans" (*Brāhmaṇavarga*) from the *Udānavarga* (xxxiii, vv. 1–2)—a text, like the *Divyāvadāna*, that is probably affiliated with the Mūlasarvāstivādins (Schmithausen 1970). These verses also occur, with minor variations, in the Pāli *Dhammapada* (Dhp, vv. 141–42) and the Buddhist Hybrid Sanskrit *Dharmapada* (Dhp-BHS, vv. 195–96). There, however, they occur in the "Chapter on Punishment."

400 Divy 339.24, *moham*. Following Pāṇini 5.2.127, understand as *mohinam*. Hiraoka (HA 17; HD 37), following GM-Saṅgh 257/44v6, *Udānavarga* xxxiii, v. 1, and the Tibetan (107b1; 108b7), reads *martyam*. The Pāli *Dhammapada* (Dhp, v. 141) and

the Buddhist Hybrid Sanskrit *Dharmapada* (Dhp-BHS, v. 195) likewise read "mortal" (*maccam* and *māccam*, respectively).

401 Following GM-Saṅgh 257/44v6, the Tibetan (107b2; 109a1), and Hiraoka (HA 17; HD 37), read *brāḥmaṇapratisaṃyuktā gathā bhāṣata iti.* Divy 339.30, *brāḥmaṇapratisaṃyuktam* (mss., *brāḥmaṇaṃ pratisaṃyuktam*) *ata ity.* Cowell and Neil (Divy 339n4) query *ity ata*; Vaidya (Divy-V 210.11) omits *ata.*

402 Here the Gilgit manuscript of the Saṅgharakṣita story (GM-Saṅgh 258/44v7–261/46r9) provides an excerpt from the *Nagaropamasūtra* that concludes with a verse. The *Divyāvadāna* only offers the verse. For more on the *Nagaropamasūtra*—a popular apotropaic text, particularly in Central Asia—see Bongard-Levin et al. 1996; *Saṃyukta-nikāya* ii, 104–7; and the *Nidānasaṃyukta* (Tripathi 1962: 5).

403 For more on the complex history of this verse, see Skilling 1994: ii, 535–36.

404 Following Speyer (1902: 343–44), GM-Saṅgh 261/46r10, Hiraoka (HA 17; HD 38), and Divy 48.15, 49.13, etc., read *cābhinirhṛtā.* Divy 340.9, *cāpi nirhṛtā* (mss., *nirhṛtāḥ*).

405 The Gilgit manuscript of the Saṅgharakṣita story (GM-Saṅgh 261/46v1–262/46v4) then extols, in detail, the five benefits of being fully intent on becoming a renunciant. Cf. Divy 302.22–303.6.

406 Divy 340.21, *-avavādena-*. Hiraoka (HA 17; HD 38), following GM-Saṅgh 262/46v6 and the Tibetan (111a8; 112b7), reads *-anubhāvena-*.

407 Following GM-Saṅgh 262/46v6, the Tibetan (111a8; 112b7), and Hiraoka (HA 17; HD 38), read *kolopamaḥ*. Divy 340.22, *laṅghanakopamaḥ*. This is conjecture, for the mss. are corrupt. The mss. (Divy 340n5) read *lakṣatako mama saṃvṛttaḥ* (ms. A, *lakṣayatako-*; ms. B, *laṅkhatako*?). Cf. Edgerton (BHSD, s.v. *laṅghanaka*).

408 In the Gilgit manuscript of the Saṅgharakṣita story (GM-Saṅgh 262/46v5–6), Saṅgharakṣita is "distressed" (*vyathitaḥ*) and responds "with a face full of sadness and pity" (*hīnadīnavadanaḥ*). He has been successful as a raft, bringing others to religious attainment (i.e., they have acquired magical powers to teleport themselves), but he himself has lagged behind. He hasn't yet arrived at the far shore that is awakening. So, in what follows, he meditates and brings himself there.

409 Divy 340.27–28, *sthānāsthāna-*. Edgerton (BHSD, *sthāna*) takes this to mean either "possibilities and impossibilities" or "sound and unsound propositions or conclusions." Vogel and Wille (GM-Saṅgh 277–78) translate it as "(discriminating) correct and incorrect conclusions." Cf. *Majjhima-nikāya* iii, 64–67; trans. in Bodhi 1995: 928–30.

410 Divy 340.28, *aparapratibaddhā cāsya bhavati avavādānuśāsanīti.* Vogel and Wille (GM-Saṅgh 278) offer this translation: "one's advice and instruction is not dependent on another." However, I don't think the meaning here is that "the instructions and admonitions one gives are not dependent on another" but that one isn't dependent on another for them. Following Nobel (1955: i, 85), they also note the possibility of "and advice and instruction therein," referring back to the previous benefit(s). Tharchin (1984: 43), translating more loosely, offers: "One no longer needs to rely on any other person for advice or teachings on their meaning."

The text appears to be deficient here in that it only lists four benefits. At Divy 567.7–10, the text enumerates a slightly different list, adding "aggregates" and "sense bases" but not including "what is possible and impossible," to total five. GM-Saṅgh 262/46v7 adds "sense bases" (*āyatana-*), which would make the present list in the *Divyāvadāna* total five, but then Vogel and Wille (GM-Saṅgh 287) add "aggregates" in their translation, following Divy 506.8. This allows "one's instructions and admonitions are not dependent on others" to be separate from the list. See also MSV i, 23.10–12, which likewise enumerates the benefits in the same way.

411 Following Divy 282.1–4 (modified accordingly). Divy 341.1, "and so on as before" (*pūrvavad yāvat*).

412 Following GM-Saṅgh 262/47r1, *bhagavatsakāśam*. Divy 341.9 (omitted).

413 Following Divy-V 211.23, read *evaṃ sthitā*. Divy 342.2, *nopasthitā*. GM-Saṅgh 263/47r6 reads *nepacchitā*. Hiraoka (HA 17; HD 38) suggests *nepatthitā*. Cf. Divy 281.27–28, and the corresponding note.

414 Following Divy 282.1–4 (modified accordingly). Divy 342.6, "and so on as before" (*pūrvavad yāvat*).

415 Following Hiraoka (HA 17; HD 38), read *taṭṭvākāran*. Divy 342.11, *khaṭvākārān*. See note 391.

416 A version of following portion of the text (Divy 342.13–343.23) occurs in the *Śikṣāsamuccaya* (57.11–59.6; trans. in Bendall and Rouse 1971: 58–60), although the wording of the latter much more closely resembles its counterpart in the Gilgit manuscripts (GM-Saṅgh 263/47v2–265/48r2).

417 Following Hiraoka (HA 17; HD 38), add *tvam*. Divy 342.17 (omitted).

418 Following Hiraoka (HA 17; HD 38), read *taṭṭvākāram*. See note 391. Divy 342.26–27, *tapvākāraṃ* (ex conj.; mss. AB, *-taḥ | kāraṃ*; mss. CD, *tathākāraṃ*). Cowell and Neil (Divy 342n9) note, "Can *tapu* mean 'a cauldron'"? As Hiraoka (HD 38) notes, Vogel and Wille "read *taṭṭuka* for *taṭvaka* ([GM-Saṅgh 264,] 47v5), on the basis of an example in the *Śikṣ[āsamuccaya]*. This is supported by Tib. *phor pa* (113b4; 115a4)." MSV iv, 45.15, "water-jar" (*ghaṭa*).

419 Divy 343.1–2, *pānakavāram uddiṣṭas tad vārakaṃ* (mss. BC, *tat pānakaṃ*) *nirmādayati*. Hiraoka (HA 18; HD 38) suggests reading *pānavārakam* for *pānakavāram*. As Hiraoka (HD 38) notes, "This seems to be a misprint. Cf. Tib. *skom gyi gtsang sbyor* (113b4; 115a5)." Hiraoka (HA 18; HD 38) also suggests reading *taṭṭukaṃ* for *tad vārakaṃ*.

420 The Gilgit manuscript of the Saṅgharakṣita story preserves quite a different reading for this passage. Vogel and Wille (GM-Saṅgh 291–92) offer this translation: "That being whom you saw having the form of a cup was a novice in charge of drinks. (When) he washed the cup(s) and guest monks came, they asked him: 'Novice, will there (still) be drink(s) for the congregation today?' His mind affected with avarice, he said: 'Don't you see (that) I have washed the cup(s)? The drink(s have been) drunk.' They became despaired at (the thought that) the time (for drinks was) over, (and) proceeded with worried and sad faces. Therefore he came to be having the form of a cup" (*yas tvaṃ satvān adrākṣīs taṭvakākārā śrāmaṇerakā āsīt* [read *yaṃ tvaṃ satvaṃ adrākṣīs taṭṭukākāraṃ sa śrāmaṇeraka āsīt*] *pānakavārikaḥ sa taṭvakaṃ* [read *taṭṭukam*] *nirmādayaty āgantunkāś ca bhikṣavo 'bhyāgatāḥ tair asau pṛṣṭaḥ śrāmaṇerādya saṃghasya pānakaṃ bhaviṣyatīti | sa mātsaryopahatacittaḥ kathayati na paśyatha mayā taṭvakaṃ* [read *taṭṭukaṃ*] *nirmāditaṃ pītaṃ pānakam iti | te vṛttaveleti nairāśyam āpannāḥ hīnadīnavadanā(ḥ) prakrāntāḥ tena taṣvakākāras* [read *taṭṭukākāras*] *saṃvṛttāḥ* | GM-Saṅgh 264/47v5–6).

421 Following Hiraoka (HA 17; HD 38), read *taṭṭvākāraḥ*. Divy 343.5, *tapvākāraḥ* (*sic* mss. ABC; ms. D, *taddhākāraḥ*).

422 Following GM-Saṅgh 264/47v8, the Tibetan (113b8–114a1; 115b1), and Hiraoka (HA 17; HD 38), read *ulūkhale stokaṃ khaleḥ*. Divy 343.9, *khalastokam* (mss. AC, *khale stokam*; ms. B, *khalu stokam*). Edgerton (BHSD, s.v. *khali*) suggests, "read *khaleḥ* [mss. *khale*] *stokam*, or with *Śikṣ*[*āsammucaya*] 58.7, 9, citation of this Divy passage, *khali-stokaṃ*, a little bit of oil-cake paste." I am unsure of what, precisely, is being ground in the mortar. Oil cake is often used as cattle feed and sometimes as manure. Cf. Marathi, *peṇḍ*.

423 Divy 343.11, *yadi rocate*. Hiraoka (HA 17; HD 38), following GM-Saṅgh 264/47v7 and the Tibetan (113b8–114a1; 115b1), reads *yadi mama kalpeta ulūkhalaṃ spraṣṭum*. That is, "if it were proper for me to touch a mortar."

424 Following Hiraoka (HA 17; HD 38), read *khaleḥ stokam*. Divy 343.12, *khalastokam* (mss., *khale stokaṃ*). Cf. note 422.

425 The Gilgit manuscript of the Saṅgharakṣita story tells a slightly different, and more provocative story. Vogel and Wille (GM-Saṅgh 293) offer this translation: "Those beings whom you saw having the form of pots were servants, waiters upon the monks. [When] they [were] unkindly addressed by the monks while decocting medicine, they got irritated and smashed the pots. Thereby they came to be having the form of pots" (*yā<ṃ>s tvaṃ satvān adrākṣī<s> sthālyākārāṃ<|>s te kalpikārā āsaṃ bhikṣūṇām upasthāyakāḥ tair bhaiṣajyaṃ kvāthayanto bhikṣubhir apyayam uktā<ḥ> taiś cittaṃ pradūṣya tās sthālyo bhinnāḥ tena sthālyākārās saṃvṛttāḥ* | GM-Saṅgh 265/47v10–48r1).

426 For Pāli and Sanskrit parallels, see *Vinayapiṭaka* i, 86.36–88.3; GM-Nāga 27–29 [MSV iv, 48.19–51.21]—translated in GM-Nāga 39–43; a Turfan fragment, and its translation, in GM-Nāga 65–69; and *Avadānakalpalatā* no. 60 (Rani 2005: 60–61 and woodcut L-3; Tucci 1949: ii, 497 and plate 118). The corresponding Tibetan can be found at P 1030 *khe* 115b6–117b6 and D 1 *ka* 117a7–119b1 [cf. Eimer 1983]. For more, see Hiraoka 2007: ii, 23; HD 36; and Grey 2000: 281.

In the *Mūlasarvastivāda-vinaya*, as Vogel and Wille (GM-Saṅgh 248) note, this story "makes up, as it were, the frame story of the *Saṃgharakṣitāvadāna*, with the tale of the present preceding and that of the past succeeding it. The aim of this superordinate avadāna is to exemplify the maxim that a so-called phantom creature—an animal able to transform itself into a human being—must be removed from the congregation."

427 Vogel and Wille (GM-Nāga 39) gloss "young nāga" here as "the metamorphic serpent-demon youth." This is the young nāga who, in the beginning of the previous story, was confronted by the group of six monks.

428 According to a nineteenth-century Tibetan scholar (Jamgön Kongtrul Lodrö Tayé 1995: 110), "Beyond Mount Meru and completely surrounding it like curtains are seven mountain ranges, each forming a square. These seven golden mountain ranges [are named according to the shape of their peaks:] Yoke, Plough, Acacia Forest, Pleasing-to-the-Eye, Horse's Ear, Bent, and Rim. The spaces between [the mountain ranges] are filled with what are known as the seven seas enjoyed [by the nāgas], the waters of which have eight qualities: cool, tasty, light, soft, clear, odorless, harmless to the throat if swallowed, and harmless to the stomach."

429 Divy 344.15, *-rāṣṭṛadhānīṣu*. Following Hiraoka (HA 17; HD 38) to fix this misprint, read *-rāṣṭra-*. Intended, perhaps, was *rāṣṭrarājadhāṇīṣu*. Cf. Divy 18.13, 18.19, etc.

430 Following Hiraoka (HA 17; HD 38), read *cācirajātakaḥ*. MSV iv, 49.13 reads likewise. GM-Nāga 27/48v8, *acirajātakaḥ*. Divy 344.16, *ca cirajātakaḥ*.

431 This incident suggests the hereditary feud between nāgas and Garuḍa—more loosely, snakes and birds. This feud is especially well represented in Gandhāran art.

432 Following Divy 282.1–4. Divy 344.24, "and so on as before" (*pūrvavad yāvat*).

433 Following Hiraoka (HA 17; HD 38), read *cācirajātakaḥ*. MSV iv, 49.13 reads likewise. GM-Nāga 28/49r2, *acirajātakaḥ*. Divy 344.16, *ca cirajātakaḥ*. Vogel (1926: 188) translates as "born to us in our old age."

434 Divy 345.4, *tādṛśaḥ suduṣṭanāgo* (mss. AB, *tādṛśasuduṣṭanāgo*; ms. C, *tādṛśaḥ suduṣṭanāgo*; ms. D, *tādṛśasuduṣṭā nāgo*) *yad*. MSV iv, 50.5, and Vaidya (Divy-V 213.20) both read the same. GM-Nāga 28/49r3, *tādṛśo 'asau duṣṭa āsīd yasya*.

435 Divy 345.18, *avalambyate*. Cowell and Neil (Divy 345n3) write "Sic mss." Vaidya (Divy-V 213.29) emends to *avalambate*. GM-Nāga 28/49r6, *nibadhyeta*.

436 Divy 345.18–19, *yo* (*sic* mss.; *sa*?) *yasmin sthāne 'ntardhāsyati tena tatra nimittam udgṛhītam* (mss. ABC, *udgrahīta*; ms. D, *udgrahītaṃ*). Cf. Divy 57.1–2. Vogel (1926: 188), reading against the grammar but nevertheless very cogently, suggests, "Mark thou the spot where thy master will vanish." GM-Nāga 28/49r6, *sa taiḥ protsāhito yatra sthāne sa riddhyā antardhīyate tatra gatvāvasthitaḥ*. That is, "Encouraged by them, he went to that place where his teacher would magically disappear and he waited."

437 Following GM-Nāga 28/49r8, read *jarayitum*. Divy 345.27, *kārayitum*. Perhaps, "handle." MSV iv, 51.5, *dhārayitum*.

438 Following GM-Nāga 28/49r8, read *śakṣyate*; otherwise, *śaknoti*. Divy 345.27, *śakyate*.

439 Divy 346.1–2, *odanamijy avatiṣṭhate*. Cowell and Neil (Divy 346n1) write, "Sic MSS; query *odanamihy* (*mihī* from *mih*) or *-mikṣy*." Citing this passage, Edgerton (BHSD) explains *mijī* as "drop, small bit." This is supported by the Tibetan (117a8; 119a3), which reads *gzegs ma*. Edgerton also notes, in an oddly petulant tone, "Prob. corrupt, but I think of no good em[endation] (those suggested in ed. note are clearly worthless)." GM-Nāga 28/49r9 reads *tasmin odanasitthako lagnaḥ*. That is, "and [some] cooked rice was stuck in it." MSV iv, 51.7, *odano 'bhiṣakto 'vatiṣṭhate*.

440 GM-Nāga 28/49r10 describes this as a "false fervent aspiration" (*mithyāpraṇidhānam*).

441 Divy 346.8–9, *tasya dṛṣṭa eva dharme ubhābhyāṃ pāṇibhyāṃ jalaṃ syanditum ārabdham*. Just prior to this, GM-Nāga 29/49r10–v1 adds *atyudīrṇaparipūrṇāni karmāṇi śarīrasy nidhanaṃ nopekṣaṃte*, which Vogel and Wille (GM-Nāga 43) translate as "[As] very intense (and) fully accomplished acts do not wait for loss of the body." In that context, I would translate *dṛṣṭa eva dharme* as "in this lifetime," my standard translation for the phrase, to emphasize the immediacy of the karmic effects of his action. Edgerton (BHSD, s.v. *dharma*) translates it as "the present state, the present life," and Vogel and Wille (GM-Nāga 43) as "in the visible (present) world." In this instance, however, I take it more loosely to mean at that very moment in his life.

Furthermore, it is unclear whether the novice is actively trickling water through his hands, or whether water is flowing from them or over them, and what this action accomplishes or indicates. Burnouf (2010: 324; cf. 1844: 332) translates this as "And immediately, the novice started to spread water with his two hands [to destroy a nāga he had chosen]." Vogel (1926: 188–89) translates it as "At the very moment water began to flow from his hands." My sense is that, as a result of his fervent aspiration, water is trickling from his hands because he is turning into a nāga; or, at least, showing signs of his future rebirth as one. Cf. the Tibetan (117b4; 119a6).

442 Divy 346.9, *śirorttiḥ* (*sic*). GM-Nāga 29/49v1 reads *śiro rujā*. Vaidya (Divy 214.11) emends to *śirortiḥ*.

443 Divy 346.13–14,

> *pravaṇībhūtam idaṃ cittaṃ na śaknomi nivārayitum |*
> *ihasthasyaiva me bhadanta pāṇibhyāṃ syandate jalam ||*

Burnouf (2010: 324–25; cf. 1844: 332) translates the verse as "This thought has possessed me; I am no longer able to free myself from it; I pour water, Lord, with my two hands during the time that I exist in this world." Vogel (1926: 189) offers this translation: "Free course hath though been allowed this thought of mine / How were I able to suppress it now? / Lo, Rev'rend Sir, e'en in my present state / From both my hands freely the waters flow." Peter Skilling (personal communication) suggests translating *pravaṇībhūtam* more idiomatically as "which has its own momentum." GM-Nāga 29/49v2 reads *dūrībhūtam* for *pravaṇībhūtam*, *nivarttitum* for *nivārayitum*, and *yasmāt* for *bhadanta*. Vogel and Wille (GM-Nāga 43) offer this translation: "Far (from my mind is) this thought, / I cannot give (it) up; / For what reason, while I am just standing here, / Water trickles from my hands." Cf. the Tibetan (117b5; 119a7), which Vogel and Wille (GM-Nāga 43n42) translate as "This thought is far (from my mind); / thus [*evam*], while I am standing here, / water trickles from my hands; / hence I cannot give (it) up."

444 Cowell and Neil (Divy 346n8) observe that "all the MSS. add here 23 (for 24?)." In the *Mūlasarvāstivāda-vinaya*, this story comes after the second installment of the *Saṅgharakṣita-avadāna*. In other words, this story would be chapter 25.

445 For Sanskrit parallels, see GM-Saṅgh 265/48r2–266/48v4 [MSV iv, 47.1–48.18]—translated in GM-Saṅgh 293–95. The corresponding Tibetan can be found at P 1030 *khe* 114b1–115b6 and D 1 *ka* 116a2–117a7 [cf. Eimer 1983]. For more, see Hiraoka 2007: ii, 23 and HD 36.

446 Following Divy 131.7–14 (modified accordingly) and GM-Saṅgh 265/48r3–4. Divy 346.23–24, "and so on as before" (*pūrvavat*).

447 Following Divy 344.5–7 and GM-Saṅgh 265/48r5. Divy 347.1, "and so on as before" (*pūrvavat*). GM-Saṅgh 265/48r5–6 then adds *sa vārāṇasīnagarīm upaniśritya viharati ṛṣivadane mṛgadāve*. That is, "He stayed near the city of Vārāṇasī in the deer park at Ṛṣivadana (Mouth of Sages)."

448 Divy 347.2, *vaiyāvṛtyakāraḥ*. GM-Saṅgh 265/48r6, *vaiyyāpṛ[ ]tyakaraḥ*. Cf. Divy 347.27–28, *dharmavaiyāvṛtyaṃ kṛtam*. For more on this term, see Silk 2008b: 50–51.

449 See too GM-Saṅgh 265–266/48r7–8, "Since I have followed the religious life for as long as I lived under the perfectly awakened Lord Kāśyapa without amassing many virtues, by this root of virtue may I go forth as a monk in the order of the young brahman named Uttara about whom the perfectly awakened Lord Kāśyapa has made the following prediction: 'Young brahman, when people live for one hundred years, you will be a perfectly awakened tathāgatha arhat named Śākyamuni.' And may I then, by ridding myself of all defilements, directly experience arhatship" (*yan mayā bhagavati kāśyape samyaksaṃbuddhe* {*yā*} *yāvadāyur brahmacaryaṃ caritaṃ na ca kaścid*

guṇagaṇo 'dhigataḥ anenāhaṃ kuśalamūlena yo 'sau bhagavatā kāśyapena samyaksaṃbuddhenottaro nāma māṇavo vyākṛto bhaviṣyasi tvaṃ māṇava varṣaśatāyuṣi prajāyāṃ śākyamunir nāma tathāgato 'rhaṃ samyaksaṃbuddha iti tasyāhaṃ śāsane pravrajya sarvakleśaprahāṇād arhatvaṃ sākṣātkuryām iti).

450 Following Divy 23.28–24.1 and GM-Saṅgh 266/48v3–4. Divy 348.3, "and so on as before" (*pūrvavat*).

451 For a translation, see Hiraoka 2007: ii, 263–75. For Sanskrit parallels, see MSV i, 68.17–79.2 (GBM 159b[987]3–162a2[992]8); Divy 76.10–80.5 [cf. Divy 465.10–469.16]; and *Mahāvastu* ii, 379.12–395.19. The corresponding Tibetan can be found at P 1030 *ge* 145b4–151a2 and D 1 *kha* 157a2–162b5. For more, see Hiraoka 2007: ii, 272 and HD 52.

452 Following Cowell and Neil's query (Divy 461n3), MSV i, 68.17, the Tibetan (145b4; 157a2; cf. Shackleton Bailey 1951: 100), Speyer (1902: 115) and Hiraoka (HA 23; HD 52), add *ānandam*. Divy 461.11 (omitted).

453 Divy 461.12–13, *cārikāṃ prakrāntaḥ*. MSV i, 68.19–20, *carikāṇ caran prakrāntaḥ*. Hiraoka (HA 23; HD 52) follows the latter reading.

454 Cf. MSV i, 69.10–11, where the brahman responds in verse.

455 Following MSV i, 69.14 and Edgerton (BHSD, s.v. *bāṣpāyati*), read *vāṣpāyamānaḥ*. Divy 462.2, *vāpyāyamānaḥ*.

456 Divy 462.5, *mahābrāhmaṇa*. Cf. MSV i, 69.16, where the Buddha addresses him as a "brahman," not a "great brahman."

457 Following Divy 71.25, add *yaṃ śrutvā*. Divy 462.11, "and so on as before" (*pūrvavad yāvad*).

458 This formulaic expression usually reads "that arises with its twenty peaks of incorrect views." Cf. Divy 46.25, 52.24–25, 71.25–26, etc.

459 Divy 462.13, *atikrānto 'haṃ bhadantātikrāntaḥ*. Hiraoka (HA 23; HD 52) suggests *bhadantāham atikrāntābhikrāntaḥ*.

460 Shackleton Bailey (1951: 100), following the Tibetan (146b6; 158a4–5), suggests adding *saṃvṛttam*. Divy 463.2 (omitted).

461 Following MSV i, 70.22, the Tibetan (146b7; 158a5), and Hiraoka (HA 23; HD 52), read *yat tavābhipretam*. Divy 463.5, *yathābhipretam* (mss., *yatrobhipretam*). Cowell and Neil (Divy 463n4) query *yat te 'bhi-*; Shackleton Bailey (1951: 100) concurs.

462 Following Divy 461.16–23 (modified accordingly). Divy 463.12, "and so on as before" (*pūrvavad yāvad*).

463 Following Divy 71.25, add *yaṃ śrutvā*. Divy 462.11, "and so on as before" (*pūrvavad yāvad*).

464 Following MSV i, 71.16, the Tibetan (147a6; 158b5), and Hiraoka (HA 23; HD 52), read *tenāñjaliṃ praṇamya*. Divy 463.22, *tenopasaṃkrāntāḥ | praṇamayya*.

465 Following MSV i, 71.16, the Tibetan (147a7; 158b6), and Hiraoka (HA 23; HD 52), read *labhema vayam*. Divy 463.23, "teach us [so that we may] . . ." (*deśaya*).

466 Following 281.23–26 (modified accordingly). Divy 463.25–26, "and so on as before" (*pūrvavad yāvat*).

467 Divy 463.26, *te panthitā*. Cowell and Neil (Divy 463.11) query *te naiva sthitā*. Vaidya (Divy-V 302.16) emends to *te avasthitā*. MSV i, 71.18, reads *naiva sthitā*. Likewise, in other instances of this stock passage, we find *naiva sthitā* (Divy 48.24), *nopasthitaḥ* (Divy 281.27–28), and *nopasthitā* (Divy 342.2), which Vaidya emends, respectively, to *evaṃ sthitā* (Divy-V 29.32), *upasthitaḥ* (Divy-V 174.19), and *evaṃ sthitā* (Divy 211.23). Here the reading may hint at *nepatthitā*, the emendation suggested by Edgerton (BHSD,

s.v. *nepatthita*) and Hiraoka (HA 23; HD 52). Nevertheless, as I do in other instances of this passage, I follow Vaidya.

468 Following Divy 281.29–282.4 (modified accordingly). Divy 463.27, "and so on as before" (*pūrvavat*).

469 Following MSV i, 58.1–3. Divy 464.4, "The Blessed One taught them the dharma with three principles—and so on as before—like when he crossed the Gaṅgā River and taught geese, fish, and tortoises" (*teṣāṃ bhagavatā tribhiḥ padārthair dharmo deśitaḥ pūrvavad yāvad yathā gaṅgāvatāre haṃsamatsyakūrmāṇām*). The corresponding passage in the *Mūlasarvāstivāda-vinaya* (MSV i, 72.1–5) is nearly identical. MSV i, 57.19–58.3, however, preserves an unabridged version of the passage, although with slightly different wording than the abridged version suggests. It reads, "Now when the Blessed One crossed over the Gaṅgā River, he was surrounded and respectfully encircled by five hundred geese, fish, and tortoises. The Blessed One taught them the dharma with three principles. 'Friends,' he said, 'everything that is conditioned is impermanent, all phenomena are without self, and nirvāṇa is peace. Cultivate faith in me and then you will escape animal existence'" (*atha bhagavān nadīṃ gaṅgām avatīrṇas tatra pañcabhir haṃsamatsyakūrmaśataiḥ parivṛtaḥ pradakṣiṇīkṛtaś ca | teṣāṃ bhagavatā tribhiḥ padair dharmaḥ deśitaḥ | iti hi bhadramukhāḥ sarvasaṃskārā anityāḥ | sarvadharmā anātmānaḥ śāntaṃ nirvāṇaṃ | mamāntike cittam abhiprasādayata | apy evaṃ tiryagyoniṃ virāgayiṣyatheti*). Hiraoka (1998: 428–29) cites this as an example of the compiler of the *Divyāvadāna* uncritically borrowing from the *Mūlasarvāstivāda-vinaya*. These three principles are part of the well-known "four seals" of Buddhism.

470 Divy 464.5, *svarbhavanam*. Shackleton Bailey (1951: 100) and Hiraoka (HA 23; HD 52), following the Tibetan (147b2–3; 159a2) and MSV i,72.4, read *svabhavanam*. That is, "their homes."

471 Divy 464.7, *kiṃ nu*. Hiraoka (HA 23; HD 52), following MSV i, 72.7 and the Tibetan (147b3; 159a3), suggests *kiṃ bhadanta*. This is part of a standard passage in the text (Divy 53.28, 191.6, 282.7).

472 Following Divy 131.7–14 (modified accordingly). Divy 464.12–13, "and so on as before" (*pūrvavad yāvat*).

473 Following Divy 344.5–7. Divy 464.15, "and so on as before" (*pūrvavat*).

474 Divy 464.22, *vihārasvāmī*. Commenting on a passage from the *Kṣudrakavastu*, Silk (2008b: 142n24) remarks that "the Chinese has 'the *dānapati* [donor] who built the monastery,' which means precisely the same thing as *vihārasvāmin*." For more on this term, see Lévi and Chavannes 1915. See too Schopen 2004: 219–59.

475 Following Divy 23.28–29.1 Divy 465.8–9, "and so on as before" (*pūrvavad yāvat*).

476 This rest of the story (Divy 465.10–469.18) also occurs, nearly verbatim, at Divy 76.10–80.9.

477 Following Divy 76.10, add *ānandam*. Divy 465.10 (omitted).

478 Following Divy 67.5–7. Divy 465.15, "and so on as before" (*pūrvavad yāvat*).

479 Divy 465.21, *pratodayaṣṭyā*. Both "The Story of the Toyikā Festival" and "The Story of a Brahman Named Indra" make use of this story, and hence this image, but in different ways. Here the associated image is the cattle prods that bruised the oxen's bodies in the previous embedded story (Divy 463.9–11). In the latter avadāna, the associated

image is the Buddha-sized "post" (*yaṣṭi*) whose discovery engendered a brahman's faith (Divy 75.14–19).

480 Following Edgerton (BHSD, s.v. *kṣūṇa*) and Divy 76n3 (ms. D), read *kṣūṇa*. Divy 465.23, *kṣaṇa*. Cf. Divy 76.25, and the corresponding note (DS 419n434).

481 Divy 465.24, *samyak pratyātmajñanadarśanaṃ* [read *-jñāna-*] *pravartate*. Cf. 76.26, which reads *pratyaya-* for *pratyātma-*.

482 Divy 465.26, *upasaṃkramya*. Cf. Divy 76.28, which reads *upasaṃkrameṇa*.

483 Divy 466.15, *draṣṭukāmaḥ*. I think *darśayitukāmaḥ* ("desired to show") would have been better. Cf. Divy 77.18–19.

484 Following Divy 78.7, MSV i, 76.2, Shackleton Bailey (1951: 100), and Hiraoka (HA 23; HD 52), read *-saṃjananārtham*. Divy 467.3, *-samjanārtham*.

485 Divy 467.21, *teṣām api cittam ājñāya*. Cf. Divy 79.21–22, which reads *teṣām api cetasā cittam ājñāya*. Hiraoka (HA 23; HD 52) follows the latter reading, which is a common turn of phrase in the text.

486 Divy 467.22, *suvarṇam ūḍham*. Vaidya (Divy-V 305.1) reads *suvarṇamūḍham*. In the *Divyāvadāna*, the term *mūḍha* usually occurs in a list of types containers and means of transport. See Edgerton (BHSD, s.v. *muṭa*). Cf. Divy 78.23, which reads *suvarṇaniṣkā*.

487 Divy 467.24–25, *muktakapuṣparāśim*. Cf. Divy 78.24, which reads *muktasupuṣparāśim*. There I understood *mukta* in the sense of *muktā*, and translated the compound as "heaps of pearls and lovely flowers." But I now prefer to read *mukta*, in the sense of "loose." There is a progression here of increasingly more valuable gifts to offer at stūpa, and "loose flowers" flows logically to "garlands." My thanks to Chris Clark for this observation.

488 Divy 467.28, *teṣām api cittam ājñāya*. Cf. Divy 77.27–28, which reads *teṣām api cetasā cittam ājñāya*. Hiraoka (HA 23; HD 52) and Shackleton Bailey (1951: 100) follow the latter reading.

489 Divy 79.10 adds "thus with their minds" (*evaṃ cetasā*). Divy 468.10 (omitted).

490 Divy 468.18, *dhvajapatākāropaṇam*. Cf. Divy 79.17, which reads *chattradhvajapatākāropaṇam*. In what follows (Divy 468.21), "umbrellas" (*chattra*) is likewise included with "flags and banners."

491 Divy 468.22, *teṣām api cittam ājñāya*. Cf. Divy 77. 27–28, which reads *teṣā[m api cetasā] cittam ājñāya*. Hiraoka (HA 23; HD 52) follows the latter reading.

492 Following MSV i, 78.3, read *eṣā hi*. Divy 468.27, *eṣāṃ hi*.

493 Following Divy 79.22, read *acintiye*. Divy 469.6, *acintiyaiḥ* (ms. C, *acintiyaḥ*).

494 Vaidya (Divy-V 306.12) omits Divy 469.6–7.

495 Divy 469.7, *apratihatadharmacakrapravartinām*. Divy 79.23, however, reads *apratihatadharmacakravartinām*. MSV i, 78.12, concurs. The present reading is more grammatically correct, yet it breaks meter. This suggests that it may be a later hypercorrection.

496 Following MSV i, 79.1, the Tibetan (151a5; 162b4), and Hiraoka (HA 23; HD 52–53), read *śrāddhaiḥ*. Divy 469.17, *sārdham*.

497 Following ms. H 179a5 and Hiraoka (HA 23; HD 53), read *pañcakārṣakaśatāvadānam*. The manuscripts used by Cowell and Neil (Divy 469.18–19) read "The Story of the Youth Sudhana" (*Sudhanakumāra-avadānam*), but this is the name of the preceding story. Vaidya (Divy-V 306.21) renames it the *Toyikāmaha-avadāna*.

498 For a translation, see Hiraoka 2007: ii, 276–94. For insightful studies of the text, see Ohnuma 2000 and Mrozik 2006. For Sanskrit parallels, see Haribhaṭṭa's *Jātakamālā* no. 6 (Hahn 1992: 51–57; trans. Ohnuma 2004b); *Jātakamāla* no. 1; *Avadānakalpalatā* no. 51 (Rani 2005: 55–56 and woodcut R-15; Tucci 1949: ii, 489 and plate 115). See Vajracarya 1977 for a modern retelling in Newari. For more, see Hiraoka 2007: ii, 289–90; HD 53; and Grey 2000: 328–29.

499 Following Divy 290.14, Cowell and Neil (Divy 470n3), and Hiraoka (HA 23; HD 53), insert *lokam*. Divy 470.8 (omitted).

500 Following Divy 290.20, which reads *saced bhikṣavaḥ*, read *evaṃ saced bhikṣavaḥ*. Divy 470.14, "and so, monks" (*evaṃ ca bhikṣavaḥ*). Cowell and Neil (Divy 470n4) query *ced* for *ca*. Cf. *Itivuttaka* 18–19.

501 Vaidya (Divy-V 307.14) omits Divy 470.15–16.

502 Divy 470.17–18, *tam api nāsaṃvibhajya pareṣv ātmanā vā paribhuñjiran*. Perhaps read *eva* for *vā*.

503 Divy 470.18, *mātsaryacittaṃ paryādāya tiṣṭheyuḥ*. Hiraoka (HA 23; HD 53), following Divy 290.25, reads *mātsaryaṃ cittaṃ paryādāya tiṣṭhet*. Cf. Divy 481.11, *tiṣṭhet*; and Divy 470.24 and 481.15, *tiṣṭhati*.

504 Divy 470.22, *kavaḍaḥ paścima*. For both terms, Cowell and Neil (Divy 470nn1–2) write "sic." Hiraoka (HA 23; HD 53) reads *kavaḍo 'paścima*. Cf. Divy 290.22–23, *apaścimaḥ kavaḍaḥ* (mss., *karadaḥ*).

505 The standard passage (Divy 62.9, 131.17, 435.6–7, etc.) adds "with plenty of food" (*ca subhikṣā*). Divy 471.2 (omitted). Hiraoka (HA 23; HD 53) suggests its addition.

506 Dimitrov (2008: 47n8) notes, "There is a certain inconsistency in the spelling of the heroine's name and consequently of the title of the legend. Apart from *rūpāvatī*, as it is given in the *editio princeps*, some MSS and modern sources cite the name as *rūpyāvatī* and more rarely *rūpavatī*." Cf. Steiner (2002), who suggests that *rūpyāvatī* is to be given preference.

507 Divy 471.7, *rūpāvatī strī*. The text refers to her throughout as the "woman Rūpāvatī," but I generally translate this simply as "Rūpāvatī." The emphasis on her gender may be a way to highlight the enormity of the change that she will undergo in what follows.

508 Divy 471.10, *prajātābhirūpam*. Hiraoka (HA 23; HD 53) suggests *prajātam abhirūpam*.

509 Divy 471.12, *svāni putramāṃsāni*. Hiraoka (HA 23; HD 53) suggests *svaputramāṃsāni*.

510 Divy 471.14, *svakāni putramāṃsāni*. Hiraoka (HA 23; HD 53) likewise suggests *svakaputramāṃsāni*.

511 Following Hiraoka (HA 23; HD 53), read *te na*. Divy 471.15, *tena*. Cf. Divy 471.17, *na me*.

512 Divy 471.22, *pṛthivī*. Hiraoka (HA 23; HD 53), following the Chinese, suggests *pṛṣṭham*. That is, "back."

513 Divy 472.7, *sthāmaṃ ca balaṃ ca vīryaṃ ca*. Regarding this passage, Susanne Mrozik (2006: 27–28) notes, "*Vīrya* can mean anything from 'valor,' 'courage,' or 'vigor,' to 'manliness,' 'virility,' and 'semen.' . . . In a story about the transition of a female Bodhisattva to a male Bodhisattva, I find most suggestive a masculine reading of *vīrya* as virility. According to such a reading, Beautiful Woman [Rūpāvatī] generates mascu-

line qualities in her body prior to becoming male." For more on *vīrya* and its connection to an idealized form of masculinity, see Whitaker 2011: 59–108.

514 Following Hiraoka (HA 23; HD 53), read *sahakṛte tenāsmin*. Divy 472.28, *sahakṛtenāsmin*.

515 Divy 473.1–2, *atityāgo 'tityāgagauravatāyā* (ms. A, *atityośātityāga-*; mss. BC, *atityāgātityāga-*; ms. D, *atibhyāśātibhyāga-*) *rūpāvatyāḥ striyāḥ kṛtaḥ*. Vaidya (Divy-V 308.28–29) emends to *atityāgo 'tityāgagauravatā yā rūpāvatyā striyā kṛtaḥ*. Perhaps read *-gauravatayā*.

516 Being Śakra, lord of the gods, is a position that one attains by accumulating large amounts of merit through the performance of meritorious deeds. Here Śakra is afraid that Rūpāvatī, as a result of her great sacrifice, will accrue enough merit to force Śakra from his post.

517 Following Divy 473.19, read *brāhmaṇa*. Divy 473.20, *brahman*.

518 Following Divy 473.19, read *brāhmaṇa*. Divy 473.22, *brahman*.

519 For accounts of Rūpāvatī's sex change, see Mitra 1981: 314 and Burlingame 1917: 451. Mitra translates this passage as follows: "I long not for kingdom, or wealth, or supremacy; I yearn for the absolute knowledge, which would enable me to rescue the fallen, redeem the lost, and restore mankind to eternal beatitude. I wish therefore to become a man."

520 Divy 475.12–13, *aṅkadhātrī maladhātrī stanadhātrī krīḍāpaṇikā dhātrīḥ*. In the *Divyāvadāna* a newborn child is usually given over to eight nurses: "two shoulder nurses, two playtime nurses, two nursemaids, and two wet nurses" (*dvābhyām aṃśadhātrībhyāṃ dvābhyāṃ krīḍanikābhyāṃ dvābhyāṃ maladhātrībhyāṃ dvābhyāṃ kṣīradhātrībhyām* | Divy 3.13–14; cf. 99.24–26, 271.18–20, etc.). Here we have "lap nurse" (*aṅkadhātrī*) instead of "shoulder nurse" (*aṃśadhātrī*), and for "wet nurse," *stanadhātrī* instead of *kṣīradhātrī*, with "breast" (*stana*) metonymically replacing "milk" (*kṣīra*). The text also reads *krīḍāpaṇika*, yet as Cowell and Neil (Divy 475n2) note, "Mss. vary between *krīḍāp-* and *krīdāy-* and between *-nikā* and *-ṇikā*."

521 Divy 475.17–18, *dakṣakāṇām* (mss., *dahukānām*). Speyer (1902: 356–57) conjectures *daharāṇām* or *daharakāṇām*. Edgerton (BHSD) conjectures *dahara(ka)* or *dahraka*. Hiraoka (HA 23; HD 53), following Speyer, suggests *daharakānām* (*sic*).

522 Divy 475.18–19, *akāyikā sakāyikā* (mss. ABD, *saṃkāyikā*) *vitkoṭikā*. Agrawala (1966: 67, 75), "mere heads without being attached to busts" (*ākāyikā*), "full figurines, complete with head, bust and legs" (*sakāyikā*), "grotesque bandylegged female dwarf figurine" (*vitkoṭikā*). Agrawala notes that Edgerton approved of these changes and said as much in a personal letter. M. G. Dhadphale (personal communication) also suggests "personal and impersonal toys" (*akāyikā sakāyikā*).

523 Divy 475.19, *syapeṭārikā*. Agrawala (1966: 75), "basket full of miniature cooking utensils." Perhaps equivalent to Hindi, *sītā-piṭārī* or *sītā kīrasoyī*.

524 Divy 475.19, *agharikā*. This is obscure. Edgerton (BHSD) simply notes that it is "a kind of toy."

525 Divy 475.19, *vāṃśaghaṭikā*. Cf. Agrawala 1966: 75. Edgerton (BHSD) thinks it may refer to a bamboo stick used in a game.

526 Divy 475.19–20, *saṃdhāvaṇikā*. This is obscure. Again Edgerton (BHSD) simply notes, "a kind of toy."

527 Divy 475.20–21, *balīvardavigrahāḥ kathayanti dhanurgrahāḥ*. The term *kathayanti* ("they say") makes little sense in this context and so has not been translated.

528 Divy 475.21–22, *kāṇḍakaṭacchupūrakūrcabhaiṣajyasthavikāś ca purataḥ parikṛṣyante*. This is obscure.

529 Following Speyer (1902: 357) and Hiraoka (HA 24; HD 53), read *eta* [= *ehi*] *dārakā*. Divy 475.28, *etad dārakā*. As Speyer translates, "Now then, boys, let all of us make up our mind to strive for Highest Wisdom."

530 Divy 476.10, *uccaṃgamaḥ pakṣī*. Here *uccaṃgamaḥ* seems to be a description—that is, "high flying"—but in what follows (Divy 480.12–13) it is said to be the name of the bird. What is clear is that it is a bird of prey, perhaps a vulture.

531 Divy 476.16, *iṣye*. Cowell and Neil (Divy 710) suggest this is a substitute for *iṣyate* [or, perhaps, *iṣṭam*]. As they note, "This dialogue [Divy 476.15–17] seems to be purposively written in a debased Sanskrit, thus *iṣye* for *iṣyate*, *pakṣi* for *pakṣin*, and *utpāṭayitu* and *muñca* for *utpāṭayitvā* and *muñces*."

532 Divy 476.17, *manye*. Hiraoka (HA 24; HD 53), following the Chinese, "tentatively" suggests *manyase*.

533 Divy 476.17–19, *sacen mama pakṣi sahasrakṛtvo* (mss., *sahasraṃ kṛtvo*) *nayanaṃ gṛhītvā utpāṭayitu* (*sic* mss.) *punar muñca na tv evāhaṃ vārayeyam*. I follow Vaidya (Divy-V 310.27) and for *pakṣi* read the nominative *pakṣī*, not the vocative *pakṣin*. Vaidya (Divy-V 310.27) likewise emends *utpāṭayitu* to *utpāṭayatu* and *muñca* to *muñca(tu)*.

534 Following Cowell and Neil's suggestion (Divy 477n1), read *mānavakaśatāni*. Divy 477.1, *māṇavakāni*.

535 Divy 477.7, *yasyedānīṃ brahmaprabha kālaṃ manyase*. See note 204.

536 Vaidya (Divy-V 311.19) mistakenly adds the following: "Having approached, he approached the two brahman sages" (*upasaṃkramya punar yena tau dvau brahmarṣī tenopasaṃkrāntaḥ*).

537 Divy 478.17, *abhidrotum*. Vaidya (Divy-V 311.31) emends to *abhidrotu(gdhu)m*, indicating the standard Sanskrit reading in parentheses. For more on loving-kindness (*maitrī*) as a means of protection from danger, see Schmithausen 1997.

538 Divy 478.19, *tatas tīkṣṇaṃ* (ms. D, *tīkṣṇāṃ*) *ca veṇupeśīṃ tīkṣṇāṃ*. Hiraoka (HA 24; HD 53) suggests emending to *tīkṣṇam asiṃ* (or *śastraṃ*) *veṇupeśīm*.

539 For more on this vow, see Ohnuma 2007: 99–100.

540 Kṣemendra's *Avadānakalpalatā* (no. 51, vv. 45–46; ii, 319.5–12), from the eleventh century, contains a near-verbatim rendering of these verses. Most likely these verses are later interpolations from Kṣemendra's text (Dimitrov 2008), although when this may have happened, or why or by whom, is very much unknown. Vaidya (Divy-V 547) argues for the converse. Elsewhere in the *Divyāvadāna* we also find verses from Kṣemendra's text, and these too are likely later insertions (Bongard-Levin and Volkova 1965: 5; Jaini 1966: 541n41 and 543–46n53). For more on the Sanskrit parallels of the *Rūpāvatī-avadāna*, see Le Coq and Waldschmidt 1928: 19 and Hikata 1954: 51a; 1978: 52a.

541 Divy 479.2, *alakṣyata*. The manuscripts, however, read *alakṣata*, as does *Avadānakalpalatā* no. 51, v. 45 (ii, 319.6).

542 Following *Avadānakalpalatā* no. 51, v. 45 (ii, 319.6) and Vaidya's suggestions (Divy-V 547), read *vikṣatāsya*. Divy 479.2, *vīkṣatārā*.

543 Following *Avadānakalpalatā* no. 51, v. 46 (ii, 319.10) and Vaidya's suggestions (Divy-V 547), read *saharṣam*. Divy 479.5, *sahasram*.

544 Concerning these verses, Cowell and Neil (Divy 710) write: "These obscure lines seem to mean something like the following—'His bosom, while torn by the sportive claws of the tigress, was seen for a moment as if possessed of bright eyes (in its wounds), while it was as it were filled, in the midst of its joyous horripilation, with the brilliance of the purest moonbeams. As he gazed with rapture on the tigress fiercely seizing his flesh and drinking his blood, his life-breath, bewildered at the crisis of an eternal parting, lingered for a moment in his throat and gave him a transient revival.'" Dimitrov (2008: 52–53) offers this translation:

> Being torn by the playfulness of the string of the tigress' claws, the wounded bosom of [his] body covered with hair standing on end seemed for a moment as if pervaded by the sprout-like beams shining [just like his] noble nature [which was] as bright as the moon.
>
> While [he was] gazing with joy at the tigress who was frantically devouring his flesh and drinking [his] blood, the faculty of his own life engaged at the time of going on a long journey [of reincarnations] fixed itself for an instant resting on [his] throat.

545 Following Divy 479.21, 479.24, 479.27–28, read *yuṣmākaṃ bhikṣavo kāṅkṣā vimatir vānyā sā*. Divy 479.17, *yuṣmākaṃ bhikṣavo 'nyā sā*. Hiraoka (HA 24; HD 54) supplies "the usual expression": *bhikṣavo yuṣmākaṃ kāṅkṣā vimatir vānyā sā tena kālena tena kalena*.

546 I understand this to be a variant of Puṣkalāvatī. As Jason Neelis (2008: 159) notes, "Puṣkalāvatī (located near Chārsada in northwestern Pakistan) was the primary urban center of Gandhāra until the capital shifted across the Kabul River to Puruṣapura (modern Peshawar) in the Kuṣāṇa period."

547 Following Divy 479.18. Divy 479.19, *utpalāvatam*.

548 Presumably this is the same Candraprabhā who is the wife of King Rudrāyaṇa in "The Story of Rudrāyaṇa."

549 A portion of text seems to be omitted here (Divy 480.22; cf. Divy-V 313n1). Some of the text can be posited on the basis of the repeated passages in the coda (Divy 479.17–480.21), but the identity of the forest remains a mystery.

550 Following Divy-V 313.13, add *vyāghrī*. Divy 480.29 (omitted).

551 Hartmann (1980: 266) offers this translation: "At that time, monks, the Bodhisattva Maitreya has been excelled by one single giving up of my throat after he had set out forty kalpas ago." Ohnuma (2007: 305–6n67) gives this one: "And thus, Monks, Maitreya Bodhisattva, who had set out on a journey [for Buddhahood] forty eons before, was outdistanced by a single gift of my throat."

552 Divy 481.9, *kavaḍaḥ paścima*. Hiraoka (HA 23; HD 54) reads *kavaḍo 'paścima*.

553 Following Divy 470.20–21, add *yathāhaṃ jāne dānasya phalaṃ dānasaṃvibhāgasya ca phalavipākam*. Divy 481.12 (omitted).

554 Divy 481.13, *kavaḍaḥ paścima*. Hiraoka (HA 23; HD 54) reads *kavaḍo 'paścima*.

555 Divy 481.13, *apareṣām*. Cf. Divy 470.22–23, which in the same formulaic passage reads *pareṣu*.

556 Hiraoka (HA 23; HD 54), following Cowell and Neil's query (Divy 481n4), reads *naśyati* for *paśyati* at Divy 481.16 and 481.17. This same reading occurs in a very similar verse at Divy 298.13–16. The present verse, however, is more opaque.

557 Divy 481.6, *purākṛtam*. Cf. Divy 298.13, which reads *pūrvakṛtam*.

558 A similar verse occurs at Divy 298.17–18.

559 For translations, see Upreti 1989: 90–91 and Hiraoka 2007: ii, 317–21. James Ware (1929) has also translated this sūtra along with Tibetan and Chinese counterparts. The corresponding Tibetan can be found at P 850 *mu* 105b5–106b7 and D 183 *tsa* 95b2–96b6. My thanks to Jason McCombs for sharing his work on the *Dānapāramitā Sūtra*, which overlaps with this sūtra. See McCombs 2014: 120–83.

Kazunobu Matsuda has located a leather folio (13.5 x 5.5 cm) among the Schøyen manuscripts (MS 2376/176), written in Gupta Brāhmī script from perhaps the fifth or sixth century, that corresponds to Divy 483.6–17. The folio—which Matsuda identifies with the *Dānānuśaṃsānirdeśasūtra*—was likely written by a monk, not a professional scribe, and the format suggests that it may have been created for ritual purposes. My thanks to Jens Uwe Hartmann for his comments on the folio, and to Kazunobu Matsuda for an image of the folio along with a transcription of the text (both of which he produced for a talk in 2003, which is as yet unpublished).

560 Following the Tibetan (105b6; 95b3) and Vaidya (Divy-V 426.2), add *bhagavān*. Divy 382.2 (omitted).

561 Ware (1929) suggests the following concordance: Verse no. 1 in the Tibetan and Chinese has no corresponding Sanskrit. The Tibetan (105b6; 95b3–4) reads, "He gives a gift with faith in order to eradicate greed." Sanskrit nos. 1–19 correspond to Tibetan and Chinese nos. 2–20; Sanskrit no. 20 has no corresponding Tibetan and Chinese; Sanskrit nos. 21–24 correspond to Tibetan and Chinese nos. 21–24; no corresponding Sanskrit for Tibetan and Chinese no. 25; Sanskrit nos. 25–36 correspond to Tibetan and Chinese nos. 26–37. So, in order to get to the "thirty-seven ways" that a wise person gives, one could follow the Tibetan and Chinese numbering or divide up the Sanskrit in some other way.

562 Divy 482.5, *trivastu pariśuddham*. The referent here isn't clear. Cowell and Neil (Divy 681) define *trivastu* as "Buddha, dharma, and saṃgha." Ware (1929: 41) explains that "the true meaning, however, is 'tho[ugh]t, word, and deed.'" Cf. Divy 489.2. Or perhaps this is a variant of *trimaṇḍalapariśuddhi*—"with the three spheres [of giver, recipient, and act of giving] fully purified." See too *Bhagavad Gītā* 17.20, "at the right time and place, and to the right person" (*deśe kāle ca pātre ca*).

563 Divy 482.7, *skandhaṃ dānam*. According to Ware (1929: 42): "It is evident from the Tib. and Chin. that we must seek for the original Skt. a reading other than the *skandha* of the present text which here is meaningless. I would suggest, therefore, that the original text read **anyadānam*. The Tib. and Chin. have both interpreted this reading. As for the present Skt. text, perhaps its history is as follows: *anyadānaṃ* > *anyaṃ dānaṃ* > *skandhaṃ dānaṃ* as the result of a poorly written manuscript." This etymology, however, isn't particularly convincing. Cf. the Tibetan (105b8; 95b5).

564 Following Divy 482.10, 11, 12, etc., read *-pratilābhasaṃvartanīyam*. Divy 482.8–9, *pratisaṃvartanīyam*.

565 Hiraoka (HA 24; HD 55), following the Tibetan (106a2; 95b7), adds *sarvatra jātiṣu*. That is, "in all lives to come." This also occurs on Divy 482.15. Divy 482.14 (omitted).

566 Following the Tibetan (106a5–6; 96a3), Divy 482.7–8, 482.9, 482.10, etc., and Hiraoka (HA 24; HD 55), add *-vipāka-*. Divy 482.23 (omitted).

567 Divy 482.25, *-viśuddha-*. Hiraoka (HA 24; HD 55) suggests emending to *viśuddhi-*. The Tibetan (106a6; 96a4), *rnam par dag pa*, could translate either.

568 Divy 483.2, *devamanuṣyābhiṣekapaṭṭabandha-*. A similar "crowning" ritual is alluded to in *Śathapatha Brāhmaṇa* V.3.23. As Eggeling (1893: iii, 86n2) explains, "The commentators do not seem to be quite in accord in regard to this particular item of the ceremony. The most natural explanation, however, seems to be this: the head-band (turban, *uṣṇīṣa*) is wound (?once) round the head and tied behind; the ends being then drawn over the shoulders so as to hang down from the neck in the manner of a brahmanical cord (or like the ribbon of an order); and being finally tucked in under the mantle somewhere near the navel." Cf. Ghurye 1966: 267–68, 283. Ware (1929: 47) explains that "since both the Tib. and Chin. have a common reading, [equivalent to Skt.] *vimokṣa*, differing from the Skt. [reading of *abhiṣeka*], I believe that the original Skt. probably read: *devamanuṣye vimokṣapaṭṭa-*. 'Garment of release' is the name given to a long robe worn by Buddhist priests." The Tibetan (106b1; 96a7) reads *rnam par grol ba*.

569 Ware (1929: 47) observes that "one of the nos. 27–29 has been lost in the Skt."

570 Divy 483.5, *sūtradānam*. Ware (1929: 48), following the Tibetan and Chinese, suggests that "the original Skt. read *snānadānaṃ* for the present *sūtradānaṃ*." The Tibetan (106b2; 96b1) reads *khrus kyi yo byad*—perhaps, "requisites for bathing" (*snānopakaraṇa*). If one were to follow this reading, one might want to follow Ware (1929: 47) and translate *samantaprāsādika-* as "perpetual beauty" and not as "instilling faith all around."

571 Divy 483.7, *pañcasāra-*. The referent here is unclear. Perhaps this is a reference to Ayurveda, where the "five essences" are milk, sugar, honey, ghee, and long pepper (*Piper longum*).

572 Divy 483.8, *maitryātmaka-*. Hiraoka (HA 24; HD 55), following the Tibetan (106b3; 96b2), suggests *maitryāśrita-*. The *Dānānuśaṃsānirdeśasūtra* (23r4) reads likewise. As Hiraoka (HD 55) explains, "From here the four *apramāṇāni* ["immeasurables"] are explained, and *-ātmaka-* is *-āśrita-* in the other three items. It is better, therefore, to read *āśrita* for *ātmaka* here too."

573 Divy 483.10, *mahāsukha-*. Ware (1929: 48) remarks that "it seems almost certain that the platitude *mahāsukha* has been substituted for the very definite *ahiṃsā*." The Tibetan (106b4; 96b2) reads *'tshe ba med pa*. Elsewhere *mahāsukha* is a technical term referring to "great bliss," an experience akin to nirvāṇa—what one scholar describes as "the ultimate reality absorbing within it all ideas of existence and extinction" (Banerjee 1979: 468).

574 Divy 483.11, *sarvathā muditānanda-*. The *Dānānuśaṃsānirdeśasūtra* (23r6) reads *anunayaprahāṇa-*. That is, "the destruction of attachment."

575 Divy 483.14, *sarvārthaparityāgam*. The *Dānānuśaṃsānirdeśasūtra* (23v4) reads *apratikāṃkṣāśritam*. That is, "free of expectation."

576 For a revised edition of part of the text (Divy 498.17–504.9), see Maue 2010: 599–605. For a translation, see Hiraoka 2007: ii, 322–97; for a partial translation, see Maue 2010: 605–11; and for a comparative study, see Lojda 2009. For Pāli and Sanskrit parallels, see *Jātaka* no. 4 [cf. Divy 498.17–504.9]; *Jātaka* no. 254 [cf. Divy 509.6–515.3]; Pāli *Vinayapiṭaka* iv, 54.1–55.10; *Dhammapada-aṭṭhakathā* i, 239.15–250.16; Sanskrit fragments from Turfan (Sander and Waldschmidt 1985: nos. 1349, 1464, and 1516; Maue 1996: 19–41); and *Kathāsaritsāgara* 15.37–16.21. The corresponding Tibetan can be found at P 1032 *ñe* 58a3–81b7 and D 3 *ja* 61a4–86b1. For more, see Ch'en 1945–47: 270–71n103; Gokhale 1977: 126–27; Clouston 1887: ii, 317–21, 491–93; Hiraoka 2007: ii, 360; HD 55; and Grey 2000: 196.

577 Divy 483.25–484.1, *vṛddhayuvatiḥ*. In "The Story of Dharmaruci," I translated the term as "madam" or "procuress." See note 85. Here, however, as Silk (2008a: 177) notes, "we have both Tibetan and Chinese translations of the source text in the *Vinayavibhaṅga* of the Mūlasarvāstivāda Vinaya. The former has *bud med rgan mo*, the lat[t]er *lăomŭ* . . . both meaning simply 'old woman.' Given this, perhaps both 'procuress' and 'midwife,' even if correct, are better understood as purely contextual meanings."

578 Following the mss. (Divy 484n1), Edgerton (BHSD, s.v. *prasavāyitā*), and Hiraoka (HA 24; HD 55), read *prasavāyitā*. Divy 484.8 reads *prasavāpitā*, following Cowell and Neil's emendation.

579 Following Divy 484.16, add *āryāṇām*. Cf. Divy 485.16. Divy 484.12 (omitted).

580 Divy 484.13, *āropayitavyaḥ*. Edgerton (BHSD) infers that the term here means "buries," but this is the only reference he cites.

581 Divy 484.17, *ciraṃ jīva*. Cowell and Neil (Divy 484n4) query *jīvatu*. Cf. Divy 484.22, 484.27, etc.

582 Divy 485.1, *asmin mahāpathe*. Hiraoka (HA 24; HD 55), following the Tibetan (59a3; 62a4) and a similar expression at Divy 485.26, reads *amuṣmin mahāpathe*. That is, "On such-and-such main road."

583 Divy 485.6–7, *bhasmagrahe*. Perhaps this refers to the appropriate way that a brahman is to receive ashes as *prasād* and smear them on his forehead or body.

584 Divy 485.7, *autkare*. Edgerton (BHSD) offers no definition, merely acknowledging that it is "some subject that was part of the education of a brahman." Perhaps this refers to knowing the proper amount to accept. MSV iv, 15.19 reads *ḍoṅkāre*. Cf. Divy 227.26, where there is a merchant named Autkarika. Hiraoka (HA 24; HD 55), following the Tibetan (59a5; 62a6), reads *karakagrahe*. That is, "use an ascetic's water pot."

585 Cf. *Manusmṛti* 10.75.

586 Vogel and Wille (1984: 312–13) offer this translation of a parallel passage in the *Mūlasarvāstivada-vinaya*: "When he had become grown up, then he thoroughly studied writing, mental, verbal, and manual arithmetic, subtraction [?], addition [?], calculation, exegesis, and recitation; [43] then he thoroughly studied the brahmins' deportment, behaviour, purity, and conduct, (their) taking ashes, taking the water-pot, and taking earth, (their) hand-gestures and hair-style, (their rules of) religious address and profane address, and the brahmins' Vedas and Vedāṅgas, (the brahmins', who are) versed in the Ṛgveda, Yajurveda, Sāmaveda, and Atharvaveda and in a brah-

min's six duties: offering sacrifices, executing sacrifices, reading, teaching, giving, and taking..." Cf. MSV iv, 15.17–16.1 and 23.18–24.1.

587 Divy 485.9, *brāhmaṇakarma*. Hiraoka (HA 24; HD 55), following the Tibetan (59a7–8; 62b1), suggests emending to *māṇavakānām*. That is, "young brahmans."

588 Divy 485.16, *āryasya*. Cf. Divy 485.21, which reads *āryāṇām*.

589 Divy 486.2–3, *tasya sīty ukte* (ms. C, *tasya tyukte*) *dham iti* (ms. A, *dham ati*; ms. D, *dhamam iti*) *vismarati*. Cf. Sander and Waldschmidt 1985: no. 1349, p. 237, v3. The Tibetan (63a2) reads *sid* + *dham* instead of *si* + *(d)dham*. As D. C. Sircar (1965: 127) notes, "Early records often begin with the auspicious word *siddham* which means the same thing as *siddhir astu*, 'Let there be success.'" Panthaka, it seems, was dumbfounded by the introductory auspicious word *siddham*, which was to be recited before beginning his studies—likely, copying syllabaries. Cf. Couvreur 1964: 112–13. Cowell and Neil (Divy 710) offer an alternate (and less convincing) suggestion: "Does this refer to some writing exercise containing the words "bud*dhaṃ sid*dham?"

590 The Tibetan (60a2; 63a3) adds, "And when he says *dham*, he's already forgotten *sid*!"

591 Following Cowell and Neil's query (Divy 486n3) and the Tibetan (63a4), add *na*. Divy 486.7 (omitted). Cf. Divy 486.13.

592 This refers to the renowned Gāyatrī mantra, which brahmans are to recite during their morning and evening prayers: *oṃ bhūr bhuvaḥ svaḥ tat savitur vareṇyaṃ bhargo devasya dhīmahi dhiyo yo naḥ pracodayāt* (*Ṛg Veda* 3.62.10).

593 Divy 486.23, *mahatā satkāreṇa*. Cf. Divy 28.2, which reads *mahatā saṃskāreṇa*.

594 Divy 487.11, *teṣām*. One would expect *tayoḥ*.

595 In the Tibetan (61a2–3; 64a3–4), Mahāpanthaka goes to the Jeta Grove, and there he sees a monk and asks him for instruction. He also promises to return at a later time. As such, Mahāpanthaka's indoctrination in the dharma seems more premeditated than serendipitous.

596 The Tibetan (62a3; 65a3–4) adds, ". . . the venerable Mahāpanthaka went forth as monk, then . . ." Divy 488.10 (omitted).

597 Following the Tibetan (62a4; 65a4) and Hiraoka (HA 24; HD 55–56), read *mahāpanthakasya*. Divy 488.11–12, *panthakasya*.

598 Following Cowell and Neil's query (Divy 488n4), the Tibetan (62a4; 65a5), and Hiraoka (HA 25; HD 56), insert *prāptam*. Divy 488.12 (omitted).

599 Divy 488.26–27, *ahaṃ cūḍaḥ paramacūḍo* (mss., *cūḍaḥ*) *dhanvaḥ paramadhanvaḥ*. As Edgerton (BHSD, s.vv. *dhanva*, *dhanvāyati*) notes, *dhanva* is a "common miswriting" for *dhandha*.

600 The Tibetan (63b1–2; 65b2–3) reads, "Are they connected with someone? Yes, they're connected with me."

601 Divy 489.6, *na vṛtta jātā*. This is a little obscure. I follow the Tibetan (62b5; 65b5), *lobs bar ma gyur to*. Cf. Divy 489.7, *pravṛttā jātā*; Divy 490.1, *anupravṛttā*; Divy 491.18, *āmukhīpravṛttā jātāḥ*.

602 Divy 489.7, *pravṛttā jātā*. This is likewise obscure.

603 Divy 489.8, *upasaṃharanti*. I follow Edgerton (BHSD) here, although perhaps *udāharanti* would have been a better word choice. The Tibetan (62b5; 65b6) reads "they showed it to him."

604 Divy 489.14–15, *svādhyāyanikāṃ paripṛcchanikāṃ ca yācanti yathādhigataṃ* (mss. ABC, *ye 'rthādhikataṃ*; ms. D, *-yerthodikatam*) *cārocayanti* (ms. A omits). Edgerton

takes *paripṛcchanikā* to mean "subject for investigation" or "subject for inquiry," but it seems more likely to mean "ask questions" or even "hold question-and-answer sessions." In what follows, the Tibetan (62b8–63a2; 66a2–4) explains that "some asked questions about the sūtras, the monastic discipline, and the abhidharma." The text seems to indicate three ways of learning: self-study, inquiry, and recitation.

605 Divy 490.1, *anupravṛttā*.

606 Following Vaidya (Divy-V 431.1), read *bhramantam*. Divy 490.10, *bhavantam*. The Tibetan (66b3–4) has Panthaka "outside the Jetavana monastery crying."

607 Divy 490.22, *bālabhāvena*. To match with the second half of the verse, one might say something like "and being aware of his ignorance"—perhaps, *bālabhāvajñaḥ*.

608 My sense is that this is less a philosophical point than a practical matter. The Buddha is busy, and teaching is time-consuming. Panthaka's previous teachers labored, first to teach him writing and then recitation, and then both gave up for lack of time. In what follows, Ānanda will do likewise.

609 Reminiscent of the verse from the *Dhammapada* quoted at Divy 339.23.

610 Following the Tibetan (64a2; 67a6) and Hiraoka (HA 25; HD 56), read *panthakam*. Divy 491.5, *ānandam*.

611 Following the Tibetan (64a3; 67a7), *Mahāvyutpatti* 8967, and Hiraoka (HA 25; HD 56), read *upānahān pūlāṃś ca poñcchitum*. Divy 491.6, *upānahān mūlāc ca* (mss., *mūlā ca*) *poñcchitum* (mss. ABD, *puñcchitum*; ms. C, *pūrṇitum*). Edgerton (BHSD, s.v. *mūla*), taking *mūla* in the sense of "foundation," suggests, "Can you clean the monks' sandals thoroughly (from the ground up)?" Likewise for Divy 491.11–12, he suggests, "He cleaned the monks' sandals thoroughly (lit., going to the very foundation?)." Hiraoka (HD 56) rightly observes that "Edgerton takes *mūlāc* as the ablative of *mūla* (as an adverb), but this cannot explain the *ca* after *mūlāc*." If one were trying to read creatively—and, like Edgerton, not try to explain the *ca*, and read a singular as a plural—one might take *mūlāt* in the sense of *pādamūlāt*, and offer this translation: "Are you able to remove the monks' sandals from their feet and wipe them clean?"

612 Read *pūlāṃś ca*. Divy 491.8, *mūlāc ca*. See previous note.

613 Divy 491.11, *anuprayacchata*. Cf. the Tibetan (64a3–4; 67b1).

614 Read *pūlān*. Divy 491.11, *mūlam*.

615 Following Divy 333.24, read *pṛṣṭhatomukhaḥ*. Divy 492.13, *pṛṣṭhato mukham* (mss., *mukha*). One could also emend to *pṛṣṭhato mukhataḥ*. Perhaps, "from behind and from all sides."

616 Following Vaidya (Divy-V 432.18), read *nipuṇapaṇḍitavijñavedanīyaḥ*. Divy 492.19–20, *'nipuṇapaṇḍitavijñavedanīyaḥ* (mss., *-puna-*). Following the example of other texts in both Sanskrit and Pāli (*Abhidharmakośavyākhyā* 103; Pāli *Vinaya-piṭaka* i, 35), one might read *nipuṇo paṇḍitavijñavedanīyaḥ*. Cf. Lojda 2009: 89n32. As the Buddha explains in the *Majjhima-nikāya* (i, 167; trans. in Bodhi 1995: 260), "This Dhamma that I have attained is profound, hard to see and hard to understand, peaceful and sublime, unattainable by mere reasoning, subtle, to be experienced by the wise" (*adhigato kho myāyaṃ dhammo gambhīro duddaso duranubodho santo paṇīto atakkāvacaro nipuṇo paṇḍitavedanīyo*).

617 Divy 492.20–21, *atredānīṃ kiṃ gambhīro 'sya yasyedānīṃ panthakaprabhṛtayaś cūḍāḥ paramacūḍā dhanvāḥ paramadhanvāḥ pravrajanti*. On account of *yasya*, which is syntactically difficult, perhaps read *pravrajitāḥ* instead of *pravrajanti*.

618 Divy 492.22–23, *mahājanakāyaḥ kṣāntim*. Hiraoka (HA 25; HD 56), following the Chinese, emends to *mahājanakāyo 'kṣāntim*. Cf. the Tibetan (65a4; 68b3), *skye bo phal po che'i tshogs kyis smras pa | mi dge ba skyed par byed kyis*.

619 Following the Tibetan (65a6; 68b5), read *saṃlakṣayati*. Cf. Hiraoka 2007: ii, 371n146. Divy 492.29, *kathayati*.

620 Following Maue 1996: 22n22, read *chandahārikāḥ*. Divy 493.3, *chandahānisaḥ* (ms. A, *-hār-*?). Cf. the Tibetan (65a8; 68b7), *gso sbyong 'bul ba*. Rhys Davids and Stede (PTSD) note that *chanda* can mean "(in the monastic law) consent, declaration of consent (to an official act: kamma) by an absentee." Cf. SWTF ii, 275, s.v. *chanda-hāraka*. Cowell and Neil (Divy 493n1) suggest *chandahāriṇyaḥ*—that is, "with little enthusiasm." Hiraoka (HA 25; HD 56) concurs.

621 Divy 493.12, *dvādaśavargīyābhiḥ*. As Edgerton (BHSD), "No such group has been discovered in Pāli; the context in Divy is my only source of knowledge of the meaning. It can hardly mean *members of the dvādaśavarga*, q.v., in the sense of *quorum for ordination*. Apparently these nuns were given to caviling and trouble-making; they object to functions assigned to (Cūḍa-)Panthaka." They are likely meant to be a counterpart to those unruly monastics known as the "group of six monks."

622 Divy 493.19–20, *yo 'smākaṃ tanusatyāni na drakṣyati tena saṃsāre ciraṃ vastavyaṃ bhaviṣyatīti*. This is obscure, if not corrupt. The Tibetan (66a2; 69b3) reads *khyed cag las gang gis der bden pa dag mthong bar ma gyur pa*. Hiraoka (HA 25; HD 56), following the Tibetan, suggests *yuṣmākaṃ tatra satyāni* for *asmākaṃ tanusatyāni*. Perhaps, "Whoever among you doesn't see the [four noble] truths will have to pass a long time in saṃsāra!"

623 Divy 493.20–21, *yena na kaścit putramoṭikāputro* (*sic* mss. except ms. B, *-ṭiko*) *'lpaśruta utsahate bhikṣuṇīr avavadetum* (*sic* mss.). Vaidya (Divy-V 433.6) reads *avavaditum* for *avavadetum*. Omitted in the Tibetan (66a3; 69b4). The nuns seems to think that if Panthaka comes to teach the nuns and finds a large crowd of laypeople there as well, he'll be shamed and will refrain from teaching. Lojda (2009: 91) offers this translation: "Zu uns wird ein solcher [Mönch] kommen, um uns zu unterweisen, der nicht [einmal] unsere wenigen Wahrheiten sehen wird. Dieser wird lange im Kreislauf der Wiedergeburten bleiben müssen. Deswegen soll nicht irgendein ungebildeter Bastard die Nonnen unterweisen."

624 Following Divy 39.19–20 and Hiraoka (HA 25; HD 56), add *śrāvastīṃ piṇḍāya caritvā*. Divy 493.27 (omitted).

625 Following Divy 39.20–21, 516.5, etc., and Hiraoka (HA 25; HD 56), read *kṛta-bhaktakṛtyaḥ paścād bhaktapiṇḍapātraḥ pratikrāntaḥ*. Divy 493.27–28, *bhaktakṛtyaḥ* (*sic* mss. BCD; ms. A omits) *paścād bhaktapiṇḍapātrapratikrāntaḥ*.

626 Divy 494.2, *pratisaṃlayanāya*. Perhaps read *pratisaṃlayanāt*.

627 Following Divy 130.9, 186.17, add *nirgatāni*. Divy 494.3 (omitted).

628 Following Vaidya (Divy-V 433.15) and Hiraoka (HA 25; HD 56), read *punaḥ parasparam*. Divy 494.6, *punaḥparasparam*.

629 Following Vaidya (Divy-V 433.16), read *purahśramaṇaḥ*. Divy 494.7, *punaḥ-śramaṇaḥ*.

630 Following Vaidya (Divy-V 433.16), read *puraḥśramaṇaḥ*. Divy 494.7, *punaḥśramaṇa*.

631 Following Hiraoka (HA 25; HD 56), read *bhavantaḥ*. Divy 494.8, *bhadanta*.

632 Divy 494.11, *vādayiṣyati*. Vaidya (Divy-V 433.18) emends to *vācayiṣyati*.

633 Divy 494.15, *prasādajātābhiḥ*. More literally, "by those who are faithful," but here there is a sense of intentionality that is mirrored by its opposite: "with the intent of doing harm" (*viheṭhanābhiprāyābhiḥ*). For more on *prasāda* and intention, see Rotman 2003 and 2009: 65–88.

634 Divy 494.17–18, *taṃ* (mss. BC, *tasmin*) *siṃhāsanaṃ yathāsthāne sthāpitam*. Cowell and Neil (Divy 688) translate *yathāsthāne* as "as at first." The Tibetan (66b4; 70a6) reads *ji ltar gnas su bzhag pa de ltar mnan nas*. Hiraoka (HA 25; HD 56), following the Tibetan, suggests *yathā sthāne sthāpitaṃ tathā avaṣṭabdham*. Perhaps, "he lowered it to the proper place."

635 Following Divy 161.3–10 (modified accordingly). Divy 494.21–22, "and so on as before" (*pūrvavad yāvat*).

636 Divy 494.25, *utsahetavyāni* (*sic* mss. ACD; ms. B, *utsaha-*). Vaidya (Divy-V 433.27) marks it with a question. Perhaps read *utsahavyāni* (*utsoḍhavyāni*). Cf. the Tibetan (67a1; 70b5).

637 Divy 494.26, *anyaiḥ padair vyañjanair arthaṃ vibhaktum*. More literally, "to analyze its meaning in terms of other words and letters." Lojda (2009: 93–94) offers this translation: "Während sieben Tagen und Nächten [wurde ich fähig] die Bedeutung [dieser] einen Strophe durch andere Worte und Silben zu erklären."

638 Following *Udānavarga* xxviii, v. 1, read *akaraṇam*. Divy 495.1, *karanam*. Vaidya (Divy-V 434.1) emends to *kāraṇam*.

639 This sentence appears to be the remnants of the venerable Panthaka's exegesis of the first half of the verse, which is included in the Tibetan (67a1–4; 70b5–71a1). See Hiraoka 2007: ii, 374–75n184.

640 Following the Tibetan (67a4; 71a1) and Hiraoka (HA 25; HD 56), read *ardhasya*. Divy 495.1, *arthasya*.

641 Following Divy 495.14, read *aprasāditaḥ*. One might even read this more strongly: "Today the venerable Panthaka will have turned a great number of people away from the faith!" See too the Tibetan (67b2–3; 71a6–7). Divy 495.11–12, *prasāditaḥ*. Lojda (2009: 95) offers this translation: "Wird heute der ehrwürdige Panthaka bei einer grossen Menge von Menschen Vertrauen [in die Lehre des Buddha] erweckt haben?"

642 Following the Tibetan (70b2; 73b5) and Divy 24.16, 87.16, etc., add *putro jātaḥ*. The Tibetan then reads, as per Divy 259.25–27, "Sexual pleasure is like salt water. The more you indulge in it, the more your thirst increases."

643 Following Cowell and Neil's query (Divy 496n2) and Hiraoka (HA 25; HD 56–57), read *andho jātaḥ*. Divy 496.4, *jātaḥ* (mss. CD, *jātāndhī-*). The Tibetan (70b2–3; 73b6) reads *mig gnyis mdongs par gyur to*.

644 Divy 496.9, *cakaṭyodanaṃ kāñjikacchiṭim*. The Tibetan (70b5; 74a1) understands them to be spoiled food—the former a kind of coarse rice (*'bras chan rtsub mo*) and the latter a kind of barley mash (*rtsabs bskol ba*). Cf. Maue 1996: 33–34, no. 19.

645 Divy 496.14, *piparikāyām* (mss. ABC, *piṭharik-*). Edgerton (BHSD) suggests reading *piṭharikāyām*.

646 Following the Tibetan (70b7; 74a4), add *anyonyam*. Divy 496.17 (omitted).

647 Divy 496.25, *paribhuktām* (*sic* mss.). This is an odd form of the verb. Cf. the Tibetan (71a1–2; 74a6).

648 Divy 497.8–10, *asmākaṃ gṛhe eva ekamukhī sthālī putrakānyeṣu geheṣu na sthālī-*

dvayaṃ tv ekamukham asmākaṃ mandabhāgyānām. The Tibetan (71a6–7; 74b4–5) reads this as a verse:

> Sons, in other households there are single pots with single mouths,
> but we, unfortunate as we are, have double pots with single mouths!

Hiraoka (HD 57) offers this reconstruction of the Sanskrit:

> *ekā ekamukhī sthālī putrakānyeṣu geheṣu* |
> *sthālīdvayaṃ tv ekamukham asmākaṃ mandabhāgyānām* ||

Maue (1996: 35, nos. 27–28) reconstructs as follows:

> *putrakānyeṣu geheṣu ekaivamukhā sthālī* |
> *asmākaṃ mandabhāgyānāṃ sthālīdvaye tv ekaṃ mukham* ||

649 Following Cowell and Neil's query (Divy 497n2) and Hiraoka (HA 25; HD 57), read *sutāḍitāḥ kṣatāḥ*. Omitted in the Tibetan. Divy 497.10, *sutāḍitākṣatāḥ*. Vaidya (Divy-V 435.11) emends to *sutāḍitāḥ*.

650 Following Cowell and Neil's query (Divy 497n3) and Vaidya (Divy-V 435.15), read *dharmatā*. Divy 497.16, *dharmā*.

651 Following the Tibetan (71b2; 74b7) and Hiraoka (HA 25; HD 57), read *madhyabhāgaḥ*. Divy 497.18, *madhye sarpaḥ*. Or, perhaps, simply emend *madhye* to *madhyaḥ*.

652 Divy 497.19, *hilimām*. Edgerton (BHSD) explains that the term is "unknown; denotes a good kind of broth or liquid food." The Tibetan (71b2; 74b7) reads *pho sha'i khu sha*. Hiraoka (HA 25; HD 57), following the Tibetan, suggests "hot" (*ahimām*) and suggests the same at Divy 497.20, 497.22, and 497.26.

653 Divy 497.23, *tasya vāṣpeṇa paṭale sphuṭite*. Or perhaps, "The steam [from the broth] dissolved the film over his eyes." Pliny, in his Natural History (1963: xxix, 38), recounts the various ways that a viper can be used to cure eye diseases, including one remedy that involves cutting off a viper's head and tail and then boiling the body to make a kind of broth. Perhaps the understanding in the *Divyāvadāna* is that the snake catcher made the snake angry before cutting off its head and tail so that the snake's poison would become medicine. This would have undermined the efforts of the twelve women to kill their father-in-law. My thanks to Dieter Maue for this reference.

654 The Tibetan (71b4; 75a3) reads, "They reflected, 'May he die quickly.' Having reflected like this, they said, 'Father, take some more. It will give you relief.'"

655 Following Speyer (1902: 128–29) and Hiraoka (HA 25; HD 57), read *parīttenāvavādenāvodya*. Divy 498.12, *parīttenāvavādena codya*. Vaidya (Divy-V 435.29–30) reads *parīttenāvādenācodya*.

656 Dieter Maue (2010) has critically reedited the following section of the story (Divy 254.3–262.6), making use of Sanskrit-Uyghur bilingual manuscript fragments as well as the Tibetan. My thanks to him for sharing his work and his insights.

657 Divy 498.17, *bhūtabhūtam* (*sic* mss.). The standard expression reads *bhūtapūrvam* (Divy 57.9, 62.7, 73.24, etc.). The Tibetan (72a2; 75b2) here reads likewise.

658 The standard formula (Divy 87.15–16, 301.7, etc.) reads "and from coupling, enjoying himself, and making love" (*krīḍato ramamāṇasya paricārayataḥ*). The Tibetan (72a3; 75b3) concurs.

659 Divy 498.21, *ṛṇaharaḥ*. Hiraoka (HA 25; HD 57) emends to *ṛṇadharaḥ*. Following the standard formula (Divy 87.18, 254.11, 301.10, etc.) and the Tibetan (72a3; 75b3), Hiraoka also adds *dhanahārakaś ca*. Maue (2010: 599§1; cf. 1996: 36, no. 33) adds *dhanaharaḥ*.

660 Following the Tibetan (72a5–6; 75b5), add *bhaktācchādāḥ parikṣīṇāḥ*. Divy 498.26 (omitted). Cowell and Neil (Divy 498n4) query *prayojanam*. That is, "If my wife needs food and clothing..."

661 Divy 499.5, *śrutam āhitaḥ* (*sic* mss.). Cowell and Neil (Divy 499n2) query *asmābhiḥ*. Also possible is [*asmākam*] *śrutam āhitaḥ*. Omitted in the Tibetan (72a8; 76a1). Cf. Hiraoka 2007: ii, 379n256 and Maue 2010: 600n30.

662 Divy 499.12, *vināsitaḥ* (*sic* mss.). Hiraoka (HA 25; HD 57), following the Tibetan (72b2; 76a3), suggests *vikraye vināśitaḥ*. Maue (2010: 600§3; cf. 615, nos. 34–36) reads *trir api... artho vināśitaḥ*, and he (2010: 606§3) offers this translation: "Dem war von einem anderen Mann <beim Handel>zwei-, dreimal <das Vermögen> geschädigt worden." In other words, the merchant, thrice-bankrupted from bad business deals, takes the boy to task for requesting a handout. Or, more creatively, one might read *prayāsaḥ vināsitaḥ*. That is, "his efforts were rejected." Cowell and Neil (Divy 499n3) query *niṣkāsitaḥ*.

663 Following the Tibetan (72b2–3; 76a3–4) and Maue (2010: 600§3; cf. 616–17, nos. 34–36), read *tasya ca gṛhāt preṣyadārikā saṃkāratalasyopari mṛtamūṣikāṃ hitvā prayacchati cchorayitum*. Hiraoka (HA 25; HD 57) reads *sthāpayitvā* instead of *hitvā* and emends *prayacchati* to *pragacchati*. Divy 499.13–14, *tasya ca gṛhāt preṣyadārikāyāḥ* (mss., *-dārikā*) *saṃkāratalasyopari* (mss. ABC, *-tarasyopari*; ms. D, *saṃkāratasyopapari*) *mṛtamūṣikāṃ dṛṣṭvā* (mss., *-kā dṛṣṭā*) *prayacchati cchorayitum*. The Tibetan reads *de'i khyim nas bu mo mngag gzhug mas phyag dar gyi steng du byi ba'i ro zhig bzhag ste phyir byung nas dor bar brtsams pa dang*. Cowell and Neil (Divy 710) note parallels with *Jātaka* no. 4 and *Kathāsaritsāgara* i, 6.

664 Maue (2010: 600§3; cf. 617, nos. 34–36), following the Uyghur, adds *tāṃ dṛṣṭvā*—that is, "having seen the mouse." Divy 499.15 (omitted).

665 Following the Tibetan (72b4; 76a5) and Hiraoka (HA 25; HD 57–58), read *saṃkāro cchoritaḥ*. Cf. Divy 585.9, *saṃkāraś choritaḥ*. Maue (2010: 600§3) reads likewise. Divy 499.20, *saṃkāre choritaḥ* (mss., *samkāracchoritaḥ*). Vaidya (Divy-V 436.21) emends to *saṃkāre choritā*.

666 Divy 499.24, *kalikāyā* (mss. AB, *kalli-*; ms. D, *kaśi*). Maue (2010: 600§4) reads *kalikayā*.

667 Following the mss. (Divy 499n13), Edgerton (BHSD), and Hiraoka (HA 25; HD 58), read *kalāvānām*. Divy 499.25, *kalāyānām*. According to *Mahāvyutpatti* 5652, *kalāva* beans are the same as *kulattha* beans. Here, however, *kalāva* seems to reference beans in general and not a particular kind of lentil.

668 Following Vaidya (Divy-V 436.26), the Tibetan (72b6; 76a7), and Hiraoka (HA 25; HD 58), read *bhrāṣṭre*. Divy 500.1, *bhraṣṭre* (mss. BC, *braṣṭe*; mss. AD, *draṣṭe*).

669 Following Edgerton (BHSD, s.v. *vardhanīya*), read *vardhanīyaṃ pūrṇam*. Divy 500.1, *vardhinīyasya pūrṇam* (ex conj.; ms. A, *vardhanīyagṛhya*; ms. B, *vardhanīya-pūrṇagṛhyāsmāt*; ms. C, *vardhanīyapūrṇagṛhyasmāt*; ms. D, *vardhanīyasya pūrṇaṃ kṛtvā*). Hiraoka (HA 25; HD 58), following the Tibetan (72b6; 76a7), reads *vardhanikāṃ pūrṇām*. Maue (2010: 600–601§5; cf. 619, no. 39.1) reads *vardhanīṃ pūrṇam*.

670 Following Speyer (1902: 357) and Maue (2010: 601§5), read *pātum*. Divy 500.6, *pātam* (*sic* mss. ACD; ms. D, *pāyam*). Hiraoka (HA 25; HD 58), following the Tibetan (72b8; 76b2), reads *pāyitam*.

671 Divy 500.7, *bhāgineya*. More literally, "nephew."

672 Divy 500.7, *kāṣṭhānām*. Hiraoka (HA 25; HD 58), following Speyer (1902: 357), reads *kāṣṭhārthī*. Also possible is *kāṣṭhānām arthāya*. The Tibetan (72b8; 76b2) reads *shing thur 'gro'o*.

673 Divy 500.8–9, *kiyatā āgamiṣyasi*. Cowell and Neil (Divy 710) offer this translation: "He replies, 'I am going for wood'; They answer, 'We went early and only got so much; starting so late, how much can you hope to get?'" Following the Tibetan (72b8; 76b2), I read *kiyatā* in the sense of *kiyatā kālena*. Cf. Maue 2010: 606n94.

674 Divy 500.10, *kāṣṭhamūlikā*. Maue (2010: 601§5; cf. 619, no. 39.2) reads *kāṣṭhapūlikā*. Likewise, at Divy 500.15, Maue (2010: 601§6) reads *kāṣṭhapūlikām* for *kāṣṭhamūlikām*.

675 Divy 500.12–13, *te kāṣṭhahārakās tathaiva tena kalāyaiḥ saṃvibhaktāḥ*. I read this in the sense of *te kāṣṭhahārakebhyaḥ tathaiva tena kalāyāḥ saṃvibhaktāḥ*.

676 Divy 500.18, *piṇḍitamūlyam*. Here the Sanskrit and English share the same idiom: "a payment" (*mūlyam*) that is "lumped together" (*piṇḍita*).

677 Divy 500.21–22, *etat pratikruṣṭataram bāṇijyānāṃ yaduta kāṣṭhabāṇijyam* (mss., *-nijyām*). The text doesn't explain why the boy thinks that this profitable business is "terrible" (*pratikruṣṭatara*)—or perhaps more accurately, "despicable" or "vile." The thought simply comes to the boy, and he acts on it. Perhaps the message here is that money brings greed or elitism, or that with money comes a sense of dissatisfaction.

678 Divy 500.23, *ukkarikāpaṇam*. Edgerton (BHSD) takes *ukkarikā* as "a kind of sweetmeat." The Tibetan (73a5; 76b7) reads *bza' bca'i zo*. Perhaps, "ration shop" or "grocery store."

679 Following the Tibetan (73a6; 76b7–77a1) and Hiraoka (HA 25; HD 58), read *tena prabhūtaḥ*. Divy 500.25, *tatprabhūtaḥ*.

680 Following the Hiraoka (HA 25; HD 58), read *tasya tena prabhūtaḥ*. Divy 501.1, *tasya prabhūtaḥ*.

681 Following Divy 500.23–25 (modified accordingly). Cf. the Tibetan (73a7–8; 77a2–3) and Maue 2010: 607n96. Divy 501.2, "as before" (*pūrvavat*).

682 Divy 501.13, *kiṃ kathayata*. Read as *kathayatha*. Cf. Edgerton 1993, vol. 1: 132, §26.11.

683 Maue (2010: 602§9; cf. 620, no. 45), following the Uyghur, adds *tair uparataiḥ*. That is, "after their deaths." Divy 501.14 (omitted).

684 Following the Tibetan (73b5; 77b2), Divy 4.12, 34.12, etc., and Hiraoka (HA 25; HD 58), add *sārthavāhena*. Divy 501.23 (omitted).

685 Following the Tibetan (73b6; 77b3) and Divy 34.16, add *sārthavāhaḥ*. Divy 501.27 (omitted).

686 Maue (2010: 602§11; cf. 620–622, nos. 46–50.1), following the Uyghur, adds

āhā<ra>ka(ḥ) nigrāhaka(ḥ), kelāyika(ḥ) ud[gr]āhaka(ḥ) karna[dhāraḥ] . . . Divy 502.1 (omitted). It is likewise omitted in the Tibetan. As Edgerton (BHSD, s.v. *pauruṣeya*) notes, this a list of the five kinds of crewmen on a ship. These terms are a little obscure; Maue offers excellent glosses.

687 Following the Tibetan (74a1; 77b6), Divy 5.11, 332.7–8, and Hiraoka (HA 25; HD 58), read *samudrataṭam*. Divy 502.1, *-samudram avatarann* (mss. ACD, *-taram*; ms. B, *-tarem*). This sentence appears to be an abbreviated form of the standard passage: "He passed through marketplaces, hamlets, villages, towns, and trading centers, one after another, until he arrived at the banks of the great ocean" (Divy 5.10–11). Cf. the Tibetan (73b7–74a1; 77b4–6).

688 Divy 502.3–3, *kathaya kathaya*. Maue (2010: 603§12; cf. 622, no. 51), following the Uyghur, reads *udghoṣaya udghoṣaya*.

689 Following Cowell and Neil's query (Divy 502n4), Divy 229.11, Edgerton (BHSD, s.v. *saubhāsika*), and Maue (2010: 603§12), read *ūrdhvagāminīm*. Divy 502.11–12, *mūrdhagāminīm*.

690 Following Divy 502.17, 229.19 and Hiraoka (HA 25; HD 58), read *udghoṣaya*. Divy 502.15, *ghoṣaya*.

691 Following the Tibetan (74a6; 78a4), Speyer (1902: 358), Hiraoka (HA 25; HD 58), and Maue (2010: 603§13), read *avarṇam*. Divy 502.16, *varṇam*. Cf. Divy 229.19.

692 Divy 502.20, *kumbhīrabhayaṃ śiśumārabhayam*. India is home to three kinds of crocodiles: the mugger crocodile, the gharial, and the saltwater crocodile.

693 Divy 502.21–22, *nīlaiḥ sitaiḥ*. The Tibetan (74a8–74b1; 78a6) agrees with the Sanskrit. Speyer (1902: 358) suggests *nīlaiḥ śītaiḥ*. That is, "with dark sails." Hiraoka (HA 25; HD 58) concurs. Maue (2010: 603–604n80), following Schlingloff (1982: 53), offers no emendation but nevertheless construes a similar meaning by taking *sita* as "white [sail]." The parallel at Divy 229.25 reads "wearing dark clothes" (*nīlavāsasaḥ*).

694 Following Divy 229.25, the Tibetan (74a8–74b1; 78a6), Huber (1906: 34n1), and Hiraoka (HA 25; HD 58), read *dhanahāriṇaḥ*. Divy 502.22, *vanacāriṇaḥ*. That is, "forest dwelling," although one expects pirates to live on ships in the ocean.

695 Divy 502.23, *priyam* (mss. AB, *priya*; ms. D, *priyayāt-*) *atmānaṃ parityaktvā* (ms. A, *-tyaktvo*; mss. BC, *-tyaktā*; ms. D, *ātmāna parityakto*) . . . *mahāsamudram*. This seems to be corrupt. Hiraoka (HA 26; HD 58–59), following the Tibetan (74b1–2; 78a7–b1) and Divy 229.25–28, suggests *parityaktum vyavasitaḥ*. Maue (2010: 604§13) reads *priyata ātmānaṃ parityaktum*.

696 Divy 503.1, *dvitri* (ms. A, omitted; ms. C, *dvitrī*). Maue (2010: 604§14) reads *dvi(tīyāṃ) tṛ(tīyām)*.

697 Divy 503.1–3, *yatas tad vahanaṃ mahākarṇadhārasaṃdhānabalavadvāyusaṃpreritaṃ mahāmegha iva saṃprasthitaḥ*. Instead of *-saṃdhānabalavad-*, Hiraoka (HA 26; HD 59), following the parallel at Divy 230.4–6 and the Tibetan (74b3; 78b2), reads *-saṃpreritaṃ balavad-*. One would also expect *saṃprasthitam* instead of *saṃprasthitaḥ*, so that it would agree with *vahanam*. Cf. Maue 2010: 609n115.

698 Following Maue (2010: 604§17), read *agre dhanikam*. Divy 503.20, *agradhanikam*. Perhaps, "main creditor." Cf. Maue 2010: 610nn126–28.

699 Divy 503.22, *dhanikaḥ kṛtaḥ*. Maue (2010: 604§17; cf. 611n129) reads *dhanikakṛtaḥ*.

700 Divy 504.2, *vānayeti* (*sic* mss.). Cowell and Neil (Divy 504n1) query *anayeti*. Hiraoka

(HA 26; HD 59), following the Tibetan (75a5; 79a5), reads *mā vārayeti*. Perhaps, "Who could turn Mūṣikāhairaṇyaka away?"

701 Following the Tibetan (75a7; 79a7) and Divy 498.25–26, add *prabhūtāḥ*. Divy 504.7 (omitted). Perhaps the money that Mūṣikāhairaṇyaka's father had entrusted to the guildmaster is now being reconfigured as a kind of bride price.

702 Following Speyer (1902: 128–29) and Hiraoka (HA 26; HD 59), read *parīttenāvavādenāvodya*. Divy 504.12, *parīttenāvavādenācodya* (ms. A, *-cādya*). Cowell and Neil (Divy 504n4) query *-vādya*.

703 Following Speyer (1902: 128–29) and Hiraoka (HA 26; HD 59), read *parīttenāvavādenāvodya*. Divy 504.13–14, *parīttenāvavādenāvādya* (*sic* mss.).

704 Following Divy 54.2–4, 131.7–9, 191.12–14 (modified accordingly), the Tibetan (75b3–4; 79b4–5), and Hiraoka (HA 26; HD 59), add *upacitāni labdhasambhārāṇi pariṇatapratyayāny oghavat pratyupasthitāny avaśyaṃbhāvīni | panthakena karmāṇi kṛtāny upacitāni ko 'nyaḥ pratyanubhaviṣyati*. Divy 504.19 (omitted). This is part of a standard passage that is not abridged elsewhere in the text. I am assuming that the missing text was elided by accident, so I have restored it.

705 Following Divy 54.7, 191.17, and Hiraoka (HA 26; HD 59), add *karmaṇi kṛtāny upacitāni*. Divy 504.21 (omitted). Cf. Divy 131.11–12 and 584.18–19, which reads only *karmaṇi kṛtāni*. This is also part of a standard passage and seems to have been inadvertently omitted.

706 Divy 505.1, *viṃśatibhir bhikṣusahasraiḥ parivāraḥ*. One would expect *parivṛttaḥ* for *parivāraḥ* or, more in the style of the text, *viṃśatibhikṣusahasraparivāraḥ*.

707 Divy 505.3, *tatra mātsaryeṇa*. Hiraoka (HA 26; HD 59), following the Tibetan (75b8; 80a2), reads *dharmamātsaryeṇa*. That is, "stingy with the dharma."

708 Divy 505.3, *bhūyaḥ* (mss., *bhūmaḥ*). The text seems be missing the rest of the story about the monk who knew the Tripiṭaka.

709 Following the Tibetan (76a1; 80a3), Vaidya (Divy-V 439.24), and Hiraoka (HA 26; HD 59), read *eva*. Divy 505.7, *evam*.

710 Divy 505.9, *jānuṣu baddhvā*. More literally, "bound them at the knees," although pigs don't have knees. The Tibetan (76a1; 80a3) simply notes that he "bound them together."

711 Divy 505.10, *bāḍitā* (mss. AC, *voḍitā*; ms. B, *vāditā*; ms. D, *voditā*). Edgerton (BHSD) reads *vāḍitā* and understands it as a substitute for *vālitā*. Cowell and Neil (Divy 687) take it to mean "sunk."

712 Following Hiraoka (HA 26; HD 59), read *āpannāḥ*. Divy 505.10, *āpannaḥ*.

713 Divy 505.15–16, *bālukāyāḥ sthalaṃ kṛtvā tatrāvamūrdhakaḥ sthāpitaḥ*. My translation follows the Tibetan (76a3; 80a5). Edgerton (BHSD), however, understands *avamūrdhaka* to mean "with head downward, upside down." As such, one could offer this translation. "Then he made a mound in the sand and stood him there upside down on his head." Edgerton also cites Divy 9.24, but there, too, *avamūrdhaka* is best understood as "face down."

714 Following the Tibetan (76a4–5; 80a6–7) and Hiraoka (HA 26; HD 59), read *yadā*. Divy 505.21, *atha*.

715 Divy 505.22–23, *sa tatrāsaṃjñikam utpādya*. The Tibetan (76a5; 80a7) reads "having generated the meditative absorption of non-consciousness" (*'du shes med pa'i snyoms par 'jug pa bskyed nas* = Skt., <*asaṃjñikasamāpattim utpādya*>).

716 Divy 505.26, *mātsaryeṇa*. Hiraoka (HA 26; HD 59), following the Tibetan (76a6; 80b1), reads *dharmamātsaryeṇa*. That is, "stingy with the dharma."

717 The Tibetan (76b1; 80b2–3) omits this opening passage (Divy 506.1–5) and instead reads as follows: "Monks, without instruction, this and other faults will also prevail. Therefore monks, without instructions one should not meditate, and if someone meditates, he commits a transgression."

718 Something is missing here, as the Buddha never accepts Jīvaka Kumārabhūta's invitation. Here the standard cliché (Divy 81.2–4, 183.9–12, 189.11–13), modified accordingly, would read: "With his silence, the Blessed One accepted the householder Jīvaka Kumārabhūta's invitation. Then, realizing that by his silence the Blessed One had accepted his invitation . . ." The Tibetan (76b6–7; 81a2–3) fills out the passage likewise.

719 Here the standard cliché—see the previous footnote—adds "venerated with his head the feet of the Blessed One."

720 Divy 506.27–28, *yathā te jīvaka kuśalānāṃ dharmāṇāṃ vṛddhir bhavati*. Cf. Divy 236.15–17 and Divy-V 317.28–29.

721 Divy 507.15, *anugantī*. Cowell and Neil (Divy 672) suggest "message" and query *anugantrī*. Edgerton (BHSD) cites the same. I follow the Tibetan (77a8; 81b4), which reads *byug ris* in the sense of "place" or "space."

722 Divy 507.16–17, *vāridhārāṃ na pratigṛhṇāti*. I understand this to mean that the Buddha wouldn't wash his hands and bowl, as he does before a meal. Cf. *Majjhima-nikāya* ii, 138. The Tibetan (77b1; 81b5) reads *chab kyi rgyun*.

723 Following the Tibetan (77b1; 81b5), Vaidya (Divy-V 441.4), and Hiraoka (HA 26; HD 59), read *pratigṛhṇāti*. Divy 507.18, *pratigṛhāṇa* (*sic* mss. AD; ms. B, *-gṛhṇāṇa*; ms. C, *-grihṇāhāṇa*).

724 Divy 507.19, *na tāvad bhikṣusaṃgha iti samagra iti*. Hiraoka (HA 26; HD 59) emends to *na tāvad bhikṣusaṃghaḥ samagra iti*. The Tibetan (77b2; 81b5–6) doesn't indicate the presence of two *iti*.

725 Following Hiraoka (HA 26; HD 59), omit *saṃghaḥ*. Divy 507.20–21, *panthako bhikṣuḥ saṃghaḥ*.

726 Following the Tibetan (77b3; 81b7) and Hiraoka (HA 26; HD 59), read *bahir | na*. Divy 507.24, *bahir na vā* (mss. AC, *bahi vārā*; ms. B, *bahiḥ cārā*; ms. D, *bahicārā*). The Tibetan reads *dge 'dun las phyi rol du gyur pa yin nam | bcom ldan 'das ma lags so*.

727 Divy 507.28, *trayodaśabhikṣuśatāni*. Hiraoka (HA 26; HD 60), following the Tibetan (77b5; 82a2), reads *ardhatrayodaśabhikṣuśatāni*. That is, "1,250 monks."

728 The Tibetan (82a2–3) offers a more detailed account:

The messenger went there and called out, "Panthaka, Panthaka."

Many monks responded, "Over here!"

The man returned and said to Jīvaka Kumāra, "I went there and called out 'Panthaka, Panthaka.' But that place, Kalandaka in the bamboo grove, was filled with monks sitting down just like it was filled with monks sitting down in the past. Then many monks called out, 'Over here!' From among these monks, whom should I address?"

729 Following the Tibetan (77b7; 82a4), *'tsho byed gzhon nus gsos kyis skabs de bcom ldan 'das la gsol ba dang*. Divy 508.3 (omitted).

730 Divy 508.11–13, *dharmatā khalu na tāvat sthavirasthavirāṇāṃ bhikṣūṇāṃ pātrāṇi*

pratigṛhyante (mss., *pratigṛhnante*) *yāvad bhagavataḥ pātrapratigrahī na bhaviṣyati*. Cf. the Tibetan (78a1–2; 82a6–7). See too PTSD, s.v. *pattagāhāpaka*.

731 Jīvaka expects that such a miracle would be performed by a senior monk (i.e., one of the monks next to him in the area of the elders). Panthaka, however, is standing elsewhere, perhaps among the novices.

732 This story bears similarity to the *Kuṇḍakakucchisindhava Jātaka* (*Jātaka* no. 254).

733 Divy 509.8, *aśvājaneyaḥ*. As Edgerton (BHSD, s.v. *ājanya*) explains, "*of noble race, blooded*, primarily of animals, esp. horses; by extension used of men, esp. Buddhas and Bodhisattvas, and very rarely (meaning *noble*) of other, inanimate entities. Tib. (e.g., Mvy 1080, 4769, etc.) regularly renders *cang shes* (*pa*), 'omniscient,' falsely interpreting the word as derived from *jña*, 'know.' In composition, the word in all its forms regularly (not always) follows the noun, e.g., *aśvajāneya*, 'a blooded horse' (orig. perhaps 'a thoroughbred of a horse'?)." Nevertheless, in what follows, this horse shows himself to be quite magical and powerful—a veritable bodhisattva among horses.

734 Divy 509.12, *sa yam eva divasam upādāya*. The Tibetan (78b4; 83a2) reads *de gang gyi nyi ma la byung ba de nyid kyi nyi ma nas*. Hiraoka (HA 26; HD 60), following the Tibetan, reads *divasaṃ jāta* for *divasam*. Cf. Divy 509.8–9.

735 Divy 509.12–13, *saṃcartum api nārabdhāḥ*. Or perhaps, "never again grazed." The Tibetan (78b4; 83a2–3) reads *sna sgra 'byin par yang mi brtson nas*. That is, "no longer whinnied."

736 Divy 509.15–16, *navayavasaṃpannayogyāśanam* (mss., *-āsanam*) *anuprayacchati*. The Tibetan (78b5; 83a3) reads *sbyin par mi byed do*—that is, "he didn't offer" her grass or even water. Hiraoka (HA 26; HD 60), following the Tibetan, reads *nānuprayacchati*.

737 Divy 509.17, *varṣārātryaḥ pratyupasthitāḥ*. Rhys Davids and Stede (PTSD) translate *vassāratta* as "time of rains" (i.e., the rainy season) and cite this passage from the *Divyāvadāna*. It is unclear, though, whether *varṣārātryaḥ* refers to the rainy season proper—roughly June to October—or simply "rain lasting some nights." The former is the more standard reading, but the latter might make better sense in context: "There he found himself in for some nights of rain."

738 Divy 509.18, *kledaṃ gamiṣyanti*. Elsewhere in the *Divyāvadāna*, *kledaṃ* + √*gam* means not simply "to get wet" but also "to go bad" or "to be spoiled" (Divy 505.6–7) and perhaps "to get wet and spoiled" or "to be spoiled from moisture" (Divy 336.25–27). This double meaning seems to apply here as well. Moisture can cause horses's hooves to crack or to develop seedy toe or stone bruises.

739 Following the (78b6; 83a4), Divy 510.7–8, and Hiraoka (HA 26; HD 60), read *tasya tatraiva*. Divy 509.19, *sa tasyaiva*.

740 Following the Tibetan (78b7–8; 83a6) and Hiraoka (HA 26; HD 60), read *tasyoccalitasya*. Divy 509.24, *tasmāc calitasya*. This sentence is obscure, if not corrupt, meaning something like "He took a lump of clay from where [the caravan leader] had walked and stood before him" (*tasmāc calitasya mṛtpiṇḍaṃ* [mss. ABC, *mṛtapiṇḍam*] *gṛhītvopasthitaḥ*). The Tibetan (78b7–8; 83a6) reads *rdza mkhan des ded dpon 'phags pa'i mdun du*. Perhaps better, although reading against the Tibetan, is "a lump of potter's clay from [home?]" (*tasmāc chilpasya mṛtpiṇḍaṃ*). There are many differences between the Sanskrit and Tibetan versions of this story; like Hiraoka (HD 60), I do my best at "keeping changes to a minimum."

741 Read *priyo 'sti*. Divy 510.1, *priyo 'si*.

742 Following the Tibetan (79a3; 83b2), Speyer (1902: 358), and Hiraoka (HA 26; HD 60), read *pacyamānānām*. Divy 510.8, *pakvamānānām*.

743 Divy 510.18, *kuṭim* (*sic* mss.). Following Edgerton (BHSD), although this is the only citation for the term. Perhaps, "fodder." The Tibetan (79a6; 83b5) reads *sran phub*.

744 Divy 510.20, *ca bahu-*. Hiraoka (HA 26; HD 60), following the standard cliché (Divy 62.8–9, 62.12–13, 131.16–17, etc.) and the Tibetan (79a6; 83b5), reads *ca kṣemaṃ ca subhikṣaṃ cākīrṇabahu-*.

745 Divy 510.21, *sāmantarājyaiḥ*. Judging by what follows, these kings were subsidiary potentates who paid homage and allegiance to King Brahmadatta, to whom they were subordinate. With the death of King Brahmadatta's thoroughbred horse—the veritable marker of the king's royal power—these kings could then assert their dominance over Brahmadatta and demand that he pay them tribute or remain under house arrest in Vārāṇasī (or be formally arrested if he left the city).

746 Read *udyānāṃ vā te nirgatasya kaṇṭhake 'nvavarodhya ānayiṣyāmaḥ*. Divy 510.22–34, *udyānāṃ vā te nirgatakaṇṭake 'nuvarodhya* (mss. AC, *-rādhvā*; ms. D, *-rodhā*) *ānayiṣyāmaḥ*. This is corrupt, and it resists any simple fix. Cowell and Neil (Divy 710) make this suggestion: "[Divy] 510, 22–23; i.e. the subject kings, hearing of the death of the royal horse, sent a message that Brahmadatta must either remit their tribute or consent to be imprisoned (qu. for *anvavarodhya*?) in a garden as a *roi fainéant*." The Tibetan (79a8–b1; 83b7) reads *yang na ni bā rā ṇa sī'i phyi rol gyi skyed mos tshal du ma byung shig | de lta mi byed na gnya' ba nas btags te bkri'o*. Hiraoka (HA 26; HD 60), following the Tibetan, and again "keeping changes to a minimum," suggests *mā nirgatavyaṃ kaṇṭake 'nubadhya* for *te nirgatakaṇṭake 'nuvarodhya*.

747 Divy 511.2–3, *ājāneyās te 'śvāḥ*. More literally, "These horses are thoroughbreds," but from context it is clear that they were trained by—or, at least, were in the presence of—a thoroughbred horse but aren't thoroughbreds themselves. Cf. the Tibetan (79b3; 84a2).

748 Following the Tibetan (79b3–4; 84a3) and Hiraoka (HA 26; HD 60), read *vaḍabām* (or, *aśvāvaḍavām*). Divy 511.3, *sārthavāham*. That is, "caravan leader."

749 Divy 511.7, *pūjitake*. Previously (Divy 509.16) the town was called Pūjita, and it is again later in the story (Divy 514.21). It isn't clear here whether the town is referred to as both Pūjita and Pūjitaka, as Edgerton (BHSD) seems to suggest, or whether the *ka* suffix might be used in the sense of the dimimutive (i.e., "the small town of Pūjita") or the pejorative (i.e., "the Podunk town of Pūjita").

750 Following Cowell and Neil's query (511n8) and Edgerton (BHSD, s.v. *kaṭi*), read *kuṭi sakaṇṭaṃ*. Divy 511.19, *kaṭi sakaṇṭaṃ*.

751 Divy 511.23, *āgatvā*. According to standard Sanskrit grammar, one would expect *āgatya*.

752 Following the Tibetan (80a4; 84b3) and Hiraoka (HA 26; HD 60), read *vā neti*. Divy 512.1, *dhārayati* (mss. AB, *dhāvayati*). Perhaps, "What does he know? This is a thoroughbred horse that supports him!"

753 Following the Tibetan (80a4; 84b4) and Divy 511.24, omit *suvarṇalakṣaṃ*. Divy 512.4, *yāvad vā suvarṇalakṣaṃ dakṣiṇena sakthnākariṣyati* (mss., *dakṣiṇe vānuśaknā-*).

754 Following Vaidya (Divy-V 443.28), read *mandurāyāṃ pratiṣṭhāpitaḥ*. Divy 512.10, *mathurāyāṃ pratiṣṭhāpitaḥ* (ms. A, *duriṣṭhāp-*; ms. B, *puriṣṭhāp-*). Hiraoka (HA

26; HD 60), following the Tibetan (80a7; 84b6) and *Mahāvyutpatti* 5610, reads *aśvaśālāyām*.

755 Divy 512.10, *paramayogyāśanam* (ms. D, *yavama-*; mss., *-āsanam*). Hiraoka (HA 26; HD 60), following Divy 513.7 and the Tibetan (80a7; 84b6), reads *yavasayogyāśanam*. That is, "nutritious (i.e., appropriate) foods mixed with barley."

756 These verses are quite opaque and corrupt. The Tibetan is helpful in deciphering them, but it often preserves readings that are sufficiently divergent such that the Sanskrit remains mysterious. As such, my translation of the verses is provisional.

757 Following Speyer (1902: 359), Vaidya (Divy-V 443.31), and Hiraoka (HA 26; 60), read *ghaṭikarasya*. Divy 512.13, *ghaṭīkarasya*.

758 Following the Tibetan (80a8; 84b7) and Hiraoka (HA 26; HD 60–61), read *vāridhānyaviprayuktām*. Divy 512.13, *iha vidhairya* (ms. A, *vucidhairya*; ms. C, *vudhairya*; ms. D, *ahaivaṃdhairya*) *viprayuktaḥ*. Cowell and Neil (Divy 512n9) query *yavārjavadhairya-*. The Tibetan reads *gang tshe ran chas chu med pa'i | rdza mkhan bres na*.

759 Divy 512.15, *-śirā-*. Speyer (1902: 359) suggests *-sirā-*.

760 Following the Tibetan (80a8; 84b7), read *mātra*. Divy 512.15, *-gātra*.

761 Divy 512.16, *na carasi bahumatas tadarthe* (ms. I, *tad ardha*). Speyer (1902: 359) suggests emending to the vocative *bahumata*. The Tibetan (80a9; 84b7) reads *mang po khyod la bsams ma gyur*.

762 Divy 512.16–17, *māsīd iha hi cara yānasahasrapūrṇayāyī* (ms. H, *-pūrṇayāḥ*). Following the Tibetan (80a9; 85a1), Cowell and Neil's query (Divy 512n12), and Hiraoka (HA 26; HD 61), read *-pūrvayāyī*.

763 Divy 512.18, *hayavasanam* (mss., *-vasam*; likewise, ms. H, *-vasam*) *idaṃ tṛṣāpanītam*. This is obscure. Vaidya (Divy-V 444.5) emends to *hyavasanam*. Cf. the Tibetan (80a9; 85a1).

764 Following ms. I, the Tibetan (80a9; 85a1), Speyer (1902: 359), Vaidya (Divy-V 444.6), and Hiraoka (HA 26; HD 61), read *sādhu pṛṣṭhaḥ*. Divy 512.19, *sādhupṛṣṭhaḥ*.

765 Divy 512.20–21, *paramayavārjavadhairyasaṃprayuktaḥ*. Following ms. I, the Tibetan (80a9; 85a1), Speyer (1902: 359), and Hiraoka (HA 27; HD 61), read *-javā-* for *-yavā-*. Or, perhaps better, read *paramajavaḥ ārjavadhairyasaṃprayuktaḥ*. That is, "The swift horse, although endowed with integrity and fortitude, became impatient..."

766 Divy 512.20, *tam akathayad amarṣitaḥ* (mss., *-ta*) *sakopam*. Here I am tempted to read against the Sanskrit. Judging from what follows, it doesn't seem that the horse "speaks angrily" but that he is "on the verge of speaking out of anger" and then composes himself. The Tibetan (80a9–b1; 85a1–2) remarks that he is "angry" then "pacified" and then he speaks.

767 Divy 512.24–25, *tvam iha vidhihitapradābhimānī* (mss. CD, *-mānāṃ;* ms. I, *-māno?* or *-mānā?*) *na ca vihito bhavato yathāvad asmi*. The Tibetan (85a2–3) reads "Here you know the virtues I have. / It isn't that you don't know me as I am" (*'dir khyod kho boi'i yon tan de nyid shes | kho bo ji bzhin khyod kyis ma rig min*).

768 Divy 513.1–2, *nidhanam aham iha prayāyam* (ms. C, *prajāyam*) *āśu na ca viduṣāya tareya pūrvyām* (ms. I, *pūrvā*). As Cowell and Neil (Divy 513n1) note, "This line is corrupt." The term *pūrvyām* is also unexpected. My translation is based in part on the Tibetan. The Tibetan (85a2–3), which is also a little unclear, reads: "If I am insulted by a wise person, it is better / if I quickly die here and not wander the earth" (*mkhas*

pas brnyas nas ste nga mi rgyu zhing | kho bo 'dir ni myur du shi yang bla). See Hiraoka 2007: ii, 394–95n481.

769 Divy 513.3, *suciram api hi na sajjanāvamānaḥ*. After *na*, Cowell and Neil (513n2) suggest omitting or reading *durjanā-*. As is, I read it in the sense of "a not-good person."

770 Following Cowell and Neil's query (Divy 513n3), read *saumya so 'vamānaḥ*. Divy 513.5–6, *nāvamānaḥ*. Cf. ms. I, 274a6.

771 Divy 513.8, *kāsyānupūrvī kṛtā*. I follow the Tibetan (80b3; 85a4) and read against tense. One might translate this more literally as "What procedures were followed for him?" but the groom doesn't answer that question in his reply.

772 Divy 513.11, *tāmrapaṭṭair badhyate*. The Tibetan (80b4; 85a5) reads *zangs ma'i glegs*. This is ambiguous. At Divy 106.13, I translate *tāmrapaṭṭa* as "copper strips," although I mention (DS 424n502) that it could also mean "pieces of tāmra wood" or "pieces of copper-colored cloth." Handurukande (1988: 15) translates the term as "copper slabs." At Divy 483.1–3, *paṭṭa* refers to the fine cloth that is used as a crown or diadem. It is royal insignia, and it is "tied," as is the *paṭṭa* in the present case. Nevertheless, my sense is that the *tāmrapaṭṭa* here is, idiomatically speaking, equivalent to a "red carpet." It is part of a royal treatment—or even coronation ceremony—as is made clear by the king in what follows (Divy 513.16).

773 Divy 513.15, *lakṣaṇena*. I follow Edgerton (BHSD). Cowell and Neil (Divy 689) suggest "spoon." The Tibetan (80b5; 85a6) reads *chol zangs*. Perhaps, "tub" or "bed pan." My sense is that it was a premodern pooper scooper.

774 Following the Tibetan (80b8; 85b2), Divy 513.10–11, and Hiraoka (HA 27; HD 61), add *sthāpyate sa pradeśaḥ*. Divy 513.19 (omitted).

775 Following the Tibetan (81a1; 85b2–3) and Hiraoka (HA 27; HD 61), read *tam anunayati ca pārthivaḥ sasūtaḥ paramasugandhivilepanānudhārī | madhuramadhurakṛtāntarānurāgā nṛpamahiṣī turagottamāya dattā*. Hiraoka (HD 61) explains, "On basis of Tib. and Chi., I take this as verse. The meter seems to be a mixture of *kṣamā* (the first half) and *praharṣiṇī* (the second half)." The Tibetan reads *sa bdag 'dul sbyong bcas pa de la chags || shin tu dri zhim byug pa mchog 'chang zhing || sa bdag btsun mo ji dngar bzang chas kyis*. Divy 513.24–26, *tam anunayati pārthivaḥ | sasṛtaparamasugandhivilepanānudhārī madhuramadhurakṛtāntarānurāgā* (ms. A, *-nānunāgo*; ms. B, *-nonugango*) *nṛpamahiṣī turagottamāya dattā* (mss., *datte*).

Here the queen is given to the horse as a kind of bride, and she is a willing participant in this coronation/betrothal for she feels, quite literally, "sweet, sweet love inside." For this one week of equine protocol, the horse is the "true" king—as the king himself acknowledged—and the king, it seems, is a temporary cuckold.

776 Following the Tibetan (81a1–2; 85b3) and Hiraoka (HA 27; HD 61), read *rājñaḥ udyānabhūmīṃ nirgantukāmasya*. Divy 513.26–27, *rājñā | udyānabhūmīṃ nirgantukāmo 'sya*. The Tibetan reads *rgyal po skyed mos tshal gyi sar 'gro bar 'dod pa la*.

777 Divy 514.6, *nālikāyām*. Following Edgerton (BHSD) and Agrawala 1966: 73.

778 Divy 514.14–15, *jīvitam anuprayacchati*. The horse has "given life back" to the king and "given his life" to him as well.

779 For translations, see Tatelman 2005: 310–423 and Hiraoka 2007: ii, 398–465. For Pāli and Sanskrit parallels, see *Suttanipāta* vv. 835–47 (cf. Hoernle 1916); *Dhammapada-aṭṭhakathā* i, 199.6–228.7, and iii, 193.3–195.4 [cf. Divy 515.13–515.4]; *Jātaka* no. 387 [cf. Divy 521.10–523.3] and no. 196 [cf. Divy 523.9–528.19]; and *Mahāvastu*

ii, 83.17–88.18 [cf. Divy 521.10–523.3], iii, 67.17–90.10 and 286.16–300.9 [cf. Divy 523.9–528.19]. The corresponding Tibetan can be found at P 1032 *te* 158b4–188b7 and D 3 *ña* 170a5–202a6. Naomi Appleton's (2006) work on Siṃhala is also very helpful, as is Benjamin Bogen's (2014) discussion of Tāmradvīpa. For more, see Hiraoka 2007: ii, 435; HD 61; and Grey 2000: 406, 465–67.

Although "The Story of Mākandika" and "The Story of Rūdrāyaṇa" are separate stories in this collection, elsewhere they form part of the same narrative. As Huber (1906: 3; cited in Waldschmidt 1973: 367) notes, "these two avadānas are only one in reality; the compiler of the *Divyāvadāna* tore the original unity in two pieces and reversed the order of the two parts, leaving a gap in between them corresponding to the six pages in the Chinese text." These stories appear in the *Mūlasarvāstivada-vinaya* as an introduction to *pātayantika* rule no. 82.

780 Perhaps, "Resident of Mākandī." The Tibetan reads *ma du*.

781 Perhaps, "Resident of Sākala." That is, modern-day Sialkot in Pakistan. Cf. Upreti 1995: 23. The Tibetan reads *bur ma*.

782 Divy 515.19, *jātīmahī* (*sic* mss.) *saṃvṛttā yāvaj* (mss. ACD, *yā jā-;* ms. B, *rājā-*) *jāta-mahaṃ kṛtvā*. Hiraoka (HA 27; HD 61), following the standard cliché (Divy 3.5–6, 301.8, etc.), emends to *jātāyā jātīmahaṃ kṛtvā*.

783 Read *bhū ratnabhāsaṃtatir asti tasya pragacchataḥ*. My reading is based on Cowell and Neil's query (Divy 516n5), *bhūratnabhāsaṃtatir asti tasya pragacchataḥ*. Tatelman (2005: 314.6, 315) follows their suggestion and offers this translation: "Being the jewel-on-earth, he leaves a trail of radiance where he walks." Divy 516.26, *bhūratnabhā santi tasya pragacchataḥ*. Hiraoka (HA 27; HD 61), following the Tibetan (159b1; 171a3–4), reads *sā bhūmir atyānamate ca*. That is, "the earth sinks low." Yet, as he notes, "Here Tib. and Chi. preserve a different tradition from the Skt." This discrepancy, which occurs throughout the story, makes it difficult to "correct" the Sanskrit based on either of those sources. The Tibetan reads "When he presses on the earth, it sinks low, and when he lifts the earth, it rises up." See too Divy 549.19.

784 Divy 516.26–27, *atyunnamate na caiva*. This is peculiar, unless one follows the Tibetan for the first part of the verse. Vaidya (Divy-V 446.30) flags it with a question mark. Tatelman (2005: 315) translates it, quite creatively, as "And it is ever perfectly level."

785 Following Divy 517.11, 517.22, etc., the Tibetan (159b1; 171a4), Hiraoka (HA 27; HD 61), and Tatelman (2005: 314.8), read *bhartā*. Divy 516.28, *bhaktāṃ*. That is, "He won't accept a maiden as a devotee" (*nāsau bhaktāṃ bhajate kumārikām*). As noted elsewhere (Rotman 2009: 139), "Mākandika's wife refers to their daughter as *kumārikā*, an affectionate, diminutive, and even desexualizing term that in the voice of a mother might be translated as 'sweet little girl.'"

786 Divy 517.1, *tvam*. Cowell and Neil (Divy 517n1) query *tvaṃ mā gamo* to extend the meter.

787 Divy 517.2, *saced drutasamadhikṛtaṃ* (ms. D, *-adhikam*) *bhaviṣyati*. Here I follow Edgerton (BHSD, s.v. *samadhikṛta*). Hiraoka (HA 27; HD 62), following the Tibetan (159b2; 171a5), emends to *vratam upāyahṛtam*. Cf. Divy 519.1, *druta-samadhikṛtam* (mss., *drutam upadhikṛtam*). The Tibetan reads *brtul zhugs thabs kyis blangs gyur na*. Also possible, with a very minor emendation, would be *saced rutaṃ samadhikṛtaṃ bhaviṣyati*; perhaps, "if things happen the way I have said."

788 Divy 517.10, *pādato gatā*. Here I follow Tatelman 2005: 317. I would expect this to mean "broken at the legs," but that only makes sense for a raised bed (e.g. Divy 12.16–17), not one made of strewn grass. Hoernle (1916: 724) translates this as "trodden by his foot." The Sanskrit fragment of the *Suttanipāta* that Hoernle analyzes (1916: 729) reads here *avakṛṣṭa*, which agrees with the Pāli recension that preserves *avakaḍḍita*.

789 Following Divy 517.1–3, 517.12–13, etc. Divy 517.24, "as before" (*pūrvavat*).

790 Divy 517.25–26, *aśrauṣīn . . . śuśrāva*. Hiraoka (HA 27; HD 62) suggests deleting *śuśrāva*, as "the repetition of the same verb is unnecessary."

791 Following the Tibetan (160a2; 171b5), read *brahmā-*. Cf. Divy 483.1. Divy 518.3–4, *brāhmaṇa-*. Otherwise, one could read *brāhmaṇa* separately as a vocative. Tatelman (2005: 319) translates this as "with a voice like a brahmin's kettledrum."

792 Following Divy 517.1–3, 517.12–13, etc. Divy 518.7, "as before" (*pūrvavat*).

793 Divy 518.14–15, *yugamātradarśī*. More literally, "seeing only a yoke's length before him." Cf. *Buddhacarita* 10.13.

794 Following Divy 517.1–3, 517.12–13, etc. Divy 518.18, "as before" (*pūrvavat*).

795 Divy 518.22–23, *yathāsya kāle sthita eva gacchataḥ*. Hiraoka (HA 27; HD 62), following the Tibetan (160a8; 172a4), reads *kāye*. Cowell and Neil (Divy 518n4) query *sthitir*, and Tatelman (2005: 320.12) emends accordingly.

796 Divy 519.3, *vaśiṣṭho ṣīramaunalāyanā*. Cowell and Neil (Divy 519n2) and Vaidya (Divy-V 448.28) both consider this corrupt. Presumably these are names of exemplary men not deluded by sensual pleasures. Uśīra could refer to Uśanas (i.e., Śukra), although the referent isn't clear. Maunalāyanā could be Maudgalyāyana, one of the Buddha's foremost disciples. Tatelman (2005: 323) understands the term of refer to two people: Mauna and Layana. The Tibetan (160b1–2; 172a5) reads *gnas 'jog gser mdog o ta la dag kyang*. That is, "Vaśiṣṭa, Kanakavarṇa (or, Suvarṇavarṇa), and Otalāyana."

797 Divy 519.3–5, *apatyahetor atatkāmamohitāḥ | dharmo munīnāṃ hi sanātano hy ayam apatyam utpāditavān sanātanaḥ*. Following the Tibetan (160b2; 172a6), read *tatkāmamohitāḥ* for *atatkāmamohitāḥ*. Otherwise, I understand Sākalikā to be the speaker, and reading *sanātanam* for *sanātanaḥ,* would translate as follows: "were not deluded by a desire for offspring | For only this eternal dharma of sages | gives birth to offspring that is eternal." Tatelman (2005: 323) offers this translation: ". . . for the sake of offspring, were deluded by desire. For the law of the sages is eternal—indeed, that eternal law has caused me to produce this child, Anupamā."

798 Divy 519.7–10,

imāṃ bhagavān paśyatu me sutāṃ satāṃ satīm[a] |
rūpopapannāṃ pramadām alaṃkṛtām |
kāmārthinīṃ yad bhavate pradīyate[b] |
sahānayā sādhur ivācaratāṃ bhavān[c] |
sametya candro nabhasīva rohiṇīm ||

[a]To preserve the meter, Thomas (1940: 655) suggests *imāṃ bhavān paśyatu me sutāṃ satīm*. That is, "Look at this virtuous daughter of mine." Thomas emends *bhagavān* to *bhavān* because "a brahmin, it is well-known, does not address the Lord as such, but as *bhavān*." For the peculiar term *satāṃ*, Cow-

ell and Neil (Divy 519n4) query *satyāṃ*. Tatelman (2005: 322.7) omits it, and I leave it untranslated.

[b]Speyer (1902: 359) suggests *rūpopapannā pramadā alaṃkṛtā kāmārthinī yad bhavate pradīyate*, which preserves *jagatī* meter. Hiraoka (HA 27; HD 62) follows Speyer.

[c]Speyer (1902: 359) likewise suggests *sahānayā sādhu cared ratiṃ bhavān*, and Hiraoka (HA 27; HD 62) again follows Speyer. Also possible is *sahānayā sādhur ivācared bhavān*.

799 Divy 519.14–15, *dṛṣṭā mayā mārasūtā hi vipra tṛṣṇā na me* (mss. omits) *nāpi tathā ratiś* (mss., *ratisva*) *ca*. Thomas (1940: 654) suggests *dṛṣṭā mayā mārasūtā hi vipra tṛṣṇā rāga cāpi tathā aratiś ca*. That is, "Brahman, I have seen Māra's daughters—Tṛṣṇā (Craving), Rāga (Passion), and Arati (Affection)." This reading corresponds to *Suttanipāta* 163/v. 839: *disvāna taṇham aratiṃ rāgañ ca | nāhosi chando api methunasmim*.

800 Following the Tibetan (160b6; 172b2), Tatelman (2005: 322.20), and Hiraoka (HA 27; HD 62), read *spraṣṭum hi padbhyām*. Cf. Divy 521.1. Divy 519.18, *praṣṭuṃ hi yattām* (mss. AC, *yakām*; mss. BE, *yabhām*). Speyer (1902: 359) suggests *spraṣṭuṃ hi dattām*. Thomas (1940: 655) suggests *spraṣṭum hi pādād*, likewise on the basis of *Suttanipāta* 163/v. 839: *kimevidaṃ muttakarisapuṇaṇaṃ | pādāpi naṃ samaphusituṃ na icchi*. Bodhi (2017: 300) offers this translation for the full verse: "Having seen Taṇhā, Aratī, and Ragā, I did not have any desire for sexual intercourse, so why then this, full of urine and feces? I would not wish to touch her even with my foot."

801 Divy 519.22–23, *viviktabhāveṣv iva kāmabhogī*. Cf. Divy 520.6–7. This is unclear. Tatelman (2005: 323), "As a sensualist feels none for those bereft of strong emotion." Hoernle (1916: 726) translates this passage as "like one (i.e., Vaśiṣṭha) did who, in the midst of his abstraction, enjoyed sexual pleasure?" Perhaps, reading against the grammar, "like someone detached from all feelings of sensual pleasure." For *viviktabhāveṣu*, the Tibetan (160b6–7; 172b3) reads *yid 'ong gzugs dag la*.

802 Following Cowell and Neil's query (519n10), the Tibetan (160b7; 172b4), Tatelman (2005: 324.4), and Hiraoka (HA 27; HD 62), read *saktām*. Divy 519.27, *śaktām*.

803 Divy 520.1, *kṛtī*. Perhaps the idea here is that he, unlike a solitary buddha, will actively engage in the world, doing what must be done. Cf. Pāli, *kataṃ karaṇīyam*. See also the Tibetan (160b8; 172b4) and Hiraoka 2007: ii, 439n53.

804 Following Cowell and Neil's query (Divy 520n2), read *na*. Divy 520.4, *ca*.

805 Following Cowell and Neil's query (Divy 520n3), Vaidya (Divy-V 449.33), and Tatelman (2005: 324.13), add *eva*. Divy 520.6–7, *viviktaḥ*. Hiraoka (HA 27; HD 62), following the Tibetan (161a1; 172b5), reads *viviktacittaḥ*. Two syllables are missing for the verse to be complete.

806 Following the Tibetan (161a2; 172b7) and Hiraoka (HA 27; HD 62), read *sthūlībhūtāsthikācabhūtākṣī*. Divy 520.10, *sthūlībhūtāryasthītikāvarībhūtekṣiṇī*. Tatelman (2005: 324.17, 325), following Cowell and Neil's query (Divy 520n4), reads *-spīthikāvarībhūtekṣiṇī*, which he translates as "and her eyes, wide open and staring, glazed over."

807 For more on the character of this old monk (*mahalla*), see Strong 1992: 68.

808 Divy 520.14, *asmatsametām*. Tatelman (2005: 325) translates this as "whom we have

encountered." Hiraoka (HA 27; HD 62), following the Tibetan (161a3; 173a1), suggests *asmabhyam etām*.

809 Divy 520.20–21, *vrajantu niṣṭhām* (*sic* ms. E; mss. ABD, *-riṣṭām*; ms. C, *-tiṣṭhām*). Hiraoka (HA 27; HD 62), following the Tibetan (161a5; 173a2), reads *vrajantu naṣṭām*. That is, "may they be destroyed!"

810 The text is ambiguous about whether the previous verse was spoken by the old monk or the Buddha. Here (Divy 520.24) the text reads *evam ukte*, which I could have translated as "thus addressed," as I did at Divy 520.18. I follow the sense of the Tibetan (161a5; 173a3), which reads *de skad ces smras ne*. Hiraoka (HA 27; HD 62), likewise following the Tibetan, emends to *uktvā*.

811 Divy 521.1–2, *evam uktasya*. One might expect this to mean "was thus addressed," but that seems incorrect. Here too there appears to be some confusion between various participial forms of √*vac*. I follow the sense of the Tibetan (161a7; 173a4), which reads *de skad ces smras pa dang*. Hiraoka (HA 27; HD 62), likewise following the Tibetan, emends to *ukte*.

812 Divy 521.7, *labhyamānā*. One might also translate this as "available for marriage" or "being married off." More literally, "being obtained." Tatelman (2005: 327) offers this translation: "although she was given to you."

813 Following Divy 24.13–16. Divy 521.11, "and so on as before" (*pūrvavad yāvat*). For variants in the expansion, see Hiraoka 2007: ii, 441n99.

814 Divy 521.19, *matpitaivāṅgīkṛtya vadati*. Perhaps the *eva* should be *evam*. The Tibetan (161b5; 173b3) seems to concur.

815 Following Edgerton (BHSD) and mss. (Divy 521n5), read *-bhaṇḍikām*. Divy 521.25, *bhāṇḍikām*.

816 Following Speyer (1902: 360), Vaidya's query (Divy-V 451.11), Tatelman (2005: 330.8), the Tibetan (174a1), and Hiraoka (HA 27; HD 62), read *vipulam*. Divy 522.7, *vipratam* (*sic* ms. A; mss. BC, *tipratam*; ms. D, *vipranam*). Cowell and Neil (Divy 522n1) query *vitatam*.

817 Tatelman (2005: 333), quite cleverly, translates the identifications as such: "Now, monks, who do think that that young man was? It was I who was he at that very time. And he who was that blacksmith? It was this very Mākandika who was him at that time."

818 Divy 523.5–6, *ayaṃ mahallako 'nupamām āgamyānayena vyasanam āpanna iti*. Cf. DS 394n108.

819 Following Divy 282.27–28. Divy 523.11, "and so on as before" (*pūrvavad yāvat*).

820 Following Divy 24.12–13. Divy 523.14, "and so on as before" (*pūrvavad yāvat*).

821 Here the Tibetan (174b5–175b1) offers an extended version of the stereotypical passage; it does much the same with similar passages throughout the beginning of this story.

822 Following Divy 441.9 and Hiraoka (HA 27; HD 62), read *uccaghoṣaṇaḥ*. Divy 523.18, *uccaghoṇaḥ* (ms. D, *-ghoṣaḥ*).

823 Following Divy 3.4–5, 26.6–7, 58.4, etc., and the Tibetan (175b2), add *jñātayaḥ saṃgamya samāgamya*. Divy 523.20 (omitted).

824 Following Hiraoka (HA 27; HD 62–63) and the standard formula (Divy 3.5, 26.7, etc.), delete the second *tasya*. Divy 523.19–20, *tasya . . . tasya jātasya*.

825 Following Divy 523.12 and Hiraoka (HA 27; HD 62–63), read *siṃhakasya*. Divy 523.22, *siṃhasya*.

826 Following Divy 58.11–20. I follow Hiraoka (HC 42) and add "the science of cloth" so that eight sciences are listed. Divy 523.25, "and so on as before" (*pūrvavad yāvat*).

827 Divy 524.17, *ādāya*. Hiraoka (HA 27; HD 63), following the standard refrain (Divy 5.9, 332.6, etc.), emends to *āropya*.

828 Divy 524.19–20, *vistareṇa rākṣasīsūtraṃ sarvaṃ vādyam*. Cowell and Neil (Divy 524n2) note that "[mss.] BC give this sentence, though C marks it as to be omitted." The Tibetan (164b1–171a7; 176b2–183b7) provides the full text of the sūtra. The corresponding account in Chinese (T. 1442, ch. 47–48; xxiii, 888a4–889c19) was summarized by Huber (1906: 23), and this summary was rendered into English by Tatelman (2005: 421–22). A version of this story also appears in the *Kāraṇḍavyūha Sūtra* (281, 284–88), and a translation from the Tibetan called *The Basket's Display* is available at http://read.84000.co/#UT22084-051-004/part%20two. See too de Jong 1968: 486; Schlingloff 1988: 256–65; Lienhard 2003; Karashima and Vorobyova-Desyatovskaya 2015: 157.

Here is Tatelman's rendering (modified slightly) of Huber's summary:

"The helmsman warned the merchants of the perils of the ocean. They provided themselves with planks and inflatable leather sacks in order to be able to escape any shipwreck. A sea monster (*makara*) smashed up the ship; those merchants who were destined not to die yet were carried by the waves to Tāmradvīpa (Ceylon), to the city of the demons (*rākṣasī*).

"On the highest tower of that city were planted two magic flagstaffs: the movement of one flag announced to the demons good fortune, the other misfortune. On that day the former began flapping and fluttering and from this the sirens concluded that shipwrecked men from India were about to reach the shore. There the sirens welcomed the men. Each merchant married one of them and lived with her in joy and luxurious comfort. To each man was born a son and a daughter. The sirens, however, forbade their husbands access to the road that led to the southern part of the city.

"Simhala, suspicious, proceeded there one night while the women were sleeping and arrived at a city enclosed by high iron walls that had no door or gate. From the interior of this city issued the sound of plaintive voices: 'Alas, India! Alas, our parents!' Simhala clambered up a *śirīṣa* tree and spoke with the prisoners. They also were shipwrecked Indians; they had been imprisoned since the day Simhala's company had landed on the island. From time to time their former wives came to devour one of them and the same fate awaited Simhala and his companions the day that a new group of shipwrecked men were cast onto the island.

"The fifteenth of each month, *upoṣadha* day, the gods gathered in the air above that sorrowful city to lament the fate of the unfortunates whom the iron walls prevented from returning to the north of the city—because on that day of the month, Bālāha, the divine horse, waited in the north of the city to offer transport to whomever wished to cross to the other shore of the ocean, which was India.

"Simhala explained to his companions what he had learned and on the fifteenth day of the lunar month they all betook themselves to the north of the city where they found Bālāha, who promised to save them, so long as they did not allow themselves to be bewitched by the sirens at the last moment, for if that were to happen, he would not be able to carry them. The horse then rose up into the air and the flag of misfortune which was driven into the ground above the city began to flutter. The sirens, more beautiful than ever, hurried to the seashore and entreated the departing men to remain or at least not to leave without their children. All except Simhala were filled with regret; they fell from the horse and were devoured by rākṣasīs . . ."

Since the editor of the *Divyāvadāna* has left out the *Rakṣasī-sūtra* but given instructions to include the "full" story "in its entirety," it seems likely that the text was well known to the reader/recitors of the day and that it was of some importance. A version of this story, in fact, is depicted in impressive fashion at the Buddhist site Ajanta in cave 17. Moreover, this was a *residential* cave for the monks, so "it is possible that the murals were intended primarily to be experienced by the Monastic Community of Ajanta" (Dehejia 1990: 392).

829 Following Hiraoka (HA 27; HD 63) and Vaidya (Divy-V 452.30), read *nirbandhaḥ*. Divy 524.26, *nibandhaḥ*.

830 Divy 525.24, *kṣudraputrāham*. Hiraoka (HA 27; HD 63), following the Tibetan (172a2; 184b2), reads *kṣudraputraṃ māñ ca*. That is, ". . . forgive his young child and me."

831 Following Vaidya's query (453.17), add *tyaja*. Cf. Divy 525.9, *parityaja*. Hiraoka (HA 27; HD 63), following the Tibetan (172a2; 184b3), suggests *kṣipa*.

832 Divy 525.26–27, *kṣudaputreyaṃ tapasvinī* (*sic* mss.). Hiraoka (HA 27; HD 63), following the Tibetan (172a2–3; 184b3), reads *kṣudaputram imāṃ tapasvinīḥ*.

833 Divy 526.12, *śrutvā*. Hiraoka (HA 27; HD 63), following Divy 525.6, 525.3, and the Tibetan (172a8; 185a1), reads *kṛtvā*.

834 Divy 526.13–14, *kṣudraputrāham* (ms., *kṣutra-*; ms. C, *kṣatra-*). Hiraoka (HA 27; HD 63), following the Tibetan (172a8–b1; 185a1), reads *kṣudraputraṃ māñ ca*. And since the word *arhasi* occurs twice in the sentence, he suggests omitting its second occurrence.

835 Divy 526.23, *āsvāpanam*. For more on the term, see Bloomfield 1920: 345.

836 Divy 527.6, *kṣamaṃ cintayata*. I take this figuratively. Tatelman (2005: 349) translates this as "consider this carefully." Hiraoka (HA 28; HD 63), following the Tibetan (173a1; 185b2), reads *upakramaṃ cintayata*. That is, "think of a plan."

837 Following the Tibetan (173a2; 185b3). Divy 527.10 (omitted).

838 Divy 527.21, *śobhanaṃ te*. Hiraoka (HA 28; HD 63), following the Tibetan (173a6; 185b7), omits *te*.

839 Divy 527.23, *āhūya*. Cowell and Neil (527n2) query *āhūyante*.

840 Following Hiraoka (HA 28; HD 63), read *āpannasthānīyaḥ*. Divy 528.1, *āpaṇasthānīyaḥ* (mss., *āpana-*). Tatelman (2005: 350.14) emends to *āpadāsthānīyaḥ*.

841 Following Hiraoka (HA 28; HD 63), read *āpannasthānīyaḥ*. Divy 528.2, *āpaṇasthānīyaḥ* (mss., *āpana-*).

842 Here, between *-tīra-* and *-m*, ms. C (Divy 528n2) adds, "That royal horse named Bālāha—the great being, the bodhisattva Avalokiteśvara—with a heart full of compassion, saved me from the danger of a great disaster and then guarded and protected me."

843 Divy 528.9, *utkīlayitvā*. Edgerton (BHSD) suggests "having opened up the city." Tatelman (2005: 351) reads "leave this city."

844 An alternate etymology for name of the island (modern-day Sri Lanka) occurs in the *Mahāvaṃsa* (Mhv 66/ vii.42). There it is said, "King Sīhabāhu, since he had slain a lion (*sīha*), was called Sīhala. And because of his ties with Vijaya's followers, they were also called Sīhala." For more on this account, see Thapar 1978: 281.

845 Divy 528.26, *deva madduhitā deva na kasyacid*. Hiraoka (HA 28; HD 63), following

the Tibetan (174a2; 186b4), adds *kasya dattā* between *madduhitā* and *deva*. Also possible is that the second *deva* should be read as *eva*.

846 Divy 529.1, *paṇyapariṇītāḥ*. This term, which only occurs once in the *Divyāvadāna*, indicates a marriage that is explicitly a commercial transaction. The wives in question were "married" (*pariṇītāḥ*) in exchange for "commodities" or "merchandise" (*paṇya*).

847 Following Vaidya (Divy-V 455.13) and Tatelman (2005: 354.3), read *tasya puṣpadantasya pariṇītā*. Divy 529.1, *tasya puṣpadantasya pariṇītāḥ*. Tatelman (2005: 355) offers this translation: "Anupama became the wife to the King's Flower-Bower Palace." Cowell and Neil (711) translate the unemended text, along with the preceding sentence, as follows: "The king had many concubines and many wives belonging to the Puṣpadanta palace."

848 Divy 529.2, *tasyāḥ puṣpadantasya prāsādasyārthaṃ dattam*. Cowell and Neil (Divy 711) offer this translation: "She had a sum of money given to her suitable to the Puṣpadanta palace." The Tibetan (174a3; 186b5) reads *-ardhaṃ* for *-arthaṃ*. That is, "She was given half of the Puṣpadanta Palace."

849 Divy 529.20, *nātra hy evam*. This is ambiguous. It could also be rendered, "It should not be otherwise." Tatelman (2005: 357) offers this translation: "not only here and now does she speak thus." The Tibetan (174b1; 187a3–4) reads "no offense has been committed here"—a translation of *nātra doṣa iti*—as it does at the corresponding passage at Divy 529.28.

850 Following Vaidya (Divy 455.32), the Tibetan (174b5; 187a7), and Hiraoka (HA 28; HD 63–64), read *sakāśam*. Divy 529.29, *sakāmam*.

851 Following the Tibetan (174b5–6; 187a7) and Hiraoka (HA 28; HD 64), read *anupamayā*. Divy 529.29, "the king" (*rajñā*).

852 Following the Tibetan (175a5; 187b6–7) and Hiraoka (HA 28; HD 64), read *śramaṇasya gautamasyārthāyāpi na kalpate devasyāpi na kalpate śramaṇasya gautamasya kalpate devasya na kalpate*. Divy 530.17–18, *śramaṇasyārthāya na kalpate devasyāpi kalpate devasya na kalpate*. Cowell and Neil (Divy 711) note, "Some words seem lost here before *devasyāpi*; we might supply, *yadi śramaṇasya kalpate*." That is, "If it's permissible to do so on behalf of an ascetic . . ." Speyer (1902: 360) suggests instead inserting *atha kalpate*. That is, "Since this is permissible . . ." Tatelman (2005: 358.27) inserts *na* between *devasyāpi* and *kalpate*.

853 Following Cowell and Neil's query (530n2), the Tibetan (175a6; 188a1), and Hiraoka (HA 28; HD 64), read *svā pariṣad*. Divy 530.21, *svopaniṣad*.

854 Divy 530.26, *mā sarveṇa sarvaṃ bhaviṣyati*. Vaidya (Divy 456.19–20) adds *na*. Tatelman's (2005: 361) translation offers an implied threat: "Don't make the next arrow fly back at you all the way." Cf. the Tibetan (175b1–2; 188a4).

855 Divy 530.27, *yakṣaṇī* (*sic* mss.). Read as, or emend to, *yakṣiṇī*.

856 Divy 531.2, *mamāntike dharmānvayam upasthāpayet*. Hiraoka (HA 28; HD 64), following the Tibetan (175b4; 188a6), reads *bhaginīsaṃjñām* for *dharmānvayam*. Perhaps, "may I be treated like a sister." I understand both readings to have a similar meaning: the king is to treat his wife chastely, as one Buddhist devotee would treat another. Tatelman (361) offers this translation: "may he arrange for me to receive regular instruction in the Dharma."

857 Following the Tibetan (175b4–5; 188a6–7) and Hiraoka (HA 28; HD 64), read *sa*

rājā 'nupamāyā sārdhaṃ ratiṃ krīḍāṃ paricaryāṃ ca pratyanubhavati. Divy 531.3, *so 'nupamāyāḥ* (*sic* mss.). Cowell and Neil (531n1) query *sakāśāt.*

858 Divy 531.3–4, *śyāmāvatyā antike dharmānvayaṃ prasādayati.* Tatelman (2005: 363) offers this translation for the full sentence: "And so the king granted the favor of regular instruction in the Dharma for Anupama and Śyāmavatī." Edgerton (BHSD, s.v. *prasādayati*) cites only this passage and suggests as a translation "grants the favor of." Also possible would be "he cultivated faith in accordance with the dharma."

859 Divy 531.5, *navartukāni* (mss., *-takāni*). Or, perhaps, "fresh seasonal flowers."

860 Following the Tibetan (176a3; 188b6), Vaidya (Divy 457.3), and Hiraoka (HA 28; HD 64), read *devenaiva.* Divy 531.19, *devenaivam.*

861 The Tibetan (176a5; 188b7–189a1) records that Mākandika, like Yogāndharāyaṇa and Ghoṣila, first refused the king's order, but after being overruled by the king three times, finally relented. Mākandika references this expurgated bit of plot in what follows (Divy 531.29).

862 Divy 531.25, *nānujānīṣe.* Tatelman (2005: 364.5) reads likewise. Hiraoka (HA 28; HD 64), following the Tibetan (176a6; 189a2), reads *tātānujānīṣe.* That is, "Father, do you know . . ." Cowell and Neil (Divy 531n4) query *nanu jānīṣe.* That is, "Surely you know . . ."

863 Divy 531.26, *nānujānīṣe.* Tatelman (2005: 364.8) reads likewise. Cowell and Neil (Divy 531n4) query *nanu jānīṣe.* Hiraoka (HA 28; HD 64) reads *tātānujānīṣe.*

864 These are two of the nine bonds to existence.

865 Divy 532.1, *bhavatu nāmāpi na gṛhītum.* Hiraoka (HA 28; HD 64), following the Tibetan (176a8; 189a3), reads *abhavat te* for *bhavatu.*

866 Following the Tibetan (176b2; 189a5) and Hiraoka (HA 28; HD 64), read *praghātayitum upāyasaṃvidhānam.* Divy 532.6, *praghātayitu yāyavidhānam* (*sic* mss. ABC; ms. D, *-yitum api bhūyā vidhānam*). Cowell and Neil (Divy 536n2) query *-yituṃ yāvad vidhānam.* Vaidya (Divy-V 457.14–15) emends to *praghātayitum upāyavidhānam.*

867 Divy 532.10–11, *atra bhūrjena prayojanaṃ tailena masinā kalamayā tūlena* (mss., *bhūlena*). Cf. Divy 535.10 and 535.20–21. Peter Skilling (2014: 502) offers this translation: "they need birchbark, oil, ink, pen, and cotton." But as Skilling (2014: 503) explains, "What about oil and cotton? Are they used for preparing the surface of the birchbark, or are they simply needed for the lamps . . . Oil and cotton are used today to clean palm-leaf manuscripts in South Asia. But it may be simpler to simply see the reference as materials needed to keep lamps burning—oil and cotton, the latter to be twisted to make wicks."

868 Divy 532.14–15, *na* (ms. A, *naḥ*; ms. B, *ne*) *bhūyo bhūyaḥ praveśitavyam.* Tatelman (2005: 367) offers this translation: "There is not much more to be brought in."

869 Hiraoka (HA 28; HD 64), following the Tibetan (176b5–6; 189b1), adds *icchāvaḥ.* That is, "want." Tatelman (2005: 367) offers this translation: "Are you here to gawk at the king's women?"

870 Following Cowell and Neil's query (Divy 532n7), Divy 535.13, the Tibetan (176b6; 189b1–2), and Hiraoka (HA 28; HD 64), read *yantrakalācāryaḥ.* Divy 532.20, *yantrakarācāryaḥ.*

871 A version of this verse and the next can be found in the *Dhammapada* (vv. 127–28). Cf. Divy 561.5–7.

872 Following the Tibetan (177a2; 189b6), Hiraoka (HA 28; HD 64), and Tatelman (2005: 368.12), read *udakabhrameṇa*. Divy 533.6, "with haste" (*sasaṃbhrameṇa*).

873 Hiraoka (HA 28; HD 64–65), following Divy 533.18, adds *dagdhāni*. Divy 533.14 (omitted).

874 Divy 533.14–15, *śrutvā ca punaḥ kauśāmbīṃ piṇḍāya praviśya* (ms. A, *prācchaṃ caritvā*; ms. B, *praviṣṭa caritvā*; mss. CE, *prācaritvā*; ms. D, *prāvaritvā*) *caritvā pratikramya*. This appears to be an abridged, and irregular, form of a standard expression. Cf. Divy 39.10–21, 552.23–25, 566.3–4. The Tibetan (177a5; 190a1–2) follows the standard form. Tatelman (2005: 369) offers this translation: "After learning that, they again entered Kauśāmbī for alms and completed their alms-round. Then they left the city."

875 Divy 533.17, *vatsarājasyāntaḥpuram*. Hiraoka (HA 28; HD 65), following Divy 533.12–13 and the Tibetan (177a8; 190a4), reads *vatsarājasya janapadān gatasyāntaḥpuram*.

876 Hiraoka (HD 65), following the Tibetan (177b3; 190a7) and parallels at MPS 9.15 and MSV i, 87.2, adds *ca tanutvāt*. Divy 533.28 (omitted). Cf. MSV ii, 87.1–2, "That monk who had rid himself of the three bonds to existence and weakened attachment, hate, and delusion will, as a result, become a once-returner" (*eṣa bhikṣus trayāṇāṃ saṃyojanānāṃ prahāṇād rāgadveṣamohānāṃ ca tanutvāt sakṛdāgāmī bhaviṣyati*).

877 Divy 534.4, *niyatasamādhiparāyaṇāḥ*. Hiraoka (HA 28; HD 65), following the Tibetan (177b4; 190b1), reads *niyatasaṃbodhiparāyaṇāḥ*. That is, "constantly focused on awakening."

878 Following the Tibetan (177b6; 190b3) and Hiraoka (HA 28; HD 65), read *prasannacittena kālam*. Divy 534.10, *prasannacittālaṃkāram*.

879 Divy 534.12, *āgamayata* (sic mss.). The Tibetan (177b7; 190b3) reads *tshur sheg*. Hiraoka (2007: ii, 452n270) queries *shog* and also points to parallels at Divy 76.10–11 and 465.10–11.

880 Tatelman (2005: 375), adjusting the formula to context, offers this translation: "We must not permit our minds to be corrupted even by such burned pillars as these, much less by bodies endowed with consciousness." Cf. DS 331 and 437n683.

881 Divy 535.2–3, *vṛttir dīyatāṃ kim apriyākhyāyino vṛttir dīyata ity ayaṃ sa kālaḥ*. This is a little obscure. Tatelman (2005: 375) offers this translation: "Then let my wages be paid." "Why have we been paying you the wages of an announcer of ill tidings all this time?" Also possible is the following: "[Previously the king said,] 'Give him a job.' [And you said,] 'Why is this bearer of bad news to be given a job?' Well now is that time."

882 Following Vaidya (Divy-V 459.10), read *kāryaṃ nivedayeti*. Divy 535.4, *kāryo nivedayati* (sic ms. E; ms. A, *niveyata*; ms. B., *niveyate*; ms. C, *nivedeti*; ms. D, *nivedayet*). Tatelman (2005: 375) offers this translation: "Tell us what to do." Hiraoka (HA 28; HD 65), following the Tibetan (178a6; 191a3), reads *ko 'nyo* for *kāryo*. That is, "who else will inform him?"

883 Following Vaidya (Divy-V 459.14) and Skilling (2014: 503n12), read *tūlamasiḥ*. Divy 535.10, *tūlam asiḥ*. Here "ink" (*masi*) is a much better reading than "sword" (*asi*).

884 Again read *tūlamasiḥ*. Divy 535.20–21, *tūlam asiḥ*.

885 Divy 536.1–2, *sa teṣāṃ lekhāṃ lekhayitvā*. Or perhaps, reading against the Tibetan (178b8; 191b5), "He had them sign their names to it."

886 Following the Tibetan (178b8; 191b5) and Hiraoka (HA 28; HD 65), add *rājñaḥ*. Divy 536.3 (omitted).

887 Divy 536.11, *apahṛtaḥ*. Hiraoka (HA 28; HD 65), to make it agree with the subject, emends to *apahṛtam*.

888 Following Hiraoka (HA 28; HD 65), read *tad gatam etat*. Divy 536.11–12, *tad gatam | etat*. Cf. Divy 272.22–23.

889 Divy 536.16–17, *ekena tāvad ahaṃ rājñā daśa diśo viśrānto 'yaṃ ca dvitīyaḥ*. This idiom is tricky. Tatelman (2005: 381) offers this translation: "Until now, by only one king in the ten directions have I been pacified—and this is the second." Cf. the Tibetan (179a5; 192a2–3).

890 Divy 536.18, *sa kaṇṭhe 'siṃ baddhvā*. Or perhaps, "He tied his sword in supplication around his neck."

891 As Waldschmidt (1973: 383n4) observes, "The method of informing somebody of remarkable events through a painted sequence of scenes is repeatedly used in Indian art and literature." Cf. Granoff 2000.

892 Following the Tibetan (179b1; 192a7) and Hiraoka (HA 28; HD 65), read *rūpyamāṇaḥ*. Divy 537.1, *ruṣyamāṇah* (mss., *rupya-*).

893 Following Hiraoka (HA 28; HD 65), read *sthāpitā*. Divy 537.23, *sthāpitaḥ*.

894 Divy 537.23, *rājñaḥ saptame divase śoko vigataḥ | sa vigataśokaḥ*. This might also refer to the observance of a mourning period. Thus, "For seven days the king observed a period of grief, and then his grief departed."

895 Divy 537.24–25, *yathāvṛttaṃ niveditam*. This could also mean, "Yogāndharāyaṇa informed him of what he had done," but this doesn't fit well with what follows. Cf. the Tibetan (180a2; 192b6–193a1). My thanks to J. R. Joshi for his thoughts on this passage.

896 Following the Tibetan (180a2; 193a1). The king's logic seems to be that with his two principal wives dead, he should now leave behind mundane affairs and become a monk. It is for just this reason, it seems, that his chief minister Yogāndharāyaṇa had his wife Anupamā imprisoned rather than killed. He doesn't want the king to renounce. Divy 537.25–27, *mākandikena* (mss., *-dike*) *śyāmāvatī praghātitā, tvayāpy anupamayā saparivārayā sārdhaṃ mayā pravrajitavyaṃ jātam iti*. This is corrupt. Perhaps, "Mākandika killed Śyāmāvatī, and you likewise [killed Anupamā]. Otherwise I would have gone forth as monk, together with Anupamā and her retinue." Tatelman (2005: 385), quite creatively, offers this translation: "Splendid! Mākandika caused Śyāmavatī's death, although you and I should send Anupamā, together with her retinue, into exile."

897 Divy 538.5, *navaśavāyā arthe*. More literally, "about the recently deceased" or "about a fresh corpse." This makes little sense in context, so I read creatively. J. R. Joshi (personal communication) suggests that, following the Pāli compound *manguracchavī* ("golden complexion"), there might have been a Middle Indic compound *navachavī* ("fresh complexion"), and that *navachaviyāya* could have produced the mis-Sanskritized form *navaśavāyāḥ*. Cf. Divy 537.29–30, *amlānaśarīrā*, and Divy 541.9, *amlānagātrī*. Or, perhaps, emend to *navaśarīrā*. Furthermore, following the Chinese version of the text, Waldschmidt (1973: 384) notes: "The king believes that a lover must have befriended her. She denies this and requests him to ask trustworthy Buddha for the explanation of her *good looks*" (emphasis added).

898 Considering that the Sanskrit here is a little obscure, Hiraoka (2007: ii, 456n334) translates from the Tibetan. The Tibetan (180a6–7; 193a4–5) reads as follows:

"Do you have faith in the Blessed One?"

"Well, I met him."

"At that time you called him 'the ascetic Gautama.' But now it seems you call him 'Blessed One.' I will not ask the Blessed One for someone like you who is so crass, but I will ask him for Śyāmāvatī's sake."

With that said, the king went before the Blessed One.

899 Read *udakabhrameṇa*. Divy 538.10, *anukrameṇa* (mss., *-brahameṇa*). See note 872.

900 Following Divy 282.11–18 (modified accordingly). Divy 538.12, "and so on as before" (*pūrvavad yāvat*).

901 Following Divy 282.27–28. Divy 538.15–16, "and so on as before" (*pūrvavad yāvat*).

902 Following Divy 133.8–9, 192.7–8, 313.14, etc., the Tibetan (181a3–4; 194a3), and Hiraoka (HA 28; HD 65), read *jvalanatapana-*. Divy 539.3, *tapana-*.

903 Read *tāpi*. Divy 539.8, *tāni* (*sic* mss.).

904 Read *-udakabhrameṇa*. Divy 539.20, *-anukrameṇa* (mss., *-bhrameṇa*).

905 Following Divy 55.9–12 (modified accordingly). Divy 529.22, "and so on as before" (*pūrvavad yāvat*).

906 Following Divy 54.2–10 (modified accordingly). Divy 539.29, "and so on as before" (*pūrvavad yāvat*).

907 Following Divy 282.26–28. Divy 540.2, "and so on as before" (*pūrvavad yāvat*).

908 The Tibetan (182a6; 195a6) translates this as *gzungs byed*.

909 Following Divy 283.2. Divy 540.8, "and so on in its entirety as before" (*iti vistaraḥ pūrvavad yāvat*).

910 Following the Tibetan (182b1–6; 195b1–5). Divy 540.12, "and so on as before" (*pūrvavad yāvat*).

911 Following the Tibetan (182b6; 195b6) and Hiraoka (HA 28; HD 65), read *bhaviṣyati*. Divy 540.12, *vinyasya*.

912 Read *māpitā*. Divy 540.14, *māpitāḥ*. Cf. Divy 59.20.

913 Following the Tibetan (182b7–8; 195b7). Divy 540.14, "and so on as before" (*pūrvavat*). Cf. Divy 59.21, *yūpasya paricārako vyavasthitaḥ*.

914 Here the Tibetan (183a3–6; 196a3–6) includes the formulaic passage that begins, "the deeds that she herself has performed and accumulated have now come together . . ." Cf. Divy 54.1–10; 131.6–14, 141.6–15, etc.

915 Divy 540.27, *taiḥ*. Hiraoka (HA 28; HD 65), following the Tibetan (183a7; 196a7), reads *tatra*. That is, "there."

916 These bracelets, it seems, are functioning as a "bowl rest" (*pātrādhiṣṭhānam*). Cf. MSV iii, 98.3–4. For more on this term, see Schopen 2004: 277–78n13.

917 Here the Tibetan (183b2–4; 196b2–5) again includes the formulaic passage that begins, "the deeds that she herself has performed and accumulated have now come together . . ." Cf. Divy 54.1–10; 131.6–14, 141.6–15, etc.

918 Divy 541.8, *yad*. Hiraoka (HA 28; HD 65), following the standard formula, reads *yena*.

919 Following the Tibetan (183b6; 196b6). Divy 541.8 (omitted).

920 Following Divy 54.2–10 (modified accordingly). Divy 541.10, "and so on as before" (*pūrvavad yāvat*).

921 Here the Tibetan (184a3–185b5; 197a5–199a1) embeds an additional narrative. The brahman girl reluctantly makes an offering to the solitary buddha as well as a negative vow. This results in her being placed in a torture chamber for seven days without food and coming out undefiled and radiant. Next is a story of a woman who, as a result of

a vow, is reborn as the daughter of Ghoṣila and given the name Śrīmatī. The Buddha explains that she was Rādhā (*mgu byed*) from a previous life. For more, see Hiraoka 2007: ii, 460nn409–10.

922 Following the Tibetan (185b6; 199a3). Divy 541.27 (omitted).

923 Following the Tibetan (185b6; 199a3) and Hiraoka (HA 28; HD 65), read *cārakam*. Divy 541.28, *dārakam*. That is, "I'm going to deliver a child."

924 Divy 542. 3, *tadātmanaḥ*. Hiraoka (HA 28; HD 66) suggests *tad ātmanaḥ*.

925 Following Cowell and Neil's query (Divy 542n1), Tatelman (2005: 402.19), the Tibetan (185b8; 199a5), and Hiraoka (HA 29; HD 66), read *kakṣāyām*. Divy 542.4, *kāyām*.

926 Following the Tibetan (186a1; 199a5) and Hiraoka (HA 29; HD 66), read *bhūmi-parikarma*. Divy 542.6, *bhūri* (*sic* ms. D; mss. ABCE, *bhūmi-*) *karma*. Otherwise, following Tatelman (2005: 403), "He had a lot of other work done."

927 Following Divy 310.9–14 (modified accordingly) and the Tibetan (186a5–7; 199b2–4). Divy 542.15, "and so on as before" (*pūrvavad yāvat*).

928 Divy 542.17, *bhagavān aupadhike sthitaḥ*. Edgerton (BHSD, s.v. *aupadhika*) notes: "*bhagavān aupadhike 'sthāt abhinirhṛtapiṇḍapātaḥ* (Divy *sthitaḥ*, omit *abhi-*), 'The Lord remained (without partaking of) the material gift (a meal which his monks received)' MSV ii, 128.3; 180.5 (Tib. *bsgrubs pa na bzhugs nas*, remained when [the meal] was supplied)." Waldschmidt (1973: 380) translates this expression as "remained behind without partaking of (and) received alms food (at his residence)." Schopen (2010: 117) suggests "to achieve an objective, remained away and had alms brought to him." He also remarks that "the expression in both languages [i.e., Sanskrit and Tibetan] is open to more than one interpretation." The Tibetan (186a8; 199b5) omits this sentence. See too a copperplate grant from the fifth or sixth century in Andhra Pradesh that includes the phrase *tyāga-paribhogānvayam aupadhikañ ca puṇyakriyāvastv*. For additional citations regarding this inscription, see Schopen 1996: 116n69 and 2004: 255n69.

929 Following MSV ii, 128.4, the Tibetan (186a8; 199b5), and Tatelman (2005: 404.15), read *abhinirhṛtapiṇḍapātaḥ*. Divy 542.19, *abhinirhṛtaṃ mantrayate sma*. Edgerton (BHSD, s.v. *abhinirharati*) offers this translation and observation: "He (Buddha) considered (reflected on) what he had undertaken (produced? realized? or initiated, taken upon himself?); but in parallel passage MSV ii, 128.3 [= 236.24–25] and 180.5 [= 262.19] *abhinirhṛta-piṇḍapātaḥ* evidently means, 'when almsfood had been produced' (entertainment provided by a layman), and I suspect a corruption in *mantrayate*." Perhaps, more loosely, "then there was a discussion about the offering of meals."

In a parallel passage in the *Mūlasarvāstivāda-vinaya* (MSV ii, 128.5–8), the five reasons are listed: "What are the five? [1] When they wish to withdraw for meditation; [2] when they wish to expound the dharma to deities; [3] when they wish to consider particular accommodations; [4] when they wish to look after the sick; [5] when they wish to instruct their disciples in the precepts of the monastic code." Cf. the Tibetan (186a8–186b2; 199b5–7).

930 Divy 542.21, *upadhivārakasya*. Elsewhere (i.e., Divy 237.17–18) I take this to mean "an acting caretaker of a monastery." Cf Silk 2008b: 85–86.

931 Divy 542.22, *smṛtim upasthāpayati* (*sic* mss.; ms. C adds *sa praviśāmayati*) *praviśā-*

mayati. Perhaps, reading creatively, "Śāriputra then established himself in a state of mindfulness [and remembered] that [the Buddha] permits others to enter [in his place]." My thanks to J. R. Joshi for this suggestion. Vaidya (Divy-V 463.27) emends to *praviśāmeti*, and I follow his emendation. The Tibetan (186b4–5; 200a2) reads *dran pa nye bar zhog shig dang 'jug par bya'o zhes*. Hiraoka (2007: ii, 462n437) suggests *smṛtim upasthāpya praviśāma iti*. That is, "Let us establish ourselves in a state of mindfulness and then enter."

932 Following Divy 310.21–25 (modified accordingly). Divy 542.25, "and so on as before" (*pūrvavad yāvat*).

933 Following the Tibetan (187a1–2; 200a6–7) and Hiraoka (HA 29; HD 66), read *kuśalamūlāni na vā*. Divy 543.1, *kuśalamūlāni | na*. Cf. Divy 331.28–29.

934 Following the Tibetan (187a3; 200b1) and Hiraoka (HA 29; HD 66), read *pratyayaṃ kṛtvā*. Divy 543.6, *pratyakṣaṃ kṛtvā*.

935 Following Divy 52.25–53.5 and Divy 310.29–311.8 (modified accordingly). Divy 543.9, "here it is to be recited in its entirety as before" (*pūrvavad yāvat sarvaṃ vādyam*). The version of this passage that occurs on Divy 52.25 and following contains verses (Divy 52.28–53.5) that I include here to create the formulaic passage "in its entirety." Tatelman (2005: 407–411) does likewise. Cf. the Tibetan (187a4–187b2; 200b2–7).

936 Following the Tibetan (201a2) and Hiraoka (HA 29; HD 66), omit *bhikṣavaḥ* (Divy 543.14). Otherwise—although this is a stretch—read *ārocayanti* for *ārocayati* and take *bhikṣavaḥ* as the subject rather than as a vocative.

937 Previously (Divy 542.19–22) it was said that "orders from four types of people are not to be refused."

938 Divy 543.18–19, *atha bhagavān śikṣākāmatayā varṇam bhāṣitvā pūrvavad yāvat pūrvikā prajñaptiḥ*. This is difficult to translate, and I find myself in agreement with Tatelman (2005: 423): "Of the dozens of places in these stories where *pūrvavad yāvat*, inserted in the text, signals that a passage has been abbreviated, this was one of the very few instances I have been unable to fill." According to the Tibetan (187b5–6; 201a3–5), "The Buddha praised those who desire training, those who respect training, and those who minimize their belongings [in respect to training]. Then the Buddha gave teachings to the monks that were in conformity, in alignment, and in accord with this. Then he said, 'Monks, the former is established [as a rule]. It is authorized. In this way my . . .'"

939 Divy 543.19, *iyaṃ cābhyanujñātā*. Tatelman (2005: 411) offers this translation: "And this regulation he certified as valid, saying . . ."

940 The rule here is nearly equivalent to the 83rd/84th *pācittiya* in the Pāli *Vinayapiṭaka* (iv, 157–64), although the introductory story differs. Cf. Schiefner 1964: 547. Interestingly, the corresponding Tibetan (201a6) leaves out *anyatra*, as it does in the commentary (201b5). For more on this passage and what it says about the relationship between the *Divyāvadāna* and the *Mūlasarvāstivāda-vinaya*, see Hiraoka 1998: 424–26.

941 Divy 543.26, *anudite*. Hiraoka (HA 29; HD 66) suggests its omission "because it is contextually unnecessary."

942 Following Divy 115.3. Divy 543.29, "and so on as before" (*pūrvavad yāvat*). Cf. the Tibetan (188a2–3; 201b1–2).

943 This phrase could be translated more literally as "a kṣatriya king who has been anointed

on the head," but as the commentary here makes clear this anointing is tantamount to a coronation ceremony.

944 Following the Tibetan (188a7–8; 201b5–7). Divy 544.10, "and so on as before" (*pūrvavat*). I cannot find the Sanskrit version of the passage to be supplied.

945 Following Hiraoka (HA 29; HD 66), although reading against the Tibetan (188b4; 202a3), read *prabhāta-*. Divy 544.14, *aprabhāta-*.

946 Following the Tibetan (188b4; 202a4) and Hiraoka (HA 29; HD 66), add *aprabhāte vaimatika āpadyate papantikām*. Divy 544.15 (omitted).

947 Following Cowell and Neil's suggestion (Divy 711), add *sarīsṛpa*. The text, otherwise, lists only seven "dangers" (*antarāya*). The Tibetan (188b6; 202a5) reads *klu*, suggesting nāgas. The Pāli *Vinayapiṭaka* (e.g., i, 112; i, 169) lists ten dangers: "kings, thieves, fire, water, humans, nonhumans, wild animals, serpents, living things, celibacy."

948 Divy 544.19–20, *anāpattir ādikarmikasyeti pūrvavat*. The Tibetan (202a5–6) reads, "When one has been called by a king, queen, prince, or minister and when one has encountered the eight obstacles—that is, kings, robbers, humans, nonhumans, wild animals, fire, water, and nāgas—then there is no offense. For the first [monk] ever to do it, the insane, the mentally disturbed, and the emotionally disturbed, there is no offense. This is the eighty-second offense: going to the palace during the night."

949 For translations, see Hiraoka 2007: ii, 466–547, as well as Burnouf 1844: 340–44, 2010: 331–34 and Strong 2002: 39–34 (Divy 546.27–549.20). For Pāli and Sanskrit parallels, see *Dhammapada-aṭṭhakathā* i, 161–231; Waldschmidt 1973; and *Avadānakalpalatā* no. 40 (Rani 2005: 46–48 and woodcut R-13; Tucci 1949: ii, 481 and plate 113). The corresponding Tibetan can be found at P 1032 *te* 95a7–125a8 and D 3 *ña* 102a7–133a2, and a translation at Tharchin et al. 1984: 7–81. For more, see Hiraoka 2007: ii, 514; HD 66; Grey 2000: 326–27. In what follows, I made extensive use of Johannes Nobel's work on the story. He edited the Tibetan version of the text, translated the Tibetan into German with very helpful notes, and compiled a Tibetan-German dictionary for the story. Based on the Tibetan, Nobel offers numerous insights and emendations to the Sanskrit text of the *Divyāvadana*; I include many of them below. Also helpful was Stephen Teiser's (2006: 104–19) analysis of the story. For more on this story, see Adaval 1970 and von Simson 1982.

In addition, Borobudur—an enormous Buddhist site in Central Java, Indonesia, built in the ninth century—contains twenty-five relief panels (nos. 64–88) that illustrate the story of Rudrāyaṇa. Although "a more elaborate version of the tale has evidently been followed than the one known to us from the *Divyāvadāna*" (Krom 1927: i, 285), the relief panels are nonetheless helpful for making sense of the story in the *Divyāvadāna*, precisely because the latter is apparently abridged. For a description of the panels, see Krom 1927: i, 282–301, or online at www.photodharma.net/Indonesia/06-Divyavadana-Level-1/06-Divyavadana-Level-1-Rudrayanas-Storyboard.htm. For a representation of the story in Tibetan art, see Hackin 1913 and 1916.

950 Roruka (sometimes Rauruka) was likely Rohri, the capital of the Ror dynasty, built in the fifth century BCE. It was located near to the modern city of Sukkur in the province of Sindh in Pakistan. Senarat Paranavitana (1969), however, identified Roruka with the sand-buried ruins of Mohenjodaro. Buddhist sources connect the city with extensive commerce (MacLean 1988: 59).

951 In what follows, Pāṭaliputra is not mentioned again, and Roruka's counterpart

becomes Rājagṛha. Cf. Nobel 1955: i, 49n3. Furthermore, both cities are described as thriving simultaneously.

952 The text generally calls the chief ministers "Hiru" and "Bhiru," although it sometimes refers them as "Hiruka" and "Bhiruka." For references, see Edgerton (BHSD, s.vv *Bhiru, Bhiruka, Hiru, Hiruka*). I use "Hiru" and "Bhiru" throughout.

953 Elsewhere, according to popular etymology, her name is said to mean "wise." Cf. PTSD and DPPN, s.v. *Vedeha*.

954 Varṣakāra (Pāli, Vassakāra) is generally understood to mean "rainmaker," but I follow Kosambi (1952: 56), who proposes "*vaśyakāra* (better *vaśyakara* or *vaśyakārin*) as the proper Sanskritization of *vassakāra*." The minister subjugates others more than he causes rain.

955 Divy 545.12, *āmātyān*. It might have made more sense here if the text read "merchants," considering that it is the "merchants" (*baṇijaḥ* | 545.16) who respond to him. Cf. the Tibetan (96a1–3; 103a2–3) and Nobel 1955: i, 51.

956 Here (Divy 546.10) the text reads, "The messenger returned" (*sa dūtaḥ pratyāgataḥ*). I follow Hiraoka (HA 29; HD 66) and omit this sentence. Cf. Nobel 1955: i, 53n1.

957 Divy 546.10, *athāpareṇa samayena*. Hiraoka (HA 29; HD 66) emends to *atha*, "because, contextually, it should not be 'another time.'"

958 Divy 546.13, *kīdṛśam*. Hiraoka (HA 29; HD 66), following the Tibetan (97a2; 104a1), emends to *svayam*.

959 Here (Divy 546.13–14) the text seems to be abridged. Cf. Nobel 1955: i, 52n3.

960 Divy 546.25, *anargho 'yaṃ dharmatā*. Nobel (1955: i, 53n3) suggests *anarghyam iyaṃ dharmatā*.

961 Here (Divy 546.28–547.1) the text is likely corrupt. The Tibetan (97b3–6; 104b2–5) preserves a quite different reading, with Varṣakāra telling the king about the special jewel that is the Buddha. See Hiraoka 2007: ii, 518n58 and Nobel 1955: i, 54–55.

962 Divy 547.8, *durāsadā*. Cf. the Tibetan (98a4; 105a2) and Nobel 1955: i, 54n2.

963 Divy 547.9, *nimittam*. Speyer (1912: 117) emends to *nirmitam* and suggests the same at Divy 547.11, 547.14, and 547.16.

964 Following the Tibetan (98a5–6; 105a3–4) and Hiraoka (HA 29; HD 66), read *evaṃ vayam śaknumaḥ*. Nobel (1955: i, 54n4) suggests *evaṃ* (?) *vayaṃ śakṣyāmaḥ*. Divy 547.10, *eva svayaṃ saṃjñapaya* (mss. BD, *saṃjñayāya*). Vaidya (Divy-V 466.15) reads *evaṃ svayaṃ saṃjñāpaya*. Perhaps, "you yourself could inform him of this [so that we may] grasp the Blessed One's appearance."

965 Cf. Nobel 1955: i, 55n1.

966 Divy 547.25, *abhyupapattiḥ*. This is a little obscure. It could also mean "beneficial counsel." The Tibetan understands it to mean "solemn promise"—what Nobel (1955: i, 55) translates as "dieses ist das feierliche Versprechen."

967 Divy 547.26, *lokasaṃvṛttiḥ*. Vaidya (Divy-V 466.27) reads *lokasaṃvṛtiḥ*. Also possible is that this is an instance of aphesis, and so *alokasaṃvṛti*—hence, "this goes beyond common understanding."

968 Following Edgerton (BHSD, s.v. *abhyutsāhatā*), the Tibetan (98b5; 105b3), and Hiraoka (HA 29; HD 67), read *abhyutsāhatā*. Edgerton suggests, "energy, energizing, instigation, encouragement." Nobel (1955: i, 55) suggests *abhyutsāhanā* and translates this is "dieses ist die Aufmunterung!" Divy 547.26, *atyutsāhatā*.

969 Cf. Nobel 1955: i, 56n3.

970 Divy 548.10–11, *na śakyaṃ tena yad vā tad vā pratiprābhṛtam anupreṣayitum.* Cowell and Neil (Divy 711) suggest, "He cannot have sent a common present in return for your former one."

971 Divy 548.11–12, *ānupūrvī tāvat kriyatām.* Cowell and Neil (Divy 711) suggest, "We shall know what course to adopt." Hiraoka (HA 29; HD 67), following the Tibetan (99a4–5; 106a3), reads *parīkṣā* for *ānupūrvī.*

972 Following Divy 391.5–6, 475.5, and Hiraoka (HA 29; HD 67), read *vipañcikaiḥ.* Divy 548.22, *vipaścikaiḥ* (ex conj.; mss. ACD, *vipañcanakaiḥ*; ms. B, *vipañcamakaiḥ*). Cf. Edgerton (BHSD, s.v. *vipañcika*) and Nobel 1955: i, 57n2.

973 Divy 548.24, *cāturaṅgair vijetā.* Cf. Divy 60.15, *caturantavijetā.* See too Divy 140.21–22, *cāturarṇavāntavijetā,* and Divy 315.28–316.1, 368.26–27, 372.22, 379.21, 402.17, *caturbhāgacakravartī.*

974 Divy 549.1, *śamena.* Hiraoka (HA 29; HD 67), following the Tibetan (99a4–5; 106b5), reads *samena.* Cf. Nobel 1955: i, 57n5. Other instances of the passage (e.g., Divy 60.22, 140.28) read *samayena.* Cf. DS 416n382.

975 Divy 549.6–7, *lokasya pravṛttinivṛttī.* Previously (Divy 547.26) *lokasaṃvṛttiḥ.* Nobel (1955: i, 57) offers this translation: "und das ist (die Formel des) Werdens und Entwerdens der Welt." Tharchin (1984: 15) translates this as "how one enters and can leave the world." Perhaps, "the origin and cessation of the world," "the arising and dissolution of the world," or even "worldly activity and renunciation."

976 Following Edgerton (BHSD, s.v. *abhyutsāhatā*), Nobel (1955: i, 57n6), and Hiraoka (HA 29; HD 67), read *abhyutsāhanā.* Divy 549.7, *atyutsāhanā* (*sic* mss.).

977 Divy 549.10, *pratiprasrabhya.* Cf. Nobel 1955: i, 58n2.

978 Divy 549.14–15, *avidyāpratyayāḥ* (mss., *-ayā*) *saṃskārā yāvat samudayo nirodhaś ca bhavati.* The second half of this sentence is unclear. The Tibetan (100a4–b2; 107a3–b1; trans. in Nobel 1955: i, 58) offers a detailed account of interdependent arising in forward and backward order. For versions of this in Pāli, see *Saṃyutta-nikāya* ii, 70, and *Udāna* 1.

979 Divy 549.19, *bhūratnena.* Nobel (1955: i, 59n2) and Hiraoka (HA 29; HD 67), following the Tibetan (100b3; 107b2), read *dūrasthena.* That is, "far away."

980 Divy 550.9, *-pātaprati-.* Hiraoka (HA 29; HD 67), following the standard formula, emends to *pātraḥ prati-.* Cf. Divy 39.21, 155.29, 199.26–27, etc.

981 Divy 550.9–10, *paribhuktaṃ śayanam.* Hiraoka (HA 29; HD 67), following the standard formula, emends to *yathāparibhuktaśayanāsanam.* Cf. Nobel 1955: i, 60n1.

982 Divy 550.17, *dātavyāni.* Cf. Divy 40.11, *anupradāpitāni* and DS 407n292. In that instance, I read the verb to mean "inspired donations of." See too Divy 550.23, *dāpitāni.*

983 Following Edgerton (BHSD, s.vv. *uccaka, kocava*) and Hiraoka (HA 29; HD 67), read *vṛṣikākocava-.* Divy 550.16, *-vṛṣikoccaka-* (ms. A, *-otvaca-*; ms. B, *-occakta-*; ms. C, *-ovaca-*; ms. D, *-ovvaka-*). Cf. DS 407n292.

984 The Tibetan preserves a more detailed account here. Nobel (1955: i, 60n4) offers this reconstruction: *[r]udrāyaṇo rājā lekhaṃ vācayitvā prītiprāmodyajātaḥ* (or, *-jāto babhuva*) | *tenārdha- . . . nagaraśobhā kṛtā caturaṅgena balakāyenānekajanaśatasahasraparivāreṇa svayam eva pratyudgamya . . .* That is, "King [R]udrāyaṇa read out the letter and was pleased and delighted. Then he made the road beautiful for two and a half leagues, made the city beautiful as well, and then personally went out to

receive him together with his fourfold army and with many hundreds and thousands of followers . . ."

985 Here the text (Divy 550.19) adds "five hundred monasteries" (*pañcavihāraśatāni*). I omit this, following the Tibetan (101b1; 108b1) and Hiraoka (HA 29; HD 67), since it is included in what follows.

986 Following the Tibetan (101b1; 108b1) and Hiraoka (HA 29; HD 67), read *anekajanaśatasahasra-*. Divy 550.19–20, *yena ekajanasahasra-*. Cowell and Neil (Divy 550n5) query *-tāny aneka-*.

987 Hiraoka (HA 29; HD 67), following the standard cliché (e.g., Divy 50.8–9) and the Tibetan (101b5; 108b4–5), adds *sākṣātkṛtaṃ kaiścit sakṛdāgamiphalam*. That is, "some directly experienced the reward of the once-returner." Divy 551.1 (omitted). See Divy 166.16–17, 209.14, 226.7–8, etc., for variants to the cliché.

988 Divy 551.12, *āryamahākātyāyana bhavato 'ntike*. Following the Tibetan (102a2; 109a2), one would expect *āryamahākātyāyanasyāntike*. Cf. Nobel 1955: i, 61n6.

989 Divy 551.15–16, *sarvasaṃskāragatīḥ*. Cf. Divy 180.23, where the same passage reads "rebirth in all realms of saṃsāra" (*sarvasaṃsāragatīḥ*).

990 Following the Tibetan (102b2; 109b2), Nobel (1955: i, 63n3), and Hiraoka (HA 29; HD 67), read *praṇayatīti*. Divy 551.27–28, *praprīṇayatīti* (*sic* ms. A; mss. CE, *prapīṇ-*; ms. D, *prīṇayatīti*; ms. B, *prapānnaiyatīti*). Edgerton (BHSD) translates this as "makes delightful."

991 Cf. Nobel 1955: i, 63n5.

992 Divy 552.17, *antaḥpuraparijanaḥ* (mss., *antaḥpuram*). Normally *parijana* would refer to "attendants," and I would translate this compound as "palace women and their attendants." In what follows (Divy 552.20), however, the text reads *antaḥpurajanaḥ*, suggesting that here *parijana* refers to the palace women themselves, perhaps denoting their low status.

993 Following Divy 550.8–9, the Tibetan (103a4; 110a4), and Hiraoka (HA 29; HD 67), add *prāvikṣat | rājagṛahaṃ piṇḍāya*. Divy 552.24 (omitted).

994 Divy 552.25, *-pātaprati-*. Hiraoka (HA 29; HD 67–68), following the standard formula, emends to *-pātrā prati-*. Cf. Divy 39.21, 155.29, 199.26–27, etc.

995 Divy 552.25, *yathāparibhuktaṃ śayanāsanam*. Hiraoka (HA 29; HD 68), following the standard formula, emends to *yathāparibhuktaśayanāsanam*.

996 Divy 552.29, *śāstrānugatā*. Nobel (1955: i, 64n1) and Hiraoka (HA 29; HD 68), following the Tibetan (103a6; 110a6), emend to *śāstrānuśastā*. That is, "recommended by the Teacher."

997 Following Edgerton (BHSD, s.vv. *uccaka, kocava*) and Hiraoka (HA 29; HD 68), read *vṛṣikākocava*. Divy 553.2, *vṛṣikocca-* (mss., *vṛmśi-* and *-dhānā-*). Cf. DS 407n292.

998 Following Divy 550.17–17, the Tibetan (103a8; 110a7), and Hiraoka (HA 29; HD 68), add *mahataḥ*. Divy 553.4 (omitted).

999 Following Divy 550.14, 550.19, etc., the Tibetan (103a8; 110b1), and Hiraoka (HA 29; HD 68), add *nagaraśobhā ca*. Divy 553.6 (omitted).

1000 Following the Tibetan (103b1; 110b1–2) and Hiraoka (HA 29; HD 68), add *-śata-*. Divy 553.6 (omitted).

1001 Divy 553.18, *durnṛtyam*. Nobel (1955: i, 65n2) suggests *durnṛttam*.

1002 Following Speyer (1912: 361), the Tibetan (103b8; 111a1), Nobel (1955: i, 65n3), and Hiraoka (HA 29; HD 68), read *ārye candraprabhā*. Divy 553.27, *āryacandraprabhā*.

1003 By "focusing her attention" (*samanvāhṛtya*), Śailā has activated her knowledge and insight—in this case, regarding the karmic condition of the queen. As it is frequently said in the text (e.g., Divy 84.6–7, 190.8, 492.9–10), "the knowledge and insight of arhats does not operate unless they focus their attention." Cf. DS 408n304.

1004 Divy 554.10, *paryuṣitaparivāsā*. Egderton (BHSD, s.v. *paryuṣita*) offers this explanation: "*having completed residence* (in heaven; said of gods reborn there after having been lower beings previously; is divine existence regarded as a kind of *probation*? prob[ably] merely *change of residence*, sc. from earth." Edgerton offers this translation: "It would not be proper that we should approach the Blessed One to see him after finishing our residence (probation?); let us, while it is still unfinished, (visit him)." The cliché also occurs in the *Avadānaśataka* (i, 259.9, 282.3). Perhaps the probationary period here concerns not her time in the realm of the gods but the fact that she never finished her ordination in the human world. Cf. Nobel 1955: i, 66n5.

1005 Following the Tibetan (104a6; 111a7), Vaidya (Divy-V 470.23), and Hiraoka (HA 29; HD 68), read *cala-*. Nobel (1955: i, 66n7) and Speyer (1902: 360) suggests *calad-*. Divy 554.13, *balad-*. Cowell and Neil (Divy 554n1) query *balavad-*.

1006 Following Vaidya (Divy-V 470.24) and Hiraoka (HA 30; HD 68), *utsaṅgam*. More literally, the term means "lap," but one only has a lap when sitting, and the goddess hasn't yet sat down. Perhaps she is cradling the flowers against her stomach. Divy 554.15, *utsargam*.

1007 Hiraoka (HA 30; HD 68), following the standard cliché and the Tibetan (104a6; 111a7), adds *-padma-*. Divy 554.14 (omitted).

1008 The Sanskrit is a little peculiar here. Nobel (1955: i, 66–67n8) suggests the following reconstruction: *pūrayitvā atikrāntavarṇā* ... (?) *rātryāṃ yena bhagavāṃs tenopasaṃkrāntā upasaṃkramya bhagavantaṃ puṣpair avakīrya bhagavataḥ pādau śirasā vanditvaikānte niṣaṇṇā apīdāniṃ candraprabhāyā devakanyāyā varṇānubhāvena sarvaṃ veṇuvanaṃ kalandakanivāsam udāreṇāvabhāsena sphuṭum abhūt.*

1009 Divy 554.15, *kārandakanivāpam*. Vaidya (Divy 470.25) emends to *kalandakakanivāpam*.

1010 Following Divy 311.5 and Divy 580.19, add *smaḥ*. Or following Divy 47.16, add *vayam*. Divy 554.27 (omitted).

1011 Divy 554.28–29, *bahuduḥkhayuktaḥ*. Nobel (1955: i, 68n1) suggests *bahuduṣṭayuktaḥ*. Cf. Divy 52.28–29, *bahudoṣaduṣṭaḥ*, and MSV iv, 59.8, *bahudoṣayuktaḥ*.

1012 Following Divy 52.29, Speyer (1912: 360), Vaidya (Divy-V471.3), Nobel (1955: i, 67–68n3), and Hiraoka (HA 30; HD 68), read *supuṇyā*. Divy 555.1, *svāpuṇyā*.

1013 Following Divy 53.1, Speyer (1912: 360), Nobel (1955: i, 67–68n3), and Hiraoka (HA 30; HD 68), read *tīrṇā ca*. Divy 555.5, *tīrṇaś ca*.

1014 Divy 555.12, *parigamya* (mss. insert *ca*) *pradakṣiṇam*. Cf. MSV iv, 601, *praṇipatya ca dakṣiṇam*. Nobel (1955: i, 68n5) therefore suggests *parigamya ca dakṣiṇam*.

1015 Following Speyer (1912: 360), Vaidya (Divy-V 471.15), Nobel (1955: i, 68n5), and Hiraoka (HA 30; HD 68), read *jitāriṃ*. Divy 555.12, *jitāraṃ*.

1016 Following Divy 462.17, Cowell and Neil's query (Divy 555n3), Speyer (1912: 360), Vaidya (Divy-V 471.17), and Hiraoka (HA 30; HD 68), read *sasya-*. Divy 555.14, *samyak* (mss. ABD, *samyasaṃ-*).

1017 Divy 555.17, *svarbhavanaṃ*. Speyer (1902: 360), Nobel (1955: i, 68n6), Hiraoka

(HA 30; HD 68), MSV iv, 60.5, and the Tibetan (104b8; 112a3), read *svabhavanaṃ*. That is, "her home." See too Divy 464.5, where I also prefer *svar-* to *sva-*.

1018 Divy 555.22, *middhāvasthalocanāparisphuṭo 'vijñātaḥ*. Nobel (1955: i, 68n9) suggests *middhāvaṣṭabdhalocano 'parisphuṭavijñānaḥ*, which he translates as "Schlaftrunkenen Auges und noch nicht bei klarem Bewusstsein." Tharchin (1984: 27) offers this translation: "his eyes and mind still clouded by sleep." Cf. Edgerton (BHSD, s.v. *middha*), which Nobel thinks needs correcting.

1019 Divy 555.26, *dṛṣṭadharmā*. Nobel (1955: i, 69n1) suggests *dṛṣṭadharme* or *dṛṣṭadharma eva*.

1020 Following the Tibetan (105a6; 112b1) and Hiraoka (HA 30; HD 68), read *saṃnidhikāraparibhogena*. Nobel (1955: i, 69n3) suggests *saṃnidhānakāraparibhogena* and offers this translation: "Es wäre nicht recht, wenn ich, nachdem mich die Göttin aufgefordert hat, als Hausherr im Hause bleibe, dem Genuss der angehäuften Schätze und den Lüsten nachgehe." Also possible is this: "It wouldn't be proper for me to remain a householder, clinging to my home, now that I've been urged by a deity [to renounce]. Should I enjoy hoarding wealth here or sensual pleasures [in heaven]? Cf. *Saṅghabhedavastu* i, 143.19–20. Divy 556.4–5, *saṃnidhānī kālaparibhogena*. This is obscure, and likely corrupt. Edgerton (BHSD), trying to make sense of *saṃnidhānin*, suggests "staying in the neighborhood, living in the same vicinity (as at present)?" The whole sentence, quite provisionally, might be rendered, "Should I stay where I am with deadly pleasures or enjoy sensual delights [in heaven]?"

1021 Following the Tibetan (105b4; 112b7) and Hiraoka (HA 30; HD 68–69), read *mayā rājyaṃ kārayatā kasyacid aparādhaṃ taṃ kṣantavyam*. Nobel (1955: i, 70n1) suggests *yan mayā rājyaṃ kārayatā kasyacit kiṃcid aparā(d)dhaṃ kṛtaṃ tat kṣāntavyam iti*. Divy 556.20–21, *bhūyaśaḥ putram āha | putra tvayā rājyaṃ kārayatā kasyacid aparādhyaṃ na* (mss., *ta*) *kṣāntavyam iti*. That is, "And to his son, he said, 'Son, while ruling the kingdom you should not forgive anyone's wrongdoing.'" These words, though sensible, don't seem correct in this context.

1022 Following Vaidya (Divy-V 472.12) and Divy 46.20–21, 101.5, 250.15, etc., add *saṃprasthitaḥ*. Divy 556.26 (omitted).

1023 Hiraoka (HA 30; HD 69), following the Tibetan (105b6; 113a2) and Divy 557.8, adds *-kumāra-*. That is, "princes." Divy 556.27 (omitted).

1024 Divy 557.15 *pauruṣān* (mss., *pauruṣāṇ*). Nobel (1955: i, 70n3) suggests emending to *pauruṣeyān*.

1025 Read *te kathayanti*. Divy 557.16–17, "he said" (*sa kathayati*).

1026 Following Divy 552.9, 552.28, 557.25, etc., the Tibetan (106b2; 113b7), and Hiraoka (HA 30; HD 69), read *priyavayasyā*. Divy 557.29, *vayasyā*. According to the Tibetan, Rudrāyaṇa prefaces his remarks by saying, "No, it isn't like that." Cf. Nobel 1955: i, 71n5.

1027 Following Nobel (1955: i, 71n6) and Vaidya (Divy-V 473.2), read *abhyunnamayya*. Divy 558.1, *atyunnamayya*.

1028 Following Nobel (1955: i, 71n8) and Vaidya (Divy-V 473.4), read *ākāṅkṣante*. Divy 558.5, *ākāṅkṣate*.

1029 Divy 558.8, *anekaśatāyā*. Hiraoka (HA 30; HD 69), following the Tibetan (106b6; 114a3), reads *anekaśatasahasrāyā*. That is, "many hundreds and thousands." Cf. Nobel 1955: i, 71n9.

1030 Divy 558.20, *-kara-*. Nobel (1955: i, 72n2) and Hiraoka (HA 30; HD 69), following

Divy 37.1–2, read *-karaka-*. See note 182. And then, following the standard cliché (Divy 37.2, 48.21, 159.10, etc.) and the Tibetan (107a3; 114a7), Hiraoka (HA 30; HD 69) adds *saptāhāvaropitakeśaśmaśruḥ*. That is, "with a week's growth of hair and beard."

1031 Following Divy-V 473.18, read *evaṃ sthitaḥ*. Divy 558.22–23, *naiva sthitaḥ*. Cf. Divy 48.24 and 159.12, *naiva sthitā*, which Vaidya (Divy-V 29.32 and 98.22) emends to *evaṃ sthitā*, and Divy 342.2, *nopasthitā*, which Vaidya (Divy-V 211.23) also emends to *evaṃ sthitā*. Nobel (1955: i, 72n3) and Hiraoka (HA 30; HD 69) suggest "clothed" (*nepatthitaḥ*). See note 183.

1032 Divy 559.6, *śatapale*. More literally, the bowls are "one hundred *palas* in size." Nobel (1955: i, 73) takes this to mean "one hundred ounces in weight," although the weight of a *pala* seems to have differed by region.

1033 Following Nobel (1955: i, 73n3) and Vaidya (Divy-V 473.28), read *rājate*. Divy 559.6, *rajate*.

1034 Following Nobel (1955: i, 73n4), read *māṃsopasecitam*. Divy 559.8, *māṃsopasevitam*. Cf. Pāli *maṃsupasecanam*.

1035 Following Edgerton (BHSD, s.v. *sparśita*), read *nivāte sparśitārgaḍe*. Divy 559.12, *nirvāte sparśitāgate*. Edgerton offers this translation: "Having slept in a secure tower with locked door-bolts, are you not tormented sitting at the roots of trees?" Also possible is that *nirvāte* (or *nivāte*) could mean "sheltered from the wind" or perhaps "with closed windows." Nobel (1955: i, 73) offers this translation: "windstill und mit Türbalken verschlossen." See too Nobel 1955: i, 73nn5–6.

1036 Following the Tibetan (107b5; 115a3–40) and Nobel (1955: i, 74), read *gavaṃ damayate yugam*. Divy 559.26, *kathaṃ damayate yugam*. This is obscure. Perhaps, "How does he subdue the yoke?" Cf. Hiraoka 2007: ii, 528n222.

1037 Following the Tibetan (107b6; 115a4) and Hiraoka (HA 30; HD 69), read *purātanam*. Nobel (1955: i, 74n4) suggests *-parāyaṇaḥ*. Divy 559.27, *-parāyaṇa*. That is, "O you who are devoted to pleasure."

1038 Divy 560.2, *dharmakāyena*. Nobel (1955: i, 75n1) and Hiraoka (HA 30; HD 69), following the Tibetan (107b7; 115a5), read *dharmaṃ kāyena*.

1039 Divy 560.3. *deva tripathanirāśī* (mss., *tṛ*; ms. C, *-nirvāṇī*). Perhaps these three paths refer to this world, the upper world (i.e., the divine realms), and the under world (i.e., the realms of hell). Nobel (1955: i, 75n2) and Hiraoka (HA 30; HD 69), following the Tibetan (107b7; 115a5) and in consideration of the meter, read *devatvam atha nirvāṇam*. Nobel (1955: i, 75) offers this translation: "Dieser wird bestimmt ein Gott werden oder in das Nirvāṇa eingehen."

1040 Divy 560.3, *dhruvaṃ tasya vidhīyate*. In Pāli, *dhuva* (= Skt., *dhruva*) can be a synonym for *nibbāna* (*Saṃyutta-nikāya* iv, 370; cf. Dhadphale 1980).

1041 Divy 560.4, *nṛpaḥ*. Hiraoka (HA 30; HD 69), following the Tibetan (107b7; 115a5), reads *nṛpa*. That is, "O king."

1042 Divy 560.7–8, *śrutvā dharmaṃ tato jñeyo* (mss., *jñeyā*) *yadi tvaṃ prītim iṣyasi*. Nobel (1955: i, 75n5) suggests *śrutvā dharmaṃ tato deva yatra* (or *yena*) *te prītir eṣyasi*. That is, "After hearing the dharma you can go where you please."

1043 Read *puruṣasyāyuḥ*. Nobel (1955: i, 75n8) suggests *poṣasyāyuḥ* or *purṣasyāyuḥ* to preserve the meter. Divy 560.11, *puruṣasyāsu*. Further emendations could also be made as the subject of this sentence is in the plural while the verb is in the singular.

1044 Following Speyer (1912: 361), Smith (1953: 125), the Tibetan (108a1; 115a7), Nobel

(1955: i, 75n9), and Hiraoka (HA 30; HD 69), read *putradāradhaneṣu*. Divy 560.12, *putraparadhaneṣu*. Also possible is *putrāparādhaneṣu*—that is, "wives, women, and money." In this case, the women are "other women" (i.e., other than one's wives).

1045 Read *putradveṣiṇīm*. Divy 560.13, *putrād vepiṇīyām* (*sic* ms. D; mss. ABCE, *vepilī*). Cowell and Neil (Divy 560n4) query *vaiparītyam*. That is, "opposition." Hiraoka (HA 30; HD 69) concurs. Vaidya (Divy-V 475.1) emends to *veṣiṇīyām*. Edgerton (BHSD, s.v. *kṛti*) suggests *vepilīyām*. The reading and meaning here isn't clear. Cowell and Neil (Divy 711) write "Does this mean that 'a spell comes through a wife'?" In their index, however, *kṛti* is defined as a "house for relics." Edgerton (BHSD, s.v. *kṛti*) refers to this as "an obscure passage where the mg. is probably also *work*, and surely not *house for relics*." Helmer Smith (1953: 126) offers detailed comments on *vepiṇīyām*—emended to *vepiliyam* by way of *vepuliyam*—and suggests this translation: "Quelle est la joie que nous donneront un fils, une épouse, des biens? D'un fils on nous promet la surproduction, l'épouse n'est, dit-on, qu'une outre, les biens sont convoités par les bandits." Cf. the Tibetan (108a2; 115b1) and Nobel 1955: i, 76n1. Nobel (1955: i, 76) offers this translation: "Wegen des Sohnes nennt man (ihn) freudig, wegen der Gattin bezeichnen sie (ihn) hochmütig."

1046 Divy 560.14, *caurā*. Vaidya (Divy-V 475.2) emends to "heroes" (*śaurā*).

1047 Divy 560.18, *ko neha* (mss., *nveha*). Nobel (1955: i, 76n2) reads *ko 'dyeha*.

1048 Following Speyer (1912: 361), Vaidya (Divy-V 475.9–10), the Tibetan (108a3; 115b2), and Hiraoka (HA 30; HD 69), read *mahānubhāvā vṛṣṇyandhakāḥ kuravaḥ pāṇḍavāś ca*. Cf. Nobel 1955: i, 76n3, *-bhāvāḥ kṛṣṇāndhakāḥ*. Divy 560.20–21, *mahānubhāvās* (mss., *-bhāvā*) *tṛṣṇāndhakāḥ kuravaś ca sapāṇḍavāś ca*. It could be said, however, that the Kurus and the Pāṇḍavas, battling each other as they do in the *Mahābhārata*, are "blinded by desire" (*tṛṣṇāndhakāḥ*).

1049 Following Speyer (1912: 361), the Tibetan (108a3; 115b2), Nobel (1955: i, 76n4), and Hiraoka (HA 30; HD 69), read *saṃpannavittā yaśasā jvalantaḥ*. Divy 560.22, *saṃpannacittā yaśaḥsamājvalantaḥ*. Vaidya (Divy V 475.11) reads *saṃpannacittā yaśasā jvalantaḥ*.

1050 Divy 560.22–23, *te na śaktā maraṇaṃ nopagantum* (mss., *nāpa-*). Nobel (1955: i, 76n5) reads *te nāpi śaktā maranam apahantum*.

1051 Divy 560.26, *vittapūgair* (ex conj.; mss. AC, *-sūgair*; ms. D, *-sagair*; mss. BE, *cittasagair*) *na* [*varair*]. Vaidya (Divy-V 475.15) does not add in *varair*. Following the Tibetan (108a3; 115b2), Hiraoka (HA 30; HD 69) reads *bhṛtyapūgaiḥ* and Nobel (1955: i, 76n7) reads *bhṛtyavargaiḥ*. That is, "by a staff of servants."

1052 Divy 561.3, *sa pṛthivīpradeśaḥ*. Nobel (1955: i, 77n1) suggests *so pṛthivīpradeśaḥ* and likewise in the next verse (Divy 561.7).

1053 A version of this verse and the next can be found in the *Dhammapada* (vv. 127–28). Cf. Divy 532.27–29.

1054 Divy 561.8, *diśo daśa* (mss. ABC, *daśaḥ*). Nobel (1955: i, 77n3) suggests *diśo diśaḥ*. This verse and the next share similarities with *Dhammapada* v. 149: *yān' imāni apatthāni alāpūn' eva sārade | kāpotakāni aṭṭhini tāni disvāna kā rati*. Cf. Nobel 1955: i, 77n4.

1055 Following Speyer (1902: 561), the Tibetan (108a5; 115b4), Hiraoka (HA 30; HD 69–70), read *apāstāni*. Divy 561.10, *upasthānāni*.

1056 Following Cowell and Neil's query (Divy 561n3), read *śārade*. The commentary to

Dhammapada v. 149 (*Dhammapada-aṭṭhakathā* iii, 112; cited in PTSD) explains *sārade* as "scattered by the autumn winds." Divy 561.10, *serabhe* (*sic* mss.). Speyer (1902: 561), the Tibetan (108a6; 115b5), and Hiraoka (HA 30; HD 70) read *śerate*. Nobel (1955: i, 77) offers extensive notes on this verse and provides this translation: "Wenn man all diese muschelfarbigen Schädel sieht, die weggeworfen sind und niedergefallenen Kürbissen gleichen, welche Freude (sollte man dann) hier (noch haben)!"

1057 Divy 561.14, *mṛtyor vaśaṃ bhuṅkte*. Nobel (1955: i, 78n1) and Hiraoka (HA 30; HD 70), following the Tibetan (108a7; 115b6), read *martyo 'śanaṃ bhuṅkte*. That is, "As long as a person eats food." Nobel (1955: i, 78n1) finds the alternative "senseless," but I've kept it anyway. The term *martyaḥ* also appears in the next verse (Divy 561.17).

1058 Following the Tibetan (108a7; 115b6), Nobel (1955: i, 78n1), and Hiraoka (HA 30; HD 70), read *anyat kṣiptam*. Nobel (1955: i, 78) offers this translation for the verse: "(Nur) solange der Mensch Speise isst, sich kleidet oder gibt, ist dieses als sein eigen zu bezeichnen; das andere wird weggeworfen und geht dahin." Divy 561.15, *anyan nityam*.

1059 Divy 561.16, *acaurāharaṇam*. Vaidya (Divy-V 476.3) emends to *aśaurāharaṇam*.

1060 Following Vaidya (Divy-V 476.10), the Tibetan (108a7; 115b6), Nobel (1955: i, 78n5), and Hiraoka (HA 30; HD 70), read *rajatajātarūpam*. Divy 561.22–23, *rajatarūpam*.

1061 Divy 561.25–26, *saced* (mss. ABDE, *sacedṛśaṃ*) *ṛṇaṃ bhavati* [to preserve the meter, read *bhoti*] *pitur mṛtasya priyāḥ sutā nāsya vahnim* [*vahanti*]. As Cowell and Neil (Divy 561n13) observe, this line is missing a verb. Following the Tibetan (108b1; 116a1) and Nobel (1955: i, 78n6)—*khyer*—add *vahanti* (or perhaps *haranti*). Nobel offers this translation: "Wenn nach dem Tode des Vaters Schulden entstehen, dann bringen die lieben Söhne ihm nicht das Feuer." Vaidya (Divy-V 476.14), less convincingly, suggests adding *viśanti*—as in, "his dear sons can't ascend his funeral pyre."

1062 Divy 561.27–28, *rāhuḥ* (ms. E, *cāhuḥ*) *pitā mama kāryateti*. This line is corrupt and requires revision. Following the Tibetan (108b1; 116a1) and Nobel (1955: i, 78n7), read *nāhuḥ* for *rāhuḥ* (ms. E, *cāhuḥ*). Otherwise, "My father is a Rāhu!" This is a more strained reading. Rāhu is a demon that tried to join the gods in drinking the immortal nectar that they had churned from the ocean. The sun and the moon exposed Rāhu as an imposter, and Viṣṇu decapitated him. But Rāhu had tasted the nectar, so his severed head became immortal. Even now, on occasion, it takes its revenge on the sun and the moon by swallowing them up as a celestial body that sometimes eclipses them. Perhaps the idea here could be that their father was the demon that swallowed the moon of their wealth.

Also problematic here is that the meter is broken—there is a missing syllable—and it isn't clear how best to understand the unattested *kāryateti*. The Tibetan (108b1; 116a1) reads *bdag gi pha 'am rjer me smra*. Perhaps, "They don't even say [he is] my father or master." Nobel (1955: i, 78) offers this translation: "Bei seinem Tode weinen sie nicht mit Tränen im Angesicht und sagen nicht: 'mein Vater, ach!'" For the missing syllable, perhaps add *kim* or *vā*, based on the Tibetan *'am*. Hiraoka (2007: ii, 530n248) suggests *kāruṇiko ti* for *kāryateti*—apparently reading *rje* in the sense of *snying rje*—but makes no emendations. Perhaps emend to *bhārteti*.

1063 Following the Tibetan (108b1; 116a1), Nobel (1955: i, 78n8), and Hiraoka (HA 30;

HD 70), read *āḍhyam tu matvāpi*. Divy 562.1, *āyantu sattvāḥ* (ms. C, *sattvā 'pi pitā*). That is, "'Come everyone!"

1064 Divy 562.3, *dūṣyair enaṃ prāvṛtam nirharanti jyotiḥ samādāya dahanti*. Vaidya (Divy-V 476.22) reads . . . [*ca taṃ*] *dahanti*. Nobel (1955: i, 79n1) reads *dūṣyeṇa taṃ prāvṛta nirharanti jyotiḥ samādāya tato dahanti*.

1065 Divy 562.4, *sa dahyate jñātibhī rudyamāna* (mss. BD, *-mānaiḥ*) *ekena vastreṇa vihāya bhogam*. Or perhaps understand *bhoga* as "property." In other words, he burns with nothing but a single sheet of cloth to his name, all his other property left behind. Nobel (1955: i, 79n1) suggests emending to *jñātibhi*, for metrical reasons, and after *bhogam* adding *kurvanti* or *bhuñjante* (Tib., *longs spyod byed*). Perhaps, "While his relatives weep, he burns with just a single cloth, and then they leave him behind and enjoy themselves."

1066 Following Vaidya (Divy-V 477.9), the Tibetan (109A1; 116b1), Nobel (1955: i, 79–80n4), and Hiraoka (HA 30; HD 70), read *visāriṇī tṛṣṇā*. Divy 562.23, *visāriṇī kṛṣṇā*. Perhaps, "the spreading black fire." Edgerton (BHSD, s.v. *visāriṇī*) offers a long note on this passage and explains that "the words *visāriṇī kṛṣṇā* perhaps corruptly represent an abl. phrase, *from his evil course*."

1067 Following the Tibetan (109a2; 116b3), Nobel (1955: i, 80n2), and Hiraoka (HA 30; HD 70), add *duṣṭasya*. Divy 563.2 (omitted). As Cowell and Neil (Divy 563n2) note, there is a "word lost" here. Vaidya (Divy-V 477.14) suggests "undigested" (*ajīrṇasya*).

1068 Following the Tibetan (109a5; 116b5), Nobel (1955: i, 80n6), and Hiraoka (HA 30; HD 70), read *nākhaṇḍitā*. Divy 563.8, *nākranditā*. Perhaps, "unless they are beaten."

1069 Hiraoka (HA 30; HD 70), following the Tibetan (109a5; 116b5), adds *na*. Divy 563.9 (omitted).

1070 Following Vaidya (Divy-V 477.20), the Tibetan (109a5–6; 116b5–6), Nobel (1955: i, 80n7), and Hiraoka (HA 30; HD 70), read *yad*. Divy 563.10, *yadi*.

1071 The Tibetan preserves additional questions about King Śikhaṇḍin's various ministers.

1072 Divy 563.28, *pracārite* (ms. D, *pravārite*). Cf. Divy 564.5, *pracāritam* (ms. D, *pravār-?*). Edgerton (BHSD) suggests "town" or "region." Nobel (1955: i, 81n3), following the Tibetan (109b2; 117a3), suggests *prati(ni)vṛttya* or *prati(ni)vartitvā*.

1073 Divy 564.18, *ko nu virodha iti*. Speyer (1902: 361), the Tibetan (110a1; 117b2), and Hiraoka (HA 30; HD 70) read *ko 'tra virodha iti*.

1074 Vaidya (Divy-V 478.27) marks this with a question mark. Nobel (1955: i, 82) reads, "Wenn Vater oder Brüder oder auch der dem eigenen Körper entsprossene Sohn sich zu den Widersachern begeben, dann muss man die Erde (mit ihnen) mehren?"

1075 Cf. Divy 448.25–26.

1076 Divy 565.10, *tapanīyam*. The Tibetan (110a8; 118a2) reads *tarkaṇīyam*. That is, "there is nothing here to consider." Cf. Nobel 1955: i, 82n4.

1077 Divy 565.11, *yad*. As Nobel (1955: i, 82n5) notes, one would expect *ye*.

1078 Divy 565.18, *hiraṇyasuvarṇa-*. Although *hiraṇya* and *suvarṇa* are often near synonyms (see note 110), here I take them as "silver" and "gold," for that reading makes the most sense at Divy 575.11. Here Nobel (1955: i, 83) translates *hiraṇya* as "Kostbarkeiten" but later (1955: i, 96n5) takes it to mean "silver."

1079 Divy 566.18, *āryaparābhavacihnakaram*. This is obscure, and Nobel (1955: i, 84n2) likewise finds it lacking sense. He suggests *āryabhāvacihnakaram*. That is, "marking your becoming a noble one."

1080 Nobel (1955: i, 84) offers this translation of the Tibetan: "Bester der Männer, was das Kennzeichen der deinem Charakter angemessenen Wesenheit des Heiligen (ausmacht), das hast du vollendet. Du Guter, was (aber) dem Charakter jenes entspricht, das wirst du jetzt sehen."

1081 Divy 567.4, *anurūpaṃ* (mss. ABC, *anuyāṃ*; mss. DE, *anurūpāṃ*) *gacchāmīti*. The Tibetan (111b3; 119a5), Nobel (1955: i, 85n1), and Hiraoka (HA 31; HD 70) read *anuprāpsyāmīti*. Nobel (1955: i, 85n1) also reads *svakārtham* for *svakāryam*.

1082 Cf. Divy 340.26–28.

1083 Following Divy 5.5, 55.1, the Tibetan (112a7; 120a3), Nobel (1955: i, 86n3), and Hiraoka (HA 31; HD 70), read *deśayāpy evaitat*. Divy 567.3, *deśayāmy etat*.

1084 Following the Tibetan 112a8; 120a3), Nobel (1955: i, 86n4), and Hiraoka (HA 31; HD 70), read *māsau sattvaḥ*. Divy 568.2, *mamāsau sattvaḥ*. Perhaps, "so that this being [who is a part] of me."

1085 Following the Tibetan (112a8; 120a4), Nobel (1955: i, 86n5), and Hiraoka (HA 31; HD 70), read *karma-*. Divy 568.3, *dharma-* (mss., *dharmo-*).

1086 Divy 568.3–4, *ṛkāro 'pi na pratibhāti prāgeva ṛddhiḥ*. This is a tricky idiom to capture. Tharchin (1984: 47) offers this translation: "'I should make use of my miraculous powers and escape, which will save this evil one from dropping into the hells.' But when he attempted to do so, his karma prevented him even from framing the required thought, much less performing the miracle." And according to Nobel (1955: i, 86): "Aber welches Zaubermittel er auch begann, das wurde auf Grund seiner Taten zunichte, und so entschwand schon die erste Silbe des Zauberspruches, um wieviel eher erst der ganze Zauberspruch!"

1087 Following Hiraoka (HA 31; HD 70), read *narakān*. Divy 568.13, *narakam*.

1088 Divy 568.29, *devān*. Understand as *devanikāyān*.

1089 This divine realm isn't mentioned in the other instances of this passage. See appendix.

1090 The following pronouncements (Divy 569.8–13) occur in a more abridged form than they do in the standard cliché (e.g. Divy 68.26–69.5, 139.6–16). I translate them in full nonetheless.

1091 Following Vaidya (Divy-V 482.12), read *dhīra buddhyā*. Divy 569.23, *dhīrabuddhyā*. And following Vaidya (Divy-V 483.13) and Hiraoka (HA 31; HD 71), read *śramaṇa jinendra kāṅkṣitānām*. Cf. Nobel 1955: i, 89n2. Divy 569.24, *śravaṇajinendrakāṅkṣitānām*.

1092 Here the Tibetan (113b7–114a1; 121b4–5) offers an account that is not preserved in the Sanskrit. Cf. Nobel 1955: i, 89n4 and Hiraoka 2007: ii, 534n317.

1093 Divy 570.6, *sāśrukaṇṭhaḥ*. Cf. Divy 173.23 and DS 433n637.

1094 Divy 570.19, *prāṇaviyogaḥ*. Nobel (1955: i, 90n1) suggests *prāṇaviyoge*.

1095 Following Nobel (1955: i, 90n4), read *sa śoka-*. Divy 570.25, *manaḥśoka-* (mss., *maśoka-*). Cf. the Tibetan (114a8; 122a5).

1096 Divy 570.25, *haritalūna*. Reading the former as "being meaningless," Speyer (1902: 361) suggests *hastalūna*. The Tibetan (114a8; 122a5) reads *sdon por brngas pa*. Nobel (1955: i, 90) offers this translation: "und welkte wie grün abgemähtes Schilfrohr dahin."

1097 Divy 571.6, *vinipātya*. Nobel (1955: i, 91n2) suggests following the Tibetan, which reads *chud gzan pa*, and translating this as "consumed." I think the idea idea here is that since they were charlatans, they "consumed" the offerings, but in doing so they also "ruined" them. Since the offerings were eaten by those unworthy of offerings, they wouldn't generate much merit for their donors. Cf. Edgerton (BHSD, s.v. *vinipātayati*).

1098 Following Speyer (1902: 361), the Tibetan (114b4; 122b2), and Hiraoka (HA 31; HD 71), read *svīkṛtya*. Divy 571.8, *kṛtvā*. Nobel (1955: i, 91n2) suggests *hṛtvā*. Cf. Divy 572.26, *māṃsapeśīm ādāya*.

1099 The queen is unnamed here, although she is called Taralikā in the *Avadānakalpalatā* (no. 40, v. 120). Śikhaṇḍin is apparently her son, and now that he has become king, she has become the principal queen, the role previously filled by Queen Candraprabhā.

1100 Divy 571.15, *prativinodayāmi* (mss., *pratinod-*). Edgerton (BHSD) defines this as "dispels, removes, gets rid of." One could also take this to mean "remove [the suffering]" or "remove [the sin]." Cf. Tharchin (1984: 51) and Nobel (1955: i, 91n5), who also suggests reading *tāvad* for *tad*. Perhaps, "I can make that go away."

1101 Divy 571.26–27, *dattaṃ bhavatu | sā kathayati | yathābhūtaṃ* . . . Hiraoka (HA 31; HD 71), following the Tibetan (115a3; 123a1), emends to *bhavatu kathaya yāthābhūtam*. Nobel (1955: i, 91n6) offers a slightly different arrangement: *dattaṃ bhavatu | (tat) kathaya yāthā bhūtam*. That is, "Your safety is guaranteed. Tell it like it is."

1102 Divy 572.1, *ekāntīkariṣyantīti* (mss. ABC, *ekākikar-*; ms. E, *akākikar*). Edgerton (BSHD, s.v. *ekāntīkaroti*), citing this passage, explains that this verb means "makes all right, makes perfect, completes." Perhaps, "they will give you the last word in the matter." Nobel (1955: i, 92n2) suggests *vyantīkariṣyantīti*. That is, "put an end to" or "get rid of."

1103 Divy 572.7, *anukūlam*. Nobel (1955: i, 92n4) strongly prefers the Tibetan (115a8; 123a5), which reads *ananukūlam*.

1104 The text here seems to be incomplete. Cf. Nobel 1955: i, 93n2.

1105 Divy 573.6, *adbhutaṃ* (mss. CD, *adbhuta*) *saṃvṛttam* (mss., *-ttāḥ*). Nobel (1955: i, 93n6), following the Tibetan (116a4; 124a2), suggests *maṅkavaḥ saṃvṛttāḥ*. That is, "were dismayed."

1106 Following the Tibetan (116a4; 124a2), Nobel (1995: 93n6), and Hiraoka (HA 31; HD 71), read *anudagrā aviśāradāḥ*. Divy 573.6, *anubhāvodagrā aviśāradāḥ*. Perhaps, "And those who were well known for their great power were unnerved."

1107 Following Nobel (1995: 93n7) read *āryasya mahākātyāyanasya*. Hiraoka (HA 31; HD 71) suggests *āryakātyāyanasya*. Cf. the Tibetan (116a4; 124a2). Divy 573.8, *āryakāśyapasya kātyāyanasya*. That is, "the noble Kāśyapa, to Kātyāyana."

1108 Divy 573.12, *vinayāpekṣayā*. Perhaps this is meant to evoke, or is a misprint for, *vineyāpekṣayā* or *vaineyāpekṣayā*—"in expectation of a new disciple." Both of these terms occur frequently in the text while this is the lone occurrence of *vinayāpekṣayā*.

1109 Following the Tibetan (116a4; 124a2), Nobel (1955: i, 94n2), and Hiraoka (HA 31; HD 71), read *duḥkhaṃ ca raṅgacchavikarma kriyate*. Divy 573.21–22, *duḥkhaṃ carad gacchati karma kriyate*. Perhaps, "that he proceeds practicing suffering; that an action will be done by him." This passage is puzzling. Cowell and Neil (Divy 711) offer this translation: "I fear lest the king should show me disfavour; misfortune is hastening to him, his fate is working, he will bespatter my cup and robes with dust." Nobel (1955: i, 94) offers this translation: "da die Arbeit des Färbens schwierig ist, wäre es nicht gut, wenn die Mönchsgewänder von Staub (Schmutz) getroffen würden."

1110 Following Speyer (1902: 361) and Hiraoka (HA 31; HD 71), read *avakariṣyatīti.* Divy 573.22, *'vatariṣyatīti.* Cf. Nobel 1955: i, 94n2.

1111 Following Nobel (1955: i, 94n2), read *mā sma cīvarāṇi.* Hiraoka (HA 31; HD 71) reads *cīvarāṇi.* Divy 573.22, *pātracīvarāṇi.*

1112 Divy 573.29–574.1, *māham asya pitṛmārakasya rajasāṃ* (ms. D, *jarasāṃ*) *pravrajyāmīti.* Following Vaidya (Divy-V 485.4), read *rajasā.* Nobel (1955: i, 94n4) reads *rajasā saṃprakṣya iti.* That is, "Let me not be touched by the dirt..."

1113 Following the Tibetan (116b6–7; 124b4) and Hiraoka (HA 31; HD 71), read *ekaikena ekaikā pāṃśumuṣṭi āyuṣmato mahākātyāyanasyopari kṣiptā | tasyopari.* Cf. Nobel 1955: i, 95n1. Divy 574.5, *ekaikayā pāṃśumuṣṭyā āyuṣmato mahākātyāyanasyopari.* That is, "With each handful of dirt, [a great pile of dirt was amassed] on top of the venerable Mahākātyāyana."

1114 Divy 574.8, *buddhyāyamānāḥ.* Cowell and Neil (Divy 711) translate this tentatively as "thinking him a Buddha," but Edgerton (BHSD, s.v. *buddhyāyate*) rejects this translation and suggests "being mentally alert." Also possible is "coming to understand the situation." Nobel (1955: i, 95n4) and Hiraoka (HA 31; HD 71), following the Tibetan (116b8; 124b5), read *avadhyāyamānāḥ.* That is, "thinking ill of him."

1115 Following Edgerton (BHSD, s.v. *adūṣin*), Nobel (1955: i, 95n6), and Hiraoka (HA 31; HD 71), read *adūṣyanapakārī.* Divy 574.11, *aduṣyanayakārī.*

1116 Divy 574.15, *kiṃ anyad bhaviṣyatīti.* Nobel (1955: i, 95n7) and Hiraoka (HA 31; HD 71), following the Tibetan (117a2; 124b7), add before this *santi karmāṇi.* That is, "These are the deeds."

1117 Divy 574.16, *mahākātyāyane* (mss. AD, *-yana*) *janakāyasahāyena.* Hiraoka (HA 31; HD 71) omits *mahākātyāyane* because it is "out of context." Nobel (1955: i, 96n2) reads *mahājanakāyasahāyena.*

1118 Following Cowell and Neil (574n5) and Nobel (1955: i, 96n2), add *vipākaḥ.* Divy 574.17 (omitted).

1119 Divy 574.21, *hiraṇya-.* Elsewhere I take this to mean "gold," particularly when it is paired with terms such as *rajata.* But here and in what follows (Divy 576.14–16), where it is paired with *suvarṇa-*, Nobel (1955: i, 96n5) takes it to mean "silver," and I follow his lead. Cf. Divy 565.18.

1120 Following the Tibetan (117b2–3; 125a7), Nobel (1955: i, 96n8), and Hiraoka (HA 31; HD 71), read *kiṃ devenārye mahākātyāyane kiṃcit kṛtam | kiṃ pāṃśunāvaṣṭabdhaḥ.* Divy 575.3–4, *kiṃ devenāryo mahākātyāyanaḥ kiṃcid uktaḥ pāṃśunā 'vaṣṭabdhaḥ.* Perhaps, "Did my lord say something about the noble Mahākātyāyana being buried by dirt?"

1121 Divy 575.7, *kānupūrvīṃ* (*sic* mss.) *kathayati.* Hiraoka (HA 31; HD 71), following Divy 574.18 and the Tibetan (117b4; 125b1), reads *kānupūrvī bhaviṣyati.*

1122 Following Hiraoka (HA 31; HD 71), omit Divy 575.14–20. I agree with Hiraoka (HD 71) that this "is unnecessarily copied from the preceding sentences (Divy 574.25–575.2)." Cf. Nobel 1955: i, 97n1.

1123 Divy 575.21–22, *samucchinnapiṇḍapātaḥ pāṃśuvarṣeṇāvaṣṭabdhaḥ sa kim anyad vaditum īdṛśaṃ vā* (*sic* mss. corrupt) *vadate devato vā pāpanaram iti.* This is obscure. Vaidya (Divy-V 486.3) reads *vadatu* for *vaditum* and marks *pāpanaram* with a question mark. I read *pāpakaram* for *pāpanaram.* Nobel (1955: i, 97nn2–3), following the Tibetan (117b7–8; 125b3–4), suggests *deva yo brāhmaṇaḥ saṃprayata-*

samucchinnapiṇḍapātaḥ sa kiṃ śobhanaṃ cintayiṣyati | sa devena pañcaśataparivāraḥ samucchinnapiṇḍapātaḥ pāṃśunāpy avaṣṭabdhaḥ | pāṃśuvarṇāvaṣṭabdhaḥ sa kim anyad vaditum īdṛśaṃ yad vadate 'to (vākyaṃ) kalyāṇataram iti. He offers this translation: "Majestät, wenn man einem Brahmanen (erst) Bettelmahlzeiten gewährt und (sie ihm nachher) eingestellt hat, was soll er Gutes denken! Der König hat ihm samt seinem Gefolge der fünfhundert (Mönche erst) Bettermahlzeiten gewährt und (sie ihm nachher) eingestellt und hat ihn auch noch mit Staub bedeckt; wie sollte er da eine andere segensreichere Rede führen als das was er sagt!"

1124 Divy 576.3, *tadā.* Hiraoka (HA 31; HD 71–72), following the Tibetan (118a5; 126a1), reads *tayā.*

1125 See Divy 213.21–24; trans. in DS 352.

1126 Hiraoka (HA 31; HD 72), following Divy 574.22, 575.11, and the Tibetan (118b3; 126a6), adds *paścād.* Divy 576.18 (omitted).

1127 Here (Divy 576.22–26) the text refers to the chief ministers as "Hiruka" and "Bhiruka," so the cities that they found are their namesakes. For more on the variability of their names, see note 952.

1128 The location of this city (if it ever existed) is unknown.

1129 This is likely the same as Bharukaccha or Bhṛgukaccha, now called Bharuch, which is on the northern bank of the Narmadā River in Gujarat.

1130 Nobel (1955: i, 98n4), following the Tibetan (118b6–8; 126b1–3), reconstructs the following portion, which is missing from the Sanskrit: *rauruke nagare uccaśabdo mahāśabdo nirgataḥ | rājā kathayati | bhavantaḥ kim eṣa uccaśabdo mahāśabdaḥ | āmātyāḥ kathayanti | deva pāṃśuvarṣaṃ patitam | rājā kathayati | bhavanto yady evaṃ paryeṣata yatra* (or *yena*) *hirukabhirukāv agrāmātyau tiṣṭhataḥ | te paryeṣitum ārabdhāḥ | yāvad etau niṣpalāyitāv upalabhante | tai rājābhihitaḥ | deva etau niṣpalāyitau | nāvatiṣṭhataḥ | tato rājā śikhaṇḍī niṣpalāyitum ārabdhaḥ | amanuṣyakair dvārāṇy avaṣṭabdhāni.* That is:

A lot of noise and commotion arose in the city of Rauruka.

"Gentlemen," the king said, "what is all this noise and commotion?"

"My lord," the ministers said, "a rain of dirt has fallen."

"Gentlemen," the king said, "if that's the case, find out where the chief ministers Hiruka and Bhiruka are staying."

The ministers began to look for them and found that the two of them had escaped. "My lord," they told the king, "the two of them have escaped! They're not here."

Then King Śikhaṇḍin tried to escape, but nonhumans blocked the gates to the city.

1131 Following the Tibetan (119a1; 126b4) and Nobel (1955: i, 99n1), read *kāṃśikām.* Hiraoka (HA 31; HD 72), following Divy 579.7, reads *kāṃśyam.* Divy 576.29, "a piece of [silk] cloth from Vārāṇasī" (*kāśikām*).

1132 Read *kāṃśikā.* Divy 576.30, *kāśikā.* See previous note.

1133 Following the Tibetan (119a1; 126b4) and Hiraoka (HA 31; HD 72), read *ardhamātreṇa ākīrṇā.* Cf. Nobel 1955: i, 99n2. Divy 576.30, *anavīkṛtā.* Edgerton (BHSD) suggests "made not fresh, i.e. stained, spoiled (with dust; of a silk cloth)," and he cites only this passage, but none of these meanings apply after emending *kāśikā* to *kāṃśikā.*

1134 Following the Tibetan (119a1–2; 126b4), Nobel (1955: i, 99n3), and Hiraoka (HA

31; HD 72), read *sāvaśeṣagocara iti.* Divy 577.1, *sāva śeṣāgocara iti.* Perhaps, "A part of it still can't be seen."

1135 Divy 577.1, *niṣkāsitā pūrṇā cūḍikābaddhā saṃvṛttā.* Hiraoka (HA 31; HD 72), having emended *kāśikā* (feminine) to *kāṃśya* (neuter), reads *niṣkāsitaṃ pūrṇaṃ cūḍikābaddhaṃ saṃvṛttaṃ.* This isn't necessary if we read *kāṃśikā.*

1136 Following Nobel (1955: i, 99n4), read *agocarībhūtā.* Divy 577.3, "It's become uninhabitable [out there]" (*agocarībhūtam*). Cf. Divy 577.1. Tharchin (1984: 65) offers this translation of the Tibetan: "This is now no place to be."

1137 Perhaps we should emend Khara to Khala (Threshing Ground), considering that in the town there is a "granary" (*khalābhidhāna* | Divy 577.12). Cf. Nobel 1955: i, 100n2. The term *khara* (donkey? heron?) doesn't make much sense in this context. The Tibetan reads *kharavana.* Cf. Nobel 1995: 100n1.

1138 Following the Tibetan (119a6; 127a1) and Hiraoka (HA 31; HD 72), read *te.* Divy 577.12, *tena.*

1139 Divy 577.14, *piṇḍapātram.* Read as *piṇḍāya.* Cf. Divy 579.14 and Nobel 1955: i, 100n2.

1140 Divy 577.21–22, *tāḍakaṃ kuñcikāṃ* (mss. ABC, *kuñcikāva*; ms. D, *kuñcikāve*) *ca.* Edgerton (BHSD) and Cowell and Neil (Divy 680) both understand *tāḍaka* to be some kind of "key." The Tibetan reads *lde mig* and *lde mig kyog po,* which Nobel (1955: i, 100) translates as "Schloss und Schlüssel." Yet, considering that all this takes place in a granary (*khalābhidhāna*)—or perhaps it's a "threshing ground"—maybe these items are "a flail and a broom," although this would stretch their traditional meanings.

1141 Divy 577.23, *gṛhītam.* Nobel (1955: i, 100n4) suggests *adhivāsitam.* That is, "accepted his request."

1142 Following Cowell and Neil's query (Divy 73n3), add *uktā.* Vaidya (Divy-V 487.15) adds *uktam.* Hiraoka (HA 31; HD 72), following the Tibetan (119b4; 127a6), suggests replacing *dattā* with *uktā.* Divy 577.27, *dattā ca.*

1143 Here one expects the verbal form *kṛtvā,* but it is absent. Nobel (1955: i, 100n7) suggests adding it. Divy 578.6 (omitted).

1144 Divy 578.8, *adhiṣṭhā bhava ihaiva.* Or, perhaps, "preside over this place." Hiraoka (HA 31; HD 72), surmising from the Tibetan (199b7; 127b1), reads *adhiṣṭhāne bhavatīhaiva.* Nobel (1955: i, 101n1) suggests *adhīṣṭā.*

1145 Following Nobel (1955: i, 101n2) and Hiraoka (HA 31; HD 72), read *mahākātyāyanaḥ.* Divy 578.10, *mahākātyāyana iti.*

1146 Divy 578.13–14, *yadi yādṛśam eva mama sthaṇḍilaṃ kārayatha tādṛśam evāryasyeti.* Nobel (1995: 101n3) suggests *yadi yādṛśam eva mama sthaṇḍilaṃ kāritaṃ kārayatha tādṛśam eva āryasya tiṣṭhāmīti.* That is, "In just the same way that you constructed an altar for me, make one for the noble one. Then I'll stay."

1147 This term *asau* in this sentence (Divy 578.17) is grammatically suspect and could be deleted.

1148 Divy 578.18, *prākārakaṇṭake.* Perhaps, "rampart." One could read this as a "rampart" or even "a battle station on a wall to the city," but the Tibetan understands it simply as "a wall."

1149 Divy 578.22, *nirāmagandhasya-.* He is, more literally, "free from the foul smell [of immorality]."

1150 Following the Tibetan (120a4; 127b6) and Hiraoka (HA 31; HD 72), read *tayā*. Divy 578.23, *tasmāt*.

1151 Divy 578.25, *saṅktum* (mss. ABD, *saktum*; ms. C, *sektum*) *ārabdhāḥ*. The Tibetan (120a5; 127b7) reads *'dom par gyur te*. Cf. Nobel 1955: i, 101n5.

1152 Following the Tibetan (120a7–8; 128a2) and Hiraoka (HA 31–32; HD 72), read *samayataḥ kṣamāmi yadi yūyaṃ yādṛśam eva mama satkāraṃ kurutha tādṛśam evāryasya mahākātyāyanasyeti*. Nobel 1955: i, 101n7 concurs except for reading *kṣamiṣyāmi* for *kṣamāmi*. Divy 578.30–579.1, *yadi yūyaṃ yādṛśam evāryasya mahākātyāyanasyeti*. As Cowell and Neil (Divy 579n1) observe, "The lost words are easily supplied from above."

1153 Following Nobel (1955: i, 102n1) and Vaidya (Divy-V 488.6), read *kṣāntam*. Divy 579.2, *kṣāntā* (*sic* mss. except ms. D, *kṣāntyā*).

1154 Following Nobel (1955: i, 102n2), read *tena tasyāḥ kāṃśikā dattā*. Hiraoka (HA 32; HD 72) reads *kāṃśyam dattam*. Divy 579.6–7, "He gave her a piece of Vārāṇasī silk" (*tena tasyāṃ kāśikā dattā*).

1155 Divy 579.7, *prakṣipya*. The Tibetan (120b2; 128a4) reads "overturned." Elsewhere "overturning the bowl" (*pātranikubjana*) signifies one's refusal to accept offerings from a particular person. Cf. Nobel 1955: i, 102n3.

1156 Following Nobel (1955: i, 102n4), read *kāṃśimaha kāṃśimaha iti*. Hiraoka (HA 32; HD 72) reads *kāṃśyamaha kāṃśyamaha iti*. Divy 579.8, "Kāśimaha—Kāśimaha (Vārāṇasī Silk Festival)" (*kāśimaha kāśimaha iti*).

1157 Divy 579.12, *lambakapāla* (sic ms. E; ms. A, *lambayākepāla*; mss. BC, *layokepāla*; ms. D, *lambakepāla*) *iti*. Cf. Nobel 1955: i, 102n7. The people there were referred to as "cowherders" (*gopālaka*) and "cattleherders" (*paśupālaka*), and now they've come to be known as a different kind of "herder" or "protector" (*pāla*)—a kind of "hanging guard." Their town is likely meant to be Lampāka, modern-day Laghman in Afghanistan.

1158 Divy 579.19, *paryaṭitum*. Nobel (1955: i, 102n8), following the Tibetan, suggests *paryeṣitum*. That is, "to search."

1159 This is equivalent to modern-day Wakhān in Afghanistan.

1160 Following Speyer (1902: 361) and Hiraoka (HA 32; HD 72), read *diṣṭyā* for *dṛṣṭvā*, and following Cowell and Neil's query (Divy 580n2), Speyer (1902: 361), Vaidya (Divy-V 488.27), Divy 580.8, the Tibetan (121a5; 128b6), and Hiraoka (HA 31; HD 72), read *cirasya* for *asya*. Divy 680.7, *dṛṣṭvāsya* (*sic* mss.). Nobel (1955: i, 103n5), also suggests *putra tvām* for *putrakam* at Divy 580.7 and 570.8.

1161 Following Divy 46.23–24, 48.13, 52.23, etc., read *caturāryasatyasaṃprativedhakī*. Divy 580.12, *caturāryasaṃprativedhikī*.

1162 Divy 580.21, *duṣkarakāriṇā*. Nobel (1955: i, 104n1), following the Tibetan (121b4; 129a4), suggests *duṣkarakāriṇyāḥ*.

1163 Following Vaidya (Divy-V 489.7) and Hiraoka (HA 32; HD 72–73), read *putra yatnena*. Divy 580.24, *putrayatnena*. Cf. Nobel 1955: i, 104n2, *suprayatnena*.

1164 Divy 580.25, *bhadrakanyām*. Burnouf (1844: 271; 2010: 76), Edgerton (BHSD), and Tatelman (2000: 78) take *bhadrakanyā* as a proper name. Here Cowell and Neil don't capitalize the name, suggesting that they don't take it as a proper name, but they do capitalize it at Divy 52.16 and 52.22. Cf. Divy 52.19 (trans. in DS 112) for an explanation of her youthful status as a "daughter" (*kanyā*). In the Pāli materials, however, her name appears to be Moggalī or Moggallāni (cf. DPPN).

1165 Divy 580.27, *kiṃcid*. Hiraoka (HA 32; HD 73) and Nobel (1955: i, 104n5), following the Tibetan (121b6–7; 129a6) and Divy 579.6 and 581.5, read *kiṃcic cihnam*. That is, "some token."

1166 Divy 580.28–581.1, *tayā stūpaṃ pratiṣṭhāpya sā tasmin pratimāropitā*. More literally, "She constructed a stūpa and in it mounted that image," but this is peculiar. One could take it to mean that the "staff" (*yaṣṭi*) is an "image" (*pratimā*): "she established a stūpa and in it mounted that image [i.e., the staff]." Also possible is that she mounted the staff in the stūpa as an image, probably of her son: "she established a stūpa and in it mounted that [staff] as an image." It is strange, though, to think of a "staff" as an "image," whether literal or figural. The term *pratimā* generally refers to something iconic, not aniconic, in the *Divyāvadāna* (e.g., Divy 300.16, 373.15, 419.3, 427.3, 547.6–7, 548.17). The Tibetan (121b7; 129a7) simply states that in the stūpa she mounted the staff. As such, Nobel (1955: i, 104n6) suggests emending *pratimāropitā* to *pratisamāropitā*, although the term is unattested in the *Divyāvadāna*. Also possible is *samāropitā* or simply *āropitā*. Panel 85 on the north wall of Borobudur features a representation of the stūpa of Vokkāṇa, but there is no staff to be seen.

1167 Following the Tibetan (122a2; 129b2) and Nobel (1955: i, 104n9), read *pūle*. Nobel (1955: i, 104) takes this to mean "lace-up shoes." Divy 581.7, *pule*. Edgerton (BHSD), citing this passage, suggests that it might be "a kind of gem."

1168 Following the Tibetan (122a2; 129b2) and Hiraoka (HA 32; HD 73), read *tasyā ete*. Divy 581.7, *tad ete* (*sic*). Cowell and Neil (Divy 581n3) query *ete te*.

1169 Following the Tibetan (122a2; 129b2) and Hiraoka (HA 32; HD 73), read *tasyā ete*. Divy 581.8, *tasyaite*.

1170 Following the Tibetan (122a3; 129b2–3), read *pūleśvara iti saṃjñā saṃvṛttā*. Divy 581.9, *itaścarasanti* (*sic* mss.) *saṃjñā saṃvṛttā*. The Sanskrit is obscure. Nobel (1955: i, 105n1), following the Tibetan, suggests *tayā sthaṇḍile kārayitvā te tatra pratiṣṭhāpite | kaiścit pūleśvara iti saṃjñā kaiścit pūlādhiṣṭhānam (?) iti saṃñā saṃvṛttā*. That is, "She built two altars and placed them there. Some people know this place by the name Pūleśvara (Lord of Shoes). Others know it by the name Pūlādhiṣṭhānam [or Pūlapada?] (Shoe Site)."

1171 Following the Tibetan (122a5; 129b5) and Hiraoka (HA 32; HD 73), read *rājñā śikhaṇḍinā raurukanivāsinā ca janakāyena*. Divy 581.14–15, *rājā śikhaṇḍī raurukanivāsī ca janakāya*. Cf. Nobel 1955: i, 105n3.

1172 Following the Tibetan (122a6; 129b6), Nobel (1955: i, 105n4), and Hiraoka (HA 32; HD 73), read *alpārthā bhikṣavaḥ*. Cowell and Neil (Divy 581n5) likewise query *bhikṣavaḥ*. Divy 581.17, *atha* (*sic* mss.) *pāthābhikṣavaḥ*.

1173 Following Hiraoka (HA 32; HD 73), read *adūṣyanapakārī*. Divy 581.18, *aduṣyanayakārī*.

1174 Hiraoka (HA 32; HD 73), following the standard formula, adds the vocative *bhikṣavaḥ*. That is, "monks." Divy 581.26 (omitted).

1175 This sentence is a conjoining of two clichés: "long ago, monks, in a time gone by" (e.g., Divy 62.7, 73.24, 98.12) and "when no lord buddhas are born, solitary buddhas can arise in the world" (e.g., Divy 88.13–14, 132.20, 191.24). My sense is that something in between them was deleted; see, for example, Divy 191.21–25 and 428.8–11. Also, in the second cliché, following Vaidya's emendation (490.3–4), Cowell and Neil's query (Divy 582n2), and the above citations, read *utpāde*. Divy 582.7, *anutpāde*.

1176 Divy 582.15, *rātriṃdivā samupāgataḥ*. Nobel (1955: i, 106n8) suggests *rātriṃnivāsam upagataḥ*. That is, "spent the night."

1177 Following Hiraoka (HA 32; HD 73), omit *taṃ karvaṭakam anuprāptaḥ*. That is, "arrived at that market town." Its inclusion here (Divy 582.16) is redundant, and it is omitted in the Tibetan.

1178 Divy 582.21, *pātrasrāvaṇam* (sic. mss.). Nobel (1955: i, 107n1) suggests *pātraparisrāvaṇam*, which is the form that occurs at Divy 582.24. Cf. Edgerton (BHSD, s.v. *parisrāvaṇa*).

1179 Divy 582.23, *pātraṃ ca*. Nobel (1955: i, 107n2) suggests emending to *prakṣālya*. That is, "washed." Hiraoka (HA 32; HD 73) suggests its omission.

1180 Following Divy 582.11, 582.13, Hiraoka (HA 32; HD 73), and Nobel (1955: i, 107n5), read *pāśālepān*. Divy 582.29, *pāśān*.

1181 Divy 583.9, *karākārasadṛśam*. Nobel (1955: i, 107n9), following the Tibetan (123a6; 130b7), queries *ānakākara-*. That is, "size of a drum."

1182 Divy 583.19, *yady atra suvarṇapalo 'pi dātavyo 'haṃ pariprāpayāmīti*. Nobel (1955: i, 108n4) and Hiraoka (HA 32; HD 73), following the Tibetan (123b2–2; 131a4), read *suvarṇapaṭṭaḥ*. That is, "golden bandage." Perhaps, "Even if a golden bandage needs to applied in this case, I'll get it for you."

1183 Following Divy 567.22, the Tibetan (123b3; 131a4), and Nobel (1955: i, 108n5), add *tat prāptam*. Hiraoka (HA 32; HD 73) suggests *prāpya*. Divy 583.20 (omitted).

1184 Divy 583.25, *nave kumbhe*. Nobel (1955: i, 108n6), following the Tibetan (123b5; 131a6), suggests *suvarṇe kumbhe* or *survarṇakumbhe*. That is, "golden pot." Cf. Divy 327.25.

1185 Following the Tibetan (123b5; 131a6), Nobel (1955: i, 108n7) suggests adding *rathyānāṃ catvare* (or *rathyācatvare*). That is, "at the main crossroads."

1186 Following the Tibetan (124a1–2; 131b2–3) and Hiraoka (HA 32; HD 73), read *enaiva ca karmāvaśeṣeṇa tasminn evodapāne pañca janmaśatāni mṛgo jātaḥ saviṣeṇa śareṇa marmaṇi tāḍito yāvad*. Divy 584.6, *tasminn api codapāne saviṣeṇa śareṇa marmaṇi tāḍitas tenaiva ca karmāvaśeṣeṇa* (mss. AB, *karmaviśeṣeṇa*; ms. C, *karmāviś-*). Nobel (1955: i, 109n3) suggests this reconstruction for the passage: *tasya karmaṇo vipākena kalpam avīcau mahānarake taptas tenaiva karmāvaśeṣeṇa pañcajātiśatāni tasminn evodapāne mṛgo bhūtvā* (or *mṛgībhūtvā*) *saviṣeṇa śareṇa marmaṇi tāḍitaḥ kālagataḥ | etary api arhattvaṃ prāptaḥ śastreṇa praghātito nirvṛtaḥ*. That is, "As a result of that action, he suffered for an eon in the great Avīci hell, and because of the karma that remained, for five hundred lifetimes, at this very pond, he was born as a deer, struck in a vital point with a poisoned arrow, and died. Even now, after obtaining arhatship, he died by the sword before entering nirvāṇa."

1187 Following Nobel (1955: i, 110n5) and Hiraoka (HA 32; HD 73), omit *yāvad anyatamaḥ pratyekabuddho janapadacārikāṃ* (mss., *-kāṃś*) *caraṃs taṃ karvaṭakam anuprāptaḥ* (Divy 584.26–27). That is, "Meanwhile a certain solitary buddha, after traveling through the countryside, arrived at that market town." Its inclusion here is redundant; the same passage occurs at Divy 585.2–3.

1188 Following the Tibetan (124b6; 132a7–b1) and Hiraoka (HA 32; HD 73), read *daivam*. Nobel (1955: i, 110n6) suggests *daivena* or *daivāt*. Divy 585.7, "It's not like that" (*naivam*).

1189 Following Divy 585.7, Nobel (1955: i, 110n7), and Hiraoka (HA 32; HD 73–74), read *āgatā*. Divy 585.8, *nāgatā*.

1190 Divy 585.10, *tadā dārikayā*. Nobel (1955: i, 111n1) and Hiraoka (HA 32; HD 74), following the Tibetan (124b7; 132b1), read *tayā dārikayā*. Divy 585.4 and 585.6 read likewise.

1191 Following the Tibetan (124b7; 132b2), Nobel (1955: i, 111n1) and Hiraoka (HA 32; HD 74), read *anyasyā*. Divy 585.11, *asyā*. Cowell and Neil (Divy 585n5) query *asya*.

1192 Following the Tibetan (125a1; 132b3) and Hiraoka (HA 32; HD 74), read *kuśaladharmau*. Nobel (1955: i, 111n4) suggests *śubhadharmakau*. Divy 585.16, *samakau*. Perhaps, "of the same status."

1193 Following Nobel (1955: i, 111n5), read *tābhyām uktam*. Divy 585.17, "they told her" (*sābhyām uktā*). The householders are addressing wrongdoers in general—note the plural vocative—not just the girl.

1194 Divy 585.17, *vardhate*. Perhaps meant to be *vartate*.

1195 Nobel (1955: i, 111n6), following the Tibetan (125a3–4; 132b5), offers this reconstruction of the Sanskrit: *yad ebhiḥ pratyekabuddhānām ṛṣīṇāṃ mātapitror upari saṃkāraś chorita*. That is, "Since they threw garbage on solitary buddhas, seers, mothers, and fathers . . ."

1196 Read *yau etau*. Divy 585.23, *yo 'sau*.

1197 Following Vaidya (Divy-V 492.11), omit *cittam*. Divy 585.28, *yadi tena na vipuṣpitaṃ cittaṃ*. Nobel (1955: i, 111n7), following the Tibetan (125a5–6; 132b7), offers this reconstruction of the Sanskrit: *yadi mahākātyāyanena bhikṣuṇā evaṃvidho guṇagaṇo nādhigato mahākātyāyano bhikṣuḥ pāṃśunāvaṣṭabdho 'nayena vyasanam āpanno 'bhaviṣyad iti*. That is, "If the monk Mahākātyāyana had not amassed a great collection of virtues, then he would have been buried under [a pile of dirt] and straightaway met with his death."

1198 The chart included here is a composite of the work of other scholars. See Collins 1998: 297–302; Gethin 1998: 112–32; Kloetzli 1997; and Kongtrul Lodrö Tayé 1995.

1199 For more on this term, see Coomaraswamy 1939: 116–117.

1200 The *Divyāvadāna* (225.10–11), however, determines that the lifespan of Śakra—the chief god of Trāyastriṃśa—is 360,000 years. See Collins 1998: 298 and Gethin 1998: 117.

1201 The Pāli equivalents for the names of these first three cold hells all seem to refer to large numbers (cf. CPD, s.vv. *abbuda, aṭaṭa*). The idea here may be that the denizens of these hells suffer for a long time.

1202 The Tibetan (Kongtrul Lodrö Tayé 1995: 247) has variant names for these last three hells. They are "Splitting Like a Blue Lotus" (*utpala ltar gas pa*), "Splitting Like a Lotus" (*padma ltar gas pa*), and "Splitting Like a Great Lotus" (*padma ltar cher gas pa*). Perhaps these names are meant to conjure an image of a lotus beaten down by the cold. This is an image not uncommon in Sanskrit literature. See, for example, Kālidāsa's *Meghadūta* (part 2, v. 23) and Bhāsa's *Svapnavāsavadatta* (book 5, v. 1).

Glossary

Āgamas. See *four Āgamas*.

aggregates (*skandha*). See *five aggregates*.

Ajātaśatru. Prince of Magadha, who became king after he killed his father, King Bimbisāra.

analytic insights (*pratisaṃvid*). There are four: with regard to dharma, meaning (*artha*), languages and linguistic usage (*nirukti*), and eloquence (*pratibhāna*).

Ānanda. One of the Buddha's main disciples and a veritable treasurer of the dharma. He was the Buddha's cousin and, for the latter stage of the Buddha's life, his personal attendant.

Anāthapiṇḍada. The Buddha's chief patron. After purchasing a park from Prince Jeta, son of King Prasenajit, he had a monastery constructed there for the Buddha to pass the rainy season.

antigod (*asura*). One of a class of demigods whose home is beneath the waters at the base of Mount Meru. Positioned just below the lowest heavenly sphere, these "not [quite]" (*a*) "gods" (*sura*) often vie with the gods above them (cf. Divy 222.23ff.).

arhat. A "worthy one," who has destroyed all of his defilements and thereby attained awakening. Often an epithet of a buddha. According to Paul Griffiths (1994: 62), it is used as a title for a buddha "to indicate both Buddha's worthiness to receive the homage (*pūjārhattva*) and offerings of non-Buddhists and, using a different etymology, Buddha's success in killing (*han-*) the enemies (*ari*) to awakening."

armed wheel-turning king (*balacakravartin*). A king who needs to use force or the threat of force to establish his dominion. For more, see Strong 1983: 49–56.

aśoka. *Saraca indica* L. (= *Jonesia asoca* Roxb). A tree that blossoms with fragrant orange-yellow flowers when, according to poetic convention, kicked by a beautiful woman.

atimuktaka. Following James McHugh (2012: 266n25), "Monier Williams [1990] says this refers to a number of shrubs 'surpassing pearls in whiteness.' Apte [1986] says that it can refer to a creeper that embraces the mango tree. Here, [it is] classed 'with other great trees,' so perhaps it is, in fact, a tree? The commentary of Bhanūji Dīkṣita on Amara[kośa] 4.26 gives a Hindi synonym as *tiniśa*, a tree, *Ougeinia oojeinensis* Hochr. (= *Dalbergia oojeinensis* W. Roxburgh)."

auspicious age (*bhadrakalpa*). An eon, such as the present one, in which five buddhas appear. In our present eon, the buddhas Krakucchanda, Kanakamuni, Kāśyapa, and Śākyamuni have already appeared, and Maitreya will be the fifth and last.

bakula. *Mimusops elengi*. A tree that is said by poets to bloom with fragrant flowers when young women sprinkle it with mouthfuls of wine.

bhadanta. A respectful term used to address Buddhist monks.

billionfold world-system (*trisāhasramahāsāhasralokadhātu*). More literally, "the great thousand third-order thousand world-system." As one nineteenth-century Tibetan commentator explains,

> The area that includes the four continents, Mount Meru, and the outer rim of mountains . . . is referred to as a four-continent world-system. An identical world-system is located in space at a distance of one thousand times the magnitude of that world-system. A total of one thousand such world-systems [evenly distributed in space], encircled by a rim, is referred to as a first-order thousand world-system. This considered as a single unit, replicated one thousand times and surrounded by a perimeter, is referred to as a second-order thousand world-system. One

thousand [second-order thousand world-systems] enclosed by a great rim is called a third-order thousand world-system. Thus, one billion four-continent world-systems is called one great thousand third-order thousand world-system. (Kongtrul Lodrö Tayé 1995: 102–3).

Bimbisāra. The king of Magadha, who reigned in Rājagṛha and who was a patron of the Buddha. He was killed by his son, Prince Ajātaśatru, who then ascended the throne.

blessed one (*bhagavān*). An epithet of a buddha. I translate *bhagavān* as "Blessed One" when it refers to Gautama Buddha, and as "lord" when it modifies a buddha (e.g., the lord Vipaśyin).

bodhisattva. One who has vowed to attain awakening as a buddha for the welfare of all sentient beings.

bonds to existence (*saṃyojana*). See *five bonds to the lower realms of existence* and *three bonds to existence*.

Brahmā. The highest deity in the world we inhabit. He lords over the "Brahmā world" (*brahmaloka*), which consists of three heavens: Mahābrahmaṇa (Great Brahmā), Brahmapurohita (Brahmā's Priests), and Brahmakāyika (Brahmā's Assembly).

Brahmā-like voice (*brahmasvara*). The twenty-eighth of the thirty-two marks of a great man. According to the *Dīgha-nikāya* (ii, 211), such a voice is "distinct, intelligible, charming, pleasant to hear, compact, concise, deep, and resonant."

Brahmā world (*brahmaloka*). The first three heavens in the form realm (*rūpadhātu*): Brahmakāyika, Brahmapurohita, and Mahābrahmaṇa. See appendix.

brahman (*brāhmaṇa*). One of the four hereditary classes (*varṇa*) according to Brahmanical Hinduism (i.e., *brahman, kṣatriya, vaiśya, śūdra*). The primary duties of this class involve ritual activity.

buddha. One who has attained the highest possible awakening—who is, literally, an "awakened one." In the *Divyāvadāna*, "the Buddha" is often used as a title to refer to Śākyamuni.

buddha vision (*buddhacakṣu*). Buddhas are said to possess five faculties of vision: the physical eye (*māṃsacakṣu*), the divine eye (*divyacakṣu*), the wisdom eye (*prajñācakṣu*), the dharma eye (*dharmacakṣu*), and the buddha eye (*buddhacakṣu*). This last quality I translate as "buddha vision."

campaka. *Magnolia champaca* (L.) Figlar (= *Michelia champaca* L). This tree, which is also known as the yellow jade orchid tree, has very fragrant flowers that are white, yellow, or orange in color.

celestial musician (*gandharva*). One of a class of beings who inhabit the lowest heaven, the realm of the Cāturmahārājika. Dhṛtarāṣṭra, one of the four great kings, is their lord. However, in the *Divyāvadāna* (Divy 202.29), Supriya is said to be their king.

community (*saṅgha*). The Buddhist order of monks (*bhikṣu*) and nuns (*bhikṣuṇī*). The text often speaks, however, of a community of monks (*bhikṣusaṅgha*).

coral tree (*mandārava, māndārava, māndāraka*). *Erythrina indica*. One of the five celestial trees. Flowers from this tree are sometimes said to rain down from heaven as a divine greeting of respect.

corruptions (*āsrava*). These negative karmic forces, which must be interrupted to escape from saṃsāra, are sometimes translated as "cankers" or "outflows." They are often equated with the *four floods*.

deadly sin (*ānantarya-karma*). There are five such sins of immediate retribution: killing one's father, one's mother, or an arhat, drawing the blood of a buddha, and creating a schism in the monastic community. For more, see Silk 2009: 21–37.

desire realm (*kāmadhātu*). The world of desire and sense pleasure, which includes the realms of hell beings, animals, hungry ghosts, humans, and the first six divine realms. See appendix.

dharmic form (*dharmakāya*). The corpus of a buddha's teachings or, as it were, a buddha embodied in the dharma.

dhānuṣkārī (or *dhātuṣkārī*). A kind of flowering tree that is perhaps a kind of jasmine. See note 53.

disciple (*śrāvaka*). A follower of the Buddha is known as a "hearer" (*śrāvaka*), signaling the importance in early Buddhism of listening to the Buddha's dharma. In the *Divyāvadāna*, however, devotees are enjoined to look, as much as to hear, for visual practices are represented as the primary means of cultivating faith.

divine hearing (*divyaśrotra*). The quality of clairaudience, one of the *superhuman faculties.*

divine sight (*divyacakṣu*). The quality of clairvoyance, one of the aspects of *buddha vision*. It is also one of the *superhuman faculties.*

dukūla. A fine cloth made from the fiber of the *dukūla* plant.

eight sciences (*aṣṭavidyā*). One list in the *Divyāvadāna* includes the sciences of elephants, horses, jewels, wood, cloth, men, women, and various commodities (Divy 100.1–3). Elsewhere, the sciences of young men and women occur instead of the sciences of men and women (Divy 58.19). In addition, there are instances in the text when some manuscripts attest to "the science of cloth" while others attest to "the science of building sites" (Divy 58.17, 100.3). The Tibetan corresponding to Divy 26.12–14 lists the sciences of objects, cloth, jewels, wood, elephants, horses, young men, and young women.

eightfold path (*āṣṭāṅgamārga*). See *noble eightfold path*.

eighty minor marks (*aśītyānuvyañjana*). The secondary characteristics of a great man. Following Robert Thurman's enumeration (1983: 156–57), these are:

> [1] fingernails the color of brass, [2] shiny [3] and long; [4] round fingers; [5] tapered fingers; [6] fingers wide-spreading; [7] veins not protruding, [8] and without tangles; [9] slender ankles; [10] feet not uneven; [11] lion's gait; [12] elephant's gait; [13] swan's gait; [14] bull's gait; [15] gait tending to the right; [16] graceful gait; [17] steady gait; [18] his body is well covered, [19] clean, [20] well proportioned, [21] pure, [22] soft, and [23] perfect; [24] his sex organs are fully developed; [25] his thighs are broad and knees round; [26] his steps are even; [27] his complexion is youthful; [28] his posture is not stooped; [29] his bearing is expansive, [30] yet extremely poised; [31] his limbs and fingers and toes are well defined; [32] his vision is clear and unblurred; [33] his joints are not protruding; [34] his belly is relaxed, [35] symmetrical, [36] and not fat; [37] his navel is deep [38] and wound to the right; [39] he is completely handsome; [40] he is clean in all acts; [41]

he is free of spots or discolorations of the skin; [42] his hands are soft as cotton; [43] the lines of his palms are clear, [44] deep, [45] and long; [46] his face is not overlong [47] and is bright as a mirror; [48] his tongue is soft, [49] long, [50] and red; [51] his voice is like an elephant's trumpet or like thunder, [52] yet sweet and gentle; [53] his teeth are rounded, [54] sharp, [55] white, [56] even, [57] and regularly arranged; [58] his nose is long [59] and straight; [60] his eyes are clear [61] and wide; [62] his eyelashes are thick; [63] the pupils and whites of his eyes are clearly defined, and the irises are like lotus petals; [64] his eyebrows are long, [65] soft, [66] evenly haired, [67] and gently curved; [68] his ears [69] are long-lobed and symmetrical; [70] his hearing is acute; [71] his forehead is high [72] and broad; [73] his head is very large; [74] his hair is as black as a bee, [75] thick, [76] soft, [77] untangled, [78] not unruly, [79] and fragrant; [80] and his feet and hands are marked with lucky signs [of the *śrīvatsa*, svastika, and *nandyāvarta*].

Thurman follows *Mahāvyutpatti* §269–348. Edgerton (BHSD, s.v. *anuvyañjana*) constructs a slightly different list. For alternate translations, see Jones 1976: ii, 40–41 and Mitra 1998: 130–31. For more on the lucky signs, see Bapat 1953.

elements (*dhātu*). "The psycho-physical constituent elements of the personality in relation to the outside world," to quote Franklin Edgerton (BHSD). There are eighteen: the six sense organs (i.e., eye, ear, nose, tongue, body, mind), the six objects of the sense organs (i.e., the visible, sound, odor, taste, tactile objects, mental objects), and the resultant six consciousnesses (i.e., eye consciousness, ear consciousness, nose consciousness, tongue consciousness, body consciousness, mind consciousness).

emptiness (*śūnyatā*). The Buddhist doctrine that all persons and things have no inherent existence.

fervent aspiration (*praṇidhāna*, *praṇidhi*). A firm vow or resolution to attain some higher form of karmic development, usually in a future life.

field of merit (*puṇyakṣetra*). Entities, such as the Buddha or the community, who are such great repositories of virtue that meritorious deeds directed toward them are especially beneficial for the donor.

five aggregates (*pañcaskandha*). These constitute the physical and mental constituents of a person. They are matter (*rūpa*), feeling (*vedanā*), recognition (*saññā*), conditioning (*saṃskāra*), and consciousness (*vijñāna*).

five [bad] qualities (*pañcāṅga*). Equivalent to the five hindrances (*pañcanīvaraṇa*). These are sensual desire (*kāmacchanda*), ill will (*vyāpāda*), tiredness and sleepiness (*styānamiddha*), excitement and lethargy (*auddhatyakaukṛtya*), and doubt (*vicikitsā*).

five bonds to the lower realms of existence (*pañcāvarabhāgīya-saṃyojana*). Defilements binding one to existence in the *desire realm*. They are the false view of individuality (*satkāyadṛṣṭi*), holding on to precepts and vows (*śīlavrataparāmarśa*), doubt (*vicikitsā*), sensual desire (*kāmacchanda*), and ill will (*vyāpāda*). In total there are ten of these bonds, which are also known as "fetters."

five good qualities (pañcāṇga) of the Buddha's voice. It is (1) deep like thunder, (2) soothing and comforting to the ear, (3) pleasant and delightful, (4) lucid and articulate, (5) suitable and consistent. See Rigzin 1997: 293–94.

five powers (*pañcabala*). Various powers to be developed by the Buddhist practitioner. These are essentially the same as the *five spiritual faculties*; perhaps thought of as their full development.

five realms of existence (*pañcagati*). The various categories of living beings. These are gods (*deva*), humans (*manuṣya*), animals (*tiryagyoni*), hungry ghosts (*preta*), and hell beings (*naraka*). Often the category of antigods (*asura*) is added between humans and hungry ghosts. See appendix.

five spiritual faculties (*pañcendriya*). These are virtues or capacities to be developed by the Buddhist practitioner. They are confidence (*śraddhā*), strength (*vīrya*), mindfulness (*smṛti*), concentration (*samādhi*), and wisdom (*prajñā*). See also *five powers*.

five superhuman faculties (*pañcābhijñā*). See *superhuman faculties*.

four Āgamas. The fourfold division of the Buddha's discourses contained in the Sūtra Piṭaka. These collections are the *Longer Sayings* (*Dīrghāgama*), the *Middle-Length Sayings* (*Madhyamāgama*), the *Connected Sayings* (*Saṃyuktāgama*), and the *Gradual Sayings* (*Ekottarikāgama*).

four assemblies. These are monks, nuns, and male and female lay devotees.

four bases of success (*caturṛddhipāda*). The bases that lead one to acquire magical power and spiritual success. These are the desire to act (*chanda*), strength (*vīrya*), mind (*citta*), and investigation (*mīmāṃsā*). For more, see Gethin 1992: 81–103.

four confidences (*caturvaiśāradya*). The confidence of being perfectly awakened to all dharmas (*sarvadharmābhisambodhivaiśāradya*), the confidence in the knowledge that all corruptions have been destroyed (*sarvāśravakṣaya-jñānavaiśāradya*), the confidence of having described precisely and correctly the obstructive conditions [to the religious life] (*antarāyikadhar-mānanyathātvaniścitavyākaraṇavaiśāradya*), and the confidence in the correctness of one's way of salvation for the realization of all good things (*sarvasampadadhigamāya nairyāṇikapratipattathātvavaiśāradya*).

four continents (*caturdvīpa*). The four continents that humans inhabit. These are Jambudvīpa (Black Plum Island, or India) to the south, Pūrvavideha (Eastern Videha) to the east, Aparagodānīya (Western Godanīya) to the west, and Uttarakuru (Northern Kuru) to the north.

four floods [*of corruptions*] (*caturogha*). These are desire (*kāma*), existence (*bhava*), ignorance (*avidyā*), and views (*dṛṣṭi*). One who has crossed these four negative flows of karma is an arhat.

four great kings (*catvāro mahārājānaḥ*). The guardians of the four directions who live in the divine realm known as Cāturmahārājika (Four Groups of the Great Kings). They are the gods Dhṛtarāṣṭra in the east, Virūḍhaka in the south, Virūpākṣa in the west, and Kubera (= Vaiśravaṇa, Dhanada) in the north. See appendix.

four means of attracting beings [*to the religious life*] (*catvāri saṅgrahavastūni*). These are generosity (*dāna*), kind speech (*priyavacana*), beneficial conduct (*arthacaryā*), and exemplary behavior (*samānārthatā*).

four noble truths (*caturāryasatya*). The classic formulation of the Buddha's teaching. It is true that there is suffering (*duḥkha*), that it has a cause (*samudaya*), that it can end (*nirodha*), and that there is a path (*mārga*) that leads to its cessation.

four stages of penetrating insight (*nirvedhabhāgīya*). These are the four stages on the path of application (*prayogamārga*). They are heat (*uṣmagata*), tolerance (*kṣānti*), summit (*mūrdha*), and highest worldly dharma (*laukikāgradharma*). The first three of these four stages are themselves divided into three stages—weak, medium, and strong—hence there are ten stages in all.

gośīrṣa. A kind of valuable sandalwood. Its name literally means "cow's head," but the significance of this name is unclear. Perhaps it may be the sandalwood found on Gośīrṣa Mountain.

great king. See *four great kings*.

great man (*mahāpuruṣa*). One who has the thirty-two marks, and as such is destined to become either a wheel-turning king ruling the four quarters of the earth or a buddha.

great snake (*mahoraga*). One of a class of celestial beings that are said to have a human body with a serpent head.

group of six monks (*ṣaḍvargika, ṣaḍvargīya*). These monks (i.e., Nanda, Upananda, Punarvasu, Chanda, Aśvaka, and Udāyin) are unruly followers of the Buddha. In the *Divyāvadāna*, they seem to be close to heretics.

guide (*vināyaka*). An epithet of a buddha.

heat stages (*uṣmagata*). See *four stages of penetrating insight*.

heavenly bird (*garuḍa*). One of a class of birdlike supernatural beings. They are said to be an enemy of the snakelike nāgas.

highest worldly dharma stage (*laukikāgradharma*). See *four stages of penetrating insight*.

impermanence (*anitya*). The Buddhist doctrine that all conditioned things inevitably undergo change.

interdependent arising (*pratītyasamutpāda*). The Buddhist doctrine of causal interdependence, which describes the cycle of existence (*saṃsāra*). By extension, the doctrine that all things are interdependent.

Jambudvīpa. The southern continent, usually identified with India. Although often translated as "Rose Apple Island," current research (Wujasyk 2004) suggests that a more accurate rendering is "Black Plum Island." See also *four continents*.

Jīvaka Kumārabhūta. Jīvaka was abandoned on a heap of trash as an infant and then rescued by Prince Abhaya, who raised him. Later he studied medicine and became a renowned physician.

kalāva. See *kulattha*.

karma. Often translated as "deed" or "action," although left untranslated when it refers to the force exerted by the results of such deeds—for example, in determining the quality of one's rebirth, present experience, or inclinations.

karmic bonds (*karmaploti*). These are the "connective threads" (*ploti*) that tie together one's karmic history.

karṇikāra. A tree from the island of Uttarakuru, where trees are said to bear perpetual fruit and foliage.

karoṭapāṇi. A class of yakṣas who act as guards for the gods, especially the gods of Trāyastriṃśa.

kārṣāpaṇa. A kind of coin in ancient India, usually of copper or silver, although gold ones also circulated.

kāśa. A kind of grass used in ritual offerings.

Kauśika. An epithet of Śakra, for he is "connected with the Kuśikas."

kinnara. A class of beings, often said to be half human and half animal, as indicated by their name—literally, "What (*kiṃ*) sort of man (*nara*)?" In the *Divyāvadāna*, we most often come across the beautiful and bewitching kinnara women (*kinnarī*), whose name might aptly be translated as "What a woman!"

kroñca maidens (*kroñcakumārikā*). These maidens are probably so called because they "scream" or "screech" (*kroñca*), just as "elephants trumpet" (*hastinaḥ kroñcanti* | Divy 251.2). Perhaps they are a kind of siren.

kṣatriya. One of the four hereditary classes (*varṇa*) according to Brahmanical Hinduism (i.e., *brahman*, *kṣatriya*, *vaiśya*, *śūdra*). The duties of this class include maintaining order and inflicting punishment.

kulattha. *Delichos biflous*. A kind of black or gray-seeded lentil known in Hindi as *kulathī*. It is sometimes referred to as "horse gram."

kumbhāṇḍa. One of a class of evil spirits who, as their name would indicate, had "testicles" (*aṇḍa*) as big as "pots" (*kumbha*). Virūḍhaka, one of the four great kings, is their lord.

kuśa. A kind of grass used in ritual offerings.

lion throne (*siṃhāsana*). A seat of honor, often for a buddha, for he is likened to a lion.

lord (*bhagavān*). See *blessed one*.

lower realms of existence (*apāyagati*). The realms of hell beings, animals, and hungry ghosts.

magical power (*ṛddhi*). A set of special powers acquired through spiritual practice; also one of the *superhuman faculties*. There are often said to be eight: (1) being one he becomes many, being many he becomes one; (2) becoming invisible; (3) passing through solid objects; (4) traveling through the earth; (5) walking on water; (6) flying through the air; (7) touching and stroking the sun and moon with one's hand; (8) ascending to the world of the god Brahmā.

Mahākātyāyana. One of the Buddha's main disciples and a master of doctrinal exposition.

Mahāmaudgalyāyana. The "great" (*mahā*) Maudgalyāyana. See *Maudgalyāyana*.

Maitreya. A bodhisattva who lives in Tuṣita heaven, awaiting his final rebirth in the human realm when he will become a buddha.

makara. A kind of hybrid sea creature, with a terrestrial form in the front (e.g., elephant, crocodile, deer) and an aquatic form in the back (e.g., fish, seal).

maṇḍīlaka. Om Prakash (1961: 288) explains that *maṇḍīlaka* is a variant of *maṇḍaka*, which designates "a loaf of bread prepared with powdered wheat or rice flour mixed with salt, milk and clarified butter." Cf. Silk 2008a: 149n100.

mantra. A ritual formula that can function as a spell or charm.

Māra. An evil figure personifying death and temptation who assails Buddhist practitioners and tries to lead them astray. He is sometimes said to be king of the Paranirmitavaśavartin gods.

master (*nātha*). An epithet of a buddha.

mātṛkā. A list of significant points of doctrine.

Maudgalyāyana. One of the Buddha's chief disciples, regarded as foremost in the attainment of psychic powers.

Middle Country (*madhyadeśa*). One of five traditional divisions of India. These are Middle Country (*Madhyadeśa*), North Country (*Uttarāpatha*), Eastern India (*Pūrvadeśa*), South Country (*Dakṣiṇāpatha*), and Western India (*Aparānta*).

minor offense (*duṣkṛta*). A minor monastic transgression.

most-treasured. See *seven treasures*.

Mount Meru. A sacred mountain, 80,000 leagues high, located in Jambudvīpa and considered to be the center of the world. On its terraces reside the gods of Cāturmahārājika and on its summit the gods of Trāyastriṃśa. See appendix.

Mount Sumeru. See *Mount Meru*.

mṛdugandhika. An unidentified species of plant that is, as its name indicates, "delicately fragrant."

nāga. A serpent, capable of taking on human form, who lives in the water and possesses miraculous powers. Although often dangerous to humans, these beings can be instructed in the dharma. Virūpākṣa, one of the four great kings, is their lord.

nāgakeśara. *Mesua ferrea* L. A tree with large Cistus-like flowers that are white and fragrant. Sometimes known as the Indian rose chestnut.

Nanda. See *group of six monks*.

Nandana Grove (*nandanavana*). Quite literally "a grove of delight" in Trāyastriṃśa heaven, which is located atop Mount Meru and ruled by Śakra.

nine bonds to existence (*navasaṃyojana*). These are attachment (*anunaya*), aversion (*pratigha*), conceit (*māna*), ignorance (*avidyā*), views (*dṛṣṭi*), clinging (*parāmarśa*), doubt (*vicikitsā*), envy (*īrṣyā*), and stinginess (*mātsarya*). The term *saṃyojana* is usually translated as "fetter," but these nine do not correspond to the standard list of fetters (e.g, ten fetters, five lower fetters, three fetters).

nine successive states of quiescence meditation (*navānupūrvavihāra*). The four meditations or contemplations (*dhyāna*) of form, the four formless spheres—i.e., the sphere of infinite space (*ākāśānantyāyatana*), the sphere of infinite consciousness (*vijñānānantyāyatana*), the sphere of nothingness (*akiñcanyāyatana*), the sphere of neither consciousness nor unconsciousness (*naivasaṃjñānāsaṃjñāyatana*)—and, lastly, the cessation of conceptualization and sensation (*saṃjñāvedayitanirodha*).

Nirgrantha. A monk who engages in practices of austerity in the hope of becoming, as the name indicates, "free from hindrances." In the *Divyāvadāna*, these monks are heretics who oppose the Buddha and his dharma. Mahāvīra, one of the founders of Jainism, originally belonged to this school.

noble eightfold path (*āryāṣṭāṅgamārga*). The proper path of conduct, which has eight aspects: right view (*samyagdṛṣṭi*), right intention (*samyaksaṅkalpa*), right speech (*samyagvāc*), right action (*samyakkarmānta*), right livelihood (*samyagājīva*), right effort (*samyagvyāyāma*), right mindfulness (*samyaksmṛti*), and right concentration (*samyaksamādhi*).

nonreturner (*anāgāmin*). One who has attained the third of four stages of religious development that culminate in arhatship (e.g., stream-enterer, once-returner, nonreturner, arhat). Such a person will have no additional rebirths as a human; he will attain awakening after being reborn in one of the higher heavens.

North Country (*uttarāpatha*). One of five traditional divisions of India. These are Middle Country (Madhyadeśa), North Country (Uttarāpatha), Eastern India (Pūrvadeśa), South Country (Dakṣiṇāpatha), and Western India (Aparānta).

no-self (*anātman*). The doctrine that individuals have no permanent or abiding self.

once-returner (*sakṛtāgāmin*). One who has attained the second of four stages of religious development that culminate in arhatship (e.g., stream-enterer, once-returner, nonreturner, arhat). Such a person will attain awakening in his next rebirth.

paṇava. A kind of drum.

pāṭalā. Stereospermum suaveolens DC. A tree that blooms with sweetly fragrant flowers at the beginning of the dry season.

path of application (*prayogamārga*). The second of the five paths of the religious practitioner—i.e., (1) the path of accumulation (*sambhāramārga*), (2) the path of application (*prayogamārga*), (3) the path of seeing (*darśanamārga*), (4) the path of cultivation (*bhāvanāmārga*), and (5) the path of no more learning (*aśaikṣamārga*).

path of cultivation (*bhāvanāmārga*). The fourth of the five paths of the religious practitioner. See also *path of application*.

path of seeing (*darśanamārga*). The third of the five paths of the religious practitioner. See also *path of application*.

perfectly awakened (*samyaksambuddha*). An epithet of a buddha. He is perfectly awakened, and hence his awakening is superior to the awakening of a disciple or solitary buddha.

perfections. See *six perfections*.

perfumed chamber (*gandhakuṭi*). A special structure in a monastery for a buddha. For more, see Strong 1977.

piśāca. A kind of demon. According to Monier-Williams (1990), "possibly so called either from their fondness for flesh (*piśa* for *piśita*) or from their yellowish appearance."

powerful fighter (*sahasrayodhin*). Quite literally, "one who can battle a thousand men." Here it designates an elite and extremely capable guard employed by the king. As Edgerton (BHSD) notes, it "seems to be a rather technical term."

powers. See *five powers*.

precepts (*śikṣāpada*). Quite literally the "rules of training" for monks, nuns, novices of both genders, and so on. Generally this refers to the five precepts observed by lay Buddhists: not to take life, not to steal, not to be engaged in sexual misconduct, not to lie, and not to take intoxicants.

punnāga. Calophyllum inophyllum L. An evergreen tree with white fragrant flowers, also known as the Alexandrian laurel.

quiescence (*śamatha*). See *tranquility*.

quinquennial festival (*pañcavarṣika*). A five-year-long gift-giving extravaganza. For more, see Strong 1983: 92–96, 265–68.

realms of existence. See *five realms of existence*.

refuges (*śaraṇagamana*). See *three refuges*.

resolute one (*dhīra*). An epithet of a buddha.

root of virtue (*kuśalamūla*). A "virtuous deed" (*kuśala*), or the merit accrued from such a deed, that functions as a "root" or "foundation" (*mūla*) for a request or aspiration.

Śakra. The chief of Trāyastriṃśa heaven, who is said to be the lord of the gods (*devendra*).

Śākyamuni. An epithet meaning "sage of the Śākya clan," used to designate Siddhārtha Gautama, the most recent buddha in our eon. See *auspicious age*.

śāla. *Shorea robusta* Gaertn.f. (= *Vatica robusta*). The sal tree, although that name is not well known in English. It has large leathery leaves and yellow flowers.

saṃsāra. The repeating cycle of life, death, and rebirth, which is characterized by suffering. In short, existence as we know it.

Śāriputra. One of the Buddha's chief disciples, regarded as foremost in comprehending the dharma.

saugandhika. A divine tree that produces, as the name indicates, a "sweet-smelling" and wondrous flower. For more, see McHugh 2012: 94–96.

sense bases (*āyatana*). There are twelve: the six senses (i.e., eye, ear, nose, tongue, body, mind) and their corresponding objects (i.e., the visible, sound, odor, taste, tactile objects, mental objects).

serious offense (*pāpāntikā, pātayantika*). A monastic transgression. The *Divyāvadāna* (544.1) explains that such a deed is called *pāpāntika* because "it burns, scorches, and torments" (*dahati pacati yātayati*). Such a deed is also known as *pātayantika*, or "downfall," because it "causes one to fall [to an evil existence, if not repented and expiated]."

seven factors of awakening (*saptabodhyaṅga*). The factors that lead one to awakening. These are the awakening factors of mindfulness (*smṛti*), dharma analysis (*dharmapravicaya*), strength (*vīrya*), joy (*prīti*), serenity (*praśrabdhi*), concentration (*samādhi*), and equanimity (*upekṣā*).

seven treasures (*saptaratnāni*). The special possessions of a wheel-turning king. They are the most-treasured wheel (*cakraratna*), the most-treasured elephant (*hastiratna*), the most-treasured horse (*aśvaratna*), the most-treasured jewel (*maṇiratna*), the most-treasured woman (*strīratna*), the most-treasured householder (*gṛhapatiratna*), and the most-treasured counselor (*pariṇāyakaratna*).

single guardian [which is mindfulness] (*ekārakṣa*). According to Pāli sources, the third of ten noble dispositions (*ariyavāsa*). The *Dīgha-nikāya* (iii, 269) explains that the single guardian is, in fact, mindfulness.

six duties (*ṣaṭkarma*). These duties of a brahman are teaching and reciting [the Vedas], sacrificing for oneself and sacrificing for others, giving and receiving. Cf. Divy 485.8–9.

six [good] qualities (*ṣaḍaṅga*). According to Pāli sources, the second of ten noble dispositions (*ariyavāsa*). The *Dīgha-nikāya* (iii, 269) explains that one who is endowed with these qualities remains equanimous and mindful in six instances: upon seeing a sight, hearing a sound, smelling a smell, tasting a flavor, touching an tactile object, and cognizing a mental object with the mind.

six perfections (*ṣaṭpāramitā*). These are virtues that are to be practiced and perfected by the bodhisattva. They are the perfection of generosity (*dānapāramitā*), the perfection of morality (*śīlapāramitā*), the perfection of tolerance (*kṣāntipāramitā*), the perfection of strength (*vīryapāramitā*), the perfection of meditation (*dhyānapāramitā*), and the perfection of wisdom (*prajñāpāramitā*).

six spheres of desire (*ṣaṭkāmāvacara*). The worlds of desire and sense pleasure inhabited by the gods of the first six divine realms. See appendix.

six superhuman faculties (*ṣaḍābhijñā*). See *superhuman faculties*.

solitary buddha (*pratyekabuddha*). One who attains awakening on his own, as would a buddha, but who does not found a community.

special knowledges (*vidyā*). There are three: the knowledge of remembering past lives (*pūrvanivāsānusmṛtijñāna*), the knowledge of the passing away and arising [of beings] (*cyutyupapādajñāna*), and knowledge of the destruction of the corruptions (*āsravakṣayajñāna*). Following *Saṅghabhedavastu* ii, 249–50. See also *Dīgha-nikāya* i, 81–85.

sphere of desire (*kāmāvacara*). See *six spheres of desire*.

spiritual faculties. See *five spiritual faculties*.

stream-enterer (*srotāpanna*). One who has attained the first of four stages of religious development that culminate in arhatship (e.g., stream-enterer, once-returner, nonreturner, arhat). Such a person will attain awakening within seven rebirths.

stūpa. A mound-like monument that generally contains relics, such as a buddha's hair and nails.

śūdra. One of the four hereditary classes (*varṇa*) according to Brahmanical Hinduism (i.e., *brahman*, *kṣatriya*, *vaiśya*, *śūdra*). The primary duty of this class, which is considered the lowest, involves serving the higher classes.

suffering (*duḥkha*). The Buddhist diagnosis that existence in saṃsāra is fundamentally unsatisfactory.

sugata. An epithet of a buddha. Often said to mean "one who has attained bliss" or "one who is fully realized."

sughoṣaka. A kind of musical instrument.

sumanā. Apte (1986), Monier Williams (1990), and Rhys Davids and Stede (PTSD) list it as the "great flowering jasmine," with Monier Williams specifying *Rosa glandulifera*, or *Chrysanthemum indicum* L.

summit stages (*mūrdhan*). See *four stages of penetrating insight*.

superhuman faculties (*abhijñā*). Powers and abilities possessed by arhats. These are clairvoyance (*divyacakṣu*), clairaudience (*divyaśrotra*), telepathy (*paracittajñāna*), remembering past lives (*pūrvanivāsānusmṛti*), and magical powers (*ṛddhi*)—for specifics, see *magical powers*. Sometimes included as a sixth faculty is the knowledge of the destruction of the corruptions (*āsravakṣayajñāna*).

supreme knowledge (*anuttarajñāna*). See *unsurpassed perfect awakening*.

sūtra. A discourse attributed to a buddha. It is also one of the three main divisions of the ancient Buddhist canon (i.e., *sūtra*, *vinaya*, *abhidharma*).

tagara. As McHugh (2012: 73–74) notes, "There is some confusion regarding the actual identity of this material, possibly the root of some fragrant Indian valerian species (*Valeriana wallichii* D.C. = *Valeriana jatamansi* Jones) or the root of the Indian rosebay (*Tabernaemontana coronaria* Willd)."

tamālapatra. *Cinnamomum tamala*. A tree in the Lauraceae family that, as its name indicates, is prized for its leaves (*pātra*). The leaves are aromatic and used for both culinary and medicinal purposes. They are sometimes called "Indian bay leaves," although the common bay leaf, which comes from the bay laurel (*Laurus nobilis*), is of a different genus, appearance, and aroma.

tathāgata. An epithet of a buddha. This term has a variety of interpretations (e.g., "thus come," "thus gone," "thus not gone") but is used only in reference to a buddha. Often it is used by Śākyamuni Buddha to refer to himself. For a more complete exegesis of the term, see Bodhi 1978: 331–44.

tenfold path of evil actions (*daśākuśalakarmapatha*). Taking life (*prāṇātipāta*), taking what is not given (*adattādāna*), sexual misconduct (*kāmamithyācāra*), lying speech (*mṛṣāvāda*), harsh speech (*pāruṣyavacana*), malicious speech (*paiśunyavacana*), idle chatter (*sambhinnapralāpa*), covetousness (*abhidhyā*), ill will (*vyāpāda*), and wrong views (*mithyādṛṣṭi*).

tenfold path of virtuous actions (*daśakuśalakarmapatha*). To abstain from the tenfold path of evil actions.

ten powers (*daśabala*). Powers by which a buddha exercises his influence. They are the power from knowing what is possible and impossible (*sthānāsthānajñānabalam*), the power from knowing the results of actions (*karmavipākajñānabalam*), the power from knowing various inclinations [of living beings] (*nānādhimuktijñānabalam*), the power from knowing [the world with its] various elements (*nānādhātujñānabalam*), the power from knowing the superiority and inferiority of the faculties [of living beings] (*indriyavarāvarajñānabalam*), the power from knowing courses of conduct that lead to all destinations (*sarvatragāmanīpratipattijñānabalam*), the power from knowing the defilement, cleansing, and emergence of contemplations, liberations, meditative concentrations, and attainments (*sarva dhyānavimokṣasamādhisamāpattisaṅkleśavyavadānavyutthānajñāna balam*), the power from remembering past lives (*pūrvanivāsānusmṛtijñānabalam*), the power from knowing the passing away and rebirth [of living beings] (*cyutyutpattijñānabalam*), the power of the destruction of the corruptions (*āśravakṣayabalam*). For a slightly different list, with helpful glosses, see *Majjhima-nikāya* i, 69–70; trans. in Ñāṇamoli and Bodhi 1995: 166.

terrible realms of existence (*apāyagati*). See *lower realms of existence*.

thirty-two marks of a great man (*dvātriṃśat mahāpuruṣalakṣaṇa*). The primary characteristics of a great man. According to the *Lakkaṇa-sutta* in the *Dīgha-nikāya* (iii, 143–45; following trans. in Walshe 1987: 441–42), these are:

> [1] He has feet with level tread. This is one of the marks of a great man. [2] On the soles of his feet are wheels with a thousand spokes, complete with felloe and hub. [3] He has projecting heels. [4] He has long fingers and toes. [5] He has soft and tender hands and feet. [6] His hands and feet are net-like. [7] He has high-raised ankles. [8] His legs are like an antelope's. [9] Standing and without bending, he can touch and rub his knees with either hand. [10] His male organ is enclosed in a sheath. [11] His complexion is bright, the color of gold. [12] His skin is delicate and so smooth that no dust can adhere to his body. [13] His body-hairs are separate, one to each pore. [14] His body-hairs grow upward, each one bluish-black like collyrium, curling in rings to the right. [15] His body is divinely straight. [16] He has the seven convex surfaces. [17] The front part of his body is like a lion's. [18] There is no hollow between his shoulders. [19] He is proportioned like a banyan-tree: the height of his body is the same as the span of his outstretched arms, and conversely. [20] His bust is evenly rounded. [21] He has a perfect sense of taste. [22] He has jaws like a lion's. [23] He has forty teeth. [24] His teeth are even. [25] There are no spaces between his teeth. [26] His canine teeth are very bright. [27] His tongue is very long. [28] He has a Brahmā-like voice, like that of the *karavīka*-bird. [29] His eyes are deep blue. [30] He has eyelashes like a cow's. [31] The hair between his eyes is white and soft like cotton-down. [32] His head is like a royal turban.

three bonds to existence (*trisaṃyojana*). These are the false view of individuality (*satkāyadṛṣṭi*), clinging to precepts and vows (*śīlavrataparāmarśa*), and doubt (*vicikitsā*). In total there are ten of these bonds, which are also known as "fetters."

three jewels (*triratna*). The Buddha, the dharma, and the community.

three objects for self-control (*tridamathavastu*). Presumably these are body, speech, and mind.

three realms (*traidhātuka*). See *three worlds*.

three refuges (*triśaraṇa*). According to the Buddhist formula for ordination, one takes refuge in the Buddha, the dharma, and the community.

three special applications of mindfulness (*trīṇyāveṇikāni smṛtyupasthānāni*). The establishing of one's attention in three ways. Being equanimous when others are being attentive (*śuśrūṣamāṇeṣu samacittatā*), being equanimous when others are being inattentive (*aśuśrūṣamāṇeṣu samacittatā*), being equanimous when others are being attentive and inattentive (*śuśrūṣamāṇāśuśrūṣamāṇeṣu samacittatā*).

three worlds (*triloka*). The three levels of existence in a world-system such as our own. These are the realms of desire (*kāma*), form (*rūpa*), and formlessness (*ārūpya*). The Buddha is said to be the teacher of the three worlds.

tilaka. Likely *Symplocos racemosa* Roxb, a small tree with yellowish flowers.

timi. A kind of sea creature or monster.

Timiṅgila. The Timiṅgila is probably so named because he "devours" or "swallows" (*gila*) other "sea creatures" (*timi*). According to Malalasekera (DPPN), Timiṅgala is "a fish, one thousand leagues long, living in the deep ocean and feeding on seaweed." He is the veritable leviathan of Buddhist literature. See note 16 as well as the cover image of this book.

Timitimiṅgila. See *Timiṅgila*.

tolerance stages (*kṣānti*). See *four stages of penetrating insight*.

tranquility (*śamatha*). A type of meditation that aims at the development of perfect and effortless concentration and leads to the attainment of magical powers.

Tripiṭaka. The "three baskets" that comprise the three divisions of the Buddhist canon: the Buddha's discourses (*sūtra*), the monastic discipline (*vinaya*), and the higher teachings (*abhidharma*).

truth. See *four noble truths*.

unsurpassed awakening (*anuttarā bodhi*). See *unsurpassed perfect awakening.*

unsurpassed perfect awakening (*anuttarasamyaksambodhi*). The complete awakening of a buddha.

Upananda. See *group of six monks.*

upoṣadha. Fortnightly periods of observance on the days of the new and full moons. Laypeople are enjoined to observe additional precepts, further restricting sexual and sensual activities. Monastic communities convene to recite the disciplinary code, confess any offenses that may have been committed, and expound the dharma.

uṣṇīṣa. A protuberance on top of a buddha's head that makes it appear to be turbanned. This is the last of the thirty-two marks of a great man. It may also be taken to mean "turban" more literally, as it is one of the five royal insignia that King Bimbisāra removes before approaching the Buddha (Divy 147.11–14).

vaiśya. One of the four hereditary classes (*varṇa*) according to Brahmanical Hinduism (i.e., *brahman*, *kṣatriya*, *vaiśya*, *śūdra*). This class is involved in agriculture, trade, and commerce.

vallabhaka. A kind of sea animal or monster.

vallarī. A musical instrument. According to the Tibetan (Mvy 5019), a kind of three-stringed lute.

varṣikā. A kind of flower likely connected to the "rainy season," as its name indicates. Edgerton (BHSD) suggests that it's a kind of jasmine; perhaps *Jasminum sambac.*

victor (*jina*). An epithet of a buddha.

view of individuality (*satkāyadṛṣṭi*). The false belief that an individual really exists. For more, see Collins 1982: 93–94, 132–33.

Viśvakarman. The chief architect, designer, and decorator of the gods who lives in Trāyastriṃśa heaven.

vow of truth (*satyavacana*). The vow of truth is a formal declaration of fact accompanied by a resolution that the desire of the speaker will be accomplished. As a trope in premodern Indian literature, it occurs in Buddhist, Hindu, and Jain materials.

wheel-turning king (*cakravartin*). One who uses the seven treasures to conquer the four corners of the earth and rule an entire world-system.

world-system (*sahālokadhatu*). See *billionfold world-system.*

yakṣa. Minor deities who possess magical powers and are associated with forests. Often depicted in the *Divyāvadāna* as helping Buddhist practitioners. Kubera (= Vaiśravaṇa, Dhanada), one of the four great kings, is their lord.

Bibliography

Abhidharmakośavyākhyā.
Edition. See Dwarikadas Sastri 1987.

Adaval, Niti. 1970. *The Story of King Udayana as Gleaned from Sanskrit, Pali, and Prakrit Sources*. Chowkhamba Sanskrit Studies 54. Varanasi: Chowkhamba Sanskrit Series Office.

Agrawala, Vasudeva S. 1966. "Some Obscure Words in the *Divyāvadāna*." *Journal of the American Oriental Society* 86 (2): 67–75.

Ali, Daud. 2003. "Gardens in Early Indian Court Life." *Studies in History* 19 (2): 221–52.

Alsdorf, Ludwig. 1955. "Der Stūpa des Kṣemaṅkara." In Otto Spies, ed. *Studia Indologica (Festschrift für Willibald Kirfel zur Vollendung seines 70)*, 9–16. Bonn: Selbstverlag des Orientalischen Seminars der Universität Bonn.

Andersen, Dines, and Helmer Smith, eds. 1965. *Suttanipāta*. London: Pali Text Society.

Appleton, Naomi. 2006. "The Story of the Horse-King and the Merchant Siṃhala in Buddhist Texts." *Buddhist Studies Review* 23 (2): 187–201.

Apte, Vaman Shivaram. 1986. *The Practical Sanskrit-English Dictionary*. Revised and enlarged edition. Kyoto: Rinzen.

Aśokāvadāna.
Edition. See Mukhopadhyaya 1963.
Translation. See Strong 1989.

Avadānakalpalatā of Kṣemendra.
Edition. See Vaidya 1959b.

Avadānaśataka.
Edition. See Speyer 1992.
Edition. See Vaidya 1958.
Translation. See Feer 1891.

Bagchi, Sitansusekhar, ed. 1967–70. *Mūlasarvāstivādavinayavastu*. 2 vols. Darbhanga: Mithila Institute.

Banerjee, Biswanath. 1979. "A Note on the Mahāsukha in Buddhism." In J. P. Sinha et al., eds. *Ludwik Sternbach Felicitation Volume*, 1:467–70. Lucknow: Akhila Bharatiya Sanskrit Parishad.

Bapat, P. V. 1953. "Four Auspicious Things of the Buddhists: śrīvatsā, svastika, nandyāvarta and vardhamāna." In B. G. Gokhale, ed. *Indica: The Indian Historical Research Institute Silver Jubilee Commemoration Volume*, 38–46. Bombay: Examiner Press.

Basu, Santona. 1968. "Lotus-Birth in Vedic and Pali Literature." *Vishveshvaranand Indological Journal* 6: 61–64.

———. 2002. *The Lotus Symbol in Indian Literature and Art*. Delhi: DK Fine Arts Press.

Baums, Stefan. 2002. "Jyotiṣkāvadāna." In Jens Braarvig et al., eds. *Buddhist Manuscripts*, 2: 287–302. Manuscripts in the Schøyen Collection 3. Oslo: Hermes.

———. 2016. "A New Fragment of the Jyotiṣkāvadāna." In Jens Braarvig, ed. *Buddhist Manuscripts*, 4:345–350. Manuscripts in the Schøyen Collection 26. Oslo: Hermes.

Bendall, Cecil, ed. 1897–1902. *Śikṣāsamuccaya*. Biblioteca Buddhica 1. St. Petersburg: Académie impériale des sciences.

Bendall, Cecil, and W. H. D. Rouse, trans. 1971 (1922). *Śikṣāsamuccaya: A Compendium of Buddhist Doctrine*. Delhi: Motilal Banarsidass.

Bénisti, Mireille. 1960. "Étude sur le Stūpa dans l'Inde ancienne." *Bulletin de l'Ecole Française d'Extrême-Orient* 50: 37–115.

Bernhard, Franz, ed. 1965. *Udānavarga*. Göttingen: Vandenhoeck and Ruprecht.

Bhagavad Gītā.
Edition and translation. See Zaehner 1973.

Bloomfield, Maurice. 1920. "Notes on the *Divyāvadāna*." *Journal of the American Oriental Society* 40: 336–52.

Bodhi, Bhikkhu, trans. 1978. *The Discourse on the All-Embracing Net of Views: The Brahmajāla Sutta and Its Commentarial Exegesis*. Kandy, Sri Lanka: Buddhist Publication Society.

———, trans. 2000. *The Connected Discourses of the Buddha: A Translation of the Saṃyutta Nikāya*. 2 vols. Boston: Wisdom Publications.

———, trans. 2017. *Suttanipāta: An Ancient Collection of the Buddha's Discourses*. Boston: Wisdom Publications.

Bogin, Benjamin. 2014. "Locating the Copper-Colored Mountain: Buddhist Cosmology, Himalayan Geography, and Maps of Imagined Worlds." *Himalaya: The Journal of the Association for Nepal and Himalayan Studies* 34 (2): 3–17. Available at http://digitalcommons.macalester.edu/himalaya/vol34/iss2/5

Bongard-Levin, G. M., Daniel Boucher, Takamichi Fukita, and Klaus Wille. 1996. "The Nagaropamasūtra: An Apotropaic Text from the Saṃyuktāgama. A Transliteration, Reconstruction, and Translation of the Central Asian Sanskrit Manuscripts." In *Sanskrit-Texte aus dem buddhistischen Kanon: Neuentdeckungen und Neueditionen*, 3: 7–131. Sanskrit-Worterbuch der buddhistischen Texte aus den Turfan-Funden 6. Göttingen: Vandenhoeck and Ruprecht.

Bongard-Levin, G. M., and O. F. Volkova. 1965. *The Kunala Legend and an Unpublished Asokavadanamala Manuscript*. Edited with an introduction. Calcutta: Maitra for Indian Studies.

Buddhacarita of Aśvaghoṣa.
Edition and translation. See Olivelle 2008.

Burlingame, Eugene Watson. 1917. "The Act of Truth (*Saccakiriya*): A Hindu Spell and Its Employment as a Psychic Motif in Hindu Fiction." *Journal of the Royal Asiatic Society* 11: 429–67.

———, trans. 1969 (1921). *Buddhist Legends Translated from the Original Pali Text of the Dhammapada Commentary* (*Dhammapada-aṭṭhakathā*). 3 vols. Harvard Oriental Series 28–30. Cambridge: Harvard University Press.

Burnouf, Eugène. 1844. *Introduction a l'histoire du buddhisme indien,* vol. 1. Paris: Imprimerie Royale. Translated as *Introduction to the History of Indian Buddhism* by Katia Buffetrille and Donald S. Lopez Jr. (Chicago: University of Chicago Press, 2010).

Carter, James Ross, and Mahinda Palihawadana, eds. and trans. 1987. *The Dhammapada*. Oxford: Oxford University Press.

Chandra, Moti. 1977. *Trade and Trade Routes in Ancient India*. New Delhi: Abhinav.

Ch'en, Kenneth K. S. 1945–47. "A Study of the Svāgata Story in the *Divyāvadāna* in Its Sanskrit, Pali, Tibetan and Chinese Versions." *Harvard Journal of Asiatic Studies* 9: 207–314.

Clarke, Shayne. 2014 *Vinaya Texts*. Gilgit Manuscripts in the National Archives of India: Facsimile Edition, vol. 1. New Delhi and Tokyo: National Archives of India and the International Research Institute for Advanced Buddhology, Soka University.

Clouston, W. A. 1887. *Popular Tales and Fictions, Their Migrations and Transformations,* vol. 2. Edinburgh: William Blackwood and Sons.

Collins, Steven. 1982. *Selfless Persons: Imagery and Thought in Therāvāda Buddhism.* Cambridge: Cambridge University Press.

Couvreur, W. 1964. "Koetsjische schrifttabellen in Slanting Gupta." *Orientalia Gandensia* 1: 111–43.

Cowell, E. B., and R. A. Neil, eds. 1886. *Divyāvadāna.* Cambridge: Cambridge University Press.

Cowell, E. B., Robert Chalmers, W. H. D. Rouse, Henry Thomas Francis, and Robert Alexander Neil, trans. 1990 (1895). *The Jātaka.* 3 vols. Delhi: Motilal Banarsidass.

Cunningham, Alexander. 1879. *The Stupa of Bharhut.* London: W. H. Allen.

Dayal, Har. 1932. The *Bodhisattva Doctrine in Buddhist Sanskrit Literature.* London: Kegan Paul, Trench, Trübner.

Dehejia, Vidya. 1990. "On Modes of Visual Narration in Early Buddhist Art." *Art Bulletin* 72 (3): 374–92.

Dhadphale, M. G. 1980. *Synonymic Collocations in the Tipiṭaka: A Study.* Poona: Bhandarkar Oriental Research Institute.

Dhammapada.

Edition and translation. See Carter and Palihawadana 1987.

Dhammapada-aṭṭhakathā.

Edition. See Norman 1906–14.

Translation. See Burlingame 1969.

Dīgha-nikāya.

Edition. See Rhys Davids and Carpenter 1890–1911.

Translation. See Walshe 1987.

Dimitrov, Dragomir. 2008. "Some Remarks on the Rūpyāvatyavadāna of the *Divyāvadāna(mālā).*" In Dragomir Dimitrov, Michael Hahn, and Roland Steiner, eds. *Bauddhasāhityastabakāvalī: Essays and Studies on Buddhist Sanskrit Literature,* 45–64. Indica et Tibetica 36. Marburg, Germany: Indica et Tibetica.

Divyāvadāna. (For additional sources, see the first footnote in each story.)

Edition. See Cowell and Neil 1886.

Edition. See Vaidya 1959a.

Translation of stories 1–17. See Rotman 2008.

Translation of stories 1–38. See Hiraoka 2007.

Dölpa, Gampopa, and Sakya Paṇḍita. 2015. *Stages of the Buddha's Teaching:*

Three Key Texts. Translated by Ulrike Roesler, Ken Holmes, and David P. Jackson. Boston: Wisdom Publications.

Durgaprasad, Pandit, and K. P. Parab, eds. 1915. *Kathāsaritsāgara*. Revised by W. S. Pansikar. Bombay: Javaji.

Durt, H. 1980. "Mahalla/Mahallaka et la crise de la communauté après le Parinirvâna du Buddha." In *Indianisme et bouddhisme: Mélanges offerts à Mgr Étienne Lamotte*, 79–99. Louvain-la-Neuve: Université Catholique de Louvain.

Dutt, Nalinaksha, ed. 1984 (1950). *Gilgit Manuscripts*. 4 vols. Delhi: Sri Satguru.

Edgerton, Franklin. 1993 (1953). *Buddhist Hybrid Sanskrit Grammar and Dictionary*. 2 vols. Delhi: Motilal Banarsidass.

Eggeling, Julius, trans. 1882–1900. *The Śatapatha Brāhmaṇa According to the Text of the Mādhyandina School*. 5 vols. Sacred Books of the East 12, 26, 41, 43, 44. Oxford: Clarendon Press.

Eimer, Helmut. 1983. *Rab tu 'byuṅ ba'i gẑi: Die tibetische Übersetzung des Pravrajyāvastu im Vinaya der Mūlasarvāstivādins*. Nach Vorarbeiten von Frank-Richard Hamm und weiteren Materialien hrsg. 2 vols. Asiatische Forschungen 82. Wiesbaden: Harrassowitz.

Fausbøll, V., ed. 1877–97. *The Jātaka Together with Its Commentary*. 7 vols. London: Trübner.

Féer, Léon, trans. 1891. *Avadana-Çataka: Cent légendes (bouddhiques)*. Annales du Musée Guimet 18. Paris: E. Leroux.

———, ed. 1884–98. *Saṃyutta-nikāya*. 5 vols. London: Pali Text Society.

Fišer, Ivo. 1954. "The Problem of the Seṭṭhi in the Buddhist Jātakas." *Archiv Orientalni* 22: 238–66.

Formigatti, Camillo A. 2016. "Walking the Deckle Edge: Scribe or Author? Jayamuni and the Creation of the Nepalese *Avadānamālā* Literature." *Buddhist Studies Review* 33 (1–2): 101–140.

Frye, Stanley. 1981. *Sutra of the Wise and Foolish*. Translated from the Mongolian. Dharamsala: Library of Tibetan Works and Archives.

Gethin, Rupert. 1992. *The Buddhist Path to Awakening: A Study of the Bodhi-Pakkhiyā Dhammā*. Leiden: E. J. Brill.

Ghurye, Govind Sadashiv. 1966 (1951). *Indian Costume*. 2nd ed. Bombay: Popular Prakashan.

Gnoli, Raniero, ed. 1977–78. *The Gilgit Manuscript of the Saṅghabhedavastu*. 2 vols. Rome: Istituto Italiano per il Medio ed Estremo Oriente.

Gokhale, Balkrishna Govind. 1977. "The Merchant in Ancient India." *Journal of the American Oriental Society* 97 (2): 125–30.

Goshima, Kiyotaka, and Keiya Noguchi. 1983. *A Succinct Catalogue of the Sanskrit Manuscripts in the Possession of the Faculty of Letters, Kyoto University*. Kyoto: Society for Indic and Buddhistic Studies, Kyoto University.

Granoff, Phyllis. 2000. "Portraits, Likenesses and Looking Glasses: Some Literary and Philosophical Reflections in Representation and Art in Medieval India." In Jan Assmann and Albert I. Baumgarten, eds. *Representation in Religion: Studies in Honour of Moshe Barasch*, 63–107. Leiden: E. J. Brill.

Grey, Leslie. 2000. *A Concordance of Buddhist Birth Stories*. 3rd ed. Oxford: Pali Text Society.

Grierson, G. A. 1913. "Duryodhana and the Queen of Sheba." *Journal of the Royal Asiatic Society* 45 (3): 684–85.

Griffiths, Paul J. 1981. "Buddhist Hybrid English: Some Notes on Philology and Hermeneutics for Buddhologists." *Journal of the International Association of Buddhist Studies* 4 (2): 7–32.

———. 1994. *On Being Buddha: The Classical Doctrine of Buddhahood*. Delhi: Sri Satguru.

Hackin, Joseph. 1913. "Sur des illustrations tibétaines d'une legend *Divyāvadāna*." *Annales du Musée Guimet: Bibliothèque de vulgarization* 40: 145–57.

———. 1916. "Les scènes figurées de la vie du Buddha d'aprés des peintures tibétaines." *Mémoires concernant l'Asie orientale, Inde, Asie central, Extrême-orient*, 2:1–117. Paris: Ernest Leroux.

Hahn, Michael. 1992. *Haribhaṭṭa and Gopadatta: Two Authors in the Succession of Āryaśūra. On the Rediscovery of Parts of Their Jātakamālās*. 2nd ed. Studia Philologica Buddhica. Occasional Papers Series 1. Tokyo: Reiyukai Library.

Hahn, Michael, and Gudrun Bühnemann. 1985. *Der Grosse Legendenkranz (Mahajjātakamālā): Eine mittelalterliche buddhistische Legendensammlung aus Nepal*. Wiesbaden: Otto Harrassowitz.

Handurukande, Ratna. 1982. "The Advantages of Image-Making." *Buddhist Studies* (Bukkyo *Kenkyū*) 11: 143–47.

———, ed. 1988. *The Supriyasārthavāhajātaka*. Indica et Tibetica 15. Bonn: Indica et Tibetica.

Hanneder, Jürgen. 2002. "The Blue Lotus: Oriental Research between Philology, Botany and Poetics?" *Zeitschrift der Deutschen Morgenländischen Gesellschaft* 152: 295–308.

———. 2007. "Some Common Errors Concerning Water-Lilies and Lotuses." *Indo-Iranian Journal* 50: 161–64.

Hartmann, Jens-Uwe. 1977. "Das Candraprabha-Avadāna: Nach dem Gilgit-Manuskript herausgegeben, übersetzt, und kommentiert." MA thesis, Ludwig Maximilian University of Munich.

———. 1980. "Notes on the Gilgit Manuscript of the *Candraprabhāvadāna*." *Journal of the Nepal Research Centre* 4: 251–66.

Heim, Maria. 2014. *The Forerunner of All Things: Buddhaghosa on Mind, Intention, and Agency*. New York: Oxford University Press.

Hikata, Ryūshō. 1954. *Honshōkyō rui no shisōshiteki kenkyū* (*A Historical Study of the Thoughts in Jātakas and the Similar Stories*). Tokyo: Toyo Bunko.

———. 1978. *Honjō kyōrui sōgō zempyō* (*Addendum: A Complete List of References Concerning Jātakas*). Revised and enlarged edition. Tokyo: Sankibō Busshorin.

Hiraoka, Satoshi. 1998. "The Relation between the *Divyāvadāna* and the *Mūlasarvāstivāda Vinaya*." *Journal of Indian Philosophy* 26: 1–16.

———, trans. 2007. *Budda ga nazotoku sanze no monogatari: Diviya avadāna zen'yaku*. 2 vols. Tokyo: Daizō shuppan.

———. 2009. "Text Critical Remarks on the *Divyāvadāna* (1)." *Sōka Daigaku Kokusai Bukkyōgaku Kōtō Kenkyūjo Nenpō* (*Annual Report of the International Research Institute for Advanced Buddhology at Soka University*) 12: 29–72.

———. 2010. "Text Critical Remarks on the *Divyāvadāna* (2)." *Sōka Daigaku Kokusai Bukkyōgaku Kōtō Kenkyūjo Nenpō* (*Annual Report of the International Research Institute for Advanced Buddhology at Soka University*) 13: 35–74.

Hoernle, A. F. Rudolf. 1916. "The Sutta Nipata in a Sanskrit Version from Eastern Turkestan." *Journal of the Royal Asiatic Society of Great Britain and Ireland* 48 (4): 709–32.

Horner, I. B., trans. 1938–66. *The Book of Discipline* (*Vinaya-piṭaka*). 6 vols. London: Pali Text Society.

Huber, Edouard. 1906. "Les sources du Divyāvadāna." *Bulletin de l'Ecole Française d'Extrême-Orient* 6: 1–43, 335–40.

Ishihama, Yumiko, and Yoichi Fukuda, eds. 1989. *A New Critical Edition of the Mahāvyutpatti: Sanskrit-Tibetan-Mongolian Dictionary of Buddhist Terminology*. Tokyo: Toyo Bunko.

Itivuttaka.

Edition. See Windisch 1975.

Translation. See Woodward 1948.

Jaini, Padmanabh. 1966. "The Story of Sudhana and Manoharā. An Analysis of the Texts and the Borobudur Reliefs." *Bulletin of the School of Oriental and African Studies* 29: 533–58.

Jamison, Stephanie W., and Joel P. Brereton, trans. 2014. *The Rigveda: The Earliest Religious Poetry of India*. 3 vols. Oxford and New York: South Asia Research.

Jātaka.
Edition. See Fausbøll 1877–97.
Translation. See Cowell et al. 1990.

Jātakamāla of Āryasūra.
Edition. See Kern 1891.
Translation. See Khoroche 1989.

Jones, J. J., trans. 1976 (1949–56). *Mahāvastu Avadāna*. 3 vols. London: Luzac.

de Jong, J. W. 1968. "The Magic Wall of the Fortress of the Ogresses: Apropos of *āsīyati* (*Mahāvastu* III, 86.3)." In J. C. Heesterman et al., eds. *Pratidānam: Indian, Iranian, and Indo-European Studies Presented to Franciscus Bernardus Jacobus Kuiper on His Sixtieth Birthday*, 484–87. The Hague: Mouton.

Kāraṇḍavyūha Sūtra.
Edition. See Vaidya 1961: 258–308.

Karashima, Seishi, and Margarita I. Vorobyova-Desyatovskaya. 2015. "The Avadāna Anthology from Merv." In Seishi Karashima and Margarita I. Vorobyova-Desyatovskaya, eds. *Buddhist Manuscripts from Central Asia: The St. Petersburg Sanskrit Fragments* 1: 145–523. Tokyo: Institute of Oriental Manuscripts of the Russian Academy of Sciences and the International Research Institute for Advanced Buddhology.

Kathāsaritsāgara of Somadevabhatta.
Edition. See Durgaprasad and Parab. 1915.

Kern, Hendrik, ed. 1891. *The Jātaka-Mālā; or, Bodhisattāvadānamālā*. Harvard Oriental Series 1. Boston and London: Ginn; Leipzig: Otto Harrassowitz.

Khoroche, Peter, trans. 1989. *Once the Buddha Was a Monkey: Ārya Śūra's Jātakamālā*. Chicago: University of Chicago Press.

Klaus, Konrad, ed. and trans. 1983. *Das Maitrakanyakāvadāna (Divyāvadāna 38)*. Indica et Tibetica 2. Bonn: Indica et Tibetica.

Kloetzli, W. Randolph. 1997 (1983). *Buddhist Cosmology: Science and Theology in the Images of Motion and Light*. Delhi: Motilal Banarsidass.

Kongtrul Lodrö Tayé, Jamgön (Kong sprul Blo gros mtha' yas). 1995. *Myriad Worlds: Buddhist Cosmology in Abhidharma, Kālacakra, and Dzog-chen*

[Selections from *Shes bya mtha' yas pa'i rgya mtsho*]. Ithaca, NY: Snow Lion.

Kosambi, D. D. 1952. "The Sanskrit Equivalents of Two Pali Words." *Annals of the Bhandarkar Oriental Research Institute* 32: 53–60.

Krom, N. J. 1927. *Borobudur: Archaeological Description*. 2 vols. The Hague: Nijhoff.

Kuiper, F. B. J. 1959. "Yūpayaṣṭi—(Divy. 244.11)." *Indo-Iranian Journal* 3: 204–5.

Kurita, Isao. 2003. *Gandharan Art*. 2 vols. Revised and enlarged edition. Tokyo: Nigensha.

La Vallée Poussin, Louis de. 1937. "*Staupikam*." *Harvard Journal of Asiatic Studies* 2: 276–89.

Lamotte, Étienne, trans. and ed. 1944. *Le traité de la grande vertu de sagesse de Nāgārjuna (Mahāprajñāpāramitāśāstra)*, vol. 1. Louvain: Bureaux du Muséon.

Langenberg, Amy Paris. 2013. "South Asian Buddhist Tales of Fertility and Child Protection." *History of Religions* 52 (4): 340–69.

Le Coq, Albert von, and Ernst Waldschmidt. 1928. *Die buddhistische Spätantike in Mittelasie*, vol. 6. Neue Bildwerke 2. Berlin: D. Reimer.

Lefeber, Rosalind. 1995. "Jain Stories of Miraculous Powers." In Donald Lopez, ed. *Religions of India in Practice*, 426–33. Princeton: Princeton University Press.

Lenz, Timothy, and Jason Neelis. Forthcoming. *Further Gāndhāran Avadānas: British Library Kharoṣṭhī Fragments 4 and 12 + 14*. Seattle and London: University of Washington Press.

Lévi, Sylvain. 1932. "Note sur des manuscrits sanscrits provenant de Bamiyan (Afghanistan), et de Gilgit (Cachemire)." *Journal Asiatique* 220: 1–45.

Lévi, Sylvain, and Edouard Chavannes. 1915. "Quelques titres énigmatiques dans la hiérarchie ecclésiastique du bouddhisme indien." *Journal Asiatique* 5: 193–223; 6: 307–10.

Lienhard, Siegfried. 2003. "A Jaina Version of the Siṃhalāvadāna." In Olle Qvarnström, ed. *Jainism and Early Buddhism: Essays in Honor of Padmanabh S. Jaini*, 504–9. Fremont, CA: Asian Humanities Press.

Linke, Elfrun. 1997. "Birds in Sanskrit Literature: Sanskrit-English Index." *Annals of the Bhandarkar Oriental Research Institute* 78: 121–41.

Liu, Xinru. 1996. *Silk and Religion: An Exploration of Material Life and the Thought of People, AD 600–1200*. Delhi: Oxford University Press.

Lojda, Linda. 2009. "*Rajo harāmi, malaṃ harāmi*: Die Geschichte der Arhats

Cūḍapanthaka und Mahāpanthaka." *Studien zur Indologie und Iranistik* 26: 83–123.

Maclean, Derryl N. 1989. *Religion and Society in Arab Sind*. Leiden: E. J. Brill.

Mahābhārata.
Edition. See Sukthankar et al. 1933–59.

Mahāvastu.
Edition. See Senart 1977.
Translation. See Jones 1976.

Mahāvyutpatti.
Edition. See Ishihama and Fukuda 1989.

Majjhima-nikāya.
Edition. See Trenckner and Chalmers 1888–89.
Translation. See Ñāṇamoli and Bodhi 1995.

Mahajjātakamālā.
Edition. See Hahn and Bühnemann 1985.

Malalasekera, G. P. 1995 (1938). *Dictionary of Pāli Proper Names*. 2 vols. New Delhi: Munshiram Manoharlal.

Manusmṛti (*Mānavadharmaśāstra*).
Edition and translation. See Olivelle 2005.

Masefield, Peter, trans. 1994. *The Udāna*. 2 vols. Oxford: Pali Text Society.

Matsunami, Seiren. 1965. *A Catalogue of the Sanskrit Manuscripts in the Tokyo University Library*. Tokyo: Suzuki Research Foundation.

Maue, Dieter. 1996. *Alttürkische Handschriften: Teil 1, Dokumente in Brāhmī und Tibetischer Schrift*. Verzeichnis der Orientalischen Handschriften in Deutschland 13/9. Stuttgart: Franz Steiner.

———. 2010. ". . . , was zusammengehört. Verstreute Fragmente eines Blattes mit der Geschichte vom Mūṣikāhairaṇyika." In Eli Franco and Monika Zin, eds. *From Turfan to Ajanta: Festschrift for Dieter Schlingloff on the Occasion of His Eightieth Birthday* 2: 595–625. Bhairahawa, Rupandehi, Nepal: Lumbini International Research Institute.

McClintock, Sara. 2017. "Ethical Reading and the Ethics of Forgetting and Remembering." In Jake H. Davis, ed. *A Mirror Is for Reflection: Understanding Buddhist Ethics*, 185–202. New York: Oxford University Press.

McCombs, Jason. 2014. "Mahāyāna and the Gift: Theories and Practices." PhD diss., University of California–Los Angeles.

McHugh, James. 2012. *Sandalwood and Carrion: Smell in Indian Religion and Culture*. New York: Oxford University Press.

Mitra, Rajendralal. 1981 (1882). *The Sanskrit Buddhist Literature of Nepal.* New Delhi: Cosmo.

———. 1998 (1853–81). *The Lalita-Vistara: Memoirs of the Early Life of Sakya Sinha (Chs. 1–15).* Delhi: Sri Satguru.

Miyazaki, Tensho, Jundo Nagashima, Tatsushi Tamai, and Zhou Liqun. 2015. "The Śārdūlakarṇāvadāna from Central Asia." In Seishi Karashima and Margarita I. Vorobyova-Desyatovskaya, eds. *Buddhist Manuscripts from Central Asia: The St. Petersburg Sanskrit Fragments,* 1:1–84. Tokyo: Institute of Oriental Manuscripts of the Russian Academy of Sciences and International Research Institute for Advanced Buddhology.

Monier-Williams, Monier. 1990 (1899). *A Sanskrit-English Dictionary.* Delhi: Motilal Banarsidass.

Mrozik, Susanne. 2006. "Materializations of Virtue: Buddhist Discourses on Bodies." In Ellen Armour and Susan St. Ville, eds. *Bodily Citations: Religion and Judith Butler,* 15–47. New York: Columbia University Press.

Mukhopadhyaya, Sujitkumar, ed. 1954. *Śārdūlakarṇāvadāna.* Santiniketan, India: Visvabharati.

———, ed. 1963. *The Aśokāvadāna: Sanskrit Text Compared with Chinese Versions.* New Delhi: Sahitya Akademi.

Ñāṇamoli, Bhikku, and Bhikkhu Bodhi, trans. 1995. *The Middle Length Discourses of the Buddha: A New Translation of the Majjhima Nikāya.* Boston: Wisdom Publications.

Näther, Volkbert. 1975. "Das Gilgit-Fragment Or. 11878A im Britischen Museum zu London: Herausgegeben, mit dem Tibetischen verglichen und übersetzt." PhD diss., University of Marburg.

Negi, J. S. 1993–2005. *Tibetan-Sanskrit Dictionary.* 16 vols. Sarnath, Varanasi: Dictionary Unit, Central Institute of Higher Tibetan Studies.

Neelis, Jason. 2008. "Historical and Geograpical Contexts for Avadānas in Kharoṣṭhī Manuscripts." In Richard Gombrich and Cristina A. Scherrer-Schaub, eds. *Buddhist Studies,* 151–167. Papers of the Twelfth World Sanskrit Conference 8. Delhi: Motilal Banarsidass.

Nobel, Johannes. 1955. *Udrāyaṇa, König von Roruka: Eine buddhistische Erzählung; Die tibetische Übersetzung des Sanskrittextes.* 2 vols. Wiesbaden: Otto Harrassowitz.

Norman, H. C., ed. 1906–14. *Dhammapada-aṭṭhakathā.* London: Pali Text Society.

Norman, K. R., trans. 1984. *The Group of Discourses* (*Suttanipāta*). With alternative translations by I. B. Horner and Walpola Rahula. London: Pali Text Society.

Ohnuma, Reiko. 2000. "The Story of Rupavati: A Female Past Birth of the Buddha." *Journal of the International Association of Buddhist Studies* 23 (1): 103–45.

———. 2004a. "A King Gives Away His Head." In Donald S. Lopez, ed. *Buddhist Scriptures*, 142–58. New York: Penguin.

———. 2004b. "Rūpyāvatī Gives Away Her Breasts." In Donald S. Lopez, ed. *Buddhist Scriptures*, 159–71. New York: Penguin.

———. 2007. *Head, Eyes, Flesh, and Blood: Giving Away the Body in Indian Buddhist Literature*. New York: Columbia University Press.

Oldenberg, H., ed. 1879–83. *Vinayapiṭaka*. London: Pali Text Society.

Olivelle, Patrick, ed. and trans. 2005. *Manu's Code of Law: A Critical Edition and Translation of the Mānava-Dharmaśāstra*. Oxford and New York: Oxford University Press.

———, ed. and trans. 2008. *Life of the Buddha by Aśvaghoṣa*. New York: New York University Press and JCC Foundation.

Panglung, Jampa Losang. 1981. *Die Erzählstoffe des Mūlasarvāstivāda-Vinaya Analysiert auf Grund der Tibetischen Übersetzung*. Tokyo: Reiyukai Library.

Paranavitana, Senarat. 1969. "Roruka: Was in Mohenjo-daro?" In K. S. Lal, ed. *Studies in Asian History: Proceedings of the Asian History Congress, 1961*, 111–16. New Delhi: Asia Publishing House.

Pliny. 1963. *Natural History*, vol. 8 (books 28–32). Translated by W. H. S. Jones. Loeb Classical Library. Cambridge: Harvard University Press.

Pollock, Sheldon. 2011. "Indian Philology and India's Philology." *Journal Asiatique* 299 (1): 423–75.

Prakash, Om. 1961. *Food and Drinks in Ancient India: From Earliest Times to c. 1200 AD*. Delhi: Munshi Ram Manohar Lal.

Prebish, Charles. 1996. *Buddhist Monastic Discipline: The Sanskrit Prātimokṣa Sūtras of the Mahāsaṃghikas and Mūlasarvāstivādins*. Delhi: Motilal Banarsidass.

Puri, B. N. 1965. *India under the Kushanas*. Bombay: Bharatiya Vidya Bhavan.

Przyluski, Jean. 1920. "La Roue de la vie à Ajaṇṭa." *Journal Asiatique* 16: 313–31.

Rani, Sharda. 2005 (1977). *Buddhist Tales of Kashmir in Tibetan Woodcuts: Narthang Series of the Woodcuts of Kṣemendra's Avadānakalpalatā*. New Delhi: International Academy of Indian Culture and Aditya Prakashan.

Rau, W. 1954. "Lotusblumen." In J. Schubert and U. Schneider, eds. *Asiatica: Fetschrift Friedrich Weller*, 505–13. Wiesbaden: Otto Harrassowitz.

Ray, Reginald. A. 1994. *Buddhist Saints in India: A Study in Buddhist Values and Orientations*. New York: Oxford University Press.

Ṛg Veda.
Translation. See Jamison and Bereton 2014.

Rhie, Marylin Martin. 1999. *Early Buddhist Art of China and Central Asia*, vol. 1. Leiden and Boston: E. J. Brill.

Rhys Davids, T. W., and J. E. Carpenter, eds. 1890–1911. *Dīgha-nikāya*. 3 vols. London: Pali Text Society.

Rhys Davids, T. W., and H. Oldenberg, trans. 1987 (1882–85). *Vinaya Texts (Vinayapiṭaka)*. 3 vols. Delhi: AVF Books.

Rhys Davids, T. W., and William Stede. 1986 (1921–25). *The Pāli Text Society's Pāli-English Dictionary*. London: Pali Text Society.

Rigzin, Tsepak. 1997. *The Tibetan-English Dictionary of Buddhist Terminology*. Revised and Enlarged Edition. Dharamsala: Library of Tibetan Works and Archives.

Roth, Gustav 1980. "Symbolism of the Buddhist Stūpa According to the Tibetan Version of the *Caitya-vibhāga-vinayodbhāva-sūtra*, the Sanskrit Treatise *Stūpa-lakṣaṇa-kārikā-vivecana*, and the Corresponding Passage in Kuladatta's *Kriyāsaṃgraha*." In A. L. Dallapiccola and S. Z. Lallemant, eds. *The Stūpa: Its Religious, Historical, and Architectural Significance*, 183–207. Wiesbaden: Franz Steiner.

———. 1985. "Remarks on the Stupa of Kṣemaṃkara." *Journal of the Nepal Research Center* 7: 183–96. Originally published in German in *Studien zur Indologie und Iranistik* 5–6 (1980): 181–92.

Rothenberg, Bonnie Lynne. 1990. "Kṣemendra's *Bodhisattvāvadānakalpalātā*: A Textcritical Edition and Translation of Chapters One to Five." PhD diss., University of Madison–Wisconsin.

Rotman, Andy. 2003. "The Erotics of Practice: Objects and Agency in Buddhist Avadāna Literature." *Journal of the American Academy of Religion* 71 (3): 555–78.

———. 2008. *Divine Stories: The Divyāvadāna, Part 1*. Classics of Indian Buddhism, inaugural volume. Boston: Wisdom Publications.

———. 2009. *Thus Have I Seen: Visualizing Faith in Early Indian Buddhism*. New York: Oxford University Press.

———. In progress. *Saving the World through Commerce? Buddhists, Merchants, and Mercantilism in Early India.*

Salomon, Richard. 2000. *A Gāndhārī Version of the Rhinoceros Sūtra: British Library Kharoṣṭhī Fragment 5B*. Seattle and London: University of Washington Press.

Saṃyutta-nikāya.
Edition. See Féer 1884–98.
Translation. See Bodhi 2000.

Sander, Lore, and Ernst Waldschmidt. 1985. *Sanskrithandschriften aus den Turfanfunden*, part 5. Stuttgart: Franz Steiner.

Saṅghabhedavastu.
Edition. See Gnoli 1977–78.

Sastri, Dwarikadas, ed. 1987. *Abhidharmakośa and Bhāṣya of Ācārya Vasubandhu with Sphuṭārthā Commentary of Ācārya Yaśomitra.* 2 vols. Bauddha Bharati Series 5–8. Varanasi: Bauddha Bharati.

Schiefner, F. Anton von. 1893. *Tibetan Tales.* Translated from the German by W. R. S. Ralston. London: Kegan Paul, Trench, Trübner.

———. 1964. "Zur Interpretation des Prātimokṣasūtra." *Zeitschrift der Deutschen Morgenländischen Gesellschaft* 113: 536–51.

Schlingloff, Dieter. 1982. "Indische Seefahrt in römischer Zeit." In H. Müller-Karpe, ed. *Zur geschichtlichen Bedeutung der frühen Seefahrt*, 51–85. Kolloquien zur Allgemeinen und Vergleichenden Archäologie 2. Munich: C. H. Beck.

———. 1988. *Studies in the Ajanta Paintings: Identifications and Interpretations*. Delhi: Ajanta Publications.

Schmithausen, Lambert. 1970. "Zu den Rezensionen des Udānavargaḥ." *Wiener Zeitschrift für die Kunde Südasiens* 14: 47–124.

———. 1997. *Maitrī and Magic: Aspects of the Buddhist Attitude toward the Dangerous in Nature.* Vienna: Österreichische Akademie der Wissenschaften.

Schopen, Gregory. 1996. "The Lay Ownership of Monasteries and the Role of the Monk in Mūlasārvāstivādin Monasticism." *Journal of the International Association of Buddhist Studies* 19 (1): 81–126.

———. 1997. *Bones, Stones, and Buddhist Monks*: *Collected Papers on the Archaeology, Epigraphy, and Texts of Monastic Buddhism in India*. Honolulu: University of Hawai'i.

———. 2000. "Hierarchy and Housing in a Buddhist Monastic Code: A Translation of the Sanskrit Text of the *Śayanāsanavastu* of the *Mūlasarvāstivāda-vinaya*—Part One." *Buddhist Literature* 2: 92–196.

———. 2004. *Buddhist Monks and Business Matters: Still More Papers on Monastic Buddhism in India.* Honolulu: University of Hawai'i Press.

———. 2006. "The Buddhist 'Monastery' and the Indian Garden: Aesthetics, Assimilations, and the Siting of Monastic Establishments." *Journal of the American Oriental Society* 126 (4): 487–505.

———. 2010. "On Incompetent Monks and Able Urban Nuns in a Buddhist Monastic Code." *Journal of Indian Philosophy* 38: 107–31.

———. 2014. AAR Centennial Roundtable: Liberation Is Only for Those Already Free: "Reflections on Debts to Slavery and Enslavement to Debt in an Early Indian Buddhist Monasticism." *Journal of the American Academy of Religion* 82 (3): 606–35.

Senart, Emile, ed. 1977 (1882–97). *Le Mahāvastu: Texte sanscrit publié, pour la première fois et accompagné d'introductions et d'un commentaire*. 3 vols. Tokyo: Meicho-Fukyu-Kai.

Shackleton Bailey, D. R. 1950. "Notes on the *Divyāvadāna*, Part 1." *Journal of the Royal Asiatic Society*: 161–84.

———. 1951. "Notes on the *Divyāvadāna*, Part 2." *Journal of the Royal Asiatic Society*: 82–102.

Sharma, Sharmistha. 1992. *Astrological Lore in the Buddhist Śārdūlakarṇāvadāna*. Delhi: Eastern Book Linkers.

Śikṣāsamuccaya of Śāntideva.

Edition. See Bendall 1897–1902.

Translation. See Bendall and Rouse 1971.

Silk, Jonathan. 2008a. "The Story of Dharmaruci: In the *Divyāvadāna* and in Kṣemendra's *Bodhisattvāvadānakalpalatā*." *Indo-Iranian Journal* 51: 137–85.

———. 2008b. *Managing Monks: Administrators and Administrative Roles in Indian Buddhist Monasticism*. New York: Oxford University Press.

———. 2008c. "*Parikarṣati Reconsidered." *Annual Report of the International Research Institute for Advanced Buddhology at Soka University for the Academic Year 2007* 2: 61–69.

———. 2009. *Riven by Lust: Incest and Schism in Indian Buddhist Legend and Historiography*. Honolulu: University of Hawai'i Press.

———. 2013. "Kern and the Study of Indian Buddhism: With a Speculative Note on the Ceylonese Dhammarucikas." *Journal of the Pali Text Society* 31: 125–54.

Sircar, D. C. 1961–62. "Some Brahmi Inscriptions." *Epigraphia Indica* 34: 207–12.

———. 1965. *Indian Epigraphy*. Delhi: Motilal Banarsidass.

Skilling, Peter. 1994. *Mahāsūtras: Great Discourses of the Buddha.* 3 vols. Oxford: Pali Text Society.

———. 2014. "Birchbark, Bodhisatvas, and Bhāṇakas: Writing Materials in Buddhist North India." In Nalini Balbir and Maria Szuppe, eds. *Scribes and Readers in Iranian, Indian and Central Asian Manuscript Traditions,* 499–521. Eurasian Studies 12. Rome: Istituto per l'Oriente Carlo Alfonso Nallino.

Smith, Helmer. 1953. "En marge du vocabulaire Sanskrit des bouddhistes." *Orientalia Suecana* 2 (2): 119–28

Speyer, J. S. 1902. "Critical Remarks on the Text Divyāvadāna." *Wiener Zeitschrift fuhr die Kunde des Morgänlandes* 16: 103–30, 340–61.

———. 1992 (1906). *Avadānaśataka: A Century of Edifying Tales Belonging to the Hīnayāna.* 2 vols. Delhi: Motilal Banarsidass.

Steiner, Roland. 2002. "Zum ursprünglichen Titel der 'Rūpyāvatī'-Geschichte." In Dragomir Dimitrov, Ulrike Roesler, and Roland Steiner, eds. *Śikhisamuccaya: Indian and Tibetan Studies,* 203–10. Collectanea Marpurgensia Indologica et Tibetologica. Vienna: Arbeitskreis für Tibetische und Buddhistische Studien Universität Wien.

Steinthal, P., ed. 1885. *Udāna.* London: Pali Text Society.

Strong, John. 1977. "Gandhakuṭī: The Perfumed Chamber of the Buddha." *History of Religions* 16: 390–406.

———, trans. 1989 (1983). *The Legend of King Aśoka (Aśokāvadāna).* Princeton: Princeton University Press.

———. 1992. *The Legend and Cult of Upagupta: Sanskrit Buddhism in North India and Southeast Asia.* Princeton: Princeton University Press.

———. 2002. *The Experience of Buddhism: Sources and Interpretations.* 2nd ed. Belmont, CA: Wadsworth/Thomson Learning.

Sukthankar, Vishnu S., et al., eds. 1933–59. *Mahābhārata.* Pune: Bhandarkar Institute.

Suttanipāta.

Edition. See Andersen and Smith 1965.

Translation. See Norman 1984 and Bodhi 2017.

Tatelman, Joel, ed. and trans. 2005. *The Heavenly Exploits: Buddhist Biographies from the Divyāvadāna,* vol. 1. New York: New York University Press and JJC Foundation.

Teiser, Stephen F. 2006. *Reinventing the Wheel: Paintings of Rebirth in Medieval Buddhist Temples.* Seattle: University of Washington Press.

Thapar, Romila. 1978. *Ancient Indian Social History: Some Interpretations*. New Delhi: Orient Longman.

Tharchin, Sermey Geshe Lobsang, Judith Chiarelli, et al., trans. 1984. *King Udrayana and the Wheel of Life (Rudrāyaṇa-avadāna)*. Hovell, NJ: Mahayana Sutra and Tantra Press.

Thomas, E. J. 1940. "Note on the Divyāvadāna." *Bulletin of the School of Oriental and African Studies* 10: 654–56.

Thurman, Robert, trans. 1983 (1976). *The Holy Teaching of Vimalakīrti: A Mahāyāna Scripture*. University Park and London: Pennsylvania State University Press.

Trenckner, Vilhelm, and Robert Chalmers, eds. 1888–89. *The Majjhima Nikāya*. 4 vols. London: Pali Text Society.

Tripathi, Chandrabhal. 1962. *Fünfundzwanzig Sūtras des Nidānasaṃyukta*. Berlin: Akademie-Verlag.

Tucci, Giuseppe. 1949. *Tibetan Painted Scrolls*. 3 vols. Rome: Libreria dello Stato.

Udāna.

Edition. See Steinthal 1885.

Translation. See Masefield 1994.

Udānavarga.

Edition. See Bernhard 1965.

Upasak, C. S. 1975. *Dictionary of Early Buddhist Monastic Terms*. Varanasi: Bharati Prakashan.

Upreti, Kalpana. 1989. "The Rationale of the Mahāyāna Sūtra *Dānādhikaraṇa-Mahāyāna-Sūtra* in the Hīnayāna Text *Divyāvadāna*." *Buddhist Studies* 13: 89–93.

———. 1995. *India as Reflected in the Divyāvadāna*. Delhi: Munshiram Manoharlal.

Vaidya, P. L., ed. 1958. *Avadānaśataka*. Buddhist Sanskrit Texts 19. Darbhanga: Mithila Institute of Post-Graduate Studies and Research in Sanskrit Learning.

———, ed. 1959a. *Divyāvadāna*. Buddhist Sanskrit Texts 20. Darbhanga: Mithila Institute of Post-Graduate Studies and Research in Sanskrit Learning.

———, ed. 1959b. *Avadānakalpalatā*. Buddhist Sanskrit Texts 22–23. Darbhanga: Mithila Institute of Post-Graduate Studies and Research in Sanskrit Learning.

———, ed. 1961. *Mahāyāna-sūtra-saṃgraha*, part 1. Buddhist Sanskrit Texts 17. Darbhanga: Mithila Institute of Post-Graduate Studies and Research in Sanskrit Learning.

Vajracarya, Mohanraj. 1977. *Rūpāvatyavadāna: Bhagavān Buddha Misājuyā Janmajūgu.* [In Newari]. Lalitapura, Nepal: Mohanarāja Vajrācārya.

Vinayapiṭaka.

Edition. See Oldenberg 1879–83.

Translation. See Rhys Davids and Oldenberg 1987.

Translation. See Horner 1938–66.

Vira, Raghu, and Lokesh Chandra. 1995. *Gilgit Buddhist Manuscripts.* Revised and enlarged compact facsmile edition. Biblica Indo-Buddhica Series 150–52. Delhi: Sri Satguru.

Visvanathan, Meera. 2009. "Writing, Gifting and Identities: Providing Contexts for Early Brahmi Inscriptions (300 BCE–250 CE)." MPhil diss., Jawaharlal Nehru University, New Delhi.

Vogel, Claus, and Klaus Wille. 1984. "Some Hitherto Unidentified Fragments of the Pravrajyāvastu Portion of the Vinayavastu Manuscript Found near Gilgit." *Nachrichten der Akademie der Wissenschaften Göttingen, Philologisch-Historische Klasse,* 299–337. Göttingen: Vandenhoeck and Ruprecht.

———. 1996. "The Final Leaves of the Pravrajyāvastu Portion of the Vinayavastu Manuscript Found near Gilgit: Part 1, Saṅgharakṣitāvadāna." In G. Bongard-Levin et al., eds. *Sanskrit-Texte aus dem buddhistischen Kanon: Neuentdeckungen und Neueditionen,* 3:241–96. Göttingen: Vandenhoeck and Ruprecht.

———. 2002. "The Final Leaves of the Pravrajyāvastu Portion of the Vinayavastu Manuscript Found near Gilgit: Part 2, Nāgakumārāvadāna and Lévi Text, with Two Appendices Containing a Turfan Fragment of the Nāgakumārāvadāna and a Kučā Fragment of the Upasampadā Section of the Sarvāstivādins." In J. Chung et al., eds. *Sanskrit-Texte aus dem buddhistischen Kanon: Neuentdeckungen und Neueditionen,* 4:11–76. Göttingen: Vandenhoeck and Ruprecht.

Vogel, Jean Philippe. 1926. *The Indian Serpent Lore; or, The Nagas in Hindu Legend and Art.* London: Probsthain.

von Hinüber, Oskar. 2016. "Some Remarks on Technical Terms of Stūpa Architecture." *Annual Report of the International Research Institute for Advanced Buddhology at Soka University* 19: 29–46.

von Simson, Georg. 1982. "Die buddhistische Erzählung von Udrāyaṇa von Roruka und ihr mythologischer Hintergrund." *Indologica Taurinensia* 10: 199–214.

Waldschmidt, Ernst. 1973. "The Burning to Death of King Udayana's 500 Wives: A Contribution to the Udayan Legend." In *German Scholars in India*, 1:366–86. Varanasi: Chowkhamba Sanskrit Series Office.

Waldschmidt, Ernst, et al. 1973–. *Sanskrit-Wörterbuch der buddhistischen Texte aus den Turfan-Funden und der kanonischen Literatur der Sarvāstivāda-Schule*. 3 vols. Göttingen: Vandenhoeck and Ruprecht.

Walshe, Maurice, trans. 1987. *Thus Have I Heard: The Long Discourses of the Buddha (Digha-nikāya)*. London: Wisdom Publications.

Ware, James R. 1929. "Studies in the Divyāvadāna II: *Dānādhikāramahāyānasūtra*." *Journal of the American Oriental Society* 49: 40–51.

———. 1938. "The Preamble to the *Saṃgharakṣitāvadāna*." *Harvard Journal of Asiatic Studies* 3 (1): 47–67.

Weller, F. 1953. "Divyāvadāna 244.7 ff." *Mitteilungen des Instituts für Orientforschung* 1: 268–76.

Whitaker, Jarrod L. 2011. *Strong Arms and Drinking Strength: Masculinity, Violence, and the Body in Ancient India*. New York: Oxford University Press.

Wijayaratna, Mohan. 1990. *Buddhist Monastic Life: According to the Texts of the Theravada Tradition*. Cambridge: Cambridge University Press.

Windisch, E., ed. 1975 (1889). *Itivuttaka*. London: Pali Text Society.

Woodward, F. L., trans. 1948. *The Minor Anthologies of the Pali Canon II: Udāna (Verses of Uplift) and Itivuttaka (As It Was Said)*. London: Pali Text Society.

Wujastyk, Dominik. 2004. "Apples or Plums? Jambudvīpa: The Continent of the Jamun Tree." In Charles Burnett, Jan P. Hogendijk, Kim Plofker, and Michio Yano, eds. *Ketuprakāśa: Studies in the History of the Exact Sciences in Honour of David Pingree*, 287–301. Leiden: E. J. Brill.

Zaehner, R. C., trans. 1973. *The Bhagavad Gita*. New York: Oxford University Press.

Zimmer, Heinrich. 1925. *Karman, ein buddhistischer Legendenkranz*. Munich: Bruckmann.

Index

A

Abhaya, Prince, 361n154
actions. *See* deeds
Āgamas. *See* four Āgamas
ages, destruction of, 6
aggregates
  karma in, 73, 112, 163, 173, 227, 272, 275, 278, 339, 342
  rising and falling of, 88, 365n208
Agrajyoti, 46–47. *See also* Jyotiṣka
Airavaṇa (elephant king), 81
Ajanta caves, 417–18n828
Ajātaśatru, Prince, 69, 70–73, 287, 362n178
Ājñāta Kauṇḍinya, 54
alms
  abstaining from, five reasons for, 280, 424n929
  in nāga realm, 159, 160
  offering single measure, 89–92
  See also community of monks
alpeśākhya, 352n47
altars. *See* shrines
ambrosia, divine, xxix, 159, 160
Ānanda, 167
  on Buddha's smile, 51–53, 324–25
  Jyotiṣka and, 61
  on Maudgalyāyana, 96–97
  Panthaka and, 210, 213, 229–30, 232
  previous life as tiger cub, 194
Anaṅgaṇa, 74–75, 76
  grief of, 79–80
  harsh speech of, 78, 82, 363–64n195
Anāthapiṇḍada, 3, 83, 176, 181, 197, 201
Anavatapta lake, 158
Andhaka kings, 310
animal realm, 43, 285, 294, 346, 354
  on five-sectioned wheel, 97, 99, 100, 101
  prediction of rebirth in, 323
  rebirth in, 17, 323
  suffering of, 95, 96
animals
  charity toward, 189, 191
  as metaphors for Buddha, 53, 54
  rebirth of, 174
  teaching dharma to, xxx, 172, 390n469
  See also birds; cattle; crocodiles; oxen; thoroughbred horse; tigress
anunayavacana, 357n106
Anupamā, xxxi
  birth of, 241
  as blacksmith's daughter, 251
  Buddha and, 247
  fresh appearance of, 271–72, 277–78
  as husband-eating demon, 259
  imprisonment of, 271, 422n896
  self-loathing of, 248
  and Śyāmāvatī, rivalry with, 260–65
antigods, 54, 83, 93, 131, 133, 181, 191, 195, 345
Aparagodānīya (continent), 97, 346
application, path of, 17
arhatship, xxvii, 58–59, 180, 216, 295, 363–64n195

of Dharmaruci, 17–18
of farmers, five hundred, 171, 172, 174
fervent aspiration for, 164–65, 388n449
of former young nāga, 158–59
of Gautama, 47
of Jyotiṣka, 72–73, 82
of Mahāpanthaka, 206–7
of merchants/monks, five hundred, 8, 9
omniscience in, 328
of one thousand noble sons, 152–53
of Panthaka, 211–12
of Rudrāyaṇa, 319–20, 339
of Saṅgharakṣita, 150–51, 163, 165
of Tiṣya and Puṣya, 296
armies
of Candraprabha, 118
fourfold, 118, 238, 271, 291–92, 294–95, 298, 304
of Śikhaṇḍin, 313, 330
See also rebellions
armor, jeweled, 289, 290
arrow, poisoned, 341, 342
aspirations, fervent, 355n69
of Anaṅgaṇa, 82
of Candraprabha, 131
of deer hunter, 342
of five hundred monks, 8–9
of guildmaster and powerful fighter, 23–24
of hut-burning palace women, 273–74
of Jyotiṣka, 82
of novice bowl-carrier, 160–61, 387n441
of Sahasodgata, 115
of Sandhāna's daughter, 277
of Saṅgharakṣita in previous life, xxx, 164–65, 388n449
of Yaśodharā in previous life, 28–29, 32–33, 355n69
assassins, 317, 318–21, 325
asthiśakala, 352n37
aśvājaneya, 409n733
Aśvajit, 54
atikrānta and *abhikrānta*, 368n245
attachment
dangers of, 267–68
freedom from, 243, 244, 245
of kings, 309
purification of, 198, 211
to sense objects, 247–48
symbol of, 97
attention, focusing, 114, 299, 334, 336, 430n1003
Avadānakalpalatā (Kṣemendra), 394n540
Avalokiteśvara. *See* Bodhisattva Avalokiteśvara
Avīci hell, 320, 321, 326, 327, 346, 443n1186. *See also* hells
awakening, seven factors of. *See* seven factors of awakening

B

Bālāha (divine horse), 254, 417n828, 418n842
Balasena, 112–14
Bandhumān, King, 74, 75–76, 77, 81, 363–64n195
Bandhumatī (capital), 74, 75, 77, 78, 81
Bandhumatīyaka Forest, 74, 75
baṇikśreṣṭhin, 352n43
banners and flags, 48, 118, 334, 391n490
at holy sites, 119, 123, 132, 341
merit from, 179
welcoming, 29, 78, 130
Bāṣpa, 54
baths, ritual, 63, 188, 199, 202, 203, 205, 304
beans of Mūṣikāhairaṇyaka, 221, 222, 404n667
beds, 307
Buddha's, 243
four-jeweled, 25
gift of, 198
specially prepared, 143, 144, 145,
beggars, as dear to Buddha, 182
beings
in realms of existence, 345, 346–47
sentient, benefiting, 190, 339
unusual forms of, 147, 153–55
Bhadraśilā (capital), 118–20, 121, 123, 124, 125–27, 129, 130, 133
Bhadrika, 54
bhagavato 'ntike, 351n20
Bhāgīrathī River, 292
Bharat Kala Bhavan, 350–51n16

Bhiru, 287, 330
escape of, 331–32, 333, 339, 342, 344, 439n1130
Śikhaṇḍin and, 303, 312–13, 314, 315, 326, 329
variant names of, 427n952, 439n1127
Bhiruka/Bhirukaccha (city), 333, 439n1129
Bhūrika, 46–47
Bimbisāra, King, 287, 361n154
Jyotiṣka and, xxviii, 58, 59, 61–63, 67–70, 361n154
Rudrāyaṇa and, xxxi–xxxii, 287–91, 293, 294, 297–98, 304–8, 312
at Śītavana, 56
Vāsava as, 34
birds
in Bhadraśilā, 118, 119
carrion-eating, 257
eagle and goose, 53
heavenly, 83, 93, 131, 133, 181, 191, 195
partridges, 261–62
to tell time, 69–70
See also Suparṇin (bird king); Uccaṅgama (bird)
blacksmith and craftsman, 249–51
blindness, curing, 219, 403n653
Bodhisattva Avalokiteśvara, 418n842
Bodhisattva Maitreya, 131, 194, 376n329, 395n551
bodhisattvas, 24, 34, 42, 87–88, 131, 188–89, 194, 376n329, 395n551, 418n842
See also Candraprabha, King
Borobudur panels, 426n949, 442n1166
bowls
begging, turning into iron hammers, 143
bracelets as rest for, 277, 423n916
brass, 333, 335–36, 441n1155
sandalwood, 62–64
types of, 64, 307
Brahmā, 54, 84, 131, 182, 189, 239
Brahmā world, 117, 129, 132
Brahmadatta, King, 235, 236, 238–39, 272, 273, 275, 410nn745–46
Brahmā-like voice, 198, 245
brahmans
blind, 217–19
duties of, 9, 158, 203, 398n586
five hundred young, 190, 205–6
education of, 202–3, 204, 398n583, 398n584
of Kṣemāvatī, 21–22
seers with Brahmaprabha, 190–91, 194
skilled in omens, 85–86, 187
verses concerning, 149
Viśvāmitra's disciples, 125–26
See also Brahmaprabha; Mahāpanthaka; Mati; Panthaka; Raudrākṣa; Sumati; Uttara
Brahmaprabha, xxx, 189–93, 194, 395n544
Brahmāvatī pond, 239
brilliance. *See* radiance
Buddha Dīpaṅkara, xxvii, 24–25, 27, 29–34
Buddha Kanakamuni, 140
Buddha Kāśyapa, xxx, 140, 157–58, 160, 173, 227, 362n165
burial site of, xxx, 175–76
disciples of, xxix, 144–46, 154–55, 382n386
five hundred monks of, 8–9, 174
prediction of, 164–65, 388n449
Buddha Krakucchanda, xxvii, 34–35, 140
Buddha Kṣemaṅkara, xxvii, 19, 20, 21
Buddha Śākyamuni, xxx, 9, 84, 140, 388n449
on actions resulting in unusual beings, 153–55
on Agrajyoti, 45, 46
alms offering, refraining from, 280, 424n928
audiences of, types of beings in, 83, 93, 133, 181, 195
beauty of, 54, 167, 170, 175
as bodhisattva, 42–43
as Brahmaprabha, 194
and Candraprabhā, discourse to, 300
as Candraprabha, 133, 193
on charity, 84, 92–93, 182, 194–95
desire, lack of, 246–48
disciples of, great, 54. *See also* Ānanda; Maudgalyāyana; Śāriputra
on fire in women's quarters, 266–67
on five-sectioned wheel, 97–98

footprints of, 244
gaze of, 245, 246
Ghoṣila and, 279–80
on gift for Rudrāyaṇa, 290–92
gift of one thousand new disciples for, 152
as guildmaster, 19–24, 226, 352n43
householder's son (Sahasodgata) and, 104, 105–6, 108, 110–12, 115
Jīvaka Kumārabhūta and, 229–33
journey to Śītavana, 52–53, 54–56
Jyotiṣka and, 61, 71–72
in Kalmāṣadamya, 242
as Kanakavarṇa, 92–93
on Maudgalyāyana, 96–97
Mahāpanthaka and, 202
as monk who knew Tripiṭaka, 42–43
on offering instructions, 283–85
omniscience of, 177, 178–79
painting of, 290–91
Panthaka and, 209–10, 213, 216–17
power of name of, 6–8
prediction about, 292–93
request to Saṅgharakṣita, 139
on requesting dharma, 136–37
rice gruel offering to, 167–69
Rudrāyaṇa and, 306, 317
as Rūpāvatī, 193
selects Kātyāyana for Roruka, 294
selects Śailā for palace women, 297
as Siṃhala, 259
similes for, 53–54, 359n134
smile of, 50, 52, 56–57, 321, 324
Timiṅgila and, 7
at Toyika, 174–76
verse of praise to, 293
as young craftsman, 251
Buddha Śikhin, 140
Buddha Suprabha, 194
Buddha Vipaśyin, xxviii, 73–77, 79, 81–82, 140
Buddha Viśvabhū, 140
Buddharakṣita, 137, 138
buddhas
abstaining from alms, five reasons for, 280, 424n929
activity of, 248, 415n803
descriptions of, 19, 24, 34–35, 73–74, 83–84, 157, 164, 173, 181–82, 227
inconceivability of, 180
mundane thoughts of, 176
presence of, 229
qualities of, 48–49, 52
seeing, never tiring of, 290
seeing, rarity of, 301
teaching methods of, 210, 400n608
vision of, 49
wonderful occurrences of, 30–31
See also solitary buddhas
Buddhism, four seals of, 51, 322, 390n469

C

Campā (city), 64
campaka tree, ever-blossoming, 130, 132, 378n328
Candraprabha, King, xxviii–xxix, 193
affection of his subjects for, 121
death and cremation of, 132–33
description of, 119
generosity of, 119–20, 122, 123, 124
rebirth as Brahmaprabha, 189
rebirth of subjects, 132, 133
Rūpāvata as, xxx, 186–89
sacrifices of, 126–32, 134, 189
Candraprabhā, Queen, 193, 287, 298–302, 395n548, 437n1099
Candraprabhabodhisattvacaryā-avadāna, xxviii–xxix, 117–34
capitals. *See* Bandhumatī; Bhadraśilā; Dīpāvatī; Kanakāvatī; Kṣemāvatī; Siṃhakalpā; Śobhāvatī; Utpalāvatī
caravan leaders, 107–8
epithet for Buddha, 53, 179
with five hundred horses, 233–34, 235, 236, 239–40
Mūṣikāhairaṇyaka as, 223–24
Siṃhaka, 252
Siṃhala as, 253–56, 257–58
caste, x, 60, 205, 284, 361n158
cats, rebirth of Tiṣya and Puṣya as, 326, 328–29
cattle, xxx, 74, 252, 272, 275. *See also* cows with golden horns; oxen
cattle prod, 175, 390n479

celestial musicians, 53, 83, 93, 131, 133, 181, 284, 347
"Chapter on Brahmans" (*Brāhmaṇa-varga*), 149, 383n399
charity
of Candraprabha, xxviii–xxix, 119–20, 122, 123, 124
in *Kanakavarṇa-avadāna*, xxviii, 90–92
result of and consequence of offering, 84, 92–93, 182, 194–95
of Rūpāvatī, xxx, 184
thirty-seven ways of offering, xxxi, 197–99, 396n561
circumambulation, 176–77, 190, 301–2, 326, 323–24, 328
cities. *See* Bhiruka/Bhirukaccha; Campā; Hirukam; Kauśāmbī; Lambakapāla; Pāṭaliputra; Puṣkalāvata; Rājagṛha; Roruka; Śrāvastī; Takṣaśilā; Vārāṇasī; Vokkāṇa
cloth, twin pieces of, 64–67
community of monks, 29, 54, 83, 117, 170, 181, 197, 295
of Buddha Kṣemaṅkara, 19
of Buddha Vipaśyin, 75-77, 79, 81-82
causing fights within, prohibition on, 144
feeding, 13, 15, 81-82, 101, 102, 104, 105–6, 107, 108, 110-11, 229–32, 279–81
offerings to, 62, 75
refuge in, 169, 283
two assemblies of, 208
See also monasticism
compassion
of Buddha Śākyamuni, 54, 152, 168, 306
of buddhas, 48–49, 54
of Candraprabha, 123, 124, 126–27, 128, 132, 134
gifts given out of, 105, 199
in Śikhaṇḍin's words, 316
of solitary buddhas, 89, 113, 114–15, 273–74, 276, 278, 340–41, 343
of Viśvāmitra, 125
confidences, four. *See* four confidences
confusion, gifts that remove, 197
Connected Sayings (*Saṃyuktāgama*), 140
constellations, 53, 85–86, 187, 364n202
continents. *See* Aparagodānīya; Jambudvīpa; Pūrvavideha; Uttarakuru
coronations, 168, 170, 238, 284, 303, 421n772, 412n775, 425–26n943
cosmology, Buddhist, 50–52, 321–24, 345–47
cotton, rain of, 92
cows with golden horns, 120
cremations, xxvii, 57–58, 82, 132, 205, 312, 341, 363–64n195, 435n1065
cremation grounds, 48, 52–53, 54–58, 189, 194, 205, 265
crocodiles, 5, 224, 406n692
crossing over, 48, 111, 131, 168–69, 192, 282–83, 368n245
crowning ritual, 199, 397n568
Cūḍāpakṣa-avadāna, xxxi, 201–40
cultivation, path of, 17
cup, beings in form of, 147, 153, 154, 385n420

D

Dānādhikaraṇa-mahāyānasūtra, xxxi, 197–99, 396n559
dangers, eight, 285–86, 426nn947–48
Daśabala Kāśyapa (monk), 63, 362n165
daughters-in-law, twelve, 217–19
dawn, stages of, 284
day laborers, xxviii, 102–4, 106, 109, 112, 114, 115, 367n230
death
cultivating consciousness of, 299
facing, 6–7
inevitability of, 310–12
as punishment, 313
signs indicating, 299
verse spoken at, 204–5
deeds, xxviii–xxix, 103, 190, 209, 311
of Anupamā, 277–78
of Candraprabhā, 299–300
of Dharmaruci, 11, 41–43
of five hundred farmers, 172–74
of five hundred merchants, 8–9
good and evil, fruits of, 195
of Jyotiṣka, 73
of Kubjottarā, 274–75, 277
leading to five realms, 99–100

maturity of, 93, 103, 112, 114, 195
meritorious, 27–28, 119, 186, 239, 303, 393n516. *See also* merit
of misbehaving monks, 143–46
of Panthaka, xxxi, 226–27
rebirth and, 99–100
in Roruka's shower of dirt, 331, 333, 342–43
of Sahasodgata, 112
of Saṅgharakṣita, 163
sinful, 208, 215–16
of solitary buddhas, 88–89, 90, 114–15, 273, 341
of Śyāmāvatī and retinue, 265, 272
See also karma; miraculous deeds
deer hunter, 340–42
deities, 6, 25, 302
of Bhadraśilā, 126–27, 129
of Gandhamādana, 124
of Kanakāvatī, 90
of Maṇiratnagarbha, 130–31, 132
of North Country, 338
requesting dharma from Saṅgharakṣita, 139, 148–50
of Roruka, 333, 334–36
in yakṣa abode, 65–66
See also gods
delusion, 97, 117, 198, 211, 266, 267, 421n876
Demon Sūtra (*Rākṣasī-sūtra*), 254, 417n828
demonesses, 5, 225, 254–57, 417n828
desire, 159
Buddha's lack of, 247
freedom from, 216
mired in mud of, 115, 273
for offspring, 246, 414n797
overcoming, 149
sexual, 26, 35–36
six spheres of, 133, 347. *See also* divine realms
for wealth, 4, 224
See also passion
desire realm, 117, 129, 345, 346–47
Devadatta, 70, 133, 377n340
Dhanada. *See* Vaiśravaṇa
dharma
discourse to nāgas, 135–36
discourse to Sahasodgata, 111–12
false, 344
followers of, qualities, 149
gift of, 198
inconceivability of, 180
inspiration through small teaching, 219–20, 226
profundity of, 212, 400n616
as protection, 310
requesting, importance of, 136–37
rewards attained upon hearing, 58–59
ruling according to, 304, 336, 364n202
stinginess with, 227, 228, 407n707
teaching to women, 297–98
with three principles, 172, 390n469
Dharmaruci, xxvii, 358n116
with Buddha, 16–17, 18–19, 24, 34, 43, 352n37
committing three deadly sins, 35–43
arhatship of, 17–18
and householder donor, 13–15, 352n39
as Mati, 25–26, 32, 33–34
as powerful fighter, 21–22, 23–24
satisfaction of, 10–11, 12–13, 15, 16, 352n39
Dharmaruci-avadāna, xxvii, 3–43
Dhṛtarāṣṭra, 53, 347. *See also* four great kings
diamonds, 4, 225, 331, 333
Dīpa, King, 25, 27, 29, 33
Dīpaṅkara. *See* Buddha Dīpaṅkara
Dīpāvatī (capital), 25, 26, 27, 31, 34
Dīrghāgama. See *Longer Sayings* (*Dīrghāgama*)
dirt, rain of, 331–32, 333, 439n1130
divine beings, unconscious, 228, 407n715
divine realms, 51, 172, 302, 322, 346, 347, 359n131. *See also* Trāyastriṃśa
divine hearing, 7
divine sight, 89, 119, 128
divine-like glory, 46–48, 55, 56, 59, 64, 67–68, 69, 73, 82
divyamānuṣīm, 358n119
dreams, 26–27, 64, 122–24
droughts, xxviii, 86–87, 275
dṛṣṭasatya, 363n195. *See also* truth, seeing
dvārakoṣṭhaka, 366n220

E

earth, 55, 60, 175, 183, 265, 310
  Buddha as jewel of, 293
  four quarters of, 119
  and gold, regarding as equal, 17, 72, 151, 153, 158, 172, 206, 211, 296, 320
  lighting up and remaining flat, 243, 713nn783–84
  protectors of, 123, 127, 134
  sacrificing, 316
  six ways of moving, 30–31
  See also elements, deeds maturing in
eight sciences, 253, 417n826
eightfold path. *See* noble eightfold path
Ekottarikā. See *Gradual Sayings* (*Ekottarikāgama*)
elements, deeds maturing in, 73, 112, 163, 173, 227, 272, 275, 278, 339, 342
eloquence, as inspired yet controlled, 136, 213, 214, 379n354
emptiness, 51, 322
encouragement, 291, 293
essences, five. *See* five essences
evil actions, tenfold path of, 99
existence
  bonds to, 264, 266–67, 420n864
  clinging to, 88
  states of, 16
  See also realms of existence; wheel of existence
eyes, sacrificing, 189

F

faculties, superhuman, 17, 27, 72, 125, 151, 153, 158, 172, 207, 212, 296, 320, 344
faith, 6
  in Buddha, 46, 108, 117, 136, 267, 271–72, 422n898
  in Candraprabha, 129, 131, 133
  duty of, 103–4, 108, 367n233
  gifts of, 145, 174
  of hell beings, 50
  inspiring, 216, 402n641
  instilled through body of solitary buddha, 113
  of Jyotiṣka, 62, 63
  of Mahāpanthaka, 206
  practices of, 176–80
  from seeing Buddha, 31, 167–68, 170
  from seeing magical image of Buddha, 50, 322
  Śikhaṇḍin's refutation of, 329
  of Suparṇin, 158
  of Udayana, 262
famine, ix, 86–87, 91, 183, 364n202
father, spiritual, 117, 133, 369n258, 377n341
fear and dread, withstanding, 139, 140, 148, 253, 380n364
filth, 210, 211
fire
  mastery over, 215
  set to hut of solitary buddha, 273–74
  set to monastery, 145
  set to Puṣpadanta Palace (women's quarters), 264–65, 268, 270
  See also elements, deeds maturing in
five [bad] qualities, 48
five essences, 199, 397n571
five hundred boys, 188, 193, 268, 269, 270
five hundred farmers, xxx, 170–74
five hundred merchants, xxix
  and householder's son (Sahasodgata), 106–7, 367n240
  ordination of, 7–9
  previous lives of, 165
  on Siṃhala's voyage, 253–54
  sons of, 138, 140, 142, 151–52
  voyage of, 3–7
five hundred seers, xxix, 147–50
five hundred students, 164, 165
five-sectioned wheel. *See* wheel of existence
five spiritual faculties, 8
flags. *See* banners and flags
flagstaffs, magic, 417n828
floor mistaken for water, 68–69, 362n176
flowers, 22, 30, 69, 78, 118, 119, 125, 132, 242, 287, 288, 300, 304, 313, 334. *See also* lotuses
  beings having form of, 147, 153, 154
  as medicine, 164
  offerings of, 23, 27–28, 31, 133, 177–79, 228

rain of, 91, 331, 332
of seven factors of awakening, 49, 198
food
appearing as molten iron, 144
equal distribution to all, 86–87
gifts of, 198, 367n240
sharing of, 182, 195
single measure of, 87, 89, 90
forgiveness, 81, 114, 213, 232–33, 240, 258, 303, 335
form and formless realms, 345, 346
four Āgamas, xxix, 138, 140–41, 142
four assemblies, 95, 96
four bases of success, 48, 198
four confidences, 48, 54
four continents, 97, 346
four floods [of corruptions], 48
four great kings, 53, 347. *See also* Dhṛtarāṣṭra; Kubera; Virūḍhaka; Virūpākṣa
four immeasurables, 199, 397n572
four means of attracting beings to religious life, 48
four noble truths, 51, 111, 168, 171, 216, 262, 265, 274, 281, 283, 294, 300, 322, 337, 338, 363–64n195
fruits, 22, 119, 125, 228, 262–63, 287, 288, 313
beings have form of, 147, 153, 154
intoxicating, 5, 225
as medicine, 164, 204
rain of, 91, 92

G

Gaṅgā River, 172, 390n469
garments
of Bimbisāra, 288–89
jeweled armor, 289, 290
Jyotiṣka's divine, 67–68
rain of clothes, 331, 332
of release, 397n568
Garuḍa, 387n431
Gautama. *See* Buddha Śākyamuni
Gāyatrī mantra, 204, 399n592
gender, 392n507, 392n513
generosity. *See* charity
Ghoṣila, 259, 263, 278–80, 332, 420n861, 423–24n921
gifts
benefits of giving, 224
of faith, 145, 174
five great, 25, 26
of new disciples, 152, 305–6
between Rudrāyaṇa and Bimbisāra, 288–92
thirty-seven ways of offering, xxxi, 197–99, 396n561
See also offerings
Gilgit Buddhist Manuscripts
Candraprabha's sacrifice in, 375n325
flowering trees of Maṇiratnagarbha in, 376n328
ill omens of Bhadraśilā in, 372n298
request for Candraprabha's head in, 375n323
Saṅgharakṣita story in, 384n405, 384n408, 384n410, 385n420, 386n425, 388n449
spiritual father, use of in, 377n341
See also *Mūlasarvāstivāda-vinaya*
gods, 6, 54–56, 83, 93, 111, 118, 124, 125, 140, 191, 195, 282, 294, 310, 345, 346–47
buddhas as teachers of, 19, 24, 35, 74, 84, 157, 164, 173, 182, 227
Candraprabhā as, 299–302
consecration by, 199
oxen reborn as, 172–73, 174
prediction of rebirth as, 323
realms of, 95, 96, 97, 99–100, 101
respect and honor from, 17, 72, 151, 153, 159, 172, 207, 212, 282, 296, 320
superiority of buddhas to, 49
See also deities; rebirth, in divine realms
gold
barley turning to, 169
and earth, regarding as equal, 17, 72, 151, 153, 158, 172, 206, 211, 296, 320
mountains, seven, 158, 386n428
offerings of, 341, 443n1182
rain of, 92, 331, 332, 333
relative merit of, 177–79
goldsmiths, 222–23

Gradual Sayings (*Ekottarikāgama*), 135–36, 141, 157, 161, 379n352, 379n357, 381n368
grain increasing in granary, 334
grass
  beds of, 243
  kāśa and *kuśa*, 137, 380n361
greed, 35, 88, 155, 396n561
guildmasters, 41, 118, 334, 352n43
  Buddha's past lives as, 19–24, 220, 221, 225–26
  Candraprabha's father, 186, 187
  Dharmaruci's father in past life, 35, 39–40
  metaphor for Buddha, 53
  Sahasodgata's appointment as, xxviii, 109

H

hair, matted, 31–32, 33, 34
hate, 42
  freedom from, 117, 266, 421n876
  purification of, 198, 211
  symbol of, 97
heads, jeweled, 122, 127
heat stage, 17, 58, 180
heavens, six. *See* six heavens
hell beings, xxix, 99, 101, 321–22, 346
hells
  Dharmaruci's rebirth in, 34, 43
  individual realms of, 144, 145, 146, 381n380
  names of, 50, 321–22, 346, 444nn1201–2
  prediction of rebirth in, 323
  rebirth in, 249, 274, 323, 324
  sufferings of, 101
hiraṇyasuvarṇa, 358n110
Hiru, 287, 330
  escape of, 331–32, 333, 339, 342, 344, 439n1130
  Śikhaṇḍin and, 303, 312–13, 314, 315, 326, 329
  variant names of, 427n952, 439n1127
Hirukam (city), 333
human realm, 159, 294, 345, 346
  on five-sectioned wheel, 97, 99, 101
  pleasures of, 100, 101–2
  prediction of rebirth in, 323
  suffering of, 95, 96, 184
hunger
  of Dharmaruci, xxvii, 10–15
  of Dharmaruci's mother, 910
  freedom from, 198
  of starving mother fed by Rūpāvatī, xxx, 183–84
  of tigress, 191
  of Timiṅgila, 9
  See also famine; hungry ghost realm
hungry ghost realm, 100, 294, 345, 346
  on five-sectioned wheel, 97, 101
  prediction of rebirth in, 323
  rebirth in, 17–18, 285, 323
  suffering of, 95, 96, 99

I

impermanence, 51, 97, 123, 124, 128, 129, 172, 322
impurity, 210, 211
incest, 35–39, 40, 41, 87
inconceivability, 47, 57, 124, 180, 210
Indra, 6, 17, 72, 81, 151, 153, 159, 172, 207, 212, 296, 320
inheritances, 78, 311–12
insults, virtue and, 237, 411n768
intentions, 184
  of buddhas, 48, 113
  of doing harm, 215, 402n633
  for heaven and liberation, 131, 133
  to renounce, 100–101
  See also aspirations, fervent
interdependent arising, 88, 150, 319. *See also* twelve links of interdependent arising

J

Jambudvīpa (Indian subcontinent), xxviii, 3, 4, 5, 119, 122, 127, 134, 224, 225, 346
  crowns falling from all heads in, 129
  depiction on five-sectioned wheel, 97
  famine in, 86, 87, 89–92
  ill omens in, 123, 124, 125–26, 372n298
  Maudgalyāyana in, 95–96
  royal pleasures in, 120–21, 123–24
  Saṅgharakṣita's return to, 142, 143–46

Siṃhala's return to, 254, 258
taxes and customs fees, exemption from, 85, 119
jealousy, xxxi, 259–64
Jeta Grove, 3, 7, 12, 13–16, 17, 18, 83, 181, 197, 201, 213, 399n595
Jīvaka Kumārabhūta, xxxi, 57–58, 229–33, 240, 361n154, 408n718, 408n728, 409n731
joy
at birth of Candraprabha, 187
of Brahmaprabha, 192, 395n544
of Candraprabhā, 301–2
gifts given out of, 199
of Kanakavarṇa, 91–92
of noble people, 232
of Rudrāyaṇa, 298, 320
of Śakra, 186
Jyotiṣka, xxvii–xxviii, 58, 59–62, 361n154
Ajātaśatru and, 70–73
as Anaṅgaṇa, 82
divine-like glory and, 64, 66–68
home of, 68–70
sandalwood bowl and, 62–64
status of, 361n159, 362n172
Jyotiṣka-avadāna, xxvii–xxviii, 45–82, 359n136

K

Kalandakanivāpa, 45, 95, 99, 229, 231, 287, 300
Kalmāṣadamya, 241, 242, 243
Kāṃśimaha festival, 336, 441n1156
Kanakavarṇa, King, xxviii, 84–87, 89–92
Kanakavarṇa-avadāna, xxviii, 83–93
Kanakāvatī (capital), 85, 89, 90
Kanakumuni. *See* Buddha Kanakumuni
Kapila, 292
karma
being overpowered by, 265, 310
destroying bad, 210–11
evil, pure, and mixed, 82, 115, 165–66, 174, 274, 344
faith and, 322
of hell beings, 50–51, 322
of Hiru and Bhiru, 331, 342–43
maturing of, 73, 112, 163, 173, 227, 272, 275, 278, 284–85, 339, 342
resulting in diverse forms, 153–55
of Rudrāyaṇa, 317–18, 319, 321, 339, 342, 443n1186
of Śikhaṇḍin, 326, 342–43
of Śyāmāka, 336
See also deeds
Kāśyapa (disciple of Buddha), 54
Kāśyapa. *See* Buddha Kāśyapa
Kātyāyana. *See* Mahākātyāyana
Kauṇḍinya, 194
Kauśāmbī (city), 259, 263, 264, 265–66, 268–69, 270, 271, 332
Kauśika. *See* Śakra
kettledrums, 118, 119, 121, 123, 124, 126
khaḍgaviṣāṇakalpa, 365n210
Khara, 333, 440n1136
khustikayā, 379n353
killing, 42
arhats, 41, 321, 327–29, 358n113
fathers, 39–40, 70, 71, 315–17, 320–21, 325–26, 339
mothers, 41
knowledge and insight, 49, 114, 175, 212, 430n1003
Kosala countryside, 205, 207
Krakucchanda. *See* Buddha Krakucchanda
krīḍitā ramitāḥ, 365n212
krośca maidens, 5, 225
Kṣema, King, 19, 20, 21
Kṣemaṅkara. *See* Buddha Kṣemaṅkara
Kṣemāvatī (capital), 19, 20
Kubera, 6, 347, 352n36. *See also* Vaiśravaṇa; four great kings
Kubjottarā, 265, 272, 274–75, 277
kulastha, 371n289
kulopakagṛha, 367n236
kumārāmātya, 360n142
kumārikā, 413n785
Kuru countryside, 241, 242
Kuru kings, 310, 433n1048

L

Lambakapāla (city), 336, 441n1157
lamplight, 264, 420n867
learning, 310

five benefits of great, 150, 319, 384n410
three ways of, 399–400n604
life span
by class of beings, 346, 347
during reign of Candraprabha, 119
during time of Buddha Kāśyapa, 157, 164–65, 173, 227
during time of Buddha Śākyamuni, 164–65, 388–389n449
of humans, 309
of Śakra, 347, 444n1200
light rays, 50–51, 52, 134, 192, 215, 321–24
lion throne, 69, 136, 214, 215, 361n159
lion's roar, 55–56
lokākhyāyikā, 367n231
Longer Sayings (*Dīrghāgama*), 140
lotuses, 118
birth in, xxvii–xxviii, 57, 360n145
hell realm imagery of, 444n1202
as metaphor for buddhas, 83, 181, 246, 248
as metaphor for growth, 59, 138, 252
offerings of, 30, 132, 300
pools and ponds of, 22, 27, 239, 273
root of, 52, 324
smell of, 232
See also waterlilies
loving-kindness, 30
of Brahmaprabha, 191
gifts given out of, 199
as protection, 191
of Śyāmāvatī and retinue, 262–63
of thoroughbred horse, 237
toward Raudrākṣa, 129, 132
lumbermen, 221–22
lunar festival, 239–40

M

madam, 35–37, 356n85, 356n90
Madhyama. See *Middle-Length Sayings* (*Madhyamāgama*)
Magadha countryside, 56, 229, 287, 305
magical powers, 326, 328
of Dharmaruci, 18
of Buddha Dīpaṅkara, 29
displaying, transgression of, 62–64
flight, 89, 90–91, 151, 159–60, 186, 191, 265, 333, 336
for food, increasing amount of, 168
invisibility, 149–50
of Jyotiṣka, 67–68
karma and, 321, 436n1086
of Mahākātyāyana, 330, 336
of nāgas, 136, 159–60
of Panthaka, 215, 231, 232, 408n728, 409n731
of Śailā, 332
of Śakra, 80–81
of Buddha Śākyamuni, 16, 17, 29, 50–51, 322
shapeshifting, 185, 254, 255
at Śītavana, 57–58
in Sumati's dreams, 26, 354n64
winning over ordinary people with, 273
See also miraculous deeds
Mahācandra, 122, 127–28, 129, 133
Mahākātyāyana, xxxii, 297, 329, 332, 338–39, 342, 365n217
buried under dirt, 330, 331, 344, 438n1113, 444n1197
flees Roruka, 333–34
journey to Roruka, 294–95
in Khara, 334–35
mother of, 337–38, 441n1164
ordains Tiṣya and Puṣya, 295–96
on Śyāmāka as king, 336
mahalla, 379n352
Mahāmaudgalyāyana. *See* Maudgalyāyana
Mahānāma, 54
Mahāpanthaka, xxxi, 213
birth and upbringing of, 201–3, 204
chastises Panthaka, 209, 212
dharma, indoctrination in, 205–7, 399n595
five hundred followers of, 207, 208
journey to Śrāvastī, 207
mahāsukha, 397n573
Mahāvaṃsa, 418n844
maheśākhyatara, 352n47
Mahīdhara, 122–23, 128, 129, 133
Maitreya. *See* Bodhisattva Maitreya
Mākandika, xxxi, 241, 249, 413n780
as blacksmith, 251, 416n817

imprisonment of, 271, 422n896
as minister to Udayana, 259
offers Anupamā to Buddha, 242–48, 413n785
sets fire to women's quarters, 264–65, 268–69, 270
Śyāmāvatī placed in care of, 263–64, 420n861
Mākandika-avadāna, xxxi, 241–85, 412–13n779
makaras, 5, 254, 256, 417n828
Māndhāta, King, 67, 332
maṇḍīlaka cakes, 39–40
Maṇiratnagarbha Park, 119, 130–31, 369n270, 376n328
mantras, 85, 187, 189–90, 204, 205, 399n592
Māra, 84, 182
Māra's daughters, 247, 415n799
marks, thirty-two major and eighty minor, 54, 167, 170, 175, 199
Mati, 25–26, 32, 33–34
Maudgalyāyana, 54, 95–97, 117, 133, 205, 414n796
Maunalāyana, 246, 414n796
Māyādevī, Queen, 194
meditation, 206, 208, 424n929
devotion to, 266–67
of Kanakavarṇa, 85
levels of existence and, 345
locations for, 157–58, 190
of Panthaka, 212, 214, 215
perfection of, 188
of pork dealer, 228, 407n715
quiescence, 49, 168, 170
tranquility and insight, 48
as transgression, 408n717
walking, 246
memory
of Ānanda, 210
of Panthaka, 208–9, 210–11
of Sākali, 242–43
skill in, 141
merit
of brahman farmers, 169, 175
from Buddha's image, 291
from circumambulation, 177
of donors, 146, 382n388
from honoring living or passed buddhas, equality of, 179–80
nāgas desire for, 159
from offerings, 177–79, 391n487
ploy using exhaustion of, 217–18
of Rudrāyaṇa, 298
of Sahasodgata, xxviii, 109
of Śakra, 393n516
of Sumati, 27–28, 31, 355n66
of twelve-year sacrifice, 25
See also deeds, meritorious
Meru, Mount, 158, 160, 179, 213, 232, 386n428
mice
dead, 221
made of jewels, 225–26
Middle Country (*Madhyadeśa*), 233, 254, 292, 338
Middle-Length Sayings (*Madhyamāgama*), 140
midwife, 201–2, 203, 398n577
mindfulness, 48, 54, 88, 148, 150, 280, 293
ministers, ix, 53, 67, 69, 83, 176, 181, 186, 278, 285, 360n142
of Bandhumān, 77, 78, 81
of Brahmadatta, 235, 236, 238, 239
of Bimbisāra, 56, 67, 287, 288, 289
of Candraprabha, xxix, 118, 122–23, 127–128, 129, 133
of Dīpa and Vāsava, 27, 29, 33, 34
of Kanakavarṇa, 85, 86, 89, 90, 91, 92
of Śikhaṇḍin, xxxii, 303, 304, 313–17, 325–30, 332–333
of Siṃhakeśarin, 256, 257, 258
of Udayana, 259–60, 263, 269, 271. *See also* Mākandika
of Rudrāyaṇa, 288, 289, 291, 293, 302, 305, 306
See also Bhiru; Hiru
miraculous deeds, 115, 273, 296, 328, 341, 368n252. *See also* magical powers
Moggalī/Moggallāni, 441n1164
Mohenjodaro, 426n950
monasteries, 42, 143–46, 174, 295, 298, 381n375, 390n474

monasticism
benefits of, 100
eligibility for, 207–8
meal customs in, 143, 144, 231, 232, 367n237, 381n377, 408n722, 424n928
teaching, regulations on, 136–37, 283–85, 425n940, 426n948
See also community of monks
monks, 181
concealed virtues of, 63
evil thoughts toward, 145
five hundred of Buddha Kāśyapa, 8–9, 174
group of six, 106, 135–36, 208–9, 379n357, 379n359, 386n427, 401n621
old, that desired Anupamā, 248–49, 259
one who knew Tripiṭaka, 42–43
prohibited conduct of, 297
qualities of, 53, 149
similes for, 53–54, 359n134
two activities of, 206
See also community of monks
mortar, beings resembling, 147, 153, 154–55
mountains, seven golden, 158, 386n428
Mṛditakukṣika Forest, 62
Mūlasarvāstivāda-vinaya, 135, 378n348–49, 412–13n779
on abstaining from alms, 424n929
on animals, teaching dharma to, 390n469
brahman's education in, 398n586
Nāgakumāra-avadāna in, 386n426, 388n444
See also *Gilgit Buddhist Manuscripts*
Mūlasarvāstivādins, 383n399
Mūṣikāhairaṇyaka,
business ventures of, 220–23, 405n677
debt of, 225–26
as maritime merchant, 223–25
musical instruments, 23, 30, 121, 123–24, 125, 132, 198, 284

N

Nāgakumāra-avadāna, xxix, 157–61, 378n348–50
Nagaropama. See *Simile of the Town (Nagaropama)*
nāgas, xxix, 83, 93, 133, 181, 191, 195, 379n356, 426nn947–48
Buddha Kāśyapa's skeleton, raising of, 176
evil thoughts toward, 160–61, 387n441, 388n443
Garuḍa and, 387n431
as shapeshifting monk, 135–37, 141, 157, 158–61, 379n352, 381n368, 386n427
Saṅgharakṣita and, 139–42
Timiṅgila's corpse and, 9
Nanda, 106, 135–36
Nandana Grove, 78
needles that float, 250–51
news, bearers of, 260, 268–71, 421n881
nīlavāsas, 352n36
nine successive states of quiescence, 49
Nirgranthas, xxvii–xxviii, 45, 48, 56–58
nirvāṇa, 97, 131, 179, 180, 186, 192, 266, 397n573
of Buddha Kṣemaṅkara, 20, 21
of Buddha Śākyamuni, 22
gift that results in, 198
path to, 282, 301
remainderless, 117, 296, 328, 341
of Rudrāyaṇa, 320, 326, 443n1186
supreme security of, 100–101, 220, 226, 309
noble eightfold path, 49
nonreturners, 17, 58, 149, 180, 216, 262, 266, 295
North Country (Uttarāpatha), 118, 133, 183, 193, 233, 235, 338
no-self, 51, 172, 322
nuns, 11, 83, 93, 96, 181, 195, 329
dharma teaching of, 297
group of twelve, 213–15, 217, 219, 401n621, 401n623
instruction by Panthaka, 213, 214–16
nurses, 59, 187–88, 252, 393n520

O

ocean journeys
of Dharmaruci, 16–17
of five hundred merchants, 3–8, 106

of guildmaster, 19
of Mūṣikāhairaṇyaka, 223–24
of Mūṣikāhairaṇyaka's father, 220
of Sahasodgata's father, 98, 107
of Saṅgharakṣita, 139–40, 142
of Siṃhala, 253–55
offerings
of Anaṅgaṇa and Bandhumān, 75–82
benefits of, 23
to Buddha, 167–69, 181
by five hundred merchants, 107–8
to Subhadra, 57, 360n148
to thoroughbred horse, 239–40
to Tiṣya and Puṣya, 326, 436n1097
worthiness of, 21
See also gifts
omens, xxix, 123, 124, 125–26, 187, 372n298
omniscience, 128, 177, 178–79, 328, 375n323
once-returners, 17, 58, 180, 216, 266
orders, not to be refused, 280, 283
ordination
of Candraprabhā, 299
denial of, 42
of Dharmaruci, 12, 43, 358n116
of five hundred farmers, 171
of five hundred seers, 150, 151–52
of Jyotiṣka, 71–72
of Mahāpanthaka, 206
of Panthaka, 207–8
of Rudrāyaṇa, 306
of Tiṣya and Puṣya, 296
oxen, 170, 172, 174

P

padma, 354n65. *See also* lotuses
Pañcakārṣakaśata-avadāna, xxx, 167–80, 391n497
Pāṇḍava kings, 310, 433n1048
Panthaka, xxxi
birth and upbringing, 203–4
as blind brahman, 219
instruction given by, 213, 214–16
Jīvaka Kumārabhūta and, 229–32, 408n728, 409n731
as Mūṣikāhairaṇyaka, 226
ordination and instruction of, 207–12, 399n589
as pork dealer, 228
reputation of, 212, 214–15
skill in transforming minds of others, 216–17
as thoroughbred horse, 240
paṇyapariṇīta, 419n846
passion, 256
buddha's lack of, 52, 54, 247, 324
casting off, 17
evil acts and, 88, 316
words of, 38, 357n106
See also desire
Pāṭaliputra (city), 287, 426n951
perfections, six. *See* six perfections
perfume, 23, 31, 178–79, 198, 222, 341
piṇḍitamūlya, 405n676
pleasures
Bimbisāra's offer of, 308
futility of, 310–11
gifts resulting in, 197–98, 199
of humans, 100, 101–2
royal, 120–21, 123–24
sexual, 39, 41, 402n642
See also sense pleasures
pork dealer, 227–28
postures, four bodily, 215
pots
beings resembling, 147, 153, 155, 386n425
with one mouth and two compartments, 218, 402–3n648
potter, thoroughbred colt and, 234, 235–36, 237
poverty, ix, 4, 89–92, 308
prabhūtasattvasvāpateya, 364n200
prakaraṇāvadāna, 116, 368n255
Prasenajit, King, 176
pratikaṇṭhukayā, 353n49
precepts, 43, 59, 137, 174, 283, 290, 291, 293
predictions
about Agrajyoti/Jyotiṣka, 45, 46, 48, 56, 59, 70
about Buddha Śākyamuni, 292–93
about Sumati, 32

by light rays vanishing into Buddha, 323
of twelve-year drought, 275
pride, 52, 54, 57, 250–51, 324
proclamations
of Brahmadatta, 275
of Candraprabha, 120–21, 123
of Mūṣikāhairaṇyaka, 223
of Rudrāyaṇa, 303
of Siṃhaka's father, 253
Strive! Go forth!, 51, 97, 291, 322–23
of Udayana, 263
psychology, cosmology and, 345
Pūjita/Pūjitaka, 233, 235, 239, 410n749
Pūleśvara site, 338, 442n1170
Purāṇa, 176
Pūrvavideha (continent), 97, 346
Puṣkalāvata (city), 193, 395n546
Puṣpadanta Palace, 259, 264–65, 266, 268–69, 270, 419nn847–48
Puṣya, 295–96, 326, 328

R

Rādhā, 423–24n921
radiance
of Brahmaprabha, 189
of Buddha, 167, 170, 175, 242, 243
of Candraprabha, 119, 187
Rāhu (demon), 434n1062
Rāhula, 193, 194
rains, 287–88
of dirt, xxxii, 331–32, 333, 439n1130
of food, cloth, and jewels, 91–92
of gold, 67, 331, 332–33
See also famine
rainy season, 155, 208–9, 253
horses in, 233, 409nn737–38
offering provisions for, 19, 74–76, 82
Rājagṛha (city), 48, 55, 56, 59, 64, 65, 98, 109, 288–89, 426–27n951
almsrounds in, 45–46, 63, 294, 298, 306
Buddha in, 62, 95, 117, 229, 287
five hundred merchants in, 106–7
marketplace at, 66–67
Rudrāyāṇa in, 303–4, 306–12, 314–15, 317
Ratnadvīpa, 4–5, 224–25
Raudrākṣa, 371n297
arrival in Bhadraśilā, 126–27
Candraprabha's head and, 124, 128–30, 132, 375n323
as Devadatta, 133
realms of existence, xxviii, 100
deeds leading to specific, 99
depiction of, 97
rebirth in, 17–19, 323
sufferings of, 95, 96, 101
types of beings in, 345
rebellions, 263, 269–70
rebirth
in animal realm, 17, 323
Buddha's predictions of, 323
cycle of, 18
in divine realms, xxviii, 34, 43, 51, 100, 101, 102, 104, 106, 108, 132–33, 267, 322
ending, 312, 319
on five-sectioned wheel, 97
in hell realms, 249, 274, 323, 324
in human realm, 51, 159, 267, 322
karma and, 73, 173
resulting from gifts, 198, 199
thoughts that arise at, 17–18, 159, 299–300
from virtuous offerings, 82
refuge, 58–59, 290–91, 293
of brahman farmer, 168–69
of Buddharakṣita, 137
of Candraprabhā, 301
of Jyotiṣka, 62
of Sahasodgata, 111
of Śrīmatī, 282, 283
renunciants
five benefits from becoming, 100–101, 366n226
non-Buddhist (*tīrthya*), 63, 202, 203, 362n163
rhinoceros, buddhas as, 88, 365n210. *See also* solitary buddhas
rice, 307
fed to blind man, 217–18, 402n644
gruel, gift of, 167–69
Rohiṇī, 247
Roruka (city), 287, 288, 295–96, 318, 329, 330–32, 333, 344, 426n950

roundabout stories, 11
royalty and rulership, 364n202
according to dharma, 304, 336, 364n202
death and, 310
desire and, 433n1048
and famine, relationship of, 364n202
symbols of, 238, 270, 410n745, 421n772
unjust, xxxii, 312–14
Ṛṣidatta, 176
Ṛṣivadana, 173, 216, 388n447
Rudrāyaṇa, King, xxxi–xxxii, 287
attainment of, 293–94, 319–21
Buddha image, receipt of, 291–93
Candraprabhā and, 299, 302
death and rebirth of, 321, 325
deeds of, 339–40
as deer, 342, 443n1186
gifts to Bimbisāra, 288, 289, 290
plot to kill, 315–17
receives Mahākātyāyana and Śailā, 295, 297, 298
refutation of kingship by, 309–12
renunciation of, 302–8, 431n1020
returns to Roruka, 317–20
Śikhaṇḍin, makes inquires about, 314
Rudrāyaṇa-avadāna, xxxi–xxxii, 287–344, 412–13n779, 426n949
Rūpāvata, xxx, 186
Rūpāvatī, xxx, 183–86, 193, 392nn506–7, 392n513, 393n519
Rūpāvatī-avadāna, xxx, 181–95

S

sābhisaṃskāreṇa, 354n61
Śacī, 81
sacrifices
of Candraprabha's head, 124, 126–32, 134
of Rūpāvatī's breasts, 184–86, 393n516
to tigress, 131, 191–92, 376n329
Sahasodgata, xxviii, 115
attainment of, 111–12
birth and upbringing of, 98–99
as day laborer, 102–104
feeds community of monks, 105–6, 110–11
as guildmaster, 109
with five hundred merchants, 106–8
monastery visit of, 99–102
Sahasodgata-avadāna, xxviii, xxx, 95–116, 368n255
Śailā, 297–99, 329, 332, 430n1003
Sākali (a.k.a. Sākalika), 241, 242–46, 413n781
Sākalika. *See* Sākali.
Śakra, 54, 79–81, 131, 185–86, 192, 347, 363n193, 393n516, 444n1200
Śākya clan, 63, 292
Śākyamuni. *See* Buddha Śākyamuni
saṃsāra, 214, 345, 401n622
arhat's understanding of, 72, 171, 296, 319
cycling through, 267, 312
deliverance from, 220, 226
suffering of, 184
virtue and, 12
Saṃyuktaka. See *Connected Sayings* (*Saṃyuktāgama*)
Sandhāna, 275–77
Saṅgharakṣita, xxix, xxx, 153–55
birth of, 137–38
deeds, maturation of, 163–66
gathers disciples for Buddha, 149–53
misbehaving monks and, 143–46
in nāga realm, 140–42
as raft, 150, 384n408
silence of, 147–48
voyage of, 138–40
Saṅgharakṣita-avadāna, xxix, 135–55, 163–66, 378nn348–50, 386n426
sārdhaṃvihārin, 365n217
Śāriputra, 54, 117, 133, 137–39, 140, 205, 280–81, 283
sarvarūpa, 352n35
sciences, eight. *See* eight sciences
seeds, selecting one variety, 109
seeing
five things one never tires of, 142
path of, 17
seers, 27, 89–90, 243, 292
five hundred, xxix, 147–50
garbage thrown on, 343–44, 444n1195
speech of, 55, 60

two brahman with Brahmaprabha, 190–91, 194
See also Viśvāmitra
sense bases, 73, 112, 163, 173, 227, 272, 275, 278, 319, 339, 342, 384n410
sense pleasures, 243, 244, 245, 246, 247, 248
sentient beings, benefiting, 190, 339
sesame oil, rain of, 92
seven factors of awakening, 8, 49, 198
seven treasures, 92, 292, 369–70n270
sex change of Rūpāvatī, 186, 393n519
shrines
acts of faith at, xxx, 177–78
bathing of, 199
for Buddha Kṣemaṅkara, 20–23, 352n47
for Mahākātyāyana, 335, 338
from Sumati's hair, 33
See also stūpas
siddham, 204, 399n589
Śikhaṇḍin, King, xxxii, 318, 342, 439n1130
consecration of, 303, 304
father of, true identity of, 327
as girl throwing garbage, 344
killing of Rudrāyaṇa and, 315–17, 319, 320, 325–26
Mahākātyāyana and, 329–32, 339
mother of, 326–27, 437n1099
as prince, 287
unjust rule of, 312–15
Śikhin. *See* Buddha Śikhin
silver, rain of, 331, 332, 438n1119
Siṃhaka, 252
Siṃhakalpā (capital), 252, 253, 255, 257
Siṃhakeśarin, King, 252, 256–57, 259
Siṃhala, 259
abandons wife, 254–56
birth and upbringing of, 252–53
consecration of, 257–58
ocean journey of, 253–55, 417n828
Siṃhaladvīpa, 258, 418n844
Simile of the Town (*Nagaropama*), 149
Sindhu, 338
single guardian, 48
sins
deadly, 34–43, 321, 326, 327
freedom from, 282, 301
rebirth and, 366–67n228
toward field of merit, 363–64n195
verses on freedom from, 208, 215–16
Śītavana cremation ground, 48, 54–58
Śiva, 6
six [good] qualities, 48
six heavens, 347
six perfections, 43, 49, 188, 209, 354n57
skeletons, 16–17, 175–76, 352n37
snake-catcher, 218–19
snakes, broth from, 219, 403n653
Śobhāvatī (capital), 35
solitary buddhas, xxviii, 23, 278, 365n210, 415n803
awakening as, 58–59, 88, 180, 216, 295, 323
Balasena's offerings to, 113–15
conditions for, 113, 273, 276, 278, 340, 343
deer hunter and, 340–41, 342
feeding one thousand, 276–77
five hundred, 228
garbage thrown on, 343–44
hut set on fire of, 273–74
with Kanakavarṇa, 89–91
meal customs of, 340
reluctant offering to, 423n921
teaching method of, 90, 114–15
speech, 203
of Buddha Śākyamuni, 55, 59–60, 244–45, 359n137. *See also* Brahmā-like voice
fault of talking too much, 147
harsh, 81, 114, 115, 155, 247, 363–64nn195–96
spiritual faculties, five. *See* five spiritual faculties
Śrāvastī (city), 34
Buddha staying at, 3, 83, 181, 197, 201, 229
Buddha's journey to, 167
Dharmaruci in, 9, 11, 18
Dharmaruci's donor from, 13–15
five hundred merchants in, 7
Mahākātyāyana in, 338–39
Mahāpanthaka in, 207
nuns announcement in, 214, 401n623
Saṅgharakṣita's birth in, 137
Śāriputra and Maudgalyāyana in, 205

Sri Lanka, 418n844
Śrīmatī, Queen, 278–83, 423–24n921
Staff Stūpa, 338, 442n1166
stinginess, 264
  charity and, 84, 92, 182, 195
  with dharma, 227, 228, 407n707
  rebirth due to, 99
story-telling, popular, 103, 367n231
stream-enterers, 17, 180, 216, 266, 295
  brahmans as, 168–69
  Candraprabhā as, 300–302
  five hundred farmers as, 171
  Mahākātyāyana's mother as, 337–38
  Rudrāyaṇa as, 293–94
  Sahasodgata as, 111–12
  Śrīmatī as, 281–83
stūpas, 341–42
  for Mahākātyāyana, 335
  at Maṇiratnagarbha, 131, 132–33
  renovation of, 22–23, 353nn48–51
  of Tiṣya and Puṣya, 296, 326, 328
  See also shrines; Staff Stūpa
Subhadra, 45–48, 57, 58, 60–62, 360n148
success, four bases of. *See* four bases of success
Sudarśana (divine city), 121, 124
Śuddhodana, King, 194
suffering, 9, 11, 87, 117, 144, 145, 146, 158, 267, 282, 322
  alone, 312
  eight types of, 134, 377n345
  ending, 51, 97, 100, 291, 299, 302, 323
  of hell, xxix, 41
  of once-returners, 266
  of realms of existence, 95, 96, 99, 101, 184, 301
  from sin, 208, 216
  truth of, 51, 322
sukhitā tvam, 383n397
sukumārī, 367n234
Sumati, 25–29, 31–34, 355n66, 355n69
Sumeru, Mount. *See* Meru, Mount
summit stage, 17, 58, 180
sun and moon, touching with hand, 26, 354n64
Suparṇin (bird king), 158, 159, 387n431
Suprabha. *See* Buddha Suprabha
sweet shops, 222, 405n678
Śyāmāka, 332, 333–37
Śyāmākarājya, 337
Śyāmāvatī, Queen, xxxi, 274, 332
  Anupamā's plot against, 263–64
  consumed in fire, 265–67, 268–69, 270, 272, 422n896
  devotion to Buddha of, 260–62

T

tadrūpo guṇagaṇo 'ahigataḥ, 351n21. *See also* virtue
Takṣaśilā (city), 133
Tāmradvīpa, 254, 255, 256, 258, 417n828
Taralikā, Queen, 326–27, 437n1099
taxes and fees, 85, 119, 169
ten powers, 49, 54, 362n165
tenfold path of virtuous actions, 100, 122, 206
theft by Ajātaśatru, 70–71
thirty-seven gifts. *See* gifts, thirty-seven ways of offering
thoroughbred horse, 409n732
  birth of, 233
  eating, refusal to, 236–37, 411nn765–66
  potter and, 234
  royal protocol for, 238, 421n772, 421n775
  sold to Brahmadatta, 235–36, 410n747
three bases, 197, 396n562
three jewels, 197
three objects for self-control, 48
three realms, 17, 72, 100, 151, 153, 158, 172, 206, 211, 296, 320, 345, 346–47. *See also* realms of existence
tigress, xxx, 131, 190–92, 194, 376n329, 395n544
Timi, 4, 224
Timiṅgila (a.k.a. Timitimiṅgila), xxvii, 4, 5–6, 7, 9, 16–17, 224, 350n16, 352n37
Timitimiṅgila. *See* Timiṅgila
tīrthya, 362n163
Tiṣya, 295–96, 326, 328
tolerance stage, 17, 58, 180
Toyikā, xxx, 174–76, 390n479
Toyikāmaha festival, xxx, 180
Toyikāmaha-avadāna, 390n479, 391n497

toys, 188, 393nn522–26
Trāyastriṃśa (divine realm), 51, 81, 121, 124, 185, 347, 444n1200
treasures, seven. *See* seven treasures
Tripiṭaka, 34, 42–43, 136, 206, 213–14, 227–28
triple path, 309, 432n1039
trivastu, 396n562
truth, seeing, 81, 111, 115, 150, 364n195
  of Candraprabhā, 300–302
  of five hundred farmers, 171
  of Mahākātyāyana's mother, 337–38
  of oxen, 174
  of Rudrāyaṇa, 293–94
  of Śrīmatī, 281–83
truth, vow of, 131, 185, 186, 191–92, 326, 328
twelve links of interdependent arising, 97, 206, 290, 293

U

Uccaṅgama (bird), 189, 194, 394n530
Udānavarga, 149, 383n399
Udayana, King, xxxi, 266
  Buddha and, 272–74
  grief of, 271, 422n894
  hears of fire and deaths, 268–71, 422n891
  lust of, 267
  ministers of, 259–60, 263
  rebellion against, 263, 269–70
  wives of, 259, 260–61, 262, 279, 419n846
umbrellas, 48, 119–20, 123, 130, 132, 198, 334, 341
  gift of, 198
  hundred-ribbed, 29, 79, 81, 238
  merit from, 179
  two cloths hidden in, 65–66
upakrama, 351n27
Upananda, 106, 135–36
Upendra, 6, 17, 72, 151, 153, 159, 172, 207, 212, 296, 320
uṣṇīṣa, 323, 397n568
Uśīra, 246, 414n796
Utpalāvatī (capital), 183, 185, 186, 189, 190, 193, 395n546
Uttara, 164–65, 388n449
Uttarakuru (continent), 97, 346

V

Vaidehī, Queen, 287, 427n953
Vaiśravaṇa (a.k.a. Kubera; Dhanada), 6, 54, 74, 112–13, 252, 275, 347, 352n36
Vārāṇasī (city), 158, 228, 388n447
  Brahmadatta at, 235, 236, 239, 272, 273, 410n745
  Buddha Kāśyapa at, 173, 227
  Sandhāna at, 275, 276,
  silk from, 120, 307, 439n1131, 441n1154, 441n1156
  turning wheel of dharma at, 216
Varṣakāra, 287, 427n954
Varuṇa, 6
Vāsava, King, 25, 26, 27, 29, 33, 34
Vaśiṣṭha, 246, 414n796
vassal kings, 53, 235, 239, 270, 410nn745–46
Vasuguta, 350n16
Vedas, 25, 203, 204, 398n586, 399n592
Vemacitri, 54, 345
views, false, 58, 329
  of individuality, 111, 168, 171, 281, 293, 294, 300, 337
  twenty peaks of incorrect, 111, 281, 293, 300, 337
vihārasvāmin, 390n474
Vipaśyin. *See* Buddha Vipaśyin
virtue
  amassing collection of, 8, 12, 351n21
  of Buddha, 83, 181–82
  of buddhas, 180
  carelessness with, 130
  of Kanakavarṇa, 85
  of monks for donor's merit, 146, 382n388
  of Panthaka, 212, 213, 232–33, 240
  roots of, 49, 58, 139, 168, 176, 207, 281, 332, 342
virtuous actions, tenfold path. *See* tenfold path of virtuous actions
Virūḍhaka, 54, 176, 347. *See also* four great kings

Virūpākṣa, 347, 359n134. *See also* four great kings
vīrya, 392n513
Viśākhā Mṛgāramātā, 176
viṣṭhā, 57, 361n162
Viśvabhū. *See* Buddha Viśvabhū
Viśvakarman, 81
Viśvāmitra, 125–26
Vokkāṇa (city), 337, 441n1159, 442n1166
vṛddhayuvatī, 356n85, 356n90, 398n577
Vṛṣṇi kings, 310
Vulture's Peak, 117

W

water
  flowing out of pork dealer's body, 228
  sacred, 202, 203
  trickling from novice's hands, 160–61, 387n441, 388n443
waterlilies, 26, 30, 31, 354nn65–66, 355n71. *See also* lotuses
wealth
  of Anaṅgaṇa, 74
  attachment to, 309
  of Balasena, 112–13
  complete sacrifice of, 199
  desire for, 4, 224
  divine, 81–82
  of Kanakavarṇa, 84–85
  in reign of Candraprabha, 120
  renouncing, 308
  of Sahasodgata, 109
  of Sandhāna, 275–77
  of Siṃhaka, 252–53
  true, 311
wheel of dharma, turning, 22, 216
wheel of existence, xxviii, 97–98, 99–106. *See also* twelve links of interdependent arising
wheel-turning kings, 53, 119, 122, 131, 186, 192, 292, 323
wind
  element of, 73, 112, 163, 173, 226, 272, 275, 278, 339, 342
  humor, excess of, 277
women
  advice never to touch, 267–68
  Buddha and, 243, 413n785
  as demons, 255, 256. *See also* demonesses
  five hundred in Śyāmāvatī's retinue, 265, 266, 274
  jealousy of, 263
  of Rudrāyaṇa's palace, 297, 429n992
  shared between fathers and sons, 38
  and solitary buddha, setting fire to hut of, 273–74
  wives, treatment of, 218, 254–56, 307–8, 309
wood, fragrant, 77–78, 132, 363n190
world-system, billionfold, 51, 132, 192–93, 323

Y

yakṣas, 54, 83, 93, 133, 181, 195
  bowl in hand (*karoṭapāṇi*), 123
  five hundred dark-clothed, 14, 352n36
  serpent, 64, 65, 362n170
  sorrow of, 129
  See also Vaiśravaṇa
Yama (god of death), 184
Yaśaḥpūrṇa, 54
Yaśodharā, 34
yathādhauta, 365n211
Yogāndharāyaṇa, 259, 263, 271, 420n861, 422nn895–96

About the Translator

ANDY ROTMAN is a professor of Religion, Buddhism, and South Asian Studies at Smith College. His publications include *Divine Stories: Divyāvadāna, Part 1* (Wisdom Publications, 2008), *Thus Have I Seen: Visualizing Faith in Early Indian Buddhism* (Oxford University Press, 2009), and a coauthored volume, *Amar Akbar Anthony: Bollywood, Brotherhood, and the Nation* (Harvard University Press, 2015). He has been engaged in textual and ethnographic work on religious and social life in South Asia for more than twenty-five years.

About Wisdom Publications

Wisdom Publications, a nonprofit publisher, is dedicated to making available books about Buddhism for the benefit of all. We publish works by ancient and modern masters across Buddhist traditions, translations of important texts, and original scholarship. We also offer books that explore East-West themes, which continue to emerge as traditional Buddhism encounters modern culture in all its complexity. Our titles are published with an appreciation of Buddhism as a living philosophy, and with a commitment to preserve and transmit important works from Buddhism's many traditions.

You can contact us, request a catalog, or browse our books online at our website. You can also write to us at the address below.

Wisdom Publications
199 Elm Street
Somerville, Massachusetts 02144 USA
Telephone: (617) 776-7416
Fax: (617) 776-7841
Email: info@wisdompubs.org
www.wisdompubs.org

Supporting the Classics of Indian Buddhism Series

The volumes in the Classics of Indian Buddhism series adhere to the highest standards of accuracy and readability, making them works that will stand the test of time both as scholarship and as literature. The care and attention necessary to bring such works to press demand a level of investment beyond the normal costs associated with publishing. If you would like to partner with Wisdom to help make the series a success, either by supporting the meticulous work of translators and editors or by sponsoring the publication costs of a forthcoming volume, please send us an email at cib@wisdompubs.org or write to us at the address above. We appreciate your support.

Wisdom is a nonprofit, charitable 501(c)(3) organization affiliated with the Foundation for the Preservation of the Mahayana Tradition (FPMT).